Charles Hudson

Genealogical Register of Lexington Families

from the first settlement of the town

Charles Hudson

Genealogical Register of Lexington Families
from the first settlement of the town

ISBN/EAN: 9783337221362

Printed in Europe, USA, Canada, Australia, Japan

Cover: Foto ©Andreas Hilbeck / pixelio.de

More available books at **www.hansebooks.com**

Charles Hudson

GENEALOGICAL REGISTER

OF

LEXINGTON FAMILIES,

FROM THE

FIRST SETTLEMENT OF THE TOWN.

BY CHARLES HUDSON,

MEMBER OF THE MASSACHUSETTS HISTORICAL, THE NEW ENGLAND HISTORIC-GENEALOGICAL, AND THE
AMERICAN ANTIQUARIAN SOCIETIES.

BOSTON:
WIGGIN & LUNT, PUBLISHERS,
221 WASHINGTON STREET,
1868.

GENEALOGICAL REGISTER

OF

LEXINGTON FAMILIES.

INTRODUCTION.

In the following notices of the Lexington families, I have been desirous to give a full genealogy of those who settled in the town early, or who have resided long in the place. Most of the families which have come into Lexington within the last twenty or thirty years, have little or no record on our town books; and hence it is impossible to give any connected view of them from our records. In such cases I have applied to the families personally or by circular, to furnish a complete record; and wherever such a record has been procured, it has been used in this volume. But many, I regret to say, have supplied no such lists. This fact is mentioned, to show that the fullest opportunity has been given to every family, to provide the means which would enable me to give them a place in this Register. It would be impossible for me to take up every modern family, and follow them through the records of the respective places where they and their ancestors may have resided, and give their genealogy. A life-time would be insufficient for such a Herculean task; especially when we consider the changing character of our population at the present day. I regret the absence of many families from this list, but the fault is not mine.

My plan has been to begin as far back as my means of information would allow, and to trace the line of descent to the family or individual who came to Lexington; and while he or they remained in town, I have endeavored to embrace in the list every member of the family. When any individual or family have left town, I have dropped their genealogy; though I have noted all important historical events, connected with the individual or family, known to me, as far as they fell within the scope of this sketch.

58

While I have endeavored to be accurate, I have not the vanity to suppose that I have avoided all errors. Every one who has had any experience in labors of this kind, knows that errors are unavoidable. The neglect of parents in having the births, deaths, and marriages in their respective families recorded, renders it impossible in many cases, to collect from the town records a correct list of a family. And this difficulty is increased by the recurrence of the same name in the different branches of a family. Where there are two or three *Williams*, or *Johns*, or *Samuels*, or *Sarahs*, or *Marys*, or *Abigails* of the same surname, and the record gives the birth, death, or marriage of a person of that name, without giving the name of the parent or the age of the individual, it is difficult, and sometimes impossible, from the record, to decide which of the individuals is intended. In all such cases I have had recourse to other evidence, and have generally satisfied myself on this subject.

Genealogists know what allowances to make. But in this case as in almost all others, those are the most difficult to please, who know the least of the embarrassments in this kind of labor. Every genealogist must make up his mind in advance that his work will be branded as unreliable, by those who have neglected to give accurate information, or have been remiss in having their children recorded.

I regret that the accounts given of some families are so meagre and imperfect; but the defect is chargeable to the record. What I have given is the fruit of much labor, study, and anxiety. I have carefully examined the records of Lexington, and most of the neighboring towns, the published genealogies of numerous families, and also the records of the Probate office and the office of the Register of Deeds for the county. From these sources I have supplied, in numerous cases, the defects of the town records, and have even supplied the record of whole families, not found upon the town records at all.

The following explanations will enable the reader to understand the genealogical tables:

ABBREVIATIONS.—b. stands for *born*; bap. for *baptized*; m for *married*; unm. for *unmarried*; d. for *died*; dau. for *daughter* or *daughters*; wid. for *widow*; r. for *resides* or *resided*; ad. for *admitted*; o. c. for *owned the Covenant*; ch. for *church*; chil. for *children*. I have also abbreviated many of the towns to which frequent reference is made, as Lex. for *Lexington*; Camb. for *Cambridge*; Wo. for *Woburn*; Wat. for *Watertown*; Con. for *Concord*; Walt. for *Waltham*; Bed. for *Bedford*, &c. All towns mentioned will be considered as being within this State, unless another State is mentioned; or the case is so clear as to exclude doubt, as *Philadelphia, Chicago, Detroit, &c.*

In the following tables, the parents' names are given in full, and are printed in SMALL CAPITALS; the children's Christian name alone is given, and is printed in *italics*. Children are separated from their parents by a short line, thus: ———. And different families, or branches of the same families, are separated from each other by a line across the page, thus:

The right hand figure on the left margin of the page, denotes the number of persons consecutively from the first named to the last of the family of that name. The first male mentioned under each general head or new family, is set down as 1, and his children as 2, 3, 4, &c., and so on consecutively through every branch of the family; and the number set against any person is considered as his number, and no one is ever brought forward again but in connection with that number. Whenever the children are first named in the series, the number of the father is brought down against them, and placed at the left hand, separated by a hyphen, thus: 1-2 or 12-41, as the case may be—the left hand figure denoting the father, and the right hand figures the children—the father's number being understood as applying to each of his children. Whenever an obelisk (†) is prefixed to a name, it denotes that the person will be taken up again; and the place where he is thus treated of may be found by following down the left margin of the page, till you find his number standing in the second place to the left of the marginal line, and the number of his father one place to the left of that, expressed thus: 1-2- or 12-41-. The numbers, of course, will vary with the position of the person in the table.

That the above explanation may be fully understood, I will illustrate it by its application to a particular family in this Register. Take the SMITH FAMILY, as an example.

John Smith, being the ancestor of the family, stands as No. 1. Against this number his personal history is given. He is separated from his children by a short rule or line. His number (1) is brought down against the name of his first child, John, who is numbered 2. The other children are numbered in succession—Francis, 3, Daniel, 4, and Thomas, 5. It is understood that the number of the parent stands against the name or number of each of the children. By inspecting the table, it will be seen that an *obelisk* is prefixed to the name of *Thomas,* No. 5. This denotes that he will be brought forward again. To find the place where he will be further treated of, follow down the left hand of the page till you find the number of the father (1) and the number of the son (5) standing together thus: 1-5-. Thomas's number (5) is brought down against his children, whose consecutive numbers are 6 to 14, inclusive. Here again you find the obelisk against the names of Thomas, John, and Joseph, denoting that each of them will be further considered where their respective numbers, and that of their fathers, are found in the margin. Take the first named in this family, viz. *Thomas,* whose number is 8. He will be

found in the table where his number is placed in the margin, standing
at the right hand of the number of his father (5) thus : 5–8–. Against
the number of Thomas (8) will be found the numbers of his children,
from 15 to 20, inclusive. In this family, Thomas, Joseph, and Benjamin have the mark prefixed to their names, showing that they will
be brought forward again and their families given. Take *Joseph* as
an example, whose number is 19. Further along in the margin, you
will find 8, the number of the father, and 19, the number of Joseph ;
there you will find his personal history, and below, against his number (19), you will find his children, numbered from 31 to 40, inclusive.
Several of the sons are marked with an obelisk, showing that more will
be said of them where their respective numbers are found in the
margin associated with 19, the number of their father. Take Hezekiah, numbered 33. By following down the margin, we find 19–33–
where Hezekiah is taken up as a father, and his history, and the
names of his children, are given. From his children, who are marked
for further consideration, we will select Joseph, whose number is 66.
Following the direction already given, we find 33–66– in the margin,
where a notice of him and his children will be found. If we should
select Billings, numbered 140, and look for his appropriate place
where his father's number (66) and his own (140) are found in the
margin, we should find among his children, Billings, our present fellow-
citizen, standing as number 204.

By following these directions, the reader can easily trace the Smiths
or any other family. This can be done backward as well as forward.
Take, for example, *Elias Smith*, who married Harriet Hastings. His
number is 152, which stands against 87, the number of his father,
Josiah. By following back the consecutive numbers, you find that 87
is the son of 40 of the same name ; and 40 is the son of 19, which is
the number of Joseph, the father ; and 19 is the son of 8 ; and 8 the
son of 5 ; and 5 the son of 2 ; and 2 the son of 1, the original ancestor.

In this way any family can easily be traced in the following register. It will be seen that each division of a family separated by
a long rule or line, presents at once three generations—the grandfather, the father, and the children—the first by number, and the last
two by name.

I have been thus particular, because people frequently complain
that they cannot understand the arrangement of genealogists, or trace
the connection between the different branches or members of a family.
The plan I have adopted is partly original, and is, I believe, more
simple than any plan in use ; and if it be followed, will enable any
person to trace the connection between the members of any family
which is presented in a tabular form.

THE ABBOT FAMILY.

ADOPTING the alphabetical order,.we must place the *Abbots* at the head of the Lexington Families. They were not among the earliest settlers, nor were they very numerous, but for a time held a very respectable position among the people of the place. By the aid of the Abbot Genealogy, we are enabled to present a connected line of descent from the original emigrant.

1   GEORGE ABBOT, with three sons, George, Nehemiah and Thomas, emigrated from England, and settled in Rowley, where he d. 1647.

1- 2   *George*, the eldest son of the emigrant, b. in England, settled in Andover, 1655, where he m. May, 1658, Sarah Farnum. He d. March 22, 1689, and she d. 1728, aged 90, the widow of Henry Ingalls.

2- 3   *George*, b. Jan. 28, 1659; d. Jan. 24, 1724, aged 65.
4   *Sarah*, b. Sept. 6, 1660; m. 1682, John Faulkner.
5   *John*, b. Aug. 26, 1662.
6   *Mary*, b. Mar. 29, 1664; m. 1687, Stephen Barker.
7   ‡*Nehemiah*, b. July 20, 1667; d. Oct. 8, 1750.
8   *Hannah*, b. Sept. 20, 1668; m. 1695, James Ingalls.
9   *Mehitabel*, b. Feb. 17, 1671; d. young.
10   *Lydia*, b. Sept. 29, 1675; m. 1695, Henry Chandler.
11   *Samuel*, b. May 30, 1678.   12 *Mehitabel*, b. April 4, 1680.

2-7-   NEHEMIAH ABBOT, m. Abigail Lovejoy, 1691. He was a deacon in Andover, and represented the town in the General Court.

7-13   ‡*Nehemiah*, b. Jan. 19, 1692; d. Feb. 17, 1767.
14   *Abiel*, b. Aug. 10, 1693; d. Jan. 21, 1758.
15   *Zebadiah*, b. April 6, 1695; d. Sept. 9, 1767.
16   *John*, b. Oct. 31, 1697; d. Nov. 25, 1779.
17   *Abigail*, b. Sept. 30, 1699; m. Benjamin Abbot, and d. Dec. 8, 1753.
18   *Mary*, b. March 24, 1701; m. James Bridges, and d. 1774.
19   *Joseph*, b. ——; d. Nov. 12, 1726.

7-13-   NEHEMIAH ABBOT, from Andover, bought, May 11, 1714, of Thomas Woolson, a house and land in Weston, known as the Stony Brook Mill Lot. He m. 1714, Sarah Foster. About 1719, he removed to Lex. where a portion of his children were born. He was ad. to the ch in Lex. Feb. 23, 1724. His name first. appears upon the Town Records in 1721. He served his fellow townsmen from time to time, as school committee man, assessor, and town treasurer. His wife probably d. 1770. He lived in the southwestern part of the town, now within the bounds of Lincoln.

13-20   *Nehemiah*, bap. in Weston, Dec. 4, 1715; d. young.
21   *Nehemiah*, bap. in Weston, March 14, 1717; d. July 13, 1785.
22   *Sarah*, bap. in Weston, Nov. 2, 1718.

23 | *Abigail*, b. Jan. 26, 1721; m. Amos Lawrence, of Groton, and died Jan. 6, 1784.
24 | *William*, b. Oct. 9, 1724; d. Jan. 2, 1798. aged 74.
25 | †*Joseph*, b. June 8, 1727; d. 1793, aged 66.

13-25—   JOSEPH ABBOT, m. March 24, 1752, Hannah White. He appears to have been the only son of the family which remained in Lex. He resided at or near the Spaulding place in Lincoln, which was taken from Lex. when Linc. was incorporated in 1754. Hence he is frequently mentioned in the Records as of Lincoln.

25-26 | †*Joseph*, b. July 10, 1752; d. 1834, aged 82.
27 | *Nehemiah*, b. 1754; d. in Linc. 1840. He m. Polly Hoar — was a soldier of the Revolution.
28 | *Abiel*, b. ——; m. Dec. 16, 1788, Polly Merriam, of Lex. and d. 1817.
29 | *Hannah*, bap. April 10, 1757; d. 1785.
30 | *Abigail*, b. ——; d. young.   31 *Sarah*, bap. Aug. 1, 1762.
32 | *Abigail*, bap. July 21, 1765.   33 *Asa*, bap. Feb. 28, 1768.
34 | *Mary*, bap. Jan. 31, 1773; m. Amaziah Fawcett.

25-26—   JOSEPH ABBOT, m. April 30, 1778, Ruth Buckman of Lex. He resided in Linc. where he had a family of children, several of whom were bap. in Lex. He subsequently moved to Sidney, Me.

26-35 | *Elizabeth*, bap. Feb. 7, 1779.   36 *John*, bap. Jan. 22, 1783.
37 | *William*, bap. June 11, 1786.   38 *Samuel*, bap. Nov. 23, 1788.
39 | *Joseph*, bap. April 24, 1790.   40 *Sarah*, bap. April 28, 1793.
41 | *Abigail*, bap. Oct. 18, 1795.   42 *Mary*, bap. Feb. 1, 1801.

THE ADAMS FAMILY.

1   GEORGE ADAMS, a glover, and his wife Frances, settled in Wat. 1645. On the 4th of Nov. 1664, he sold to John Chenery his house and land in Wat. and moved to Camb. Farms, now Lex. probably about the time of this sale. The birth of *only* two of his children is recorded; though he had five or six at least.

1-2 | *John*, b. April 6, 1645; d. young.
3 | †*George*, b. 1647; d. Jan. 27, 1732, aged 85.
4 | *Daniel*, b. ——. Executor of his father's will.
5 | *John*, b. Mar. 6, 1657.
6 | *Mary*, bap. and o. c. Nov. 21, 1686, in Wat.

1-3—   GEORGE ADAMS, m. Jan. 20, 1684, Martha Fiske, dau. of John and Sarah (Wyeth) Fiske, of Camb. Farms. She was bap. in Wat. Nov. 21, 1686, and he was bap. and o. c. June 19, 1698. Both George Adams, and George Adams, Jr., were taxed in Camb. Farms in 1693, for the minister's salary, and for the purchase of the land which laid the foundation of the Ministerial Fund. He was an assessor in 1702; constable in 1715.

3-7 | †*George*, born Ap. 28, 1685. He was bap. in Wat.
8 | *Martha*, b. June 10, 1686; bap. in Wat. the May following.
9 | †*John*, b. Sept. 6, 1688; m. Mary Flagg, of Wat. Oct. 27, 1714.
10 | *Nathaniel*, bap. June 12, 1698. Supposed to be the Nathaniel of Grafton, who m. Nov. 20, 1738, Eunice Stearns, of Waltham.
11 | *Sarah*, bap. June 12, 1698.
12 | †*Benjamin*, b. Dec. 20, 1701; m. Eunice ——.

3-7-   George Adams m. about 1705, Judith ——. He was a physician, and resided in Lex. till about 1720, when he removed to Waltham, where he d. Feb. 8, 1767, aged 82.

7-13 *Lydia*, b. July 9, 1706; m. Oct. 13, 1731, Caleb Pond, of Dedham.
14 *Jonas*, b. Jan. 6, 1708; d. June following.
15 *Judith*, b. Sept. 15, 1709; m. —— Boyden.
16 *Elizabeth*, b. July 8, 1712; m. Feb. 26, 1744, Robert Baker, of Con.
17 *Hannah*, b. Feb. 9, 1715; m. Dec. 4, 1734, Barachias Lewis, of Rox.
18 *Seth*, b. March 25, 1717; d. 1730.
19 *Josiah*, b. June 13, 1719; m. Grace Hager; had children in Weston.
20 *Deborah*, b. June 13; d. June 16, 1719; a twin with Josiah.
21 *Abigail*, b. in Walt. May 6, 1721; d. May 26, 1740.
22 *Daniel*, b. in Walt. May 2, 1724; m. Nov. 22, 1743, and had Elizabeth, Jonas, and Seth.

3-9-   John Adams m. Oct. 27, 1714, Mary Flagg. He was probably the John Adams who m. Nov. 24, 1743, Mary Sanderson, of Walt. He was chosen to the dignified office of hog-reeve in 1715, showing that he was an inhabitant at that time, and that he had recently assumed another important relation. His last wife d. July 21, 1786, aged 95.

9-23 *Mephibosheth*, b. July 4, 1715; m. May 2, 1734, Jane Derby.
24 *John*, b. Feb. 22, 1717; probably settled in Linc. where he m. Elizabeth ——, and had a family of 11 children. He d. 1774.
25 *Micah*, b. Aug. 14, 1718; d. Aug. 23, 1747.
26 *Mary*, b. Feb. 27, 1722.
27 *Abigail*, b. June 3, 1723.
28 *Prudence*, b. April 1, 1727.
29 †*Sampson*, b. Aug. 25, 1730; d. Aug. 26, 1785.
30 †*George*, b. May 17, 1733; m. July 18, 1758, Abigail Prentice, of Newton.
31 *Susanna*, b. March 21, 1735.
32 *Lucy*, b. Dec. 27, 1738.   33 *Jane*, b. June 3, 1740.

3-12-   Benjamin Adams m. Eunice ——. Their first two children were bap. in Walt. He and his wife were ad. to the ch. in Lex. Sept. 26, 1736.

12-34 †*Benjamin*, b. Feb. 5, 1727; d. Oct. 27, 1790, aged 64.
35 *Micajah*, b. Feb. 11, 1728.   36 *Eunice*, bap. June 3, 1731.
37 *Israel*, b. June 2, 1732.   38 *Simon*, b. Oct. 15, 1734.
39 *Ebenezer*, b. July 25, 1736; d. young.
40 *Nathaniel*, b. Oct. 5, 1738; d. Dec. 17, 1738.
41 *Ebenezer*, b. May 23, 1740.   42 *Abraham*, b. Aug. 24, 1742.
43 *Solomon*, b. April 6, 1744.
44 *Martha*, b. Nov. 2, 1746; d. May 7, 1747.
45 *Mary*, b. Nov. 25, 1748.

9-29-   Sampson Adams m. Mary ——, and had Anna, b. Nov. 20, 1775. His wife d., and he m. Nov. 11, 1779, Katharine Bacon, of Wo. They had Zedekiah, bap. Oct. 3, 1784. Sampson Adams d. Aug. 26, 1785. She d. April 25, 1829, aged 84. His family record is imperfect. He had a son Thomas in the Revolution.

9-30-   George Adams m. July 18, 1758, Abigail Prentice, of Newton. She d. Jan. 2, 1760, leaving two children; and he m. March 18, 1762, Elizabeth Crosby. He d. Feb. 8, 1814, aged 84 years.

30–46 | *Abigail*, b. Jan. 3, 1759.   47 *Anna*, b. Dec. 24, 1760.
48 | *Elizabeth*, b. Feb. 15, 1763.
49 | *George*, b. Sept. 25, 1764; d. Dec. 10, 1764.
50 | *Samuel*, b. Feb. 12, 1766,   51 *Eunice*, b. Aug. 21, 1767.
52 | *George*, b. Oct. 2, 1769; d. March 31, 1793.
53 | *Rebecca*, b. Dec. 13, 1771; d. Dec. 1772.
54 | *Micah*, b. April 9, 1774.   55 *Phinehas*, b. Oct. 11, 1776.
56 | *Stephen*, b. Dec. 9, 1778.

12–34– | BENJAMIN ADAMS m. —— ——. He d. Oct. 27, 1790. The only record is a baptismal one, which reads as follows: " Oct. 30, 1791, bap. Benjamin Adams, Eliphalet Adams, and Nathaniel Adams, — children of Benjamin Adams, deceased."

There have been other Adamses in town: Samuel Adams, b. in West Camb. Sept. 28, 1790; m. May 22, 1822, Ann Whittemore. He came to Lex. 1827. He d. Sept. 16, 1866; she d. May, 1862. They had four children: Annas, b. June 5, 1823; m. April 2, 1867, John Beals; W. Frank, b. April 16, 1829; m. Emma C. Balles, of N. Jersey; Robinson, b. Nov. 24, 1832; went to N. Y.: d. 1866; Georgia, b. June 6, 1839; m. May 10, 1857, Albert Griffith, of W. Camb. She d. May, 1859.

ALLEN OR ALLINE.

In 1783, on the 24th of March, Ezekiel Allen, of Lex., and Sarah Abbot, of Line., were united in marriage. Ezekiel Allen was taxed in Lex. from 1778 to 1783, when his name disappears. Phinehas Allen was taxed in town as a resident in 1783. Ezekiel Allen, or Alline, as the name is sometimes spelt, was in the first eight months' service of the Revolution from Lex. in 1775.

1 | GALEN ALLEN, b. Aug. 19, 1802, Acworth, N. H. Was a son of Galen Allen, formerly of Bridgewater, Mass. He came to Lex. a single man about 1835, and m. April 4, 1839, Lavinia Munroe, dau. of John Munroe, b. Oct. 16, 1823. He d. June 29, 1864, and she d. April 22, 1865. He filled the office of selectman for several years.

1– 2 | *Harriet A.*, b. Jan. 7, 1840; m. April 17, 1856, John D. Bacon; and d. March 22, 1865.
3 | *Annette A.*, b. June 8, 1842; m. March 23, 1862, Abraham B. Smith.
4 | *John G.*, b. Jan. 31, 1845.   5 *Lavinia M.*, b. July 14, 1848.
6 | *Jonas M.*, b. Jan. 22, 1854.

THE ANGIER FAMILY.

1 | JOHN ANGIER, of Malden, m. March 2, 1794, Mary Simonds, of Lex., dau. of John and Mary (Tufts) Simonds. He must have established himself in town immediately after his marriage, for his name appears soon after upon the tax bills. He resided on Burlington Street, near what was called Bull Hill Meadow.

1– 2 | *John*, b. March, 1794. He was in the war of 1812 and in the Mexican war; went to Wis.
3 | *Daniel*, b. Aug. 24, 1796; m. June 15, 1823, Sally Davis, of Con. Chil.: Marshall, b. Oct. 26, 1823; Charles D., b. Jan. 26, 1825; Rufus H., b. July 8, 1828; Sarah L. H., b. Aug. 31, 1830; Har-

riet M., b. Aug. 5, 1832; Eustis, b. Sept. 16, 1834; M. W., b.
Oct. 3, 1838; Cyrus L., b. May 3, 1845.

4 *Abigail*, b. Feb. 11, 1798; m. Nov. 3, 1821, Samuel C. Simonds, of
Burlington.

5 *Amos*, b. Dec. 27, 1802; m. Nov. 3, 1828, Esther R. Winn, of
Salem, dau. of Benjamin and Susan (Estabrook) Winn, formerly
of Bur. Chil.: Amos M., b. Feb. 28, 1831; m. May 31, 1857,
Sarah F. Blaisdell, of Charlestown; Lucius B., b. May 14, 1833.
He served in Mass. Vols. in the late rebellion; Louisa, b. Sept.
27, 1835; Henry A., b. Apr. 30, 1838. He was in the first three
months' vols., was wounded and taken prisoner at the first Bull
Run battle, and confined at Richmond. He is married, and resides
at Somerville; Everett M., b. Dec. 1841.

ARMS.—RICHARD ARMS, sometimes spelled Orms, was ad. to the
ch. in Lex. Apr. 10, 1709. He m. Oct. 28, 1714, Sarah Carley, of
Lex. No record of children. Rev Mr. Hancock made the following
entry in the ch. record, Mar. 24, 1752: " Baptized Sarah Arms at her
house, she being above eighty years old, and confined; I preached
there at the same time." She d. July 8, 1760, aged 88. He d. Apr.
26, 1736. He was constable in 1728, and committee to provide for
the schools in 1733, and subsequently. He was a shoemaker by
trade, and resided on the hill west of the residence of the late Col.
Merriam. The names of Arms and Carley have long since become
extinct in Lex.

THE BABCOCK FAMILY.

LEONARD GARDNER BABCOCK, b. May 28, 1841; m. Dec. 25,
1864, Frances C. Chalmers, of Galesburg, Ill. He is son of Dr.
Aaron G. and Anna (Blashfield) Babcock, of Princeton, Mass., who
was a descendant of Malachi Babcock, of Sherburn. At the breaking out of the Rebellion, being at St. Louis, he entered the 11th Ill.
Reg. for three years. He was in several battles, and at Fort Donel-
son received six wounds, several of them very severe. He came to
Lex. where he had relatives, in May, 1866. In Apr. 1867, he was
appointed Postmaster. He has one child, Frederick G., b. Nov. 1,
1865.

THE BACON FAMILY.

1 NATHANIEL BACON and his wife Abigail were in Lex. in 1729,
when we find the birth of one of their children. He d. Oct. 19,
1773, aged 74. His wife survived him many years. The record of
their family is meagre.

1- 2 *Abigail*, b. Sept. 20, 1729.
3 *Jacob*, b. Mar. 14, 1738; m. Feb. 13, 1776, Katharine Davis, Bed.
4 *Oliver*, b. Ap. 14, 1740; m. Dec. 6, 1770, Sarah Reed.
5 *Ruth*, b. June 23, 1746; m. Apr. 30, 1771, James Gleason.
Jacob and Oliver must have left town about the time of their marriages, as their names disappear from the tax bills the years following.

There has recently been another family of this name in town—
John D. Bacon, son of George, of Bil. b. Sept. 14, 1832, came to
Lex. 1854, and m. Apr. 17, 1856, Harriet A. Allen, dau. of Galen
Allen. She died Mar. 22, 1865, and he m. June 20, 1867, Hattie E.

Grant, of Acworth, N. H. He had Carrie A., b. May 14, 1857; George H. b. Dec. 30, 1860, d. Mar. 1861; Annette A., b. Apr. 6, 1862, d. May, 1865.

THE BAILY FAMILY.

1 JAMES BAILY, b. in Greenfield, N. H. Jan. 6, 1792; m. Sept. 27, 1818, Abigail Simonds, dau. of David, of Lex. He died Sept. 9, 1865. She d. Aug. 9, 1853.

1- 2 *Lydia Ann*, b. Feb. 17, 1820; m. Apr. 30, 1837, Charles Hutchinson. They have three children, Abigail Angeline, m. 1862, Henry Capell; Lydia Ann Addia, m. 1867, R. L. Woodbury; Elvira Augusta, m. 1864, Charles A. Grover.

3 *James B.*, b. Oct. 23, 1822, m. Nov. 17, 1855, Rachel E. Marston.

4 *Frederick P.*, b. June 29, 1824; m. Nov. 1851, Dorcas Ann Skelton.

5 *Chellus B.*, b. Oct. 26, 1828; m. Apr. 19, 1855, Ellen E. Hartwell, of Lin. They have George H., Nellie L., and Estella A.

6 *Edward B.*, b. June 28, 1833; m. June 28, 1860, Sophia L. Gould, of Lex. dau. of Thomas Gould.

7 *Nathaniel*, b. Feb. 29, 1836.

THE BATE FAMILY.

1 BENJAMIN BATE and his wife Mary were 'ad. to the ch. in Lex. Oct. 31, 1703, " by a letter of dismission from the church of Christ at Hingham." May 27, 1716, Benjamin Bate confessed to the ch. that " through the temptations of the Devill and his own corrupt heart, he had been led into many sins, particularly Sabbath breaking, which is a leading sin to other hainous sins; therefore, being easily taken by the Devill at his will, fell into the sin of killing John Lawrence's cow yᵉ night before yᵉ last, leaving yᵉ ax sticking in its body."—A solemn warning surely to resist the ' Devill,' and avoid Sabbath breaking.

1- 2 *Solomon*, bap. Dec. 10, 1702.   3 *Lydia*, d. Oct. 24, 1703.

4 *John*, bap. Oct. 7, 1705; d. young. 5 *Benjamin*, bap. Jan. 17, 1716.

6 *John*, bap. Dec. 3, 1717.

7 *Mary*, bap. July 20, 1719, d. 1723. 8 *Joseph*, bap. July 2, 1721.

8 *Charity*, bap. Jan. 20, 1722; d. Jan. 29, 1723.

THE BARRETT FAMILY.

HUMPHREY BARRETT came from Eng. and settled in Con. 1640. He d. 1662, and his wife d. 1663. They had 4 sons, one of whom, Thomas, was drowned in Con. River. *Oliver* Barrett, a *grandson* of the emigrant, m. Oct. 24, 1754, Anna Fiske, dau. of Ebenezer and Grace (Harrington) Fiske, of Lex. and settled in Chelmsford. About 1770, he moved to Westford, and afterwards entered the army, and d. at Albany, leaving 7 children. One of their sons, viz. Benjamin Barrett, b. Jan. 16, 1770, m. Betsey Gerrish, dau. of Samuel Gerrish, of Westminster. He d. in Springfield, N. Y., to which place he had removed, Oct. 21, 1844. He had 11 children, of whom 4 received a collegiate education, and 3 of them were clergymen. The late Samuel Barrett, D. D., of Boston, was one of them.

Rev. FISKE BARRETT, son of Benjamin, was b. in Springfield, N. Y., Mar. 1, 1816; grad. at Union College, 1842. After being

Principal of Hallowell Academy, Me., he entered the ministry, and was settled in Lex. Sept. 1849. In 1852, he was dismissed at his own request, and has subsequently been settled in Scituate and Stoneham. He m. June 8, 1853, Ann E. T. Henchman, dau. of David Henchman, of Boston. She is not living.

THE BEALS FAMILY.

JOHN BEALS was b. in Salem, Jan. 20, 1801, where his father resided. His mother was a Bacon from Bedford. He came early to Lex. to reside with his grandmother Bacon, and in 1825 m. Mary S. Brown, dau. of John D. Brown. She d. Apr. 4, 1865, and he m. Apr. 2, 1867, Eleanor Adams, dau. of Samuel Adams. He had one child, George, b. May 13, 1827; d. Mar. 16, 1828.

THE BENNETT FAMILY.

1   MOSES BENNETT, of Groton, m. Aug. 11, 1719, Anna Blanchard. They had the following children.

1- 2	*Abigail*, b. Aug. 31, 1720.	3	*Stephen*, b. Oct. 16, 1723.
4	*Moses*, b. Aug. 15, 1726.	5	*David*, b. May 15, 1729.
6	*Eunice*, b. Mar. 27, 1731.	7	*Jonathan*, b May 17, 1733.
8	†*James*, b. Dec. 5, 1736.	9	*Anna*, b. Nov. 8, 1739.

1-8-   JAMES BENNETT, of Groton, m. —— ——, and had 7 children. His wife d. and he m. Dec. 14, 1784, Olive Shattuck, dau. of John and Elizabeth Shattuck; she was b. Jan. 27, 1753, and hence was 17 years younger than her husband. He settled in the northwest corner of Ashby, near Watatick Mountain, adjoining the bounds of Ashburnham and New Ipswich. He d. Aug. 9, 1808, aged 71 years, 4 mo. and 4 days. He was in the army of the Revolution. In 1775, he was stationed at Lechmere's Point, East Cambridge, and was in the battle of Bunker Hill; he was in other battles, and had the command of a company. His wid. m. Jan. 25, 1816, Nehemiah Hardy, of Hollis, N. H. Capt. Bennett had by his 2d wife the following children.

8-10   *Eliab*, b. Jan. 13, 1789; d. in Pepperell of a fever, May 4, 1815, on the day appointed for his marriage, aged 26.
11   †*James Harvey*, b. Nov. 22, 1791; m. Winifred Knowles.
12   *Sarah*, b. Aug. 7, 1795; m. in Boston, 1816, Williams Wright, b. in Pepperell, Apr. 6, 1788. He had been a merchant in Boston. They had six children.

8-11-   JAMES H. BENNETT m. Oct. 22, 1820, Winifred Knowles, b. in Truro, June 21, 1800. He commenced business in Boston in 1822, and continued his residence there till 1845, when he came to Lex. and soon after closed his business in the city. He was in the West India goods trade. After he closed his business in Boston, he opened a store in Lex. where he traded several years.

11-13   *James Knowles*, b. July 20, 1821; m. Martha Stimpson, Jan. 2, 1853.
14   *Mary Winifred*, b. Apr. 22, 1823; m. Apr. 26, 1843, Peter McIntire, a merchant in Boston.
15   *Charles Hawes*, b. Mar. 23, 1836; m. Mar. 27, 1862, M. E. Kendall. He d. July 8, 1864. He was in trade in Lexington.

THE BLANCHARD FAMILY.

GEORGE BLANCHARD was early in Lex. and m. about 1707, Sarah Munroe, dau. of the original emigrant. They were ad. to the ch. Jan. 18, 1708, when their first child was bap. There seem to have been others of the same name, as Lydia, Nathaniel, Mary, and William were bap. about the same time. They may have resided in Wo.— At a later day, *Elhanan Blanchard* and his wife Betsey E., had Betsey, b. Sept. 2, 1809; Mary Ann, b. Nov. 8, 1811; John W., b. Dec. 2, 1813; Alanson, b. June 2, 1816; James P., b. Dec. 13, 1821, d. young; James P., b. Dec. 20, 1824; George W., b. Feb. 27, 1828.

THE BLASDEL FAMILY.

The Lex. records giving no information of the family, our record is necessarily brief and imperfect. ABNER BLASDEL, of Portsmouth, N. H., m. Judith Powers, and had five children. She is now residing in Lex. in her 78th year, with her dau. Sarah Adelaide, who was b. Dec. 27, 1825, and m. Feb. 7, 1847, George N. Dexter. They have been in Lex. several years.

JOHN C. BLASDEL, the oldest son of Abner and Judith, was b. 1809, and m. Joanna Chase Perkins, of Gardiner, Me. They resided in Boston several years, when he moved to Lex. about 1851. He purchased the mansion house, built by Capt. Daniel Chandler, which he has adorned and improved. He was chosen in Nov., 1867, to represent the District in the Legislature. They have no children.

There is another family of the same name, viz. EBENEZER BLASDEL, but the absence of a record compels us to omit an account of them.

THE BLINN FAMILY.

JAMES BLINN m. a Miss Gilmore, of Woolwich, Me., by whom he had a family of ten children. *James*, one of his sons, m. Abigail De Lans, of Plymouth, Mass. They had a large family of children.

1   RICHARD D. BLINN, one of their sons, m. Harriet Gragg. They resided in Wiscasset, Me. He followed the sea, and was master of a vessel.

1- 2   { †*Richard D.*, b. July 31, 1832, m. Charlotte Piper.
   3   } *William H.*, b. July 31, 1832.
   4   *John F.*, b. July 10, 1834.

1-2-   RICHARD D. BLINN, m. Apr. 26, 1855, Charlotte Piper, of Bed. He came to Lex. from Bed. in 1852, and went upon the railroad as brakeman or baggage master. In about two years he was promoted to the place of conductor. He has been for the last two or three years president of the road.

2- 5   *Harriet E.*, b. Feb. 20, 1857.
   6   *Helen Josephine*, b. Apr. 4, 1861.

THE BLODGETT FAMILY.

1   THOMAS BLODGETT, the ancestor of the greater part of the Lex. Blodgetts, was from Wo. He was a son of Samuel Blodgett, and was b. 1660. He m. Nov. 11, 1684, Rebecca Tidd, dau. of John and Rebecca Tidd, then of Wo., but afterwards of Lex. A portion of their children were b. in Wo. and the remainder in Lex. Mr. Blodgett was a subscriber to the meeting house in the Precinct in 1692, but does not appear to have been a taxable inhabitant till 1694. He and his wife were ad. to the ch. in Lex. Mar. 5, 1699, by a letter of dismission from the Wo. ch. Mr. Blodgett, or Capt. Blodgett as he is generally designated, became a useful and prominent man in the town. He was an assessor in 1710, and after the town was incorporated, he filled almost every place of honor and trust. In 1714, he was chosen one of the selectmen — an office to which he was often re-elected. He also represented the town in the General Court. He resided on Adams street, near its intersection with North street. He d. Sept. 29, 1740, aged 80. She d. July 3, 1716.

1- 2 †*Thomas*, b. in Wo. Aug. 5, 1686; m. Mary ———.
   3 *Rebecca*, b. in Wo. June 5, 1689.
   4 †*Joseph*, b. ———; m. Nov. 5, 1719, Sarah Stone, of Con.
   5 *Abigail*, bap. in Lex. Nov. 13, 1698.
   6 †*Samuel*, bap. in Lex. June 17, 1702; m. Mary Russell.

1-2-   THOMAS BLODGETT, m. Mary ———. She was ad. to the ch. in Lex. Feb. 18, 1728, with 22 others. She died about 1753. He d. Mar. 1, 1771. He resided with or near his father.

2- 7 *Rebecca*, b. Feb. 15, 1716.
   8 †*Thomas*, b. Apr. 29, 1717; m. Charity Raymond.
   9 *Ebenezer*, b. Mar. 4, 1721. He was in the French war, 1760.
  10 †*Amos*, b. July 1, 1723.
  11 †*Phinehas*, b. Mar. 8, 1726; m. Joanna Locke.
  12 †*Jonathan*, b. June 28, 1729.

1-4-   JOSEPH BLODGETT, m. Nov. 5, 1719, Sarah Stone, of Con. She was ad. to the ch. June 9, 1728. He d. Jan. 7, 1731.

4-13 *Joseph*, b. Ap. 7, 1721.   14 *Sarah*, b. Nov. 12, 1722.
  15 *Anna*, b. Ap. 10, 1724.   16 *Abigail*, b. July 24, 1726.
  17 *Ruth*, bap. Mar. 10, 1728.

1-6-   SAMUEL BLODGETT, m. June 26, 1726, Mary Russell, dau. of James and Mary Russell, b. Jan. 1, 1706. He d. Jan. 23, 1773, aged 71.

6-18 *Samuel*, b. Ap. 30, 1727.
  19 †*Simeon*, b. June 5, 1730; m. Susan Skilton.
  20 *Joseph*, b. Feb. 10, 1732; d. Jan. 7, 1733.
  21 *Mary*, b. June 20, 1733; m. Jonathan Perry.
  22 *Ruth*, b. Aug. 29, 1735; m. Oct. 25, 1759, Henry Harrington.
  23 †*Josiah*, b. Dec. 28, 1737; m. Ap. 24, 1760, Jane Thorn.
  24 †*Timothy*, b. Aug. 7, 1740; m. Millicent ———
  25 †*Isaac*, b. Feb. 1, 1744; m. Ap. 20, 1769, Mary Locke.

2-8-   THOMAS BLODGETT, m. Charity Raymond, dau. of Jonathan and Charity, b. Sept. 15, 1724. He was in the French and Indian War in the campaign of 1760, under Capt. Clapham. She d. Jan. 28, 1771, and he m. again in 1773. He d. Feb. 4, 1800, aged 83.

8–26 | *Sarah*, b. Dec. 22, 1745; m. July 24, 1766, Levi Parker, Billerica.
27 | *Mary*, b. Ap. 5, 1747.
28 | ‡*Nathan*, b. July 7, 1749; m. Jan. 3, 1791, Deborah Robbins.
29 | *William*, b. Ap. 25, 1751; d. July 13, 1773.
30 | *Abijah*, b. Dec. 16, 1762.   31 *Ruth*, b. Dec. 23, 1764.
32 | *Aaron*, b. Dec. 2, 1769; m. May 1, 1798, Patty Lane. They had a child b and d. 1799.

2–10– | AMOS BLODGETT, m. Margaret ———.

10–33 | *Rebecca*, b. Jan. 31, 1752.   34 *Bette*, b. June 17, 1754.
35 | *Amos*, b. Aug. 25, 1756.   36 *Sally*, b. Dec. 14, 1758.
37 | *Nanne*, b. Dec. 25, 1760.
38 | *James*, b. June 5, 1763; m. Sept. 1, 1786, Ruth Fowle, of Wo.

2–11– | PHINEHAS BLODGETT, m. Oct. 10, 1753, Joanna Locke. He was one of the patriotic band which marched, 1757, to the relief of Fort William-Henry.

11–39 | *Benjamin*, b. Aug. 13, 1754.   40 *David*, b. Dec. 26, 1756.
41 | *Joseph*, b. June 10, 1758.   42 *Ebenezer*, b. Ap. 28, 1761.

2–12– | JONATHAN BLODGETT, m. ———.

12–43 | *Molly*, bap. Oct. 5, 1760.   44 *Thaddeus*, bap. June 26, 1763.

6–19– | SIMEON BLODGETT, m. Dec. 24, 1761, Susan Skilton, dau. of Thomas and Ruth Skilton, of Wo., b. July 24, 1737. They were ad. to the ch. Jan. 2, 1763.

19–45 | *Simeon*, b. Oct. 4, 1762.
46 | *Joseph*, b. May 22, 1764; m. Abigail Munroe, July 8, 1788.
47 | *Susanna*, b. Sept. 28, 1765.   48 *Lydia*, bap. June 12, 1768.
49 | *Ruth*, bap. Aug. 25, 1771.   50 *Sarah*, bap. Oct. 16, 1774.

6–23– | JOSIAH BLODGETT, m. Ap. 24, 1760, Jane Thorn. They o. c. Ap. 12, 1761. He was one of the brave men who repaired to Camb. on the 17th of June, 1775, under Capt. Parker. He had been in the French war.

23–51 | *Azubah*, b. Feb. 3, 1761.   52 *Salmon*, b. Ap. 21, 1766.

6–24– | TIMOTHY BLODGETT, m. Millicent ———. They were ad. to the ch. Feb. 3, 1767.

24–53 | *Timothy*, bap. Ap. 5, 1767.   54 *Thaddeus*, bap. June 12, 1768.
55 | *Levi*, bap. Aug. 5, 1770.   56 *Lucy*, bap. Ap. 4, 1773.

6–25– | ISAAC BLODGETT, m. Ap. 20, 1769, Mary Locke. He d. July, 1830, aged 89. He was a soldier in Capt. Parker's company on the 19th of April, 1775.

25–57 | *Polly*, b. July 24, 1769.   58 *Lucinda*, b. Mar. 8, 1772..
59 | *Sarah*, b. Nov. 27, 1775.
60 | *Isaac*, b. Nov. 3, 1777; d. Nov. 28, 1815.
61 | *Simeon*, b. June 21, 1780.
62 | *Samuel*, b. Aug. 5, 1783; d. May 25, 1820, aged 37.
63 | *Patty*, b. June 5, 1786; d. probably May 14, 1805.

8-28- NATHAN BLODGETT, m. —— Severs, by whom he had one child. She d. Nov. 30, 1790, and he m. Jan. 31, 1791, Deborah Robbins. He died Feb. 6, 1825.

28-64 *Nathan*, b. before 1790; m. Ap. 25, 1805, Susanna Frost, Camb.
65 *Billy*, b. Dec. 8, 1791.
66 *Lydia*, b. Ap. 27, 1793; m. Samuel Downing.
67 *John*, b. Oct. 7, 1794; went West and d.
68 *Aaron*, b. Jan. 8, 1796; went West and d.
69 †*Peter*, b. Mar. 22, 1799; m. Tryphena Caldwell.
70 *Sarah C.*, b. Dec. 8, 1800; m. Billings Smith, Nov. 19, 1820.
71 *Sullivan*, b. Mar. 29, 1806.
72 *Stephen R.*, b. Dec. 24, 1811; d. Ap. 3, 1815.

28-69- PETER BLODGETT, m. Dec. 14, 1823, Tryphena Caldwell, dau. of Thomas and Anna (Merriam) Caldwell, of Woburn, who removed to Lex. about 1803. Peter Blodgett d. May 8, 1856, aged 57.

69-73 *John*, b. Ap. 4, 1825; d. Aug. 24, 1825.
74 *Tryphena*, b. Sept. 4, 1827, d. Nov. 11, 1836.
75 *Sarah*, b. Dec. 30, 1829; m. Samuel Barnes, and r. in Manchester, N. H.
76 *John*, b. Feb. 18, 1832; m. Mar. 2, 1856, Almira Meserve, of Charlestown.   77 *Peter*, b. June 25, 1834.

There has been another family of Blodgetts in Lex. not traceable on our records, though undoubtedly of the same parent stock with the family above.

1 JAMES BLODGETT, m. Ruth Hadley. He d. Mar. 23, 1836, aged 73. She d. June 23, 1818, aged 59.
There being no record of the family, the children may not be arranged in the order of their birth.

1- 2 †*James*, who m. Rhoda Winn, of Bed.
3 *Nancy*, m. Amos Stearns.   4 *Lucy*, m. Benj. M. Nevers.
5 *Charles*, m. Mary Ann Dizer; and Eliza Smith, Mar. 29, 1831.
6 *Amos*, m. and was drowned at Neponset.
7 *Darius*, m. Ann Tileston, went West and d.
8 *Clarissa*, m. Josiah Johnson, of Wo. He d. and she m. Mar. 3, 1818, Nath'l Bryant, of Boston. They are now residing in Lex.
9 *Ruth*, m. Wm. Tileston. They moved to the West.

1-2- JAMES BLODGETT, m. Rhoda Winn, of Bed. He d. Jan. 3, 1839. She d. Aug. 6, 1854. They had 10 children.

2-10 *Mary Ann*, b. Aug. 9, 1809; m. Elias Dupee, June 18, 1830.
11 *Clarissa*, b. Feb. 17, 1811; m. Oct. 11, 1835, Joseph Butterfield, Bed.
12 *Rhoda*, b. May 7, 1813; m. May 31, 1835, Amos Locke.
13 *Elizabeth*, b. Ap. 30, 1815; m. Ap. 4, 1837, Solomon Estabrook.
14 *James*, b. Mar. 2, 1816; m. Sarah Jackson, res. E. Cam.
15 *Almira*, b. Mar. 30, 1821; m. Sidney Butters.
16 †*Charles*, b. Ap. 16, 1818; m. Maria Winn, of Salem.
17 *Elias*, b. Oct. 13, 1822; m. Eliza Brown, r. E. Camb.
18 *Susan*, b. May 8, 1824; m. Amos Richardson, of Med.
19 *Lucy*, b. July 8, 1829.

2-16-   CHARLES BLODGETT, m. Maria Winn, of Salem.

16-20 *Charles S.*, b. Sept. 10, 1848.   21 *Walter*, b. Sept. 19, 1850.
   22 *Emily M.*, b. Dec. 10, 1854.

THE BOND FAMILY.

This family came originally from Wat., and are the descendants of William Bond, who came to this country about 1630. He settled in Wat. where he m. Feb. 7, 1649, Sarah Briscoe, by whom he had nine children. Thomas, their third son, b. Dec. 22, 1654; m. Sept. 30, 1680, Sarah Woolson of that town. His 3d son, John, b. July 14, 1695, was by calling a tailor. He m. Sarah Mason, by whom he had six children. She dying, he m. Ruhamah Whittemore, wid. of Benjamin Whittemore, of Con. His first three children were born in Wat., the others in Lex., to which he had removed. In 1726, he bought two houses and lands, and a wood lot in Lex. for £480.

1   JOHN BOND appears to have been the first of the name within our borders.

1- 2 †*Joshua*, b. Nov. 24, 1720; d. Feb. 18, 1790, aged 70.
   3 *Ezekiel*, b. June 19, 1722; d. young.
   4 *Sarah*, b. Sept. 22, 1723; d. 1731.
   5 *Lovice*, bap. in Lex. Mar. 26, 1727.
   6 *Elizabeth*, bap. in Lex. Feb. 23, 1729; d. June 30, 1759.
   7 *Mary*, bap. in Lex. Dec 5, 1731; d. 1733.
   8 *Lucy*, b. ——.
   9 *Ruhamah*, b. ——; d. July 25, 1746.

1-2-   JOSHUA BOND, m Millicent Russell, dau. of Philip and Sarah Russell, who was b. Dec. 29, 1720. He was a tailor by trade. He d. Feb. 18, 1790, and she d. Ap. 28, 1795, aged 75. There seems to have been a little opposition, or at least distrust, on the part of her father, who, though he gave her the usual outfit of that day, was careful to loan the articles to her, so that he could reclaim them in case of necessity.

2-10 *Sarah*, bap. Ap. 8, 1744.
   11 *Joshua*, bap. Oct. 13, 1745. He was a saddle and harness maker, and had his house and shop burned by the British, Ap. 19, 1775. His property destroyed was valued at £190.
   12 *Millicent*, b. July 12, 1747; m. Ap. 24, 1777, Josiah Nelson, of Lin.
   13 *Joseph*, b. Jan. 8, 1749; d. in infancy.
   14 *Mary*, bap. July 27, 1750; d. 1753.
   15 *John*, bap. Ap. 19, 1752; d. Dec. 25, 1753.
   16 *Phebe*, bap. Nov. 30, 1755.   17 *Joanna*, bap. June 15, 1757.
   18 *Mary*, bap. Oct. 7, 1759.   19 *Joseph*, bap. May 13, 1761.
   20 *Abel*, bap. Oct. 19, 1762; d. 1783.

Though this family was quite numerous, consisting of eleven children, by the early death or removal from town of the sons, the name soon disappeared.

THE BOWMAN FAMILY.

1   NATHANIEL BOWMAN, of Watertown, was the progenitor of those of that name who settled at Cambridge Farms. Mr. Bowman was one of the early proprietors of Wat.—his name being on the records in 1636-7. He removed early to Cambridge Farms, and settled on

lands purchased of Edward Goffe, situated in the southeasterly part of the town, near Arlington line. His wife, Anna, probably died first, as no mention is made of her in his will. He d. Jan. 21, 1682. His will bears date Oct. 21, 1679, and was proved Apr. 4, 1682. He gives to his son Francis the farm on which he lived,—Francis to pay Nathaniel £25, and in case he should die without issue, it was to revert to the children of Francis. His real estate was inventoried as follows: House and 10 acres of land, £120; 20 acres of meadow, £50; 70 acres of upland unimproved, £70. His children, as far as known, were as follows:

1- 2 †*Francis*, admitted freeman, 1652.
3 *Mary*, buried Jan. 1, 1638. 4 *Joanna*, buried Nov. 20, 1638.
5 *Dorcas*, buried Feb. 6, 1639, aged 7 days.
6 *Nathaniel*, b. Mar. 6, 1641; probably d. in Lex. 1694; was taxed 1693, but not in 1694.
· 7 *Joanna*, b. Nov. 20, 1642; probably mother of Hannah Turner, mentioned in her father's will as a grandchild.
8 *Dorcas*, m. Benjamin Blackleach, and afterwards m. —— March.

1-2-   Francis Bowman, m. Sep. 26, 1661, Martha Sherman, b. Feb. 21, 1641. He resided at Cambridge Farms, where he d. Dec. 16, 1687, aged 57 years.

2- 9 †*Francis*, b. Sept. 14, 1662; d. Dec. 23, 1744.
10 *John*, b. Feb. 19, 1665.
11 *Martha*, b. Mar. 2, 1667; d. Dec. 1667.
12 †*Nathaniel*, b. Feb. 9, 1669; d. June 30, 1748.
13 †*Joseph*, b. May 18, 1674; d. Apr. 8, 1762.
14 *Anna*, b. Sept. 19, 1676; d. Sept. 26, 1700.
15 *Samuel*, b. Aug. 14, 1679. He resided in Cambridge, where he was Dea. He m. first, Nov. 2, 1700, Rebecca Andrews, who d. Nov. 18, 1713, and he m. second, Deborah ——. He had 14 children.

2-3-   Francis Bowman, m. first, June 26, 1684, Lydia, dau. of Dea. Samuel and Sarah Stone of Camb., second, Ruth, dau. of Rev. Samuel Angier. By a will, dated 1744, he directed his wife Ruth "to take as her own proper estate forever three of my negro servants, viz. Battiss, Philliss, and Pompy, so named. Also I give to my granddaughter, Ruth Bowman, full power at my decease to take my negro boy Domini to be her own forever,—she paying her brother Francis £20 old tenor at the time of receiving Domini." He mentions in his will, wife Ruth, son Isaac, and dau. Mary Morse, Lydia Simonds, and Sarah Russell. Francis Bowman was among the most prominent men in the township, filling from time to time every office in the gift of the people. In 1693 he was on the committee to purchase land for the support of the ministry, and was on the first board of selectmen and assessors under the town organization, to which posts he was frequently re-elected. He also represented the town in the General Court, 1720, '22, '26, '27, '32, '33. He was also one of the Royal Magistrates first appointed in 1720. He appears to have been much respected; for in "seating the meeting house" he was one of the three who were permitted to sit at the table; and his wife was "plaste in ye fore seatt in ye body of seats."

9-16 *Francis*, b. about 1685. 17. *Mary*, b. —; m. —— Morse.
18 *Lydia*, b. ——; m. Jonathan Simonds.
19 †*John*, b. July 14, 1689; m. Mary Stone.
20 *Sarah*, b. ——; m. Phillip Russell.
21 †*Isaac*, b. 1693; d. July 18, 1785.

2-12   NATHANIEL BOWMAN, m. at Camb. Farms, Dec. 16, 1692, Anna Barnard, of Wat. She d. Sept. 15, 1757; and he d. June 30, 1748.

12-22 *Mary*, b. Dec. 22, 1693; m. Samuel Garfield, of Wat.
23 *Anne*, b. Sept. 6, 1696; m. Nathaniel Bright.
24 *Elizabeth*, b. Nov. 13, 1698; d. Feb. 25, 1748, unm.
25 *Abigail*, b. 1700; m. Mar. 22, 1720, Matthew Bridge, of Lex.
26 *Nathaniel*, bap. May 31, 1702; d. Dec. 26, 1723, leaving a wid. and a dau. Mary, b. Dec. 19, 1723, and d. May 24, 1727.
27 *Grace*, bap. Oct. 1, 1704; m. Mar. 10, 1726, Nathaniel Cooledge.
28 *Sarah*, bap. May 25, 1707; m. Feb. 3, 1731, Samuel Stearns.
29 *Jane*, b. ——; m. Jan. 21, 1734, James Brown, of Lex.

2-13-   JOSEPH BOWMAN, m. Phebe ——. She d. Dec. 20, 1757, and he d. Apr. 8, 1762, aged 88. He was one of the leading and influential men of the town, both in municipal and church affairs. He filled the office of town clerk, assessor, and selectman repeatedly. He was on the board of selectmen fifteen years, and a representative six years. He was also a justice of the peace for many years.

13-30 *Joseph*, b. Sept. 16, 1697.
31 *Hannah*, b. Nov. 11, 1699; m. Mar. 26, 1719, Joseph Estabrook.
32 *James*, b. Sept. 11, 1701.
33 *Jonathan*, b. Feb. 22, 1703; grad. H. C. 1724; united with the ch. at Lex. 1726; was ordained at Dorchester, Nov. 5, 1729; and d. May 30, 1775.
34 *Francis*, b. June 10, 1705; d. 1750, unm.
35 *Edmund*, b. Mar. 5, 1709; grad. at H. C. 1728; established himself as a merchant at Portsmouth, N. H.
36 †*Thaddeus*, b. Sept. 2, 1712; m. Dec. 2, 1736, Sarah Loring.
37 ‡*William*, b. Sept. 2, 1715; m. May 5, 1753, Mary Reed.
38 *Martha*, b. Sept. 8, 1718; m. Apr. 27, 1738, Samuel Bridge.

9-19-   JOHN BOWMAN m. Mary Stone. They were ad. to Lex. ch. June 22, 1718. He d. Apr. 30, 1726, and she d. June 28, 1757.

19-39 †*John*, b. Dec. 5, 1713; m. Feb. 19, 1736, Susanna Cooledge.
40 †*Jonas*, b. Feb. 3, 1717; m. Abigail Russell.
41 *Francis*, b. Apr. 2, 1718; m. June 24, 1756, Sarah Simonds. He resided in Bedford.
42 *Ebenezer*, b. Apr. 2, 1720; m. and moved to W. Camb., where they had Abigail, bap. in Lex. May 27, 1750, and a son Ebenezer, bap. at West Camb. 1752.
43 *Ruth*, b. Dec. 23, 1723; ad. to the ch. Oct. 18, 1741.

9-21-   ISAAC BOWMAN m. Mar. 28, 1716, Elizabeth Harrington. She d. June 8, 1741, and he m. Sarah Munroe, wid. of William Munroe. Isaac Bowman and his wife Elizabeth united with the ch. Feb. 18, 1728. He d. July 18, 1785, in the 92d year of his age. His wife Sarah d. a few months before him, viz. Apr. 13, 1785. He filled every office in town, from field-driver to representative. He was a magistrate for many years.

21-44 *Elizabeth*, b. July 25, 1717; m. —— Sutton, of Boston.
45 ‡*Francis*, b. Nov. 26, 1752; m. Susanna Chamberlain.

13-36-   THADDEUS BOWMAN m. Dec. 2, 1736, Sarah Loring, b. about 1715, dau. of Dea. Joseph and Lydia Loring. She d. Dec. 23, 1747. He m. Feb. 8, 1753, Sybil Woolson, widow of Isaac Woolson, of

Weston. Thaddeus and Sarah united with the ch. Dec. 6, 1741. He enjoyed the confidence of his townsmen, and was often called to fill offices of honor and trust. He was also captain of a company.

36–46 | *Sarah*, b. Oct. 2, 1737; d. Oct. 3, 1742.

47 | *Edmund*, b. August 4, 1739; m May 8, 1760, Esther Hoar, of Linc. She d. July 22, 1780, and he m. Eunice Mead, of Stow.

48 | *Joseph*, b. Feb. 13, 1741; m. Nov. 22, 1764, Catharine, dau. of William and Sarah (Mason) Munroe. He soon after removed to New Braintree. He was an ensign of a company of fifty men from that small town, who marched to Boston on the report of the attack upon the company at Lex. on the 19th of April. He soon after joined the army, and commanded a battalion at the Battle of Bennington, and the other battles which resulted in the capture of Burgoyne. Maj. Bowman was not only a leading man in the town of New Braintree, but his family uniting the blood of the Bowmans and Munroes of Lex. became one of the most influential in that part of Worcester County. His daughters intermarried with the Delanos, Woods, Fields, &c., in New Braintree and the neighboring towns. His son Joseph, b. Sept. 10, 1771, represented the town of New Braintree in the General Court fourteen years, between 1807 and 1839. He was a Senator from the County of Worcester in 1828 and 1829, and was a member of the Governor's Council in 1832, '33, and '34. He was also President of the Hampshire Manufacturer's Bank, chosen annually for twenty-one consecutive years. Few men retained the confidence of the public as long as did Hon. Joseph Bowman.

Isaac Bowman, another son of Maj. Joseph Bowman, moved to Wilkesbarre, Penn., about 1795, where he soon acquired the confidence of the people, was chosen General, and promoted to other offices of power and trust.

49 | *Thaddeus*, b. Feb. 10, 1743; m. Nov. 7, 1764, Elizabeth Lawrence, b. Dec. 13, 1741, dau. of Jonathan and Elizabeth (Swain) Lawrence. He was a member of Capt. Parker's company in 1775, and was the messenger who brought the first reliable intelligence of the near and rapid approach of the British upon Lex. on the morning of the 19th of April, 1775. On the year following, Thaddeus and his wife Elizabeth were dismissed from the Lex. ch. to that of Winchendon, to which place they had removed.

50 | *Solomon*, b. Feb. 10, 1743, a twin of Thaddeus; d. June 6, 1744.

51 | *Solomon*, b. June 2, 1745. He was a Lieutenant in the 25th Regiment of the army of 1775, was in the battle of Bunker Hill, and was killed at the battle of Monmouth, in 1778.

52 | *Joshua*, b. Jan. 22, 1747. He went to Wilkesbarre, Penn., and from thence to Ohio, where his descendants are still living.

53 | *Samuel*, b. Dec. 2, 1753. (Samuel and the following children were by Thaddeus's second wife.) Samuel Bowman enlisted at the commencement of the Revolution, and became a captain in the Continental line, and served to the close of the war. It is said that he was with Maj. Andre the night before his execution, and commanded the guard which conducted him to the gallows. He m. in Philadelphia, Nov. 3, 1784, Eleanor Ledlie, whose parents were from Ireland. About 1789, he moved to Wilkesbarre, Penn., where his wife had a large estate, and where he had a family of children, some of whom have become quite distinguished.

54 | *Sarah*, b. July 4, 1755.

55 | *Ebenezer*, b. July 31, 1757; grad. H. C. 1782; studied law, and established himself at Wilkesbarre, Penn.

56 | *Gideon*, b. Sept. 30, 1759; d. Oct. 20, same year.

57 | *Lucy*, b. Jan. 21, 1761; m. in Walt., June 17, 1790, Rev. Richard
R. Elliott, of that town, as his second wife.

58 | *Sybil*, b. Aug. 2, 1764; d. Dec. 2, 1765.

13-37- | WILLIAM BOWMAN m. May 5, 1753, Mary Reed, of Lex. Previous to his marriage he resided in Narraganset No. 2, (now Westminster,) in which settlement his father had an interest. He was dismissed from the ch. of Lex. and recommended to that of Narraganset, Sept. 26, 1742. We find in a pamphlet history of Westminster, published in 1832, the following well authenticated anecdote of William Bowman.*

"In 1748, William Bowman, from Lexington, who had been in the township five or six years, and who garrisoned, if not resided, with Capt. Hoar, was mowing one day in the field, some distance from Hoar's fort, when he discovered some Indians in the adjacent woods. They had placed themselves in such a position as to cut him off from his fort; and no doubt felt sure of their victim. Bowman very adroitly concealed his agitation, and, as though he had made no discovery, kept at work, but moving at the same time in a direction from the fort and his insidious foe, until he had gained the declivity of a hill, when he dropped his scythe, and made for Grave's fort in another part of the town about two miles distant, with such speed as to elude the grasp of his fleet-footed pursuers. Bowman soon after this occurrence left the place, having no desire, it would seem, to continue his band with adversaries trained to every art of guile, and every method of cruelty and torture."

After leaving Westminster, he returned to Lexington, and married as before stated. He at last moved to West Cambridge. He d. Oct. 12, 1793, aged 78 years. His wife d. Oct. 27, 1802, aged 76.

37-59 | *Mary*, b. Feb. 28, 1754; m. June 27, 1775, Joel Viles.
60 | *Hannah*, bap. Jan. 4, 1756; m. James Walker, of Burlington.
61 | *Phebe*, bap. June 19, 1757; m. Feb. 22, 1781, Jonathan Bridge.
62 | *Martha*, bap. Nov. 19, 1758; m. May 8, 1788, Abraham Smith.
63 | *Betty*, bap. Oct. 28, 1759; m. William Bridge, of Walt.
64 | *Lydia*, bap. Dec. 14, 1766; m. John Davis, of Methuen.

19-39- | JOHN BOWMAN m. Feb. 19, 1737, Susanna Cooledge, dau. of Capt. Joseph and Elizabeth (Bond) Cooledge of Wat. They owned the covenant in Lex. Dec. 4, 1737. He d. Apr. 21, 1760.
The Records do not enable us to fill out the following families.

39-65 | *Susanna*, b. Jan. 19, 1738; m. Dec. 16, 1779, Bezaleel Learned.
66 | *Josiah*, b. Mar. 21, 1740.   67 *Mary*, b. Aug. 1, 1742.
68 | *Elizabeth*, b. Nov. 4, 1744.   69 *Ruth*, bap. Oct. 5, 1746.
70 | *Benjamin*, bap. June 5, 1757; d. Feb. 17, 1776.
71 | *John*, bap. July 15, 1759.

19-40- | JONAS BOWMAN m. May 19, 1739, Abigail Russell. June 17, 1739, he owned the covenant.

40-72 | *Jonas*, b. July 19, 1739; m. May 18, 1758, Susanna ——, of Wat., and had Abiathar b. Feb. 18, 1759.
73 | *Abigail*, b. Jan. 19, 1741.   74 *Lydia*, b. Jan. 14, 1743.

21-45- | FRANCIS BOWMAN m. Aug. 11, 1788, Susanna Chamberlain. She d. 1855.

45-75 | *Salle*, b. June 7, 1789; m. June 30, 1808, Wm. Clapp, of Boston.
76 | *Isaac*, b. July 27, 1790.   77 *Francis*, b. Apr. 23, 1792.

---

* See Hudson's History of Westminster.

THE BRADSHAW FAMILY.

The name of Bradshaw is but rarely found on the Lex. records. Those of that name probably came from Camb. or Med. where the Bradshaws were somewhat numerous.

ABRAHAM BRADSHAW, by wife Abigail, had Abigail, b. Feb. 14, 1749; Jonathan, b. July 19, 1751; Susanna, b. Ap. 26, 1759.

THE BRIDGE FAMILY.

The Bridges, who were among the earliest settlers in what now comprises the town of Lexington, were the descendants of Deacon John Bridge of Camb. He came from Essex County, England, in what was called Hooker's Company, and settled in Camb. in 1632. Hooker and a great part of his company, as we have already seen, removed to Conn. and commenced the settlement of Hartford; but Mr. Bridge remained, and connected himself with Mr. Shepherd's church — of which he was for many years a leading member and officer. He was ad. a freeman in 1634. He was an influential and prominent man, not only in the church, but in the town and in the Colony. He filled almost every office of honor and profit within the gift of his fellow citizens. He represented them in the General Court in 1637, '38, '39, and '41, and served them as selectman eleven years from 1635 to 1652. He was also often employed by the General Court to lay out lands, serve on committees, and perform other important duties. He was a large landholder, not only in Camb. but in other parts of the Colony. He was one of the first to whom lands were granted at the "Farms," as this part of Camb. was then called. As early as 1643, he had a lot granted him on Vine Brook in Lex. and this lot was described as bounding upon his other and earlier improved lands.

He had a daughter Sarah, b. Feb. 16, 1649, who probably died in early infancy. His son Thomas d. 1656 The inventory of his estate was dated Dec. 1, 1656, and was returned by his father Jan. 10, 1657. Thomas left a widow, Dorcas, and a daughter of the same name. His wid. m. Jan. 3, 1666, Daniel Champney, of Camb. The will of John Bridge, proved Oct. 3, 1665, mentions his wife Elizabeth, his son Matthew, daughter-in-law Dorcas, and sister Betts. His wife, it is said, had previously been the wife of Roger Bancroft, and of Martin Saunders; and after the decease of Dea. Bridge, she had a fourth husband, Edward Taylor, of Boston. She was living in 1683.

There can be no question but that the Bridges of Lex. may with certainty trace their pedigree to

1 DEA. JOHN BRIDGE, of Cambridge, who d. Apr. 1665.

1-2- MATTHEW BRIDGE, son of John Bridge, was a lad when he came to this country. In 1643, eleven years after he came to the Colony, he was a member of the Ancient and Honorable Artillery Co. About the same time, viz. 1643 or 4, he m. Anna Danforth, dau. of Nicholas Danforth, formerly of Framingham, Suffolk, England. He d. Apr. 28, 1700; and she survived him about four years, and d. Dec. 2, 1704. We have no means of knowing the exact time when Matthew Bridge took up his abode at Cambridge Farms; but as his father owned lands on Vine Brook, within the territory, and these lands were cultivated, so far at least as to cut the grass, as early as 1643, it is probable that he removed to the place soon after. He was in the place at the organization of the Parish in 1692, and had previously subscribed towards the erection of a meeting-house. He was a large landholder; and in the first parish tax in 1693, he stood higher on the list than any other man except Samuel Stone, Sen. William Munroe, Sen. and Benjamin Muzzy. Though quite advanced in life, he was appointed on a committee to wait upon Mr. Hancock, and make the necessary arrangements for his ordination in 1698. As a mark of distinction, he was seated at the table in the meeting-house by the order of the Parish.

2- 3 *John*, b. Mar. 16, 1644.
4 *Anna*, b. ——, m. June 4, 1668, Samuel Livermore of Wat.
5 *Martha*, b. June 19, 1648; d. Jan. 15, 1650.
6 †*Matthew*, b May 5, 1650; d. May 29, 1738, aged 88.
7 *Samuel*, b. Feb. 17, 1654; died Feb. 25, 1692.
8 *Thomas*, b. June 1, 1656; d. Mar. 28, 1673.
9 *Elizabeth*, b. Aug. 17, 1659; m. June 19, 1678, Capt. Benjamin Garfield of Wat. He d. Nov. 28, 1717, and she m. Oct. 25, 1720, Samuel Harrington.

2-6-   MATTHEW BRIDGE m. 1687, Abigail Russell, dau. of Joseph and Mary Russell of Camb. who d. Dec. 14, 1722, aged 55. His will, dated and proved in 1738, mentions sons Matthew, John and Samuel, and daughters, Abigail Whitney, Elizabeth and Martha. He was either b. in Camb. Farms, or came here in early infancy. He was a soldier in the Narragansett war, and served in the ill-fated Canada expedition from July to Nov. 21, 1690. He was a subscriber for the first meeting-house in Lex. 1692, and was clerk of the precinct eight or ten consecutive years. He enjoyed in a great degree the confidence of his townsmen, who conferred upon him with a liberal hand their temporary honors. He was chosen, at their first organization as a town, first selectman, treasurer, and clerk — to which offices he was reëlected on the following year. He served many years as Treasurer, and filled almost every town office from time to time. He was also a prominent member of the church to which he was admitted Dec. 7, 1718.

6-10 *Mary*, b. June 19, 1688; m. Capt. William Russell, of Camb.
11 *Anna*, b. Sept. 12, 1691; m. Isaac Watson, of Camb.
12 †*Matthew*, b. Mar. 1, 1694; d. Mar. 25, 1761, in Walt.
13 *Abigail*, b. Apr. 1, 1696; m. Benjamin Whitney, then of Marlborough, but afterwards of Boston, about 1730. She was his second wife, and had five children,—making in all fourteen children b. to Benjamin Whitney. She d. Aug. 1, 1767.
14 †*Joseph*, b. July 8, 1698; m. Nov. 18, 1722, Abigail Cutler.
15 †*John*, b. Sept. 1, 1700; d. Mar. 8, 1776, aged 76 years.
16 *Elizabeth*, b. Nov. 30, 1703; d. Nov. 24, 1751, unm.
17 †*Samuel*, b. May 2, 1705; d. June 8, 1791, aged 86.
18 *Martha*, b. Sept. 20, 1707; d. Ap. 20, 1752, aged 44, unm.

6-12-   MATTHEW BRIDGE m. Mar. 22, 1719, Abigail Bowman. He resided in Lex. till 1748, when he moved with his family to Walt., to the ch. of which place he and his wife, together with Nathaniel and Sarah Bridge, were dismissed from the ch. of Lex. Like his father, he filled the office of selectman, town clerk, treasurer, and assessor before leaving his native place. She d. Dec. 13, 1797, aged 92.

12-19 †*Matthew*, b. July 18, 1721; grad. H C. 1741.
20 *Anna*, b. Sept. 21, 1723; m. —— Brooks.
21 *Nathaniel*, b. July 8, 1725; d. Dec. 19, 1794.
22 *Sarah*, b. Sept. 30, 1728 m. —— Pierce.

6-14- | JOSEPH BRIDGE m. first, Nov. 18, 1722, Abigail Cutler, and, second, about 1730, Mary ———. He d. Nov. 11, 1778, aged 79.

14-23 | *Thomas*, b. July 8, 1723; went to Spencer and m. 1745, Mary Harrington, of Brookfield. He removed to Shutesbury in 1771, and was living there in 1795. He had a family of eight children between 1745 and 1764.

24 | *Abigail*, b. Sept. 28, 1726; m. Mar. 26, 1750, Jacob Fox.

25 | *Benjamin*, b. Nov. 15, 1728; by his wife Anna he had Benjamin, who d. June 4, 1758.

26 | †*Joseph*, b. May 9, 1731; d. Sept. 11, 1775, aged 45.

27 | *Jeremiah*, b. Dec. 28, 1734; he was a soldier at Lake George.

28 | *Millicent*, b. Apr. 16, 1738; d. July 24, 1753.

6-15- | JOHN BRIDGE m. June 4, 1730, Anna Herrick, of Wenham, who d. in childbed, Dec. 14, 1730, aged 22, and he m. Sarah Tidd, dau. of Joseph and Mary, who d. Mar. 14, 1754, aged 42; and he m. Oct. 14, 1756, Mary Porter, of Wo., for his third wife. He was selectman in 1746 and 1756.

15-29 | *Anna*, b. Dec. 7, 1730; d. in early infancy.

30 | *Mary*, b. Apr. 9, 1733; m. Apr. 22, 1754, Isaac Reed.

31 | *Sarah*, b. Dec. 21, 1735; m. Apr. 11, 1754, Oliver Reed.

32 | †*John*, b. Dec. 17, 1737; he was twice married.

33 | *Josiah*, b. Dec. 28, 1739; grad. H. C. 1758; ordained as a clergyman at East Sudbury (now Wayland) Nov. 4, 1761. He d. June 21, 1801. He was quite distinguished in his profession. He preached an election sermon. He m. Martha, dau. of Rev. Aaron Smith, of Marlborough, and had a family of six children. His youngest son, Josiah, m. Eunice Morse and moved to Lancaster, where he had, among other children, William F., who was b. Feb. 15, 1821, grad. H. C. 1846, studied theology, and was settled in East Lex. 1849. It is a remarkable fact that though Rev. William F. Bridge came to Lex. a stranger, he, through the line of his ancestors, had been only one generation from the town.

34 | *Ebenezer*, b. Feb. 3, 1742; grad. H. C. 1756; d. 1814. He m. in Framingham Nov. 3, 1763, Mehitabel Wood.

6-17- | SAMUEL BRIDGE m. Susanna Reed, who d. in childbed Jan. 16, 1735, aged 24 years, and he m. Apr. 27, 1738, Martha Bowman, dau. of Joseph and Phebe. She d. June 10, 1793, aged 76, and he d. June 8, 1791, aged 86. Samuel Bridge appears to have been very unfortunate in his family, losing a large number of his children in their infancy.

17-35 | *Samuel*, b. Jan. 6, 1735.

36 | *Edmund*, b. Aug. 8, 1739; m. Sept. 6, 1764, Phebe Bowman. He united with the ch. in Lex. in 1764. He moved to Pownalborough, Me., afterwards called Dresden, to the ch. of which he and his wife were dismissed from Lex. June 26, 1801. He was appointed by Gov. Hancock sheriff of Lincoln co., an office which he held about thirty years. He d. Sept. 10, 1826, aged 87. He had several sons, who were quite distinguished. His oldest son, James, was grad. H. C. 1787, studied law with Judge Parsons, and established himself at Augusta, Me. He filled the office of judge and counsellor, and was offered by John Quincy Adams, his old class-mate, a mission to Russia, which he declined on account of ill health. He d. 1834. Edmund, a brother of James, was a distinguished merchant at Wilmington, N. C., where he d. 1822. Nathan, another brother, was

a lawyer in Gardner, Me. He d. 1828. Samuel, another brother, was a merchant in Boston, and for a time was partner of the late Robert G. Shaw. He moved to Dresden, Me., where he d. 1822. His son, Samuel J. Bridge, b. 1812, was appointed in 1841 an appraiser in the Boston custom house, where he remained twelve years, when he was appointed appraiser-general for the Pacific Coast, and resides at San Francisco. William, another brother of James, Edmund, &c., was a merchant at Augusta, and afterwards moved to New Orleans, where he d. 1818. Joseph Bowman Bridge, the last of the brothers, resided in Me., where he filled various offices. He was an elector for President in 1848, when Gen. Taylor was chosen.

37 *William*, b. Apr. 19, 1741; m. Oct. 17, 1765, Mary Porter, of Lex. He settled in Rutland, where he d. Feb. 9, 1804.

38 *Nathan*, bap. Mar. 20, 1743; d Sept. 14, 1771, aged 28.

39 *Francis*, bap. Dec. 29, 1745; d. Nov. 20, 1747.

40 *Francis*, bap. Aug. 28, 1748; m. Feb. 11, 1773, Eunice Brown. He resided many years in Winchendon. They had one child, *Lucy*, bap. in Lex. 1789. He d. Apr. 28, 1796. He had other children, among whom was Ruhamah, who m. Feb. 6, 1810, James Tyler, of Charlestown.

41 ‡*Matthew*, bap. Mar. 11, 1753; m. Apr. 29, 1779, Alice Parker.

42 *Joshua*, bap. Dec. 29, 1754; d. Dec. 20, 1760.

43 *Phebe*, bap. June 6, 1756; m. Nov. 11, 1789, Stephen Barrett of Con.

44 *James*, bap. Nov. 13, 1757; d. Oct. 9, 1760.

45 ‡*Jonas*, bap. Sept. 2, 1759; m. Susanna Reed.

46 *Joshua*, bap. Sept. 12, 1760; d. 1761.

12-19-   MATTHEW BRIDGE grad. H. C. 1741. He studied Divinity and settled in Framingham, Feb. 19, 1746. He m. Anna Perkins, of Bridgewater, dau. of Rev. David Perkins. He d. Sept. 2, 1775, and his wid. m. Rev. Timothy Harrington, of Lancaster. At the breaking out of the Revolution, Mr. Bridge, in common with other patriotic clergymen, volunteered his services as Chaplain to the American Army, which was stationed at Cambridge. While in the discharge of his duty, he was seized with an epidemic disease which prevailed in the camp, to which he fell a sacrifice in a week or two after he returned home.

14-26-   JOSEPH BRIDGE m. May 3, 1757, Eliot Reed, dau. of William and Sarah Reed, who was b. Apr. 28, 1731. They were ad. to the ch. July 23, 1758. He d. Sept. 11, 1775, aged 45. They were severely afflicted in the loss of their children.

26-47 ‡*Jonathan*, b. Sept. 20, 1758; m. Feb. 22, 1781, Phebe Bowman, of Camb.

48 *Eliot*, b. May 3, 1761; d. young.

49 *Eliot*, b. Apr. 28, 1763; m. Feb. 7, 1786, David Blanchard, of Wo.

50 *Isaac*, b. ———, 1765; d. Feb. 5, 1769.

51 *Joseph*, b. Feb. 27, 1767; d. Sept. 3, 1775.

52 *Isaac*, b. Dec. 5, 1768; d. Feb. 1, 1769.

53 *Sarah*, bap. Aug. 8, 1773.

15-32-   JOHN BRIDGE m. Apr. 14, 1761, Hannah Reed, dau. of William and Sarah, who was b. Oct. 21, 1740. She d. Oct. 26, 1782; and he m. Mary Moore. She d. Apr. 1, 1788, leaving an infant one year old. He was a soldier under Capt. Blodgett, who marched for the relief of Fort William-Henry, in 1757, and was several times called into active service during the Revolution. He was a member of Capt. Parker's company, and was at the battle of Bunker Hill. He rose to the rank of Maj. in the militia. He filled many posts of honor in the town, and was for a long time a leading magistrate, and solemnized more marriages than any other Justice in the town.

32–54 *John*, b. July 12, 1762; went to the State of Maine, where he m. Rachel Flagg, of Boston. They resided in Wiscasset, where they had four children, Hannah, Fanny, John, and Rachel. John d. young, and Rachel m. Mar. 24, 1814, Joseph Veazie. They r. in Boston.

55 *Eliab*, b. July 2, 1764; d. young.

56 *Hannah*, b. Ap. 30, 1771; m. Sept. 29, 1791, Joseph Chandler. He d. Oct. 26, 1807, and she m. June 7, 1810, Dr. Thomas Whitcomb, of Lex. and had Elizabeth, who m. —— Gerry.

57 *Mary*, bap. Jan. 14, 1776; d. Sept. 4, 1778.

58 *Sarah*, b. June 20, 1780; d. Dec. 1, 1780.

59 *Mary*, bap. May 6, 1787; m John Bridge, of Bil.

17–41– MATTHEW BRIDGE m. Apr. 29, 1779, Alice Parker. He moved to Charlestown, where he became a prominent merchant. He and his partner, T. K. Jones, are said to have owned the first copper-bottomed ship which sailed out of Boston.

41–60 *Alice*, b. Nov. 18, 1779; m. Ebenezer Baker, of Charlestown.

61 *Nathan*, b. Apr. 18, 1782; m. Betsey Bartlet, of Charlestown.

62 *Sally*, b. ——; m. Seth Knowles.

63 *Samuel*, b. ——; grad. H. C. 1816; d. 1830, unm.

17–45– JONAS BRIDGE m. Susanna Reed, dau. of Joshua and Susanna (Houghton) Reed. She d. Aug. 1830.

45–64 Their first child b. Jan. 16, and d. Jan. 17, 1784.

65 *Patty*, b. June 3, 1785; d. Feb. 19, 1788.

66 *Susanna*, b. Jan. 24, 1787; d. unm.

67 *Patty*, b. Apr. 24, 1788; d. unm.

68 *Betsey*, b. Apr. 23, 1790; d. Mar. 27, 1793.

69 *Jonas*, b. Aug. 26, 1792; d. July 5, 1813.

70 *Samuel*, b. Nov. 12, 1793; d. Sept. 30, 1795.

71 *Bowman*, b. June 18, 1795; went to St. Louis, where he d.

72 †*Samuel*, b. Dec. 12, 1796; m. Hannah Maria Wellington.

73 *Betsey*, b. Jan. 7, 1799; d. unm.

74 *Caroline*, b. July 28, 1800; d. unm.

26–47– JONATHAN BRIDGE m. Feb. 22, 1781, Phebe Bowman, of Camb. They were ad. to the ch. Mar. 30, 1785. He was one of a detachment of Capt. Parker's Co., which marched to Cambridge on the memorable 17th of June, 1775. He d. 1849, aged 91.

47–75 *Joseph*, bap. Apr. 9, 1783.

76 *Nancy*, b. Sept. 12, 1785; d. unm.

77 *Phebe*, b. Nov. 7, 1789; m. —— Sargent, of Malden.

78 *Eliot*, b. Oct. 20, 1793.

79 *Jonathan*, b. Feb. 1798; m. —— Smith, of Charlestown.

45–72– SAMUEL BRIDGE m. June 15, 1836, Hannah Maria Wellington, dau. of Nehemiah Wellington, b. Nov. 17, 1809.

72–80 *Caroline Eliza*, b. June 3, 1837; m. Sept. 2, 1858, George O. Davis.

81 *Jonas Francis*, b. June 27, 1839; d. Sept. 4, 1845.

82 | *Amelia Maria*, b. Dec. 23, 1841; d. Aug. 24, 1842.
83 | *James Bowman*, b. Feb. 26, 1843; d. Apr. 13, 1843.
84 | *Annie Marie*, b. Sept. 8, 1846; m. Nov. 16, 1865, George Lyman
    Stratton, of Boston; r. in Lex.

THE BRIGHAM FAMILY.

There has been a family of the name of Brigham in Lexington, the extinction of which is so remarkable as to deserve notice.

AARON BRIGHAM b. 1785, son of Ithamar Brigham, of Marlboro', m. 1808, Comfort Valentine, by whom he had three children, Catharine, William, and Sophia. *Catharine* was an invalid, and for years could not dress herself, or get off from her bed without help. Her father, after doing business in Boston, and acquiring a comfortable property, purchased a small farm, and came to Lex. in 1853, hoping that the country air might prove beneficial to his feeble daughter. Mr. and Mrs. Brigham were very domestic, and seemed to make the comfort of their invalid daughter the great object of their care; and the daughter often expressed the hope that she should not survive her parents. Though Mr. Brigham enjoyed good health for a man of his years, he was taken down with a fever, and d. Oct. 3, 1863, aged 78 years. His wife d. suddenly Dec. 19, 1863, aged 80 years; and Catharine, the invalid daughter, as if she had nothing on earth to live for, d. Dec. 29th of the same year, aged 54 years. Thus, in less than three months, the whole family in Lex. became extinct.

WILLIAM BRIGHAM b. Mar. 27, 1805, came to Lex. about 1830. He m. Aug. 4, 1835, Abby Ann Muzzey, dau. of Rev. William and Anna Muzzey. He is a dea. of the Unitarian church, and takes a lively interest in religious affairs. They have but one child, *Laura Muzzey*, b. July 20, 1836.

Dea. Brigham is a son of *Elijah* and Mary (Gleason) Brigham, of Sudbury, who had a family of eleven children. Elijah was born Oct. 13, 1776, and was a direct descendant from John Brigham, the second son of Thomas who came to this country in 1635, in the ship Susan & Ellyn, and settled in Wat.

THE BROWN FAMILY.

The name of Brown is so common, that in tracing the line of family descent, we are in great danger of confounding one person with another, and of becoming bewildered among the William Browns and John Browns, as we should be if we fell into the labyrinths of the John Smiths. But being favored by the labors of one of the family, I have been materially aided in giving a connected view of the Lex. Browns. The original ancestor of this family, who came to this country, was

1 | JOHN BROWN, who was baptized at Hawkedon, Eng. Oct. 11, 1601. He was son of John, an elder brother of Richard Brown; he arrived in New England in the ship Lion, Sept. 16, 1632, and settled in Wat. He was ad. freeman in 1634, and d. June, 1636, aged 36. By his wife Dorothy, he had three children, one of whom must have been born abroad.

1- 2 | †*John*, b. in England, 1631.   3 *Hannah*, b. Sept. 8, 1634.
4 | *Mary*, b. Mar. 24, 1636.

1-2-   JOHN BROWN, m. Apr. 24, 1655, Esther, or as it is sometimes written, *Hester* Makepeace, of Boston. They had eleven children— the first four of whom were born in Camb. and the remaining seven in Marlborough, to which place he had removed. He sold out his place in Marl. to Thomas Rice, and removed to Falmouth, and from thence to Wat. His Will, dated at Wat. Nov. 20, 1697, in which he is designated as "late of Falmouth," mentions his wife Hester; sons John, Thomas, Daniel, and Joseph; dau. Deborah Meacham; sons-in-law John Gustin, John Adams, Thomas Darby, and John Hartshorne.

    2- 5 *Joseph*, b. Feb. 8, 1656; killed by a cart Sept. 24, 1671.
       6 *Elizabeth*, b. Mar. 26, 1657.   7 *Sarah*, b. July 8, 1661.
       8 *Mary*, b. Dec. 19, 1662.   9 *John*, b. Nov. 27, 1664.
     10 *Hester*, b. and d. 1667.   10½ *Ruth*, b. Dec. 8, 1668.
     11 *Thomas*, b. 1669.   12 *Daniel*, b. 1671.
     13 *Deborah*, b. 1673; m. —— Meacham.
     14 *Abigail*, b. 1675.
     15 †*Joseph*, b. 1677; d. Jan. 11, 1764, aged 86.

2-15-   JOSEPH BROWN m. in Wat. Nov. 15, 1699, Ruhamah Wellington, dau. of Benjamin and Elizabeth (Sweetman) Wellington, of that place. He probably settled at Wat. Farms, (now Weston,) as he sold a place there in 1709, soon after which he removed to Lex. On the 31st of May, 1713, he and his wife were ad. to the ch. in Lex. and a few weeks after one of their children was baptized. He was a prominent member of the ch. and was chosen dea. in 1727, which office he held till his death in 1764. His services were also appreciated in the town. While in Wat. he was constable, selectman, and town clerk; and after he came to Lex. he was called to fill similar offices, being assessor, and selectman. He d. in Lex. Jan. 11, 1764, aged 86. She d. July 1, 1772, aged 91. They lived together, husband and wife, 64 years.

  15-16 *Ruhamah*, b. in Wat. July 15, 1701.
     17 †*Daniel*, b. in Wat. Dec. 21, 1703.
     18 *John*, b. in Wat. Jan. 6, 1706; d. Jan. 21, 1730.
     19 †*Joseph*, b. in Wat. Sept. 2, 1708
     20 *Jonas*, b. in Wat. May 3, 1711.
     21 †*James*, bap. in Lex. July 26, 1713; d. June 11, 1768.
     22 *Josiah*, bap. in Lex. Aug. 12, 1715; was ad. to the ch. Mar. 11, 1730. He settled in Sterling. He was grad. at H. C. in 1735, preached in Sterling, and d. Mar. 4, 1774.
     23 ‡*Benjamin*, bap. July 3, 1720; d. 1801, aged 81.
     24 *William*, bap. Apr. 28, 1723. He removed to Framingham, where he was a dea. of the ch. and selectman of the town. He d. Dec. 12, 1793, and his widow d. Feb. 1810. They had a family of eight children.

15-17-   DANIEL BROWN m. Eliot —— about 1728. They were ad. to the ch. in Lex. Mar. 15, 1734   She d. July, 1735, and he m. July 16, 1736, Anne Bright, of Wat.

  17-25 *John*, bap. Nov. 30, 1729; d. young.
     26 *Ruhamah*, b. Apr. 7, 1731; m. Jan. 18, 1753, John Reed.
     27 †*Nathaniel Bowman*, b. July 1, 1737.
     28 *Abisha*, bap. Aug. 13, 1738.   29 *Anna*, b. Apr. 29, 1739.
     30 *Daniel*, b. Dec. 20, 1741.
     31 *Esther*, b. Aug. 12, 1743; m. Aug. 16, 1770, Nathaniel Tottingham, Westminster.

32 *Jerusha*, b. Mar. 18, 1746; m. Oct. 13, 1766, Abisha Brown, Con.
33 *Martha*, b. June 18, 1749; m. Nov. 27, 1766, Zachariah Brown, Con.
34 *John*, b. Apr. 12, 1751; killed on the Common, April 19, 1775.
35 *Hannah*, b. Apr. 8, 1756.   36 *Mary*, b. May 5, 1758.

15-19-   JOSEPH BROWN, ad. to Lex. ch. Feb. 18, 1727; removed to Holliston, where he was dea. of a ch.; m. Lydia Twitchel, and had a
family.

15-21-   JAMES BROWN m. Jan. 21, 1735, Jane Bowman, dau. of Nathaniel
and Anne Bowman. She d. May 8, 1761, and he m. Elizabeth, wid.
of Hezekiah Smith, of Lex., May 18, 1762. James Brown and Jane
were ad. to the ch. Oct. 19, 1735; he was chosen dea. 1756, and
filled that office till June 11, 1768, when his earthly labors ceased.
His wid. d. Dec. 29, 1774.

21-37 *Mary*, b. Aug. 13, 1735; m. Sept. 3, 1753, Samuel Thacher, of Wat.
38 †*Francis*, b. Jan. 22, 1738; d. Apr. 21, 1800, aged 62.
39 *Joseph*, b. Apr. 14, 1741; grad. H. C. 1763; was ad. to the ch. in
Lex. May 7, 1765. He m. May 7, 1765, Sarah Smith; was dismissed from the ch. at Lex. to the ch. of Winchendon, over which
he was ordained May 24, 1769. He d. 1811.
40 *James*, b. Jan. 3, 1744; d. Jan. 22, 1749.

15-23-   BENJAMIN BROWN, m. Dec. 22, 1742, Sarah Reed, dau. of William
Reed, Esq. and Sarah (Poulter) his wife. He was chosen dea. Oct.
14, 1768. He was justice of the peace. He d. Mar. 4, 1802.

26-41 *Benjamin*, b. Jan. 1, 1744; m. June 12, 1769, Esther Whittemore,
of Lex. They were dismissed to the ch. in Templeton, Apr. 26,
1772,—since Phillipston.
42 †*Thaddeus*, b. Mar. 12, 1745; m. Nov. 16, 1769, Bethiah Muzzy.
43 *Sarah*, b. Mar. 24, 1747; m. Nathaniel Page, of Bed.
44 *Eunice*, b. Jan. 20, 1751; m. Francis Bridge, Feb. 11, 1773.
45 *Oliver*, b. July 25, 1753; moved to Virginia and settled on the Ohio
River, and gave his name to the place, viz., *Brownville*.
46 *Solomon*, b. Jan 15, 1757. He was not only one of the heroes of the
19th of Apr. 1775, but he commenced his patriotic labors the day
preceeding. He was the first who brought the intelligence into
Lex. that a number of British officers were on their way from
Boston; and when they had passed above Lex. he was one who
volunteered to follow them and watch their movements. He was
taken prisoner and detained several hours on the evening of the
18th, which of course prepared his mind for the events of the following day. Subsequently he removed to Vt.
47 †*James*, b. Oct. 13, 1758; m. May 30, 1780, Betty Reed.
48 *Ruhamah*, b. Apr. 23, 1761; m. Sept. 20, 1780, Thaddeus Wellington, of Walt.
49 *Susanna*, b. June 17, 1764; m. June 19, 1783, Samuel Downing.
50 *Nathan*, b. Sept. 5. 1766; m. Lydia Muzzy. Dec. 25, 1788.
51 *Lucy*, b. Jan. 17, 1770; m. Joseph Converse, of Bed.

17--27   NATHANIEL B. BROWN m. Abigail ———. They were ad. to the
ch. Oct. 6, 1765, and dismissed 1783 to the ch. in Lunenburg.

27-52 *Susanna*, bap. Oct. 24, 1766.   53 *Abigail*, bap. Apr. 26, 1767.
54 *Nathaniel*, bap. Mar. 26, 1769.   55 *Anna*, bap. Feb. 3, 1771.

21-38- FRANCIS BROWN m. Feb. 16, 1764, Mary Buckman, dau. of John and Mary (Fiske) Buckman, of Lex. b. Dec. 27, 1749. They were ad. to the ch. Nov. 24, 1765. He was one of that gallant band which boldly stood before the British troops on the memorable 19th of April, 1775. He met the enemy in the morning, and on their flight from Concord they were again met by Capt. Parker's co. in Lincoln, where Brown received a very severe wound,—a ball entering his cheek, passed under his ear, and lodged in the back part of his neck, from which it was extracted the year following. But notwithstanding this severe casualty, he commanded the Lex. co. in 1776, and lived about twenty-five years after the event.

38-56 *Mary*, b. Dec. 2, 1765 ; m. Charles Harrington, Dec. 18, 1786.
57 *Elizabeth*, b. Dec. 30, 1770; m. 1799, Samuel Stearns, of Walt.
58 †*James*, b. July 23, 1773; m. Pamela Munroe.
59 *Sarah*, b. Aug. 20, 1775; m. Nov. 5, 1798, Thomas Stearns, of Walt.
60 *Rebecca*, b. Feb. 10, 1778; m. James Perry, of West Camb.
61 †*John*, b. Apr. 15, 1779; m. Nancy Stearns, of Walt.

23-42- THADDEUS BROWN m. Nov. 16, 1769, Bethiah, dau. of Amos and Esther (Green) Muzzy. They resided in Lex. till 1785, when they removed to Templeton, to the ch. of which they were dismissed.

42-62 *Thaddeus*, b. in Lex. Sept. 30, 1770.
63 *Ashbel*, b. in Lex. Oct. 11, 1772; d. unm.

23-47- JAMES BROWN m. May 30, 1780, Betty Reed, dau. of Hammond and Betty (Simonds) Reed, b. Dec. 12, 1757. They were ad. to the ch. Apr. 4, 1781. He was subsequently a dea. of the ch. It is a singular fact that he was the fourth Brown who filled that office in Lex. ch.

47-64 *James*, b. Apr. 22, 1781; d. Oct., 1785.
65 *Betty*, b. June 30, 1783; m. Sullivan Burbank, 1803.
66 †*James*, b. Oct. 4, 1786; m. Betsey Dudley, of Con.
67 †*Leonard*, b. Jan 3, 1788; m. Dorcas Munroe.
68 *Eliab*, b. Sept. 4, 1790; m. Mary White; no issue.
69 *Nabby*, b. Dec. 1793; d. Sept. 1794.
70 *Nabby*, b. June 27, 1795; m. Ebenezer Pierce.
71 *Hiram*, b. Feb. 12, 1798; d. about 1824, unm.
72 *Madison*, b. May 1, 1802; d. about 1832, unm; was found dead in his bed.

23-50- NATHAN BROWN, m. Dec. 25, 1788, Lydia, dau. of William Muzzy. They moved to Phillipston, where they had a family Their first two children were born in Lex. Nathan, bap. Aug. 29, 1790, and Lydia, bap. Jan. 10, 1793.

38-58- JAMES BROWN, m. Oct. 19, 1799, Pamela, dau. of Edmund and Rebecca Munroe. They were ad. to the ch. May 2, 1813, and five of their children were baptized the next Sabbath.

58-73 *Pamela*, b. July 29, 1800; m. May 18, 1823, Jonas Stone Fiske.
74 †*Francis*, b. Aug 29, 1802; m. Caroline M. Kuhn.
75 *Harriet*, b. Sept. 28, 1804; m. Oct. 10, 1832, Edmund A. Chapman.
76 *Charlotte*, b. Nov. 11, 1806; m. Oct. 10, 1832, William Gleason.
77 †*Edmund M.*, b. Feb. 13, 1809; m. Harriet Whitney.
78 *Charles*, b. June 3, 1812, d. Jan. 1, 1813.
79 †*Charles*, b. May 2, 1816; m. Sarah Ann Sumner.

38-61- | JOHN BROWN, m. Nancy Stearns of Waltham.

61- 80 | *Caroline*, b. June 5, 1802.
    81 | *Mary S.*, b. May 9, 1804; m. July 28, 1825, John Beals.
    82 | *John S.*, b. Sept. 14, 1806.
    83 | *Susanna W.*, b. May 24, 1808; m. Apr. 23, 1831, Wm. Proctor.
    84 | *Horatio*, b. July 24, 1809; m. Apr. 22, 1832, Susan H. Johnson.
    85 | *Ann*, b. Oct. 16, 1811.
    86 | *Louisa Amanda*, b. Sept. 14, 1813.
    87 | *Hannah E.*, b. Nov. 10, 1816.   88 *Jane I.*, b. Nov. 23, 1822.

47-66- | JAMES BROWN, m. Elizabeth Dudley of Concord, June 9, 1811.

66- 89 | *Benjamin*, b. Aug. 23, 1813,   90 *Oliver*, b. July 28, 1817.
    91 | *Lucy E.*, b. Feb. 20, 1820; m. —— Rogers of Manchester, N. H.

47-67- | LEONARD BROWN, m. Nov. 25, 1810, Dorcas, dau. of Nathan and Elizabeth (Harrington) Munroe, b. Mar. 31, 1788.

67- 92 | *Elizabeth*, b. June 15, 1811; d. Mar. 2, 1820.
    93 | *Mary*, b. May 9, 1814; d. Mar. 3, 1820.
    94 | *Leonard*, b. Mar. 19, 1818; d. Sept. 4, 1819.
    95 | *Leonard*, b. Feb. 24, 1821; m. Sarah Ann Goodnow of Stow, resides at Lowell.
    96 | *Elizabeth*, b. Mar. 8, 1823; m. Elias V. Blodgett.
    97 | *Mary*, b. July 30, 1825; m. George Patch of Littleton.
    98 | *Hiram*, b. July 20, 1827; m. Cyntha Farrar of Walt. resides in Arlington.
    99 | *Nathan*, b. Feb. 8, 1830; m. Hannah E. Fiske, Mar. 7, 1852.

58-74- | FRANCIS BROWN, m. Jan. 1, 1833, Caroline Matilda Kuhn, dau. of John and Sarah of Boston, b. Dec. 15, 1812. He is a merchant in Boston, has represented the city in the General Court, and in the city government, and has for a long period held by appointment of Governor, the office of Inspector of butter and lard. They have had at least two children Francis H., b. Aug. 8, 1835; grad. at H. C. 1857; and Horace S., b. Aug. 9, 1847; d. May 30, 1848.

58-77- | EDMUND M. BROWN, m. May 1, 1835, Harriet Whitney of Wat. b. Nov. 15, 1812.

77-100 | *Edmund M.*, b. Oct. 30, 1837.   101 *James H.*, b. Oct. 26, 1839.
   102 | *William H.*, b. Jan. 2, 1841.

58-79- | CHARLES BROWN, m. May 9, 1839, Sarah Ann Sumner, dau. of James and Sally Sumner. She was b. Jan. 27, 1820. He represented the town in the General Court, 1854.

79-103 | *Charles F.*, b. Oct. 9, 1842; d. same day.
   104 | *Ellen Maria*, b. Nov. 28, 1843.

THE BRYANT FAMILY.

1 | JOSIAH BRYANT, son of Josiah and Lydia (Green) Bryant, of South Reading, was. b. June 20, 1778. He m. Aug. 28, 1803, Sally Withington, of Dorchester, dau. of Edward and Eunice (Tucker) Withington, b. Mar. 24, 1778. He probably came to Lex. about the time of his marriage, as his wife was ad. to the ch. the year after. He d. Nov. 14, 1837.

1- 2 | *Susanna T.*, b. July 11, 1804; m. May 18, 1834, William D. Phelps.
3 | *Cynthia*, b. Oct. 7, 1806; m. Oct. 11, 1830, Benjamin Shurtleff, Jr.
4 | *Sally*, b. July 13, 1809; m. Feb. 8, 1830, Charles Ellms.
5 | †*Albert Withington*, b. Feb. 16, 1814; he has been twice married.

1-5-   ALBERT W. BRYANT m. May 9, 1838, Elizabeth Wellington, dau. of Marshall and Elizabeth Wellington. She d. July 15, 1840, and he m. Aug. 23, 1841, Nancy W. Wellington, sister of his first wife. He has filled the office of selectman and assessor, and has been town clerk 23 years. He also has a commission of justice of the peace.

5- 6 | *Josiah*, b. Mar. 13, 1839. He was in the service nine months in the late rebellion.
7 | *Albert W.*, b. Jan. 4, 1844; d. Oct. 25, 1847.
8 | *Arthur W.*, b. July 20, 1847.   9 *Edwin P.*, b. Aug. 31, 1850.
10 | *Anna Elizabeth*, b. Nov. 12, 1856.
11 | *Clifford W.*, b. Oct. 11, 1859.

THE BUCKMAN FAMILY.

Though the Buckmans were somewhat connected with the history of Lexington in 1775, they were not among the early settlers. When they came to Lex. I have not ascertained with certainty. John Buckman was in the town, and was chosen to the office of hog constable in 1740, which might imply that he had just settled in the world, and the date of the birth of his first child rather confirms us in that opinion. From what place he came, I am not able to say; but as the Buckmans, or Bucknams, as the name was at first generally spelled, were very numerous in Malden, it is highly probable that the Lex. Buckmans originated there.

1   JOHN BUCKMAN m. 1739, Mary Fiske, dau. of Dr. Robert. They were ad. to the ch. in Lex. May 15, 1745. He d. Feb. 17, 1763, aged 51; she d. Feb. 10, 1768, in the 48th year of her age.

1- 2 | *Mary*, b. Dec. 27, 1740; m. Feb. 16, 1764, Francis Brown.
3 | †*John*, b. Apr. 2, 1745; m. July 21, 1768, Ruth Stone.
4 | *Sarah*, b. Jan. 3, 1748; m. June 12, 1766, Jonas Stone.
5 | *Elizabeth*, b. Jan. 11, 1753.   6 *Ruth*, b. Dec. 30, 1755.

1-3-   JOHN BUCKMAN, m. July 21, 1768, Ruth Stone, dau. of Samuel and Jane Stone. He resided in the house now occupied by Rufus Merriam, which he kept as a public house. It was here that Capt. Parker, and his patriotic men assembled on the evening of the 18th of April, 1775; and from this house they issued on the approach of the British the next morning. Shots were fired from this house upon the British, after they had attacked the Americans upon the Common, and some of the clapboards to this day give evidence that the fire was returned. John Buckman stands enrolled as a member of Capt. Parker's company. He had but one child by his first wife, who d. Sept. 8, 1778, aged 33. He m. as a second wife, Sept. 28, 1784, Sarah Weld, who d. Nov. 16, 1801, aged 43. He d. Dec. 21, 1792, aged 48.

3- 7 | *John*, b. Sept. 12, and d. Sept. 22, 1771.
8 | *Sarah*, b. Feb. 19, 1785.   9 *John*, b. May 7, 1787.
10 | *Henry*, b. Aug. 6, 1788.   11 *Polly*, b. Apr. 19, 1790.

There were several other Buckmans mentioned in our records at
an earlier date than those mentioned above; but it is doubtful
whether they resided here permanently. We will give the record
as we find it.

Paul Buckman, bap. Apr. 26, 1734.

Benjamin, son of Joseph Buckman, bap. June 12, 1737.

Jacob Buckman, m Elizabeth Munroe, Jan. 1, 1787. They had
Bowen, b. Apr. 19, 1788; and Dennis and Willis, twins, b. May
13, 1794.

THE BURBANK FAMILY.

Col. Burbank came to Lexington in 1801. His father, *Samuel
Burbank*, had two wives, by whom he had twelve children. His first
wife died; and he married Eunice Kendall, of Sherborn. She was a
daughter of Benjamin Kendall of that town, who originated in Lex.
being a son of Thomas Kendall, who resided in this town. Samuel
Burbank was a soldier of the Revolution. He was a Lieutenant at
the Battle of Bunker Hill. He afterwards commanded a company
which marched to Rhode Island, where he served under General
Sullivan, for whom his oldest son was named. After the birth of
Sullivan, he moved from Holliston to Fitchburg, and subsequently
to Cavendish, Vt. where he died. Daniel, one of his sons, was
killed accidentally at a military muster in Westminster.

SULLIVAN BURBANK, the oldest son of Samuel and Eunice (Kendall) Burbank, was b. in Holliston, Oct. 8, 1776, and m. 1803,
Betsey, dau. of James Brown, of Lex. He came to Lex. 1801, and
opened a store in the village. In 1812 he received a commission as
Lieutenant of infantry in the United States service. He acted at
first as a recruiting officer in Lex. and Boston; but marched in
August to Plattsburg, and on the winter following was again detailed
on the recruiting service. In April, 1813, he marched with about
one hundred recruits first to Greenbush, N. Y., and then to Sackett's
Harbor; and arrived at that post just in season to assist in repelling
the attack of Sir George Provost, on the 29th of May. Remaining
at Sackett's Harbor during the summer, he moved with the army
under Gen. Wilkinson down the St. Lawrence in November, 1813,
and was in the action at Cristler's Fields on the 11th of that month,
and went into winter quarters at French Mills. Early in the spring,
he returned to Sackett's Harbor, and thence to Buffalo. On the 3d
of July, 1814, he crossed with the troops into Canada, was in the
battle of Chippeway on the 5th of that month, and at the more sanguinary battle of Niagara on the 25th. Being in Col. Miller's regiment, he was one of the gallant spirits who stormed the enemy's
battery, which commanded the field, and thus turned the fortunes of
that desperate struggle. In this charge, rendered memorable by the
noble daring of the regiment, and the modesty of Col. Miller, who,
when asked if he could silence that battery, meekly replied, "*I will
try, Sir,*" Capt. Burbank received a severe wound in the shoulder.
For his bravery and good conduct in that action, Capt. B. received
the brevet rank of Major.

On the reduction of the army in 1815, consequent upon the term-
ination of the war, Brevt. Maj. Burbank was retained in the service,
a Captain in the 5th Regiment of infantry. On the peace establishment, Maj. B. has served at almost every part on the frontier from
the St. Lawrence to the Sabine. He was stationed first at Detroit,
then at Fort Gratiot at the outlet of Lake Huron, then at Fort

Snelling at the junction of the Minnesota and Mississippi, under the gallant Colonel in honor of whom the Post was named. He was then detached to Fort Armstrong, (Rock Island,) where he had the command about four years. In 1828, he was stationed at Jefferson Barracks, Mo., thence he was given the command at Fort Mackinaw. About this time he was promoted to the rank of Major in the 7th Regiment, and ordered to Fort Gibson, Arkansas; thence to Fort Towson on the Red River; thence to Fort Jessup, La., and thence again to Fort Gibson. At this time he was promoted to the rank of Lieut. Col. and ordered to Fort Winnebago, near Portage City, Wis. After this Col. Burbank was ordered to New York to act as general superintendent of the recruiting service for the army. Feeling the infirmities of age, Col. Burbank, in 1839, resigned his commission, and being honorably discharged, he retired to private life. He was highly respected as a man and a citizen. He represented the town of Lex. in the General Court in 1846, and 1847. He died Sept. 30, 1862, aged 86. She d. Mar., 1860, aged 77.

1- 2 | *Lorenzo*, b. Feb. 28, 1804; m. Mary Ann Alexander, of Charlestown. They resided in Somerville, and subsequently in Lex.
3 | *Daniel*, b. August 29, 1805; d. June 14, 1810.
4 | *Sidney*, b. Sept. 26, 1807. He was graduated at West Point in 1829 as a Lieut. and entered the service of the United States. He served in the Florida War, and during the war with Mexico was in command of Fort Scott. He was promoted to the rank of Capt., and then to that of Major. He was also in the service of his country in the late rebellion, being true to the old flag. He m. at West Point, Isabella Slaughter, dau. of Sheriff Slaughter, of Culpepper Co., Va., by whom he has several children.
5 | *Ophelia*, } b. Dec. 27, 1809; { d. 1818.
6 | *Paulina*, } { m. ——, Pelatiah P. Peirce, of Lex.
7 | *Octavia*, b. Apr. 18, 1812; m. ——, 1837, Charles Sumner Jacobs, of Medford. She d. Jan. 20, 1857.

THE BURDOO FAMILY.

As God has made of one blood all nations of men, there is no reason why we should not notice a very respectable colored family, which resided many years in town, and discharged all the duties of citizens.

1 | PHILIP BURDOO resided on the Bedford road, nearly opposite the old Simonds Tavern House. His wife was ad. to the ch. Dec 26, 1708. The record of the family, though probably incomplete, is as follows.

1- 2 | †*Philip*, bap. Apr. 10, 1709; m. Mary ——, about 1738.
3 | *Eunice*, bap. Apr. 10, 1709; d. Feb. 28, 1720.
4 | †*Moses*, bap. Apr. 9, 1710; m. Feb. 13, 1754, Phebe Banister, Con.
5 | *Aaron*, bap. July 27, 1712.   6 *Phinehas*, bap. July 31, 1715.

1-2- | PHILIP BURDOO, m. Mary ——.

2- 7 | *Philip*, bap. Oct. 21, 1739.   8 *Mary*, bap. Feb. 18, 1742.
9 | *Silas*,? and a child which d. Oct. 13, 1755.

1-4- | MOSES BURDOO, m. Phebe Banister of Con. and had *Eli*, bap. July 20, 1755, and probably other children. Tradition says that some of this family moved to Vt. where they were highly respected, and some of them promoted to public office.

THE BUTTERS FAMILY.

1   JOSHUA BUTTERS was b. in Wilmington; m. Susanna Peters, b. in Burlington. They resided in Boston, where their children were born. He d. 1840; she d. 1824.

1- 2   *Joshua*, b. ——.
3   †*Charles A.*, b. May 7, 1808; m. Sarah A. Viles.
4   *George W.*, b. ——.
5   *Susan*, b. ——; m. John Tidd, of Wo.
6   †*Sydney*, b. May 22, 1817; m. Almira R. Blodgett.

1-3-   CHARLES A. BUTTERS m. Oct. 3, 1834, Sarah A. Viles, b. Mar. 17, 1810, dau. of John Viles of Lex.

3- 7   *Frank V.*, b. Apr. 8, 1837; m. May 4, 1862, Lizzie Hastings, of Con. They have Alice H., b. Nov. 11, 1864; Charles A., b. Oct. 6, 1867.
8   *Sarah Louisa*, b. July 3, 1839.   9 *Ella F.*, b. Sept. 15, 1844.

1 6-   SYDNEY BUTTERS m. Apr. 28, 1844, Almira R. Blodgett, dau. of James. He was nine months in service in the late rebellion.

6-10   *George S.*, b. May 2, 1845.   11 *Jason W.*, b. Jan. 29, 1848.
12   *Josephine Augusta*, b. Nov. 11, 1849.
13   *James Francis*, b. Mar. 17, 1852; d. Apr. 15, 1854.
14   *Charles Francis*, b. Mar. 23, 1854.
15   *William Henry*, b. Aug. 31, 1856; d. July 17, 1857.
16   *Willietta*, b. May 17, 1858; d. May 19, 1858.
17   *Willie*, b. May 13, 1859.
18   *Freddy Ellsworth*, b. July 1, 1862.

THE BUTTRICK FAMILY.

1   ISAAC BUTTRICK, b. in Pepperell, Dec. 8, 1809, went to Con. in 1825, where his ancestors probably resided. From Con. he came to Lex. in 1830, and m. 1834, Abigail Locke. He was a Captain in the militia.

1- 2   *Matilda*, b. Aug. 17, 1835; d. Aug. 31, same year.
3   *Isaac F.*, b. Mar. 31, 1836. He enlisted for 3 years, was wounded and discharged.
4   *Charles F.*, b. June 8, 1838; m. Aug. 6, 1861, Eunice L. Glacier, Som. He was 3 years in the army of the Potomac.
5   *Mary H.*, b. Oct. 4, 1840.
6   *Lydia*, b. Sept. 30, 1842; d. July 18, 1858.
7   *Jonas M.*, b. Feb. 10, 1845.
8   *William*, b. Jan. 11, 1847; d. Nov. 4, 1863.
9   *Ella*, b. Sept. 20, 1848.   10 *Volney*, b. Mar. 25, 1850.
11   *Eugene*, b. Sept. 25, 1851; d. Sept. 26, 1854.
12   *Eugenia*, b. Mar 9, 1854; d. May 25, 1856.
13   *Oscar*, b. Aug. 12, 1857.

THE CALDWELL FAMILY.

There are a few instances in which the name of Caldwell appears on Lex. records. They probably came from Wo.

ADAM CALDWELL by wife Phebe had Phebe, b. Mar. 26, 1743;

Sybil, b. May 16, 1745, m. Feb. 1, 1767, Samuel Fletcher; Mary, b. Mar. 6, 1747; Ruth, b. Feb. 7, 1749.—There were a few of the same name some fifty or sixty years later, who were from Burlington.

THE CAPELL FAMILY.

1   CURTIS CAPELL, b. Nov. 17, 1806; m. May 2, 1832, Mary Augusta Brown, b. Apr. 2, 1812.

1- 2 *William C.*, b. Feb. 10, 1833.
3 *Mary E.*, b. Nov. 23, 1834; m, Sept. 1, 1855, Sylvester S. Crosby.
4 *Henry*, b. Apr. 27, 1838; m. Nov. 26, 1862, Augustine Hutchinson.
5 *Jonas F.*, b. Mar. 6, 1842. He enlisted in the service of the United States in 1861, in the 16th Mass. Reg., was made sergeant, promoted to 2d Lieut., 1st Lieut, Capt., and Maj. by brevet.
6 *Francis H.*, b. Sept. 6, 1844. He enlisted in the 9 months' service in the late rebellion, and subsequently entered the regular army.

THE CARLY FAMILY.

WILLIAM CARLY was taxed in Lex. in 1695. He d. May 12, 1719, aged 86. Mrs. Jane Carly, probably his wife, d. July 12, 1719, aged 70. Elizabeth Carly d. June 3, 1719, aged 34. Rachel Carly, an insane woman, had a guardian, and was taken care of by the town. She d. Sept. 11, 1725. Sarah Carly m. Oct. 28, 1714, Richard Arms.

THE CHANDLER FAMILY.

The Chandlers, though a prominent family in Lexington for the last century, were not among the early settlers of the town. They came here from Con. about 1757. An impression has prevailed in the family that they descended from John Chandler, one of the early proprietors of Con.; but I am satisfied that this is not the fact.

The Chandlers who came to Lex. were from a different stock. Shattuck, in his valuable history of the town of Concord, tells us that the Chandlers of that town were the descendants of Roger Chandler, who was one of a co. most of whom were from Plymouth, which had a grant of land in Con in 1658; that Roger Chandler was employed by Dolor Davis to build a house there. Dolor Davis was originally from the Plymouth Colony, and represented Barnstable in the General Court of that colony. He afterward came to Cambridge, and was one of the original proprietors of Groton. Dolor Davis was the ancestor of a large number of Davises, among whom was the late Governor Davis of Worcester.

Who Roger Chandler was I cannot state with certainty. We find in the early records of Plymouth Colony the names of Dolor Davis, Roger Chandler, John Chandler, Edmund Chandler, and Samuel Chandler. The latter was in 1637 warned to appear before the court, to answer for the heinous crime of "shooting off three guns in the night tyme, as if it were an alarum." These Chandlers had grants of land in and about Duxbury, where that name has been common. Roger must have d. before 1665, as the Court of that year made a grant of land to his children, "he being deceased." The Roger who settled in Con. was undoubtedly a son of some of these Chandlers, and most likely of Roger, of Plymouth; and he probably came to Con. with Dolor Davis, the old friend of his father.

But be this as it may, the Con. records clearly show that Roger was the ancestor of the Con. Chandlers, and that the Lex. Chandlers were a branch of the same stock. They were considerably numerous, and were highly respected in Con.

1   ROGER CHANDLER was one of a company of twenty persons, mostly from Plymouth, which had a grant of land in Con. in 1658. He m. in 1671, Mary Simonds, of Con. He d. 1717; and she d. 1728. They left several children. In his will, dated 1705, and proved 1717, he speaks of Samuel as his only son, and of his daughter Mary Heald, Abigail Brown, and of his youngest dau. Hepzibah Jones.

1- 2 *Mary*, b Mar. 3, 1672; m. John Heald, of Con.
  3 †*Samuel*, b. Mar. 3, 1673; m. 1695, Dorcas Buss.
  4 *Joseph*, b. Aug. 7, 1678; d. Dec. 4, 1679.
  5 *Abigail*, b. Mar. 31, 1681; m. Ebenezer Brown.
  6 *Hepzibah*, b. ——; m. first, —— Jones, second, Joseph Fletcher.

1-3-   SAMUEL CHANDLER m. Dec. 11, 1695, Dorcas Buss. He d. 1745. His will, proved that year, mentions sons Samuel, James, and Joseph, and dau. Mary, Huldah, and Rebecca. He was engaged in the land speculation so common at that day,—being one of the petitioners, in 1726, for the large tract lying between Turkey Hill (now Lunenburg) and Rutland. He was also one of the proprietors of the town of Grafton. He was town treasurer from 1723 to 1727, and representative from 1729 to 1736.

3- 7 *Elizabeth*, b. Apr. 6, 1696; d. Oct. 18, 1720, unm.
  8 *Mary*, b. Sept 22, 1699; m. Joseph Dudley, Oct. 2, 1718.
  9 *Joseph*, b. Oct. 11, 1701; d. Jan. 31, 1746.
 10 †*Samuel*, b. Oct. 19, 1704; m. Dinah ——.
 11 *John*, b. Jan. 11, 1707; d. May 3, 1730.
 12 *Huldah*, b. July 5, 1709; m. Sept 28, 1731, Ebenezer Flagg.
 13 *Rebecca*, b. Dec. 2, 1711; m. —— Davis.
 14 *James*, b. Aug. 28, 1714. He m. first, in 1737, Mary Flagg; she d. and he m. second, in 1756, Mary Whittaker, of Carlisle; she d., and he m. third, in 1765, Mary Melvin. Among his children were James, Joseph, and Jonathan. James settled in New Ipswich, N. H., where he became a prominent citizen, and for thirty years was a deacon of the church. His descendants settled in different parts of the country. His son Roger settled in New Ipswich, and was the father of Rev. Seth Chandler, of Shirley. Joseph was for many years a dea. of the Con. ch., and a prominent citizen in the place. He represented the town from 1799 to 1808. He d. Jan. 19, 1813, of a cancer, aged 64.

3-10-   SAMUEL CHANDLER m. Dinah —— about 1730. His will, proved Nov. 17, 1754, mentions wife Dinah, sons Samuel, Jonas, Nathan, and Daniel, and dau. Elizabeth and Mary. Son John appointed executor.

10-15 †*John*, b. Nov, 26, 1731; m. Beulah Merriam, of Lex.
 16 *Samuel*, b. May 29, 1734.   17 *Jonas*, b. Feb. 27, 1737.
 18 *Nathan*, b. July 12, 1739. He was a soldier in the French war in 1760; d. 1760.
 19 *Daniel*, b. Jan. 23, 1741.
 20 *Ebenezer*, b. Mar. 21, 1743; d. Dec. 21, 1752.
 21 *Mary*, b. Mar. 21, 1746; m. William Muzzey, of Hubbardston.
 22 *Elizabeth*, b. Oct. 4, 1749.

10-15- JOHN CHANDLER, m. July 12, 1757, Beulah Merriam, dau. of Joseph and Mary (Brewer) Merriam, of Lex., who was b. Aug. 2, 1730. The Chandlers spoken of above were all of Con. John probably resided in that part of Con. which was included in Lincoln, when it was erected into a town in 1754, as his marriage is recorded as of Lin. He came to Lex. and erected a house on the present Lincoln st., near his father-in-law's, where he spent his days. He held a commission under Gov. Bernard as "Cornet of His Majesty's Blue Troop." His sword, holsters, and a part of his commission are preserved by the family, and were in the hands of his grandson, the late Samuel Chandler. Though he held a commission under the royal governor, he was not false to his native colony. He belonged to the Spartan band headed by Capt. Parker in 1775. He was a prominent man in town for a long period, and filled many offices. He was one of the board of selectmen in the eventful period of the Revolution, was a member of the committee of correspondence, and filled other responsible stations. He was many years treasurer of the Ministerial Fund, which he managed with great wisdom and fidelity. He d. Nov. 22, 1810, aged 79, and she d. Feb. 9, 1813, aged 83. He was ad. to the ch. 1758.

15-23 †*John*, b. Dec. 31, 1758; m. Peggy Mack, of Salem.
24 †*Nathan*, b. Feb. 24, 1762; m. Ruth Tidd.
25 *Sarah*, b. Feb. 27, 1764; m. Oct. 26, 1786, Hammond Reed.
26 *Samuel*, b. Feb. 16, 1766; was grad. H. C. 1790, studied theology, and was ordained over the Second Church in Kittery, afterward Eliot, N. H., Oct. 17, 1792. He m. May 30, 1793, Lydia Spring, dau. of his predecessor in the parish, by whom he had a family. One son, Alpheus S. Chandler, was a physician in Columbia, Me. He d. 1829, aged 63.
27 †*Joseph*, b. Sept 2, 1768; m. Hannah Bridge.
28 *Abiel*, b. June 2, 1771; was grad. H. C. 1798; d. Feb. 11, 1799, unm.

15-23- JOHN CHANDLER, m. Jan. 12, 1786, Peggy Mack, of Salem, at which place he was residing at the time; but the year following they removed to Lex. They were ad. to the ch. Jan. 9, 1791. He d. Oct. 19, 1804, aged 46; she d. Apr. 27, 1853, aged 87. He was a member of Capt. Parker's company, and was on the Common on the 19th of April. He was also in a detachment of the co. which were called to Cambridge on the 10th of May, and in another detachment which marched to Cambridge on the 17th of June, 1775. In 1779, John Chandler, Jr., Joseph Loring, and Burdoo, a colored man from Lex., entered the marine service under Commodore Tucker. Being on the southern coast, they were included in the capitulation of Charleston, S. C., by Gen. Lincoln, in 1780, and were confined as prisoners of war until they were exchanged. After enduring severe sufferings from confinement and want of provisions, they were exchanged, and Chandler and Loring, without money, and almost without clothing, wended their way as best they could to their native home, depending upon the charity of the people, and reached Lex. in a destitute and wretched condition, after having been absent about one year. Such severe trials, though hardly known to the present generation, were common in those days, and show the price our fathers paid for freedom. Such sacrifices on their part should inspire their descendants with true patriotism.

After the close of the war, he was actively engaged in the militia; was elected captain in 1790, and promoted to the office of major in 1796. He was one of the selectmen in 1796, '97, '98.

23-29 | †*John*, b. Nov. 6, 1786; m. Susanna Whitmore Reed.
30 | †*Daniel*, b. Oct. 14, 1788; m. Susanna Downing.
31 | *Sally*, b. Ap. 20, 1791; d. Mar. 15, 1815, unm.
32 | *Peggy*, b. Jan. 15, 1793; m. May 9, 1833, Joseph Eaton,—no issue.
33 | *Mary*, b. Feb. 20, 1794; d. Oct. 19, 1818, unm.
34 | ‡*Samuel*, b. Oct. 26, 1795; m. first, Lydia Muzzey, and second, Abigail Muzzey.
35 | *Jonas*, b. June 23, 1797; d. Apr. 5, 1814.
36 | *Abiel*, b. Mar. 21, 1799; d. in Taunton about 1862.
37 | *Thomas*, b. May 9, 1801; d. Sept. 2, 1838.
38 | *Leonard*, b. June 9, 1803; d. July 6, 1825.

15-24- | NATHAN CHANDLER, m. Oct. 24, 1785, Ruth Tidd, only child of Lieut. William and Ruth (Munroe) Tidd, who was b. Oct. 11, 1767. He lived on Hancock street, where Nathan Chandler now resides, it being the homestead of his father-in-law. He was a lieutenant in the Lex. artillery in 1793. He was selectman fifteen years, assessor eleven years, town clerk eight years, and treasurer thirteen years, representative eight years, and a senator and councillor four years, and was for a long time one of the principal magistrates in the town. Thus for many years he was one of the most popular and influential citizens in the place. He d. Mar. 14, 1837, aged 75, and she d. Sept. 15, 1846, aged 80.

24-39 | *Polly*, b. Jan. 3, 1787; m. May 22, 1806, Nathaniel Mulliken.
40 | ‡*William*, b. Oct. 4, 1788; m. first, Elizabeth Harrington, and second, Mrs. Mary La Bart.
41 | †*Nathan*, b. Mar. 3, 1792; m. Dec. 7, 1821, Maria H. Mead.

15-27- | JOSEPH CHANDLER, m. Sept. 29, 1791, Hannah Bridge, dau. of Major John and Hannah (Reed) Bridge, who was b. Apr. 30, 1771. He d. Oct. 26, 1807, aged 39, and she m. June 7, 1810, Dr. Thomas Whitcomb, who d. Oct. 8, 1813, aged 48. About three weeks before his death, Joseph and his wife o. c. at his residence, and his four children were dedicated to God in baptism.

27-42 | *Hannah*, b. June 26, 1794; d. Jan. 20, 1809, unm.
43 | *Sarah*, b. May 1, 1796; d. Feb. 10, 1800.
44 | *Joseph*, b. Feb. 26, 1801; d. Nov. 16, 1822.
45 | *John B.*, b. Dec. 11, 1806; d. Nov. 10, 1807.

23-29- | JOHN CHANDLER, m. June 7, 1815, Susanna Whitmore Reed, dau. of Nathan and Mary (Page) Reed. He d. Feb. 28, 1817, aged 30. He was ardently devoted to the military, was chosen Captain when he was 23, and rose to the rank of Lieut. Col. and obtained his discharge when he was only 28 — a thing uncommon, especially at that period. He had but one child, viz. *Sarah Chandler*, b. Feb. 27, 1816, who is now living. His wid. d. Dec. 1863, aged 77 years.

23-30- | DANIEL CHANDLER, m. May 19, 1817, Susanna Downing, dau. of Samuel and Susanna (Brown) Downing. He entered the U. S. service as an ensign in Mar. 1812, and on the breaking out of the war of 1812, marched in August to the frontier in Col. Tuttle's regiment; wintered in 1812–13 at French Mills, and was at Plattsburg in 1813. While on a hunting excursion he was severely wounded by the accidental discharge of a gun, and being unable to perform active duty, he was detailed on the recruiting service till 1814, when he returned to the frontier. On the return of peace he resigned his commission, and returned to Mass. While attached to the army he was promoted to a Lieutenancy. He was five years superintendent of the Farm School on Thompson's Island in the harbor of Boston; and was afterwards appointed superintendent of the House of Industry, and also of the House of Reformation in the city of Boston. He erected the house in Lex. where J. C. Blasdel now resides, and was about to move into it, when he was attacked by the ship fever, and d. June 16, 1847, aged 59. His wid. d. Apr. 15, 1866, aged 77.

30-46   *Mary Jane Mack*, b. Mar. 6, 1818; m. Hamilton Hutchins.
47   *Susan D.*, b. Dec. 6, 1819; d. Nov. 23, 1843, unm.
48   *Daniel*, b. Sept. 8, 1822. He r. at Buffalo, N. Y.
49   *Delia, twin of Daniel*, b. Sept. 8, 1822; m. Sept. 28, 1846, Ansel W. Putnam, by whom she had 2 children, Mary H., b. Sept. 20, 1847, and Clara D., b. Mar. 4, 1849. She d. Oct. 15, 1850.
50   *Patrick Henry*, b. Mar. 9, 1824, r. in Boston.
51   *Sarah R.*, b. Sept. 30, 1826; d. Aug. 27, 1846, unm.
52   *Leonard*, b. Aug. 4, 1828; m. Jan. 1848, Lucy Le Baron. He d. in San Francisco, Mar. 22, 1848.
53   *John G.*, b. Dec. 31, 1831. He grad. at West Point, 1854, and entered the service of the United States as a Lieut. of Artillery; he has continued in the service to the present time, passing through the various grades to that of a Coloneley in the regular army. He has served in California and in divers positions through the rebellion.

23-31-   SAMUEL CHANDLER, m. Oct. 29, 1818, Lydia Muzzey, dau. of Amos and Lydia (Boutelle) Muzzey. She d. Aug. 12, 1830, and he m. Sept. 11, 1834, Abigail Muzzey, sister to his first wife. She d. April 24, 1840. He had 5 children by his first wife, and 3 by his last. Having rather a hereditary taste for military matters, he entered the service of the United States as an Ensign in 1814, and repaired to the cantonment at Pittsfield; from thence he was detailed to conduct a body of British prisoners to Canada on exchange, and returned to Pittsfield. Soon after, the troops at that place were ordered to the Niagara frontier and arrived at Buffalo the latter part of July, the day before the battle of Lundy's Lane. But though this corps were not upon the lines in season to take part with the gallant Scott, Porter, and Ripley, on the field of Bridgewater, they were in season to pass through another fiery ordeal more trying than any single battle however sanguinary. They were ordered to Fort Erie, which was early in August besieged by the British under General Drummond, and kept in a close state of investment about two months. During this period there were two desperate battles in which Lieut. Chandler participated — an assault by Drummond upon the Fort on the 15th of August, and a sortie from the Fort on the 17th of September, which induced Drummond to raise the siege. The severity of the engagements may be understood from the fact that the American loss was returned at 595, and that of the enemy about 1700, including nearly 400 taken prisoners. After some slight skirmishes on the Niagara frontier, the army were ordered to proceed by forced marches to Sackett's Harbor, from an apprehension that that post might be attacked by the enemy. On the return of peace, Lieut. Chandler was discharged, after a short but active and trying campaign, in which for five months in succession he and others never slept but with their clothes on. Though he held a commission as Lieut., during the greater part of the campaign he had the command of a co., and during his term of service was promoted from a 3d to 1st Lieut. He was subsequently Major General in the Militia, and held the office of Sheriff of the County ten years. He also represented the County in the Senate of the State, and held the office of Justice of the Peace and Trial Justice. He was many years an active member of the Middlesex Agricultural Society. He d. July 20, 1867, in his 72d year.

34-54 | *John L.*, b. Oct. 6, 1820; m. Abby M. Kimball, dau. of Porter Kimball, of Fitchburg. He resides at Memphis. He was in Mo. at the breaking out of the rebellion, when he entered the service, where he continued till the troops were discharged. He commenced as a Lieut., was in several severe battles, and for gallantry was advanced from time to time, till he reached the rank of Lieut. Col. He was on Fremont's staff, and afterwards Provost Marshal at Little Rock, Ark.

55 | *Amos M.*, b. Nov. 26, 1821; d. Oct. 10, 1825.
56 | *Almira M., B.* Feb. 12, 1824.
57 | *Amos M.*, b. Dec. 21, 1825; d. Aug. 11, 1836.
58 | *Joseph*, b. July 29, 1829; m. Oct. 27, 1865, Eleanor Ball.
59 | *Henry L.*, b. Oct. 31, 1835. He went to Calcutta, where he spent some 8 years. Was there during the rebellion against British authority.
60 | *Samuel E.*, b. Sept. 2, 1837; m. 1864, Laura J. Alley.
61 | *Edward T.*, b. Feb. 28, 1840.

Joseph, Samuel, and Edward, were in the service of the U. S. in the late rebellion. Joseph was taken prisoner at the 2d Bull Run battle. Samuel was wounded and taken prisoner at the 1st Bull Run battle, and was carried to Richmond, where he was confined about 6 mo. He reënlisted into the 12th Reg., was made Quartermaster Sergeant, and was discharged to accept the office of 1st Lieut. in the 7th Mo. Cavalry, and served as Adjutant. He should have been mentioned among the Lex. promotions in p. 308.

24-40- | WILLIAM CHANDLER, m. Oct. 17, 1813, Elizabeth Harrington, dau. of Nathan and Elizabeth (Phelps) Harrington, of Woburn. Though Nathan Harrington resided within the bounds of Woburn, he was of the Lex. family, and his associations were with the Lex. people. She d. Sept. 30, 1847, aged 59, and he m. June 15, 1848, Mrs. Mary La Bart, of Lowell. She was a Munroe of the Lex. stock, and a granddau. of John Munroe. With a sort of family instinct he enlisted into the Rifle company, and in 1826 became the commander of that co. He has filled almost every office in the gift of the town, having been selectman, and many years assessor. He has represented the town in the Legislature, and has been for many years one of the principal magistrates in the place.

40-62 | *Tryphena Harrington*, b. Mar. 8, 1814; d. Mar. 2, 1830.
63 | *William Tidd*, b. June 17, 1816; m. Eliza Ann West, of Charlestown, where they reside. They have had seven children, four of whom are now living.
64 | *Mary*, b. May 22, 1819; m. Oct. 18, 1848, Warren Duren, then of Wo. but now of Lex. She was his 2d wife. No issue.
65 | *Elizabeth*, b. July 8, 1822; m. Abijah Blanchard, of Charlestown, where they reside. They have three children.
66 | *J. Quincy Adams*, b. Sept. 17, 1824; m. Mar. 26, 1866, Sarah P. Dudley. They have one child.
67 | *Nathan*, b. Mar. 22, 1827; m. first, Dec. 17, 1852, Mary Jane Francis. She died, leaving one child, and he m. second, Jan. 16, 1855, Mrs. Clara Wyman Kimball, of Winchester. He resided in Boston, and had two children, one by each wife. He d. June 27, 1861.

24-41- NATHAN CHANDLER, m. Dec. 7, 1821, Maria H. Mead, dau. of Josiah Meade. He resides on the old Tidd place on Hancock st. where his grandfather Tidd resided. He has no children. True to the spirit of the family, he was somewhat devoted to the military, having been captain of the Rifle company.

THE CHILD OR CHILDS FAMILY.

The family of this name have been very numerous in Watertown, Waltham, and several other neighboring towns; but none of them were permanently in Lex. till about the middle of the last century. Abijah Child appears to have been the first who permanently located in the place. He came from Walt. about the time of his marriage in 1763, and was a descendant of one of the early settlers of Wat., of which Walt. was then a part. *Joseph Child,* of Wat., m. July 3, 1654, Sarah Platts, by whom he had several children, among whom was Joseph, b. June 6, 1659. *Joseph Child* was a carpenter by trade, and m. Sept. 23, 1680, Sarah Norcross. She dying, he m. July 25, 1705, Ruth Maddock. He had eight children, four sons and four dau. His youngest son, *Isaac,* m. July 2, 1729, Eunice Pierce. She d. Sept 19, 1793; he d. Feb. 7, 1789. They had eight children, five sons and three dau. Their fifth son, *Abijah,* settled in the south part of Lex.

1 ABIJAH CHILD m. Oct. 27, 1763, Sarah Cutler, dau. of Benj. and Mary Cutler, of Lex. The record of the marriage speaks of them as "both of Lex.," by which we infer that he came here, a young man, before he married. He and his wife were ad. to the ch. Oct. 14, 1764. Mr. Child was a respectable citizen, and filled several town offices. They had seven children, and were called to pass through a scene of affliction which rarely falls to the lot of parents. Six of their children were taken from them by death in the short space of twelve days. These children were interred in the old grave yard, and one long stone tells the sad tale of human mortality and parental affliction, well calculated to produce sober reflection and awaken sympathetic emotions in every parental breast. He d. Aug. 30, 1808; she d. Mar. 3, 1812; he in his seventy-first, and she in her seventy-eighth year.

1- 2 *Sarah,* b. Dec. 17, 1764; d. Aug. 28, 1778.
3 *Eunice,* b. May 15, 1766; d. Aug. 23, 1778.
4 *Abijah,* b. Aug. 1, 1767; d. Aug. 29, 1778.
5 *Abigail,* b. June 18, 1771; d. Aug. 29, 1778.
6 *Benjamin,* b. Nov. 16, 1773; d. Aug. 24, 1778.
7 *Moses,* b. Sept. 1, 1776; d. Aug. 19, 1778.
8 *Isaac,* b. Oct. 11, 1777; d. Nov. 20, 1811.
This branch of the family became extinct.

There have been Childs in town since that period, who belong to the same original family. Some of them have spelt their name with an *s,* Childs, but they are without doubt from the same stock. As in the preceding family, Joseph Childs, of Wat., by wife Sarah Platts, had *Joseph,* b. 1659, who m. 1680, Sarah Norcross, and had *Joseph,* b. June 21, 1685. He m. Mary Thatcher, and had, among other children, *Jonathan,* b. July 3, 1714, who by his wife Elizabeth had five children. *Joseph,* his youngest son, b. Dec. 1761, m. Oct. 3, 1782, Lucy Parminter. *Moses,* son of Joseph and Lucy, b. June 13, 1787, m. Aug. 5, 1810, Mary B., dau. of Thomas and Mary (Ball) Williams, of Marlborough, b. Apr. 4, 1786. Thomas Williams was a direct descendant from Abraham Williams, one of the proprietors of Marlb. Moses Childs d. Feb. 14, 1811, and his wife Sept. 21, 1807, each aged 51.

1   LUKE CARTER CHILDS, a son of Moses and Mary, was b. Mar. 16, 1811. He had one sister, Elizabeth W., b. Dec. 22, 1812. He m. Dec. 10, 1835, Rebecca A. Hale. He did business in Boston several years, and came to Lex. in 1849, and settled upon a farm. He built a neat rural cottage in a central part of his farm, which presents a fine appearance from the street.

1- 2 | *Caroline R.*, b. Dec. 3, 1836; d. Feb. 21, 1838.
3 | *Henry M.*, b. May 17, 1839; d. Nov. 16, 1844.
4 | *Ellen R.*, b. Oct. 17, 1841; d. Sept. 14, 1849.
5 | *Mary E.*, b. Sept. 19, 1843.
6 | *Edward H.*, b. Apr. 23, 1846; d. Sept. 12, 1849.
7 | *Frank C.*, b. Apr. 21, 1849.

There is still another Lex. family of the same name, and from the same parent stock. AUGUSTUS CHILDS, son of Isaac and Betsey Childs, of Walt., was b. Oct. 9, 1818; m. Mar. 9, 1854, Eliza Ann Blodgett, dau. of Charles and Eliza Blodgett. She d. May 20, 1865, and he m. May 10, 1867, Mary Cunningham. He had by first wife, *Charles A.*, b. Jan. 21, 1855; d. Oct. 18, 1861. *Carlton A.*, b. May 20, 1865.

THE CLAFLIN FAMILY.

The name of CLAFLIN scarcely appears on the records of Lex., and yet it seems that there was at an early day a family of that name in the place. *Antipas Claflin* and *Sarah*, his wife, were ad. to the
1   ch. July 31, 1709; and the town records show that they had the following issue.

1- 2 | *Sarah*, b. Nov. 1, 1706. | 3 *Robert*, b. Mar. 13, 1708.
4 | *Noah*, b. Apr. 12, 1710. | 5 *Nehemiah*, b. Sept. 28, 1713.

THE CLARKE FAMILY.

We have had occasion to speak frequently of the Rev. Mr. Clarke, the devoted priest and ardent patriot, whose life and services are interwoven with the history of Lexington. We will now present a genealogical view of the family. His ancestors were respectable, and possessed those stern qualities which form the basis of the New England character, to which we are indebted for much that is valuable in society, even at the present day.

1   HUGH CLARKE, the ancestor of Rev. Jonas, came to this country early, and settled in Wat., where he had three children. He afterwards moved to Rox. He was admitted a freeman May 30, 1660, and was a member of the An. and Hon. Artillery Co. 1666. He d. in Rox. July 20, 1693. His wife, Elizabeth, d. 1692.

1- 2 | ‡*John*, b. in Wat. Oct., 1641.
3 | *Uriah*, b. June 5, 1644; was made freeman in 1685, and d. in Framingham, Feb. 24, 1725.
4 | *Elizabeth*, b. June 31, 1648; m. Joseph Buckminster, of Rox.

1-2-   JOHN CLARKE resided first in Rox. and afterwards moved to Newton. He probably had three wives, though the name of the first

I am unable to give. He m. second, Lydia Buckminster in 1680, and m. third, Elizabeth Norman in 1684.

———

2- 5 | †*John*, of Newton, m. 1697, Ann Pierce, of Dorchester.
6 | *William*, b. June 20, 1686; d. 1737.
7 | *Ann*, b. 1688; m. Apr. 24, 1712, John Billings, of Con.
8 | *Martha*, b. 1690.   8½ *Esther*, b. 1692.
9 | *Hannah*, b. 1693.   9½ *Moses*, b. 1695.

2-5- | JOHN CLARKE m. Ann Pierce, of Dorchester, in 1697.

5-10 | *Mary*, b. 1698.
11 | *John*, b. Sept. 22, 1700; d. in Walt. May 31, 1773.
12 | †*Thomas*, b. 1704; m. 1728, Mary Brown; d. at Hopkinton, June 30, 1775.
13 | *Isaac*, b. 1707; m. first, Experience Wilson; moved to Hop., had a second wife and numerous children.
14 | *Atherton*, m. Patience ———; settled in Hop. and had children.

5-12- | THOMAS CLARKE m. 1728, Mary Bowen, b. Dec. 1704. He d. at Hop. 1775, to which place he and his two brothers had removed. He was a captain when that office gave distinction and commanded respect.

12-15 | *Peter*, b. 1729.
16 | †*Jonas*, b. Dec. 14, 1730; grad. H. C. 1752; settled at Lex.
17 | *Thomas*, b. June 8, 1732.
18 | *Pennel*, b. Mar. 18, 1734; d. 1736.
19 | *Mary*, b. 1736; d. same year.   20 *Mary*, b. Oct. 11, 1737.
21 | *Pennel*, b. July 5, 1739; d. 1742.
22 | *Sarah*, b. and d. 1742.

12-16- | JONAS CLARKE m. Sept. 21, 1757, Lucy Bowes. She was a dau. of Rev. Nicholas Bowes, of Bed. Her mother was Lucy Hancock, dau. of Rev. John Hancock, of Lex. Mr. Clarke was ordained at Lex. Nov. 5, 1755. In taking charge of the church and society in Lex. he became the immediate successor of his grandfather on the side of his wife. He d. Nov. 15, 1805, in the seventy-fifth year of his age, and the fifty-first of his ministry. She d. Apr. 27, 1789.
We have spoken so fully of the life and services of Rev. Jonas Clarke in the civil and ecclesiastical history of the town, that it is unnecessary to extend a notice of him in this place. He had a family of twelve children, several of whom were distinguished in themselves and descendants, as will be seen by the following brief sketch.

———

16-23 | *Thomas*, b. July 6, and d. Nov. 13, 1758.
24 | *Thomas*, b. Sept. 27, 1759; he moved from Lex. to Boston, and engaged in trade. He m. Sally Conant. In 1809 he was chosen town clerk, and continued in that office thirteen years. In 1822, Boston was converted into a city, and Mr. Clarke was chosen Clerk of the Common Council, an office which he held till his death, which happened in 1832. He held the two offices of town clerk and clerk of the common council twenty-three consecutive years, and died in office, in the seventy-third year of his age. The President of the common council, at a meeting of that board, June 1, 1832, announced the death of Thomas Clarke, Esq., and paid the following tribute to his memory: "His private virtues and his long-tried and faithful public services are too well known and too highly appreciated by you to require any eulogium from me. He

has gone down to the grave in the fullness of years, and his memory
is honored by the universal respect of his fellow-citizens."

25 *Jonas*, b. Nov. 27, 1760. He moved, when a young man, to Kenne-
bunk, Me., where he m. Sally Watts. He enjoyed the confidence
of the public, and was called to fill places of honor and trust. He
was collector of the port, and judge of probate for the county
of York.

26 *Mary*, b. May 4, 1762; m. Mar. 31, 1789, Rev. Henry Ware, of
Hingham. He received the appointment of Hollis Professor of
Divinity in Harvard University, and moved to Camb. and entered
upon the discharge of his duties in 1805. He was a man of distinguished ability and of great moral worth, and adorned the office he
was called to fill. He received from the University the honorary
degree of Doctor of Divinity. She d. July 13, 1805, about the
time he moved to Camb. and was buried in the family tomb at
Lex. By his wife, Mary Clarke, Dr. Ware had ten children —
three sons and seven dau. four of whom d. in infancy. *Henry
Ware, Jr.* their oldest son, grad. H. C. 1812, was ordained over
the Second Church in Boston, 1817; but his health failing him, he
left his society and visited Europe. On his return, he was appointed Professor of Pulpit Eloquence and Pastoral Care in Harvard University. He d. Sept. 22, 1843, greatly lamented by all
who knew him.

William Ware, another son of Henry and Mary (Clarke) Ware,
studied theology and settled first in New York city, and afterwards at Walt. and West Camb., Mass. He was also distinguished as a writer.

John, of Henry and Mary, turned his attention to the healing art,
and settled in Boston, where he became one of the most distinguished in his profession. He long filled the office of Professor
of the Theory and Practice of Physic in the Medical Department
of Harvard University.

Lucy Ware, of Henry and Mary, m. Rev. Joseph Allen, D.D., of
Northborough, by whom she had several children, two of whom,
viz. Joseph H. Allen and Thomas P. Allen, are clergymen. *Harriet Ware*, sister of Lucy, m. Rev. Dr. Hall, of Providence, R. I.
She d. June, 1838. One of their sons has entered the ministry.

27 *Elizabeth*, b. June 24, 1763. She united with her father's church
Apr. 25, 1784. She d. Dec. 5, 1843, unm. aged 80.

28 *William*, b. June 20, 1764. He engaged in commercial pursuits in
Boston, and in the prosecution of his business went to Amster-
dam. He was subsequently appointed Consul to Emden, the
chief seaport of the kingdom of Hanover, and d. at Porto Rico in
1822, in the fifty-ninth year of his age. He was never married.

29 *Peter*, b. Nov. 25, 1765. He commenced mercantile business in
Berwick, Me., where he m. his first wife; from Berwick he moved
to Portsmouth, N. H. In the prosecution of the business of his
calling, he sailed for Cadiz; on the voyage he was captured by the
French, and thrown into prison at Guadaloupe, where he contracted a disease of which he died on his passage home. He m.
for his second wife, Nancy Harris, of Concord, N. H.

30 *Lucy*, b. May 2, 1767; m. June 17, 1787, Rev. Thaddeus Fiske, of
West Cambridge, a faithful and popular clergyman.

31 *Lydia*, b. Mar. 20, 1768; m. Aug. 13, 1789, Rev. Benjamin Green,
of Medway. He subsequently left the ministry and entered the
legal profession. He moved to Maine, where he was appointed
Judge of one of their Courts, and afterwards Marshal of the
District.

32 | *Martha*, b. Oct. 28, 1770; m. Nov. 3, 1791, Rev. William Harris, of Salem. He was a clergyman of the Episcopalian Church. He was invited to the city of New York, and finally made President of Columbia College in that city.

33 | *Sarah*, b. Nov. 10, 1774. She united with the church, May 17, 1807, and d. unm. Jan. 28, 1843, aged 69.

34 | *Isaac Bowen*, b. June 29, 1779. He commenced business in Boston, and d. suddenly, July, 1800.

35 | *Henry*, b. Nov. 29, 1780; m. May, 1812, Susan Grafton, of Salem. He commenced business in Boston, and afterwards moved to Kennebunk, Me., where he was cashier of a bank. In 1834, he returned to Boston, where he is now living in his 89th year. Mr. Clarke long held a commission as Justice and Notary. He has had but two children, both of whom are now living. *Henry Grafton* was born May 14, 1814. He studied medicine, and resides in Boston, occupying a good position in his profession. *Jonas Bowen*, b. Jan. 16, 1816, was grad. at Dartmouth, 1839. He entered the ministry, was first settled in Conn.; but his health failing him, he returned to Massachusetts, and was settled in Swampscot.

From this glance at the subject, it will be seen that but few families can boast of distinction such as has fallen to the lot of Rev. Jonas Clarke's.

OTHER PERSONS BY THE NAME OF CLARKE.

There were several persons by the name of Clarke in the town at different times, whose lineage we have not ascertained. In 1725, the selectmen laid out a "way for the accommodation of the farms that Daniel Hoar and Judah Clarke live on." In the earliest tax bill now extant, 1729, we find Judah Clarke and Judah Clarke, Jr., taxed, the former having two houses, and the latter one. They lived in a part of the town now included in Lin.

We will give what our records contain in relation to the Clarkes, without attempting to classify them.

Richard Clarke, of Richard and Mary, b. Feb. 3, 1719.
Mary Clarke, of James and Jerusha, b. July 19, 1733.
Ruth Clarke, admitted to the ch. by a recommendation from the Pastor of Rowley, Nov. 7, 1725.
Mary Clarke, ad. to the ch. Feb. 8, 1728.
Jonathan Clarke, bap. July 15, 1733, his parents o. c.
Mary Clarke, of James, bap. July 22, 1733.
Hannah Clarke, bap. Jan. 19, 1735.
Eunice Clarke, ad. to the ch. May 30, 1736, and dismissed to Harvard, Aug. 9, 1741.
James Clarke, dismissed to the ch. at Medfield, Jan. 18, 1746. He married Jerusha Bullard of Medfield, Nov. 19, 1730. Mary and probably Hannah, in the preceding list, were their children.
Judah Clarke, of Lex. m. Nov. 21, 1752, Mary Dudley, of Con.

THE COMEE FAMILY.

1 | JOHN COMEE was in Camb. Farms at the organization of the Precinct in 1693, and was taxed to pay the minister for that year; and also for the purchase of the ministerial land the same year. In

1697 he was on a committee to look after that land, and in 1711 was a subscriber to pay for the land purchased for a Common. He m. Jan. 21, 1688, Martha Munroe, eldest dau. of William and Martha Munroe. His wife was ad. to the ch. Feb. 1, 1699, and he o. c. shortly after; and on the 26th of Feb. 1699, four of their children, John, David, Hannah, and Martha, were bap. We have no record of their births. He is probably the John Comee who d. July 20, 1723. She d. Mar. 27, 1730. He was of Con. in 1688, where he was m.

1- 2 *John*, b. ———; m. Ruhama ———.
3 †*David*, b. ———.
4 *Hannah*, b. ———; d. May 26, 1770, unm.
5 *Martha*, b. ———; m. July 9, 1713, Benj. Smith, and d. Nov. 19, 1749.
6 *Elizabeth*, bap. Feb. 1706.   7 *Abigail*, bap. Oct. 26, 1707.

1-3-   DAVID COMEE m. Ruhama Brown? We have found no record of the marriage, but presume it was about 1719, from the birth of their first child, and from the other significant fact, that he was, in 1720, called to the responsible office of looking after the swine — a custom long prevailing of giving this honor to a newly married man. She was ad. to the ch. Aug. 14, 1720, and d. 1730. He m. second, Sarah ———, by whom he had most of his children. The record of the family is not perfect. It seems that they buried at least two children in early infancy, one in 1720, and one in 1730. Whether they were some which are mentioned below is not perfectly clear. Sarah, his second wife, was ad. to the ch. May 28, 1738.

3- 8 *David*, b. July 30, 1719; d. 1720.   9 *John*, bap. Sept. 26, 1725.
10 †*Joseph*, bap. Aug. 4, 1728.
11 *Benjamin*, b. Nov. 15, 1733; m. Mar. 25, 1762, Hannah Watts, of Chelsea.
12 *Sarah*, b. Sept. 11, 1735; m. Dec. 4, 1755, Isaac Parkhurst, Wat.
13 *Martha*, b. Apr. 11, 1737.   14 *Ezekiel*, b. Apr. 27, 1740.
15 *Ruhama*, b. Apr. 15, 1742.
16 †*David*, b. Apr. 21, 1744; d. Mar. 8, 1826, at Gardner, aged 81.
17 *Jonathan*, b. Apr. 4, 1746.

3-10-   JOSEPH COMEE m. Mary ———. Joseph Comee was one of that patriot band who appeared in arms on the 19th of April, 1775. At the time of the approach of the British, he and two others were in the church to replenish their horns with powder. Seeing that the British were about to surround the house, Comee, in attempting to escape amid a shower of balls, was wounded in the arm.

10-18 *Ezra*, } probably twins, { bap. Oct. 27, 1751.
19 *Mercy*,
20 *Joseph*, b. July 1, 1753.   21 *Mary*, b. June 22, 1755.
22 *Aaron*, b. Aug. 15, 1757.   23 *Betty*, b. Mar. 23, 1760.
24 *Ruhama*, bap. Nov. 14, 1762.   25 *Benjamin*, bap. July 7, 1765.

3-16-   DAVID COMEE went to Camb.; m. first, Christiana Maltman, of Boston, and m. second, Hannah Maltman. He had fifteen children. He was in the battles of Lex., Bunker Hill, and Bennington. He moved to Gardner, where he d. Mar. 8, 1826, aged 81. His descendants are in Gardner and Fitchburg at the present day.

THE COOLEDGE FAMILY.

JOHN COOLEDGE, the ancestor of Rev. Josiah Cooledge, came to this country about 1630, and settled in Wat., of which he was a proprietor, and a leading citizen. By his wife Mary he had eight chil. *Nathaniel*, his fifth son, m. 1657, Mary Bright, and d. 1711. They had thirteen chil. *Thomas*, son of Nathl., b. Apr. 24, 1670, m. 1699, Sarah Eddy, who d. 1711; and he m. 1713, Mary Smith. They moved to Sherborne. He d. 1737. He had by his first wife three chil. *David*, the only son of Thomas, was b. June 25, 1705; m. Mary Mixer, and had six chil. *David*, the oldest child of the preceding, was b. Sept. 3, 1738, and d. of small-pox, 1788. He m. 1765, Dorothy Stearnes. They r. in Wat., and had eleven chil. *Peter*, the youngest son of David, was b. July 2, 1787, m. June 28, 1813, Mary T. Munroe, of Camb. She d. Jan. 24, 1823, and he m. July 1, 1824, Mary P. Fiske, of Framingham, where he resided. He had six children.

1   JOSIAH COOLEDGE, the second child of Peter, was b. Oct. 20, 1816, and m. May 1, 1844, Mehitable A. Fowle, of Boston. He entered the ministry and preached for a time in Shirley and other places, and was settled over the Universalist Society in Lex. in 1849. where he remained about four years. After leaving Lex. he moved to Melrose. He d. Oct. 5, 1865.

1- 2	*Julia*, b. Mar. 11, 1845; d. Sept. 11, 1847.
3	*Helen M.*, b. Mar. 5, 1847.
4	*Anna Hall*, b. June 3, 1850. ⎫ twins.
5	*Julia*, b. June 3, 1850. ⎭
6	*Henry*, b. June 14, 1853; d. Oct. 8, 1854.

THE COOPER FAMILY.

There was a family of Coopers in Lex. whose lineage we have not traced, who probably came into the place about 1700. They may have come from Camb.

1   JOHN COOPER m. Elizabeth ———. He sold his house and land in Lex. to John Palfrey, in 1719, and undoubtedly left town about that time. He lived in the southwest part of Lex.

1- 2	*Elizabeth*, b. May 9, 1699.	3	*Hannah*, b. Dec. 29, 1702.
4	*Sarah*, b. Apr. 9, 1704.	5	*Timothy*, b. Apr. 9, 1706.
6	*Joshua*, b. June 25, 1709.	7	*Abigail*, b. July 10, 1711.
8	*Ruth*, b. Sept. 23, 1714.		

CROSBY, is a name which appears a few times upon our records; but there appears to have been no permanent family of that name in Lex.

Sampson Crosby, son of Sampson and Lucy, b. June 5, 1761.
Joel,   "   "   "   "   "   " b. Feb. 9, 1763.
George Adams and *Elizabeth Crosby*, both of Lex. m. Nov. 18, 1762.
Ephraim Cook, Camb. and *Hannah Crosby*, of Lex. m. Jan. 20, 1778.

They may have belonged to the Crosby family living in Bedford. Some of the name have been in town temporarily at later periods.

THE CROWNINSHIELD FAMILY.

1   Abraham W. Crowninshield, son of William and Sarah (Plumer) Crowninshield, was b. in Portland, Dec. 16, 1801. He m. Nov. 9, 1823, Sarah Byles Peters, b. in Portland, July 16, 1804. They settled in Charlestown, where their children were born. He was engaged in the furniture and upholstery business. In 1846 he came to Lex. and purchased a small farm, still continuing his business at Charlestown some years. He has filled the office of assessor several years, and has represented the district in the General Court.

1- 2 *Sarah*, b. Aug. 28, 1824; d. Sept. 20, 1824.
3 *Caleb S.*, b. Nov. 17, 1825; m. Jan. 1, 1862, Julia H. Christy. They r. in Brighton.
4 *Mary P.*, b. Feb. 3, 1828; m. Sept. 3, 1850, William H. H. Reed, of Lex. They have had several children, some of whom they have buried. They r. in Charlestown.
5 *William B.*, b. July, 1830; d. Jan. 2, 1838.
6 *Charles F.*, b. Aug. 6, 1834; d. Dec. 9, 1837.
7 *George W.*, b. Dec. 23, 1836; d. Dec. 12, 1837.
8 *Sarah C.*, b. Apr. 23, 1839; m. June 20, 1865, Henry M. Loring, of Charlestown.

THE CUTLER FAMILY.

The Cutlers, always somewhat numerous in Lex., were among the earliest settlers in the place. They came to Lex. from Wat., and were the descendants of James Cutler. There is a tradition in the family, and English records, if they do not confirm, rather favor the position, that Sir Gervase Cutler, who married a daughter of the Duke of Bridgewater, was the ancestor of the Cutlers who came to America. 1 But be this as it may, we feel assured that as early as 1635, James Cutler was in Wat., and was an original grantee of land in the northerly part of Wat., on the road to Belmont, and in 1649, James Cutler and Nathaniel Bowman purchased of Edward Goffe 200 acres of land in Cambridge, adjoining Rock-meadow, near the Wat. line. In 1651, he sold his share to Bowman for £39. This was probably the land on which Bowman settled, near the present line of Arlington. It is probable that Cutler, and perhaps Bowman, moved from Wat. about this date. Cutler settled at Camb. Farms, near Concord, now Bed., line. A part of this farm was owned till recently by the wid. of John and heirs of Leonard Cutler. His house was situated in the lot back of the present house,—the door step and appearances of the cellar still remain. This must have been one of the first houses erected in the precinct.

He was b. about 1606, and probably married before he came to this country. His wife, Anna, was buried Sept. 30, 1644; and he m. second, Mar. 9, 1645, Mary King, wid. of Thomas King, of Wat., who d. Dec. 7, 1654. He m. third, Phebe Page, dau. of John, about 1662. He d. May 17, 1694, aged about 88. His will, dated Nov. 24, 1684, presented by his sons John and Thomas, and proved Aug. 20, 1694, mentions children James, Thomas, John, John Collar, Richard Park's wife, John Parmenter's wife, Sarah Wait, Mary Johnson, Hannah Winter, Joanna Russell (Philip's wife), Jemima, Samuel, and Phebe. "This list includes two children of my wife, formerly wife of Thomas King, one of whom was Mary Johnson." (The Mary here alluded to was b. Feb. 2, 1643, and was m. Oct. 19, 1659, to John Johnson.)

1- 2 | †*James*, b. Nov. 6, 1635; m. June 15, 1665, Lydia Wright.
3 | *Hannah*, b. July 26, 1638; m. John Winter, Jr.
4 | *Elizabeth*, b. Jan. 28, 1640; d. in infancy.
5 | *Mary*, b. Mar. 29, 1644; m. John Collar.
6 | *Elizabeth*, b. July 20, 1646; m. about 1667 John Parmenter, 3d, of Sud.
7 | †*Thomas*, b. about 1648; m. Abigail ——.
8 | *Sarah*, b. about 1653; m. Thomas Waite, of Camb. Farms; ad. to the ch. in Wat. Feb. 2, 1690; d. in Weston, Jan. 17, 1744.
9 | *Sarah*, b. —; m. Richard Park, and d. previous to 1690. She was a dau. of Thomas and Mary King, probably.
10 | *Joanna*, b. about 1660; m. Apr. 19, 1680, Philip Russell, and d. Nov. 26, 1703, in her forty-second year.
11 | *Jemima*, b. ——.
12 | †*John*, b. May 19, 1663; d. Sept. 21, 1714.
13 | *Samuel*, b. Nov. 18, 1664.
14 | *Phebe*, b. ——.

1-2- | JAMES CUTLER, of Camb. Farms, m. June 15, 1665, Lydia Wright, wid. of Samuel Wright, of Sud., and dau. of John Moore, of that town. He d. July 31, 1685, aged 50. His will, dated July 28, and proved Oct. 6, 1685, mentions wife Lydia, and chil. James, Samuel, Thomas, and Ann, and refers to other children without naming them.

2-15 | *James*, b. May 12, 1666; d. Dec. 1, 1690.
16 | *Ann*, b. Apr. 20, 1669; m. Sept. 26, 1688, Richard Blaise, of Wat.
17 | *Samuel*, } b. May 2, 1672; { d. at Lex. Nov. 20, 1700.
18 | *Joseph*, } { probably d. Sept. 22, 1738.
19 | †*John*, b. Apr. 14, 1675. He removed to Killingly, Ct.
20 | †*Thomas*, b. Dec. 15, 1677; m. Sarah Stone.
21 | *Elizabeth*, b. Mar. 14, 1681.

1-7- | THOMAS CUTLER m. Abigail ——. They united with the ch. in Wat. July 31, 1687, and when a ch. was gathered in Lex. in 1696, they removed their relation to it. He was a subscriber for the erection of the first meeting house, in 1692, and was chosen one of the assessors in 1694; and in 1700, when the parish performed what was formerly considered a very important duty, that of "seating the meeting house," David Russell, John Mason, and Thomas Cutler, "were plast in ye second seat in y^o front gallereye." He was a valuable and honored citizen, and was often employed in town business,—was an assessor, constable, and selectman. He was also honored in the public records with the title of lieutenant, no mean designation at that day. He d. July 13, 1722.

7-22 | *Abigail*, b. Oct. 31, 1674.
23 | *Thomas*, b. Jan. 19, 1678; probably the Thomas who had a son James, bap. Mar. 17, 1706.
24 | *Mary*, b. Mar. 15, 1681; m. about 1698, William Munroe, Jr., of Lex.
25 | *Hannah*, b. May 7, 1683; d. Feb. 25, 1704.
26 | †*James*, bap. in Wat. Jan. 9, 1687.
27 | *Jonathan*, bap. in Wat. June 17, 1688; moved to Killingly, Ct.
28 | †*Benjamin*, b. in Lex. July 4, and bap. in Wat. Oct. 3, 1697.

1-12- | JOHN CUTLER m. Jan. 1, 1694, Mary Stearns, dau. of Isaac and Sarah (Beers) Stearns, who was b. Oct. 8, 1663. He owned the covenant Nov. 1, 1702, when four of his children were baptized. He was in the place, and was taxed in 1693 for the purchase of the

ministerial land, and was assigned a place "in yᵉ front gallerye," in
1700, when they seated the meeting house. He must have resided
on what is now Weston street, over the brook, on the southerly side
of the old Concord turnpike. As early as 1714, John Merriam and
Matthew Bridge were appointed a committee to lay a road to accommodate Nathaniel Stone, Joseph Stone, Robert Merriam, and John
Cutler; and the description of the road leaves no doubt of the general situation of John Cutler's residence. It ran from Nathaniel
Stone's house by various bounds to the "great rock," thence across
the brook to Cutler's house. He d. Sept. 21, 1714; she d. Feb. 24,
1733.

12-29   *Samuel*, b. Dec. 20, 1694; probably d. May 12, 1742.
  30   †*John*, b. June 3, 1696; m. Jan. 9, 1724, Abigail Stone.
  31   *Ebenezer*, b. July 24, 1700. Probably the Capt. Ebenezer Cutler of
      Weston, who m. Mar. 3, 1724, Anna Whitney, of Con., and d. in
      Lincoln, Jan. 17, 1777.
  32   *Mary*, b. Apr. 3, 1702; m. Feb. 7, 1724, Capt. Samuel Bond, of
      Weston, afterwards of Linc.
  33   *Sarah*, b. Nov. 20, 1704; probably d. Jan. 12, 1749.

2-19-   JOHN CUTLER m. Hannah Snow, of Wo., Feb. 6, 1700. She was
  ad. to the ch. by letter from the ch. of Wo., July 5, 1702. They
  moved to Killingly, Ct., about 1713. They had eight children born
  and baptized in Lex.

19-34 *Hannah*, bap. Nov. 30, 1701.   35 *Mary*, bap. July 4, 1703.
  36   *Seth*,   } twins, bap. July 29, 1705.
  37   *Timothy*, }
  38   *Hezekiah*, bap. Apr. 20, 1707; father of Manasseh, D. D.
  39   *Dinah*, bap. Sept. 4, 1709.   40 *Jemima*, bap. May 27, 1711.
  41   *Uriah*, bap. May 29, 1713; went to Morristown, N. J., about 1740.

2-20-   THOMAS CUTLER m. Sarah Stone, dau. of Samuel and Dorcas
  Stone. She d. Jan. 10, 1750, in her sixty-ninth year. He o. c.
  June 6, 1703, and she joined the ch. July 4, 1708. He was constable
  in 1719, and selectman, 1729, '31, '33, '34.

20-42 *Abigail*, b. June 2, 1703; m. Nov. 18, 1722, Joseph Bridge.
  43   †*David*, b. Aug. 26, 1705.   44 *Amity*, b. Dec. 19, 1707.
  45   *Sarah*, b. Jan. 17, 1710.   46 *Mary*, b. Nov. 8, 1714.
  47   *Hannah*, b. May 13, 1717; d. June 2, 1724.
  48   †*Thomas*, b. Apr. 30, 1719; d. 1760, of small pox.
  49   *Millicent*, bap. July 29, 1722; d. Jan. 2, 1741.

7-26-   JAMES CUTLER m. Alice ———. He o. c. Apr. 17, 1715.

26-50 *James*, b. Apr. 3, 1715; may have been the James C. who d. at
      Salem 1795, aged 80.
  51   *William*, bap. Apr. 7, 1717.
  52   *Thankful*, (?) bap. Mar. 22, 1719.

7-28-   BENJAMIN CUTLER m. Mary ———. They o. c. June 28, 1724
  and she was ad. to the ch. Feb. 18, 1728. After living together
  more than fifty years he d. Nov. 3, 1776, aged 79 years, and she
  survived him only three days, and d. Nov. 6, 1776, aged 75. Their
  names are both borne on one stone in the Lex. grave yard. He was
  constable in 1739 and 1741.

28-53 | *Abigail*, b. June 4, 1724; d. young.
54 | †*Benjamin*, } twins, { b. Sept. 4, 1725.
55 | *Mary*, } { b. Sept. 4, 1725; d. Jan. 26, 1808, aged 83.
56 | *Hannah*, b. Dec. 27, 1729; d. Oct. 1, 1805, aged 76.
57 | *Elizabeth*, b. May 11, 1732; m. Apr. 7, 1761, Jacob Kendall, of Dunstable.
58 | *Sarah*, b. June 17, 1734; m. Oct. 27, 1763, Abijah Child.
59 | *Lydia*, b. Aug. 31, 1736; d. in 1740.
60 | *Nathan*, b. Aug. 18, 1738. 61 *Lydia*, b. Feb. 26, 1746.

12-30- JOHN CUTLER m. Jan. 9, 1724, Abigail Stone, dau. of John and Mary Stone, b. 1698. They made their confession to the ch. Sept. 27, 1724. He was ad. to the ch. Feb. 10, 1734, and she was ad. Sept. 12, 1742. They moved to Brookfield, to the ch. of which they were dismissed May 10, 1752. He was selectman in 1733, and assessor same year.

30-62 | *John*, b. July 7, 1724; m. 1749, Susanna Hastings, resided several years in Shrewsbury, moved to New Ipswich; d. 1771.
63 | *Isaac*, b. May 31, 1726; d. Oct. 24, 1745, at Cape Breton.
64 | *Robert*, b. Apr. 30, 1728; m. Sept. 3, 1751, Elizabeth Fiske.
65 | *Abijah*, b. May 25, 1730. 66 *Josiah*, b. Aug. 9, 1732.
67 | *Thaddeus*, b. Mar. 15, 1735.
68 | *Joseph*, b. July 26, 1737; d. Nov. 1738.
69 | *Joseph*, b. Aug. 9, 1739. 69½ *Samuel*, b. Mar. 7, 1744.

20-43- DAVID CUTLER m. Mary Tidd, dau. of Joseph and Mary Tidd. They were ad. to the ch. Apr. 14, 1728. He resided on the old homestead near Bedford line. He was constable in 1746, and selectman in 1749, '50, '51.

His will, dated Sept. 13, 1758, and proved Feb. 9, 1761, mentions wife Mary, sons David, to whom he gave the farm in Western (now Warren) on which he then lived, Joseph, to whom he gave the place in Western on which he then resided, Solomon, to whom he gave the southerly part of the homestead, and Thomas, to whom he gave the rest of the home farm; and dau. Abigail Hodgman and Mary Page. He was a man of good property — his inventory of personal property being £373 13s. He made ample provision for his widow, providing that Solomon and Thomas should supply her with a horse, two cows, and furnish her annually with twelve bushels of corn, four of rye, one bushel of malt, sixty pounds of beef, one hundred and twenty pounds of pork, three barrels of cider, and ten cords of wood, cut up and fit for the fire. He d. Dec. 5, 1760 of small pox; she d. May 25, 1797, aged 93.

43-70 | *Abigail*, b. May 1, 1728; m. May 7, 1755, Samuel Hodgman of Western.
71 | *David*, b. July 15, 1730; m. Oct. 15, 1751, Dorcas Reed, dau. of Capt. Benjamin and Rebecca Reed of Lex. He resided for a time in Western, but afterwards moved to Bennington, Vt., and perhaps went South.
72 | *Joseph*, b. May 31, 1733; m. May 6, 1755, Rebecca Howe of Linc. She d., and he m. Mary Reed of Western, and settled there.
73 | *Isaac*, b. June, 1736; d. Jan., 1737.
74 | *Mary*, b. Aug. 12, 1738; m. Sept. 15, 1758, John Paige of Hardwick.
75 | ‡*Solomon*, b. May 15, 1740; m. Rebecca Page of Bedford.
76 | ‡*Thomas*, b. May 5, 1742; m. Abigail Reed of Western.
77 | *Elizabeth*, b. Aug. 5, 1745; m. May 3, 1768, Benj Moore of Lex.

78 | *Amity*, b. July 15, 1748; m. Nov. 6, 1766, Nathan Leonard, of Hardwick.

20-48- | THOMAS CUTLER m. Sarah ———. They united with the ch. Dec. 6, 1741. She d. Jan. 12, 1749, and he m. second, Apr. 10, 1750, Lydia Simonds. May 17, 1752, Thomas Cutler and his wife were dismissed to the church at Western. They both d. 1760, of small pox.

48-79 | *Amos*, b. Sept. 28, 1742.   80 *Sarah*, bap. Apr. 7, 1745.
81 | *Ebenezer*, bap. May 3, 1747.   82 *Bethia*, bap. July 22, 1750.

28-54- | BENJAMIN CUTLER m. Elizabeth Buttrick of Harvard, Nov. 23, 1758. They were ad. to the ch. Aug. 5, 1759.

54-83 | *Dolly*, b. May 13, 1759.   84 *William*, b. Feb. 10, 1761.
85 | *Betty*, b. Jan. 16, 1763.

43-75- | SOLOMON CUTLER m. Feb. 23, 1762, Rebecca Page of Bed. They were ad. to the ch. Mar. 10, 1765. They moved to Rindge, N. H., about 1772, to the ch. of which they were dismissed Feb. 14, 1773.

75-86 | *Amos*, b. Sept. 20, 1762.   87 *Rebecca*, b. May 20, 1765.
88 | *Sarah*, b. Oct. 7, 1768.   89 *Polly*, b. Apr. 16, 1770.

43-76- | THOMAS CUTLER m. Abigail Reed of Western, (now Warren). They were admitted to the ch. June 30, 1765. She d. Sept. 26, 1784, aged 33. He m. Feb. 2, 1786, Elizabeth White, wid. of Ebenezer White. Her maiden name was Harrington, dau. of Moses Harrington. He d. July 3, 1812, aged 70; she d. Sept. 21, 1834, aged 86. His will, dated Dec. 18, 1805, and proved Aug. 12, 1812, mentions wife Elizabeth, sons John, Jonas, Amos, Leonard, and Nathaniel, and dau. Nabby Simonds, Polly, Alice, and Betsey. His real estate was inventoried at $6,980, and his personal at $1,442. Thomas Cutler was a member of Capt. Parker's company in 1775.

76-90 | *Isaac*, b. Aug. 9, 1765; m. Sophia Brown, and settled in Ashby. He d. May 6, 1826. He had six children.
91 | †*Thomas*, b. Mar. 18, 1769; m. Rebecca Earl.
92 | *Abigail*, b. May 2, 1771; m. June 5, 1794, Joshua Simonds. She d. Aug. 8, 1837, aged 66.
93 | †*Nathaniel*, b. June 19, 1773; m. Anna Child, Waltham.
94 | *Mary*, b. July 10, 1775; d. May 16, 1819, unm.
95 | †*John*, b. May 10, 1777; m. Almira Flagg, of Mason, N. H.
96 | *Alice*, b. June 1, 1779; m, Nathaniel Searle, of Mason, N. H. She d. Mar. 1815.
97 | *Jonas*, b. Mar. 3, 1782; m. Martha, dau. of Amos Marrett. He settled in Westminster; d. Jan. 29, 1830, aged 48, leaving three children.
98 | †*Amos*, b. Nov. 9, 1786; m. Rachel Flagg, of Mason, N. H.
99 | *Betsey*, b. Oct. 27, 1789; m. Dec. 13, 1815, John Bacon, of Bed. She was living, 1858.
100 | †*Leonard*, b. Apr. 21, 1791; m. Maria Cutter.

76-91- | THOMAS CUTLER m. Alice Niles. He settled in Ashby. What time he left Lex. is not exactly known. He was taxed in Lex. 1799, and his name was placed upon the tax bill in 1800, and then his name and tax are erased. Probably they left town early that year. The births of his two oldest children are recorded in Lex. Records as children of Thomas Cutler and *Ellis* his wife. Two years after the birth of his second child, the church records associate *Rebecca* with him as his wife; from which we infer that he buried his wife Ellis, or Alice, and m. Rebecca Earl about 1798. He d. in Bedford, Feb. 14, 1833, aged 64.

91-101   *Charles*, b. Feb. 3, 1795; m. Prudence Holden, in Ashby.
102   *Abigail*, b. Aug. 27, 1796; m. —— Green.
103   *Marshall*, b. ——; m. Catharine Wood; d. at Mobile.
104   *Thomas C.*, b. ——; m. first, Maria Wood, second, Louisa Wheat. Lives in Bedford.
105   *Rebecca*, b. ——; d. unm. aged 21.
106   *Nathaniel*, b. ——; m. first, Susan Lane; second, —— Wheeler; third, wid. Clemens. Lives in Bedford.
107   *Leonard*, b. ——; d. unm. aged 21.
108   *Alice Searle*, b. ——; m. —— Hassington?

76-93-   NATHANIEL CUTLER m. Apr. 4, 1799, Anna Child, dau. of Abijah Child, of Waltham, b. Nov. 14, 1775. He purchased the White place in the south part of Lex. on what is now Concord Avenue, where he d. Sept. 3, 1849, aged 76. She d. Mar. 22, 1863, aged 87.

93-109   *Isaac*, b. Mar. 30, 1800; m. Nov. 24, 1825, Lydia Braman, of Norton. He settled in Con. in 1839, moved to Camb. was alderman, 1855, '56, and '57. They had five children, viz. first, George Henry, b. 1826; m. Mary Ann Rice, and second, Lydia Ann Holbrook. Second, Wm. Francis, b. 1828; m. Margaret Scolley; d. 1857. Third, Lydia, b. 1830. Fourth, Edwin Braman, b. 1831. Fifth, Frances, b. 1839.
110   †*Thomas*, b. Nov. 15, 1801; m. Sarah Smith, Dec. 28, 1828.
111   †*Curtis*, b. Jan. 1, 1806; m. Clarissa W. Morrell.
112   *Eliza Ann*, b. Oct. 14, 1813; m. May, 1839, Theo. P. Wood, of Gardner. He d. June 15, 1843, and she m. Dec. 25, 1844, Francis Richardson, of Gardner.

76-95-   JOHN CUTLER m. Jan. 19, 1813, Almira Flagg, of Mason, N. H. He lived on the homestead, and d. Mar. 12, 1828. She was living on the old place in 1858.

95-113   *Emily*, b. Sept. 10, 1813; m. D. C. Chamberlain, of Somerville.
114   *Alice*, b. Feb. 19, 1815; m. G. C. Hawkins, Lex., second, E. C. Mann, Somerville.
115   *Cynthia*, b. June 16, 1816; m. J. Lathrop; went to Wisconsin.
116   *John Reed*, b. Sept. 20, 1819; r. at Napoleon, Ark.
117   *Hiram*, b. Sept. 21, 1821; m. Rebecca Hawkins, and r. at Northwood, N. H.
118   *Artemas*, b. Nov. 12, 1823; m. Mary J. Batchelder, and r. at East Cambridge.
119   *Marcellus*, b. July 23, 1826; d. Mar. 23, 1839.
120   *George Martin*, b. Oct. 27, 1828; m. Lucy A. Burrell; r. in Illinois.

76-98-   AMOS CUTLER m. Rachel Flagg, of Mason, N. H., where he d. Dec. 1823.

98-121   *Frederick P.*, b. Oct. 26, 1813; r. in Brattleboro', Vt.
122   *Elbridge*, b. Mar. 3, 1815; died young.
123   *David A.*, b. Apr. 12, 1816; m. Martha Nutting.
124   *Lucy Ann*, b. ——; m. —— Flanders.
125   *Edward W.*, b. ——; m. —— Foss.

126 | *Rebecca J.*, b. ——— ; m. Addison Parker.
127 | *Amos Elbridge*, b. ——— ; m. Belinda Johonnot, Woburn.

76–100– | LEONARD CUTLER m. May 21, 1826, Maria Cutter, of West Cambridge, and settled on a part of the homestead. He d. 1853.

100–128 | *Cornelia Maria*, b. 1828 ; m. Samuel R. Duren, Wo.
129 | *Abby Sarah*, b. 1830 ; m. Joseph R. Kendall.
130 | *Anna Bacon*, b. 1832, m. Lewis Spaulding, of Bedford.
131 | *Isabella*, b. 1834.   132 *James Russell*, b. 1838.
133 | *Cyrus Morton*, b. 1841.   He was in the Army of the Potomac.
134 | *Ella Adine*, b. 1843.
135 | *Alfred Dennis*, b. 1848 ; was in the service in the 6th Mass. V. M.

93–110– | THOMAS CUTLER m. Dec. 28, 1828, Sarah Smith, of Waltham, b. Nov. 30, 1806. They reside on Concord Avenue, on the farm formerly occupied by his father. She d. Sept. 26, 1864, aged 57.

110–136 | †*Thomas Everett*, b. Apr. 1, 1830 ; m. Melinda W. Houghton.
137 | *Albert Curtis*, b. Mar. 26, 1831 ; m. Apr. 9, 1853, Eliza M. Tyler, of Waltham, where he resides.
138 | *Sarah Ann*, b. Jan. 11, 1835 ; d. Aug. 29, 1859.
139 | *Franklin*, b. Oct. 11, 1837 ; d. Jan. 15, 1860.
140 | *Eliza Wood*, b. Aug. 10, 1840 ; m. Apr. 30, 1865, F. D. Wellington, of Lincoln.
141 | *Charles*, b. June 10, 1842 ; d. Aug. 29, 1862, of disease contracted in the army.
142 | *Clara*, b. July 4, 1846.

93–111– | CURTIS CUTLER was grad. at H. C., 1829, studied theology, and was settled in Gardner, Oct. 30, 1833 ; m. May 19, 1835, Clarissa W. Morrell, dau. of Ambrose Morrell, Lex. He left Gardner, 1839, and was installed at Peterboro', N. H., Jan. 30, 1840, as colleague with Abiel Abbot, D. D. In 1848, he left Peterboro' and moved to Lex. In 1850, in consequence of a bronchial affection, he gave up his profession, and engaged in mercantile pursuits with the firm of Wm. Underwood & Co., Boston. In 1855, he represented the town in the General Court, and in the autumn of that year moved to Camb. To him we are indebted for much of the information concerning this family.

111–143 | *Sarah M.*, born in Gardner, Apr. 14, 1838.
144 | *Annie C.*, b. in Peterboro, N. H., Mar. 12, 1845.

110–136– | THOMAS EVERETT CUTLER m. Aug. 20, 1861, Melinda W. Houghton, dau. of Samuel Houghton. They have Charles F., b. Nov. 2, 1862, Ida Warren, b. Oct. 12, 1864, Edward Everett, b. May 12, 1866.

It has been difficult in some cases to distinguish the name from that of Cutter, which is found in a few instances upon the Lex. records. There are several other families mentioned on Lex. records, but probably they resided there only temporarily.

THE CUTTER FAMILY.

RICHARD CUTTER, of Cambridge, ad. freeman, June 2, 1641 ; d. June 18, 1693, aged about 72. He had two wives, by whom he had fourteen children, among whom was NATHANIEL, b. Dec. 11, 1663.

He m. Oct. 8, 1688, Mary Fillebrown. She d. May 14, 1713, and he married Elizabeth. He had seven children, among whom was JOHN CUTTER, bap. Apr. 23, 1704. What time he came into Lex. we are not able to say. His name is found on our first tax bill extant, viz., 1729. His name continues on the tax bill till 1747, when we find the name of wid. Cutter. He probably d. 1747. He m. Rachel ———, and had several children. Among them were Abigail, b. Aug. 15, 1735, and Benjamin, b. Apr. 24, 1738.

THE DAMON FAMILY.

There have been a few persons of this name in town from time to time, but no permanent residents till recently.

JOHN DAMON, b. in England, 1621, came to this country from Reading, Eng., and settled in Reading, Mass., where he was dea. of the ch. and where he d. Apr. 8, 1708. He had six children. *Samuel*, his son, b. June 23, 1656, m. Mary ———, who d. Nov. 29, 1727, aged 71, and he d. June 12, 1724, aged 68. They had nine children. *Ebenezer*, son of Saml. b. Aug. 9, 1686; m. Elizabeth ———, and had seven children. *David*, son of Ebenezer, b. Mar. 2, 1710; m. Apr. 7, 1731, Esther Gowing, and had ten children. *Benjamin*, son of David, b. June 6, 1759; m. Dec. 13, 1782, Anar Pratt. He settled in Ashby, where he d. Sept. 24, 1832, aged 73; she d. Oct. 14, 1838, aged 84. They had eight children. *Isaac*, second son of Benj., b. Mar. 31, 1785; m. Lucy Houghton, who d. and he m. Ruth Shattuck. He d. Apr. 1848, aged 63. He had three children by his first wife, who d. Apr. 20, 1826.

1   ISAAC NEWTON DAMON, the oldest child of Isaac, b. in Ashby, Dec. 14, 1812; m. Lucy K. Wright, dau. of Isaac Wright, b. Dec. 27, 1817. He came to Lex. in 1836, where he has since resided. He has filled the office of selectman, treasurer, &c., is a justice of the peace, and an assistant assessor in the internal revenue service.

1- 2   *Lusanna Phelps*, b. Sept. 28, 1843.
   3   *Myron Bates*, b. June 27, 1854.
   4   *Florence Maria*, b. Apr. 28, 1856.

DANFORTH.—DANFORTH is a name which appears occasionally on Lex. records. In 1738 we find this record,—"Amos Merriam and *Hannah Danforth*, both of Lex., were joined in marriage." There were Danforths in Camb. and in Bil. at an early day, and some from these families probably came to Lex. for a short time. In 1774, *Benjamin Danforth*, wife, and three children, among them Benjamin, Jr., came to Lex. from Bedford. As their names appear upon the tax bill up to 1785, and then disappear, it is probable that they left town about that time.

THE DAVIS FAMILY.

JOSEPH DAVIS, son of Thomas Davis of Holden, and Lattice his wife, was b. May 5, 1794, and m. May 31, 1823, Betsey G. Babcock, dau. of Amos and Betsey (Gardner) Babcock, of Princeton; b. Oct. 18, 1799. His father was a soldier in the Revolution, and was in the battles of Bunker Hill, Bennington, White Plains, &c. Joseph resided in Princeton, where he kept a public house. In 1833 he moved to Lex. and resumed his occupation as an inn-holder, which he continued about ten years. Most of his children were b. in Princeton. He was several years one of the overseers of the poor in Lex.

———

1- 2 *Horace B.*, b. May 10, 1824; m. June 2, 1852, Annie Stevens, dau. of William and Nancy Stevens. They have Frank S., b. June 7, 1857, and William Henry, b. Dec. 11, 1862.

3 *Charles E.*, b. Sept. 1, 1826; m. May, 1860, Eliza J. Tilton; r. in Brooklyn, N. Y.

4 *George O.*, b. Feb. 15, 1832; m. Sept. 2, 1858, Caroline E. Bridge, dau. of Samuel and Maria (Wellington) Bridge. They have Frederick G., b. Aug. 8, 1859, Charles B., b. Jan. 2, 1861, Harry W., b. Feb. 28, 1863. He has been some fifteen years in the Boston Custom House.

5 *Agnes*, b. in Lex. Dec. 3, 1834; d. unm. Dec. 7, 1859.

———

1 JOHN DAVIS, son of Amos and Elizabeth Davis, of Gloucester, b. Oct. 15, 1794; m. Oct 13, 1819, Mary F. Phelps, b. Oct. 1, 1795, dau. of Henry and Mary Phelps. He came to Lex. 1831. He held the office of postmaster twenty-five years — good evidence of his fidelity.

———

1- 2 *Mary A. E.*, b. Oct. 29, 1824; m. her cousin John Davis, Nov. 20, 1844. They have had Mary E., b. in Charlestown, Jan. 12, 1846, d. 1862; Ellen Amelia, b. Mar. 18, 1848; Florence W., b. in Lex. Oct. 16, 1852; Alice P., b. Apr. 19, 1855; Edith F., b. Jan. 9, 1858, d. 1859; John H., b. June 21, 1860; Hannah E., b. June 26, 1863; Frank W., b. June 9, 1866.

3 *John W.*, b. July 1, 1829; d. Feb. 19, 1832.

4 *Eliza J.*, b. July 1, 1834.

———

DIAMOND.—WILLIAM DIAMOND came to Lex. from Boston in 1772, and in 1783 m. Rebecca Simonds. He was taxed in town for several years, but I find no record of any children.

———

THE DORR FAMILY.

JOSEPH DORR came to this country from Eng., 1670. *Edward*, his son, m. Elizabeth ———, about 1682. They r. in Roxbury, and had seven children. *Ebenezer*, their second son, b. Jan. 25, 1687, m. Feb. 16, 1709, Mary Boardman, b. May 16, 1689. They had ten children. *Ebenezer*, second son of Ebenezer, b. Feb. 2, 1712, m. Mar. 5, 1714. They had thirteen children. He d. Aug. 8, 1782, aged 70. *Ebenezer*, second son of Ebenezer, b. Mar. 20, 1738, m. Jan. 7, 1762, Abigail Cummings, b. July 11, 1739. They had twelve children. He d. Sept. 29, 1809, aged 71. *John*, fourth son of Ebenezer, b. Oct. 2, 1770, m. Dec. 11, 1793, Esther Goldthwait, dau. of Benjamin G., and Sarah White (Dawes) Goldthwait. She d. July 28, 1840. He d. Aug. 10, 1855, aged 85. He more than sustained the character of the family — having had ten sons and nine daughters, all by one wife.

1 THEODORE HASKELL, the 16th child of John and Esther, b. Aug. 13, 1815, m. May 30, 1839, Nancy Caroline Richards, dau. of Joseph and Alice Richards, b. Jan. 10, 1817. He graduated at H. C., 1835, entered the ministry, and was settled at Billerica, May 28, 1839, left in 1843; settled in East Lex., July 2, 1845, left in 1849; settled at

Winchendon, June 2, 1852, left 1853; settled at Sherborne, Dec. 3, 1854, left May, 1863. After leaving Sherborne he came to Lex., where he now resides.

1- 2   *Esther G.*, b. July 2, 1840; m. May 9, 1860, E. R. Paul, of Sherborne.
   3   *Theodore H.*, b. Apr. 16, 1842; d. 1849.
   4   *John*, b. June 18, 1844. He entered the service of the U. S., 1862, as a sergeant for nine months, and served in N. C. Afterwards for one hundred days as first lieut.
   5   *Joseph Richards*, b. Nov. 7, 1848. 6 *Dudley A.*, b. Nov. 20, 1850.
   7   An infant, b. Dec. 28, 1854; d. same day.
   8   *Arthur*, b. Sept. 14, 1857.

THE DOWNING FAMILY.

1   SAMUEL DOWNING probably came to Lex. about 1777. From what place he came the records do not determine. He was first taxed in Lex. in 1778. He m. June 19, 1783, Susanna Brown, dau. of Benjamin and Sarah (Reed) Brown, who was b. June 17, 1764. She d. May 1, 1843, aged 79.

1- 2   *Polly*, b. Oct. 21, 1783; m. June 1, 1805, Samuel Butterfield of West Camb.
   3   *Oliver*, b. Mar. 10, 1785; resides in Boston.
   4   ‡*Samuel*, b. Oct. 30, 1787; m. first, Lucy Learned, and second, Lydia Blodgett, Nov. 11, 1819.
   5   *Susanna*, b. Nov. 20, 1788; m. May 19, 1817, Daniel Chandler.
   6   *Sally*, b. Nov. 23, 1790; m. Daniel Rhodes of Boston, where she d.
   7   *Lewis*, b. June 23, 1792; m. Lucy Wheelock of Con. He moved to Concord, N. H., where he has become famous as a coach manufacturer.
   8   *William*, b. Sept. 1796. He entered the service of the United States in the war of 1812, and was mortally wounded at the battle of Lundy's Lane, and d. the day following, July 26, 1814.

1-4-   SAMUEL DOWNING m. Lucy Learned of Wat. She d. Oct. 1, 1816, aged 28, and he m. second, Nov. 11, 1819, Lydia Blodgett, dau. of Nathan Blodgett.

3- 9   *Learned*, b. Jan. 26, 1810. He is a trader in Charlestown.
  10   *Susan*, b. Sept. 25, 1811.
  11   *William*, b. June 14, 1815; is a merchant at St. Louis.
  12   *Edward*, b. Nov. 29, 1820; resides in Boston.
  13   *Lucy Ann*, b. May 27, 1827; is a teacher.
  14   *Theodore*, b. Sept. 14, 1832.

ANDREW J. DOWNING, of Newburg, N. Y., who perished on board the Henry Clay at New York, July 28, 1852, and who was distinguished throughout the country as a horticulturalist and landscape gardener, and who was well known across the Atlantic by his publications on those subjects; was a near relative of the first-named Samuel Downing.

DRAPER.—WILLIAM DRAPER came to Lex. from Roxbury in 1782, and the same year m. Sarah Barnes, "both of Lex." He probably left soon after. Oct. 5, 1783, *Jonas Draper*, their child, was bap. She was ad. to the ch. Oct. 1, 1775.

THE DUDLEY FAMILY.

This family was never very numerous in Lex., nor were they among the early settlers — the name appearing on the records in 1779, for the first time. The family was first located in Concord, and from thence may have moved to Sudbury.

1   FRANCIS DUDLEY, a supposed relation of Gov. Thomas Dudley, was b. in England, and, emigrating to this country, settled in Con. perhaps about 1663. He m. Sarah Wheeler, of Con., Oct. 26, 1665, and probably remained in that town till his decease. His wife d. Dec. 12, 1713.

1- 2 | *Mary*, m. Joseph Fletcher.
3 | †*Joseph*, m. Abigail Gobble.
4 | *Samuel*, b. 1668; m. first, Abigail King, and second, Lydia ———.
5 | *Sarah*, d. 1701.
6 | *John*, m. Hannah Poulter, of Medford, May 16, 1697.
7 | *Francis*, m. first, Sarah ———, and second, Abigail ———.

1-3-   JOSEPH DUDLEY m. 1691, Abigail Gobble, and d. at Con., Nov. 3, 1702, where his children were all born.

3- 8 | *Abigail*, } b. June 11, 1692; { m. Dec. 17, 1713, John Davis.
9 | *Sarah*,
10 | *Jane*, b. Mar. 26, 1693.   11 *James*, b. ———.
12 | †*Joseph*, b. Apr. 20, 1697.
13 | *Benjamin*, b. Mar. 20, 1698.   14 *Mary*, b. Feb. 8, 1700.
15 | *Sibella*, b. Sept. 22, 1702; m. Jonathan Brown, Sept. 5, 1718.

3-12-   JOSEPH DUDLEY m. Oct. 2, 1718, Mary Chandler, dau. of Sam'l and Dorcas Chandler. Their three last children were b. at Sud., the others in Concord.

12-16 | †*Joseph*, b. July 24, 1719.   17 *Eliza*, b. Feb. 14, 1721.
18 | *Mary*, b. Jan. 17, 1723.   19 *Samuel*, b. Mar. 7, 1725.
20 | *Lucy*, b. Apr. 1, 1727; m. Dec. 6, 1744, John Perry.
21 | *Abigail*, b. about 1730; m. Apr. 12, 1759, Samuel Howe.
22 | *Ebenezer*, b. about 1735.   23 *William*, b. about 1740.
24 | *Sarah*, b. Oct. 13, 1754.   25 *Nahum*, b. May 4, 1757.
26 | *Daniel*, b. Feb. 22, 1763.

12-16-   JOSEPH DUDLEY m. Jan. 16, 1741, Mary Brown. They moved from Concord to Sudbury.

16-27 | *Benjamin*, b. Nov. 25, 1741.   28 *Joseph*, b. Sept. 16, 1743.
29 | *Samuel*, b. Sept. 29, 1746.   30 *Mary*, b. Aug. 4, 1749.
31 | †*Nathan*, b. June 17, 1755.
32 | *Abishai*, b. July 24, 1758.   33 *Abigail*, b. June 13, 1761.
34 | *Rebecca*, b. Aug. 28, 1763.   35 *Submit*, b. Aug. 16, 1765.
36 | *Moses*, b. Jan. 31, 1769.   37 *Luther*, b. May 5, 1772.
   The last three were b. in Sudbury.

16-31-   NATHAN DUDLEY m. first, Sarah Munroe, of Lin., June 24, 1786. They came into Lex. in 1779; he was first taxed in 1780. He and his wife Sarah were ad. to the ch. Jan. 27, 1790. She d. Jan. 16, 1801, and he m. second, Mrs. Hannah Lane, and d. July 17, 1835, aged 80 years. The last two children were by his second wife. He was a lieut. in the Lex. artillery.

31-38 | *Sally*, b. Oct. 16, 1786; m. John Viles, Jan. 12, 1806.
39 | *Nathan*, b. Apr. 3, 1789; d. Feb. 3, 1795.
40 | †*John*, b. Nov. 18, 1790.
41 | *Polly*, b. Sept. 18, 1792; m. Thomas Johnson, of Wo., Sept. 8, 1811.
42 | *Rebecca*, b. Aug. 14, 1794; d. Apr. 12, 1795.
43 | *Betsey*, b. June 1, 1798; m. Solomon Harrington.
44 | *Rebecca*, b. Dec. 31, 1808; m. William Shaw, of Wo.
45 | *Nathan*, b. July 29, 1810.

31-40— JOHN DUDLEY m. Esther E. Smith, of Sterling. He left Lex. before his marriage, and returned for a short time. His first and second child were born while here. He moved to Rox., where he r.

40-46 | *John W.*, b. and d. at Lex.
47 | *Eliza*, b. at Lex.; m. George W. Fowle.
48 | *Sarah D.*, b. ——, m. Rev. Joshua B. Holman.
49 | *Martha A.*, b. ——. 50 *Nathan A.*, b. Aug. 20, 1825.
51 | *Caroline M.*, b. ——. 52 *Andrew J.*, b. ——; d. young.
53 | *Charles H.*, b. ——. 54 *John E.*, b. ——.

THE DUNKLEE FAMILY.

The name of Dunklee appears on the town and church records as early as 1701. We cannot give a connected view of this family; though it appears that Nathaniel Dunklee and wife were received into the church by a letter of dismission from the church at Watertown, Aug. 25, 1705. Mr. Dunklee appears to have been an ardent man — a great saint and a great sinner. He in his weakness violated the eighth commandment by taking the property of others; but then he made a public confession which would throw the penitential psalms of the king of Israel nearly into the shade. He confesses his repeated thefts, and that he has no cause to complain of those who brought him to justice, — declaring that when the righteous smite him, it shall be a kindness to him, promises to give glory to God by confession and reformation, and hopes that his great sins may be the means of preserving himself and all others from temptation. On a confession thus full and penitent, thus submissive and prayerful, he was of course restored to his standing in the church, which he appears to have regarded as the very gate of heaven. The reader will join with us in the hope that he was never afterward " led into temptation."

We are not quite sure, but presume that the following are the 1 | children and descendants of NATHANIEL DUNKLEE, and Mary his wife.

1- 2 | *David*, bap. Sept. 21, 1701. 3 *Elnathan*, bap. Apr. 11, 1703.
4 | *Jonathan*, bap. Jan. 7, 1705. 5 *Hannah*, bap. May 8, 1707.
6 | †*Hezekiah*, bap. Nov. 21, 1708.
7 | *Robert*, bap. Apr. 9, 1710, and ad. to the ch. Jan. 7, 1728.

1 6— HEZEKIAH DUNKLEE m. Nov. 17, 1734, Damaris Wilson. He probably left town about the first of 1743, as his wife at that time was dismissed to the ch. at Billerica.

2- 8 | *Hezekiah*, b. Sept. 17, 1735. 9 *Nathaniel*, b. Feb. 23, 1737.
10 | *Damaris*, b. Mar. 16, 1739.

THE DUPEE FAMILY.

1 ELIAS DUPEE, b. Jan. 22, 1806; m. June 20, 1830, Mary Ann
Blodgett, dau. of James Blodgett. He was b. in Boston.

———

1- 2 *George C.*, b. Dec. 29, 1832; m. Nelly Tibbitts, r. in Boston and
N. Y.
3 *Lyman S.*, b. Feb. 17, 1834.
4 *Elias A.*, b. Apr. 20, 1836; m. Susan Winn, r. in Arlington.
5 *Charles S.*, b. June 18, 1842; m. Hattie Shattuck, r. in Arlington.
6 *Theodore D.*, b. Nov. 16, 1849.

THE DUREN FAMILY.

JOHN DUREN, or *Durant*, as the family formerly spelt the name,
was in Billerica at an early day, and m. Susanna Dutton, Nov. 16,
1670. They had at least four children, two of each sex. He d. in
prison in Camb. Oct. 27, 1692, a victim of the witchcraft delusion.
John, the eldest son of John, was b. July 31, 1672; m. Aug. 10,
1695, Elizabeth Jaquith. He d. Feb. 25, 1757, aged 85. They had
eight children. *Abraham*, the youngest son of John, was b. Apr. 1,
1709; m. May 20, 1736, Rachel Manning. They had nine children
b. in Billerica where they resided. *Abraham*, the eldest son of
Abraham, b. Oct. 4, 1737; m. Nov. 1, 1764, Lydia Gould, of
Chelmsford. He d. Nov. 6, 1776. An anecdote is told of his wife
which shows the energy of the woman, and the spirit of the times.
On the 18th of April, 1775, her husband being in feeble health, she
mounted their horse, and with her *panniers* set out for market at
Boston, a distance of twenty miles or more; and having accomplished
her business at Boston, returned as far as Arlington, and stopped
for the night. While she was there, she saw the British troops pass
on their way to Lex. and Con. The next morning she started for
home, and stopping at Lex. she went into the meeting-house to see
the slaughtered men killed by the British a few hours before. Such
were the women of the Revolution.—*Abraham* and Lydia had four
children. *Abraham*, the youngest child, was b. Sept. 16, 1776;
Oct. 25, 1801, Mary Russell, dau. of Jesse Russell, of Wo., where
he settled. He d. Oct. 14, 1822, and she d. May 28, 1864. The
neighborhood where he resided bears the name of *Durenville*, in
honor of him. He had five children. Samuel R., b. May 29, 1803;
m. Sybil Spaulding and Ann Searl. He d. Oct. 6, 1862; Lydia, b.
Dec. 13, 1805; m. Joseph Kendall; Warren, b. Apr. 14, 1809; he
has been twice married; William, b. June 5, 1813; m. Feb. 4, 1845,
Rebecca A. Locke; Abraham, b. Nov. 21, 1815; m. Apr. 5, 1842,
Prudence Simonds.

WARREN DUREN, the second son of Abraham mentioned above,
m. June 2, 1833, Mary Ann Marrett, dau. of Rev. Daniel and Mary
(Muzzy) Marrett, of Standish, Me. She d. Oct. 4, 1839, and he
m. Oct. 18, 1848, Mary Chandler, dau. of William Chandler, Esq.,
of Lex. He had one child by his first wife, viz. Caroline Augusta,
b. Oct. 25, 1835, and d. May 13, 1852, aged 17 years. He moved
to Lex. Sept. 1850. He has served several times on the board of
overseers of the poor.

THE ESTABROOK FAMILY.

Though the Estabrooks were not among the first settlers of Lexington, they came here quite early, and became prominent, both in the church and in the town. Lexington's first minister, and two of her early deacons, bore that name. The Estabrooks appear to have been a ministerial family. Their ancestor, Rev. Joseph Estabrook, came from England in 1660, with two brothers, one of whom settled in Con., and the other in Swanzey. Joseph entered H. C., where he was graduated in 1664, and was settled in Con. in 1667, as colleague with Rev. Mr. Buckley, where he continued till his death, which happened in 1711.

1   Rev. Joseph Estabrook had four sons, as follows:

1- 2   †*Joseph*, b. 1669; d. in Lex. Sept. 23, 1733.
3   †*Benjamin*, b. Feb. 24, 1671; d. in Lex. July 22, 1697.
4   *Samuel*, b. 1674; was grad. at H. C. 1696, and settled as a clergyman in Canterbury, Connecticut, where he d. in 1727.
5   †*Daniel*, b. Feb. 14, 1676; d. at Sudbury, 1735.

1-2-   Joseph Estabrook m. first, Dec. 31, 1689, Millicent Woodis, or Woodhouse, dau. of Henry Woodhouse, of Con. She d. Mar 30, 1692, and he m. second, Aug. 25, 1793, wid. Hannah Loring, of Hingham. He first settled in Hingham, where he and his wife united with the ch. from which they were dismissed to the ch. in Lex. in 1710. He was an active and influential member of the Lex. ch. and represented it on many public occasions. He was elected dea. in 1716, and remained in that office till his death, Sept. 23, 1733. He was highly respected as a townsman, and filled almost every office within their gift. He commanded a military company, and filled the office of town clerk, treasurer, assessor, selectman, and representative to the General Court. He was a man of more than ordinary education for that day, was often employed as a surveyor, and was engaged to teach the first man's school in the town. I cannot state the precise time when he removed to Lex., but as he bought two hundred acres of land in the precinct in 1693, and was elected to office in 1696, it is probable that he came into the place between those periods. He bought his farm of Edward Pelham, then of R. I., and it is described in the deed as being bounded northeasterly by the Cook farm, and southwesterly by the Concord road, till it comes to Vine Brook. This included the places now occupied by Mrs. L. Turner, extending to the brook in front, and back to or beyond the place owned by Mr. Hayes under the hill.

2- 6   †*Joseph*, b. Oct. 10, 1690; d. Aug. 19, 1740.
7   †*John*, b. July 28, 1694: m. Oct. 27, 1720, Prudence Harrington.
8   *Solomon*, b. Dec. 22, 1696; d. July 7, 1697.
9   *Hannah*, b. Mar. 2, 1698; m. May 23, 1717, Joseph Frost.
10   *Millicent*, b. Mar. 21, 1699.   11 *Elijah*, b. Aug. 25, 1703.

1-3-   Benjamin Estabrook was grad. at H. C. 1690, and was settled over the first church at Cambridge Farms, (now Lex.,) Oct. 6, 1696. But his ministry was of short duration. On the 22d of July, 1697, he was removed from his earthly labors by death, after a ministry of only nine months. He m. Nov. 29, 1693, Abigail Willard, dau. of Rev. Samuel Willard, of the Old South Church, Boston. She was one of a family of twenty children. Rev. Mr. Estabrook d. greatly lamented by his people. He left two children, Benjamin, b. Dec.

66

13, 1695, and Richard, b. July 5, 1697, but a few days before the death of his father. His wid. m. Rev. Samuel Treat, of Eastham, a son of Gov. Treat, of Connecticut. She d. Dec. 27, 1745, aged 82. By Mr. Treat she had three children, one of whom, Eunice, m. Rev. Thomas Paine, of Weymouth, and had, among other children, Robert Treat Paine, who was one of the signers of the Declaration of Independence, Attorney-General of this State, and one of the Justices of the Supreme Court.

1-5-   DANIEL ESTABROOK m. Abigail Flint, of Con. He first settled in Lex., where he had several children. Subsequently they removed to Weston, and, in 1715, he and his wife were ad. to the ch. in that place. He afterwards moved to Sudbury, where he d., 1735. He had Abigail, bap. in Lex. Sept. 27, 1702. David and Samuel, bap. in Lex., Jan. 21, 1705, and Aug. 20, 1710, were probably his children.

2-6-   JOSEPH ESTABROOK m. July 8, 1713, Submit Loring, his step-sister. She d. Mar. 31, 1718, in childbed, and he m. Mar. 26, 1719, Hannah Bowman. Like his father, he was captain of the company, and dea. of the ch., and like him filled almost every important office in town — assessor, treasurer, clerk, and selectman. He d. Aug. 19, 1740, and his wid. m. July 19, 1753, Capt. Benj. Reed, and d. Apr. 15, 1774, aged 72 years.

6-12 *Joseph*, b. June 27, 1714; d. July 17, 1714.
13 *Joseph*, b. Mar. 16, 1718; d. Mar. 18, same year.
14 *Joseph*, b. Apr. 9, 1720; d. Dec. 7, 1747.
15 *Hannah*, b. Sept. 22, 1725; d. Sept. 29, 1728.
16 *Benjamin*, b. Oct. 9, 1727; d. Sept. 29, 1728.
17 †*Benjamin*, b. Dec. 20, 1729; m. May 9, 1757, Hannah Hubbard.
18 *Hannah*, b. Oct. 6, 1731; m. May 7, 1752, Ebenezer Hubbard.
19 *Solomon*, b. June 10, 1733; d. Oct. 1, 1733.
20 *Samuel*, b. June 25, 1735; entered H. C.; d. July 14, 1754.
21 *Millicent*, b. July 25, 1738; m. July 4, 1758, Jas. Barrett, of Con.
22 *Ebenezer*, b. Sept. 21, 1740; m. Dec. 13, 1759, Ruth Reed, b. Nov. 7, 1741, dau. of Capt. Isaac and Rebecca Reed. They had Molly, bap. in Lex. June 3, 1760. They removed to Holden. Their descendants at the present day are found in that town and vicinity.

2-7-   JOHN ESTABROOK m. Oct. 27, 1720, Prudence Harrington. He was constable, 1737, and 1738. He d. June 19, 1742, and his wid. m. 1748, Benjamin Munroe, of Weston, the youngest son of Wm. Munroe, the original emigrant, who settled in Lex. She was his second wife, and d. 1778.

7-23 *Grace*, b. Aug. 13, 1721; m. ——— Hurd.
24 *Prudence*, b. Mar. 28, 1724; m. Richard Winship.
25 *Millicent*, b. July 11, 1727; m. ——— Harris.
26 *John*, b. Oct. 20, 1729; probably he is the John Estabrook who settled in Westminster, and had by his wife Anna fourteen children.
27 *Abigail*, b. Mar. 11, 1731; m. ——— Hunt.
28 *Elizabeth*, b. Nov. 21, 1734.
29 †*Nehemiah*, b. Mar. 2, 1738; m. Mar. 1, 1759, Elizabeth Winship.
30 *Anna*, b. Feb. 11, 1740; m. ——— Kidder.

6-17-   BENJAMIN ESTABROOK m. May 9, 1757, Hannah Hubbard, of Con. They were ad. to the ch. in Lex. June 22, 1758. He d. Mar. 8, 1803, aged 74; she d. Jan. 12, 1803, aged 67. He was many years a coroner and a justice of the peace. He was in the campaign to Ticonderoga in 1776.

17-31 | *Joseph*, b. Mar. 4, 1758; grad. at H. C. 1782. He entered the ministry, and was ordained at Athol, Nov. 21, 1787. He d. Apr. 30, 1830, in the eighty-first year of his age, and the forty-third year of his ministry.

32 | *Hannah*, b. Jan. 20, 1760; m. Dea. Ebenezer Lawrence, of Wo.

33 | †*Benjamin*, b. Mar. 23, 1762; m. Esther Russell.

34 | *Samuel*, b. Nov. 15, 1764; he m. first, Polly Creasy, and second, Nabby Warren. He lived in Brookline, but at last returned to Lex., where he d. July 20, 1814.

35 | *Martha*, b. June 22, 1765; m. Edmund Walden, and moved to Sterling, where she d. Mar. 1822.

36 | †*Attai*, b. June 14, 1769; d. Sept. 29, 1836.

37 | *Nathan*, bap. May 10, 1772; m. Sarah Smith, and moved to Ashby.

38 | *Solomon*, b. Dec. 18, 1774; m. Lucy Davis, of New Ipswich, where he resided for a time, when he returned to Lex. and d. Aug. 12, 1825, without issue.

39 | *Millicent*, b. June 8, 1777; m. Wm. Stearns, of Walt., and d. 1844.

7-29- | NEHEMIAH ESTABROOK m. Mar. 1, 1759, Elizabeth Winship, dau. of Samuel and Hannah Winship, b. May 23, 1740. He was a soldier from Lex. in the French war in 1755, and hence was well qualified to aid in the Revolutionary struggle. He left Lex. about 1777, moved to Lunenburg, afterwards went to West Camb., and d. in Hopkinton, while on a visit to his children.

29-40 | *Samuel*, b. Aug. 31, 1760; d. Oct. 29, 1778.

41 | *Nehemiah*, b. Mar. 3, 1762; m. in Lunenburg, where he lived some years.

42 | *Bettie*, b. Apr. 9, 1764; m. William Blanchard, of Medford.

43 | *Lydia*, b. May 28, 1766; m. Samuel Jones, and lived in West Camb.

44 | *Eliakim*, b. July 10, 1768; d. young.

45 | *Grace*, b. May 27, 1770; m. Nathaniel Trask, of Charlestown.

46 | †*Eliakim*, b. Oct 18, 1772; m. Hannah Cook, of West Camb.

47 | *John*, b. May 7, 1775; m. Anna Russell, and lived in West Camb.

48 | *Joseph*, b. Feb. 23, 1777; he settled in Hopkinton.

49 | *Samuel*, b. May 13, 1779; m. Lucy Jones, and lived in W. Camb.

50 | *Rebecca*, b. Mar. 4, 1781; she was living (1859) in Charlestown, unm.

17-33- | BENJAMIN ESTABROOK m. Esther Russell. He d. Oct. 29, 1819, aged 57. She d. Jan. 3, 1813, aged 49. We find no record of his family, but obtain the following from his relatives. He resided for a time in Danvers.

33-51 | *Susan*, b. Aug. 20, 1783; m. Benjamin Winn, and lived in Salem.

52 | *Benjamin*, b. in Danvers, June 7, 1785; d. in Topsham, Vt.

53 | *Walter*, b. Nov. 22, 1787.

54 | *Hannah*, b. 1789; d. in six months.

55 | *Hannah*, b. Mar. 11, 1791; d. in Salem, Apr. 19, 1811.

56 | *William*, b. 1793; d. in Lex. 1858.

17-36- | ATTAI ESTABROOK m. Polly Pierce. She d. Nov. 6, 1826, and he d. Sept. 29, 1836, aged 67.

36-57 | *Benjamin*, b. ———; d. Nov. 1826, aged about 20, by an injury received from the rebound of a gun.

58 | *Hannah*, b. ———; m. George Simonds.

59 | *Solomon*, b. Apr. 1, 1815; m. Apr. 3, 1837, Elizabeth C. Blodgett. They have Henry D. and George D., (twins,) b. May 19, 1838; Lyman, b. Feb. 26, 1849. Henry D. m. Jan. 16, 1866, Sarah A. Cummings. George D. m. July 2, 1865, Emma S. Fowle.

60 *Abigail*, b. Dec. 16, 1819; m. Apr. 7, 1846, Luke W. Wright.
61 *Joseph*, b. May 4, 1821; m. Nancy Raymond, of Littleton, and r. in Acton.
62 *Elizabeth*, b. Dec. 1, 1823; d. June 23, 1848.

29-46- ELIAKIM ESTABROOK m. Sept. 7, 1793, Hannah Cook, of West Camb., b. Sept. 15, 1778. He resided most of the time in West Camb., though he returned to Lex., where he d. Apr. 17, 1835. She was in 1859, living in Lex. Though they were mostly b. in West Camb., the number of the children induces us to give them a place here.

46-63 *Ender*, b. Feb. 24, 1795; m. Aug. 27, 1818, Lydia Adams, of West Cambridge.
64 *Louisa*, b. Sept. 8, 1797; m. Apr. 1819, Ebenezer Hovey, of West Cambridge.
65 *Joseph*, b. Apr. 17, 1799; m. Aug. 11, 1817, Nancy Page.
66 *Lovell*, b. Nov. 8, 1800; m. May 12, 1824, Mary Stearns, of Waltham.
67 *Hannah*, b. Feb. 4, 1802; m. May 9, 1818, Wm. Benjamin, of Lin.
68 *Matilda*, b. May 4, 1805; m. Oct. 13, 1833, Wm. Hooper, of Boston.
69 *Eliakim*, b. Oct. 16, 1806; m. Feb. 9, 1849, Augusta Fay, of Fitchburg.
70 *Eleanor*, b. Feb. 12, 1807; m. Apr. 25, 1826, John Norcross.
71 *Elizabeth*, b. July 10, 1808; m. May 7, 1832, Jas. Bryant, of N. H.
72 *Clarinda*, b. Aug. 13, 1810; m. Oct. 2, 1832, George Foster, of West Cambridge.
73 *Nehemiah*, b. Feb. 21, 1812; d. young.
74 *Mary A.*, b. Mar. 14, 1814; d. Dec. 5, 1843, unm.
75 *John B.*, b. Apr. 8, 1816.
76 *Lucy E.*, b. Nov. 10, 1818; d. Mar. 24, 1839, unm.
77 *Francis H.*, b. June 1, 1821; m. July 25, 1852, Louisa Jones, of Walpole, N. H. They reside in Lexington. Children, first, John Henry, b. Nov. 1854, d. young; second, George Lovell, b. Dec. 1856; third, Anna Louisa, b. Sept. 30, 1857.

We cannot close this table without doing justice to PRINCE ESTABROOK, a black man in the family of Benjamin Estabrook. He was among the patriots of the Revolution on the Common on the 19th of April, 1775, when he was wounded: we find his name among the soldiers in almost every campaign during the war. He, though a slave, fought the battles of freedom.

THE FAIRFIELD FAMILY.

About 1733, there was a family of Fairfields came to Lex. probably from Wenham, as *Walter*, *Judith*, and *Remember* were dismissed from the ch. in that place, to Lex., where they were ad. Aug. 4, 1734. On the same day, Rebecca, probably dau. of Walter and Judith, was bap. Walter, probably son of the same, was bap. Jan. 18, 1736, and Mary, Nov. 9, 1740.

There appears to have been more than one family of the name, as *Stephen*, and Hannah his wife, were ad. to the ch., he in 1734, and she in 1737. We have also the record of two of their children, Judith, b. May 30, 1736, and Rebecca, b. Dec. 26, 1738. I also find *Moses* of *Daniel*, bap. in 1738. *Walter* and *Daniel* were taxed in Lex. 1735, '36, and '37. In 1743, *Walter*, *Judith*, and *Mary*, and *Stephen* and *Hannah*, were dismissed from the Lex. ch. to the ch. at Cold Spring. They probably had left town before that time, as the name had disappeared from the tax bills.

THE FARLEY FAMILY.

The Farleys were never numerous in Lexington. George Farley settled in Roxbury, removed early to Woburn, and from thence to Billerica, before 1656, and d. there Dec. 27, 1693. He had a number of children, some of whom settled in Billerica, where the name has been quite common, as it has also been in Hollis, N. H. It is highly probable that the Lexington Farleys were from the same stock. The following imperfect sketch is all that our records furnish.

John Farley, son of John and Mary, b. Oct. 31, 1714.
Hannah Farley, dau. of Benjamin and Joanna, b. Jan. 31, 1757.
Sarah Farley, " " " " " b. Sept. 28, 1761.
Samuel Hasselton, Hollis, N. H., m. *Molly Farley,* of Lex., June 2, 1761.
Israel Putnam, of Bedford, m. *Rebecca Farley,* of Lex., Jan. 5, 1763.
Benjamin Farley, of Lex. was in the French war in 1757.

THE FARMER FAMILY.

EDWARD FARMER, son of John Farmer, of Ansley, Warwickshire, Eng., came to this country as early as 1672, and settled in Billerica, where he d. May 27, 1727, aged 87. Mary his wife d. Mar. 26, 1719, aged 78.

The name appears on Lex. records about 1748, when Nathaniel Farmer was taxed.

1 NATHANIEL FARMER m. May 28, 1755, Hannah Fessenden, dau. of Thomas and Hannah (Prentice) Fessenden. He was a member of Capt. Parker's company, and like a true patriot was on the ground on the 19th of Apr. 1775. He received a severe wound on the morning of that memorable day. A ball struck his right arm, and so fractured the bone, that he was disabled for a long time;—pieces of bone were extracted from the arm several months afterwards. The Legislature made him a grant of £15 15s. for loss of labor and expense of surgical attendance.

1- 2 †*John,* b. July 18, 1757; m. Mar. 27, 1783, Lucy Reed.
3 *Hannah,* b. Jan. 28, 1760; m. May 6, 1777, Jacob Kilburn, of Lancaster.
4 *Isaac,* b. Oct. 8, 1762; d. young.
5 *Ruth,* b. Aug. 15, 1765.   6 *Abigail,* b. Nov. 6, 1768.
7 *Sally,* } twins; b. Dec. 19, 1771; { m. Feb. 12, 1794, Samuel
8 *Rebecca,* }   { [Pierce, of Groton.
9 *Thomas Shattuck,* bap. Sept. 10, 1775.
10 *Isaac,* b. Dec. 31, 1779.

1-2- JOHN FARMER m. Mar. 27, 1783, Lucy Reed, of Camb. He was a soldier in the war of the Revolution from the town of Lexington.

THE FASSETT FAMILY.

The Fassetts came to this country from Scotland. John Fassett was made freeman in 1654. Nathaniel Fassett was taxed in Concord in 1666. There were one or more families of this name in Billerica at an early day. It is probable that the Lex. Fassetts descended either from the family in Con. or Bil., as they resided near the corner of these towns — their residence being at what is known as the

Page place, in Bed., which was formerly a part of Lex. The Fassetts were never numerous in Lex., though one individual was at one time prominent and influential.

1   JOSEPH FASSETT, and his wife Mary, were in Lex. in 1701, having made their peace with the church at that time. In 1708, he was chosen one of the assessors in the precinct, and in 1714, one of the assessors in the town. Subsequently he became quite popular, filling various offices. He was one of the assessors nine years, filled the office of selectman about as long, and for several years represented the town in the General Court. We find no record of any
2   children of theirs except *Joseph*, who was born Dec. 6, 1701. Joseph Fassett, and his wife Mary, both died about 1753 or 4. She was dau. of William Munroe, the ancestor of the Lex. Munroes.

1-2-   JOSEPH FASSETT m. Amity ———, about 1726. He d. Aug. 14, 1755, and she m. June 15, 1756, John Page, of Bed. In his will, dated 1755, he mentions wife Amity, sons Joseph, John, and Jonathan, and dau. Sarah and Amity Newton. He filled several town offices.

2- 3   *Joseph*, b. Jan. 18, 1727; d. same day.
4   *Mary*, b. Aug. 18, 1729; d. Oct. 12, same year.
5   †*Joseph*, b. Mar. 21, 1730; m. Dorothy Pollard, of Bed.
6   *Amily*, b. Feb. 1, 1732; m. Nov. 14, 1754, Simon Newton, of Bed.
7   *Mary*, b. May 9, 1736.   8 *John*, b. Dec. 7, 1739.
9   *Jonathan*, b. Mar. 15, 1742.   10 *Sarah*, bap. Jan. 22, 1744.

2-5-   JOSEPH FASSETT m. May 6, 1756, Dorothy Pollard, of Bedford. He was a lieut., and d. at the Lake in the French war, Sept. 16, 1758, aged 29 years. She m. Feb. 21, 1760, Ebenezer Page, of Bedford, son of her father-in-law.

5-11   *Joseph*, b. Apr. 10, 1757.   12 *Calley*, b. June 21, 1758.

THE FESSENDEN FAMILY.

The Fessendens were probably not in the precinct, till about the time it was erected into a town, in 1713; though they were in old Cambridge much earlier. *John Fessenden* came from Kent Co., Eng., and settled in Cambridge about 1635. He was ad. a freeman in 1641. He was a member of the ch., and was selectman in 1656, '61, '63, and '65. He d. Jan. 13, 1666, leaving no children. His wife Jane d. Jan. 13, 1682, aged 80. His relative, Nicholas Fessenden, came over from England at his request, it is said, and inherited his estate, which was very considerable for that day. Nicholas is supposed to have been a nephew of John.

1   NICHOLAS FESSENDEN m. Margaret Cheney. He was b. in England about 1650. He resided in Cambridge, where he had a numerous family, and d. Feb. 24, 1719, in his 69th year. She d. Dec. 10, 1717, in her 62d year.

1- 2   *Jane*, b. Nov. 28, 1674; d. Aug. 24, 1676.
3   *Hannah*, b. July 27, 1676; d. Aug. 4, 1676.
4   *John*, b. Nov. 4, 1678; m. Sarah ———.
5   *Nicholas*, b. Jan. 21, 1681; grad. at H. C. 1701, was distinguished as a teacher in Camb. He m. Sarah Cooledge, wid. of Stephen.
6   *Thomas*, b. Jan. 4, and d. Jan. 28, 1682.

7 †*Thomas*, b. Aug. 12, 1684; he was three times married.

8 *Margaret*, b. Jan. 22, 1687; d. unm.

9 *Jane*, b. Apr. 22, 1688; m. Jan. 10, 1712, Samuel Winship, who was high sheriff of Middlesex county.

10 *Mary*, b. Oct. 28, 1689; m. June 15, 1712, Joshua Parker.

11 *William*, b. 1694; m. first, Oct. 10, 1716, Martha Wyeth, and second, Jan. 4, 1728, Martha Brown. He d. May 26, 1756. He resided in Camb., had a family of eleven children, the youngest of whom, *Thomas*, was bap. July 15, 1739, grad. at H. C. 1758, was ordained at Walpole, N. H., 1767. He m. Elizabeth Kendall, and had a numerous family, the eldest of whom was well known in this community. *Thomas G. Fessenden* grad. at Dart. C. 1796; he was a lawyer, a wit, and a poet, whose writings left a sting behind. He was author of a satirical poem entitled, "Terrible Tractoration," which in its day made many laugh, and a few wince. He was distinguished as an agriculturalist, and edited for some years "The New England Farmer." He d. in Boston.

Through another branch of the family of William Fessenden, (No. 11 in this table,) descended G. Samuel Fessenden, an eminent lawyer of Portland, Me., who has represented his district in Congress, and who was father of Hon. William Pitt Fessenden, the distinguished senator in Congress from Maine at this time.

12 *Joseph*, b. ———; m. Mindwell Oldham, Dec. 6, 1733?

13 *Benjamin*, b. Jan. 30, 1701; grad. at H. C. 1718, was ordained at Sandwich, Sept. 12, 1722, and d. there Aug. 7, 1746, leaving a family.

14 *Hannah*, b. ———; m. John Chipman, Sandwich? She d. 1758.

15 *Ebenezer*, b. ———; m. probably Elizabeth Barrett, and afterwards Alice Babcock. He lived and d. at Cambridge.

1-7-   THOMAS FESSENDEN m. 1708, Abigail Poulter, dau. of Jonathan and Elizabeth Poulter, of Lex., b. Sept. 5, 1692. She d. April 25, 1719, aged 27; and he m. Jan. 8, 1720, Abigail Locke, dau. of Joseph Locke, of Lex. She d. June 12, 1736, and he m. Anne Phillebrown, Dec. 2, 1737. He d. Mar. 6, 1738. He probably came to Lex. about the time of his first marriage; he o. c. in 1709, when their first child was baptized.

7-16 †*Thomas*, b. Dec. 9, 1709; m. 1735, Hannah Prentice, of Camb.

17 †*Samuel*, b. Aug. 11, 1711; m. May 21, 1740, Elizabeth Allen.

18 *Abigail*, b. July 13, 1713; m. ——— Wellington.

19 *Mary*, b. Jan. 17, 1716; m. Wm. Brown, of Walt., moved to Conn.

20 *Elizabeth*, b. Mar. 8, 1721; m. Apr. 27, 1758, Samuel Hutchinson.

21 *Jonathan*, b. Apr. 28, 1723; m. June 4, 1747, Martha Crosby, of Quincy, where he lived.

22 *Hannah*, b. June 18, 1725; d. same year.

23 *Hannah*, b. Apr. 21, 1727; d. Apr. 21, 1729.

24 *John*, b. Apr. 27, 1729; m. Nov. 23, 1769, Elizabeth Wyman, r. in Rutland.

25 *Timothy*, b. May 6, 1731; m. Elizabeth Pierce, dau. of Jonas Pierce, of Lex. They r. in Westminster, where he d. Mar. 1, 1805, æt. 74.

26 *Benjamin*, b. Jan. 9, 1734; was twice m., resided in Milton, Braintree, Watertown, and Boston, where he d. Apr. 30, 1801.

27 *Submit*, b. May 28, 1736.

7-16-   THOMAS FESSENDEN m. June 19, 1735, Hannah Prentice, of Camb. They were ad. to the ch. in Lex., Oct. 16, 1737, when their first child was bap. He d. July 22, 1768.

16-28 | *Hannah*, b. Aug. 9, 1736; m. May 20, 1755, Nathaniel Farmer.
29 | *Abigail*, b. Sept. 7, 1738; d. July 13, 1741.
30 | †*Thomas*, b. July 10, 1741; m. Elizabeth Apthorp, and Lucy Lee.
31 | *Aaron*, b. Dec. 30, 1744; m. Sarah Locke. They resided a short time in Cambridge, and then removed to Townsend, where they d.
32 | *Nathaniel*, b. June 7, 1746; m. first, Lydia Bemis, about 1770, who was killed by the chance shot of a gun, holding at the time her only son (Ichabod) in her arms. He m. second, Elizabeth Webb, of Danvers, r. in Medford.
33 | †*Nathan*, b. Apr. 10, 1749, m. Sarah Winship, Oct. 17, 1771.
34 | *Sarah*, b. Aug. 9, 1753; m. Mar. 4, 1773, Isaac Winship, brother of Sarah above.
35 | *Isaac?* bap. Oct. 23, 1757.

7-17- | SAMUEL FESSENDEN m. May 21, 1740, Elizabeth Allen. He was ad. to the ch. in Lex., May 10, 1746. He d. Nov. 1, 1771. She d. Sept. 4, 1802, aged 91 years.

17-36 | *Elizabeth*, b. May 6, 1741.
37 | *Amity*, b. June 15, 1743; m. Dec. 15, 1773, Solomon Pierce.
38 | *Abigail*, b. July 20, 1747; m. Jan. 22, 1765, John Hill, of Bil.
39 | *Samuel*, bap. July 6, 1749; m. Sarah Pierce, sister of Solomon, Nov. 21, 1771.

16-30- | THOMAS FESSENDEN m. Mrs. Elizabeth Apthorp. She d. and he m. Dec. 7, 1775, Lucy Lee, of Con. He d. Feb. 25, 1804. She d. June 19, 1820, aged 66.

30-40 | *Nelly*, b. Apr. 10, 1769?
41 | *Thomas*, b. June 5, 1772; d. Mar. 7, 1807, aged 35.
42 | *Lucy*, b. Apr. 2, 1777; d. young.
43 | *William*, b. June 13, 1779; m. Apr. 26, 1802, Eunice Frost, and moved to N. H.
44 | *Lucy*, b. Sept. 16, 1782; d. about 1804.
45 | *Betsey Apthorp*, b. Sept. 8, 1787; m. Elias Viles.
46 | *John*, b. Mar. 13, 1794.

16-33- | NATHAN FESSENDEN m. Oct. 17, 1771, Sarah Winship. He d. Apr. 24, 1797.

33-47 | †*Nathan*, b. Apr. 25, 1772; m. Jane Goodrich.
48 | *Isaac*, b. Apr. 12, 1776; m. Mary Doane, of Boston, r. there.
49 | *Jonathan*, b. May 18, 1779; r. in Portland, m. Betsey Drinkwater.
50 | *Lydia*, b. May 28, 1782; m. Elisha Tainter, of Med., r. there.
51 | *John*, b. Dec. 25, 1784; went to Portland, where he r. He d. Aug. 7, 1849.
52 | *Sally*, b. Oct. 13, 1788; m. William Lovejoy, of Milford, N. H., r. there.
53 | *Nathaniel*, b. Jan. 6, 1791; d. 1821, unm.

33-47- | NATHAN FESSENDEN m. June 11, 1801, Jane Goodrich, of Lunenburg. He d. Feb. 26, 1866, aged 93 years. She d. Feb. 10, 1849, aged 70 years.

47-54 | *Elizabeth*, b. May 20, 1802; m. Darius Fillebrown. She d. Nov. 16, 1849.
55 | *Caroline*, } b. May 4, 1804; { m. Oct. 8, 1835, William Grover.
56 | *Maria*, } {

57 *Harriet*, b. Sept. 8, 1806; m. Nov. 4, 1841, James Ingals, of Town-
    send.
58 *Nathan*, b. June 15, 1808. He r. on the old homestead, has for
    several years filled the office of assessor.
59 *Albert F.*, b. Aug. 23, 1810; m. Eliza Johnson. No issue.
60 *Charles*, b. Nov. 5, 1812; he went to Fitchburg, where he m. Mar-
    tha Newton. She d. 1851, and he m. he rsister Sarah C. He r.
    in Fitchburg.
61 *Levi G.*, b. Oct. 30, 1814; m. Sarah Stratton, Oct. 22, 1849, r. in
    Ohio.
62 *Hannah*, b. June 2, 1817; m. Jan. 6, 1851, Darius Fillebrown.
63 *Jane*, b. Mar. 30, 1820; m. Dec. 14, 1847, Chas. G. Davis, of Wo.

THE FISKE FAMILY.

    "There was," says Bond, in his history of Watertown, "a consid-
erable number of early immigrants of the name of *Fiske*, who settled
in Massachusetts; and there is good reason to believe that they were
all descendants of Robert and Sibil (Gold) Fiske, who lived at
Broad Gates, Loxfield, near Framingham, county Suffolk, Eng."

1   DAVID FISKE, probably came over to America in 1636, and settled
in Wat. where he was admitted freeman, Mar. 1637. He was selectman in Wat. 1640, and '43. His will, dated Sept. 10, 1660, and
proved Jan. 22, 1662, mentions no wife, but one dau. *Fitch*, and one
son *David*, "sole executor and residuary legatee, giving him his
house, lands, cattle and chattels." Aug. 6, 1673, his son sold his
homestead and two other lots of land in Wat. to John Cooledge.

1– 2   DAVID FISKE b. 1624. He was a "planter," and was ad. freeman, May 26, 1647; he settled either at first, or soon after, at Camb.
Farms, in which place he became a prominent citizen. He m. first,
Lydia Cooper, perhaps step-dau. of Dea. Gregory Stone, by whom
he had three children. He m. second, Seaborn Wilson, dau. of
William Wilson, of Boston. He d. Feb. 14, 1710. His will, dated
Jan. 22, 1708, and proved Dec. 20, 1711, mentions, wife Seaborn,
son Nicholas Wyeth, my dau. being dead, children David, Elizabeth,
and Abigail, cousin Samuel Stone, son of Dea. Samuel Stone. Inventory of his estate, £405 17s. 6d. Oct. 16, 1676, he and wife
Seaborn, sold Samuel Page, one hundred and forty-nine acres in
Wat. granted to his father David Fiske. David Fiske, or David
Fiske, Sen., as he was designated in our early records, was not only
one of the first settlers, but became one of the most prominent and
useful men in the precinct. He headed the subscription for a meeting-house in 1692, and on the organization of the parish the year
after, he was chosen clerk, and one of the selectmen or assessors.
He was also chosen chairman of a committee to purchase of the town
of Camb. a lot of land for the support of the ministry. These and
similar offices he frequently held under the parish. He was also a
member of the ch. organized 1696, and his wife immediately after
removed her relation from the ch. in Camb. to the ch. gathered in
the precinct. He not only served his fellow-citizens in a civil and
religious, but also in a military capacity, as appears by the prefix
Lieut. which is often in the records connected with his name. He was
also often employed by the colony as a surveyor. He resided on
Hancock st. near the present residence of Joseph F. Simonds.
    A handsome monument was erected in 1856, by Benj. Fiske, Esq.,
with this inscription: "In memory of DAVID FISKE, who died Feb.
14, 1710, and his descendants."

2- 3 | *Sarah*, d. 1648.
  4 | *Lydia*, b. Sept. 29, 1647 ; d. unm.
  5 | †*David*, b. Sept. 1, 1648 ; d. Oct. 23, 1729, aged 81.
  6 | *Seaborn*, d. young.
  7 | *Elizabeth*, b. ———— ; m. John Russell, Camb.
  8 | *Anna*, (Hannah,) m. Timothy Garter, son of Rev. Thomas Carter, first of Watertown, afterwards of Woburn.
  9 | *Abigail*, m. Henry Baldwin, of Woburn.

2-5- | DAVID FISKE m. Sarah ————, who d. April 22, 1729, aged 75. He d. Oct. 23, 1729. David Fiske, like his father, was a subscriber to the first meeting-house in 1692, and, like his father, was ready to sustain the institutions of religion, and was elected to the dignified office of tythingman.

5-10 | *David*, b. Jan. 5, 1675 ; m. Elizabeth ————.
  11 | †*Jonathan*, b. May 19, 1679.
  12 | ‡*Robert*, b. May 8, 1681 ; d. April 18, 1753.
  13 | *Anna*, b. April 2, 1683.
  14 | *Lydia*, b. May 14, 1685 ; m. Joseph Loring, of Lexington.
  15 | *Sarah*, b. June 16, 1687.
  16 | *Abigail*, b. May 20, 1689 ; d. Aug. 13, 1691.
  17 | †*Ebenezer*, b. Sept. 12, 1692 ; m. ———— ————.

5-11- | JONATHAN FISKE m. Abigail ————. His name first appears upon the Lex. parish records in 1707, when Corp'l Jonathan Fiske was chosen one of the assessors. He was also a subscriber for the purchase of the Common in 1711 ; though the ch. records show that his dau. Abigail was bap. in 1704, when he o. c. He and his wife Abigail united with the ch. Oct. 24, 1708. He had a family of fourteen children, five of whom were born in Lex. and the rest in Sudbury, to which place he removed about 1713, where he was a deacon. He and his wife were dismissed to the Sudbury ch. in 1718. His will, dated Nov. 13, 1742, mentions wife Abigail, five sons and seven dau., two of his children probably having died before that period.

11-18 | *Abigail*, bap. July 23, 1704 ; m. Samuel Parris.
  19 | *Jonathan*, bap. June 9, 1706 ; not mentioned in his father's will.
  20 | *Kezia*, bap. Aug. 8, 1708 ; m. ———— Noyes.
  21 | *Lydia*, bap. April 16, 1710 ; m. ———— Patterson.
  22 | *Mary*, bap. June 30, 1712 ; m. Feb. 1, 1739, Nathaniel Fiske, of Weston.
  23 | *Hepzibah*, b. Oct. 30, 1713.   24 *Bezaleel*, b. Aug. 21, 1715.
  25 | *Samuel*, b. May 3, 1717 ; m. and lived in Newton.
  26 | *Beulah*, b. Nov. 1, 1718 ; m. first, Benjamin Stone, and second, 1747, Benjamin Eaton, of Framingham.
  27 | *William*, b. Sept. 4, 1720.
  28 | *Sarah*, b. Dec. 6, 1722 ; m. ———— Heard, of Sudbury.
  29 | *Anna*, b. 1724.   30 *David*, b. Sept. 1, 1726.
  31 | *Benjamin*, b. March 28, 1730.

5-12- | ROBERT FISKE m. May 27, 1718, Mary Stimpson, of Reading. In 1711, he was a subscriber for the purchase of the Common. He was ad. to the ch. 1736. His residence was on Hancock st. at or near the spot where Joseph F. Simonds now resides. Here his father David lived before him ; and hence this must have been one of the first settled places in the township. The present, which is probably the second house on this spot, was erected in 1732. Robert Fiske was a physician, and probably the first of the profession in the place.

His wife survived him a few years, and d. Feb. 11, 1757. He d. April 18, 1753. The inventory sheds light upon the manners and customs of the age. Among other things, we find the following: "Hat and wig, 100s. Arms — yellow stock gun, £8 10s.; little gun, £5; carbine, 50s.; brass pistols, 50s.; rapier and belt, 12s.; three staves, 20s.; two cans and two piggens, 15s.; one loom, quill wheel and warping bars, 50s.; two pair of snow shoes, 30s. Books — General Practice of Physic, 30s.; English Dispensatory or Synopsis of Medicine, 30s. The Structure and Condition of Bones, 15s." By these items, it will be seen that the doctor was quite as well armed for the art of war as for the art of healing.

12-32 | *Mary*, b. Feb. 8, 1719; d. same day.
33 | *Mary*, b. March 16, 1720; m. John Buckman, and lived in Lex.
34 | †*Robert*, b. Jan. 23, 1722; m. Betty ——.
35 | *Lydia*, b. June 23, 1724; m. James Wilson, of Bedford.
36 | †*Joseph*, b. Oct. 18, 1726; m. Hepsibah Raymond.
37 | *Ruth*, b. Nov. 15, 1729; m. —— Farmer.
38 | *John*, b. Nov. 8, 1731. He studied medicine, but it is doubtful whether he practiced to any extent. We find no account of his marriage, or children, or death. He was of Lex. in 1757, when Joseph Fiske, and John Fiske, physicians, heirs of Dr. Robert Fiske, sold land to Jonas Parker. John Fiske, of Lex. was in the French and Indian war, 1754.
39 | *Jonathan*, b. March 20, 1734; m. Sept. 4, 1755, Abigail Locke, of Woburn. She was dau. of William and Jemima (Russell) Locke, who resided near the line of Lexington. We find no account of Jonathan Fiske, or family. He was of Lex. in 1752, when for a consideration he relinquished his right to his mother's thirds.
40 | †*David*, b. March 8, 1737; m. Elizabeth Blodgett.

5-17- | EBENEZER FISKE m. Dec. 4, 1718, Grace Harrington, of Wat., by whom he had a child, which d. Aug. 25, 1721, and she d. four days after, aged 26. He m. second, Bethia Muzzy, dau. of Benj. and Sarah Muzzy. She d. Nov. 19, 1774, aged 74; and he d. Dec. 19, 1775. The monumental stone in the Lex. old yard, has the honorable prefix of *Lieut.* to the name of Ebenezer Fiske. He appears to have been popular in his day, having been called to fill many offices in the town. He was selectman ten years between 1739 and 1758: He resided on the road to Concord, a little more than a mile from the Common, at the easterly side of a large swell of land, which from his residence and ownership has taken the name of " Fiske Hill." It was at this house that the gallant Hayward, of Acton, met a British soldier coming from the well, between whom shots were exchanged, with fatal effect on both sides.

17-41 | *Sarah*, bap. Nov. 24, 1723.
42 | *Ebenezer*, b. March 5, 1826. He was a physician, and settled at Epping, N. H.
43 | *Bethia*, b. Aug. 1, 1729; m. —— Oliver, of Boston.
44 | *Elizabeth*, b. May 7, 1731; m. —— Ellis.
45 | *Jane*, b. May 2, 1733; m. Josiah Hadley.
46 | *Anna*, b. July 29, 1735; m. Oct. 24, 1754, Oliver Barrett, of Con. She was grandmother of the late Rev. Dr. Barrett, of Boston, and Rev. Fiske Barrett, once settled at Lexington.
47 | *Benjamin*, b. May 4, 1737; d. young.
48 | *Samuel*, b. Oct. 5, 1739. He grad. at H. C. 1759, and was an Episcopal clergyman in South Carolina. He d. 1777.
49 | †*Benjamin*, b. Aug. 10, 1742; d. Feb. 1, 1785.

12-31-   ROBERT FISKE m. Betty ——. She d. Dec. 14, 1770. There is
no record of his death; but as he was in Lex. in 1764, and she was a
wid. in 1767, he must have d. between those periods. In 1767 wid.
Betty Fiske bought eighty acres of land in Lex. bounded easterly on
Wo. line, and westerly by land of Lemuel Simonds. Her will, dated
Dec. 4, 1770, and proved Sept., 1771, mentions sons Robert, John,
and David, and dau. Betty and Ruth. The record of this family is
very defective. Robert Fiske, like his father, was a physician by
profession, and appears to have led rather a wandering life. In
1760 he was in the French war, in 1757 he was in Wo., and in 1764,
he came to Lex., when we find this entry, "Dr. Fiske and family
came last from Woburn."

31-50 | Robert, b. 1756.   51 †David, b. Nov. 23 1760.
52 | Ruth, b. Oct. 30, 1765.   53 John.   54 Betty.

12-36-   JOSEPH FISKE m. Dec. 13, 1751, Hepzibah Raymond. He d.
Jan. 8, 1808, aged 81. She d. Oct. 9, 1820, at the advanced age of
91. He was a physician, and successor to his father, who d. about
the time he commenced practice. He administered upon his father's
estate, and resided in the same house. He probably had other
children besides those named below, as the imperfect records speak
of the death of at least one of his infant children.

36-55 | †Joseph, b. Dec. 25, 1752; d. Sept. 25, 1837, aged 85.
56 | Ruth, b. April 20, 1758; m. May 7, 1795, John ——.
57 | Hepzibah, b. June 22, 1765; m. John Le Baron and went to Lit.

12-40-   DAVID FISKE m. June 22, 1760, Elizabeth Blodgett. He was a
weaver, and, to distinguish him from others of the same name, he
was called "Weaver David." He was famous as a hunter. Though
the wild game was not very plenty in his day, he contributed greatly
to thin off the deer, bears, &c. He ran down and killed a stately
buck on the hill over which the Burlington road ran, and hence it
has taken the name of "Buck's Hill." He has left no record of his
family; though from tradition, and intimations in the records, he
must have had at least three children. He d. July 20, 1815.

40-58 | Betsey, b. ——; m. April 14, 1788, Joseph Webber. They had
Joseph, b. Feb. 19, 1789, Susanna, b. July 9, 1791, and moved to
Bedford.
59 | †David, b. 1756.   60 Benjamin.

17-49-   BENJAMIN FISKE m. May 14, 1767, Rebecca Howe of Concord.
He d. Feb. 1, 1785, aged 42, and his wid. m. Mar. 28, 1786, Lieut.
William Merriam of Bedford.

49-61 | †Benjamin, b. Aug. 20, 1774.
62 | Elizabeth, b. Apr. 7, 1783; m. May 29, 1802, William Whitney of
Shirley, son of Rev. Phineas Whitney of that town. She d. Feb.
24, 1810, leaving two children, William F. and George H.

34-51-   DAVID FISKE m. Abigail Harrington, dau. of Robert and Abigail
(Mason) Harrington. He was a physician, and resided at the
corner of Elm avenue and Bedford street, where Mr. James Gould
now resides, which place, consisting of a house and an acre of land,
he bought of Mrs. Ruth Harrington in 1777. He d. Nov. 20, 1803,
and was buried in masonic order, being a member of that fraternity.
I find no record of his family worthy of mention.

51–63 | *Robert*, b. ——— ; m. Sally Robbins of West Camb.
64 | *Abigail*, b. ——— ; d. young.
65 | *Betsey*, b. Oct. 17, 1782 ; m. Nov. 29, 1810, Joseph Newell of New Ipswich, N. H.
66 | *John*, b. ——— ; m. Lydia Pierce ; resided in Winchester, and d. 1858.
67 | *Mary*, b. ——— ; d. young.
68 | *Chloe*, b. ——— ; scalded Feb. 16,1794.   69 *Peter*, b. ———.

36–55–   JOSEPH FISKE m. July 31, 1794, Elizabeth Stone, b. Nov. 13, 1770. She d. Mar. 6, 1842. He was a surgeon in the continental service during almost the entire Revolution — was at the capture of Burgoyne, the surrender of Yorktown, and many of the intermediate battles. Dr. Fiske was one of the original members of the Society of Cincinnati, formed by the officers at the close of the war in 1784, — a society whose benefactions have gladdened the heart of many a widow and orphan. His son, Joseph, had in his possession the certificate of membership, with the sign manual of George Washington, president, and Gen. Knox, secretary. He was also a member of the Massachusetts Medical Society. He d. May 4, 1860, aged 63.

55–70 | *Elizabeth*, b. June 15, 1795 ; m. Dec. 5, 1819, Richard Fisher of Camb.
71 | *Joseph*, b. Feb. 9, 1797 ; m. Nov. 12, 1829, Mary Gardner Kennard of Eliot, Me. Their children are Joseph Alexander, b. Mar. 8, 1830, and m. Love Langdon Dodge of Methuen, and lives at Lawrence ; Timothy Kennard, b. Aug. 5, 1833, and m. Dec. 25, 1857, Barbara Peters.
72 | *Jonas Stone*, b. May 9, 1799 ; m. May 8, 1823, Pamela Brown, dau. of James Brown. They had two children, Mary Elizabeth, b. June 2, 1824, and James Francis, b. Dec. 31, 1825. They reside in West Camb. Jonas Stone Fiske d. Mar. 23, 1828.
73 | *Sarah*, b. May 18, 1802 ; d. Dec. 27, 1825, unm.
74 | *Franklin*, b. Oct. 16, 1804 ; m. Oct. 3, 1839, Hannah Peters of Newport, N. H. They have two children, Charles A., b. Dec. 25, 1842 ; he was in the army and was severely wounded ; Joseph H. R., b. Sept. 8, 1843.
75 | *Almira*, b. June 24, 1808 ; m. Mar. 5, 1828, Zadoc Harrington. She d. Jan. 22, 1834.

40–59–   DAVID FISKE m. Apr. 26, 1784, Sarah Hadley. She d. May 21, 1804, and he m. second, Wid. Ruth Trask, May 6, 1806. He d. Aug. 17, 1820, aged 61. He had ten children by his first wife, and three by his second. He entered the service as a fifer in the company of Capt. Edmund Munroe, and served to the close of the war. For the sake of distinction he was denominated "Fifer David." There is no record of his family, and but little information can be obtained concerning them. He d. Aug. 17, 1820, aged 61.

59–76 | *Ruth*, b. ——— ; m. 1804, Philip Thomas of Rindge, N. H.
77 | †*Jonathan*, b. April 15, 1786 ; m. Rowena Leonard.
78 | *Sarah*, b. ——— ; m. Henry Spear and went to New York.
79 | *David*, b. ——— ; m. Aug. 25, 1820, Chloe Trask.
80 | *Samuel*, b. ——— ; d. unm. aged about 30.
81 | †*Benjamin*, b. April 27, 1798 ; m. Sarah Daland.
82 | *Anna*, b. ——— ; m. Sept. 10, 1820, Oliver Winship.
83 | *Charles*, b. ——— ; went to sea and never returned.
84 | *Patty*, b. ——— ; m. Daniel Gray and moved to Keene.
85 | *Betsey*, b. ——— ; m. Samuel Clarke and went to Glover, Vt.

86 | *Ichabod*, b. ——— ; went to Surry, N. H., on a visit, and d. there.
87 | *William*, b. ——— ; resides in Boston.
88 | *John*, b. ——— ; resides in Boston.
89 | *Frederic*, b. ——— ; resides in Boston.

49–61– | BENJAMIN FISKE m. May 16, 1797, Elizabeth Bridge, dau. of Rev. Mr. Bridge of Chelmsford. She d. Oct. 20, 1814, and he m. second, Nancy Adams of Westford. He moved to Boston in 1808, and was engaged in navigation till 1848. In 1843 he returned to Lex. and located himself on a large farm situated on Lowell street, where he d. He served as alderman in Boston in 1843, and as representative from 1833 to 1838. He held a justice's commission. He d. Feb. 2, 1858, aged 84.

64–90 | *John Minot*, b. July 15, 1798; m. Eliza Winn of Salem. He was grad. H. C. 1815, studied law, and d. in Chelmsford, Aug., 1841.
91 | *Louisa*, b. May 30, 1801; m. Dr. Cyrus Briggs of Augusta, Me.
92 | *Charles*, b. Nov. 17, 1807; m Nov. 8, 1831, Abigail Hayden of Boston. She d. March 28, 1859, aged 47. He m. again. Children, Frances Albertine, b. Nov. 1, 1832, m. June 8, 1852, Thomas B. Davenport of Hop.; Charles, b. May 27, 1834, m. April 4, 1855, Adeline W. Shaw of Augusta, Me.; William B., b. June 23, 1836, m. Oct. 15, 1855, Henriette S. Lyford of Boston. Henry A., b. April 23, 1840; Marion, b. Jan. 28, 1846, d. Jan. 12, 1864; Abbie Josephine, b. Nov. 18, 1848. The last three children were b. in Lex., and first three in Maine, where he then resided.
93 | *Benjamin*, b. Oct. 15, 1811; d. June 18, 1812.
94 | *Benjamin*, b. Nov. 20, 1820; m. Oct. 21, 1842, Maria Spear of Boston. He resided in New York city for a time, now resides in Medford, Mass.

59–77– | JONATHAN FISKE m. Rowena Leonard.

77–95 | *Eliza*, b. 1806; m. ——— Pierce and went to Cavendish, Vt.
96 | *George*, b. ——— ; d. about 1830, unm.
97 | *Maria*, b. ——— ; m. Dr. Haley and moved to Philadelphia, where he d. She m. again and went to Texas.
98 | *Sarah*, b. ——— ; r. in Boston.
99 | *Caroline*, b. about 1821; r. in Boston.
100 | *Rowena*, b. 1825; m. David Massy and resides in Boston.
101 | *John*, b. Nov. 6, 1827; m. Julia Denow, March 13, 1856, resides in Billerica. They have one child. She was of Lincolnville, Me.

59–81– | BENJAMIN FISKE m. Sarah Daland of Westford. She was b. Jan. 18, 1806.

81–102 | *Benjamin Ichabod*, b. Oct. 6, 1828; m. Caroline Wood of Leominster and r. in West Cambridge.
103 | *Louisa D.*, b. Feb. 21, 1830; m. George Reed of Auburn, N. H.
104 | *Frederic C. D.*, b. Oct. 3, 1831; killed at the second Bull Run battle.
105 | *Hannah E. D.*, b. June 5, 1834; m. Nathan Brown and r. in Walt.
106 | *Dan Gray*, b. Dec. 6, 1836.
107 | *Charles Henry*, b. April 23, 1838; killed in the army.
108 | *Sarah Lovina*, b. April 2, 1841.
109 | *Mary Maria*, b. March 16, 1843; m. March 24, 1861, Geo. G. Wheeler.
110 | *Oliver O.*, b. April 3, and d. April 5, 1845.

There was another family of Fiskes in Lexington having no connection with the David Fiske family.

1　SAMUEL FISKE was b. in Salem, Sept. 30, 1789. He came to Lex. when a child, and resided with John Chandler, and by him was presented for baptism, May 29, 1803. He m. Jan. 25, 1818, Ardelia L. Tufts of Charlestown, b. Jan. 7, 1795. She d. April 15, 1853. He resided in Lex. till about 1835, when he removed to Shirley, and from thence to Worcester, where he now resides. He represented Lex. in the General Court in 1828, '29, and '30.

1- 2　*Lucy Ann*, b. in Kinderhook, N. Y., May 7, 1819; m. Oct. 12, 1841, Joseph P. Hale of Bernardston.
3　*Ammi B.*, b. in Charlestown, Sept. 28, 1820; m. Dec. 28, 1846, Phebe James of Newburyport.
4　*Augusta*, b. in Lex. Dec. 31, 1822; m. Sept. 3, 1848, Timothy W. Wellington. They moved to Shirley, and from thence to Wor.
5　*Lucretia*, b. July 12, 1825; m. Oct. 19, 1845, William Hudson of Lex. They resided first in Lex., and in 1851 removed to Wor. He entered the service of the United States in 1861, was in Burnside's expedition to North Carolina, attached to the signal corps, where he d. of disease Aug. 20, 1862. He left two children, John A., b. Dec. 26, 1846, and William F., b. Oct. 3, 1848.
6　*Ardelia L.*, b. April 20, 1827; m. April 20, 1847, Lucius W. Pond of Worcester.
7　*Maria*, b. Dec. 20, 1828; m. April 21, 1853, William C. Pinkerton of Lancaster, Pa.
8　*Lydia C.*, b. July 27, 1830.
9　*Samuel*, b. March 23, 1833. He went to Lancaster, Pa., and m. Sept. 26, 1856, Amanda Stoddart of Philadelphia.

THE FITCH FAMILY.

ALBERT FITCH b. Feb. 14, 1817, was the son of Almond Fitch of Bed. He came to Lex. in 1851, with his family. He m. Nov. 24, 1841, Almira Cutler, dau. of Samuel Cutler, of Bed. b. Nov. 21, 1818. He has been several times one of the overseers of the poor. They have had three children: *Frederic A.*, b Dec. 5, 1842; *Ellen Maria*, b. Sept. 2, 1846, d. Aug. 4, 1848; *Ella Almira*, b. Jan. 16, 1849.

THE GAMMELL FAMILY.

The first of this family came to this country about 1740, and settled in Boston. He had at least two sons, *John* and *William*. JOHN GAMMELL was b. prior to 1750. He took an active part in many important events which preceded the Revolution. He was engaged in the destruction of the tea, and also of the stamp office. Immediately after the investment of Boston, he moved his family, consisting of a wife and one child, to Lex. On the 18th of June, 1775, he enlisted into the Revolutionary army.

1　WILLIAM GAMMELL, b. 1750, in Boston, where he lived till he was fourteen years old, when he moved to Chelmsford. Like his brother he was an ardent patriot, and joined the Revolutionary army. He m. Thankful Keyes, of Chelmsford, and moved to Hillsborough, N. H. about 1779. He had a family of seven children.

1- 2 | JOHN GAMMELL, son of William, was b. in Hillsborough, Nov. 12, 1785. He came to Lex. in 1806, and m. May 17, 1810, Rhoda Robinson, dau of Joseph Robinson, of Lex. He d. Oct. 1, 1866, aged 81, and she died —— ——.

2- 3 | *John*, b. Jan. 13, 1812; m. 1846, Martha A. Lakin, dau. of Samuel.
  4 | *Eliza*, b. Aug. 21, 1813; d. Jan. 14, 1848.
  5 | *Franklin*, b. May 29, 1815; m. 1839, Emily C., dau. of Joseph F. Andrews, of Charlestown. He d. Feb. 22, 1842, — leaving one child, Joseph F., b. July 6, 1840.
  6 | *Eben*, b. March 7, 1817; m. July 13, 1845, Elvira Wiley, of Charlestown. She d. and he m. Nov. 3, 1850, Mary A. Butterfield, of Lex. He has had two children by his first wife, and eight by his second, viz. *Lucy A.*, b. Oct. 29, 1846, d. Aug. 26, 1849; *Eldora E.*, b. Dec. 1848, d. Aug. 29, 1849; *Edwin H.*, b. Sept. 17, 1850, d. Aug. 29, 1857; *Howard A.*, b. Dec. 19, 1852; *Lucy E.*, b. Dec. 5, 1854, d. Feb. 18, 1863; *Abbie M.*, b. Sept. 28, 1856, d. Feb. 16, 1863; *Minnie*, b. Nov. 5, 1858, d. Jan. 14, 1863; *George R.*, b. Sept. 13, 1860; *Annie G.*, b. Nov. 5, 1862, d. Sept. 6, 1863; *Nellie M.*, b. Feb. 6, 1866. A remarkable instance of mortality.
  7 | *Margaret A.*, b Nov. 1, 1818; d. Nov. 12, 1850.
  8 | *Jonas*, b. Oct. 10, 1820. He has served on the board of overseers of the poor, and six or seven years as a member of the school committee.
  9 | *Lucy*, b. Jan. 1, 1822.

GLEASON. — There have been from time to time persons in town by the name of GLEASON, but no permanent family till recently. *George Gleason* came to Lexington from Holden in 1753. *Jonas Gleason* m. April 30, 1771, Ruth Bacon, both of Lex. In 1772, *Jonas* was ad. to the ch., and his dau. Ruth bap. In 1795, he was dismissed to the ch. of Bedford. In 1776, *Benjamin Gleason* was taxed both for personal and real estate. There are two families of *Gleasons* in town at the present time, but the records do not furnish a connected list of the families, and no list being furnished us we are obliged to omit them.

THE GODDARD FAMILY.

1 | EDWARD GODDARD was a wealthy farmer in Norfolk, England.

1- 2 | WILLIAM GODDARD, the seventh son of Edward, m. Elizabeth Miles, dau. of Benj. Miles. They resided in London, where they had six children, three of whom d. young. He and his wife, with their three remaining children, William, Joseph, and Robert, came to N. E. in 1665, and settled in Watertown, where he was made freeman in 1677, and ad. to the ch. in 1688, and d Oct. 6, 1691. She d. Feb. 8, 1698. He must have been a man of more than ordinary education, for he was employed by the town to " teach such children as were sent to him to learn the rules of the Latin tongue." They had five children b. in Watertown, two of whom d. young.

2- 3 | EDWARD GODDARD, the youngest child of William, was b. in Watertown, March 24, 1675; m. June, 1697, Susanna Stone. He was a schoolmaster, and taught successively in Watertown, Boston, and Framingham. He was a prominent man, and filled almost every place of honor and profit in the town of Framingham, where he took up his final residence; and the period during which he filled the different offices, furnishes the best evidence of his ability and fidelity. He was town clerk eighteen years, selectman ten years, town treasurer two years, representative eight years, and a member of the executive council three years. He was also a justice of the peace, and the captain of a company of horse. He d. Feb. 9, 1754, aged 79. They had nine children.

3- 4   DAVID GODDARD, the third son of Edward, b. Sept. 26, 1706, grad. at H. C. 1731. He studied theology and settled at Leicester, June 30, 1769. He m. Aug. 19, 1736, Mercy Stone, of Watertown. She d. Jan. 4, 1753, and he m. Dec. 20, 1753, Martha, wid. of Joseph Nichols, of Framingham. He visited Framingham during the prevalence of an epidemic, known there as the "great sickness," contracted the disease, and d. Jan. 19, 1754, within less than a month of his marriage. His father and mother fell a prey to the same disease about the same time. His ministry was prosperous and happy. He had nine children.

4- 5   WILLIAM GODDARD, the second son of David, was b. April 21, 1740, grad. at H. C. 1761, and was settled as a minister at Westmoreland, N. H., 1764. He m. Aug. 14, 1765, Rhoda Goddard, dau. of Edward and Hepzibah Goddard, his cousin. He was dismissed from Westmoreland on account of ill-health in 1775, removed to Orange, Mass., 1778, thence to Petersham, 1779, where he d. June 16, 1788, aged 48; she d. Dec 7, 1820, aged 80 years. They had eleven children — nine born in Westmoreland and two in Petersham.

5- 6   ASAHEL GODDARD, the youngest son of William, b. in Petersham, May 6, 1780, m. Jan. 1, 1808, Nancy Keyes, of Reading, Vt., b. June 7, 1787. They resided in Reading, where all their children but the youngest were born. He d. June 1, 1859.

6- 7   *Eliza*, b. Nov. 4, 1808; m. Jan. 25, 1848, Homer H. Hammond, widower of her sister Nancy.
8   *Amelia*, b. April 6, 1810; d. Nov. 13, 1828.
9   †*Alonzo*, b. May 27, 1814; m. April 8, 1841, Elizabeth N. Smith.
10   *Nancy Maria*, b. April 27, 1817; m. Sept. 22, 1844, Homer H. Hammond.
11   *Marcia*, b. July 26, 1819.
12   *Lucia*, b. Feb. 6, 1822; m. Dec. 2, 1852, Carlos Wardner.
13   *Asahel*, b. June 8, 1827; d. Oct. 14, 1847.
14   ‡*Solomon Keyes*, b. at Windsor, Vt., Oct. 3, 1831; m. Elizabeth M. Keyes.

6-9-   ALONZO GODDARD m. April 8, 1841, Elizabeth N. Smith, dau. of Ebenezer and Anna (Underwood) Smith. He has for several years served as one of the selectmen. He came to Lexington to reside permanently about 1850.

9-15   *Ellen E.*, b. April 29, 1845; m. May 31, 1863, Everett S. Locke. They have *Alonzo E.*, b. Oct. 13, 1863; *Martha C.*, b. Oct. 20, 1867.
16   *Alonzo A.*, b. April 1, 1847.

6-14-   SOLOMON K. GODDARD m. May 31, 1858, Elizabeth M. Keyes, dau. of Solomon and Sophronia (Darly) Keyes. He came to Lexington, 1852, where he is now in trade. They have but one child —
17   *Mina Keyes*, b. Nov. 2, 1864.

GODDING. — HENRY GODDING and his wife Sarah confessed, and were ad. to the ch. in Lexington, May 1, 1761, and their first child *Samuel*, was bap. They were in 1766, dismissed to Rowley, Canada. *John* and *Thomas* Godding were in the French war from Lexington, 1762.

GOODWIN. — PHILIP GOODWIN, by wife Elizabeth, had *Margaret*, b. Jan. 25, 1700; *Abigail*, b. June 28, 1707; *John*, b. Oct. 28, 1710.

THE GOULD FAMILY.

1   JAMES GOULD was b. in Boston, 1749. Being a wheelwright, he supplied wagons for the army during the revolution. He m. Anna Lawrence, who was b. 1742, and d. 1824, aged 82. He d. in 1789. They had five children, three of whom married, viz., Thomas, Abigail, and Mary.

1- 2   THOMAS GOULD was b. in Bridgewater, 1785; m. 1806, Sophia Lovis, who d. 1812, leaving three children. He m. Lydia Pierce, b. 1790, dau. of Jonas and Lydia (Prentice) Pierce.

2- 3   THOMAS GOULD, JR., b. in Boston, 1808; m. 1829, Lydia Ann W. Teel, b. in Newburyport, 1805. They resided in Boston till 1840, when they removed to Lex.

3- 4   *Ann Maria*, b. 1831; d. 1832, aged 7 months.
    5   *Thomas W.*, b. 1834; m. 1855, Caroline Goddard of Boston, where they reside.
    6   *Charles W.*, b. 1836; d. 1865.
    7   *Sophia Lovis*, b. 1838; m. 1861, Edward B. Bailey of Waltham.
    8   *Anna Matilda*, b. 1841.
    9   *Lucy M. R.*, b. 1843; m. 1864, Frank Whiting.

1   JAMES GOULD, from the same parent stock, m. March 26, 1826, Caroline W. Brooks, dau. of Calvin Brooks of Ashburnham. They resided in Charlestown till about 1845, when they moved to Lex.

1- 2   *Francis J.*, b. Jan. 24, 1828; grad. H. C. 1850; m. Sept. 26, 1859, Martha A. Rice. He is a physician, r. in Georgia.
    3   *Mary Caroline*, b. July 10, 1830; d. May 24, 1864.
    4   *Catharine Ann*, b. Jan. 26, 1833; m. Jan. 13, 1860, Peter W. Hyndman of Prince Edwards Island, r. there.
    5   *Rebecca Hicks*, b. April 13, 1835; m. Jan. 5, 1862, Leonard A. Saville.
    6   *Charles A.*, b. Oct. 10, 1837. He served in the army, and rose to the rank of captain—is now in Louisville, Ky.
    7   *Arthur Frederic*, b. July 30, 1841; he served nine months in the army in the rebellion.
    8   *Sarah B.*, b. Dec. 17, 1843.
    9   *Ellen Maria*, b. Oct. 12, 1847; d. Dec. 16, 1866.

THE GRAHAM FAMILY.

HUGH GRAHAM, b. in Putney, Vt., Dec. 6, 1804, was a son of Alexander Graham, who was son of Alexander Graham, one of the early settlers of Amherst, N. H. He came to Lex. about 1830. He

m. April 6, 1837, Hepzibah Marshall of Lunenburg. They have
had four children: *Mary Jane*, b. March 19, 1843; *Martha A.*, b.
Oct. 6, 1845, d. June 4, 1865; *Sarah M.*, b. Aug. 16, 1851; *George
A.*, b. Oct. 14, 1854.

THE GREEN FAMILY.

1   This name has never been common in Lexington. SAMUEL GREEN
m. Esther ——. They probably came from Wo., where the Greens
were numerous; and his wife was ad. to the ch. in Lex. Aug. 24,
1724, by a letter of dismission from the ch. in Wo. They came to
Lex. about 1718, as their first child was bap. in Lex. that year. He
held some subordinate town office in 1724. There is but little known
of this family. They probably resided near the middle of the town,
as he was employed in 1720 to ring the bell, sweep the meeting
house, and keep the key. He d. Aug. 10, 1759, aged 63.

1- 2   *Esther*, b. Sept. 7, 1718; m. Sept. 26, 1734, when she was only 16,
Amos Muzzy. He d. June 26, 1752, and she m. May 4, 1758,
Thomas Prentice, Esq., of Newton, who d. March 3, 1760.
3   *Phebe*, b. April 22, 1721; d. Aug. 9, 1722.
4   †*Samuel*, b. April 17, 1723.
5   *Elizabeth*, b. June 22, 1727; ad. to ch. Nov. 7, 1742; d. June 10,
1750.
6   *Benjamin*, b. Dec. 2, 1732; probably went to Waltham and m. 1756,
Martha Brown, and in 1770 m. Eunice Smith. This may have
been the Benjamin Green who d. in Lex. Oct. 26, 1822.

1-4-   SAMUEL GREEN m. April 3, 1750, Kezia Smith. There is little
or nothing known of this family.

4- 7   *Samuel*, bap. Aug. 16, 1752; perhaps the Samuel Green who was
dismissed to the ch. in Charlemont, March 28, 1779.

There were other Greens in Lex. from time to time, but whether
they were connections of the Samuel Green family, I have no means
of knowing.
Thomas Green came to Lex. from Camb. 1782.
William Green and family came from Wo. 1792.
Lucy Clark Green d. in Lex. Oct. 28, 1793.
Benjamin Green was taxed in Lex. in 1784 and 1785, and subse-
quently as a non-resident.
Isaac Green, of Lex., m. Sept. 5, 1778, Eleanor Tufts of Medford.

THE GREENLEAF FAMILY.

The Greenleaf family of Lex. probably descended from Edmund
Greenleaf of Newbury, who settled there 1635. He had a son,
Stephen, who m. Sarah Kent, and had among other children *Stephen*,
who m. Elizabeth Gerrish in 1676. They had a large family, and
among them *Stephen*, b. Oct. 21, 1690. This *Stephen* was probably
the Stephen Greenleaf of Medford, who m. Mary, and had six children. *Gardiner*, their first child, b. Jan. 9, 1726, m. Jan. 21, 1748,
Catharine Thompson. He d. Nov. 21, 1808.
1   JONATHAN GREENLEAF, the fourth child of Gardiner, b. June 9,
1754, m. May 5, 1778, Joanna Manning.

1- 2 | *Jonathan*, b. Feb. 16, 1784.
3 | *Joanna*, b. Dec. 28, 1786; m. Amos Locke of Lex.
4 | *William*, b. Oct. 7, 1788.
5 | †*Thomas*, b. Aug. 1, 1791; m. Oct. 2, 1822, Phebe Reed.
6 | *Mary M.*, b. Dec. 28, 1792; d. unm. aged 17.
7 | *Joseph*, b. Jan. 31, 1794; d. unm.
8 | *Sarah*, b. Oct. 25, 1797; m. —— Upson.

1-5-   THOMAS GREENLEAF m Oct. 2, 1822, Phebe Reed, dau. of Joshua and Susanna (Leathers) Reed. He d. Sept. 29, 1862, aged 70. He resided in Lex.

5- 9 | *William*, b. Oct. 25, 1825; m. Esther Horton of Gorham, Me.
10 | *Thomas*, b. Dec. 17, 1826.
11 | *Mary*, b. Sept. 12, 1830; d. May 17, 1848.

THE GRIMES FAMILY.

There were Grimeses in Lex. at the time the town was incorporated. The earliest record of any of the name is June 28, 1713, when Jonathan Grimes was bap., but the name of the parents is not given, nor have I ascertained from what place they came. George Grimes d. in Lex. July 28, 1716, aged 76. He could hardly have been the father of Jonathan. I am inclined to believe that William is the ancestor of the Lex. family. It is most likely he had other children, but I will set down the family as follows:

1   WILLIAM GRIMES m. Mary, who was ad. to the ch. June 30, 1717. He d. June 1, 1719, aged 43. His gravestone is in the old yard in Lexington.

1- 2 | †*William*, b. 1706.   3 *Mary*, b. ——.
4 | *Jonathan*, bap. June 28, 1713.   5 *Joseph*, bap. Aug. 21, 1715.
6 | *Elizabeth*, bap. June 30, 1717.   7 *Ruth*, bap. May 13, 1719.

1-2-   WILLIAM GRIMES m. Bethia ——. He d. Dec. 3, 1766, aged 60, and she d. March 15, 1772, aged 49.

2- 8 | †*William*, b. Sept. 19, 1744; m. Jan. 21, 1766, Abigail Reed.
9 | *Joseph*, b. Oct. 22, 1746; d. March 26, 1750.
10 | *John*, bap. Dec. 25, 1748; d. March 28, 1750.
11 | *Mary*, bap. July 28, 1751; m. Sept. 18, 1770, Samuel Ditson of Bil.
12 | *Sarah*, bap. Aug. 14, 1753.

2 8-   WILLIAM GRIMES m. Jan. 21, 1766, Abigail Reed, dau. of William and Abigail (Stone) Reed, b. Sept. 22, 1744. They were ad. to the ch. Nov. 8, 1767. He was a member of Capt. Parker's company, was on the Common on the 19th of April, 1775, and was also in a detachment of that company called to Camb. May 10 and June 17 of the same year. He also did other service in the revolutionary war. He resided in the north part of the town, near where Mr. Cummings now resides, on Grove Street, which place still retains the name of its original owner and occupant. They were dismissed to the ch. at Littleton, Jan. 20, 1793, to which place they had removed.

8-13 | *William*, b. May 22, 1768.   14 *Nabby*, bap. June 24, 1770.
15 | *Nathan*, bap. Dec. 20, 1772.

THE GROVER FAMILY.

John and Antipas Grover came to Lexington from Grafton in 1789. The family have not been numerous, but remain in town to the present time. John and Antipas are believed to be brothers. Their father's name is said to be Benjamin, and hence we shall set down as the head of the family BENJAMIN GROVER, probably of Grafton.

1-2-   JOHN GROVER m. Aug. 12, 1790, Polly Pierce. He resided in the part of the town commonly known as Scotland. She was b. Oct. 12, 1770, and d. Oct. 15, 1854, aged 74.

2- 3   *John*, b. April, 1792. He m. Sarah Merriam, of Bedford. They resided a few years in Lexington, where they had three children born, viz. Mary Ann, Edward, and John; they then moved to Boston, where he died.

4   *Nathaniel*, b. June 4, 1794. He went to Boston, m. Katharine Biscom, of Charlestown. They now reside in Chelsea.

5   *William*, b. Oct. 17, 1796; m. Oct. 13, 1829, Lucy Harrington, and second, Oct. 8, 1834, Maria Fessenden, dau. of Nathan Fessenden. They reside on Lowell street, near Woburn street. They have the following children.

5- 6   *William Henry*, b. April 21, 1837.
7   *Caroline M.*, b. Sept. 6, 1838. She is a teacher in Boston.
8   *Charles A.*, b. March 24, 1841.
9   *Mary Jane*, b. Aug. 29, 1843; d. June 25, 1847.
10   *Alice Jane*, b. Feb. 17, 1846.

ANTIPAS GROVER m. May 27, 1794, Sarah Pierce. They lived on Lowell street near where George Munroe now resides. They had one child born in Lexington, as seen by the record — Nathan Grover b. Jan. 1, 1795. They buried an infant Feb. 4, 1796. They moved to Fitzwilliam, N. H.

THE HADLEY FAMILY.

The Hadleys, or Headleys, as the name is sometimes spelt in our records, first appear about 1740; from what place they came we have not ascertained. The records of the family are very imperfect, and tradition but poorly supplies the defect.

1   THOMAS HADLEY m. April 15, 1741, Ruth Lawrence, dau. of Samuel and Elizabeth Lawrence. He d. July 15, 1788, in his 75th year, hence must have been born 1712. She d. May 26, 1819, at the advanced age of 94. He was a member of the gallant band who appeared under Capt. Parker in 1775. He was probably a son of Benjamin and Mehitable Hadley, of Groton, b. Aug. 11, 1712.

1- 2   *Elizabeth*, b. May 11, 1742; d. April 18, 1832, unm. aged 90.
3   *Thomas*, b. July 3, 1744; d. in early infancy.
4   †*Samuel*, b. July 9, 1746; killed on the Common, April 19, 1775.
5   *Ruth*, b. May 15, 1749; d. in infancy.
6   *Ebenezer*, b. May 5, 1751; m. May 11, 1779, Phebe Winship.
7   †*Thomas*, b. July 8, 1754.
8   †*Benjamin*, b. July 25, 1756.
9   *Ruth*, b. June 1, 1759; m. Nov. 30, 1780, James Fowle, of Camb.
10   †*Simon*, b. July 26, 1761; m. Jan. 27, 1791, Olive Porter, of Bed.

11 | *Sarah*, b. Nov. 26, 1764; m. April 26, 1784, David Fiske, 3d.
12 | *Mary*, b. May 20, 1767 ; d. in Boston, unm.
13 | *John*, b. Aug. 6, 1770; d. in Cambridge.

1-1- SAMUEL HADLEY m. Betty Jones. He was of the number who died for freedom on the first morning of the Revolution, and whose memory is embalmed in the hearts of his countrymen. After his death his widow m. again.

4-14 *Lucy*, bap. April 22, 1772.
15 | *Betty*, bap. May 24, 1772; m. Dec. 25, 1793, William Blackington, of West Cambridge.
16 | *Samuel*, bap. May 8, 1774.

1-7- THOMAS HADLEY m. Sept. 16, 1773, Alice Newton, of Bedford. She united with the ch. in Lexington, July 16, 1778. In September of the same year, three of their children, Amity, Alice, and Calley, were baptized. He probably d. about 1784, and she m. Feb. 21, 1785, Samuel Merriam, of Bedford. The record of the marriage has this addendum : " Said Alice Hadley married in a borrowed suit of cloathes." We find no record of the birth of his children ; but find the marriage of Thomas Statson, of Boston, and Amity Hadley, of Lexington, Feb. 26, 1792, who was probably his daughter. The singularity of her wedding suit probably arose from a notion which formerly prevailed, that if a man married a wife, and had no property with her, he could not be held responsible for any of her debts. Hence he took her without even the clothing she had on.

1-8- BENJAMIN HADLEY m. Lucy Dean, of Wilmington. He was a member of that patriot band commanded by Capt. Parker in 1775.

8-17 *Benjamin*, b. ———. He went to Charlestown, m. Martha Ireland, and d. 1852.
18 | *Samuel*, b. March 30, 1785; d. in the army, 1813.
19 | *John*, b. Aug. 10, 1788 ; m. Jan. 1, 1822, Susan Harrington.
20 | *Thomas*, b. ——— ; m. Thankful Whitney, went to N. Y.
21 | *Jonas*, b. ——— ; m. Mary Ann Whitney.
22 | *Martha*, b. ——— ; m. Joseph Littlefield, lived at Somerville.
23 | *Lucy*, b. ——— ; m. Joseph Miller, lives at Sandwich.
24 | *Eliza*, b. ——— ; d. Aug. 1857, unm. in Lexington.

As we have no record of this family, they may not be arranged in chronological order.

1-10- SIMON HADLEY m. Jan. 27, 1791, Olive Porter, of Bedford. Previous to his marriage, we find this entry upon the town record : "Betsey Hadley, dau. of Simeon Hadley and Betty Locke, born April 11, 1784"; from which we infer that he may have had two wives, and that Olive Porter was his second wife.

There are several families of Hadleys in town at the present day, but the imperfect records, and the want of the necessary information in the families on this subject, prevent a proper classification, or a connection of them with the Hadleys mentioned above. The following is all that has been obtained.

SEWELL HADLEY, thought to be the son of Samuel, m. Lovina Hall, of West Camb. She d. May 14, 1841, aged 39. They had the following children, viz. *Lorina*, b. Aug. 31, 1819; m. Dec. 25, 1844, George Stearns; *Sewell Thomas*, b. ——; *Benjamin*, b. Apr. 12, 1828; *Mary Ann*, twin with Benjamin.

SEWELL THOMAS HADLEY m. Nov. 30, 1846, Millicent A. D. Lakin, dau. of Samuel. They have had *Charles S.*, b. Sept. 22, 1850; d. Jan. 7, 1855; *Avery T.*, b. May 25, 1853; *Millicent A.*, b. Aug. 28, 1855; *Adelle C.*, b. Jan. 12, 1858; *Florence E.*, b. Jan. 3, 1861; *L. Evelyn*, b. July 22, 1863.

BENJAMIN HADLEY m. Anna Hall, July 4, 1852. They have four chil. *Gilbert P.*, b. July 16, 1853; *Warren*; *Charles*; *Anna*.

JONAS HADLEY, son of Benjamin, b. 1809; m. April, 1841, Mary Ann Whitney, of Wat. dau. of Jonathan Whitney. They have *Jonas H.*, b. Nov. 1, 1845; *Mary Eliza*, b. Jan. 6, 1850.

THE HALL FAMILY.

AMMI HALL, son of Ebenezer Hall of West Camb., b. Jan. 16, 1798; m. April 21, 1834, Eliza Crandall of Salem. He came to Lex. when a young man, and d. here April 10, 1867, aged 70 years. They have had but one child, *Eliza A.*, b. Jan. 25, 1835.

THE HAM FAMILY.

WILLIAM HAM, b. at Grampound, County of Cornwall, Eng., Nov. 21, 1818. He came to this country in 1837, and settled in Charlestown, where he remained till 1855. In 1856, he settled in Lex. Though he left old Eng. in 1837, the remembrance of early acquaintance induced him to revisit his native country, and take Mary Grose as a wife. They were m. Jan. 21, 1846. They have had six children. *William F.*, b. Aug. 2, 1846; he has served three years in the U. S. army; *Walter T.*, b. July 17, 1848; *Lucy Ann*, b. Feb. 21, 1850; *Joseph F.*, b. Feb. 14, 1853; *Mary P.*, b. April 11, 1855, d. April 15, 1865; *Jane T.*, b. Sept. 11, 1857.

THE HANCOCK FAMILY.

Though we have had occasion to speak of Rev. John Hancock, the second minister of Lex., and of several members of that family, I will, in accordance with the plan I have adopted, give a connected view of the family.

1 NATHANIEL HANCOCK was in Camb. as early as 1635. He m. Jane, and had a large family of children. His oldest child may have been born before he came to this country. He d. 1652.

1- 2 *Mary*, b. Nov. 3, 1634.   3 *Sarah*, b. March 3, 1636.
4 †*Nathaniel*, b. Dec. 13, 1638; m. Mary Prentice, March 8, 1664.
5 *John*, b. April ——; d. April 2, 1642.
6 *Elizabeth*, b. March 1, 1644.   7 *Lydia*, b. July 2, 1646.
8 *Abigail*, b. ——; d. May 7, 1672.
9 *Ann*, b. ——; d. Oct. 5, 1672.

1-4-   NATHANIEL HANCOCK m. March 8, 1664, Mary, dau. of Henry
Prentice of Camb. He was a dea. of the ch., and appears to have
enjoyed the confidence of his fellow-citizens. He d. April 12, 1719,
in his eighty-first year.

4- 9 *Nathaniel*, b. Feb. 28, 1665; d. same year.
  10 *Mary*, b. May 6, 1666.   11 *Sarah*, b. Aug. 23, 1667.
  12 *Nathaniel*, b. Oct. 29, 1668. He m. Prudence, who d. July 15,
1742, aged 72. He had five children, among whom was Nathaniel,
b. Jan. 14, 1701, grad. at H. C. 1721, settled as a clergyman, and
d. 1744.
  13 *Abigail*, b. Dec. 22, 1669; d. young.
  14 ‡*John*, b. Dec. 1671; grad. H. C. 1689.
  15 ‡*Samuel*, b. June 2, 1673; m. Dorothy ——.
  16 *Abigail*, b. Aug. 25, 1675.   17 *Elizabeth*, b. Aug. 25, 1677.
  18 *Ebenezer*, b. March 28, 1681; m. Susanna Clark, Jan. 14, 1702.
  19 *Joseph*, b. April 28, 1683.
  20 *Thomas*, b. 1685; m. Oct. 30, 1712, Susanna Fethergill.
  21 *Solomon*, b. ——.

4-14-   JOHN HANCOCK grad. H. C. 1689, and settled in Lex. He m.
Elizabeth Clark, dau. of Rev. Thomas and Mary Clark of Chelmsford. Mr. Clark was b. in Boston about 1652, grad. H. C. 1670,
settled in Chelmsford, 1677, d. Dec. 7, 1704. His wife, Mary, d.
Dec. 2, 1700, and Mr Clark m. Elizabeth Whiting of Billerica.
Mr. Hancock probably resided in that part of Camb. which is now
Newton. In the church record kept by Rev. Mr. Hancock, we find
this entry. "Oct. 16, 1698. I was received into full communion
with the church of Christ in this place (Lexington) by virtue of a
letter of dismission from the ch. of Christ in Newtowne." He was
ordained at Lex. Nov. 2, 1698. He d. Dec. 5, 1752, in the eighty-
first year of his age, and in the fifty-fifth of his ministry. His wife d.
Feb. 13, 1760, I have had occasion to speak of *Bishop* Hancock, as
he was familiarly called, in all the relations of life, and have done it
so fully that it is entirely unnecessary to add anything more in this
place. His remains rest in a tomb in Lex. with those of his wife and
son Ebenezer, together with those of his successor, Rev. Jonas
Clarke, and his family.

14-22 ‡*John*, b. June 1, 1702; m. Mrs. Mary H. Thaxter.
  23 ‡*Thomas*, b. July 13, 1703; m. Lydia Henchman.
  24 *Elizabeth*, b. Feb 5, 1705; m. Rev. Jonathan Bowman of Dorchester. She was bap. the day of her birth.
  25 *Ebenezer*, b. Dec. 7, 1710. He was grad. H. C. 1728, was settled a
colleague with his father Jan. 2, 1734, and d. Jan. 28, 1740, without issue. He was highly esteemed by the people of the parish.
  26 *Lucy*, b. April 20, 1713; m Rev. Nicholas Bowes of Bedford. It is
a singular fact that Lucy Hancock, the daughter of a clergyman,
married a clergyman, and her daughter, Lucy, became the wife of
Rev. Jonas Clarke of Lex., and that from them clergymen have
proceeded as streams from a fountain.

4-15-   SAMUEL HANCOCK m. Dorothy ——. He probably came to Lex.
about the time of his brother's settlement, as his son John was bap.
here in Sept. 1699. He was ad. to the ch. in Lex. April 10, 1715.

17-27 *John*, bap. Sept. 10, 1699; d. in Camb. March 18, 1776, aged 77.
  28 *Mary*, bap. April 19, 1702; probably m. James Thompson of Wo.
  29 *Solomon*, bap. June 18, 1704.

30| *Samuel*, bap. July 21, 1706; d. June 14, 1716.
31| *Hannah*, bap. Feb. 27, 1709.   32 *Sarah*, bap. Feb. 17, 1712.

14-22-   JOHN HANCOCK grad. at H. C. 1719, and was ordained at Braintree, Nov. 2, 1728, and d. May 7, 1744. He m. Mary H., widow of Samuel Thaxter of Braintree. He was a divine of more than ordinary ability, and, though he d. young, had arisen to distinction in his profession, and so gave weight to the character and celebrity of the name.

22-33| †*John*, b. Jan. 23, 1737; m. 1775, Dorothy Quincy.
34| *Ebenezer*, b. Nov. 26, 1741; m. Eliza Lowell.
35| *Mary*, b. ———; m. Richard Perkins, and d. 1779.

14-23-   THOMAS HANCOCK m. Nov. 5, 1730, Lydia Henchman. He was a merchant in Boston, was eminently successful, and accumulated a large fortune. He d. 1764, without issue, and gave the great mass of his property to John, his nephew, a son of his brother John of Braintree, deceased. He built a house in Lexington for his honored father about 1735, which afterward became the property and residence of Rev. Jonas Clarke, his father's successor. The house is now standing, and is revered for its age and associations.

22-33-   JOHN HANCOCK m. at Fairfield, Conn., Sept. 4, 1775, Dorothy Quincy, dau. of Edmund Quincy of Boston. The relations which John Hancock sustained to the town of Lex.—the birthplace of his father, and the residence of some of his near relations and esteemed friends; the place where he had spent some seven years of his boyhood, and where he was boarding temporarily at the opening of the Revolutionary drama—will justify us in going a little beyond our ordinary course, and noticing somewhat in detail the character and services of this Revolutionary patriot. John Hancock was left an orphan by the death of his father, when he was but seven years of age. His education was intrusted to the care of his relatives, and he spent the greater portion of his boyhood with his grandfather in Lex. He was graduated at Harvard College in 1754. He entered the store or counting house of his uncle Thomas as a clerk, where he acquired a knowledge of business, and learned the importance of commerce to the colony. He made such proficiency in business, that in 1760 he was sent abroad to look after the affairs of the house; and was in England, and present at the funeral of George II., and at the coronation of George III., — pageants not uncongenial to his taste. Soon after his return to this country, and about the time that the oppressive policy of the British ministry began to develop itself, he came into possession of the princely fortune left him by his uncle. It is well known that great efforts were made by the Royalists to engage him on the side of the mother country. Standing, as he did, almost at the head of the merchants of Boston, it was a great object to enlist him in the Royal cause. The safety of his large property, the flattering offers of promotion and place, would naturally have their influence on a young man of Hancock's taste and temperament, coming at once into possession of such an estate; and it was at one time suspected that he was inclined to join the royal party. But happily for him and for America, there were other influences which were brought to bear upon him. That stern and inflexible patriot, Samuel Adams, who in a manner held the fortunes of the colony in his hand, contributed in no small degree to the wise choice which Hancock made. There was another influence, more silent but more controling, which contributed to the formation of his character.

Rev. Jonas Clarke of Lexington, his old college acquaintance, had married a cousin of Hancock's. Mr. Clarke was then residing in the house erected by Thomas Hancock of Boston for a residence of his venerable father. In this mansion young Hancock had spent a portion of his early life. All these circumstances would naturally draw him to Lexington. And it is well known that there was a peculiar intimacy between him and Mr. Clarke, whose devotion to the interests of the Colony was well known and acknowledged. The dignity of character, the urbanity of manners, and the commanding talents of the patriotic priest, must have impressed the mind of the pliant and generous young merchant. And those who know the character and talents and patriotic devotion to the cause of liberty of Mr. Clarke, will not doubt that his influence upon his nephew must have been great and controlling, and all in the right direction.

Under such influences John Hancock chose the better part, and devoted himself and his all to the cause of his country. Having made his choice, no man in the community was more decided, and no man had more at stake. With his large property in the town of Boston at the mercy of the enemy, he declared himself perfectly willing, if it was thought the best policy, to lay the place in ashes. At a meeting of the "North End Caucus," an association of patriots of which he was a member, the question of the best mode of expelling the regulars from Boston being under discussion, he exclaimed, "Burn Boston, and make John Hancock a beggar, if the public good requires it." In a letter to Washington, dated Dec. 22, 1775, informing him that Congress had authorized him to attack the British in the town of Boston, if he thought it expedient, Hancock employs this patriotic language,—"I heartily wish it, though personally I may be the greatest sufferer." No one can doubt the patriotism of John Hancock. He came in direct contact with Royal authority, and was ever found true and reliable. The manner in which he was treated by the crown officers shows that they regarded him as hopelessly lost to their cause. He was elected a representative from Boston, and also a member of the Council, but was rejected and spurned by the royal prerogative. In 1767 Gov. Bernard sent him a lieutenant's commission, but he tore it in pieces in presence of the citizens. He was captain of the cadets, the Governor's body guard, and was removed by Gage. He also received several personal indignities from the British troops stationed in Boston before the breaking out of hostilities. The fact that he was coupled with Samuel Adams in the proclamation of Gage immediately after the battle of Lexington, and proscribed as beyond the pale of executive clemency, shows the light in which he was viewed by the minions of power.

In 1774, John Hancock was selected as the orator to deliver the address on the anniversary of the Boston massacre, and the bold, independent manner in which he spoke of the rights of the people, gave great offence to the friends of Parliament. John Adams, who was present, says of this performance, "the composition, the pronunciation, the action, all exceeded the expectations of everybody. They exceeded even mine, which were very considerable." In the same year John Hancock was elected to represent the town of Boston at a General Court, which was called at Salem. And although Gage subsequently to the election issued a proclamation excusing their attendance, many of the representatives assembled, and after waiting one day, they organized themselves into a convention, and elected John Hancock chairman; and when the same body resolved themselves into a Provincial Congress, they organized by choosing John Hancock President, and adjourned to Concord. During the session measures were adopted looking directly to open resistance, and no one of that band of patriots was more firm and decided than he who presided over their deliberations. He was elected chairman of the Committee of Safety, and also of the committee to take into consideration the state of the Province — the two most important committees. During the same Congress he was chosen a delegate to the Continental Congress, which met at Philadelphia, May 10, 1775. Having taken a seat in that august body, he found that his fame had preceded him, for on the third day of the session he was chosen unanimously to succeed Peyton Randolph, as President. He was President of Congress in 1776, and when the Declaration of Independence was first circulated among the members of that body, it bore the name of John Hancock alone, as President of the Congress, he being the first to affix his name to an instrument which would have proved the death-warrant of the signers, if the cause of the Colonies had not succeeded; and it is said that the bold and striking characteristics of his signature served to inspire confidence and confirm the doubtful. He resigned his station as President in October, 1777, owing to ill-health.

In 1780, John Hancock was elected a member of the Convention which framed the State Constitution, and was the first Governor of Massachusetts after its adoption, to which office he was several times reëlected. As a man and a public servant, he was noted for his benevolence and hospitality — spending his money freely to entertain distinguished guests, or to relieve the distresses of the poor and unfortunate.

Gov. Hancock was elected a delegate to the State Convention on the adoption of the Federal Constitution, and was made President of that body. For a time it was exceedingly doubtful whether the Constitution would be ratified or rejected. Hancock favored the scheme of adopting it, and at the same time proposing certain amendments to obviate the objections which had been made to it. This plan was adopted, and the Constitution was ratified by a small majority. It was thought at the time that without his influence it would have been lost. On taking the question he said, "I should have considered it one of the most distressing misfortunes of my life to be deprived of giving my aid and support to a system which, if amended, as I feel assured it will be, according to your proposals, cannot fail to give the people of the United States a greater degree of political freedom, and eventually as much national dignity as falls to the lot of any nation on earth. The question now before you is such as no nation on earth, without the limits of America, has ever had the privilege of deciding." Thus are we in a manner indebted to John Hancock for the blessed Constitution under which we live, and which has fully verified his prediction.

The public mind has been somewhat divided in its estimate of the talents of John Hancock, and of the importance of his public services. In point of ability he held a highly respectable rank. His talents were of a popular and showy, rather than of a profound character. Though he had not the far-reaching sagacity of Samuel Adams, or the logical acumen of Joseph Hawley or John Adams, or the active, stirring energy of Warren, yet he filled a place among the patriots of that day which no other man could fill, and exerted an influence highly beneficial to the great cause of freedom — operating in commercial circles where the motive of interest strongly tended to the royal cause. He may have been *vain*, but vanity can be pardoned when it can justly boast of making so great a sacrifice for the benefit of coming generations. He may have been *ambitious;* but his ambition was of a public character. He desired promotion that he might further a good cause — he sought place that he might

dispense his liberal fortune, and show that the hospitalities and even
the graces and refinements of life were not of necessity confined to
princes, and that those "who wore soft raiment are not" always, "in
kings' houses." Whatever blemishes of character a fastidious criti-
cism may discover in John Hancock, we are satisfied that but few
men, in this or any other country, can point to acts more noble, and
to sacrifices more disinterested than those which appear in his character; and few men ever gave greater evidence of active devotion
to their country's welfare.

And when we say that in point of talent and influence he fell below
Samuel Adams, we only say of him what would be true of any other
man of that day; for in reference to talents in the broadest sense of
that term, Samuel Adams had no equal. Others may have been more
learned, or may have excelled him in some particulars; but in his
knowledge of the science of human government, and of the great
principles of rational liberty — in his knowledge of men and the
springs of action in the human heart, he certainly had no superior.
And when we consider that this knowledge was ever under the con-
trol of that lofty patriotism, that unconquerable fidelity to principle,
that calm and indomitable will for which he was always distinguished,
we can truly say of him that he was the founder of civil liberty in
Massachusetts — in New England — in America. The author of
the "Life of Samuel Adams," has shown that he was second to
no man among us; and his memory will be cherished as long as civil
liberty has an enlightened devotee.

John Hancock resided in Boston, in what was then regarded as a
princely mansion on Beacon street, fronting upon, and overlooking
the Common. The house stood till 1863, when it was taken down.
An effort had been made by the State to purchase the property and
preserve the mansion for the residence of the successive Governors
of the Commonwealth; that they might show their respect for the illus-
trious patriot who first graced and adorned it; and that his disinterested patriotism might warm the breast of those who might be
called to fill the high office first filled and adorned by JOHN HANCOCK.

Mr. Hancock always cherished a fond recollection of Lexington,
as the birth-place of his father, the residence of his grandfather, and
the place where he spent the playful portion of his boyhood. He
also revered it as the place where he took counsel with Rev. Jonas
Clarke on matters of awful moment; and the place where under his
own direction the patriotic men of Lexington stood firmly before the
invaders of their rights. This attachment to Lexington he manifested by gifts to the church and society.

We have said before, that John Hancock m. September 4, 1775,
Dorothy Quincy of Boston, dau. of Edmund Quincy. He d. Oct.
8, 1793, aged 56. She m. July 28, 1796, James Scott, the master of
a London packet, formerly in the employ of her first husband. She
outlived Capt. Scott many years, and retained her faculties to the
last. She was a lady of superior education and accomplishments,
and was gifted with wonderful powers of conversation. She was one
of the first persons sought by Lafayette, when he visited this country
in 1824. "Those who witnessed this hearty interview, speak of it
with admiration. The once youthful chevalier and the unrivalled
belle met, as if only a summer had passed since they had enjoyed
social interviews in the perils of the Revolution." She d. Feb. 3,
1830, aged 83 years.

33-36 | *Lydia*, b. and d. in Philadelphia, 1776.
37 | *John George Washington*, b. 1778, and was killed at Milton, when
skating on the ice, Jan. 27, 1787. Thus the family of John
Hancock became extinct.

THE HARRINGTON FAMILY.

The name of Harrington is found in almost every town in New England; and it is probable that most, if not all of them, descended from or at least were relatives of Robert Harrington of Watertown, who was in that town as early as 1642. He had a numerous family, who were widely dispersed. He came from England where many of his children were born.

1   GEORGE HARRINGTON, from whom our Lexington Harrington descended, was probably a son or brother of Robert. He m. Susanna ——, and had, as was common in those days, a large family of thirteen children. He resided in Watertown. Two of his grandchildren settled in Lexington.

1- 2   *Susanna*, b. Aug. 18, 1649; m. Feb. 9, 1661, John Cutting.
3   †*John*, b. Aug. 24, 1651; d. Aug. 24, 1741.
4   *Robert*, b. Aug. 31, 1653; probably d. young.
5   *George*, b. Nov. 24, 1655. He belonged to Capt. Wadsworth's company, and was killed by the Indians at Lan. 1675.
6   †*Daniel*, b. Nov. 1, 1657; ad. freeman 1690.
7   *Joseph*, b. Dec. 28, 1659; ad. freeman 1690.
8   *Benjamin*, b. June 26, 1662; d. 1724.
9   *Mary*, b. Jan. 12, 1664; m. about 1680, John Bemis, and had fourteen children.
10   *Thomas*, b. April 20, 1665; ad. freeman 1690.
11   *Samuel*, b. Dec. 18, 1666.
12   *Edward*, b. March 2, 1669.
13   *Sarah*, b. March 10, 1671; m. Nov. 24, 1687, Joseph Winship of Cambridge.
14   *David*, b. June 1, 1673; d. March 11, 1675.

1-3-   JOHN HARRINGTON m. Nov. 17, 1681, Hannah Winter, dau. of John Winter, Jr., of Watertown, but afterwards of Camb. Farms. She d. July 17, 1741, and he d. Aug. 24, 1741, in that part of Watertown now Waltham.

3-15   *Hannah*, b. Aug. 9, 1682; m. April 29, 1703, Eleazer Hammond of Newton.
16   †*John*, b. Oct. 1684; m. Ap. 12, 1705, Eliz. Cutter of Camb. Farms.
17   *Mary*, b. May 11, 1687; m. March 8, 1709, Thomas Hammond.
18   *Lydia*, bap. March 2, 1690.
19   *James*, bap. April 2, 1695.   19½ *Patience*, bap. Oct. 10, 1697.

1-6-   DANIEL HARRINGTON m. Oct. 18, 1681, Sarah Whitney. She d. June 8, 1720, and he m. second, Oct. 25, 1720, Elizabeth, wid. of Capt. Benjamin Garfield, and dau. of Matthew and Anna Bridge of Cambridge.

6-20   *Daniel*, b. Feb. 24, 1684; d. young.
21   †*Robert*, b. July 2, 1686; m. Nov. 15, 1711, Anna Harrington.
22   *Daniel*, b. July 10, 1687.
23   *Jonathan*, b. March 21, 1690; m. Feb. 28, 1724, Elizabeth Bigelow.
24   *Joseph*, b. Feb. 4, 1691.
25   *Sarah*, b. Oct. 28, 1693; m. June 11, 1711, Nathaniel Livermore.

3-16-   JOHN HARRINGTON m. April 12, 1705, Elizabeth Cutter, then of Camb. Farms, but now Lex., where he settled. His name appears upon our records for the first time in 1713, when John Harrington appeared before the selectmen, and offered on certain conditions, to give the right of way across his land. His residence must have been easterly of *Hancock Hill*, near the residence of the late Joseph Fiske. He d. Nov. 29, 1750. Some articles in the inventory of his estate, show the fashions of the day — " Leather britches, a new dark wigg, sundry old wiggs, yarn leggens, pistols, warming pan, wooden plates."

16-26 ‡*Richard*, b. Sept. 26, 1707.
    27 ‡*Moses*, b. Jan. 6, 1710; d. Jan. 11, 1787.
    28 †*Henry*, b. Jan. 8, 1712.
    29 *John*, b. March 22, 1714; d. Aug. 29, 1750.
    30 *Hannah*, bap. in Watertown, Feb. 20, 1715.
    31 *William*, b. Feb. 4, 1717; d. Sept. 28, 1717.
    32 *Abigail*, b. Dec. 4, 1718; m. Mar. 1, 1738, John Palls of Townsend.
    33 *Caleb*, b. July 13, 1721; d. 1747.

6-21-   ROBERT HARRINGTON m. Nov. 15, 1711, Anna Harrington of Watertown, dau. of Samuel and Grace Harrington. He was a blacksmith, and settled in Lexington on the main street, near the present residence of P. P. Pierce. His name first appears upon our church records in 1712, when Samuel Harrington was bap., his father Robert owning the covenant. He was chosen a *fence viewer* in 1713, so he must have been a permanent resident at that time. He d. Feb. 5, 1774, aged 89, and she d. Oct. 16, 1777, aged 85. He was cousin to John, who came to Lexington from Watertown about the same time. These two were the ancestors of the numerous family of Harringtons which afterwards appear on our records.

21-34 *Samuel*, b. July 28, 1712; d. Sept. 29, 1712.
    35 *Samuel*, b. April 15, 1714.
    36 *Anna*, b. June 2, and bap. in Watertown, June 10, 1716. She m. her cousin, Rev. Timothy Harrington. He was settled at Swanzey, N. H. That town was destroyed by the Indians, April 2, 1747, and he was the next year settled at Lancaster, Mass., where he d. May 17, 1778.
    37 ‡*Robert*, b. April 26, 1719; m. Abigail Mason.
    38 ‡*Jonathan*, b May 21, 1723.
    39 *Grace*, bap. Dec. 4, 1729; d. April 10, 1759, unm.

16-26-   RICHARD HARRINGTON m. Abigail ——. He resided on Adams street, near where George F. Chapman now resides.

26-40 *Ebenezer*, b. March 16, 1733; probably d. young.
    41 *Thankful*, b. Jan. 16, 1734; d. unm.
    42 *Thaddeus*, b. Sept. 9, 1736. Enrolled in Capt. Parker's co. 1775.
    43 *Hannah*, b. March 8, 1738.
    44 *Ephraim*, b. March 2, 1739; d. Oct. 20, 1742.
    45 *Nathan*, b. Dec. 25, 1740.   46 *Ebenezer*, b. March, 16, 1743.
    47 *Solomon*, b. Jan. 27, 1746; d. Nov. 12, 1750.
    48 *Stephen*, b. May 23, 1748.   49 *Simeon*, b. July 8, 1750.
    50 *Seth*, b. Oct. 30, 1752.   51 *Abigail*, b. Aug. 9, 1754.

16-27-   MOSES HARRINGTON m. Martha ——? who was ad. to the ch. June 2, 1734. We learn by tradition that he had several children, though the records are silent upon the subject. He d. Jan. 11, 1787. It is said that he had *Moses*, *Betsey*, and *Caleb*, the latter of whom was the CALEB HARRINGTON who was killed on the Common on the 19th of April, 1775. He is said to have been about twenty-five years of age at the time of his death. Betsey m. first, Ebenezer White, and, second, Thomas Cutler.

16-28-   HENRY HARRINGTON m. June 4, 1735, Sarah Laughton, dau. of Dea. John and Sarah Laughton. She d. in childbed, May 16, 1760, and he m. second, Abigail ——, the widow of Ebenezer Blodgett. She lived to a great age, and was a woman of great peculiarities. Henry Harrington resided under the hill, near the residence of Mr. Hutchinson. He d. Dec. 25, 1791, aged 80; she d. Jan. 23, 1820, aged 94.

    28-52 *Sarah*, b. Sept. 17, 1735; m. May 28, 1755, Thomas Winship.
     53 †*Henry*, b. Aug. 27, 1737; m. Oct. 25, 1759, Ruth Blodgett.
     54 †*Jeremiah*, b. about 1741; m. Dec. 21, 1769, Sarah Locke.
     55 †*John*, b. about 1743; m. Mary Wootten.
     56 †*Jonathan*, b. about 1745; m. Ruth Fiske.
     57 †*Thomas*, b. about 1748; m. Lucy Perry.
     58 *Elizabeth*, b. Sept. 17, 1750; m. Nathan Munroe.
     59 *William*, b. Mar. 18, 1752; d. June 20, 1778, in small pox hospital.
     60 †*Moses*, b. March 22, 1754; m. Mary Reed.
     61 *Mary*, b. Ap. 19, 1756; m. Newell Reed of Wo. prec., Oct. 16, 1777.
     62 †*Ebenezer*, b. May 15, 1760; m. Sept. 4, 1788, Mrs. Sarah Johnson.

21-37-   ROBERT HARRINGTON m. Abigail Mason, dau. of Daniel and Experience Mason of Newton. They were ad. to the ch. in Lex. Aug. 11, 1745. She d. Aug. 25, 1778, aged 57, and he m. April 16, 1781, widow Chloe Trask. He d. May 30, 1793, aged 74. He filled many town offices, and bore the dignified title of *Ensign* Harrington. He was one of the selectmen in 1752, and was re-elected to that station some twelve or fourteen years, and was chairman of the board in the eventful period of the Revolution, when many important duties devolved upon him. He was also many years a magistrate, and represented the town four years in the General Court.

    37-63 †*Thaddeus*, b. Sept. 9, 1736; m. Sept. 20, 1764, Lydia Porter of Wo.
     64 †*Daniel*, b. May 25, 1739; m. Anna Munroe.
     65 *Annaritte*, bap. Aug. 12, 1744; probably d. young.
     66 *Betty*, b. May 23, 1745; d. Oct. 27, 1745.
     67 *Elizabeth*, b. Sept. 6, 1747; m. Samuel Smith.
     68 *Abigail*, b. Dec. 23, 1749; d. young.
     69 *Abigail*, b. Aug. 9, 1754; m. Dr. David Fiske.
     70 †*Abijah*, b. Feb. 7, 1761; m. first, Polly Raymond, and second, widow Locke.

21-38-   JONATHAN HARRINGTON m. Aug. 1, 1750, Mrs. Abigail Dunster. She d. June 30, 1776, and he m. second, Mrs. Lydia Mulliken, wid. of Nathaniel Mulliken. He d. Sept. 14, 1809, aged 87; and she d. Nov. 13, 1783, aged 57. He was several years selectman, and was one of the committee of correspondence in 1778, in the midst of the Revolution. He was a true son of liberty, and was found on the 19th of April at the post of danger.

    38-71 *Rebecca*, b. Feb. 17, 1751; m. Aug. 31, 1769, Edmund Munroe.
     72 *Mary*, b. April 11, 1753.
     73 *Anna*, b. Feb. 19, 1756; m. April 21, 1778, Cally Newell.
     74 †*Jonathan*, b. July 8, 1758; m. Nov. 19, 1777, Sally Banks.
     75 *Charles*, b. Nov. 15, 1760; d. Dec. 24, 1761.
     76 †*Charles*, b. March 24, 1763; m. Dec. 18, 1786, Mary Brown.
     77 †*Solomon*, b. Feb. 22, 1766; m. Polly Bent.
     78 †*Peter*, bap. July 26, 1772; m. Lydia Loring.

28-53- | HENRY HARRINGTON m. Oct. 25, 1759, Ruth Blodgett, dau. of Joseph Blodgett. They were ad. to the ch. June 2, 1763. He was a soldier in the French war, in 1756 and 1758.

53-79 | †*Henry*, b. May 25, 1760; m. March 13, 1783, Amity Pierce.
80 | *Rebecca*, b. July 12, 1762; m. Amos Stickney of Tewksbury.
81 | †*Samuel*, b. Oct. 3, 1764; m. Aug. 27, 1788, Mary Stimpson.
82 | †*Isaac*, b. Aug. 11, 1766; m. Polly Farrer of Lin.
83 | *Sarah*, b. May 16, 1769; d. unm.
84 | *Polly*, b. Aug. 10, 1771; m. John Dunkley of Charlestown.
85 | *Ruth*, b. Aug. 30, 1773; m. Nov. 20, 1795, Robert Mullett of W. Camb.

28-54- | JEREMIAH HARRINGTON m. Dec. 21, 1769, Sarah Locke, dau. of Joseph and Sarah Locke, b. Aug. 23, 1746. She d. Jan. 12, 1813; He d. Dec. 11, 1818. He served in the French war in 1762. Tradition says he had three dau., but there is no record of their birth. *Sally Harrington*, one of them, m. Dec. 30, 1792, Edward Blackington of Camb.

54-86 | †*Joseph*, b. Feb. 16, 1770; m. Lucy Russell.
87 | *Benjamin*, b. May 4, 1772; m. Oct. 1, 1792, Elizabeth Frost of W. Camb. and moved to Bedford, where he d.
88 | *Jonathan*, b. Oct. 27, 1777; m. Nov. 10, 1799, Ruth Britton of Shrewsbury. He d. June 9, 1721. They resided in Medford.

28-55- | JOHN HARRINGTON m. Dec. 3, 1763, Mary Wootten, dau. of John Wootten, an Englishman. Capt. Wootten was a shipmaster, and made twenty-two voyages to Surinam. He was of Capt. Parker's company, and met the British on the 19th of April. He was subsequently a lieutenant in the militia. He moved with his family to Deering, N. H., about 1783. His children, being young, left town with him.

55-89 | *Abigail*, b. March 3, 1763; m. 1781, Wm. Munroe, Jr.
90 | *Sarah*, b. Feb. 17, 1766.   91 | *John*, b. Feb. 1, 1770.
92 | *Stephen*, b. Nov. 22, 1774.   93 | *William*, b. Nov. 21, 1779.
94 | *Rebecca*, b. May 3, 1781.

28-56- | JONATHAN HARRINGTON m. Feb. 13, 1766, Ruth Fiske, dau. of Dr. Robert Fiske by wid. Grover. After the death of her husband she m. Feb. 18, 1777, John Smith of Boston. He was one of the gallant band who stood forth in defence of freedom on the 19th of April, 1775, and was one who fell that morning, a victim to British oppression. See History, p. 181. He was about thirty-two years of age at the time of his death.

56-95 | *Jonathan*, b. Oct. 25, 1766; d. Oct. 14, 1776.

28-57- | THOMAS HARRINGTON m. Lucy Perry of Bed. July 4, 1771. We find no record of his family except the birth of one child. He is said to have " moved into the country." What time he left Lexington we cannot say; his name is upon the tax bill in 1776, but is omitted in 1778.

57-96 | *Elizabeth*, b. Dec 19, 1773.

28-60- | MOSES HARRINGTON m. April 28, 1774, Mary Reed, dau. of William and Susanna Reed. They were ad. to the ch. June 15,

1776. She d. Oct. 22, 1822, aged 71. He was one of the minute men who served with the gallant Parker at the first dawn of Independence.

60- 97   *Sarah*, bap. Aug. 25, 1776; m. Thaddeus Hall of Chelmsford.
98   *Mary*, bap. June 21, 1778; m. Nov. 30, 1792, Joseph White.
99   *Caleb*, b. July 6, 1779; went to Charlestown, m. Dorcas Frost.
100   *Betsey*, b. April 26, 1782; d. unm.
101   *Moses*, b. May 2, 1785; d. unm. May 11, 1821.
102   *William*, b. Sept. 7, 1789.
103   *Oliver*, b. April 26, 1791; d. in the poor house, unm., Oct. 25, 1834.
104   *Edmund*, b. Feb. 21, 1794; left town and never returned.

28-62-   EBENEZER HARRINGTON m. Sept. 4, 1788, Mrs. Sarah Johnson. She d. Nov. 29, 1819, aged 65. He d. May 7, 1846, aged 86.

62-105   *Ebenezer*, b. June 22, 1789; d. unm.
106   *Hannah*, b. Feb. 24, 1791; m. —— Pierce of Acton.
107   *Simeon*, b. Feb. 27, 1793; d. unm. at the South.
108   *Kezia*, b. Aug. 30, 1795; m. April 8, 1815. Otis Locke.
109   *Susanna*, b. July 24, 1798; m. Jan. 1, 1823, John Hadley.

37-63-   THADDEUS HARRINGTON m. Sept. 20, 1764, Lydia Porter of Wo. They were ad. to the ch. April 22, 1771. He was one of the brave men who was an actor in the battle of Lexington. She d. Jan. 1821.

63-110   *Thaddeus*, b. Jan. 3, 1765; d. young.
111   *Fanny*, b. June 20, 1769; d. young.
112   *Arethusa*, bap. Oct. 20, 1771; m. Feb. 25, 1792, George Whitehead.
113   *Fanny*, bap. April 23, 1772; m. June 26, 1796, Seth Reed.
114   *Robert*, bap. May 28, 1775; moved to Boston, d. in Cambridgeport.
115   *Asa*, bap. May 4, 1777; went to New York.
116   †*Lewis*, bap. May 30, 1779; m. Sarah Dudley of Con.
117   *Lydia*, bap. March 11, 1781; m. Seth Reed, husband of her sister Fanny, deceased.
118   *Andrew*, b. ——; lived in Boston, and d. there, aged 44.

37-64-   DANIEL HARRINGTON m. May 8, 1760, Anna Munroe, dau. of Robert and Ann (Stone) Munroe, who was b. Aug. 30, 1740. She d. Oct. 19, 1811, aged 71; he d. Sept. 27, 1818, aged 79. Daniel Harrington was clerk of Capt. Parker's company, and participated with them in the dangers and glories of the memorable 19th of April, 1775. He was a prominent man in the place, and filled various posts of honor and trust. He was selectman 1779, '85, '86.

64-119   †*Levi*, b. Nov. 9, 1760; m. July 27, 1784, Rebecca Mulliken.
120   †*Nathan*, b. April 29, 1762; m. Elizabeth Phelps; d. June 28, 1837.
121   *Daniel*, b. Oct. 17, 1764; d. young.
122   *Anna*, b. Feb. 3, 1766; m. Thomas Winship, and d. July 13, 1821, aged 55.
123   *David*, b. June 10, 1768; d. July 26, 1795, aged 27.
124   *Grace*, b. March 17, 1770; m. Abner Pierce, July 22, 1792, d. Aug. 1842.
125   *Betty*, b. Feb. 1, 1772; m. Jan. 25, 1799, James Bruce of Woburn.
126   *Eusebia*, b. Jan. 20, 1774; d. Oct. 5, 1775.
127   *Eusebia*, b. Feb. 13, 1776; m. March 7, 1800, Joseph Underwood, and d. Dec. 22, 1859, aged 82.
128   *Isanna*, bap. Jan. 31, 1779; m. Jan. 11, 1801, Timothy Page of Bed.
129   *Lydia*, bap. Dec. 10, 1780; d. unm. Sept. 26, 1803, aged 23.

37-70-   ABIJAH HARRINGTON m. April 21, 1784, Polly Raymond. She d. Feb. 27, 1822, and he m. Dec. 14, 1823, Mary Locke, wid. of Asa B. Locke. He d. without issue, Dec. 31, 1852, aged 91. Though Abijah Harrington was too young (being but 13 years of age) to take part in the events of the memorable 19th of April, 1775, he was attracted by the march of the king's troops, and came to the Common immediately after their departure for Concord, and saw in the road where the British troops stood at the time of the firing, a quantity of blood upon the ground, and so is a good witness that the fire of the British was returned, and with effect, by the Americans. See Deposition appended to Phinney's History.

38-74-   JONATHAN HARRINGTON m. Nov. 14, 1782, Sally Banks. She d. July 28, 1847, aged 85. Though a lad of only 16 years of age, he was a *fifer* in that phalanx of freemen which appeared on Lexington Common on the 19th of April, 1775. He lived to a great age, and related almost to the time of his death, the leading events of that day. He said he was aroused early that morning by a cry from his mother — "Jonathan, get up, the regulars are coming, and something must be done." He arose and repaired to the place of parade, and was with the company on the approach of the British. "SOMETHING MUST BE DONE," exclaimed the patriotic mother. And *something was done* on that memorable day. The shrill notes of that stripling's fife, not only warmed the bosoms of the gallant band on Lexington Common, but enkindled a fire extinguished only by the acknowledgment of our Independence. *Something was done.* The firm resistance to the British on that occasion inspired every patriotic bosom, and called the people to arms. *Something was done* which taught the haughty oppressors that freemen in defence of their homes and firesides, their wives and little ones, were not to be intimidated by veteran troops, though led on by rash and daring commanders. *Something was done* which has given to *Lexington* a name which will be remembered as long as the spirit of liberty finds a resting place in the human breast.

    Jonathan Harrington was one of the youngest defenders of his country's rights on the opening of the Revolutionary drama, and one of the last, if not the very last of the survivors of that opening scene, who lived to partake of the blessings of freedom and to witness the growing greatness of his country. Mr. Harrington lived to a great age, and was treated with much respect and attention by the whole community. At the age of ninety-one he attended the 75th anniversary of the 19th of April, celebrated at Concord. The writer of this waited upon him to give him an invitation to attend the celebration, and give a sentiment. At first he thought he should not be able; but a recurrence to the events of the day to be commemorated, soon roused the energy of the venerable patriarch, and with a countenance lighted up with patriotism, he consented to attend. And when he was asked to give a sentiment, he gave from the fullness of his heart a sentiment, which he was requested to commit to paper, that it might be presented at Concord in his own handwriting. The next day he forwarded the following:

    "THE 19TH OF APRIL, 1775. — *All who remember that day will support the Constitution of the United States.*"

    After living to the advanced age of 95 years, 8 months, and 18 days, the venerable patriot died, March 27, 1854. The death of the last survivor of the battle of Lexington, produced a marked sensation in the whole community. The Governor ordered out two companies, the Davis Guards of Acton, and the Concord Artillery, to do escort duty at his interment. And such was the public feeling, that General Jones invited his brigade to be present on the occasion, which invitation was promptly responded to by the corps. Several other companies not belonging to the brigade volunteered — all anxious to show their regard to the memory of one who had come down from a generation of patriots, and had stood the sole representative of the first battle of freedom in America. The Governor, the Lieut. Governor and the Honorable Council, and a great part of the Legislature, which was then in session, honored the event by their presence. The Masonic fraternity, of which he was a member, attended with their regalia; and a large concourse of people from the neighboring towns filled Lexington to overflowing. The spectacle was truly imposing.

The procession was formed by Gen. Samuel Chandler of Lexingington, who acted as chief marshal on the occasion. The military moved in the following order:

First Regiment of Artillery, Lieut. Col. Gibbs, consisting of three companies.

Fourth Regiment of Light Infantry, Col. J. D. Green, consisting of four companies.

Fifth Regiment of Light Infantry, Col. B. F. Butler, consisting of four companies.

And three volunteer companies.

From the Common they moved down Main street to the Town Hall, where they received the body guard, the Concord Artillery, Captain Culbertson, and the Davis Guards, Captain Holden ; Hiram Lodge of West Cambridge, and the Grand Lodge of Massachusetts, with the body of the deceased, attended by the pall-bearers and relatives, and followed by the chief marshal, chaplain, and the committee of arrangements, consisting of some of the principal citizens of the town. These were followed by Governor Washburn and suit, Lieut. Governor Plunkett, and the Council, members of the Senate and the House of Representatives, officers of the militia, citizens of Concord and citizens generally.

From this point, it being almost the identical spot at which Lord Percy received the British fugitives in their flight from Concord on the 19th of April, 1775, the procession moved up Main street by the Common to the church, where solemn religious services were performed, and an appropriate address was delivered by Rev. Dr. Randall, Grand Master of the Grand Lodge of Massachusetts. After the services at the church were concluded, the remains were removed to the old burying-ground in the rear of the church, and deposited in the family tomb. The Masonic burial service was read at the tomb by Grand Master Randall of the Grand Lodge, and a volley was fired over the grave by the Concord Artillery and the Davis Guards. This closed the funeral solemnities of the day.

The history of the world furnishes no case more striking or sublime than this! Thousands of persons of all ages and conditions in life, flock together from one common impulse, and with one general feeling! What motive actuated the vast concourse and brought them to Lexington at that time? The season of the year was uninviting, the traveling bad, and the day inclement; and everything external would seem to forbid any gathering of the people in large numbers in the open air, — but still they came. And for what purpose? Not to obtain any direct advantage personal to themselves —not to witness any feat of art, listen to any distinguished orator, or partake of a sumptuous feast — not to behold any distinguished lord or prince from a foreign country, or any celebrated statesman from our own — not to greet a living friend surrounded with wealth and splendor, or to follow in the funeral train of a deceased President or high officer of state. No — they came to worship at the shrine of *Liberty* — to show their respect to the memory of a humble and unpretending individual, who had stood for years the sole representative of that body of freemen who rallied for their country on the 19th of April, 1775.

74-130   *Harry*, b. March 10, 1783.   He was a sea captain, and sailed out of Providence.
131   *Polly*, b. May 23, 1786; m. June 22, 1811, Payson Perrin, of Boston.
132   *Abigail*, b. Nov. 13, 1787; d. March 23, 1858, unm.
133   *Pitt*, b. July 6, 1790.   He entered the army 1812, and never returned.
134   *Jonathan*, b. June 4, 1793; d. March, 1856, unm.
135   *William*, b. March 12, 1797; d. unm.
136   *More*, b. June 23, 1801; d. Sept. 16, 1802.

38-76-   CHARLES HARRINGTON m. Dec. 18, 1786, Mary Brown, dau. of Francis Brown.   He d. Jan. 28, 1856, aged 93; she d. Jan. 9, 1843, aged 77.

76-137   *Mary*, b. Jan. 9, 1787; m. June 5, 1811, Stephen Robbins, Jr.
138   *Susanna*, b. Sept. 4, 1789; d. ——, 1857, unm.
139   *Betsey*, b. Jan. 10, 1796; m. Walter R. Mason; lived at Camb., then moved to N. H.
140   †*Charles*, b. April 10, 1798; m. Sarah H. Wade, Sept. 6, 1840.
141   *Elmira*, b. Sept. 6, 1801; m. Nov. 28, 1824, Hazen Elliott.
142   *Clarissa*, b. ——; m. Dec. 3, 1835, S. H. Elliott, brother of her sister's husband.

38-77-   SOLOMON HARRINGTON m. Polly Bent, dau. of David Bent.   She d. May 19, 1809, aged 40.   He d. May 9, 1845, aged 79.

77-143   *Charles*, b. Dec. 25, 1787.   He followed the sea, where he prob. d.
144   †*David*, b. Jan. 2, 1790; m. Dec. 6, 1810, Elizabeth Francis.
145   *James*, b. Aug. 4, 1792; d. unm.
146   †*Solomon*, b. Feb. 13, 1795; m. Feb. 6, 1820, Betsey Dudley.
147   *Abigail More*, b. Feb. 12, 1801; m. David Constantine and r. at Bed.
148   *Irene*, b. Dec. 1, 1803; m. James Haywood and r. at Billerica.

38-78-   PETER HARRINGTON m. Lydia Loring.   He d. Jan. 23, 1816, aged 43.   He lived in Lex. till about 1811, when he moved to Salem, where he d.   He was captain of the Lex. artillery, and was promoted to the lieut.-coloneley.

78-149   *Matilda*, b. April 5, 1799; m. —— Hastings, and d. at Springfield.
150   *Isaac B. Clarke*, b. Sept. 2, 1800.   He left town and d. unm.
151   *Adeline*, b. Sept. 24, 1802.   She r. at East Cambridge.
152   *Lorenzo*, b. Aug. 10, 1804.   He r. at East Cambridge.
153   *Peter*, b. Sept. 21, 1807; he d. at East Cambridge.
154   *Emeline*, b. Dec. 21, 1809; m. Benj. Reed. and r. in Chelsea.
155   *Julian*, b. March 29, 1812; m. —— Bowsway, was killed by falling down stairs at East Cambridge.
156   *Elizabeth*, b. ——; m. George Dale, and r. at East Cambridge.

53-79-   HENRY HARRINGTON, 3d, m. March 13, 1783, Amity Pierce. They had several children.   They resided first at Boston, and afterwards moved to New Orleans.

53-81-   SAMUEL HARRINGTON m. Aug. 29, 1788, Mary Stimpson.   He probably left town at the time of his marriage, as his name, which

Jona Harrington

was on the tax bill in 1788, disappears the following year. Neither the town or church records make any mention of him or his family after his marriage.

53-82- ISAAC HARRINGTON m. Oct. 21, 1798, Polly Farrer of Lincoln. He d. April 2, 1863, aged 97 years 8 months. The record of the family is very imperfect.

82-157 *Isaac*, b. March 7, 1799. He enlisted in the United States service in the war of 1812, went to Louisiana and never returned.
158 *Betsey*, b. Nov. 22, 1800; m. Emory Garfield. He d. and she m. second, Benjamin Gleason.
159 *Hiram*, b. May 23, 1802; m. Sarah Fiske.
160 *Maria*, b. Sept. 9, 1803; m. Isaiah Tay of Bur.
161 *Zadock*, b. ———; m. Almira Fiske. She d. and he m. second, Almira Morton; she d. and he m. third, Hannah Russell. He r. in Billerica.
162 *Almira*, b. ———; m. William Alurt and moved to Vt.
163 *Daniel*, b. ———; m. in Billerica, where he resides.
164 *Abel*, b. ———; m. in Billerica, where he resides.
165 *Sally*, b. ———; m. ——— Richardson, moved to Andover and d.
166 *Priscilla*, b. ———; d. young.

54-86- JOSEPH HARRINGTON m. March 27, 1792, Lucy Russell, dau. of Philip Russell. He d. Jan. 12, 1829.

86-167 *Susan*, b. Nov. 23, 1792; d. Dec. 14, 1792.
168 *Joseph*, b. May 1, 1794; he went to Con. when a lad, where he m. May 3, 1821, Mary Snow, and had issue.
169 *John*, b. June 6, 1796; d. June 4, 1804.
170 *Lucy*, b. Nov. 28, 1798; m. Oct. 20, 1829, William Grover.
171 *Jonas*, b. Nov. 7, 1800; d. Sept. 16, 1802.
172 *Mary*, b. Sept. 19, 1803; d. Aug. 4, 1828, unm.
173 *Lydia*, b. Feb. 10, 1806; m. Feb. 10, 1828, Daniel Kinneston.
174 *Nehemiah*, b. March 14, 1808; m. Dec. 11, 1845, Sophia Woodbury of N. H. He r. in Lex.
175 *Emily*, b. Aug. 13, 1810; d. March 22, 1828.
176 *Stephen*, b. May 9, 1812; m. March, 1832, Maria E. Hall, and r. in Somerville, and d. Jan. 21, 1868.

63-116- LEWIS HARRINGTON m. Aug. 31, 1806, Sarah Dudley of Con. He d. Sept. 1829, aged 50; she d. Nov. 10, 1858, aged 71.

116-177 *Lucy Ann*, b. ———; m. Seth S. Bennett, March 19, 1826. They moved to Providence, where she d.
178 *Mary R.*, b. ———; m. William Wyman of Wo., r. in Medford.
179 *Jonas*, b. 1810; m. Susan Pierce, dau. of Ebenezer and Nabby (Brown) Pierce. He d. July 5, 1857; she d. April 16, 1856. They left two children, first, Emma I., b. 1845, second, Oren C., b. May 31, 1851.
180 *Sarah E.*, b. ———; m. Elijah Gossom, and d. Sept. 3, 1858.
181 *Hannah M.*, b. ———; m. George Todd of Charlestown.
182 *Cyrus D.*, b. 1820; m. Rebecca Frost of W. Camb., where he d.
183 *Frances A.*, b. ———; m. April 23, 1846, Loring S. Pierce.

64-119- LEVI HARRINGTON m. July 27, 1784, Rebecca Mulliken, dau. of Nathaniel and Lydia. She d. Sept. 5, 1820; he d. July 26, 1846, aged 86. They were ad. the ch. April 22, 1787.

119-184	†*Nathaniel*, b. Jan, 3, 1786; m. Nov. 30, 1815, Clarissa Mead.
185	*Nancy*, b. Jan. 3, 1788; now, 1867, living unm.
186	*Fanny*, b. April 1, 1792; m. Horace Skilton of Bed., Oct. 29, 1820.
187	*Rebecca*, b. Oct. 28, 1794; m. Dan'l Hastings of Boston, Nov. 4, 1823.
188	*Dennis*, b. Oct. 7, 1796; d. Aug. 11, 1840, unm.
189	†*Hiram*, b. May 15, 1799; m. Jan. 22, 1825, Julia A. Lane.
190	*Sophia*, b. Aug. 25, 1801; m. Dec. 12, 1822, Harrison G. O. Munroe of Boston.
191	†*Bowen*, b. Aug. 6, 1803; m. Dec. 20, 1832, Elizabeth P. Ward.

64-120-	NATHAN HARRINGTON m. Elizabeth Phelps of Andover. He lived many years in Wo., then returned to Lex., where he d. Sept. 27, 1818.
120-192	*Betsey*, b. April 27, 1788; m. Oct. 17, 1813, William Chandler.
193	*Dorcas*, b. June 25, 1790; m. Joshua P. Frothingham, Charlestown.
194	†*Nathan*, b. Feb. 29, 1792; m. Martha I. Mead.
195	*Tryphena*, b Aug. 26, 1794; d. Nov. 12, 1853, unm.
196	†*Daniel*, b. Aug. 26, 1796; m. Hannah Jacobs.
197	*Anna*, b. Nov. 24, 1799; m. Addison Gage, Dec. 27, 1832. He r. in West Camb., and is extensively engaged in the ice trade.
198	*Increase S.*, b. Sept. 6, 1802; m. Dec. 12, 1826, Eliza Maynard. He d. Feb. 18, 1848.
199	*Abijah*, b. Sept. 3, 1804; he lives in Lex., unm.

76-140-	CHARLES HARRINGTON m. Sept. 6, 1840, Sarah H. Wade of Lowell, b. Sept. 6, 1810. He has no children.

77-144-	DAVID HARRINGTON m. Dec. 6, 1810, Elizabeth Francis.
144-200	*Sylvester*, b. May 1, 1811; m. May, 1841, Mary Ann Robinson, dau. of Jacob and Hannah (Simonds) Robinson.
201	*Mary B.*, b. Jan. 18, 1816; m. May 14, 1835, Charles J. Adams. They reside at East Cambridge, where he is the keeper of the house of correction.
202	*Charles S .*, b. Nov. 10, 1831; d. Jan. 4, 1838.

77-146-	SOLOMON HARRINGTON m. Feb. 6, 1820, Betsey Dudley, dau. of Nathan and Sarah Dudley, b. June 1, 1798. He resided in Lex., then moved to Boston, and subsequently to Brookline, where he d. June 5, 1858.

119-184-	NATHANIEL HARRINGTON m. Nov. 30, 1815, Clarissa Mead, dau. of Josiah. He d. Jan. 8, 1839, and she d. Feb. 16, 1866, aged 76.
184-203	†*Franklin M*, b. June 6, 1817; has been twice married.
204	*Ellen M.*, b. July 1, 1819.
205	*Edwin*, b. Feb. 21, 1821; m. Nov. 27, 1845, Eunice E. More of Sudbury, b. April 29, 1824. They reside in Sudbury.
206	*Clarissa*, b. Dec. 8, 1822; m. April 29, 1845, Samuel B. Rindge of East Cambridge, where they reside.
207	*Nathaniel*, b. Sept. 23, 1824.
208	*Larkin*, b. April 17, 1826; m. Nov. 23, 1851, Mary W. Langley. He r. in Medford, now r. in N. H.
209	*Andrew*, b. April 12, 1828; m. Dec. 29, 1853, Mary J. Rainey, r. at Galesburg, Ill.
210	*Rebecca*, b. June 12, 1830; d. May 7, 1832.
211	*Elizabeth W.*, b. Oct. 14, 1833.

119-189-	HIRAM HARRINGTON m. Jan. 22, 1825, Julia A. C. Lane. They had three children, first and second d. young, third, *Hiram Augustus*. He moved to Illinois, where he d. March 16, 1859.

119-191-   Bowen Harrington m. Dec. 20, 1832, Elizabeth P. Ward of Boston, dau. of William and Mary Ward, b. Dec. 20, 1811. She d. May 9, 1863, aged 51. He is a justice of the peace.

191-212 *Mary W.*, b. Nov. 24, 1834; m. June 9, 1864, Gershom Swan, and has Charles Ward, b. July 26, 1866.
213 *Charles B*, b. Jan. 23, 1837. He enlisted in 1861 in the Mass. volunteers for three years, came home on a furlough, being in ill health, and d. of disease contracted in the service, Sept. 5, 1862.
214 *William H.*, b. May 30, 1840. He resides in Illinois.
215 *George D*, b. July 17, 1843. He served three years in the army of the Potomac, in the late rebellion.

120-194-   Nathan Harrington m. Feb. 1, 1824, Martha I. Mead, dau. of Josiah Mead. She d. June 26, 1835. He d. Nov. 14, 1843. He was a captain in the Lexington artillery.

194-216 *Caroline M.*, b. Oct. 1, 1829.
217 *Elvira M.*, b. Feb. 18, 1832.

120-196-   Daniel Harrington m. Dec. 15, 1824, Hannah Jacobs. He d. Oct. 5, 1826, aged 30. She m. ——— Brooks.

184-203-   Franklin M. Harrington m. June 2, 1847, Susan Wiley of Ashby. She d. Feb. 20, 1858, and he m. April 16, 1859, Mrs. Susan Turner.

203-218 *Fannie W*, b. Dec. 29, 1851.   219 *Martha M.*, b. Dec. 8, 1853.
220 *Ellen E.*, b. Feb. 15, 1856.

THE HARRIS FAMILY.

1   Henry Harris, of Lexington, is a lineal descendant of Thomas Harris, who was born in Shrewsbury, England, came to Massachusetts in 1631, went with Roger Williams to Rhode Island, and settled at Providence. His descendants settled in Smithfield in that State, where they lived several generations. Henry was the son of Abner, b. 1779, and Martha (Farmer); he was the grandson of Abner, and the great-grandson of Jonathan; he was born in Providence, 1809, and married in Boston, Feb. 6, 1832. Emeline Bryant. They resided in Boston, where most of their children were born. They came to Lexington in 1853. He is engaged in the clothing business in Boston.

1- 2 *Henry F.*, b. 1835.   3 *Frederick B*, b. 1837.
4 *Emeline F.*, b. 1839; m. Nov. 1, 1863, George M. Wethern.
5 *William A.*, b. 1841.   6 *Martha A.*, b. 1843.
7 *George A.*, b. 1845; d. 1848.
8 *Charles B.*, b. 1847.   9 *Ellen M.*, b. 1849.
10 *Georgiana W.*, b. 1855.   11 *Addie L.*, b. 1857, d. 1857.

THE HARTWELL FAMILY.

The Hartwells came to Lexington from Bedford.

1   William Hartwell, b. June 25, 1770; d. May 8, 1819, aged 49. He m. Oct. 13, 1796, Johanna Davis of Bedford. She d. and he m. 1809, Mary Lake. He had several children.

1-2-   WILLIAM HARTWELL, the oldest son of the foregoing, b. Jan. 12,
1797; m. Nov. 30, 1826, Ruhamah Webber, dau. of Asa and Eliot
(Lane) Webber, b. April 14, 1802. They resided first at Concord,
and came to Lexington about 1839.

2- 3 *William W.*, b. Oct. 2, 1827.   4 *Johanna*, b. Nov. 1, 1829.
  5 *Lydia E.*, born March 15, 1835.

THE HASTINGS FAMILY.

The name *Hastings* is of Danish origin. In the early days of the
British kingdom, the Danes made frequent incursions into that part
of Britain bordering on the North Sea. In one of these incursions
Hastings, a Danish chief, made himself formidable to Alfred the
Great, by landing a large body of men upon the coast. He took
possession of a portion of Sussex; and the castle and seaport were
held by his family, when William the Conqueror landed in England;
and they held it from the crown for many generations.

Several of the name of Hastings were raised to a peerage. Sir
Henry and George Hastings, grandsons of the Earl of Huntingdon,
had sons who became Puritans, and were obliged by persecution to
leave their native land, and find homes in the new world. As early
as 1634, Thomas Hastings and wife, and soon after, John and his
family, came to New England, but no one of the family came to Lexington till about 1720.

1   THOMAS HASTINGS, aged 29, and his wife Susanna, aged 24, embarked at Ipswich, England, April 10, 1634, in the Elizabeth, William Andrews, master, for New England, and settled in Watertown,
where he was admitted freeman, May 6, 1635. He was selectman
from 1638 to 1643, and from 1650 to 1671; clerk three years, and
representative in 1671. He also held the office of deacon. His wife
Susanna died Feb. 2, 1650, and he married April, 1651, Margaret
Cheney, dau. of William and Martha Cheney of Roxbury. She was
the mother of all his children. He died 1685, aged 80. In his will,
dated March 12, 1685, and proved Sept. 7, 1685, he gave his son
Thomas only £5, saying, "I have been at great expense to bring
him up a scholar, and I have given him above threescore pounds to
begin the world with." To his sons John, Joseph, Benjamin, Nathaniel, and Samuel, and to his daughter Hepzibah Bond, he gave
£40 each, and to Hannah £3. Between 1652 and 1666, he had eight
children.

1- 2 *Thomas*, b. July 1, 1652; d. July 23, 1712. He was a physician at
  Hatfield.
  3 †*John*, b. March 4, 1654; m. June 18, 1679, Abigail Hammond.
  4 *William*, b. Aug. 8, 1655; drowned, Aug. 1669, aged 14 years.
  5 *Joseph*, b. Sept. 11, 1657; m. 1682, Ruth Rice of Sudbury.
  6 *Benjamin*, b. Aug. 9, 1659; m. 1683, Elizabeth Graves.
  7 *Nathaniel*, b. Sept. 25, 1661; m. Mary Nevinson of Watertown.
  8 *Hepzibah*, b. Jan. 31, 1663; m. 1680, Dea. William Bond of Wat.
  9 *Samuel*, b. March 12, 1665; m. first, 1687, Lydia Church; and sec-
    ond, 1694, Elizabeth Nevinson; third, 1701, Sarah Cooledge of
    Watertown.

1-3-   JOHN HASTINGS m. June 18, 1679, Abigail Hammond of Watertown, dau. of John and Abigail, b. June 21, 1656. She d. Sept. 7,
1718, and he d. March 28, 1718. He lived in that part of Watertown which was afterwards Waltham.

3-10 | *Abigail*, b. Dec. 8, 1679; m. 1699, John Warren of Weston.
11 | *John*, bap. Dec. 4, 1687; m. first, 1702, Susanna, dau. of John and Mary Bemis; second, 1706, Sarah Fiske; moved to Lunenburg.
12 | *Elizabeth*, bap. Dec. 4, 1687; m. April 14, 1714, Hopestill Mead.
13 | *Hepzibah*, bap. Dec. 4, 1687; m. April 14, 1714, Nathaniel Shattuck. He d. 1718, and she m. 1721, Benj. Stearns of Lexington.
14 | *William*, bap. July 13, 1690; m. Abigail ———, d. before 1723.
15 | †*Samuel*, b. 1693; m. Bethia Holloway of Malden.
16 | *Thomas*, b. Sept. 26, 1697; m. Sarah White, and settled in Lex., where six of his children were born, when he removed to Littleton.
17 | *Joseph*, bap. 1698; m. first, 1716, Lydia Brown; second, 1769, Elizabeth Stearns.

3-15- | SAMUEL HASTINGS m. in Medford, May 29, 1719, Bethia Holloway of Malden. He was a tailor, and resided in that part of Watertown now Waltham. He was selectman several years. She died in Lexington, June 1, 1774, aged 80.

15-18 | †*Samuel*, b. March 30, 1721; m. Jan. 16, 1755, Lydia Tidd, b. July 6, 1732, dau. of Daniel and Hepzibah (Reed) Tidd of Lexington.
19 | *Thaddeus*, b. Oct. 15, 1723; m. March 29, 1763, Mary Stratton. He settled in Lexington, where he and his wife died, leaving two young sons, who left town.
20 | *Mary*, b. Dec. 15, 1725.
21 | *Abigail*, b. March 8, 1728; m. April 2, 1747, Sam'l Brooks of Med.
22 | *Abijah*, b. May 9, 1730; m. Jan. 2, 1759, Martha Ingraham.
23 | *Philemon*, b. April 2, 1732; settled in Vermont.
24 | *Anna*, b. March 8, 1734.   25 *Martha*, b. March 23, 1736.

15-18- | SAMUEL HASTINGS m. Jan. 16, 1755, Lydia Tidd, daughter of Daniel and Hepzibah (Reed) Tidd. He settled in the southwest part of Lexington. He was one of the men who, on the 19th of April, 1775, stood firm in the cause of freedom on Lexington Green, and was also with the army at Cambridge, when Gen. Washington took command. He d. Feb. 8, 1820, aged 99; his wife d. Nov. 10, 1802, aged 71. He was often elected to places of honor and trust in the town.

18-26 | †*Isaac*, b. in Lex. Dec. 26, 1755; m. Mary Stearns.
27 | †*Samuel*, b. July 11, 1757; m. Lydia Nelson of Lincoln.
28 | *Lydia*, b. Nov. 29, 1759; d. July 22, 1788, unm.
29 | *Bethia*, b. March 25, 1761; d. Aug. 3, 1765.
30 | *Hepzibah*, b. July 3, 1762; m. 1781, John Swan of Waltham. He d. and she m. Jonas Wyeth of Cambridge, and d. 1789, aged 27.
31 | †*John*, b. July 13, 1764; d. June 5, 1789, aged 25.
32 | *Bethia*, b. June 25, 1766; d. July 26, 1786.
33 | *Abigail*, b. April 20, 1768; d. May 10, 1788.
34 | *Thomas*, b. April 25, 1772; d. Sept. 8, 1775.

18-26- | ISAAC HASTINGS m. 1781, Sarah Stearns, b. Dec. 29, 1761, dau. of Phinehas and Mary (Wellington) Stearns. He and his wife were ad. to the ch. Feb. 10, 1782. In 1808, he was chosen deacon and became a leading member of the ch. He was on the Common with Capt. Parker on the 19th of April, 1775, was at the capture of Burgoyne, and was also detailed to guard the prisoners at Prospect Hill, Charlestown, now Somerville. He lived upon his father's homestead, the site on the hill now owned by Mrs. Cary, his youngest dau. He d. July 2, 1831, aged 76, and his widow d. March, 1834, aged 73.

26–35   *Sophia*, b. Oct. 17, 1781; m. June 18, 1809, Isaac S. Spring of Standish, Me. They removed to Somerville, where she d. Nov. 1841.

36   *Isaac*, b. Nov. 3, 1783; lost at sea.

37   *Thomas*, b. Feb. 12, 1786; m. Mary Baker, in Vt., moved to Montreal, where he d. July, 1855, leaving a family.

38   *Abigail*, b. May 20, 1788; m. Dec. 9, 1821, Jonathan Cary of Boston. They moved to Lex. 1827, and took up their abode on Lincoln street, on a place known as the "Peak Place." He d. April 17, 1855, aged 86. He had no children by his last wife.

39   †*John*, b. July 21, 1790; has been twice married.

40   *Phinehas S.*, b. Oct. 13, 1792; m. Elizabeth Bowles of Portsmouth, N. H.

41   *Leonard*, b. Sept. 6, 1794; d. Nov. 10, 1802.

42   *Samuel*, b. Sept. 24, 1798; m. 1827, Lucy R., dau. of Sweethern Reed.

43   *Maria*, b. March 1, 1801; m. May 4, 1828, William H. Cary, a distinguished merchant in Brooklyn, N. Y. The old homestead of the Hastings, having passed out of the family, Mr. Cary purchased it, and fitted it up for a summer residence, where he and his wife passed the warm season of the year. The site is truly rural, as will be seen by the engraving. During his life he had caused the farm to be greatly improved, and had expressed an intention of making a tender of this place to the State, if they would establish an Agricultural school upon the premises; but dying suddenly he had made no will. His widow and his heirs however, knowing his wishes, have generously made the tender, and have also with great liberality made several other liberal grants in conformity with the intentions of Mr. Cary, as expressed in his lifetime.

The immediate and multiplied connections of the Hastings family with the CARYS, will justify a brief notice of the latter. JONATHAN CARY of Boston, b. 1768, m. first, Jemima Green of Groton. She d. and he m. second, Polly Harris of Boston; she d. and he m. third, Abigail Hastings, as stated above. In 1827, Mr. Cary retired from business, and located himself in Lexington, where he d. 1855, at the advanced age of 87. His children who are living, are by his second wife. He had seven children; *Samuel*, *William H.*, mentioned above, who m. Maria Hastings, *Nathaniel*, who resided for a time in Lex., *Isaac*, *George*, and *Maria M.*, b. March 4, 1810, who m. John Hastings as his second wife.

18–27–   SAMUEL HASTINGS m. Oct. 1, 1778, Lydia Nelson of Lincoln, dau. of Thomas and Lydia (Scott) Nelson. He was on the Common with Capt. Parker on the 19th of April, 1775; he soon after volunteered into the service, and was detailed one of Gen. Lee's life-guard, and was taken prisoner with him at Long Island. A British officer at the time of his capture, wounded him in the neck with a sword. "His queue," he used to say, "saved his life, as it broke the force of the blow, though he received a severe wound." He was paroled, but never exchanged. He was chosen Major of the Lexington Artillery. He resided in the borders of Lincoln, but being near the line of Lex. he attended ch. here, and his remains and those of his wife rest in the Lex. graveyard, where his children have erected a handsome marble monument to his memory. He d. Jan. 8, 1834, aged 76. She d. April 5, 1829, aged 71.

27–44   *Lydia*, b. Feb. 20, 1780; m. Nehemiah I. Ingraham, Boston.

45   *Samuel*, b. Dec. 15, 1781; d. Sept. 1798.

46 | *Jonathan*, b. Aug. 17, 1783; m. Nancy Adams, settled in Brighton.
47 | *Dorcas*, b. June 27, 1786; m. 1810, Rev. Daniel Marrett of Standish, Me.
48 | *Thomas*, b. May 22, 1787; m. first, Mary Robbins and second, Martha Livermore. He was a trader in East Camb., where he d. 1865, in his 79th year.
49 | *Polly*, b. April 10, 1789.; m. May 20, 1811, Benj. O. Wellington, Lex.
50 | *Oliver*, b. May 16, 1791; m. first, Eliza Bemis and second, Mrs. Huldah Trabo. He is a dealer in lumber in East Camb.
51 | *Hepzibah*, b. May 24, 1793; m. May 24, 1813, Peter Wellington, brother of her sister Polly's husband.
52 | *Harriet*, b. July 12, 1795; m. Aug. 8, 1819, Elias Smith.
53 | *James*, b. Oct. 5, 1797; m. Oct. 11, 1821, Sally Mead, dau. of Josiah Mead of Lex. He settled on his father's homestead, where most of his children were born. After some years he moved to Brattleborough, Vt., but has returned to Lex., where he now resides. They have had nine children: *Charles*, b. July 7, 1822, m. Martha Tuttle; *Emily M.*, b. March 15, 1824, m. E. F. Davis, lives in Ill.; *James W.*, b. April 9, 1826, d. June 12, 1848; *Maria C.*, b. April 16, 1828, m. L. C. Pratt of Brattleborough, Vt.; *Sarah M.*, b. Oct. 15, 1829, d. June 22, 1848; *Oliver*, b. Aug. 8, 1831, went to Kansas; *Alonzo*, b. Aug. 25, 1833, m. Eliza G. Weed, lived in Kansas; *Adelaide*, b. Oct. 15, 1836, m. J. W. Wood, and resides in Galesburg, Ill.; *Ellen A.*, b. March 2, 1841, d. March 4, 1866.

18-31- | JOHN HASTINGS m. Oct. 7, 1784, Esther Lawrence, dau. of Bezaleel and Sarah (Muzzy) Lawrence, b. June 30, 1765. He settled in Lex., where he d. June 25, 1789, aged 25. His widow d. Oct. 24, 1794, in her 30th year.

31-54 | *Nancy*, b. Jan. 28, 1785; m. June 13, 1812, Joseph Bailey of Standish, Me.
55 | *Bethia*, b. March 15, 1787; d. unm. 1820, aged 33.
56 | *Hepzibah*, b. Jan. 23, 1789; d. April 28, 1789.

26-39- | JOHN HASTINGS m. first, Dec. 9, 1834, Mrs. Sarah Riggs, dau. of Benjamin and Hannah West of Boston; she d. Sept. 16, 1860, aged 72. He m. second, Aug. 28, 1862, Maria M. Cary, dau. of Jonathan Cary of Boston, who m. his sister Abigail. He settled first in Augusta, Me., then returned to Lexington, and improves his father's homestead. They have no children.

THE HENDLEY FAMILY.

SAMUEL W. HENDLEY, son of Samuel, of Carlisle, was b. Dec. 22, 1823. His grandfather, *Charles Hendley*, was a deserter from the British army in the Revolution, who enlisted into the American service. Samuel W. Hendley m. Oct. 19, 1848, Emeline Skilton, dau. of David Skilton of Bur. They have three children, *Wallace*, b. Nov. 27, 1850; *David Eugene*, b. Oct. 3, 1854; *Howard R.*, b. Dec. 22, 1866.

THE HEWES FAMILY.

1 | JOHN HEWES, or HUES, as the name is sometimes written in Lex. records, was at Cambridge Farms at the organization of the precinct in 1693, and was taxed as a resident. He was from Wat.;

he m. March 9, 1677, Ruth, dau. of Richard Sawtel. He had several children before he came to Lex. The last two were bap. in the precinct. He d. Dec. 13, 1721, and she d. July 4, 1720. He and his wife were ad. to the ch. Aug. 1699. He r. near Capt. William Reed. He was assessor in 1705.

1- 2 | *John*, b. Feb. 15, 1678.
3 | *Samuel*, b. Oct. 27, 1679; d. young.
4 | *Elizabeth*, b. Jan. 27, 1681; d. Jan 12, 1720.
5 | †*Jonathan*, bap. in Lex. Sept. 10, 1699; probably a lad.

1-5- | JONATHAN HEWES m. ———.

5- 6 | *Jonathan*, bap. June 20, 1710.   7 *Elizabeth*, bap. Sept. 23, 1711.
8 | *Edmund*, bap. Sept. 21, 1712.

THE HOAR FAMILY.

The ancestor of this family, according to tradition, was a wealthy banker of London, and d. soon after his arrival in this country. Mrs. Joanna, probably his wife, d. at Braintree, 1661. She had two dau. and three sons, viz., *Daniel*, who went to England in 1653; *Leonard*, grad. H. C. 1650, was President of H. C. from 1672 to 1675, when he d.; and

1 | JOHN HOAR, who was a lawyer, distinguished for bold, manly independence. He lived in Scituate from 1643 to 1655. About 1660 he settled in Con., and d. April 2, 1704. His wife, Alice, d. June 5, 1697.

1- 2 | *Elizabeth*, b. ———; m. Dec. 22, 1675, Jonathan Prescott.
3 | *Mary*, b. ———; m. Oct. 21, 1668, Benjamin Graves.
4 | †*Daniel*, b. ———; m. first, Mary Stratton, and second, Mary Lee.

1-4- | DANIEL HOAR, of Con., m. first, July 19, 1677, Mary Stratton; second, Oct. 16, 1717, Mary Lee.

4- 5 | *John*, b. Oct. 24, 1678; m. Ruth ——, settled in Sud.
6 | *Leonard*, b. ———. He was a captain; d. April, 1771, aged 87, in Brimfield, where a part of his descendants now reside,— some of whom have taken the name of Homer.
7 | †*Daniel*, b. 1680; m. Sarah Jones.
8 | *Jonathan*, b. ———; d. at the Castle, Oct. 26, 1702.
9 | *Joseph*, b. ———; d. at sea, 1707.
10 | *Benjamin*.
11 | *Mary*, b. March 14, 1689; d. June 10, 1702.
12 | *Samuel*, b. April 6, 1691.   13 *Isaac*, b. May 18, 1695.
14 | *David*, b. Nov. 14, 1698.   15 *Elizabeth*, b. Feb. 22, 1701.

4-7- | DANIEL HOAR m. Dec. 20, 1705, Sarah Jones, dau. of John and Sarah Jones, and lived in the south-easterly past of Con., where he d. Feb. 8, 1773, aged 93.

7-16 | †*John*, b. Jan. 6, 1707. He was twice married.
17 | *Jonathan*, b. June 6, 1707; grad. H. C. 1740; was an officer in the Provincial service, during the war of 1744 to 1763. In 1755 he went, a major, to Fort Edward, the next year was lieut.-colonel in Nova Scotia, and aid to Major-Gen. Winslow at Crown Point. After the peace of 1763 he went to England, and was appointed

Governor of Newfoundland and the neighboring provinces, but d. on his passage thither, in 1771, aged 52.

18 *Daniel*, entered H. C. 1730, but did not grad. He m. Nov. 2, 1743, Rebecca Brooks. He moved ·to Narraganset No. 2, (Westminster,) where he d., leaving two sons and two dau.

19 *Lucy*, b. ———; m. John Brooks.

20 *Elizabeth*, b. ———; m. —— Whittemore of W. Cambridge.

21 *Mary*, b. ———; m. Zachariah Whittemore.

7-16-

JOHN HOAR m. in Lex., June 13, 1734, Esther Pierce, by whom he had two children. She d., and he m. in Wat., Aug. 21, 1740, Elizabeth Cooledge. He d. in Linc. May 16, 1786, and his wid. d. March 20, 1791. He lived successively in Lex., Wat., Lex., and Linc. This was partly owing to his changing the place of his residence, and partly from alterations of town lines, which annexed a part of Lex. to Linc. What time John Hoar became an inhabitant of Lex., we are not prepared to say. He was taxed in town both for personal and real estate in 1729, and had a seat assigned him in the meeting house in 1731, when they reseated the house. He was chosen one of the committee to provide for the schools in 1743. He subsequently filled the office of constable, assessor, and selectman. He resided in the south-westerly part of the town, at or near the present residence of Leonard Hoar, in Lincoln, – that place being set off from Lex. when Lincoln was erected into a town.

16-22 *Rebecca*, b in Lex. July 1, 1735; m. May 6, 1755, Joseph Cutler.

23 *Esther*, b. in Wat. Jan. 28, 1739; m. May 8, 1760, Edmund Bowman.

24 *John*, b. in Lex. July 14, 1741; d. young.

25 *Samuel*, b. in Lex. Aug. 23, 1743; he was a magistrate in Lincoln, frequently represented that town in the House of Representatives, and was a senator from the county of Middlesex from 1813 to 1816. He m. Susanna Pierce, and had a family of ten children, five sons and five dau. *Samuel*, his oldest son, b. May 18, 1778, grad. H. C. 1802, received the degree of LL.D. 1838. He was a lawyer and resided in Con., where he d., much lamented, in 1857. He was not only distinguished in his profession, but was called to fill many important stations. He was a senator from Middlesex county, and represented his district in the Congress of the United States. He was a man of talents and of great moral worth, leaving a spotless reputation as a rich legacy to his children, some of whom have also become distinguished. His oldest son, Ebenezer Rockwood Hoar, b. Feb. 21, 1816, grad. H. C. 1835, commenced the practice of law in Con. 1839; appointed judge of the Court of C. P. 1849. He has also, like his father and grandfather, represented his native county in the senate of Mass. He is now on the bench of the Supreme Court. He received the degree of LL.D. from Williams Coll. 1861. Edward Sherman, his third son, grad. H. C. 1844, is a lawyer in New York. His youngest son, George Frisbie, grad. H. C. 1846, commenced the practice of law in Worcester; was a senator from that county in 1857.

26 *Elizabeth*, b. in Lex. Oct. 14, 1746.

27 *Mary*, b. in Lex. Oct. 5, 1750; d. young.

28 *Sarah*, b. in Lincoln after her father's place was set off to that town, June 9, 1755; m. Nehemiah Abbot.

29 *Leonard*, b. in Linc. June 20, 1758; was twice m.

30 *Rebecca*, b. in Linc. Oct. 18, 1761; m. Joseph White, Lancaster.

31 *Mary*, b. June 17, 1764; m. March 27, 1788, Thomas Wheeler.

32 *Joseph*, b. July 30, 1767.

THE HOBBS FAMILY.

JOSIAH HOBBS, the emigrant ancestor of the family of that name in New England, came to this country in 1671, in the ship Arabella, Sprague, master, in July. He resided in Boston till 1690, when he removed to Camb. Farms. He m. in 1683, and had a son, Josiah, b. in Boston 1684. After 1690, he resided in Lex., (except for a short period, when he was in the westerly part of Wo.) till his death, which happened May 30, 1741, aged 92 years. He was a subscriber for the meeting house in 1692, and was taxed for the support of the minister the year following. Aug. 1699, he and his wife, Tabitha, were ad. to the ch. In September of the same year *Josiah, Tabitha,* and *Mary,* three of their children, were bap. In Oct. 1700, *Matthew* and *Susanna* were bap. The record of this family is very imperfect. They may have had other children. Most of the children d. in infancy, or before marriage.

1　JOSIAH HOBBS m., and resided in Lexington till about 1714. In 1713 he was chosen to "take care of ye swine." About this time he removed to Boston, where he resided many years, and late in life moved with his family to Weston, where the name has been common down to the present day. The Hobbses in Worcester county are descendants from this stock. Josiah Hobbs was married before he left Lex., and had several children bap.

1- 2　*Ebenezer,* bap. Jan. 8, 1709; his father owning the covenant.
　　3　*Elizabeth,* bap. March 23, 1712; her mother, Mary, making due confession to the church.
　　4　*Tabitha,* bap. April 13, 1712.

This name is generally spelled *Hubbs* in Lex. records.

THE HOLMES FAMILY.

1　DR. HOWLAND HOLMES and his wife came to Lex. from W. Camb. in the autumn of 1851. He is a son of Howland Holmes of Bridgewater, and grandson of Elias, and great grandson of Elisha Holmes of Plymouth. He was b. Jan. 16, 1815, and m. Aug. 28, 1849, Maria, dau. of William Cotting of West Camb., b. Mar. 3, 1818. He grad. at H. C. in 1843, and at the Mass. Medical School in 1848, and became a member of the Mass. Medical Society the same year. Before graduating from the medical school, he spent a portion of 1846 and 1847 traveling in Europe, but mostly in studying in the hospitals at Paris and London. He has served several years on the school committee in West Camb. and in Lex. He holds a commission of justice of the peace.

1- 2　*Mary Eddy,* b. in West Camb. Aug. 14, 1850; d. next day.
　　3　*Carrie Maria,* b. in Lex. April 3, 1852; d. June 21, 1857.
　　4　*Francis Howland,* b. Sept. 13, 1853.
　　5　*Sarah Eddy,* b. Sept. 15, 1855.
　　6　*Charlotte Bronte,* b. April 20, 1857; d. Feb. 25, 1865.

THE HOUGHTON FAMILY.

LEVI HOUGHTON, of Lancaster, b. 1736, m. Susan Richardson of that town. He d. 1818, aged 82; she d. 1814. Levi was probably a descendant of John Houghton, or his cousin Ralph, who settled in Lan. about 1652. Levi, by his wife, Susan, had seven children.

They resided at one time in Worcester. *Levi*, one of their sons, b. in Wor. about 1772, m. Elizabeth Stearns of Lunenburg about 1803, where he resided. He d. Jan. 27, 1865, aged 93; she d. 1828, aged 47. He was twice married after the death of his first wife, by whom he had his children, nine in number.

1   SAMUEL A. HOUGHTON, son of Levi and Elizabeth, b. Jan. 4, 1807, m. Sept. 3, 1834, Martha W. Haywood of Townsend. They resided in Boston till March, 1839, when they removed to Lex.

1- 2 *Elizabeth Stearns*, b. June 14, 1835; m. Jan. 19, 1858, Ralph W. Shattuck of West Cambridge.

3 *Melinda W.*, b. Aug. 31, 1840; m. Aug. 20, 1861, Thomas Everett Cutler.

4 *Henry M.*, b. Sept. 22, 1842.   5 *Clara G.*, b. Dec. 27, 1845.

THE HOVEY FAMILY.

DANIEL HOVEY and Rebecca, his wife, came to this country and settled in Ipswich 1637. They had nine children; *Joseph*, their fifth son, b. about 1652, m. Hannah Pratt and settled in Hadley. They had five children. *John*, b. 1684, m. first, Abbia Watson of Camb. Their family consisted of six children. Their oldest son, *John*, b. 1707, m. Elizabeth Muzzy, dau. of John Muzzy of Lex. He grad. H. C. 1725, was a clergyman, d. 1773. He m. second, Susanna Lovett. *Ebenezer*, the fourth son of John and Abbia, b. 1714, m. Elizabeth Mason of Wat. They had but one child, *Thomas*, b. at Newton, Aug. 14, 1740; m. Elizabeth Brown, dau. of Dea. Josiah Brown. They had fifteen children; all but one lived to grow up. *Ebenezer*, their fourth son, b. June 8, 1769, m. Sally Greenwood, dau. of Nathaniel Greenwood of Brighton. He d. May 5, 1831, and she d. June 27, 1863. They had twelve children,—thus sustaining the fruitfulness of the family.

1   THOMAS G. HOVEY, their fifth son, b. Jan. 23, 1816, m. Nov. 3, 1841, Ann Maria Hoping of Camb., b. Nov. 13, 1822.

1- 2 *Emma Maria*, b. Dec. 26, 1842. 3 *Ellen Amanda*, b. Jan. 1, 1844.

4 *Thomas Ebenezer*, b. June 23, 1845.

5 *Walter Sewall*, b. May 7, 1847. 6 *Georgianna*, b. Feb. 7, 1849.

7 *Stilman Southwick*, b. April 15, 1850.

8 *Frank Pierce*, b. Dec. 3, 1852.

Mr. Hovey resided in Cambridge till about 1850, where his first five children were b., when he came to Lex., where the last two were born.

THE HUDSON FAMILY.

The Hudsons were among the early settlers of New England. William, Francis, and Ralph, were in and about Boston before 1636, and were among the prominent citizens. But it is doubtful whether the Lancaster Hudsons were from either of these families.

1   DANIEL HUDSON came to this country about 1639. He was in Wat. 1640, and settled in Lancaster, 1665, where he purchased a town right for £40. His wife's name was Johanna, by whom he had eleven children. One of his daughters m. Abraham Joslin. When the Indians attacked Lancaster in 1675, Joslin and his family took

refuge in the garrison house of Rev. Mr. Rolandson. After a most vigorous defence, the house was set on fire, when the only alternative left was to perish in the flames or fall into the hands of the merciless foe. Joslin was killed while defending the inmates of the house; but his wife and daughter were taken captive, with Mrs. Rolandson, carried away and barbarously murdered in the wilderness. The fate of his daughter Anna but prefigured that of her parents; for in 1697, Daniel Hudson and his wife, one daughter, and two children of his son Nathaniel, were killed by the Indians in their incursion into that ill-fated town. His oldest son *Daniel* m. and settled in Bridgewater, and his son *William* soon followed him.

1- 2   NATHANIEL HUDSON, another son of Daniel, appears to have been rather migratory, for he is at one time in Lancaster and at another in Billerica. He m. Rebecca Rugg. We have found no record of his children, except that three of them, viz. *Seth, Nathaniel,* and *Abigail,* were bap. in Lexington, April 22, 1705. This was probably when he was residing in Billerica; for he deeded a lot of land in Lincoln to a Mr. Buss, about that time, and signed himself as of Billerica. He is also believed to be the father of *John,* who with Seth and Nathaniel settled in Marlborough.

2- 3   JOHN HUDSON, b. 1713, m. Eliz. McAllister of Northborough. She d. May 16, 1786, aged 66, and he m. March 28, 1787, Bethia Wood, who survived him. He d. in Berlin, Aug. 6, 1799, aged 86. He resided first in Marlborough, and afterwards in Berlin. There is one peculiarity in the whole family. They seem to have had a taste for a military life. Few families of the same number have furnished as many soldiers for the old French and Indian wars, and the Revolutionary war, as the Hudsons. And in searching for their genealogy, the army rolls will furnish as much information as the parish registers. John Hudson and two of his sons were in the service in the French war, and he and his eight sons were in the service during some period of the Revolutionary war.

3- 4   *Elisha,* b. ——— ; m. Oct. 4, 1770, Susanna Brigham of Marlborough. He was in the French war in 1756, '58, and '60. He was also in the Revolutionary army. After the war he removed to Canada, where he d.

5   *Elijah,* b. ——— ; m. Hannah Goodnow. He was in the French war in 1758, and '59; and also in the Revolution.

6   *Miriam,* b. 1746; m. Jonas Babcock of Northborough, where she d.

7   *Moses,* b. Jan. 4, 1749. He was five years in the Revolutionary army; d. unm.

8   *Aaron,* b. Aug. 24, 1750. He was in the Lexington alarm, 1775.

9   *Hannah,* b. July 20, 1752; d. in Berlin, unm.

10   *Ebenezer,* b. May 16, 1755; d. in the Revolutionary army.

11   *John,* b. May 9, 1757; moved to Oxford; was three years in the Continental army.

12   *Charles,* b. ———, 1759; he was a three years' man in the Continental service, and when his time was about expiring, he was accidentally killed by our own men. Two scouting parties met in the night-time, and mistaking each other for the enemy, they fired, and killed him, and another man.

13   ‡*Stephen,* b. June 12, 1761; he was three years in the Continental service.

14   *Elizabeth,* b. ——— ; m. Nov. 18, 1779, Levi Fay of Marlborough.

3-13-   STEPHEN HUDSON m. Feb. 10, 1791, Louisa Williams, dau. of Larkin and Anna (Warren) Williams. He d. March 21, 1827, aged

68, and she d. Oct. 7, 1837, aged 70. He enlisted into the Continental army at the age of 16, and after the expiration of his three years, he entered on board a privateer, which crossed the Atlantic, and cruised on the coast of Great Britain, Spain, and Portugal, and returned to the United States about the time peace was concluded. After the war was over he enlisted for a Western campaign against the Indians; but some reverses at the West induced a change of policy, and the company to which he belonged proceeded no farther than West Point, where they remained till their term of service expired. While in the army and on board of the privateer he was in several severe actions. While the army was in the Jerseys, he and others volunteered to scour the country around Philadelphia, to cut off the supplies which the British were drawing from the people. While in that service they were captured, carried into Philadelphia, and thrown into prison, where for several months, in the heat of summer, they suffered extremely from the closeness of their confinement, the want of provision, and the wanton cruelty of the guard. The " Philadelphia Jail," and the "Jersey Prison-ship," will stand as lasting monuments of British cruelty and American suffering, nearly approaching the barbarity and suffering at Andersonville. When these prisoners were exchanged, they were so feeble and emaciated that they were scarcely able to walk, and yet they were turned out without money, without rations, and almost without clothing, to beg their way to their respective regiments. He resided in Marlboro', where his children were born.

13-15   *Nancy*, b. July 8, 1791; d. unm. Sept. 30, 1853, aged 62.
16   *Elizabeth*, b. Aug. 28, 1793; m. Sept. 5, 1814, Thomas Cooledge. She had ten children, and d. Feb. 25, 1835, aged 42.
17   ‡*Charles*, b. Nov. 14, 1795; he has been twice married.
18   *Louisa*, b. May 3, 1798; m. Joseph Shurtleff. She survived her husband, and d. June 17, 1825.

13-17—   CHARLES HUDSON m. July 21, 1825, Ann Rider of Shrewsbury, dau. of John and Mercy (Brigham) Rider, b. July 4, 1806. She d. Sept. 19, 1829, aged 23 years; and he m. May 14, 1830, Martha B. Rider, sister of his first wife. He studied theology and was settled in Westminster, where he resided twenty-five years. He represented the town four years in the House of Representatives, the county of Worcester six years in the Senate, and three years in the Executive Council, and the District eight years in Congress. On leaving Congress he was appointed Naval Officer in the Boston Custom House, a place he held four years. He was also eight years a member of the Board of Education, and four years an Assessor of Internal Revenue for the Sixth Collection District of Mass. He has also filled other public stations. He has published several books and tracts on theological and other subjects. Among his publications is a History of Marlboro', his native town. He is a member of several Historical Societies. In 1849, he removed from Westminster to Lexington, where he now resides. His children were born in Westminster.

17-19   *Harriet Williams*, b. Aug. 18, 1827; d. July 26, 1828.
20   *Harriet Ann*, b. Sept. 13, 1829; m. Sept. 4, 1854, Henry M. Smith. They reside in Chicago, Ill., where he is editor of a daily paper.
21   *Martha B.*, b. April 10, 1832; d. April 25, 1832.
22   *Charles Henry*, b. July 10, 1833; grad. a civil engineer at the Lawrence Scientific School, Harvard University, 1855. He went West

in 1855, where he has been engaged in his profession. He m. Jan. 1, 1862, Frances H. Nichols of Boston. They reside at Burlington, Iowa.

23 *John Williams*, b. July 10, 1836; m. March 25, 1865, Sophia W. Mellen, dau. of Hon. Edward and Sophia (Whitney) Mellen of Wayland. He grad. H. C. 1856, taught a high school, read law, and is in practice in Boston. In the late Rebellion, he served with 35th Regt. Mass. Vols. in the Army of the Potomac, and in Kentucky, Mississippi and East Tennessee. He was lieut. col. of his regiment. He has held several town offices.

24 *Mary Elizabeth*, b. March 31, 1839.

There has been another family of Hudsons in Lexington, who came from Boston, and probably were the descendants of William or Francis, who were in Boston or its immediate vicinity at the first planting of the colony.

1   JOSEPH HUDSON m. Dec. 24, 1764, Sarah White. She d. and he m. second, 1782, Elizabeth Brown. She d. in Boston, June, 1820. He had *Joseph*, b. June 15, 1770; *William*, b. in Cohasset, June 15, 1775; *Benjamin*, b. Feb. 27, 1783; *John*, b. March 19, 1786.

1- 2   JOHN HUDSON, the last named son of Joseph, m. March, 1808, Lucy Crocker. She d. Aug. 1837, and he m. April 19, 1838, Alice Frost. She d. Nov. 7, 1867. He is living in his 81st year. He came to Lexington in 1843.

2- 3 *Eliza J. C.*, b. Dec. 4, 1808; d. Oct. 21, 1810.
   4 *Eliza J. C.*, b. Nov. 23, 1812; d. July 13, 1832.
   5 *Mary*, b. March 14, 1815; d. March 22, 1816.
   6 *John*, b. Nov. 22, 1818; d. May 22, 1840.
   7 *William*, b. March 17, 1822; m. Oct. 19, 1845, Lucretia Fiske, dau. of Samuel and Ardelia L. (Tufts) Fiske, b. July 12, 1825. He resided first in Lex. and then in Worcester. He entered the service in 1861, served under Burnside in North Carolina, was attached to the signal corps, and d. of disease Aug. 20, 1862. He left two children, John A., b. Dec. 26, 1846; William F., b. Oct. 3, 1848.

THE HUFFMASTER FAMILY.

ISAAC HUFFMASTER, son of Andrew and Abigail Huffmaster, b. in Wo. July 13, 1793. He came to Lex. in 1827, and m. Dec. 1827, Frances Wier, b. in Medford, Sept. 27, 1801. He d. Nov. 21, 1865, aged 72. They had three children,—*Frances Moria*, b. July 9, 1829; m. April 11, 1854, A. Leonard Jewell of Walt. She d. Jan. 9, 1860, leaving one child, Frank, b. Dec. 30, 1859. Mr. Jewell was killed by the falling of a staging, June 26, 1867. *Isaac*, b. June 23, 1832, d. Oct. 6, 1832; *Isaac*, b. Aug. 19, 1838.

THE HUNT FAMILY.

ISAAC HUNT was one of the assessors in 1711, and a subscriber for the purchase of the Common. His record is so meagre that we cannot trace him. The following are probably his children: *Thomas*, bap. April, 1701; *Mary*, bap. Sept. 5, 1703; *Henry*, d. Nov. 11, 1705; *Ebenezer*, bap. April 16, 1708; *Samuel*, bap. June 27, 1710; *John*, bap. March 9, 1712.

INGERSOLL.—JONATHAN INGERSOLL came to reside in Lexington in 1755 from Holliston. In 1757, *Jonathan* and *Nathaniel Ingersoll* were in the French war as soldiers from Lex. *Hannah Ingersoll* was ad. to the ch. in Lex. Oct. 14, 1759. *Dorcas Ingersoll* was bap. Oct. 21, 1859.

THE JENNISON FAMILY.

JOSIAH JENNISON, b. Jan. 22, 1730, was the son of Nathaniel Jennison of Weston, who m. Oct. 23, 1729, Abigail Mead, dau. of Hopestill and Elizabeth Mead. She d. and he m. Feb. 12, 1756, Mary Tidd, dau. of Joseph and Dorothy (Stickney) Tidd of Lex., b. Jan. 7, 1732. They were admitted to the ch. Nov. 13, 1757. They had eight children, *Mary*, bap. Nov. 13, 1757, d. young; *Betsey*, bap. Nov. 13, 1757, ad. to the ch. April 5, 1777; *Josiah*, bap. Sept. 9, 1759; *Mary*, bap. Nov. 1, 1761; *Nathan*, bap. Oct. 28, 1764; *John*, bap. Oct. 30, 1768; *William*, bap. Sept. 2, 1770.

THE JOHNSON FAMILY.

The Lexington records open with the name of four *Johnsons*, John, William, Thomas, and Obadiah, all of adult age, tax payers, and hence residents. The Johnsons were so numerous among the early emigrants, that it is impossible to trace them with accuracy. JOHN JOHNSON of Wo., probably a son of Capt. Edward, m. April 28, 1657, Bethia Reed, and had among other children *John*, b. Jan. 24, 1658; *William*, b. Sept. 29, 1662; *Obadiah*, b. June 15, 1664. These were probably the Johnsons found at Camb. Farms. John, William, and Thomas were subscribers for the meeting house, 1692, and John, William, and Obadiah were taxed in 1693. John and William are continued on the tax list 1695 and 1696.

JOHN JOHNSON had a wife, and probably children, at that time. Mary, his wife, was ad. to the ch. before 1698, and on April 9, 1699, Mary, Prudence, and Rebecca were bap., and on the next Sabbath Sarah and Esther were bap. On the 4th of May, 1699, Mary was bap., and on the 10th of Sept., 1704, Abigail was bap. From these fragmentary records it is not possible to classify the families, and the following records of deaths at that period increases the perplexity; Thomas Johnson, d. Dec. 4, 1690; Mary Johnson, d. July 16, 1691; Mary Johnson, sen., d. Dec. 29, 1694; John Johnson, d. March 8, 1698; Sarah Johnson, d. July 1, 1708. Some of these were probably the children of John.

John Johnson was one of the parish assessors in 1712, and the year following he was consulted relative to a road to pass through his land, and in 1715 he was paid for the land so taken. He must have resided in the northerly part of the town, in the neighborhood of the Lockes and the Blodgetts.

The Lancaster records give the marriage of *William Johnson* and Ruth Rugg, both of Lexington, Feb. 11, 1725; and the Lex. records contain the following: " *William Johnson*, son of William and Ruth Johnson, b. April 2, 1725." After this there is no mention of the name for more than half a century.

MUNSON JOHNSON came from Wo. to Lex. in 1795, and David Johnson in 1797. They were brothers, and sons of Francis Johnson of Wo., who was son of Francis, of the same town. *Munson* m. Betsey Munroe, dau. of Nathan. They had two children b. in Lex., Charlotte and Adelia.

DAVID JOHNSON m. Feb. 2, 1804, Philena Munroe, dau. of John. They had no issue. He d. Oct. 26, 1860, aged 80 years and 5 months. She is living, in her 86th year. He took an active part in the militia, and rose to the rank of major.

There was another branch of Francis Johnson's family which settled in Lexington.

1   THOMAS JOHNSON, son of Frederick, and grandson of Francis, came to Lex. the latter part of the last century, to learn a trade of Seth Reed, and m. Sept. 1811, Mary Dudley, dau. of Nathan and Sarah Dudley. He d. July 1, 1830, aged 45; she d. Dec. 3, 1862, aged 70. He left four dau., all of whom m. and have resided in Lex.

1- 2 *Mary D.*, b. Nov. 11, 1812; m. Jan. 16, 1836, Cotesworth P. Wheeler. They have had Mary Henrietta, b. July 22, 1838, d. July 9, 1866; Clara Ellen, b. Oct. 14, 1840; Theodora Elizabeth, b. Oct. 4, 1844. He d. May 14, 1866.
3   *Sarah Maria*, b. April 22, 1816; m. Feb. 13, 1840, James Sumner.
4   *Emily*, b. July 27, 1818; m. May 30, 1850, William E. Cogswell, and had one son, Willie, b. Jan. 15, 1853, and d. Sept. 7, 1853. He d. Feb. 12, 1860, aged 40.
5   *Susan Sprague*, b. July 4, 1824; m. Dec. 30, 1846, David A. Tuttle.

There has been another family of Johnsons in Lex., the pedigree of which we have not been able to trace.

1   JOHN JOHNSON m. Nov. 12, 1810, Eunice Pierce of Weston. He d. June 1, 1856, aged 76. He was son of Obadiah Johnson, who m. Sarah Loring, dau. of John Loring. Tradition says that he had John and Sarah. Who Obadiah Johnson was, whence he came, and whither he went, we have not been able to ascertain. John lived and d. on East street, near Lowell street.

———

1- 2 *Elbridge*, b. April 11, 1811; d. April 12, 1811.
3   *John E.*, b. Sept. 11, 1812; d. June 27, 1826.
4   *Susan A.*, b. April 17, 1815; m. April 2, 1831, Horatio Brown.
5   *Thomas S.*, b. Oct. 3, 1817; m. Aug. 15, 1844, Margaret Sweney of Charlestown, where he d. 1858.
6   *Nancy A.*, b. Aug. 28, 1820; d. Oct. 20, 1822.
7   *Ann M.*, b. March 23, 1823; m. Aug. 30, 1843, Abel Jones of Acton.
8   *Sarah J.*, b. March 13, 1825; m. June 11, 1842, Alfred Laws of Westford.
9   *Almira*, b. Ap. 30, 1827; m. Ap. 19, 1850, Wyman Skilton of Bur.
10 *John H.*, b. Sept. 18, 1830.
11 *Andrew*, b. Feb. 11, 1833; m. Oct. 19, 1866, Sarah Cheney of Orange.

There is still another family of the name. CHARLES W. JOHNSON, b. in Wayland, June 5, 1805, m. April 12, 1832, Martha S. Miles of Con. He moved to Lex. in 1848. They have four children; *Charles E.*, b. Nov. 12, 1833; m. Nov. 29, 1859, Kitty M. Hadlock; *Joseph M.*, b. Aug. 10, 1835; *Martha M.*, b. July 18, 1838, m. June 19, 1863, Albert F. Nurse; *William R.*, b. Mar. 2, 1842.

THE KENDALL FAMILY.

Though the Kendalls have never been numerous in Lex., there was one family in town about the time of its incorporation. They came from Wo., where Francis Kendall was, as early as 1640, and was made freeman 1647. He m. Dec. 24, 1644, Mary Tidd of that town, and had *John*, b. 1646, *Thomas*, b. 1648, *Samuel*, b. 1659, besides several daughters. Francis Kendall was the ancestor of most of the Kendalls in Massachusetts, and indeed of New England. His son Thomas, m. Ruth, and had among other children Thomas, b. May 19, 1677. He was the first of the name in Lex.

1   THOMAS KENDALL probably m. March 30, 1696, Abigail Brough-   *6* ton of Wo. as his first wife, and about 1701, m. second, Sarah, dau. of Rev. Thomas Cheever of Chelsea. She d. in Framingham, May 2, 1761, aged 75. They probably came to Lex. about 1710. In 1715, in the quaint language of the record, " discourse being on foot concerning highways, Capt. William Reed offered to give for the peace and quiet of the town," a highway for Thomas Kendall and the neighborhood westerly of him, through his land to the town road. From this time there was a long, bitter controversy about Thomas Kendall's road, which was settled by Mr. Kendall's giving a bond to the town in 1730, binding himself and his heirs to save the town harmless from all expense in maintaining the road forever. It is difficult to fix the exact locality of the residence of Mr. Kendall, but it would seem that he resided south and west of the great meadow, near the brook running into the same, and probably near what is now known as the Thorning Place.

Thomas Kendall and his wife were ad. to the ch. in Lex. 1728. He was constable in 1718, and filled several other subordinate town offices. In 1745, he and his wife were dismissed to the ch. in Framingham, to which place they had removed. Their first four children were born in Wo., and the rest in Lexington.

1- 2 | *Sarah*, b. Sept. 7, 1702.
    3 | *Thomas*, b. July 30, 1704. He was ad. to the ch. in Lex. 1726.
    4 | *Abigail*, b. Aug. 10, 1706; ad. to the ch. in Lex. Nov. 29, 1724.
    5 | *Benjamin*, b. Feb. 25, 1708. He went to Sherb., where he m. Jan. 24, 1733, Kezia Leland, and had a family in that place.
    6 | *Joshua*, b. Aug. 7, 1713; m. 1745, Sarah Dewing of Natick, and resided in Framingham.
    7 | *Ezekiel*, b. Dec. 21, 1715.   8 *Elizabeth*, b. March 4, 1718.
    9 | *Ruth*, b. June 13, 1720.   10 *Jane*, b. Nov. 14, 1722.
11 | *Elijah*, ⎰ b. Jan. 30, 1725; ⎰ m. May 24, 1750, Jemima Smith, Sud.
12 | *Elisha*, ⎱   ⎱ probably d. young.

There were other Kendalls in Lex. at a somewhat early day, probably relatives of Thomas. *Eleazer*, of Eleazer and Hannah Kendall, bap. April 2, 1714; *William*, bap. May 6, 1716, ad. to ch. Oct. 16, 1737. Daniel Fiske of Walt. m. April 7, 1763, *Sarah Kendall* of Lexington.

OLIVER W. KENDALL was son of Capt. Oliver and Lucy Kendall of Ashby. He was b. Sept. 17, 1805; m. Feb. 8, 1831, Mary, dau. of Paul and Elizabeth Gates of Ashby, b. May 13, 1807. They came to Lex. immediately after their marriage. He has filled the office of constable about twenty years. They have two children: *Frank O.*, b. Jan. 18, 1834; m. Jan. 15, 1860, Estelle Ditson of Boston. They r. in Marlborough. He was in service nine months in the late rebellion. *Mary Elizabeth*, b. Sept. 4, 1836; m. March 27, 1862, Charles Hervey Bennett. He d. July 8, 1864.

KIBBE.— In 1710, SHEREBRIAH KIBBE and Elizabeth Kibbe, probably his wife, were ad. to the ch. in Lex. From what place they

came, we have not learned. He subscribed, in 1711, for the purchase of the Common, and in 1713 was appointed sealer of leather.
The following is found upon the church records: *Seth Kibbe*, bap.
Feb. 17, 1711; *Sarah Kibbe*, bap. April 23, 1713; Sept. 9, 1722,
bap. *Samuel, Ebenezer, Elizabeth*, and *Mary Kibbe*,—all of whom
owned the covenant but Ebenezer. *Esther Stone*, dau. of Sherebriah
Kibbe, and *Hannah Kibbe*, were also bap.

THE LAUGHTON FAMILY.

John Laughton, and his wife Sarah, came to Lex. from Reading
about 1720. The first mention of them is the baptism of their dau.
Hannah, Nov. 6, 1720. They were ad. to the ch. in Lex. from the
church of Reading, Jan. 24, 1723. He resided on Monument street,
at or near the place recently occupied by Samuel A. Houghton. In
1733, John Laughton was chosen deacon, and became a prominent
man both in the church and in the town. In 1722, he was chosen
one of the assessors, and filled that office nine years. He was also
one of the selectmen in 1738. July 1, 1744, he and his wife and his
son Jeremiah were dismissed to the ch. at Harvard, to which place
they had removed a short time before. ,They had four children bap.
in Lex. — *Hannah*, b. Oct. 30, 1720; *Jeremiah*, b. July, 1723, d.
soon after birth; *Jeremiah*, b. Aug. 4, 1725, moved to Harvard;
Hepzibah, bap. July 27, 1735, m. Feb. 9, 1758, Edward Winship.

There were other Laughtons in Lex. about that period. THOMAS
LAUGHTON, and his wife Abigail, were in town, and had two children
bap. viz. *Sarah*, bap. Dec. 10, 1735, and *Thomas*, Nov. 15, 1737.
Thomas, the father, was ad. to the ch. April 14, 1728. He may have
been a brother of Dea. John. Both left town about the same time.

THE LAWRENCE FAMILY.

Though the Lawrences were not among the earliest settlers in
Lex., the name appears on our records as early as 1693; and for a
considerable period they were among the prominent citizens. They
were the descendants of JOHN LAWRENCE, an early settler in Wat.
This family dates back to the early period of 1190. It commenced
with Sir Robert Lawrence, who was present at the seige of Acre,
1191. The immediate descendants of Sir Robert married into the
family of Washington, and thus the name of Lawrence was continued
in the family down to the grandfather of Gen. Washington. The
grandson of Sir Robert m. Matilda, dau. of John de Washington.

1   JOHN LAWRENCE was probably in Wat. as early as 1635, as his
eldest child was born there March 14, 1636. He was admitted freeman April 17, 1637. He had two wives, and fifteen children. By
his first wife, Elizabeth, he had thirteen, and by his last, Susanna
Batchelder, he had two. The history of this family is very obscure,
but little being known of the children except their names.

1- 2 | *John*, b. March 14, 1636.
3 | *Jonathan*, b. ———; buried April 6, 1648.
4 | †*Nathaniel*, b. Oct. 15, 1639.
5 | *Joseph*, b. March, and d. May, 1642.
6 | *Joseph*, b. May 30, 1643.
7 | *Mary*, b. July 16, 1645; m. Inego Potter of Charlestown.
8 | *Peleg*, b. Jan. 10, 1647.   9 *Enoch*, b. March 5, 1649.

10 *Samuel*, mentioned in his father's will.
11 *Isaac*, b. ———; m. April 19, 1682, Abigail Bellows.
12 *Elizabeth*, b. May 9, 1655.
13 *Zechariah*, b. March 9, 1659. 14 *Abigail*, b. Jan. 9, 1666.
15 *Susanna*, b. July 3, 1667, eight days before the death of her father.

1-4-   NATHANIEL LAWRENCE of Groton m. in Sudbury, March 13, 1661, Sarah Morse, dau. of John and Hannah of Dedham. She d. in Groton 1684. He was ad. freeman in 1672, was early chosen Dea., was a representative, and was much employed in public business. After the death of his wife, Sarah, he m. Hannah ———. She d. after 1701, for her signature is set to a deed at that date. In advanced life he moved to Lex., where he d. April 14, 1724, aged 85. His will, dated Aug. 4, 1718, and proved May 4, 1724, mentions sons Nathaniel and John, dau. Hannah Houlden and Mary Wheeler, son Samuel Page, dau. Elizabeth Harris and dau. Deborah, and grandson Lawrence. What time he came to Lex. is uncertain; not however till after 1701. His son had preceded him, as he was in Lex. in 1693, his name being upon the tax bill of that year. He probably came to reside with his son John.

4-16 *Nathaniel*, b. in Sud. April 4, 1661; m. Ann ———.
17 *Sarah*, b. in Sud. Jan. 1, 1663; d. young.
18 *Hannah*, b. July 3, 1664; d. young.
19 †*John*, b. July 29, 1667; d. in Lex. March 12, 1746.
20 *Mary*, b. March 3, 1670; d. early.
21 *Sarah*, b. May 16, 1672; she was probably the first wife of Samuel Page, who moved to Southboro.
22 *Elizabeth*, b. July 6, 1674; d. Oct. 20, 1675.
23 *Elizabeth*, b. ———; m. Abner Harris of Medford.
24 *Hannah*, b. April 26, 1687; m. Samuel Holden.
25 *Mary*, b. Oct. 16, 1690; m. Zebadiah Wheeler.
26 *Jonathan*, b. June 14, 1796.

4-19-   JOHN LAWRENCE, a blacksmith and a farmer, m. in Groton, Nov. 9, 1687, Anna Tarbell. He moved to Camb. Farms in 1693, where he and his wife were admitted to the ch. Feb. 9, 1699. He resided on the Bedford road, near the Bedford line. He was chosen one of the parish assessors in 1702, constable in 1705, selectman in 1717, '19, '26, '27, and '31. He was often employed by the town on important committees, and was a highly respectable and useful citizen. He d. March 12, 1746, aged 79; she d. Dec. 19, 1732, aged 63.

19-27 †*John*, b. June 10, 1688; d. Jan. 22, 1752.
28 *Thomas*, b. ———; resided in Groton.
29 *William*, b. 1697; of Groton.
30 *Samuel*, b. July 9, 1700.
31 *Anna*, bap. Oct. 1, 1702, in Lex.; m. Capt. Benjamin Bancroft of Charlestown. She d. July 21, 1787, in Groton.
32 †*Jonathan*, bap. Feb. 24, 1706; m. Elizabeth Swain.
33 *Sarah*, bap. June 20, 1708; m. Josiah Fiske.
34 †*Benjamin*, bap. May 31, 1713; m Jane Russell, 1735.
35 †*Amos*, bap. Feb. 19, 1716; he removed to Groton.

19-27-   JOHN LAWRENCE m. May 18, 1710, Elizabeth Stone, b. June 19, 1693, dau. of Dea. Samuel and Dorcas (Jones) Stone. Though he was married in Lex. and his children were baptized there, he resided within the bounds of Wo., and took an active part in the affairs of the precinct, when the northern part of Wo. was made a distinct parish. He had eight children, one of whom, Rebecca, m. June 27, 1751, Thomas Locke of Lexington.

19-32-   JONATHAN LAWRENCE m. Feb. 26, 1727, Elizabeth Swain of Lex., b. 1707. He d. March 19, 1773, aged 68, and his widow d. July 4, 1790, aged 85. He first settled in Sudbury, afterwards in Framingham, and returned about 1740, as one of his children was bap. in Lex. in 1741. The same year he was elected to town office. In 1743, he and his wife united with the church in Lex., by a letter of recommendation from the East Church in Sudbury. He was frequently employed in public business by the town, having filled the office of highway surveyor, tythingman, constable, &c.

32-36   *Elizabeth*, b. in Lex. Feb. 19, 1728; d. Jan. 16, 1733.
     37   *Mary*, b. in Framingham Nov. 30, 1729; m. Abijah Smith of Lex., Jan. 1750.
     38   *Sarah*, b. in Fram. Dec. 15, 1731; m. Jan. 30, 1752, Jonathan Reed, son of Benjamin and Rebecca Reed of Lex. He settled in Littleton.
     39   *Jonathan*, b. in Fram. Feb 5, 1734. He went to Wo., where he m. Elizabeth Johnson; afterwards moved to Ashby.
     40   †*Bezaleel*, b. probably in Fram., April 13, 1736.
     41   *Micah*, b. March 15, 1739, and bap. in Lex. He grad. H. C. 1759, was ordained a minister at Winchester, N. H., Nov. 14, 1764, and d. Jan. 1794, aged 55.
     42   *Elizabeth*, b. Dec. 13, 1741, bap. in Lex.; m. Nov. 7, 1764, Thaddeus Bowman of Lex.
     43   *Anna*, b. March 19, 1746; d. July 18, 1753.
     44   *John*, b. June 5, 1748; went to Ashby, where he was deacon.
     45   *Benjamin*, b. Sept. 13, 1750; d. June 9, 1753.

19-34-   BENJAMIN LAWRENCE m. Feb. 12, 1735, Jane Russell, b. July 19, 1711, dau. of Jonathan and Elizabeth. He was ad. to the ch. June 29, 1735, she being a member before. They were dismissed in 1737 to the church in Westborough, and from that church to Boston.

19-35-   AMOS LAWRENCE, who was bap. in Lex. Feb. 19, 1716, m. Nov. 17, 1749, Abigail Abbott, b. Jan. 25, 1721, dau. of Nehemiah and Sarah (Foster) Abbott of Lex. At what time he left Lex. is uncertain. He moved to Groton, where his children were born. He had four sons, *Amos, Nehemiah, Samuel,* and *Asa,* born between 1750 and 1757. *Samuel,* his third son, became quite distinguished. He m. 1777 Susanna Parker of Groton. He was a dea. of the church, justice of the peace, and filled other important offices. He was one of those who rallied at Concord to oppose the progress of the British troops. He was one of the founders of the academy in Groton, which now bears his name. He was highly esteemed by his townsmen, and respected by all who knew him. He had six sons, five of whom lived to grow up, and became very distinguished. *Luther,* b. 1778; *William,* b. 1783; *Amos,* b. 1785; *Abbott,* b. 1792; *Samuel,* b. 1801. The first of these was a lawyer, and mayor of Lowell, the other four were merchants in Boston, well known and respected in the community. Abbott represented the country, as Minister Plenipotentiary, at the Court of St. James.

32-40-   BEZALEEL LAWRENCE m. Oct. 19, 1758, Sarah Muzzy, dau. of Amos and Esther (Green) Muzzy, b. March 30, 1737. He was ad. to the ch. March 26, 1758. He d. Feb. 6, 1796, and she d. Feb. 4, 1819, aged 80.

40-46 | *Sarah*, b. Sept. 3, 1759; m. Nov. 15, 1781, John Smith of Lex.
47 | *Anna*, b. May 17, 1761; d. April 4, 1845, aged 84.
48 | *Bezaleel*, b. April 12, 1763. He went to Leominster, where he became one of their prominent citizens.
49 | *Esther*, b. June 30, 1765; m. Oct. 7, 1784, John Hastings.
50 | *Bethia*, b. Sept. 25, 1767; d. April 19, 1801, aged 34.
51 | †*Jonas*, b. Feb. 27, 1770; d. Jan. 8, 1835, aged 65.
52 | †*Jonathan*, b. Sept. 11, 1774; d. 1840.

40-51- | JONAS LAWRENCE m. 1789, Dorcas Wood of Woburn.

51-53 | *Dorcas*, b. Oct. 29, 1790.   54 *Edmund*, b. Dec. 7, 1794.
55 | *Jonas*, b. Feb. 4, 1796.   56 *Lurena*, b. July 19, 1798.
57 | *Lucy*, b. Jan. 12, 1801.   58 *John*, b. June 17, 1803.
59 | *Emeline*, b. Dec. 7, 1805.   60 *Joseph B. V.*, b. Aug. 31, 1807.

40-52- | JONATHAN LAWRENCE m. April 12, 1798, Polly Reed of Bedford.

52-61 | *Polly*, b. April 28, 1799.   62 *Esther*, b. April 23, 1801.
63 | *Abigail*, b. Nov. 8, 1803; d. Dec. 23, 1826.
64 | *Elizabeth Swain*, b. Sept. 10, 1807.

There has been another family of Lawrences in town more recently, which originated from Wat., but it is thought by those well informed, that there was no relationship between them. *John* Lawrence and *George* Lawrence were both early settlers in Wat. Bond, in his genealogies of Watertown, says, "The will of John Lawrence furnishes no reason for supposing that he and George were nearly related. All the families of this name in Wat., Walt., and Weston, after the removal of John and his family to Groton, appear to be descendants from George.

The preceding families descended from John, and the following families from George.

GEORGE LAWRENCE, of Wat., was b. 1637; m. Sept. 29, 1657, Elizabeth Crispe, who d. 1681; and he m. 1691, Elizabeth Holland. He had fourteen children: *George*, his third son, b. June 4, 1668, m. Mary, and had eight children. *John*, the second son of George, was b. Feb. 20, 1704, and d. 1770. He r. in what is now Walt., and m. Jan. 24, 1734, Mary Hammond. His youngest son, *Phinehas*, b. Feb. 19, 1749, m. Nov. 5, 1770, Elizabeth Stearns. He was a deacon and selectman, 1781-1786. He had eleven children,

1 | PHINEHAS LAWRENCE, the oldest son of the preceding Phinehas, was b. Feb. 19, 1775, and m. Dec. 22, 1796, Polly Wellington, dau. of William Wellington. He resided in Walt. about four years after his marriage, when he settled in Lex., 1800. He d. June 9, 1864, aged 89, and she d. June 9, 1847.

1- 2 | †*Isaac W.*, b. in Walt. Jan. 30, 1797; m. Sept. 11, 1822, Mary Parker; he d. 1843.
3 | *Louisa*, b. in Walt. Sept. 10, 1798; m. Oct. 23, 1821, Marshall Brown; r. in Western.
4 | *Maria*, b. in Lex. April 3, 1800; m. April 23, 1822, Joshua S. Smith. She is still living.
5 | *Adeline*, b. Dec. 19, 1801; m. Nov. 21, 1822, Thomas Barnes, Walt.
6 | †*William H.*, b. Nov. 28, 1803; m. May 9, 1835, Eliza Eaton.
7 | *Sybil*, b. Sept. 4, 1805; m. Dec. 24, 1824, —— Bass of Peterborough, N. H. They had two chil. b. in Lex.; *Almira*, who m. Prescott Bennett; and *Addison*, who m. Hannah Hopping.

73

8 | ‡*Sydney*, b. Dec. 24, 1806; m. Ap. 9, 1829, Anna Maynard of Walt.
9 | *Charles*, b. Sept. 30, 1808; d. 1811.
10 | ‡*Phinehas*, b. Sept. 4, 1810; m. July 3, 1831, Catharine Pierce.
11 | *Charles*, b. June 21, 1812; drowned June 17, 1832. He was the first buried in the new cemetery in Lexington.
12 | *Franklin*, b. June 17, 1814; d. Sept. 2, 1817, unm.
13 | *Mary W.*, b. April 13, 1816; m. April 28, 1842, Willard Evans; she d. 1848.
14 | *Leonard*, b. Feb. 25, 1820; m. April 19, 1845, Elizabeth Lord of Portsmouth, N. H.; r. in Providence.

1-2- | ISAAC W. LAWRENCE m. Sept. 11, 1822, Mary Parker, dau. of Robert Parker. He d. Nov. 18, 1843. His widow is still living.

2-15 | *Albert*, b. ——.
16 | *Henry L.*, b. ——; r. in Arlington.
17 | *Parker*, b. ——; r. in Boston.
18 | *Theodore*, b. ——; r. in Boston.

1-6- | WILLIAM H. LAWRENCE m. May 9, 1835, Eliza Eaton.

6-19 | *Ann Eliza*, b. ——; m. —— Comee; r. in Boston.
20 | *Charles H.*, b. ——; m. in Boston, where he resides.
21 | *George Bancroft*, b. ——; r. in St. Louis.
22 | *Abbott*, b. ——; r. in Boston.
23 | *Wesley*, b. ——; r. in Boston.

1-8- | SYDNEY LAWRENCE m. April 9, 1829, Anna Maynard of Walt., dau. of Antipast Maynard, b. Oct. 27, 1809.

8-24 | *Julian*, b. June 1, 1830; m. Sydney Butterfield.
25 | *Charles*, b. Aug. 6, 1832; m. Georgiana Robinson; r. in E. Camb.
26 | *William Webster*, b. Sept. 15, 1834; m. Judith C. Smith; r. in East Cambridge.
27 | *Waldo E.*, b. Dec. 15, 1836; r. in Boston.
28 | *Francis M.*, b. Jan. 15, 1838; m. Mrs. Mary Thayer of Camb.; r. there.
29 | *George H.*, b. Feb. 28, 1841; m. Oct. 1865, Mary Marsh of Belmont, and r. in Boston.
30 | *Almira A.*, b. Sept 28, 1843; d. Oct. 1, 1865.
31 | *Bernard W.*, b. June 15, 1846; r. in Boston.
32 | *Sydney M.*, b. June 12, 1853.

1-10- | PHINEHAS LAWRENCE m. Catharine Pierce, dau. of Loring Pierce.

10-33 | *Leander*, b. ——; killed in the late war.
34 | *William W.*, b. ——; r. in Providence.
35 | *Sophia*, b. ——; m. Maxwell Reed; r. in Providence.

THE LIVERMORE FAMILY.

Though the name of Livermore rarely appears upon our records, the fact that Leonard J. Livermore was one of our clergymen for nine years, will justify the following notice of the family.

JOHN LIVERMORE came to New England, 1634, when 28 years of age, and settled in Wat. 1642. He was ad. freeman 1635. He was frequently elected selectman in Wat. By his wife Grace he had nine children. *Samuel*, one of his sons, was ad. freeman, 1671. He m.

Anna Bridge, and d. Dec. 5, 1690. She d. Aug. 28, 1727, aged 81. They had twelve children. *Jonathan*, their sixth child, b. April 19, 1678; m. Nov. 23, 1699, Rebecca Barnes. He d. Nov. 8, 1705, and she d. Dec. 9, 1765, aged 85. They had four children. *Jonathan*, their oldest child, b. Aug. 16, 1700; m. June 23, 1723, Abigail Ball. About two years after their marriage they moved to Northboro', of which he was the first town clerk. His wife dying, he m. Nov. 16, 1775, Jane Dunlap. He lived to the remarkable age of one hundred years and seven months. He had eleven children by his first wife. *Jonathan*, their fifth child, b. Dec. 7, 1729, grad. at H. C. 1760. He was settled as a clergyman in Wilton, N. H. He m. Sept. 14, 1769, Elizabeth Kidder, who d. his widow, Dec. 12, 1822. He d. July 30, 1809, aged 80. They had ten children.

1   SOLOMON K. LIVERMORE, the fifth child of Rev. Jonathan, was b. March 2, 1779; grad at H. C. 1802, studied law and settled in Milford, N. H. He m. July 6, 1810, Abigail A. Jarvis of Camb. He repeatedly represented the town in the Legislature.

1- 2   *Leonard Jarvis*, b April 15, 1811; d. Nov. 28, 1822.
3   *Henry Lee*, b. Aug. 3, 1812; was a merchant in Baltimore.
4   *Thomas A.*, b. Feb. 7, 1814; a surgeon dentist at Galena, Ill.
5   *Elizabeth*, b. Dec. 12, 1815; d. June, 1817.
6   *Elizabeth A.*, b. March 28, 1818.
7   *Rebecca P. J.*, b. Dec. 31, 1819; m. Aug. 24, 1841, Joseph C. Manning of Baltimore.
8   ‡*Leonard Jarvis*, b. Dec. 8, 1822; grad at H. C. 1842.
9   *Mary*, b. Sept. 18, 1825.

1-8-   LEONARD J. LIVERMORE m. March 18, 1847, Mary Anne C. Perkins, dau. of Aaron Perkins. He was installed at Lex. Oct. 4, 1857; left the Society, Nov., 1866; r. in Cambridge.

8-10   *Allena M.*, b. April 1, 1848, at East Boston.
11   *Clara P.*, b. May 27, 1851, at Groton.
12   *Joseph P.*, b. Feb. 19, 1855, at Clinton.
13   *Henry Jarvis*, b. May 27, 1865, at Lexington.

THE LOCKE FAMILY.

The Lockes have been a numerous family in Lex. from its early settlement. In 1634, among others

1   WILLIAM LOCKE, a lad only six years of age, came to this country with his relative Nicholas Davis, in the ship Planter, Nicholas Trarice, master. They came to Woburn, then a part of Charlestown. William Locke was b. at Stepney Parish, London, Eng , Dec. 13, 1628; m. Dec. 27, 1655, Mary Clarke of Wo., dau. of William and Margery. She was b. at Wat., Dec. 20, 1640, and d. at Wo. July 18, 1715, aged 74 years and 7 months. He d. June 16, 1720, aged 91 years and 6 months. He was a large land holder in different parts of Wo. and several lots bounding upon Camb. (now Lex.) line. He was a dea. of the ch.

1- 2   *William*, b. Dec. 27, 1657; d. Jan. 9, 1658.
3   ‡*William*, b. Jan. 18, 1659; m. Sarah Whitmore and Abigail Haywood.
4   ‡*John*, b. Aug. 1, 1661; m. Elizabeth Plympton and Mary Wyman.
5   ‡*Joseph*, b. March 8, 1664; had three wives.
6   *Mary*, b. Oct. 16, 1666; m. March 30, 1692, Samuel Kendall.

7 †*Samuel*, b. Oct. 14, 1669; had two wives.
8 †*Ebenezer*, b. Jan. 8, 1674; was twice married.
9 *James*, b. Nov. 14, 1677; m. Dec. 5, 1700, Sarah Cutter.
10 *Elizabeth*, b. Jan. 4, 1681; m. Oct. 14, 1700, James Markham.

1-3-   WILLIAM LOCKE, JR. m. May 29, 1683, Sarah Whitmore, dau.
of Francis and Isabel (Park) Whitmore of Camb. She d. and he
m. June 8, 1698, Elizabeth ———. He d. July 8, 1738, aged 79;
she d. 1748 or 49. He was chosen deacon 1709, was selectman in
1704 and 1732. He resided in that part of Wo. which was afterward
Burlington. After his decease, on petition of Thomas Locke, his
grandson, a part of this estate, including the house, was set to Lex.
This was the house on Lowell street, known as the Hammond Locke
place.

3-11 †*William*, b. June 28, 1684; was twice married.
12 *Francis*, b. July 25, 1690;   "   "   "
13 *Daniel*, b. July 9, 1693;   "   "   "
14 †*Ebenezer*, b. ———; by second wife, Elizabeth.
15 *Abigail*, b. June 22, 1710; m. Oct. 3, 1728, Jonas Merriam.
    These children were born in Woburn, but now Lexington.

1-4-   JOHN LOCKE m. May 31, 1683, Elizabeth Plympton, dau. of
Thomas and Abigail Plympton of Sudbury, who was an emigrant
from England, and was killed by the Indians at Sudbury, April 18,
1676. She d. Feb. 23, 1720, and he m. Nov. 30, 1720, widow Mary
Wyman, who was dau. of Increase Winn of Wo., who was the first
white child b. in that town. He lived in Wo. but probably d. at
Lancaster, about 1756. They had seven children.

1-5-   JOSEPH LOCKE m. Mary ———, who d. April, 1707, and he m.
Margaret Mead, dau. of Israel Mead. He resided in that part of
Camb. which is now Lex. His farm probably joined his brother William's. In 1695, his father gave him twenty acres at a place called
"Cambridge ffarmes," containing a mansion house and barn, and
"out-housing, orchard, fields, &c., bounded S. E. by Capt. Cook's
farm, W. by Joseph Simonds; also four acres at 'Bull Meadow,'
bounded by Cambridge line S. W."

5-16 *Mary*, b. ———; m. George Traluddia, (?) July 15, 1727.
17 *Abigail*, b. ———; m. Jan. 8, 1720, Thomas Fessenden.
18 *Lydia*, b. ———.
19 *Sarah*, b. July 14, 1696; m. June 10, 1718, Samuel Snow.
20 †*Joseph*, b. March 19, 1699; m. Sarah ———.
21 *Elizabeth*, b. March 15, 1703; m. Aug. 13, 1725, John Seatto. (?)
22 *Huldah*, b. March 28, 1705; m. May 28, 1743, Timothy Reed.
23 *Margaret*, b. May 6, 1710; m. Nov. 5, 1730, John Russell.
24 *Joanna*, b. Feb. 2, 1713; m. Jan. 3, 1734, Jonas Munroe.
25 *Ruth*, b. May 9, 1715.
26 †*Stephen*, b. Jan. 26, 1718; m. Mehitabel Raymond.

1-7-   SAMUEL LOCKE m. Ruth ———. She was a member of the ch.
in Lex. before 1698, and d. Dec. 14, 1714. He m. Mary Day of
Ipswich. He possessed a large landed property, and resided about
half a mile from Lex. Common on the county road to Bed. He had
but one child, *Samuel*, b. July 5, 1718. He lived on his father's
place, before spoken of, and d. there unm. His father left him a
large property in real and personal estate, including several slaves;
this property he contrived to spend, and d. poor, about 1800. This
branch of the Locke family became extinct.

1-8-   EBENEZER LOCKE m. Oct. 18, 1697, Susannah Walker of Wo.
She d. June 13, 1799, and he m. Oct. 14, 1701. Hannah Mead, dau.
of David and Hannah of Camb. He d. Dec. 24, 1723, aged 49; she
d. July 24, 1739, aged 63. He resided on his father's homestead.

8-27   †*Ebenezer*, b. April 28, 1699; m. Mary Merriam.
28   *Samuel*, b. Aug. 24, 1702; m. March 2, 1730, Rebecca Richardson.
29   *Josiah*, b. March 15, 1705. He resided in Woburn.
30   *Joshua*, b. Aug. 21, 1709. He was twice m. and resided in Woburn,
     Southboro', and Westboro'.
31   *Nathan*, b. March 30, 1713; d. 1723.
32   *Hannah*, b. April 11, 1716; m. 1739, Asa Richardson.

3-11-   WILLIAM LOCKE m. Mary ———, who d. Feb. 21, 1711, aged 21;
he m. second, Jemima Russell, dau. of Philip Russell. He resided
in the second precinct of Wo. which was incorporated as Burlington,
1799; but that portion of his farm on which his house stood, was the
same year annexed to Lex. This is the place situated on Lowell
street, before spoken of. He owned the covenant at Lex. Sept. 9,
1716. He d. Jan. 20, 1767, aged 83, and she d. Nov. 16, 1782,
aged 90.

11-33   *A son*, b. and d. March 1, 1710.
34   *A dau.* b. ———; d. Feb. 21, 1711, mother d. same time.
35   *Mary*, b. Sept. 7, 1716; m. April, 1746, Joseph Perry.
36   *Jemima*, b. July 4, 1718; m. Oct. 28, 1736, Ebenezer Brooks.
37   †*William*, b. Feb. 2, 1721; m. 1747, Grace Newell.
38   †*Thomas*, b. Oct. 27, 1722; m. June 27, 1751, Rebecca Lawrence.
39   *Jonas*, b. Jan. 13, 1727; m. ——— Dwight.
40   *Joseph*, b. April 23, 1729; m. Mary Ayres.
41   *Ebenezer*, b. Nov. 3, 1732; was twice married.
42   *Joanna*, b. Feb. 27, 1735; m. Oct. 10, 1753, Phineas Blodgett.
43   *Abigail*, b. Feb. 5, 1737; m. Sept. 4, 1755, Jonathan Fiske.

3-14-   EBENEZER LOCKE m. Elizabeth ———. They owned the covenant in Lex. April 20, 1717. He probably resided in Wo. though
they attended meeting in Lex. where their children were baptized.

14-44   *Ebenezer*, bap. April 28, 1717; d. March 22, 1720.
45   *Elizabeth*, bap. June 19, 1720; m. 1747, Ebenezer Merriam.
46   *Sarah*, bap. Aug. 11, 1723; m. Oct. 11. 1744, Timothy Wyman.
47   *Hannah*, bap. June 13, 1725; m. 1746, Timothy Newton.
48   *Abigail*, bap. April 28, 1728.
49   *Phebe*, bap. March 7, 1731; m. Ebenezer Merriam, Jr.
50   *Ebenezer*, bap. March 2, 1735; m. Feb. 27, 1759, Lucy Wood.

5-20-   JOSEPH LOCKE m. Sarah ———, who d. May 28, 1777; he d.
Jan. 13, 1785, aged 86. He resided in Lex. on his father's homestead, in the west half of the house. He served in the French war,
1754.

20-51   †*Joseph*, b. March 28, 1734, m. May 7, 1761, Sarah Baldwin.
52   *Benjamin*, b. Oct. 10, 1735; d. of disease contracted in the French
     war, Nov. 12, 1755, aged 20.
53   *Nathan*, b. Dec. 2, 1737; d. May 19, 1761, aged 24.
54   †*Amos*, b. Dec. 24, 1742; m. Oct. 19, 1769, Sarah Locke.
55   *Sarah*, b. Aug. 23, 1746; m. Dec. 21, 1769, Jer. Harrington.
56   *Mary*, b. May 31, 1749; m. April 20, 1769, Isaac Blodgett, who d.
     July, 1830, aged 88.

5-26-   STEPHEN LOCKE m. Mehitabel Raymond, dau. of Jonathan of
            Lex. He d. April 22, 1772, aged 53, and his wid. d. Oct. 29, 1815,
            aged 94. They resided in Lex.

26-57   *Mehitabel*, b. Aug. 17, 1747. She was living in Lex. in 1773.
    58 †*Reuben*, b. March 16, 1749; m. Jerusha Richardson.
    59 *Stephen*, b. March 29, 1750; m. 1780, Sally Hopkins; went to Deer-
            ing, N. H.
    60 *Elizabeth*, b. June 14, 1753; d. unm. 1816, aged 64.
    61 †*Benjamin*, b. May 7, 1756; m. Aug. 10, 1784, Betsey Wyman.

8-27-   EBENEZER LOCKE m. Mary Merriam, dau. of Thomas and Mary
            Merriam. In 1715, when he was sixteen years of age, " he of his
            own free will and accord put himself apprentice to Joseph Loring of
            Lex., house carpenter and joiner, to learn his art, trade, or mystery
            after the manner of an apprentice." At the close of the indentures
            is this memorandum: " It is to be understood yᵗ yᵉ said apprentice
            is bound to Lydia Loring, yᵉ now wife of yᵉ above said Joseph
            Loring, and she to him in all things to be performed what is above
            written." He had land in Townsend and Ashby. He moved first to
            Hopkinton, where he had three children bap., and from thence to
            Oxford about 1738.

11-37-   WILLIAM LOCKE m. 1747, Grace Newell of Camb. They resided
            in Lex., and perhaps for a short time in Wo. and Walt. He was a
            soldier of the Revolution; was in the battles of Ticonderoga and
            White Plains, and d. in the army in 1776, aged 56. His wid. at one
            time resided at Walt., but at a later period with her son Jonas at
            Lex., where she d. Dec. 31, 1790, aged 63. She was buried in the
            grave-yard at East Lexington.

37-62   *Mary*, bap. at Lex. June 12, 1748; d. young.
    63 *William*, b. ———; d. young.
    64 *William*, b. ———; was a soldier in the Revolution for several
            years; was like his father in the battles of Ticonderoga and White
            Plains, and at other places, and d. in the army after 1779, unm.
    65 *Edmund*, b. ———; was in the army of the Revolution nearly all
            through the war, and d. at Lex. of disease contracted in the army,
            May 16, 1786, unm.
    66 *Jemima*, b. ———; d. Sept. 6, 1781, unm.
    67 *Mary*, b. Aug. 1759; d. unm. 1848, aged 89.
    68 *Nathan*, b. March 2, 1762; m. June 21, 1785, Anna Bond.
    69 †*Jonas*, b. ———. He was three times married.
    70 *Joshua*, b. Aug. 1769. He was living at Walt., unm., 1852.

11-38-   THOMAS LOCKE m. June 27, 1751, Rebecca Lawrence, dau. of
            John of Wo. He d. Feb. 21, 1792, aged 70, and his wid. m. Jan.
            13, 1795, Noah Eaton, and d. March 14, 1814, aged 86. He was a
            carpenter, and resided on the old homestead, which was set to Lex.
            He was in the army of the Revolution.

38-71   †*Thomas*, b. Aug. 29, 1756; m. Nov. 5, 1778, Lydia Reed.

20-51-   JOSEPH LOCKE m. May 7, 1761, Sarah Baldwin of Billerica, who
            d. Feb. 19, 1824, aged 84. He d. April 27, 1791, aged 57. He
            resided in Lex. He was in the French and Indian war in 1756 and
            1760; was a sergeant in the last year.

51-72   *Nathan*, b. Dec. 7, 1761; m. 1784, Mary Howard. She d. 1797;
            he d. 1800.

73 †*Asa Baldwin*, b. Mar. 3, 1764; m. Mary Wellington, Dec. 31, 1789.
74 *Sarah*, b. May 27, 1766; m. May 12, 1789, Josiah Mead.
75 *Joseph*, b. ———; m. first, Martha Ingersoll, and second, widow Mary Foster.
76 *Edwin*, b. Sept. 13, 1771; m. Sept. 10, 1794, Matilda Trask.

20-54-   AMOS LOCKE m. 1769, Sarah Locke. She was an orphan, whose true name is now lost, who was adopted and brought up by Thomas Locke, whose name she took. He d. July 27, 1828, aged 87; she d. July 1835, aged 84. He resided in the north part of Lex., on the farm now owned by William Locke, on North street. He was one of Capt. Parker's company, and met the British on the Common on the 19th of April, 1775,— for which he was prepared by service in the French war in 1762.

54-77 †*Benjamin A.*, b. Dec. 31, 1769; he was twice married.
78 †*Stephen*, b. March 23, 1778; m. April 11, 1804, Betsey Nichols.
79 *James*, b. Dec. 22, 1785; m. Feb. 26, 1811, Lucy Nichols.
80 *Amos*, b. ———; m. March 27, 1805, Joanna Greenleaf.

26-58-   REUBEN LOCKE m. Jerusha Richardson, dau. of Reuben, who m. Esther Wyman. He d. Jan. 28, 1823, aged 74, and his wid. d. Nov. 15, 1833, aged 88. He was a soldier in the Revolutionary war, and was taken prisoner, and was confined in the prison at Forton, Eng. His farm was a part of that now owned by William Locke, on North street.

58-81 *Jerusha*, b. Jan. 16, 1774; m. David Simonds, July 23, 1795.
82 *Mehitabel*, b. March 27, 1775; d. unm. Oct. 2, 1841, aged 66.
83 *Lydia*, b. March 23, 1777; d. unm.
84 *Betsey*, b. Sept. 1, 1780; m. Jan. 25, 1798, James Wyman, Jr.
85 *Reuben*, b. Jan. 15, 1782; m. Feb. 2, 1804, Polly Wiley.
86 †*Loa*, b. June 5, 1783; m. March 15, 1805, Mary Foster.
87 †*Charles*, b. June 16, 1786; m. Abigail Nichols, Dec. 8, 1812.
88 *Stephen*, b. Sept. 27, 1791; m. Sukey Wiley; resided in Reading.

20-61-   BENJAMIN LOCKE m. Aug. 10, 1784, Betsey Wyman, dau of Reuben of Wo. He resided at Burlington and Lex. most of his life; afterward in Boston, where he d. June 4, 1842, aged 85. His wife d. in Lex. Oct. 1, 1831, aged 70. He was one of the heroes who encountered the British on the 19th of April, 1775. He was also in the detachment which marched to Camb. May 6, 1775, and likewise on the 17th of June of that year.

61-89 *Betsey*, b. Feb. 10, 1785; m. 1805, Timothy Tileston, Jr.
90 *Benjamin*, b. March 19, 1787; d. young.
91 *Ruth*, b. June 6, 1790; m. June 6, 1811, Harvey Tileston.
92 *Lucy*, b. Sept. 17, 1792; d. young.
93 *Benjamin*, b. May 17, 1795; m. Oct. 9, 1823, Susan Tileston.
94 *Lucy*, b. Aug. 3, 1797; m. James Wallis of Camb.
95 *Levi*, b. Dec. 1, 1798; m. Dec. 1, 1829, Susan Simonds.
96 *Luseba*, b. Jan. 26, 1802; m. Aug. 5, 1824, Lambert Maynard.

37-69-   JONAS LOCKE m. Dec. 21, 1781, Sarah Russell, dau. of Philip and Lydia (Dodge) Russell. She d. and he m. second, Nov. 2, 1800, Eunice Winship. She d. Sept. 29, 1825, aged 68, and he m. third, wid. Deborah Blodgett, Feb. 28, 1828. He resided in Lex., where he d. Aug. 23, 1833, aged 71. Like his father and his brothers, he was a patriot and soldier of the Revolution; he served about four years.

69- 97 | *Jonas*, bap. April 28, 1782; m. Sept. 26, 1807, Abigail White of Westminster.
98 | *William*, bap. May 25, 1783; m. Mary Welch of Boston; r. in Newton.
99 | *Sally*, bap. April 9, 1786; m. March 8, 1808, Eli Whitney. She d. 1847.
100 | *Lydia*, bap. June 3, 1792; m. May 29, 1817, Emory Whitney. They resided first at Wat. then at Le Roy, N. Y.
101 | *Martin*, bap. Aug. 1, 1799.
102 | *Edmund*, b. ———; d. unm., aged about 21.

38-71- | THOMAS LOCKE m. Nov. 5, 1778, Lydia Reed, dau. of Hammond Reed. She was b. July 14, 1760, and d. Sept. 7, 1825, aged 65; and he d. April 20, 1819, aged 63. They resided on the old Locke Place, which was set to Lex. from Burlington.

71-103 | *Lydia*, b. March 8, 1779; m. Timothy Temple; lived in Providence.
104 | *Lucy*, b. March 4, 1781; m. Amos Hills of Hudson, N. H.
105 | *Rebecca*, b. March 25, 1784; m. Oct. 1, 1820, Thaddeus Munroe.
106 | *Thomas*, b. Nov. 5, 1786; m. April 27, 1813, Lucy Rhodes. He d. Nov. 2, 1829, aged 43. She is living.
107 | †*Hammond*, b. July 13, 1790; m. Jan. 27, 1814, Rebecca Nevers.
108 | *Sally*, b. May 21, 1792; m. 1820, Abel Fitz.
109 | *Nancy*, b. Aug. 20, 1794; m. April 8, 1827, John Winning.
110 | *Harriet*, b. May 10, 1800; d. April 6, 1809.

51-73- | ASA BALDWIN LOCKE m. Mary Wellington, Dec. 31, 1789. He d. Nov. 25, 1821, aged 57, and his wid. m. Abijah Harrington, Dec. 14, 1823.

73-111 | *Oliver*, b. April 25, 1790; m. April 1, 1816, Joanna Jacobs. He was a captain in the militia, and was killed Oct. 1825, by the accidental discharge of a gun in the hands of an intimate friend. His wid. m. Nov. 28, 1832, William Smith. Capt. Locke had *Faustina Mulliken*, b. Aug. 24, 1819, m. Dec. 3, 1846, David A. Gage, and d. Dec. 4, 1850; and *Joan Sophia*, b. Oct. 3, 1825, m. June 16, 1852, Eli F. Davis.
112 | *Nathan*, b. Aug. 1792; d. 1806.
113 | *Darius*, b. Dec. 1, 1793; d. 1808.
114 | *Mary*, b. ———; m. Feb. 21, 1822, William Burgess.
115 | *Baldwin*, b. Jan. 10, 1805; m. Adeline Josline, Nov. 18, 1830. He had six children; *Oliver B.*, b. Sept. 17, 1831, *William B.*, b. Aug. 13, 1833, *Lorenzo*, b. Sept. 2, 1835, *Samuel J.*, b. Aug. 25, 1837, *Martha W.*, b. April 19, 1839, *Mary*, b. Oct. 21, 1841.
116 | *Abigail*, b. Nov. 15, 1806; m. July 30, 1837.

54-77- | BENJAMIN AMOS LOCKE m. Betsey Lawrence 1808. She d. March 16, 1822, and he m. June 23, 1823, Sally Marrett. He r. in Lex., on School street. He d. Oct. 19, 1829, aged 61. She d. Sept. 4, 1863.

77-117 | *Sarah Elizabeth*, b. Feb. 3, 1824; m. Jan. 1, 1849, Jeduthan Richardson.
118 | *Benjamin F.*, b. July 3, 1825; m. Oct. 31, 1849, Anne E. Hill. He has several children.
119 | *Albert A.*, b. Aug. 8, 1828. He left Lex. a few years since, and is in South America.

51-78- | STEPHEN LOCKE m. April 11, 1804, Betsey Nichols, dau. of Capt. Noah Nichols of Cohasset. He d. May 10, 1839, aged 61.

78–120 | †*William*, b. Sept. 2, 1805; m. Nov. 5, 1838, Harriet Locke.
121 | *Stephen*, b. Feb. 18, 1807; m. 1832, Priscilla Wellington. He d. 1861.
122 | *Nichols*, b. March 20, 1810; m. Jan. 5, 1838, Bloomy Davis.
123 | †*Amos*, b. Sept. 30, 1813; m. May 31, 1834, Rhoda Blodgett.
124 | *Elizabeth*, b. Feb. 15, 1823; d. Oct. 18, 1826.

54–79– | JAMES LOCKE m. Feb. 26, 1811, Lucy Nichols, dau. of Adna Nichols of Lex. He d. April, 1848. He resided on Grove street, near the Ebenezer Simonds place.

79–125 | *Sally*, b. April 29, 1811; m. Thomas C. Gould, Nov. 8, 1832.
126 | *James Adna*, b. Sept. 18, 1814; d. April 5, 1817.
127 | *James Adna*, b. March 14, 1819; m. Harriet Stearns, dau. of Amos Stearns; resides at Charlestown.
128 | *Benjamin*, b. Dec. 7, 1821; m. March 11, 1856, Mary H. Skilton, dau. of Horace and Fanny (Harrington) Skilton. He resides in Charlestown.

58–86– | LOA LOCKE m. March 15, 1805, Mary Foster, who was b. Oct. 3, 1784. He d. Dec. 4, 1865, aged 82; she d. Jan. 21, 1851, aged 66.

86–129 | *Loa*, b. Oct. 12, 1805; resides at the South.
130 | *Romanus*, b. Jan. 4, 1807; d. 1833, aged 26.
131 | *George*, b. April 21, 1811; m. Abby Smith Casey.
132 | *Lydia*, b. Dec. 26, 1813; m. Aug. 2, 1738, Ebenezer B. Tuck. They resided and d. in Croyden, N. H.
133 | *Stephen*, b. Oct. 24, 1816; m. Eliz. J. Casey. and r. in Saxonville.
134 | *Mary Ann*, b. Feb. 15, 1819; m. Oct. 1, 1843, Ebenezer Lakeman. He r. in Charlestown, and has several children; the first, Lydia S., was b. in Lex. Aug. 11, 1844.

58–87– | CHARLES LOCKE m. Dec. 8, 1812, Abigail Nichols of Cohasset, who was b. Dec. 15, 1791. They reside in the northerly part of Lex.; he was a deacon of the Baptist Church.

87–135 | *Charles Burrell*, b. Dec. 2, 1813; m. July 25, 1835, Lucy A. Crosby, resided in Boston, and d. about 1863.
136 | *Lewis*, b. Nov. 21, 1815; was twice m.; went to California, where he d. Aug. 23, 1864.
137 | *Abigail*, b. April 22, 1817; m. Aug. 22, 1839, William M. Roberts. They reside at Weston.
138 | *Elmira*, b. Feb. 27, 1819; d. April 27, 1828.
139 | *Elizabeth N.*, b. Nov. 15, 1828.

71–107– | HAMMOND LOCKE m. Jan. 27, 1814, Rebecca Nevers, dau. of Samuel and Ann Nevers of Bur. He resided on the farm of his ancestors in Lex. He was drowned July 15, 1843, aged 53.

107–140 | *A Daughter*, b. March 5, 1815; d. same day.
141 | *Harriet*, b. Jan. 22, 1817; m. Nov. 5, 1838, William Locke.
142 | *Marshall H.*, b. Feb. 14, 1819; d. Feb. 7, 1822.
143 | *Marshall H.*, b. Feb. 12, 1822; m. Dec. 27, 1848, Lucy A. Wyman. He has moved to Somerville.
144 | *Augusta B.*, b. March 14, 1824; m. Feb. 4, 1845, William Duren.
145 | *Adeline*, b. June 14, 1826; m. Henry Mulliken.
146 | *Theodore Lyman*, b. Feb. 22, 1829; was killed at Charlestown, April 16, 1851, while riding in his wagon, by the falling of the steeple of the Bunker Hill Baptist church, in a violent gale.

78-120- WILLIAM LOCKE m. Nov. 5, 1838, Harriet, dau. of Hammond Locke. He resides in Lex., on the farm of the first Joseph Locke.

120-147 *Emily*, b. May 3, 1841.   148 *Jane*, b. May, 1844.
149 *Austin W.*, b. June 8, 1852.

78-123- AMOS LOCKE m. May 31, 1834, Rhoda Blodgett, dau. of James, b. May 6, 1813.

123-150 *Elizabeth Augusta*, b. Aug. 16, 1835; m. Sept. 28, 1857, George F. Marvin.
151 *William Henry*, b. June 17, 1838; m. June 8, 1864, Helen F. Elliott.
152 *Warren Edgar*, b. May 28, 1841; m. June 30, 1862, Eliza C. Dawes.
153 *Henrietta M.*, b. Aug. 27, 1842.   154 *Gardner H.*, b. Nov. 10, 1851.

There was another family of Lockes in Lex.; *Micajah*, son of Josiah of Wo., b. Dec. 4, 1786, m. Sept. 20, 1812, Almira Russell. He resided in the East Village, and d. Dec. 23, 1842; they had eight children; *Josiah*, b. April 4, 1813, m. Sept. 20, 1841, Sarah Cotton; *Almira R.*, b. June 8, 1815, m. Jeremiah Evans, and —— Gould; *Frances Ann*, b. May 25, 1817, m. April 6, 1839, Loring Cummings; *Mary R.*, b. Jan. 31, 1819, m. Edward Divols; *Jonathan*, b. Nov. 20, 1820; *Eliza S.*, b. Nov. 10, 1822, m. Dec. 5, 1845, Otis Locke; *Rebecca A.*, b. Oct. 13, 1824; *Amos R.*, b. Oct. 8, 1826; *Susan A.*, b. April 8, 1829; *Matilda L.*, b. Aug. 21, 1831; *William M.*, b. Oct. 27, 1833; *George W.*, b. Aug. 21, 1836. This family must generally have left town.

THE LORING FAMILY.

Dea. Thomas Loring and his wife Jane (Newton), came to this country 1635, and settled in Hingham. They were from Axminster, Devonshire, Eng. His son John, b. in Eng. Dec. 22, 1630, m. 1657, Mary Baker of Hing., by whom he had several children. *Joseph*, his second son, was b. March 10, 1660. His descendants I give below, so far as they relate to Lex.

1 JOSEPH LORING of Hingham m. Oct. 25, 1683, Hannah Leavitt. He d. Feb. 19, 1692, and she m. Aug. 25, 1693, Joseph Estabrook, then of Hingham, but afterwards of Lex., where he became a very prominent man. He d. Sept. 23, 1733, and she d. Oct. 25, 1728.

1- 2 †*Joseph*, b. Sept. 29, 1684. He settled in Lexington.
3 *Nehemiah*, b. June 27, 1686.
4 *Joshua*, b. Sept. 21, 1688. He came to Lex. with his brother Joseph, was ad. to the ch. in 1708, and dismissed to the First Church in Boston, June 8, 1712.
5 *Submit*, b. Aug. 11, 1691; d. Jan. 8, 1740, unm. Mr. Hancock, in his church record, under date of Jan. 4, 1740, makes this entry: "*Submit Loring* I baptized after meeting at Mr. Loring's house, and this is the first I ever baptized in private. She was very sick."

1-2- JOSEPH LORING m. Lydia Fiske, dau. of David Fiske of Camb. Farms, b. May 17, 1685. He probably came to Lex. from Hingham about 1706. He bought ninety acres of land in Camb. Farms, in 1706, of John Poulter. The deed designates Joseph Loring as "of Hingham." In 1711, he was one of the subscribers for the purchase of the Common. He and his wife Lydia were ad. to the ch. July 4, 1708; and of course they were m. before that time. He was chosen one of the deacons in 1743, and d. July 4, 1746, aged 63. She d. Oct. 4, 1758. He was a valuable citizen; was constable in 1714, and town treasurer in 1725 and 1726.

2- 6 | *Lydia*, bap. June 21, 1711; m. June 11, 1731, John Mason.
7 | †*Joseph*, bap. Aug. 21, 1713; m. Kezia Gove.
8 | *Sarah*, bap. July 17, 1715; m. Dec. 2, 1736, Thaddeus Bowman.
9 | *John*, bap. Aug. 11, 1717; d. Dec. 13, 1717.
10 | *Hannah*, bap. Sept. 20, 1719; m. March 22, 1735, Samuel Winship.
11 | *Abigail*, } twins, bap. Jan. 7, 1722; }
12 | *Mary*, } } m. Jan. 30, 1760, Sam'l Allen.

2-7- JOSEPH LORING m. Jan. 1, 1736, Kezia Gove. He d. Sept. 13, 1787, aged 74, and she d. Sept. 16, 1789, aged 75. He was chosen dea. May 20, 1756, and held that office thirty-one years. He was often employed on important committees in the town. He resided on Main street, on the place opposite the Town Hall. His house was pillaged and destroyed by the British on the 19th of April, 1775. The account made out by Deacon Loring at the time, shows the amount of his suffering, and the wantonness of the enemy. He sets down his loss as follows:

A large mansion house and barn seventy feet long, and a corn barn, all burnt, £ 330 00
Household goods and furniture, viz., eight good feather beds and bedding; a large quantity of pewter and brass ware; three cases of drawers; two mahogany tables, with furniture for eight rooms, 230 00
All the wearing apparel of my family, consisting of nine persons, 60 00
All my husbandry tools and utensils, with a cider mill and press, with five tons of hay and two calves, 72 00
About two hundred rods of stone wall thrown down, 5 00
Specie, 3 00

£ 720 00

N. B. The above-mentioned buildings were the first that were destroyed in the town, and were near the ground where the brigade commanded by Lord Percy met the detachment retreating under Lt.-Col. Smith. It does not appear that any of the militia were in or near these buildings, neither could they in any way either oppose or retard the British troops in their operations; therefore the destruction must be considered as brutal, barbarous, and wanton.

JOSEPH LORING.

7-13 | *John*, b. June 28, 1742; m. June 8, 1765, Elizabeth Howe of Con.
14 | *Lydia*, b. Aug. 27, 1745; m. Nov. 26, 1776, Capt. Wm. Chambers, of N. H.
15 | †*Joseph*, b. Dec. 27, 1747; m. Nov. 26, 1772, Betsey Pollard of Bed.
16 | †*Jonathan*, b. Feb. 7, 1749; was twice m.
17 | *Sarah*, b. Feb. 27, 1755; m. Obadiah Johnson.

7-15- JOSEPH LORING m. Nov. 26, 1772, Betsey Pollard of Bed. They were ad. to the ch. Feb. 27, 1774. He was one of Capt. Parker's company, and also marched to Camb. on the memorable 17th of June, 1775. Subsequently he entered into the marine service with John Chandler, Jr., and being on the Southern coast, under Commodore Tucker, was included by Gen. Lincoln in the capitulation of Charleston, S. C. After remaining for some time a prisoner, during which he suffered severely, he was exchanged, and, amid destitution and comparative nakedness, was compelled to beg his way home to Lex., amid the taunts and sneers of the tories.

15-18 | *Betsey*, b. April 15, 1774; m. Abel Smith, moved to Jaffrey, N. H.
19 | *John Hancock*, b. Nov. 24, 1775; m. Polly Penny, and removed to Groton, where he settled.
20 | *Lydia*, b. Feb. 8, 1779; m. Peter Harrington.
21 | *Thomas*, b. Feb. 15, 1782; d. a young man.
22 | *Susy*, b. June 30, 1784; m. Nathan Munroe of Concord.
23 | *Joseph*, bap. April 12, 1792.

7-16- | JONATHAN LORING m. Rhoda ——. She d. Oct. 22, 1809, and he m. Feb. 13, 1812, Mrs. Hannah Danforth of Lex. He was a member of the gallant band commanded by Capt. Parker, and was upon the Common on the 19th of April. He was also with the detachment which marched to Camb. on the 6th of May, and also on the day of the battle on Bunker's Hill. He was also at Cambridge two months in the campaign of 1776. He not only performed his duty after the war had commenced, but he performed an important duty introductory to the affairs of the 19th of April. On the evening of the 18th, when it was known that certain British officers had gone up toward Concord, Jonathan Loring and two others volunteered to go up and watch their movements. He was taken prisoner and kept several hours, till on the return of these officers he was set at liberty near Lexington Common, about daylight in the morning. This family acted a conspicuous part on that memorable occasion. The church plate was kept at the house of Dea. Loring, and fearing that the British soldiers in their vandalism might destroy it, Lydia Loring, a sister of Jonathan, took the precaution to secrete it under some brush not far from the house, and so prevented it from being destroyed or carried off with the rest of the property of the family. He moved with his family to Mason, N. H.

16-24 | *Lucy*, bap. Oct. 8, 1786; m. Dec. 27, 1813, Levi Baxter.
25 | *Rhoda*, bap. Oct. 8, 1786.   26 *Polly*, bap. Nov. 22, 1789.
27 | *Joshua*, bap. Nov. 11, 1792.   28 *Thomas*, bap. Oct. 23, 1796.

MANN.—This name appears a few times on Lex. records. JAMES MANN m. Sept. 29, 1736, Mary Simonds. He was taxed in Lex. 1738, for both real and personal estate, and his name appears on the tax bill for a number of years. He was a soldier from Lex. in the French war, in 1759 and 1760. They had five children, viz., *Mary*, b. March 29, 1737, d. Nov. 4, 1738; *Benjamin*, bap. Nov. 4, 1739, probably went to Walt., where he had a family by his wife Martha; *Sarah*, b. Aug. 17, 1743; *Joanna*, b. April 12, 1747; *Mary*, b. 1749, d. Dec. 23, 1764.

THE MARRETT FAMILY.

The Marretts were early in the country, though they did not come to Lex. till about 1770.

1 | THOMAS MARRETT is supposed to have come to New England in 1635. He settled in Camb., where he was made a freeman in 1636. He was a dea. of the church. He m. Susan, in Eng., where *John*, the only child of whom we have any knowledge, was b. Thomas d. June 30, 1664.

1- 2| JOHN MARRETT came to this country with his father, and succeeded to his estate. He probably m. after he came to this country. His wife was Abigail Eddeson, b. in Cheshire, Eng. His will, dated 1696, mentions wife Abigail, sons Amos and Edward, and dau. Hannah and Mary. He also makes mention of Abigail Rice and Susan Amsden, two married daughters.

2- 3| *Thomas*, b. about 1655; he was killed by the Indians at Sudbury, April 20, 1675, unm.

4| *Amos*, b. 1657; m. Nov. 2, 1681, Bethia Langhorn. She d. Nov. 20, 1730, aged 70, and he m. second, Mrs. Ruth Dunster of Camb. He d. Nov. 17, 1739, aged 82, without issue. His will. dated April 12, 1735, and proved Dec. 16, 1739, mentions wife Ruth, *brother Edward*, and *sisters Abigail Crashburn and Mary Hovey*. He makes his nephew Amos the principal heir of his estate. He was dignified with the title of *Lieutenant*.

5| *Susan*, b. June 19, 1659; m. —— Amsden.

6| *John*, b. Jan. 29, 1661; d. Nov. 6, 1663.

7| *John*, b. June 3, 1664; d. at sea, unm.

8| *Abigail*, b. Aug. 6, 1666; m. first, —— Rice of Sudbury, and second, —— Crashburn.

9| *Hannah*, b. Aug. 17, 1668; m. Samuel Hastings of Cambridge.

10| ‡*Edward*, b. Aug. 2, 1670; m. Hannah Bradish.

11| *Mary*, b. March 7, 1672; m. Dec. 10, 1702, Joseph Hovey of Camb. He d., and she m. Nathaniel Parker of Newton.

12| *Lydia*, b. Feb. 22, 1674; d. young.

2-10-| EDWARD MARRETT m. Hannah Bradish of Camb. She d. April 9, 1754, in her 85th year, and he d. April 11, 1754, in his 84th year. Dying within two days of each other, they were buried the same day, in the same grave, and one monumental stone marks their resting place.

10-13| *Amos*, b. ——; d. aged about three years.

14| *John*, b. ——; d. in Boston of small pox, aged about 18.

15| *Susanna*, b. 1698; m. Sept. 27, 1722, John Pierce of Boston. They moved to Stow, where he d. and she m. Samuel Witt of Marlborough, a prominent citizen of that town, who represented them several years in the General Court. She d. in 1794, at the remarkable age of 96 years.

16| *Abigail*, b. 1700; m. June 13, 1724, Judah Monis, Hebrew Professor of Harvard College. She d. Oct. 27, 1760, aged 60. He was an Italian by birth. After the death of his wife, he left his professorship, went to Northborough, and lived with his brother-in-law, Rev. Mr. Martyn, where he d. His monumental stone bears an inscription so peculiar, that I will transcribe it, poetry and all.

Here lie buried the Remains of
Rabbi Judah Monis, A. M.
Late Hebrew Instructor
at Harvard College in Cambridge,
In which office he continued 40 years;
He was by birth and religion a Jew,
But he embraced the Christian faith
And was publicly baptized
At Cambridge, A. D. 1722,
And departed this life
April 25, 1764,
Aged eighty-one years, two months
and twenty-one days.

> A native branch of Jacob see,
> Which once from off its olive broke,
> Regrafted from the living tree,   Rom. 11 : 17, 24.
> Of the reviving sap partook.
>
> From teeming Zion's fertile womb,   Isai. 66 : 8.
> As dewy drops in early morn,   Psalm 110 : 3.
> Or rising bodies from the tomb,   John 5 : 28, 29.
> At once be Israel's nation born.   Isai. 66 : 8, 29.

17 †*Amos*, b. Sept. 5, 1703; m. Mary Dunster.

18 *Hannah*, b. ———; m. Joseph Lawrence of Camb. Afterwards moved to Connecticut.

19 *Edward*, b. ———; m. Mary Wyatt, by whom he had five children; one of them, Thomas, grad. H. C. 1761, and was a trader at Cape Ann. Edward m. as a second wife, Mrs. Susan Foster of Boston. He was a captain of a company in Camb. He d. Sept. 13, 1787.

20 *Mary*, b. ———; m. John Martyn of Boston. He was afterwards settled as a clergyman at Northborough.

10-17-   AMOS MARRETT m. Sept. 21, 1732, Mary Dunster, dau. of Henry Dunster of Camb. He d. Nov. 1747.

17-21 *Amos*, b. ———; d. in infancy.

22 *Abigail*, b. Aug. 25, 1733; d. young.

23 *Ruth*, b. April 30, 1735; d. in Newton, May 2, 1766, unm.

24 †*Amos*, b. Feb. 4, 1738; m. Abigail Tidd of Lex.

25 *Mary*, b. Aug. 20, 1740; d. 1754.

26 *John*, b. Sept. 10, 1741; grad. H. C. 1763. He studied divinity, and was settled over the second parish of Wo. (now Burlington), Dec. 21, 1774. He m. Martha Jones, dau. of Rev. Thomas Jones, his predecessor in the same parish. Mr. Marrett had but one child who lived to grow up, viz., Martha, b. Nov. 3, 1783. She m. Jan. 1, 1818, Rev. Samuel Sewall, who succeeded her father as pastor of the parish. Mr. Sewall is a son of the late Chief Justice Sewall, and is distinguished as an antiquary.

17-24-   AMOS MARRETT m. Dec. 14, 1760, Abigail Tidd, dau. of Daniel and Hepzibah (Reed) Tidd of Lex. He m. as of Cambridge, where he probably resided some five or six years after his marriage, when he moved to Lex. They were ad. to the Lex. ch., Sept. 15, 1771, from the First Church in Camb. He d. March 24, 1805, aged 66. He was a soldier in Capt. Parker's company in 1775, and was in the Jerseys three months the year following.

24-27 †*Amos*, b. in Camb. Oct. 4, 1763; m. Nov. 28, 1786, Patty Reed.

28 *Abigail*, b. in Camb. June 4, 1765; m. Oct. 6, 1788, Jonathan Smith.

29 †*Daniel*, b. in Camb. July 18, 1767; m. July 24, 1796, Mary Muzzy.

30 *Ruth*, b. Nov. 12, 1768.

31 *Betsey*, bap. Nov. 28, 1773; d. Nov. 3, 1797, aged 24.

32 *John*, bap. July 9, 1775; d. Dec. 17, 1797, aged 22.

33 *Thomas*, bap. July 20, 1777; d., a student in H. C., July 6, 1798.

24-27-   AMOS MARRETT m. Dec. 28, 1786, Patty Reed, dau. of Hammond and Betty (Simonds) Reed, b. Dec. 5, 1765. He d. Nov. 10, 1824, aged 61; she d. Oct 16, 1849, aged 85.

27-34 *Patty*, b. Sept. 9, 1787; m. Jonas Cutler. They moved to Westminster, where they had three children, who are now residing in that town. Jonas Cutler and his wife are both dead.

35 | *Sally.* b. Oct. 1, 1789; m. June 15, 1823, Benjamin Locke, Jr.
36 | *Hannah*, b. Dec. 24, 1792.
37 | *Nabby*, b. Aug. 18, 1795; d. April 6, 1854, unm., aged 58.
38 | *Betsey*, b. July 4, 1798; m. April 30, 1826, Amos Towne.
39 | *Mary*, b. March 18, 1801; m. April 1, 1827, Joel Adams.
40 | *John*, b. Oct. 17, 1803; d. 1858, unm.
41 | *Emily*, b. Dec. 26, 1806; m. Nov. 17, 1830, KING GEORGE. Surely this was a royal alliance.
42 | *Harriet*, b. Sept. 13, 1809; m. April 22, 1842, Ivory Sanborn. They have had several children. No record.

24–29– DANIEL MARRETT was graduated at H. C. 1790, and was ordained as minister in Standish, Me., Sept. 21, 1796. He m. July 24, 1796, Mary Muzzy, dau. of William and Lydia (Reed) Muzzy of Lex. She d. and he m. second, Oct. 8, 1810, Dorcas Hastings, dau. of Samuel and Lydia Hastings of Lincoln. He d. 1836.

THE MASON FAMILY.

The Masons have never been very numerous in Lex., though they occupied for a time a highly respectable position in town.

1 HUGH MASON of Wat. was one of the first settlers of that town, where he enjoyed in a high degree the confidence and esteem of his fellows. He was ad. freeman in 1635, and represented the town ten years, from 1644 to 1677. He was selectman two years, between 1639 and 1678. He was also appointed by the General Court a commissioner to try " small causes." He d. Oct. 10, 1678, aged 73.

1– 2 | *Hannah*, b. Sept. 23, 1636; m. Oct. 17, 1657, Joshua Brooks, Con.
3 | *Ruth*, b. ———; d. Dec. 17, 1640.
4 | *Mary*, b. Dec. 18, 1640; m. May 20, 1668, Rev. Joseph Estabrook of Concord.
5 | †*John*, b. Jan. 1, 1645; m. Elizabeth Hammond.
6 | *Joseph*, b. Aug. 10, 1646; ad. freeman 1690; d. July 22, 1702.
7 | *Daniel*, b. Feb. 19, 1649; grad. H. C. 1666.
8 | *Sarah*, b. Sept. 25, 1651; m. May 20, 1668, Capt. Andrew Gardner of Brookline. He was lost in the expedition to Canada, 1690.

1–5– JOHN MASON m. Elizabeth Hammond, dau. of Lieut. John and Sarah Hammond of Wat. She d Nov. 13, 1715; he d. about 1730.

5– 9 | †*John*, b. Jan. 22, 1677; m. Elizabeth Spring.
10 | *Daniel*, b. ———. He was a farmer in Newton.
11 | *Elizabeth*, b. ———; m. Thomas Brown, innholder, Boston.

5–9– JOHN MASON m. Oct. 18, 1699, Elizabeth Spring, dau. of Lieut. John and Hannah Spring of Wat. He came to Lex. about the time of his marriage. In seating the meeting house in 1699, "John Mason was plast in ye second seat in ye front gallereye." He and his wife were ad. to the ch. Dec. 19, 1708. He was one of the assessors in 1702, and a subscriber for the purchase of the Common in 1711, and was constable in 1714. He was town clerk 1729, '31, '34, '35, and '36, and selectman about the same period. His name upon the record is also dignified by the title of *Ensign*. He lived on the Main street, a little below the old Munroe Tavern, and hence the name of "Mason's Hollow."

9–12 | †*John*, b. Aug. 8, 1701; m. June 17, 1731, Lydia Loring.
13 | *Elizabeth*, b. Aug. 30, 1703.   14 *Millicent*, b. April 24, 1705.

15 *Thaddeus*, b. Dec. 27, 1706; grad. H. C. 1728; clerk of the court; d. 1802.

16 *Jonas*, b. Oct. 21, 1708.

17 *Katharine*, b. Aug. 5, 1710; d. in Holliston, May 7, 1733.

18 *Esther*, b. Jan 2, 1713; d. Aug. 3, 1713.

19 *Sarah*, b. June 7, 1714; m. Jan. 3, 1733, William Munroe, son of William, Jr. and Mary. He d. Aug. 18, 1747, and she m. second, Francis Bowman, Esq., in 1748.

20 *Mercy*, b. Nov. 12, 1716: d. Nov. 30, 1717.

21 *Samuel*, b. Oct. 9, 1720.

9-12—   JOHN MASON m. June 17, 1731, Lydia Loring, dau. of Dea. Joseph and Lydia Loring. He d. Jan. 20, 1787, aged 87; she d. Feb. 18, 1790, aged 80. He was selectman in 1755.

12-22 *Lydia*, b. March 31, 1732; d. unm. April 24, 1813, aged 82.

23 *Katharine*, b. Oct. 29, 1733; m. April 23, 1754, Daniel Edes of Charlestown.

24 *John*, b. April 9, 1735.

25 †*Joseph*, b. July 29, 1736; m. Elizabeth Peak.

26 *Jonas*, b. March 2, 1738; m. March 23, 1762, Submit Whittemore.

27 *Elizabeth*, b. June, 1739; d. young.

28 *Sarah*, bap. Oct. 26, 1740.

29 *Hannah*, bap. Sept. 6, 1747; m. a Mr. Bull of Watertown.

30 *Samuel*, bap. May 14, 1749.

31 †*Daniel*,   ⎫ twins, ⎧ bap. July 21, 1751; m. June 6, 1793, Sarah Cheney of Newton.

32 *Elizabeth*, ⎭   ⎩ bap. July 21, 1751.

12-25—   JOSEPH MASON m. Oct. 19, 1769, Elizabeth Peck. He was in the French war 1762, and was one of the gallant band which met the British on the Common at the opening scene of the Revolutionary drama. He was town clerk from 1770 to 1790. He d. Oct. 3, 1814, aged 78, and she d. Jan. 20, 1829, aged 87. He was somewhat noted as a school-master in his day.

25-33 *Mary*, b. June 24, 1770; m. Daniel Underwood.

34 *John*, b. Sept. 8, 1772; d. May 3, 1795, unm.

12-31—   DANIEL MASON m. June 6, 1793, Mrs. Sarah Cheney of Newton. He resided near the rail road crossing on Woburn street. He died without issue. He belonged to the Spartan band which refused to lay down their arms on the 19th of April, 1775, not fearing "the King's commandment."

THE MEAD FAMILY.

There is considerable difficulty in tracing the Meads. The first of the name appear to be migratory, and are found in different places. Savage informs us, that Gabriel Mead of Dorchester was made a freeman in 1638, and d. 1666, aged 79; that his will mentions several daughters, and that he had a son, Israel, b. 1639, who lived in Wat., moved to Dedham, and perhaps to Wo. Israel, probably son of the preceding, is sometimes spoken of as of Wo., and sometimes as of Camb., but it is undoubtedly the same person, and from him the Lexington Meads in part descended.

1   ISRAEL MEAD, sometimes of Camb., m. Feb. 26, 1669, Mary Hall, dau. of widow Mary Hall. He was appointed in Camb. in 1683,

" viewer of wood." Whether he resided at that time in the old town
or at the Farms, we are unable to say; but in 1693, when the North
precinct was organized, he must have been within its territory, as he
was taxed for ministerial land purchased at that time. The same tax
bill bears the name of his son, Thomas Mead. Israel Mead was one
of the original members of the ch. organized 1696, and Thomas was
ad. 1699, and his wife, Hasaniah, was admitted in August of the same
year. During the same season two of Thomas's children, Hannah
and Sarah, were bap. The record of Israel's wife's death is among
the first of the obituaries on the parish records, being Sept. 1, 1692.
Israel was one of the committee to seat the gallery of the meeting
house in 1700. He d. Sept. 6, 1714. His will, dated April 2, 1713,
and proved Sept. 20, 1714, mentions particularly sons Thomas, John,
Stephen, and Ebenezer, and dau. Margaret Locke, Mary, and Ruth.
He also makes a bequest to four grandchildren,—the oldest child of
Thomas, John, Stephen, and Margaret Locke. He also remembers
his faithful spiritual teacher. " I give to Mr. John Hancock, the rev-
erend pastor of the church of Christ in Lexington, twenty shillings."

1- 2 | †*Thomas*, b. about 1670.
3 | †*John*, b. about 1672.
4 | *Hannah*, b. about 1674; d. Jan. 28, 1702.
5 | *Margaret*, b. Jan. 20, 1676; m. Joseph Locke, as his second wife.
6 | †*Stephen*, b. about 1679; lived and d. in Concord.
7 | *Mary*, b. Feb. 10, 1682.
8 | *Ruth*, b. Aug. 10, 1684; probably d. Nov. 3, 1726, unm.
9 | *Ebenezer*, b. May 11, 1686.

1-2- | THOMAS MEAD m. Hasaniah ——. He was in the North pre-
cinct in 1693, and he and his wife were ad. to the ch. in 1699. In
1700, when they " seated the meeting house," he had a seat assigned
him in the " front side galery." He was constable in 1704 and in
1714. It is doubtful whether any of his sons, except Israel and Cornelius, lived permanently in Lex., as we do not find their names upon
the tax bills extant.

2-10 | *Hannah*, bap. May 8, 1699; d. 1723.
11 | *Sarah*, bap. May 8, 1699.
12 | *Thomas*, bap. Sept. 1700; probably went to Littleton.
13 | *Jonathan*, bap. Sept. 6, 1702.
14 | †*Israel*, bap. Aug. 16, 1704; m. Sarah ——.
15 | †*Samuel*, bap. May 3, 1706; went to Harvard.
16 | *Mary*, bap. March 3, 1709.   17 *James*, bap. April 8, 1711.
18 | †*Cornelius*, bap. June 3, 1714; m. Hannah Hadley.

1-3- | JOHN MEAD m. Rebecca ——. He probably moved to Weston.
He owned the covenant in Lex. Feb. 23, 1707, when " John Mead,
the first-born of John," was baptized. Rebecca was admitted to the
ch. July 31, 1709. He probably left town soon after the birth of his
children named below, as his name is not found upon the tax bill
in 1729.

3-19 | *John*, bap. Feb. 23, 1707.   20 *Joseph*, bap. Feb. 13, 1709.
21 | *Lydia*, b. April 7, 1714.   22 *Israel*, b. Aug. 27, 1716.
23 | *Rebecca*, b. March 1, 1719.   24 *Hannah*, b. Aug. 13, 1721.

1-6- | STEPHEN MEAD. The Lex. records give no information of him
or his family. By the Probate records I learn that in 1717, Thomas
Mead (No. 2 in this table) was appointed guardian of Joseph Mead,

the only child of his brother Stephen, late of Concord; and in 1734, Joseph Mead of Bedford settled with his uncle Thomas, his late guardian.

2-14- | ISRAEL MEAD m. Sarah ——. She d. June 22, 1745, aged 37, and he m. Mary Robbins, Feb. 21, 1751. He was ad. to the ch. March 28, 1742.

14-25 | *Sarah,* b. Aug. 14, 1732; m. Dec. 26, 1753, Nathan Pierce.
26 | *Hannah,* b. Jan. 3, 1734.
27 | *John,* b. June 2, 1745.　　　28 *Mary,* bap. Sept. 17, 1747.

2-15- | SAMUEL MEAD was ad. to the ch. 1742, and dismissed to the ch. in Harvard, July 1, 1744, where he resided and had a family. Samuel, one of his sons. grad. H. C. 1787, studied divinity, and settled at Alstead, N. H. He d. 1822. William O. Mead of Belmont, a broker in Boston, is a son of Rev. Samuel.

2-18- | CORNELIUS MEAD m. Oct. 15, 1751, Hannah Hadley. He d. 1759, and his wid. administered upon his estate.

18-29 | *Sarah,* b. Sept. 20, 1753; m. Nov. 11, 1779, Thomas Jones of Con.
30 | *Abner,* b. Dec. 15, 1754. He served in the Revolutionary war.
31 | *Benoni,* b. May 1, 1756; d. Aug. 4, 1766.
32 | *Susanna,* b. Jan. 26, 1758.

There is another branch of the Mead family, which should be kept distinct, though it is believed that they were all of the same original stock.

1 | DAVID MEAD of Camb., perhaps son of Gabriel, m. at Wat. Sept. 24, 1675, Hannah Warren, and had David, Hannah, John, and probably Hopestill, and other children. David admitted freeman 1683.

1- 2 | *Hannah,* b. Sept. 1676.
3 | ‡*David,* b. 1678; m. Feb. 5, 1708, Hannah Smith of Wat., where he settled.
4 | ‡*Hopestill,* b. 1681; m. Aug. 22, 1707, Elizabeth Hastings.
5 | *John,* b. 1685.　　　6 *Sarah,* b. 1688.　　　7 *Susanna,* b. 1690.

1-3- | DAVID MEAD m. Feb. 5, 1708, Hannah Smith, dau. of Joseph and Hannah (Tidd) Smith. He settled in Watertown, (which then included Waltham,) probably near the line of Lex. In the record of a public meeting in Lex. Feb. 23, 1712, is this entry,—" David Mead of Watertown did request that he, paying twenty shillings, might be interested in the meeting house for himself and family. Voted in the affirmative " She united with the ch. in Lex. June 22, 1718, and in October of that year their first four children were bap. She d. in childbed, Oct. 4, 1723. He d. in Walt. Feb. 25, 1767, aged 89.

3- 8 | *Lydia,* b. Dec. 1, 1710.
9 | *Moses,* b. Oct. 21, 1712; ad. to the ch. 1742.
10 | ‡*Joshua,* b. Nov. 9, 1715; m. March 24, 1750, Lucy Parker.
11 | ‡*Matthew,* b. Aug. 9, 1717; m. Martha Danforth.
12 | *Susanna,* b. Aug. 1, 1719; m. Dec. 14, 1738, Jacob Bigelow, Walt.
13 | *Hopestill,* b. Sept. 7, 1721; m. March 13, 1750, Sarah Pierce, Walt.
14 | *David,* b. Sept. 23, 1723; m. Oct. 16, 1747, Mary Bond. settled in Line. He and his wife were ad. to the ch. in Lex. June 19, 1748, and dismissed to Line. April 26, 1767.

1-4- HOPESTILL MEAD m. Aug. 22, 1707, Elizabeth Hastings. He d. Aug. 9, 1750, aged 69. In his will, dated Aug. 7, 1750, and proved Sept. 24, 1750, he mentions wife Elizabeth, kinsman Benjamin Hastings, dau. Abigail Jennison, grandson Josiah Jennison. He makes Joshua Mead of Waltham, whom he designates as his kinsman, executor of his will. As he mentions no child but Abigail, and looks among his kinsmen for heirs, it is probable that he had no other child living at that time. Though he probably lived within the limits of Waltham, his associations were with Lex., and he attended church here. He was ad. to the ch. in Lex. Sept. 12, 1742, and was dismissed to Waltham, Sept. 1, 1750.

4-15 *Abigail*, bap. Aug. 30, 1713; m. Oct. 23, 1729, Nathaniel Jennison.

3-10- JOSHUA MEAD m. March 24, 1750, Lucy Parker, dau. of Andrew and Sarah (Whitney) Parker, b. April 4, 1731. They were ad. to the ch. Dec. 8, 1751. Though Joshua Mead united with the ch. in Lex., and a part of his children were bap. here, he resided within the limits of Waltham.

10-16 *Lucy*, bap. Jan. 19, 1752; d. December of the same year.
17 *Mary*, b. May 1, 1753; m. Dec. 3, 1772, Abraham Whitney.
18 *Moses*, b. Dec. 2, 1754; m. May 22, 1777, Lizzy Viles. He was in the Revolutionary war.
19 *Lydia*, b. May 17, 1756; m. June 1, 1775, Joseph Adams of Newton.
20 *Elijah*, b. Sept. 30, 1758; m. Abigail ——.
21 *Jacob*, b. Oct. 30, 1760; d. 1816.

3-11- MATTHEW MEAD m. Jan. 23, 1754, Martha Danforth of Billerica. He was ad. to the ch. 1742, and d. April 1, 1796, aged 78; she d. Aug. 8, 1792, aged 63. He resided near the town hall, where Mr. Russell now resides. His house was ransacked by the British, April 19, 1775. He was frequently elected to office, as constable, school committee, and tythingman.

11-22 *Ward*, b. Dec. 16, 1755.
23 *Martha*, b. Aug. 10, 1756; d. young.
24 *Rhoda*, bap. July 9, 1758; m. Sept. 13, 1786, Philemon Munroe, as his second wife.
25 †*Levi*, bap. Aug. 14, 1759; m. Betsey Converse.
26 †*Josiah*, b. Oct. 18, 1761; m. Sally Locke.
27 *Elias*, bap. May 29, 1763; d. June 1, 1765.

11-25- LEVI MEAD m. Betsey Converse of Bed. They were ad. to the ch. May 30, 1784. He served in the war of the Revolution, and was, in 1796, a captain in the militia. He moved with his family, about 1801, to Chesterfield, N. H.

25-28 *Levi*, bap. Aug. 8, 1784.   29 *Joseph*, b. ——; d. young.
30 *James*, b. Oct. 26, 1788.   31 *Bradley*, bap. Oct. 18, 1792.
32 *Larkin*, bap. Oct. 18, 1795.   33 *Elias*, bap. March 17, 1799.
34 *Marshall*, b. in Chesterfield, N. H.
35 *Betsey*, b. in Chesterfield, N. H.

11-26- JOSIAH MEAD m. May 12, 1789, Sally Locke, dau. of Joseph and Sarah (Baldwin) Locke, b. May 27, 1766. He d. July 5, 1829, aged 68; she d. Sept. 2, 1839, aged 73. He was a trader in the town, and occupied the place where Mr. Saville now trades.

26-36 | *Clarissa*, b. June 10, 1790; m. Nov. 30, 1815, Nathaniel Harring-
ton. She d. 1866.
37 | *Maria Howard*, b. June 12, 1792; m. Dec. 7, 1821, Nathan Chandler.
38 | She is living in Lex. in her 76th year.
39 | *Sally*, bap. April 13, 1794; d. in infancy.
40 | *Martha J.*, b. June 6, 1797; m. Feb. 1, 1824, Nathan Harrington.
41 | She d. June 26, 1835, leaving two children.
Sally, bap. Feb. 22, 1801; m. Oct. 11, 1821, James Hastings of Linc.
They are both living in Lex.
Franklin, bap. Aug. 23, 1803; d. Oct. 1805.

The name of Mead has become extinct in Lex. In the early records the name is often spelled with an *s*, *Meads*, though in later years the *s* has been dropped.

THE MERRIAM FAMILY.

The Merriams were very numerous in Lexington during the first seventy-five years of her history. They came from England, and settled in Concord, where they were among the prominent families. Shattuck, in his history of Concord, tells the old story, which he thinks may be true in this case, of three brothers coming over together, Robert, George, and Joseph. Robert was town clerk in Con. for a long period, and also a representative. He d. without issue, Feb. 15, 1681. George m, and had a family; but Joseph was the ancestor of the Concord families. The descendants of Joseph constituted the Lexington Merriams. The imperfect records render it impossible to trace this family with entire accuracy.

The Merriams from this stock became numerous in several towns in Worcester county, and in other parts of the State.

1 | JOSEPH MERRIAM took the freeman's oath, March 14, 1638. He d. Jan. 1, 1641. We have found no mention of his wife's name, and no full record of his children.

1- 2 | †*Joseph*, b. ——, 1630; m. July 12, 1653, Sarah Stone.
3 | *William*, b. ——; m. Sarah —— and moved to Lynn.
4 | †*John*, b. ——, 1639; m. Mary Cooper.
5 | *Sarah*, b. ——; m. Oct. 14, 1658, William Hall.

1-2- | JOSEPH MERRIAM m. July 12, 1653, Sarah Stone, dau. of Dea. Gregory. He took the freeman's oath, May 22, 1651, and d. April 20, 1677, aged 47. His tombstone is the oldest one in Concord. His wife survived him nearly thirty years, and d. Ap. 5, 1704, aged 71.

2- 6 | *Sarah*, b. Aug. 2, 1654; m. Samuel Fletcher.
7 | *Lydia*, b. Aug. 3, 1656; d. Dec. 29, 1690, unm.
8 | †*Joseph*, b. May 25, 1658; d. May 31, 1727, in Lexington.
9 | *Elizabeth*, b. May 20, 1660; m. Isaac Wood.
10 | †*John*, b. May 30, 1662; d. 1736.
11 | *Mary*, b. June 4, 1664; m. Isaac Stearns.
12 | †*Robert*, b. Dec. 17, 1667; d. Feb. 11, 1717, in Lex.
13 | †*Thomas*, b. 1672; m. Mary Haywood of Concord.
14 | *Ruth*, b. ——; m. Nathaniel Stone.
15 | *David*, b. ——; d. 1744, at Townsend.

1-4- | JOHN MERRIAM m. Oct. 21, 1663, Mary Cooper at Concord. He was made freeman, May 12, 1675. She d. March 5, 1731, aged 85; he d. Feb. 2, 1704, aged 65.

4-16 | *John*, b. Sept. 3, 1666.
17 | *Anna*, b. Sept. 7, 1669; m. Aug. 9, 1692, Daniel Brooks.
18 | *Nathaniel*, b. Dec. 10, 1672.   19 *Joseph*, b. Aug. 20, 1677.
20 | *Samuel*, b. July 25, 1681.
21 | *Ebenezer*, b. ———; m. Nov. 8, 1711, Elizabeth Brooks.
22 | *Sarah*, b. ———; m. Edward Wheeler.

2-8- | JOSEPH MERRIAM m. Charity ———. Like his brothers, he was early at Cambridge Farms, and was a subscriber to the first meeting house in 1692, and in the following year was assessed in the first tax bill of the precinct; and hence was a resident there at the time. He was not called so frequently to places of honor and trust, as some of his kinsmen, though he was elected to the dignified office of tything-man, which in that day was conferred upon none but the most respectable citizens. He d. May 31, 1727.

8-23 | *Ruth*, bap. Nov. 6, 1698; d. April 20, 1749, unm.
24 | *Joseph*, bap. 1717; d. 1747.

2-10- | JOHN MERRIAM m. 1688, Mary Wheeler of Con. What time he came to Camb. Farms, does not appear, but probably about the time of his marriage. His name is borne upon our earliest records, being a subscriber for the meeting house in 1692. He was one of the original members of the church in 1696, and was chosen deacon at that time. He became one of the most prominent men in the parish and in the town. He frequently represented the church in ecclesiastical councils. He was chosen an assessor in 1700 and 1711, under the parish organization; and when the precinct was erected into a town, he was elected one of the selectmen,—an office to which he was often re-elected. He enjoyed, in a great degree, the confidence of his fellow citizens. He resided in the southwesterly part of the town. The record of his family is very imperfect; there being no account of any children from 1689 to 1701, though it is probable they had children during that period. He d. May 21, 1727; she d. Dec. 26, 1747, aged 75.

10-25 | *Mary*, b. Feb. 6, 1689.
26 | †*Benjamin*, bap. Jan. 1701; m. Mary ———.
27 | †*Jonas*, bap. Jan. 12, 1704; m. Abigail Locke, Oct. 3, 1728.
28 | *Ebenezer*, bap. May 30, 1706; he moved to Oxford about 1729.
29 | *Joshua*, bap. Feb. 22, 1708.
30 | *William*, b. Sept. 1712; d. June 21, 1735.
31 | †*Amos*, bap. July 25, 1715; m. Nov. 9, 1738, Hannah Danforth.

2-12- | ROBERT MERRIAM m. Abigail ———. He was a subscriber for the meeting house in Lex. in 1692; but probably was not a permanent resident, as he was not taxed in 1693 or 1696. In 1700, he was one of the assessors, and in 1711 was one of the subscribers for the purchase of the Common. He and his wife were ad. to the ch. in 1698. He d. Feb. 11, 1717, and she d. June 16, 1717.

12-32 | †*Joseph*, b. May 3, 1697; m. Mary Bruce of Weston.
33 | *Abigail*, b. Oct. 3, 1699.
34 | *Hannah*, b. April 16, 1701; m. John Bruce, Oct. 9, 1718.
35 | *Robert*, b. July 15, 1703; d. 1713.
36 | *Jonathan*, b. July 25, 1705; d. Feb. 20, 1738.
37 | *Hezekiah*, b. May 30, 1707.
38 | *Sarah*, bap. July 2, 1710; d. July 8, 1713.
39 | *Mary*, b. Dec. 11, 1712.
40 | *Sarah*, bap. July 2, 1716; m. Isaac Allen of Weston, 1739.

2-13- THOMAS MERRIAM m. Dec. 23, 1696, Mary Haywood of Concord. The record of his marriage speaks of him as of Cambridge; but Lex. at that time was a part of Camb., and as he was one of the original members of the church formed in 1696, he was probably residing here at the time of his marriage. His wife was dismissed from Con. to the ch. in Lex. in 1698. Thomas Merriam and others were permitted to "build a seat for their wives on the back side of the meeting house, from goodwife Reed's seat to the woman's stayers." He was a constable in 1716, and a selectman, 1718, '22, '25. He d. Aug. 16, 1738, aged 66, and she d. Sept. 29, 1756, aged 81. The early Merriams all resided in the southwest part of the town.

13-41 †*Thomas*, bap. April 21, 1700; m. Tabitha Stone.
42 *Lydia*, bap. Aug. 1, 1703; m. Nathaniel Eaton, and r. in Reading.
43 †*Nathaniel*, bap. Dec. 9, 1705; m. Esther Muzzy, dau. of Benjamin Muzzy.
44 *Simon*, bap. Nov. 28, 1708; d. Feb. 8, 1747.
45 *David*, bap. Sept. 2, 1711; d. Dec. 15, 1743, in Townsend.
46 *Isaac*, bap. July 11, 1714; m. and had two children, one of whom d. 1740. He d. Sept. 1741.

10-26- BENJAMIN MERRIAM m. Mary ——. He d. Aug. 28, 1773, aged 74, and she d. Jan. 18, 1763. He was one who marched to the relief of Fort William-Henry in 1757.

26-47 *Mary*, b. April 4, 1733.
48 *Elizabeth*, b. March 10, 1735; m. June 22, 1758, Jonas Brown of Waltham.
49 †*Benjamin*, b. June 8, 1737; m. Feb. 28, 1762, Ginger Porter.
50 *Baron*, b. Sept. 21, 1740; d. Jan. 3, 1741.

10-27- JONAS MERRIAM m. Oct. 3, 1728, Abigail Locke, dau. of Dea. William of Wo. They were ad. to the ch. July 1, 1729. She d. Dec. 5, 1755, and he m. June 22, 1758, Mrs. Sarah Winship. She d. March 15, 1773, and he d. July 23, 1776, aged 73. He filled several town offices, and was treasurer in 1747.

27-51 *John*, b. July 28, 1729.
52 †*William*, bap. Dec. 17, 1732; m. Sarah ——.
53 †*Abraham*, b. Dec. 23, 1734; m. Sarah Simonds.
54 *Silas*, b. March 5, 1737.   55 *James*, b. April 10, 1739.
56 *Abigail*, b. June 11, 1741.
57 *Eunice*, b. June 29, 1743; d. before 1746.
58 *Ebenezer*, b. Nov. 2, 1745; d. Dec. 11, 1745.

10-31- AMOS MERRIAM m. Nov. 9, 1738, Hannah Danforth. He was ad. to the ch. April 4, 1736.

31-59 *Amos*, b. Aug. 24, 1739.
60 *Jonathan*, } b. May 16, 1741; { d. Jan. 5, 1823, unm.
61 *Hepzibah*, }   { d. young.
62 *Hannah*, b. Feb. 9, 1744; m. James Townsend.
63 *Sarah*, bap. April 20, 1746; m. William Lincoln.
64 *Lucy*, bap. Sept. 4, 1748; m. William Whitcomb.
65 *Levi*, b. Feb. 3, 1756; m. Abigail Fife.
66 *Abigail*, b. March 31, 1758; m. Uriah Mores.

12-32- JOSEPH MERRIAM m. Aug. 9, 1718, Mary Bruce of Weston. He and his wife were ad. to the ch. Sept. 13, 1719. He was constable, 1738, and tythingman, 1741.

32-67 | *Joseph*, bap. July 13, 1718; d. April 22, 1725.
68 | *Elizabeth*, b. June 13, 1721. 69 *Abigail*, b. ———.
70 | *Robert*, b. 1725; d. June 11, 1729.
71 | *Mary*, bap. June 23, 1728.
72 | *Beulah*, b. Aug. 2, 1730; m. Aug. 7, 1757, John Chandler of Linc., but afterwards of Lexington.
73 | *Joseph*, b. July 10, 1732. 74 *Robert*, bap. June 11, 1738.

13-41- | THOMAS MERRIAM m. Tabitha Stone. He was ad. to the ch. Aug. 2, 1721. She d. June 22, 1760; he d. June 4, 1752.

41-75 | †*Samuel*, b. Dec. 21, 1723; m. June 4, 1752, Anna Whitney.
76 | *Nathan*, b. April 7, 1725; m. March 26, 1755, Mary Hosmer.
77 | *Mary*, b. June 15, 1727; m. David Whitney of Waltham.
78 | *Hannah*, b. Aug. 7, 1729; d. Feb. 14, 1730.
79 | *Thomas*, b. Aug. 24, 1731; m. Sarah Wilder.
80 | *Tabitha*, b. May 10, 1733; m. Nathan Whitney of Waltham. They moved to Westminster, and had Nathan, b. 1765; David, b. 1767, d. March 25, 1867, aged 99 years, 7 months, and 9 days; and John, b. 1769; besides six other children, who d. young.
81 | *Lydia*, b. Oct. 28, 1734; m. March 27, 1755, Josiah Cutting of Westminster.
82 | *Hepzibah*, b. Feb. 24, 1737; d. Aug. 10, 1740.
83 | *Elizabeth*, b. July 27, 1738; m. Nov. 5, 1755, Moses Sawtell of Con.
84 | *Eunice*, b. June 30, 1740; d. April 27, 1741.

13-43- | NATHANIEL MERRIAM m. Esther Muzzy, dau. of Benjamin and Patience Muzzy.

43-85 | *Esther*, b. Oct. 23, 1734; m. Nov. 27, 1760, Samuel Jones.
86 | *Nathaniel*, b. April 16, 1737. 87 *Mary*, b. Oct. 3, 1739.
88 | *Abigail*, b. March 11, 1744; m. June 27, 1765, Bartholomew Richardson of Woburn.
89 | *Simon*, b. Jan. 3, 1749. 90 *Sarah*, bap. Sept. 18, 1751.

26-49- | BENJAMIN MERRIAM, JR., m. Feb. 28, 1762, Ginger Porter. He d. in Pelham, Feb. 1, 1806, aged 69; she d. March 7, 1817, aged 76.

49-91 | †*Rufus*, b. Oct. 28, 1762; m. Jan. 12, 1785, Martha Simonds.
92 | *Benjamin*, b. March 23, 1764; d. March 22, 1817, aged 53, unm.
93 | *Edith*, b. Aug. 20, 1765; m. Feb. 5, 1787, Stephen Winship.
94 | *Mary*, b. July 5, 1767; m. Abiel Abbott of Lincoln.
95 | *Anna*, b. June 10, 1769; m. Oct. 26, 1797, Thomas S. Caldwell, who moved to Manchester, N. H.
96 | *George*, b. May 7, 1771. He went into business in Boston, afterwards went to Kentucky, from thence to Natchez, where he died.
97 | *Rebecca*, b. June 19, 1773; d. unm. March 10, 1835.
98 | *Tryphena*, b. Feb. 25, 1775; m. —— Brooks, and moved to Farmington, Me.
99 | *Phila*, b. April 23, 1777; d. Aug. 5, 1778.
100 | *Nathan*, b. Oct. 3, 1780. He went to Louisiana, where he was first made a sheriff, afterwards judge, then President of the Senate.
101 | *William*, b. ———. He was a trader in Cambridgeport.

27-52- | WILLIAM MERRIAM m. Sarah ———.

52-102 | *William*, b March 23, 1771. 103 *Jonathan*, b. Aug. 25, 1772.
104 | *Jonas*, b. Nov. 6, 1773. 105 *Abel*, b. March 13, 1775.
106 | *Sarah*, b. Aug. 14, 1776. 107 *Rebecca*, bap. 1786.

27-53- ABRAHAM MERRIAM m. April 22, 1756, Sarah Simonds. They were ad. to the ch. May 6, 1757. They afterwards moved to Wo,, where their last three children were born.

53-108 *Abraham*, bap. May 29, 1757.   109 *Ezra*, b. June 15, 1760.
110 *Silas*, b. Feb. 2, 1762.
111 *Sarah*, b. at Wo. Oct. 10, 1766.
112 *Jonas*, b. at Wo. July 31, 1769.
113 *Abigail*, b. at Wo. May 13, 1771.

41-75- SAMUEL MERRIAM m. June 4, 1752, Anna Whitney. They were ad. to the ch. April 11, 1756, and were dismissed, Sept. 6, 1772, to the ch. in Westminster, to which place they had removed.

75-114 *Anna*, b. Oct. 10, 1753.   115 *Eunice*, b. June 22, 1755.
116 *Samuel*, b. March 25, 1757.   117 *Ruth*, bap. Feb. 25, 1759.
118 *Tabitha*, bap. Dec. 28, 1760.   119 *Nathan*, bap. April 29, 1764.
120 *Jonathan*, bap. Feb. 22, 1767.

49-91- RUFUS MERRIAM m. Jan. 12, 1785, Martha Simonds, dau. of Joshua and Martha (Bowers) Simonds, who was b. Oct. 1, 1766. He d. May 7, 1847, and she d. May 8, 1849. He was the first post-master of Lex. He kept a public house for a long series of years.

91-121 *Martha*, b. July 21, 1787; d. June 8, 1863, unm.
122 *Rufus*, b. Sept. 11, 1789; he is living, in his 79th year.
123 *John Parkhurst*, b. July 4, 1791; d. June 25, 1863, unm. He was interested in the militia, and rose to the rank of colonel.
124 *Eliza*, b. Feb. 23, 1793.   125 *Mary*, b. Jan. 1, 1798.
126 *Emily*, b. Aug. 16, 1800.
127 *Julia Ann*, b. Oct. 12, 1804; m. Aug. 22, 1827, Rev Caleb Stetson.

MILLS.—SAMUEL MILLS of Dedham, b. 1622, was made freeman 1645. His son, *William*, was b. 1682, and his grandson, *John*, was b. 1715. *Oliver*, son of John, was b. 1742, and *Oliver, Jr.*, was b. 1780. He was the father of *Oliver P. Mills*, now residing in Lex. He was b. in Boston, Sept. 8, 1810, m. Anna A. Adams of Lex., dau. of Samuel. They have had four children : *Emily Ida*, b. Sept. 28, 1846, d. Sept. 29, 1847; *Arthur Perry*, b. April 15, 1848; *Carlton Wadsworth*, b. April 1, 1853; *Gracie Constance*, b. Sept. 13, 1862.

MITCHELL.—PATRICK MITCHELL was b. July 8, 1819, in the parish of Moor, county of Roscommon, Ireland. He was son of Daniel Mitchell. In 1834, Patrick, with his parents, came to this country and setted in Roxbury, where he remained till 1842, when he came to Lex. and established himself as a leather dresser. He m. May 6, 1845, Sarah A. Snow, dau. of Daniel and Rebecca (Abbott) Snow of Cavendish, Vt. They have had four children, *Oliver*, b. March 18, 1846; *James Alpheus*, b. Aug. 21, 1847, he was in the United States' service in the late rebellion; *Mary Rebecca*, b. Jan. 4, 1849, d. Sept. 16, 1856; *Abbott Stanton*, b. Nov. 21, 1860.

THE MOORE FAMILY.

There was a family by the name of Moore found on Lex. records about 1720. We have not ascertained the line of descent of this family. The name was common in most of the early settlements.

1| THOMAS MOORE and his wife Mary appear before the church in 1724, and had their first child bap. He d. July 19, 1767, and she d. Nov. 8, 1782, aged 81.

1- 2| *Mary*, b. July 5, 1724.   3 *Thomas*, b. Sept. 10. 1725.
4| *Elizabeth*, b. Sept. 15, 1727.   5 *Abigail*, b. April 30, 1729.
6| *Lydia*, b. Jan. 18, 1731; m. May 22, 1755, John Parker, who commanded the Lex. company in 1775. He d. Sept. 17, 1775, and she m. Nov. 5, 1778, Ephraim Pierce of Waltham.
7| *Charles*, b. Aug. 14, 1733.   8 *Robert*, b. Feb. 26, 1736.
9| *Isaac*, b. May 24, 1738.

There are a few others of the name, but they are so far between that I can give no connected view of them. Benjamin Moore m. May 3, 1768, Betsey Cutler, and had children, we believe, but neither the town or the parish records contain the names or birth.

THE MORRELL FAMILY.

1| AMBROSE MORRELL was b. in France about 1780. He received his early education in a convent, and was probably designed for the church. He was conscripted into the French army, and served in Napoleon's second campaign in Italy. He was in the famous battle of Marengo. He afterwards went to Holland, and from thence came to America, about 1798. He took up his residence in Lex. and m. Jan. 7, 1805, Sarah Holbrook of Sherborne, aged 19. He d. April 27, 1862. He was engaged in the fur dressing business. He was frequently appointed on important committees, represented the town two years in the legislature, and was a justice of the peace.

1- 2| *Sarah*, b. Jan. 12, 1807; m. Abraham Millett, June 2, 1833, no issue.
3| *Clarissa*, b. March 18, 1808; m. May 19, 1835, Rev. Curtis Cutler.
4| *Elizabeth*, b. Dec. 3. 1810; d. young.
5| *Elizabeth*, b. May 20, 1814; m. July 19, 1836, Otis H. Dana. He has been a merchant in Boston. They have one child, Ellen B., b. May 1, 1838.
6| *Mary A.*, b. July 18, 1820; m. April, 1842, George Marsh.

THE MULLIKEN FAMILY.

1| BENJAMIN MULLIKEN came to this country from Glasgow, Scotland, when he was a young man, and settled in Bradford. He was twice married. By his second wife he had Nathaniel, Samuel, and Mary. *Nathaniel* was b. 1722. He was a clock maker by trade; and according to the custom of that day, carried his clocks round for a market. In the pursuit of his calling he visited Lex., and set up one of his time pieces at Dea. John Stone's. It would seem that the family were well pleased with the beating of the clock; and the heart of their youngest daughter beat so in unison with that of the maker, that she was willing to leave the time-piece in her father's house, and place herself in a situation where she should know more of the clocks and their maker.

1- 2| NATHANIEL MULLIKEN m. June 6, 1751, Lydia Stone, dau. of John and Mary (Reed) Stone. He probably came to Lex. to reside about the time of his marriage; for his name appears upon the tax bill of 1752. She was ad. to the ch. Aug. 2, 1752. He was chosen tythingman in 1754,—a position showing that he was a man of sobriety of character. He d. Nov. 23, 1767, aged 45, and, after remaining a wid. about ten years, she m. Nov. 18, 1777, Jonathan Harrington, as his second wife. She d. Nov. 13, 1783. While she remained a wid., she was rendered houseless by having her dwelling burned by the British on the 19th of April, 1775. She lost on that occasion, in buildings and other property, £431. Her residence was near the late residence of Dea. Nathaniel Mulliken on Main street.

2- 3 *Nathaniel*, b. March 30, 1752 ; d. unm. Feb. 6, 1776, aged 24 years. He was a member of Capt. Parker's company.
  4 *Lydia*, b. July 11, 1753 ; m, Joseph Burrell of Haverhill.
  5 †*John*, b. Dec. 23, 1754 ; m. Lydia Whiting.
  6 *Samuel*, b. July 4, 1756 ; d. 1807, unm., in South Carolina.
  7 *Mary*, b. Dec. 4, 1757 ; m. Jan. 2, 1781, Abijah Sanderson of Salem.
  8 *Rebecca*, b. Dec. 10, 1762 ; m. July 27, 1784, Levi Harrington.
  9 *Joseph*, b. April 9, 1765 ; d. at Concord, where he resided, Feb. 4, 1802. He m. Hepzibah Hunt of that place.

2-5-   JOHN MULLIKEN m. Lydia Whiting, dau. of Thomas Whiting of Con. They were ad. to the ch. April 22, 1787. He d. March 9, 1840, aged 85 ; she d. Nov. 15, 1825, aged 68. He filled the office of selectman nineteen years, town clerk twelve years, treasurer eight years, and was a magistrate.

5-10 †*Nathaniel*, b. May 17, 1781 ; was twice married.
  11 †*John*, b. April 26, 1783 ; m. Susanna Reed.
  12 *Lucy*, b. March 30, 1785 ; d. July 6, 1805, aged 20.
  13 *Lydia*, b. Aug. 6, 1787 ; d. Oct. 14, 1811, aged 24.
  14 †*Isaac*, b. June 1, 1789 ; m. Mary Nelson.
  15 *Samuel*, b. April 20, 1791 ; grad. H. C. 1819, studied medicine, and established himself at Dorchester. He m. Mary L. Payson, and d. Feb. 19, 1843.
  16 *Faustina*, b. April 20, 1793 ; d. April 25, 1815, aged 22.

5-10-   NATHANIEL MULLIKEN m. May 22, 1806, Mary Chandler, dau. of Nathan and Ruth (Tidd) Chandler. She d. Oct. 27, 1817, aged 34, and he m. May 6, 1819, Lydia Sanderson of Salem. He d. June 28, 1865, aged 84 years. He was a deacon in the first church, and filled the most important offices in the town. He was selectman, assessor, town clerk, and treasurer,—and the last-named office he filled fifteen or sixteen years, and the former offices from five to nine years. He was also a justice of the peace.

10-17 *Lucy*, b. Aug. 26, 1806 ; m. Nov. 1, 1838, Joseph F. Daland of Wo.
  18 *John William*, b. Sept. 12, 1809. The town record has this entry connected with the record of his birth: "This child at his birth had four great-grandparents and four grandparents, all living in Lex., also bears the Christian name of two great-grandparents, one grandparent, and two uncles." He m. Sarah Jane Hunt of Camb. He moved to Charlestown, where he d. Sept. 19, 1854.
  19 *Mary*, b. May 17, 1811 ; m. Dec. 26, 1831, Luther Farnsworth, and had *Mary*, b. Oct. 15, 1832 ; *Rebecca S.*, b. Oct. 30, 1833 ; and *Emily M.*, b. Aug. 9, 1835, who d. May 11, 1863. Mr. Farnsworth d. Dec. 16, 1863, and his wife d. Nov. 8, 1861.
  20 *Nathaniel*, b. May 2, 1813 ; m. Nov. 15, 1836, Sarah Holt of Camb., where they resided for a time. He is now in Minnesota.
  21 *Nathan Chandler*, b. Feb. 19, 1815 ; m. Sept. 10, 1839, Faustina Roberts of Salem. They reside in Charlestown, where he is engaged in the ice business.

22 | *Eliza*, b. Jan. 31, 1820; m. 1845, Edwin Pierce. They have two chil., Eliza J., b. June 29, 1846; Edwin W., b. Dec. 16, 1849.
23 | *Ephraim*, b. March 24, 1822; m. 1849, Mary Ann Horton of Canton; they r. in Roxbury.
24 | †*Emery Abbott*, b. March 21, 1823; m. Avis M. Wellington.
25 | *Elijah S.*, b. June 30, 1824; m. Sept. 4, 1854, Helen S. Munyan of Hopedale, Milford; r. in Rhode Island.
26 | *Joseph W.*, b. June 14, 1825; d. Feb. 5, 1829.
27 | *Lydia W.*, b. Aug. 3, 1827; m. May 30, 1849, George F. H. Horton.
28 | *Augusta W.*, b. Aug. 18, 1829.

5–11– | JOHN MULLIKEN m. Nov. 30, 1813, Susanna Reed of Con. They were ad. to the ch. July 3, 1814. He d. Aug. 5, 1855, aged 72, and she d. Aug. 21, 1863. He filled the office of selectman, town clerk, and representative to the General Court.

11–29 | *Susan*, b. Sept. 19, 1814; m. May 7, 1835, Joseph F. Simonds.
30 | *Charles*, b. Oct. 8, 1816; d. Dec. 8, 1821.
31 | *Lydia*, b. Jan. 3, 1819; m. Sept. 20, 1861, Levi Bacon of Lowell. He was lost on board the Golden Gate, near California, 1862.
32 | †*George*, b. March 15, 1821; m. April 23, 1847, Charlotte Munroe.
33 | *Elizabeth R.*, b. Nov. 5, 1823; d. Aug. 18, 1825.
34 | *John*, b. April 26, 1826; is in business in Boston.

5–14– | ISAAC MULLIKEN m. Dec. 7, 1815, Mary Nelson, dau. of Josiah and Millicent (Bond) Nelson of Linc. He d. March 17, 1859, aged 69; she d. Dec. 8, 1861. He represented the town in the legislature three years, and filled important town offices.

14–35 | *Faustina*, b. April 17, 1817; m. May 17, 1854, William W. Clement.
36 | *Elizabeth*, b. March 16, 1819; d. Nov. 6, 1820.
37 | †*Henry*, b. Aug. 16, 1821; m. Adeline M. Locke.
38 | *Edward*, b. Nov. 25, 1823; m. Nov. 7, 1850, Harriet Smith of Stow.
39 | *Mary Caroline*, b. Jan. 8, 1826; m. Feb. 2, 1848, Wm. W. Clement.
40 | *Elizabeth*, b. Jan. 16, 1828; m. May 18, 1848, Hollis Gerry, and lives in Chelsea.
41 | *Joseph*, b. May 24, 1831; d. April 28, 1860.
42 | *Helen S.*, b. May 16, 1833; m. July 5, 1854, Elbridge G. Locke; r. in New York.

10–24– | EMERY ABBOTT MULLIKEN m. Oct. 17, 1850, Avis M. Wellington, dau. of Nehemiah and Anna (Stearns) Wellington.

24–43 | *Ann Eliza*, b. Nov. 9, 1851.   44 *John E. A.*, b. Sept. 8, 1856.
45 | *Amelia M.*, b. Sept. 15, 1858.
46 | *Alice W.*, b. Oct. 1862; d. Jan. 23, 1863.

11–32– | GEORGE MULLIKEN m. April 23, 1847, Charlotte Munroe, dau. of John and Charlotte Munroe. He resides in Somerville. His wife d. Dec. 8, 1861, and he m. again.

32–47 | *Charlotte M.*, b. April 27, 1848; d. July 4, 1855.
48 | *George Francis*, b. Oct. 6, 1851; d. Sept. 24, 1854.
49 | *Charles Henry*, b. Oct. 28, 1853.   50 *Clarence M.*, b. Oct. 13, 1855.
51 | *Harriet M.*, b. Feb. 6, 1858; d. 1866.

14–37– | HENRY MULLIKEN m. July 13, 1853, Adeline Matilda Locke, dau. of Hammond and Rebecca (Nevers) Locke, b. June 14, 1826.

37–52 | *William Henry*, b. June 30, 1854. 52 *Everett M.*, b. Mar. 26, 1857.

THE MUNROE FAMILY.

The Munroes, who acted a conspicuous part on the 19th of April, 1775, and were among the first settlers in Lexington, and who have from time to time filled some of the principal offices in the town, were of Scotch descent; though it is said that they came to Scotland from Ireland at a remote period. Dr. Doddridge, in his Life of Col. Gardner, has given an interesting account of the ancient family of Munroes, (of whom the Lexington Munroes were descendants,) from which account this notice is mostly taken.

The family of Munroes of Fowlis is among the most ancient and honorable families in the north of Scotland, and has generally been remarkable for a brave, martial, and patriotic spirit. They have intermarried with many of the best families and nobility in the North of Scotland; and, what is more to their honor, they were among the very first in those parts, who embraced the Reformation, which they zealously supported.

According to Buchanan, it was in the beginning of the eleventh century, and about the time of the conquest of England, when Malcolm, the second of that name, King of Scots, first distributed, or as it was expressed, *few-ed* out, or *fee-ed*, the lands in Scotland to the principal families, on account of their eminent services in his battles with the Danes. According to tradition, it was on that occasion that the country between the Borough of Dingwall and the waters of Alness in the shire of Ross, was given to Donald Munroe. A part of these lands were afterwards by the King erected into a Barony, called the *Barony of Fowlis*. Some of the Munroes were lords of this barony from its first erection; but we shall commence with them about the time they became Protestants.

George Munroe, IX Baron of Fowlis in a direct line from the above-mentioned Donald, the first Baron, was slain at the memorable battle of Bannockburn, fought by Robert Bruce of Scotland against Edward II, of England, in 1314. And George, X Baron of Fowlis, son of the former, was also slain, with a great many other of his name, at the battle of Hollydon Hill, near Berwick, where the Scots were defeated, July 22, 1333. Robert Munroe, XVII Baron of Fowlis, was slain at the battle of Pinkie, near Edinburgh, with many of his name, when the Scots were again defeated, in 1547. The first Protestant of this family was Robert Munroe, XVIII Baron of Fowlis, son of the last-mentioned, who came to the assistance of Mary, Queen of Scots, when she was involved in trouble at Inverness. He d. in 1588, and was succeeded by his son, Robert, XIX Baron of Fowlis, who d. the same year with his father. The next Baron was his brother Hector Munroe, who d. 1603.

Robert Munroe, son of Hector, was the XXI Baron. He flourished at the time that Gustavus Adolphus of Sweden was engaged in a Protestant war with Ferdinand II, in defence of the civil and religious liberties of Germany. The Baron, moved with pity and patriotism, joined Adolphus, with a great many of his clan of the same name, where they gained great distinction as soldiers. Robert became so eminent, that he was made colonel of two regiments, one of foot and the other of horse, at the same time. He d. of a wound received in crossing the Danube, in 1633. He was succeeded by Sir Henry Munroe, XXII Baron of Fowlis, the next male heir of the family, who was also a colonel in the same service, and upon crossing over into Britain, he was created a Baronet, in 1633. He d. at Hamburg two years after. His son, Sir Hector Munroe, was the XXIII Baron of Fowlis, and d. without issue 1651. Sir Robert Munroe, XXIV Baron of Fowlis, being the next of kin, succeeded him.

Up to this time there were three generals, eight colonels, five lieut.-colonels, eleven majors, and above thirty captains of the name of Munroe, besides a great number of subalterns,—all of the same original stock ; the descendants of Donald Munroe. Some of the family were for a long period in considerable military command in Sweden and many parts of Germany, and even in India.

General Robert Munroe, uncle to Sir Robert, the XXIV Baron, was in 1641, appointed by Charles II, major-general of the Scotch forces that were sent to Ireland to suppress the rebellion there. In 1644, at the head of 14,000 of the Scotch and English Protestants, he fought and defeated 22,000 of the Irish in Ulster. In 1645, he was surprised and taken prisoner by Col. Monk, and d. soon after. The general was succeeded in command by his nephew, Sir George Munroe, who had served under him in Ireland. He was made major-general by Charles II, and had a body of troops under him at Kendall, when James, Duke of Hamilton, was defeated by Cromwell at Lancaster in 1648. Upon this defeat, Sir George returned to Scotland, and defeated the Earl of Argyle. He afterwards went to Holland and joined his master, Charles II, at whose restoration he was made lieut.-general, and commander-in-chief in Scotland.

Sir John Munroe, XXV Baron of Fowlis, succeeded his father, Sir Robert, in 1668. He was a member of the Estates of Scotland at the Revolution, and a zealous promoter of that happy event. He was also a zealous Presbyterian, and being remarkable for size and corpulency, he was nick-named "the Presbyterian *mortar piece.*" He suffered both by fines and imprisonment for his devotion to the cause of religion, and d. 1696. Sir Robert Munroe, who succeeded his father in the barony as the XXVI of the family, was a pious and benevolent man, much beloved by the people. His son, Sir Robert, the XXVII Baron, succeeded him in 1729. He went early from the university to the camp, where he served seven years in Flanders, being for some time captain of the Royal Scots. On his return to England he was elected to Parliament, where he continued thirty years. He was greatly distinguished, like others of the family, for his military services. In 1715, he with his clan, in conjunction with the Earl of Sunderland, kept the Earl of Seaforth with a much larger force from joining the Rebel camp for near two months. Being made Governor of Inverness, Sir Robert kept four hundred men of his clan and name regularly paid and disciplined, and so rendered important service to his country.

He afterwards greatly distinguished himself at the battle of Fontenoy. He had obtained leave of His Royal Highness the Duke of Cumberland, to adopt his own mode of warfare, and employ his own regiment where and how he pleased. He was early in the field, and at every point of danger ; and wherever the Munroe regiment moved, victory followed its banner. He would march near the enemy, and when the French were about to fire, he would order his men to throw themselves upon the ground, and receive their fire ; and as soon as they drew the enemy's fire, he would order them to spring up and rush upon the foe, reserving their own fire till they had nearly closed with them, so that every shot would tell with dreadful effect. These attacks were repeated with the most marked success several times during the day, to the admiration of the whole army. It was observable that when he commanded his whole regiment to drop to the ground, he himself stood upright, exposed to the whole fire of the enemy. On being questioned afterwards, why he did this, he replied that though he could throw himself down as readily as younger and leaner men, his great bulk and corpulency would not suffer him to rise sufficiently early to rush upon the enemy with his men ; and the commander would not allow himself to be behind his men in such an emergency.

For his distinguished services at Fontenoy his Majesty was pleased to appoint him to succeed Gen. Ponsonby, who was slain that day in command of his troops. They were afterwards ordered to Scotland, and in the battle of Falkirk, being on one of the wings with his new regiment, they shamefully left their brave commander with five or six of his officers, to be cut to pieces by the enemy. According to the account of the rebels themselves, Sir Robert defended himself against six of them, and killed two of their number, but a seventh coming up, shot him through the body. At this fatal moment his brother, Doctor Munroe, who was near at hand, rushed to the rescue, and was slain near his brother. Doctor Munroe was not only a man of great bravery, but was highly distinguished in his profession, and much respected as a man. Scarcely less distinguished was another brother, Capt. George Munroe. He enjoyed the advantages of a liberal education, but turned his attention mainly to the profession of arms. He was in many engagements, in which he displayed great gallantry, and in one was severely wounded. He however recovered, and afterwards fell by the hands of a cowardly assassin.

"Thus," said the correspondent of Dr. Doddridge, "died these three worthy men, to the irreparable loss of their country; all of them remarkable for a brave spirit, full of love to their native land, and of distinguished zeal for religion and liberty; faithful in their promises, steadfast in their friendship, abundant in their charity to the poor and distressed; moderate in their resentments, and easy to be reconciled; and especially remarkable for their great and entire love to each other, so that one soul seemed, as it were, to actuate all the three."

Though we have brought this sketch down to 1746, we must go back about a century, to trace the history of the Munroes who came to America. The date of their emigration to this country is uncertain. Their history here, like that of many of the early settlers in this country, is handed down to us by tradition, and not by full and reliable records. As near as we can learn, they came to America about 1650. Being a young man without a family, and destitute of property, the name of the first emigrant, WILLIAM MUNROE, does not appear upon the public records till some time afterwards.

It is highly probable that the Munroes who settled in New England were prisoners of war taken by Cromwell, and sold as slaves or apprentices, as the term was. The custom was this: these prisoners were sold in England to shippers for a small sum, who sent them to this country, where they were sold into service of from three to ten years, to pay the first purchase, the cost of the passage, and such profits as the dealers in flesh and blood might be able to make. The Munroes were probably some of those who were taken at the battle of Worcester, where Cromwell was victorious. In 1651, a cargo of prisoners was consigned to Thomas Kemble of Boston. The list of prisoners contains the names of four *Munrows*, as the name was there spelled, viz., Robert, John, Hugh, and another whose first name is obliterated. This is supposed to be *William*, the ancestor of the Lex. Munroes. One of this number settled at Bristol, then in this State, but now in Rhode Island. The Munroes of Bristol were relatives of those of Lex., but how near it is impossible to say with certainty.

There is a tradition in the family that William Munroe was sold or bound out to a farmer by the name of Winship, who resided in that part of Cambridge called Menotomy (now Arlington), and that when his indentures expired, and he set up for himself, he went farther back into the woods, and procured a tract of land within the present limits of Lex., on a section now known by the name of *Scotland*, in honor of the native place of the first settler.

The name on the Lex. records in the first instances was spelt Munro or Munroe; but in a few years the first syllable was dropped, and many of the family spelled their name *Roe*. In fact, for a time Roe and Munroe seem to have been used interchangably, so that we find such entries as this: " bap. Mary *Roe*, daughter of William *Munroe*." Ultimately a better fashion prevailed, and the present orthography was adopted.

The record of the Munroes is extremely defective; the early settlers of that name being less given to letters than to arms.

1   WILLIAM MUNROE, the ancestor of all the Munroes of Lex. and this vicinity, was born in Scotland in 1625, and descended from the Munroe clan in Scotland, of which we have already spoken. He came to America in 1652, and consequently was at that time twenty-seven years of age. The first mention of him which I find in the Cambridge records is in 1657, when " Thomas Rose and William Row " were fined for not having rings in the nose of their swine. If he was sold as an apprentice when he was first brought over, his apprenticeship must have been rather a short one for those days, for he must have been his own man in 1657. He settled at Cambridge Farms about 1660, in the northeasterly part of the town, bordering on Woburn. His house was near the Wo. line, on what is now Woburn street, not far from the present residence of Hugh Graham.

Several of his sons lived with or not far from him at first; and it was said by Mrs. Sanderson, his great-granddaughter, who d. 1853, aged 104 years, that his old house looked like a rope-walk, so many additions had been made to it to accommodate his sons, as they settled in life. By adopting the custom of the Scottish clans, he in a manner confined the Munroes together, and made them for some time, as it were, a distinct people. A considerable portion of their original possessions still remain in the Munroe family.

Though he came to the country under unfavorable circumstances, and set up for himself rather late in life, he appears to have been quite successful in his worldly affairs, and to have been blessed with a large, prosperous family. He was made freeman in 1690. He was in the parish at its first organization, and was one of the committee to purchase a tract of land for the support of the ministry, with David Fiske, sen., Samuel Stone, sen., Ephraim Winship, Benjamin Muzzy, and John Tidd. In the subscription for building the meeting house, William Munroe's name is found, and his subscription of £2 shows that in public spirit and in pecuniary means he was among the first seven in the parish, and the subsequent tax bills, from 1693 to 1696, show that in point of taxable property he stood among the first half dozen men in the parish; thus showing conclusively that he was a man of enterprise and force of character. In 1694, he was one of the selectmen of Cambridge, of which Lex. was then a part; and subsequently his name appears in connection with several other important offices in the parish. He was ad. to the ch. in Lex. Feb. 1, 1699. He was three times married, though I have not been able to find the record of the marriages, or learn the family name of his first two wives. He was probably forty years old when he married, and still he reared a family of thirteen children. He m. about 1665, Martha ——, by whom he had four children, and second, m. Mary ——, about 1672, by whom he had nine children. His second wife, Mary, d. Aug. 1692, aged 41, consequently she must have been twenty-six years younger than her husband. He m. third, Mrs.

Elizabeth Wyer, wid. of Edward Wyer of Charlestown. She d. Dec. 14, 1715, aged 79, and he d. Jan. 27, 1717, at the advanced age of ninety-two. Though he married his last wife when he was well stricken in years, he must have married for love and not for money, for in the papers connected with the settlement of his estate, we find an inventory of the property which belonged to her, consisting of one bed, one bolster, one pillow, one chest, one warming pan, one pair of tongs, and one pewter platter.

His will, dated Nov. 14, 1716, mentions sons John, William, George, Daniel, Joseph, and Benjamin, and dau. Eleanor Burgess, to whom he gave the sole use of his house, Martha Comee, Hannah Pierce, Elizabeth Rugg, and Mary Fassett.

1- 2   †*John*, b. March 10, 1666; m. Hannah ——.
   3   *Martha*, b. Nov. 2, 1667; m. Jan. 21, 1688, John Comee of Con. He came to Lex., where he lived and reared a family of children. She d. April 13, 1729, aged 62.
   4   †*William*, b. Oct. 10, 1669; m. Mary Cutler.
   5   †*George*, b. ——; m. Sarah ——.
   6   †*Daniel*, b. Aug. 12, 1673; m. Dority ——.
   7   *Hannah*, b. ——; m. Dec. 21, 1692, Joseph Pierce, whose first wife was Ruth Holland, and whose third wife was Beriah, wid. of Daniel Child; by Hannah he had eight children.
   8   *Elizabeth*, b. ——; m. Thomas Rugg, by whom she had eleven children born between 1691 and 1714.
   9   *Mary*, b. June 24, 1678; m. about 1700, Joseph Fassett. They lived on what is called the Page Place, now in Bedford, but then in Lexington.
  10   *David*, b. Oct. 6, 1680; not mentioned in his father's will.
  11   *Eleanor*, b. Feb. 24, 1683; m. Aug. 21, 1707, William Burgess of Charlestown. She had four children, whose births are recorded in Lexington.
  12   *Sarah*, b. March 18, 1685; m. George Blanchard, about 1707.
  13   †*Joseph*, b. Aug. 16, 1687; m. Elizabeth ——.
  14   †*Benjamin*, b. Aug. 16, 1690; was twice married.

1-2-   JOHN MUNROE m. Hannah ——. He was ad. to the ch. Feb. 1, 1699, together with his father, and sisters Martha Comee, Elizabeth Rugg, and Hannah Pierce. He was a subscriber for the meeting house in 1692, and was taxed for the purchase of the ministerial land in 1693. He was one of the assessors in 1699, 1714, and 1720; was constable in 1700, selectman in 1718, '19, and '26, and treasurer 1718, '19, and '20. He d. Sept. 14, 1753, aged 87; she d. April 14, 1716, aged 42. He was employed many years to ring the bell and to sweep out the meeting house, which shows that he did not consider it derogatory to perform any honest labor. He also illustrated the truth of the old ballad, that "there are sweepers in high life as well as in low"; for in addition to sweeping the meeting house, he filled most of the important offices in the town.

In consequence of the number of the Munroes, and the repetition of the names *William* and *John* and *George* and *Mary* and *Sarah* and *Hannah*, we find it very difficult in some cases to trace the families. This difficulty was felt by themselves and their contemporaries, and consequently, when speaking of the individuals, they had recourse to certain other designations. A specimen of this is embodied in the following not very elegant couplet, preserved by one of the descendants.

> "Lieutenant John and Ensign Roe,
> Sergeant George and Corporal Joe."

It will be seen by these titles that the family, true to their instincts, were given to the military, and that John was honored with the office of *Lieutenant*. We also learn that John Munroe and others had nine hundred acres of land granted to them in 1735, for services rendered in the Indian fight at Lamprey River, June 6, 1690.

2-15 | *John*, bap. 1699; probably m. Rachel ——.
16 | *Hannah*, bap. 1699; d. April 14, 1716.
17 | *Constance*, bap. 1699.
18 | *Jonathan*, bap. March 12, 1699; d. Aug. 20, 1724.
19 | †*William*, bap. Feb. 1, 1701; was twice married.
20 | *Elizabeth*, bap. March 5, 1703.
21 | *Susannah*, bap. July 1, 1705; m. June 16, 1724, Ebenezer Nichols.
22 | †*Jonas*, bap. Nov. 22, 1707; he was twice married.
23 | *Martha*, b. Dec. 6, 1710.
24 | †*Marrett*, b. Dec. 6, 1713; m. April 17, 1737, Deliverance Parker.

1-4- | WILLIAM MUNROE m. Mary Cutler, dau. of Thomas. She d. June 26, 1713, aged 33, and he m. Johanna Russell, dau. of Philip and Johanna Russell, about 1716. He d. Jan. 2, 1759, aged 91, and she d. Sept. 17, 1748. He had seven children by his first wife, and two by his last. He was an ensign in the colonial militia, and hence was denominated "Ensign Roe." He was ad. to the ch. April 9, 1699, and his wife Mary was ad. April 30 of the same year, and his wife Johanna was ad. Dec. 24, 1727. He was constable, 1708, assessor, 1713, and selectman, 1724, '30, '34, and '35.

4-25 | *Mary*, b. April 3, 1699. 26 *Abigail*, b. June 28, 1701.
27 | †*William*, b. Dec. 19, 1703; m. June 3, 1733, Sarah Mason.
28 | †*Thomas*, b. March 19, 1706; m. Elizabeth ——.
29 | †*David*, b. Sept. 28, 1708; m. Abigail Wellington.
30 | *Ruth*, b. March 16, 1711. 31 *Hannah*, b. March 19, 1713.
32 | †*Philip*, b. Feb. 26, 1718; m. Mary ——.
33 | *Johanna*, b. Oct 21, 1726; d. Jan. 23, 1749, unm.

1-5- | GEORGE MUNROE m. Sarah ——. He was generally designated "Sergeant George." He was a tythingman, 1719, and selectman, 1728. He d. Jan. 17, 1749, aged 73, and she d. Dec. 4, 1752, aged 75.

5-34 | †*William*, b. Jan. 6, 1700; m. May 6, 1735, Rebecca Locke of Wo.
35 | *Sarah*, b. Oct. 17, 1701.
36 | *Dorothy*, b. Nov. 19, 1703; d. April following.
37 | *Lydia*, b. Dec. 13, 1705.
38 | †*George*, b. Oct. 17, 1707; m. Sarah Phipps.
39 | †*Robert*, b. May 4, 1712; m. July 28, 1737, Anne Stone.
40 | †*Samuel*, b. Oct. 23, 1714; the record adds, "He was the first bap. in the new meeting house."
41 | †*Andrew*, bap. June 4, 1718; m. May 26, 1763, Mrs. Lucy Simonds.
42 | *Lucy*, b. Aug. 20, 1720; m. —— Watson of Camb.

1-6- | DANIEL MUNROE m. Dority ——. He was ad. to the ch. Feb. 18, 1728, and d. Feb. 26, 1734, aged 61. His widow administered upon his estate.

6-43 | *Daniel*, b. June 27, 1717.
44 | †*Jedediah*, b. May 20, 1721; m. Abigail Loring.
45 | *Sarah*, b. June 21, 1724. 46 *Dorothy*, b. June 21, 1728.
47 | †*John*, b. May 30, 1731; m. Anna Kendall of Woburn.

1-13-   JOSEPH MUNROE m. Elizabeth ——. He was known by the cognomen of "Corporal Joe."

13-48   ‡*Joseph*, b. May 13, 1713; m. Hannah ——.
49   *Elizabeth*, b. June 12, 1715.
50   *Nathan*, b. Sept. 7, 1716; m. Nov. 23, 1738, Mercy Benjamin. He moved to Con., where he had a family of seven children. Several of his sons settled in Northboro', Shrewsbury, Worcester, and Spencer in Worcester County.
51   *Joshua*, b. Dec. 22, 1717; m. Ruth ——, resided in Concord.
52   *Nathaniel*, b. Nov. 17, 1719. He embarked in 1740 in the expedition to Cuba, and d. before his return.
53   *Amos*, b. April 21, 1721; d. July 7, 1765.
54   *Abigail*, b. Jan. 21, 1723.   55 *Mary*, b. Jan. 21, 1726.
56   *Eleanor*, b. June 13, 1727.   57 *Kezia*, b. Oct. 16, 1731.
58   *Hannah*, b. Nov. 29, 1733; m. July 26, 1760, Gershom Williams. He d. at West Camb., at the remarkable age of 100 years.

1-14-   BENJAMIN MUNROE m. Abigail ——. She d. and he m. 1748, Mrs. Prudence (Harrington) Estabrook, wid. of John Estabrook of Lex. She d. 1778. He resided in Linc., and d. April 6, 1765. His will, dated April 1, and proved April 22, 1766, mentions wife Prudence and dau. Rebecca Sawin, Abigail Brown, Sarah Cutler, Martha Stone, Mary Parker, Anna Matthis, Eunice Wheeler, and children of Lydia Williams, deceased, and son Benjamin.

14-59   *Lydia*, b. March 7, 1718; m. Oct. 19, 1740, Joseph Williams, Camb.
60   *Abigail*, b. Oct. 5, 1719; m. Feb. 7, 1745, Joseph Brown of Weston.
61   *A child*, b. ——; d. Nov. 9, 1721.
62   *Benjamin*, b. June 21, 1723; m. Mary Merriam of Lex.; lived in Lincoln.
63   *Rebecca*, b. Aug. 24, 1725; m. Manning Sawin of Marlb., May, 1746.
64   *Sarah*, b. July 26, 1727; m. May 12, 1750, Josiah Parks of Lincoln. He d. and she m. Dec. 22, 1753, Elisha Cutler of Lexington.
65   *Martha*, b. March 18, 1729; m. Sept. 8, 1748, Isaac Stone of Lex.
66   *Mary*, twin of the above; m. Josiah Parker, Jr.
67   *Anne*, b. March 4, 1732; m. —— Matthis.
68   *Eunice*, b. Apr. 9, 1734; m. June 26, 1756, Edmund Wheeler, Linc.
69   *Kezia*, b. April 22, 1736; not mentioned in her father's will, probably died before that period.

2-19-   WILLIAM MUNROE m. Phebe ——. She d. Jan. 15, 1742, and he m. May 29, 1745, Mrs. Tabitha (Hobbs) Jones of Weston. He had six children by his first wife, and four by his last. He is frequently denominated the *black-smith*, to distinguish him from others of the same name, one of whom was denominated the *shoemaker*, for the same reason. His will, dated March 25, 1777, and proved June 4, 1783, mentions wife Tabitha, dau. Phebe Caldwell, Dorcas Parker, Bridget Maxwell, Sarah Barker, Lucy Hobbs, and Susanna, and son Oliver.

19-70   *Phebe*, b. April 28, 1726; m. Adam Caldwell of Bedford.
71   *Jonathan*, b. April 1, 1729; d. June 17, 1739.
72   ‡*William*, b. May 12, 1730; not mentioned in his father's will.
73   *Edmund*, b. May 3, 1732; d. April 4, 1735.
74   *Bridget*, b. April 27, 1735; m. Nov. 4, 1760, Hugh Maxwell, then both of Bedford.
75   *Susanna*, b. ——; m. April 27, 1780, Isaac Reed of Woburn.
76   *Hannah*, b. Dec. 15, 1742; not mentioned in the will.

77 | *Sarah*, b. April 18, 1746; m. —— Barber.
78 | *Oliver*, b. Feb. 9, 1748: m. and lived in Wat., where he d.
79 | *Dorcas*, b. Nov. 14, 1750; m. Dec. 2, 1772, Ebenezer Parker.
80 | *Lucy*, b. Sept. 19, 1752; m. Nov. 24, 1774, Samuel Hobbs of Weston.

2-22-

JONAS MUNROE m. June 3, 1734, Joanna Locke, dau. of Joseph and Margaret (Mead) Locke, b. Feb. 2, 1713. She d. Sept. 17, 1748, aged 35, and he m. about 1750, Rebecca Watts of Chelsea. He d. Nov. 9, 1765, and his wid. m. April 19, 1773, John Muzzy of Lex., grandson of the first settler, and his second wife. Jonas Munroe was honored with the title of *Lieutenant.*

22-81 | *Jonas*, b. Nov. 2, 1734; d. June 3, 1760. He was in the French war.
82 | †*John*, b. Feb. 1, 1737; m. April 13, 1762, Lydia Bemis of Weston.
83 | †*Stephen*, b. Oct. 25, 1739; m. July 8, 1766, Nancy Perry of Wo.
84 | *Jonathan*, b. May 25, 1742; m. Abigail Kendall of Woburn.
85 | *Joanna*, b. April 12, 1747; m. July 9, 1771, John Adams.
86 | †*Ebenezer*, b. April 29, 1752; m. May 10, 1781, Lucy Simonds, Wo.
87 | *Rebecca*, b. June 17, 1755; m. May 22, 1777, John Muzzy, Jr.
88 | *Martha*, b. Sept. 12, 1758; d. at Ashburnham, 1793, unm.

2-24-

MARRETT MUNROE m. April 17, 1737, Deliverance Parker, dau. of Lieut. Josiah Parker, b. May 18, 1721. He d. March 26, 1798, aged 85, and she d. Aug. 9, 1799, aged 78. His will, dated Feb. 18, 1789, and proved May 1, 1798, mentions wife Deliverance, sons Josiah, Nathan, and Thaddeus, and dau. Rachel, Mary Underwood, Bethia, Deliverance Winship, Elizabeth Buckman, and a child of dau. Ann Nurse, deceased. He was selectman, 1762, '63, '64, and '67. He resided near the Common, on the place now occupied by Mr. John Hudson.

24-89 | *Rachel*, b. Nov. 29, 1737; d. unm. in Boston, where she lived.
90 | *Josiah*, b. June 29, 1742; d. June 12, 1743.
91 | †*Josiah*, b. Feb. 12, 1745; m. Nov. 15, 1768, Susan Fitch of Bed.
92 | †*Nathan*, b. Aug. 9, 1747; m. Oct. 3, 1769, Elizabeth Harrington.
93 | *Mary*, b. March 3, 1749; m. March 21, 1771, Joseph Underwood.
94 | *Bethia*, b. Jan. 22, 1753; lived at Bellows Falls; d. unm., aged 93.
95 | *Deliverance*, b. July 22, 1755; m. John Winship.
96 | *Anna*, b. June 23, 1758; m. Josiah Nurse of Framingham.
97 | *Thaddeus*, b. Oct. 26, 1760; traded in South Carolina, where he died, unmarried.
98 | *John*, b. and d. April 3, 1763.
99 | *Elizabeth*, b. Oct. 4, 1765; m. July 1, 1781, Jacob Buckman, father of Hon. Bowen Buckman, of Woburn.

4-27-

WILLIAM MUNROE m. June 3, 1733, Sarah Mason, dau. of John and Elizabeth (Spring) Mason, b. June 7, 1714. She was ad. to the ch. May 4, 1735. It is stated, in a paper left by one of the family, that he had just been engaged as a committee man to enlarge the burying yard, and taking a sudden cold while haying in his meadow, he was attacked with a violent fever, which in a few days proved fatal; and that he was the first to be laid in the new portion of the yard he had so recently procured. This account is confirmed by his grave stone, which has this inscription : " William Munroe d. Aug. 18, 1747, aged 44 years. The first buried in this (the new portion) yard." She m. Feb. 27, 1753, Isaac Bowman, Esq., and d. April 13, 1785, aged 71.

27-100 †*Edmund.* b. Feb. 2, 1736; m. Aug. 31, 1768, Rebecca Harrington.
   101 *Sarah,* b. May 1, 1738; m. Dec. 2, 1762, William Tidd of Lex.
        They moved to New Braintree, where they died.
   102 *Catharine,* b. Sept. 29, 1740; m. Nov. 22, 1764, Joseph Bowman of
        Lex. They moved to New Braintree.
   103 †*William,* b. Oct. 28, 1742; he was twice married.
   104 *Abigail,* b. Feb. 24, 1744; m. Daniel Spooner, Esq., of Hartland,
        Vt., where she d. 1816, at the remarkable age of 102 years.
   105 *Nehemiah,* b. July 1, 1747; m. Dec. 5, 1771, Avis Hammond. They
        moved to Roxbury, where he d. Aug. 2, 1828, aged 81.

4-28-   THOMAS MUNROE m. Elizabeth ——. He moved to Con., where
        his children were born. They had nine children. *Thomas,* his
        oldest son, b. May 4, 1731, m. for his second wife, Dec. 29, 1763,
        Mrs. Hepzibah Raymond of Lex., wid. of Jonathan Raymond. His
        second son, John, b. May 4, 1753, grad. H. C. 1751; studied divinity
        but was never ordained. He taught school in Con., and moved to
        Harvard in 1772, where he d. THOMAS MUNROE, the father, was a
        captain.

4-29-   DAVID MUNROE m. Feb. 29, 1733, Abigail Wellington, dau. of
        Benjamin and Lydia (Brown) Wellington, b. July 14, 1715. He
        was a member of Capt. Blodgett's company, which marched to the
        relief of Fort William-Henry, in 1757. He was also in the French
        war in 1760, and was a corporal. He d. June 13, 1764, aged 55.

29-106 *David,* b. 1734; m. Oct. 17, 1765, Elizabeth Foye of Charlestown.
   107 *Benjamin,* bap. Sept. 12, 1736; d. in Stow, without issue.
   108 *Abraham,* b. Aug. 14, 1738; m. Lois Chapen of Stow. He was a
        lieutenant in the French war. He afterward moved to Northboro',
        where he kept a public house.

4-32-   PHILIP MUNROE m. Mary ——. They o. c. Nov. 16, 1740, when
        their oldest child was bap. They had six children in Lex., and
        moved to Shrewsbury, where their last three children were bap. The
        Shrewsbury ch. record says, "they being in covenant relations with
        the ch. in Lex."

32-109 *Mary,* b. Dec. 4, 1740; d. young.   110 *Lois,* b. Dec. 11, 1742.
   111 *Jonathan,* b. Dec. 28, 1744.   112 *Prudence,* bap. May 27, 1747.
   113 *Mary,* bap. April 10, 1757.   114 *Lemuel,* bap. March 4, 1759.
   115 *Abraham,* bap. at Shrewsbury, ⎱ Sept. 4, 1763.
   116 *Abigail,*   "   "   ⎰
   117 *Sarah,* bap.   "   Oct. 14, 1764.

5-34-   WILLIAM MUNROE m. May 6, 1736, Rebecca Locke, dau. of James
        and Sarah (Cutter) Locke, b. Nov. 11, 1711. He was killed July
        10, 1778, by a cart falling upon him, aged 78. His wid. d. Nov. 19,
        1798, aged 87. Her thirds were distributed, in 1799, to James,
        Philemon, William, and the heirs of Isaac, deceased.

34-118 *James,* b. Dec. 12, 1735; m. Aug. 18, 1763, Lucy Watson of Camb.
        She d. July 10, 1783, and he m. Mrs. Sarah Hancock. He resided
        in Camb., where he was a deacon, and d. 1804. He was appointed
        armorer by the Provincial congress in 1775, and acted in that
        capacity for some time. He was a blacksmith by trade.
   119 *Isaac,* b. Sept. 11, 1737. He m. Dec. 25, 1760, Mary Hutchinson
        of Charlestown. She d. and he m. June 16, 1791, Mrs. Lydia
        Caldwell of Wo. He resided in West Camb., and was deacon of

the Baptist church there. He d. July 17, 1791, from the sting of a bee, leaving his second wife for the second time a widow, after a marriage of twenty-one days.

120 *Asa*, b. Dec. 29, 1739; d. Feb. 20, 1825, aged 85, unm. He was in the battle of Lex., being a member of Parker's company. He was in the campaign at White Plains, in 1776.

121 *Rebecca*, b. Jan. 12, 1742; d. unm. Sept. 6, 1767, aged 26.

122 *Lydia*, b. Feb. 21, 1744; m. June 23, 1768, Phinehas Parker of Reading, afterwards of Pepperell; d. 1781, without issue.

123 *Amos*, b. May 31, 1746; d. July 5, 1765.

124 *Mary*, b. Oct. 10, 1748; m. 1772, Samuel Sanderson, and d. Oct. 15, 1852, at the remarkable age of 104 years, 5 days.

125 *Hannah*, b. Sept. 26, 1751; m. Jan. 4, 1774, William Porter.

126 †*Philemon*, b. Oct. 20, 1753; he was twice married.

127 †*William*, b. Aug. 29, 1756; m. Abigail Harrington.

5-38-   GEORGE MUNROE m. Nov. 25, 1731, Sarah Phipps. He d. June 24, 1743, aged 37. His wid., Sarah, administered upon his estate. Timothy Wellington was appointed, March 7, 1747, guardian of Timothy, Thaddeus, and Elizabeth, under fourteen years of age, and of George, fifteen years of age.

38-128 †*George*, bap. May 13, 1733; m. Anna Bemis.

129 †*Timothy*, bap. April 20, 1735; settled in Lynn.

130 *Thaddeus*, bap. Aug. 20, 1738.   131 *Elizabeth*, bap. Mar. 23, 1740.

5-39-   ROBERT MUNROE m. July 28, 1737, Anne Stone, dau. of John and Mary (Reed) Stone. He was a soldier in the French war, was the standard bearer at the taking of Louisburg, in 1758, and was also in the service in 1762. Having served the colonies against the French and Indians, we might naturally suppose that he would be true to the family instinct, and to the calls of patriotism in defending the colonies against any other foe. And so he was. Being the ensign of Parker's gallant co., he was on the Common on the 19th of April, 1775, and stood manfully at his post; and fell, one of the first victims of British oppression, on the very field where he was posted by his gallant commander. He was in the 64th year of his age at the time of his death.

39-132 *Ebenezer*, b. Feb. 5, 1737; d. June 25, 1740.

133 *Anna*, b. Aug. 13, 1740; m. May 8, 1760, Daniel Harrington.

134 *Ruth*, b. July 26, 1742; m. Jan. 9, 1766, William Tidd, who was lieutenant in Capt. Parker's co., and was wounded in the battle of Lexington.

135 ‡*Ebenezer*, b. Nov. 15, 1744; m. May 2, 1771, Martha Smith.

136 ‡*John*, b. June 15, 1748; m. Dec. 3, 1772, Rebecca Wellington.

5-40-   SAMUEL MUNROE m. Abigail ——. There is no record of his family except Jonathan; but there are indications on the records of his having other children. I set down the following as the most probable. He was in the service five months at Ticonderoga, in 1776, and three months at Dorchester, the same year. He probably moved to Townsend, about 1780.

40-137 *John*, b. ——.   138 *Jonathan*, b. July 15, 1759.

139 *Eunice*, b. ——; m. first, Thaddeus Winship, and second, Ebenezer Steadman.

140 *Levi*, b. Feb. 21, 1771.

5-41- ANDREW MUNROE m. May 26, 1763, Mrs. Mary (Mixer) Si-
mouds, wid. of Daniel Simonds. He was in the French war, in
1758, '59, and '60. He d. Sept. 15, 1766, and his wid. settled his
estate.

41-141 *Andrew*, b. March 13, 1764.
142 *Ishmael*, b. Oct. 9, 1766, after the death of his father. This was the
second posthumous child his mother had,—one by each husband.
He m. Feb. 27, 1794, Elizabeth Skilton, both of Woburn.

6-44- JEDEDIAH MUNROE m. Abigail Loring. dau. of Joseph and Lydia
(Fiske) Loring. She was a twin with Mary, and a sister of Dea.
Joseph Loring. He was a member of Capt. Parker's co., and rallied
with his townsmen in defence of freedom on the 19th of April, 1775.
He was wounded in the morning; but his devotion to the cause was
too deep-seated to be quenched by the first flow of blood. He
marched with the co. toward Con. to meet the British on their re-
treat, and was killed in the afternoon, aged 54.

44-143 *Daniel*, b. Sept. 29, 1744; m. Abigail Parker of Roxbury, where he
lived and died.
144 *Jedediah*, b. ——; m. Sarah Parker, and lived in Boston.
145 *Solomon*, b. ——; m. and lived in Boston.
146 †*Joseph*, bap. Dec. 4, 1757; m. July 22, 1783, Rhoda Leath of
Woburn.
147 *Dolly*, bap. March 30, 1760; d. unm.
148 *Zacharias*, } twins, bap. July 1, 1764; } d. young.
149 *Elizabeth*, }
150 *Elizabeth*, b. ——; m. March 23, 1789, Abel Walker of Woburn.

6-47- JOHN MUNROE m. Dec. 23, 1747, Anna Kendall of Wo. He
marched to the relief of Fort William-Henry, 1757. He was a member of Capt. Parker's company, and took part in the affairs on the
19th of April, marched to Cambridge with the company on the day
of the battle of Bunker Hill, and was in the campaign, in 1776, in
the Jerseys. They were ad. to the ch. in Lexington on confession,
in 1757. He probably resided in Wo. a portion of his life.

47-151 *Anna*, b. Nov. 18, 1759.   152 *Sarah*, bap. July 21, 1767.
153 *John*, bap. July 21, 1767.   154 *Lydia*, bap. July 22, 1767.

13-48- JOSEPH MUNROE m. Hannah ——. He was in the French war,
1755. He moved to Concord, and resided in that part of the town
which was set off to form the town of Carlisle, and was one of the
members of the ch. organized there in 1781. He had a family of six
children, b. between 1742 and 1755, who settled in Carlisle and
Acton; except Joseph, who settled as a physician at Hillsboro',
N. H., and d. Feb. 24, 1798.

19-72- WILLIAM MUNROE d. 1755, aged 25 years, probably unm. His
will, dated April 4, 1755, and proved Oct. 13, 1755, mentions brother-
in-law Adam Caldwell of Bedford, and sisters Bridget and Hannah.
He was a sergeant in the French war, in 1754 and 1755.

22-82- JOHN MUNROE m. April 13, 1762, Lydia Bemis of Weston, dau.
of John and Hannah Bemis. He was a member of the Lex. company
in 1775. The record of his family is extremely defective. We find
the mention of only one child, though he may have had more. He
marched to Cambridge on the 17th of June, 1775.

82-155 | *Lydia*, bap. May 17, 1767; m. Jan. 16, 1783, Jonathan Page of Lincoln. He afterwards resided in Charlestown, where he kept a tavern of some note. He rose to the rank of colonel in the militia; and during the war of 1812 was stationed in Boston Harbor, and superintended the erection of some of the fortifications.

22-83- | STEPHEN MUNROE m. July 8, 1766, Nancy Perry of Wo. He was in the French war, 1762, was in the battle of Lex. 1775, and marched to Camb. on the 17th of June, at the time of the battle of Bunker Hill. He perhaps resided for a time in Wo.; also in the State of Maine. He d. July 30, 1826, aged 87.

83-156 | *Nancy*, b. ———; m. —— Caldwell of Woburn.
157 | *Stephen*, b. ———; r. in Concord.
158 | *Joanna*, b. ———; m. Daniel Russell.
159 | *James*, b. ———; he was feeble-minded. He was an inmate of the almshouse, and disappeared mysteriously, leading to the suspicion that he might have been murdered. Human bones were found in the woods some twelve months afterwards, supposed to be his. The mystery was never revealed.

22-86- | EBENEZER MUNROE m. May 10, 1781, Lucy Simonds of Wo. He was a member of the Lex. minute men, and ready on the 19th of April to do battle in freedom's cause. He was wounded in the elbow in the morning, but mounted his horse and rode from town to town, alarming the people and rousing them to action, until quite exhausted by the loss of blood. He claimed to have fired the first gun on the American side. That he did return the fire is abundantly proved by the testimony of others. His own account is as follows: " After the first fire (of the regulars) I received a wound in my arm; as I turned to run, I discharged my gun into the main body of the enemy. Another ball passed between my arm and my body, and just marked my clothes; one ball cut off a part of my ear locks, which were pinned up. The balls flew so thick, I thought there was no chance of escape, and that I might as well fire my gun, as stand still and do nothing." Deposition taken April 2, 1825. Ebenezer Munroe performed other duties in the Revolution, being one of the number who joined in the campaign in the Jerseys in 1776.

He moved to Ashburnham soon after the close of the war, where he was a lieutenant and a respectable citizen. He d. at Ashburnham 1825, and his wid. m. John Adams as his second wife. Ebenezer Munroe was half-brother to Mr. Adams's first wife. Mr. Adams spent his youth in West Camb., went to Ashburnham previous to the Revolution, lived there till he was nearly 100, when he went to live with a son in Penn., and d. 1849, aged 104 years, 1 mo., 5 days. He retained his faculties to the last, and is said to have made a pair of shoes the day he was 104.

88-160 | *Charles*, b. ———.   161 | *Lucy*, b. ———.
162 | *Ebenezer*, b. ———.   163 | *Jonas*, b. ———.
164 | *John*, b. ———.   165 | *Rebecca*, b. ———.
166 | *Herrick*, b. ———.

24-91- | JOSIAH MUNROE m. Nov. 16, 1768, Susan Fitch of Bed. He was in the French war in 1762. He also served three months in the Jerseys, in 1776. He then entered the Continental Line, and served two and a half years. After the close of the war he drew land in what was afterward Ohio. He settled in Marietta in that State, where he was for a time post-master. He had at least one child b. in Lex. viz., *Susanna*, bap. Nov. 10, 1771. They had another dau. and a son b. in Bedford, before he moved to Ohio.

24-92-

NATHAN MUNROE m. Oct. 3, 1769, Elizabeth Harrington, dau. of Henry and Sarah (Laughton) Harrington, b. Sept. 17, 1750. He was a member of Parker's minute men, and took part in the battle of Lex. in 1775. He resided on Monument street, where Mr. John Hudson now resides. His house received several balls, which were taken out subsequently, when the house was repaired. She d. Dec. 24, 1812.

92-167 *Dolly*, b. Nov. 18, 1769; m. Jan. 28, 1788, Elijah Pierce.
168 *Arethusa*, b. Mar. 10, 1773; m. June 20, 1793, William Fox of Wo.
169 *Betsey*, b. April 5, 1776; m. March 20, 1798, Munson Johnson.
170 *John*, b. June 15, 1778; m. a Macy in Nantucket, and r. there.
171 †*Nathan*, b. Oct. 23, 1780; m. Susanna Loring.
172 †*Jonathan*, b. May 26, 1783; m. Feb. 13, 1812, Rhoda Johnson.
173 *Polly*, b. March 11, 1785; m. June 13, 1811, Thomas Hunnewell of Charlestown.
174 *Dorcas*, b. March 31, 1788; m. Nov. 29, 1810, Leonard Brown.
175 *Thaddeus*, b. Sept. 14, 1790; r. at Quincy, Ill.
176 *Harris*, b. May 29, 1793; d. in Dedham, 1829.

27-100-

EDMUND MUNROE m. Aug. 31, 1768, Rebecca Harrington, dau. of Jonathan and Abigail Harrington, b. Feb. 17, 1751. She was sister to Jonathan Harrington, who d. 1854, the last survivor of the battle of Lex. Edmund Munroe was distinguished as a military man. Entering the Provincial service at an early age, he was promoted to an ensign in a corps of rangers commanded by Maj. Rogers, which performed signal service in the French war. In 1761, he was acting adjutant in Col. Hoar's regiment at Crown Point. In 1762, he received a commission from Gov. Bernard, as a lieutenant in His Majesty's service, and continued with the troops at Crown Point, Ticonderoga, and vicinity, till the peace of 1763. His kinsmen Robert and Abraham were officers in the same service with him. He not only served in the French and Indian war, but being enrolled in the company of Lex. minute men, he met the enemy on the 19th of April, and shared in the dangers of that day. But his devotion to the cause of the colony did not permit him to cease from effort when the oppressors were driven from his native village. Having served under Rogers and Hoar, the companions and co-laborers with Wolf and Barre and Putnam, he was not willing to confine his efforts to a limited field. As early as August, 1776, we find him on his way to meet the British on the same fields where he had toiled with them in subduing the French and Indians. He was commissioned as lieutenant on the 12th of July, 1776, in Capt. Miles's co. and Col. Reed's regiment. On the 16th of the same month he was appointed quartermaster and destined to the northern frontier. In a letter addressed to his wife, dated Charlestown, N. H., Aug. 5. 1776, he says, " I have been used very well by the field officers of the regiment. We shall march from this place for Ticonderoga this day."

On the first of January following, he received his commission as captain in Col. Bigelow's regiment. He was with the Northern army under Gates, at Stillwater, Saratoga, and Bennington; and so distinguished himself that after the capture of Burgoyne he was presented by his superior officers with a pair of candle-sticks,—a part of the traveling equipage or tent ornaments of Gen. Burgoyne.

The capture of Burgoyne transferred the seat of war to the Middle

States; and Capt. Munroe repaired to the Jerseys, and joined the army under Washington, where, on the 28th of June, 1778, he was slain on the field of Freehold, commonly called the Battle of Monmouth. The same cannon ball which deprived the country of the services of the gallant captain, killed George Munroe, his kinsman, and maimed for life Joseph Cox of Lexington, who was a wheelwright by trade, and worked at that business in Roxbury, in 1790. He wore a wooden leg.

The Burgoyne candlesticks of which we have spoken, together with a sword, a curious beaded Indian powder horn, several bead belts, pistols, &c., used by Capt. Munroe in the French war, were left by his widow, in 1834, to her son Edmund.

When Capt. Munroe entered upon the command of a co. in the Continental line, he had in his co. fifteen men from Lex., viz., Nehemiah Estabrook, David Fiske, Pomp Blackman, Samuel Crafts, Jupiter Tree, Thaddeus Munroe, Amos Russell, George Munroe, Joseph Cox, David Simonds, Ebenezer Hadley, James Fowle, Thomas Hadley, Levi Mead, and Seth Read.

Among these original papers left in the family is the oath of office, bearing the signature of Capt. Munroe, and that of the Baron de Kalb. We will give this document entire, with a fac-simile of their hands.

I, Edmund Munroe, Captain in Col. Bigelow's regiment, do acknowledge the United States of America to be Free, Independent, and Sovereign States, and declare that the people thereof owe no allegiance to George, the Third, King of Great Britain; and I renounce and abjure any allegiance or obedience to him; and I do swear that I will to the utmost of my power support, maintain, and defend the said United States against the said King George the Third, his heirs and successors, and his or their abettors, assistants, and adherents; and will serve the said United States in the office of Captain, which I now hold, with fidelity, according to the best of my ability, skill, and understanding.

Edm. Munro Capt

Sworn to, Camp at
Valley Forge, May 18, 1778. }

The Baron de Kalb
Maj Gl.

Capt. Munroe was deliberately brave, without enthusiasm. Some of his letters evince this coolness. Writing to his wife from Valley Forge, May 17, 1778, he says, "I am going on command to-morrow morning down to the enemy's lines. There are two thousand going on the command. I am of the mind, we shall have *a dispute with them before we return.*" He was forty-two years old at the time of his death. He was, like most men at that day who devoted themselves to the public service, comparatively poor. He left a wid. and four children. She moved to West Camb., where she d. April 6, 1834, aged 83. Honorable mention was made of her in an obituary notice, in the Boston Daily Advertiser of April 11, 1834, from which we extract the following: "The worthy lady who is the subject of this notice, with other families in Lexington, fled on the 19th of April, 1775, with their children, to the woods, while their husbands were engaged with the enemy, and their houses were sacked or involved in flames. Her husband was killed at Monmouth in New Jersey, June 28, 1778. On his bereaved partner, in the midst of discouragement, sorrows, and the privations of the times, devolved the task of rearing an infant family. The long life of this venerable lady was a pattern of domestic duties and virtue."

100–177 | *Pamelia*, b. Sept. 17, 1769; d. Sept. 29, 1770.
178 | *Rebecca*, b. June 27, 1771; m. 1795, —— Fessenden.
179 | *Pamelia*, b. Sept. 20, 1773; m. Jan. 19, 1800, James Brown.
180 | *Edmund*, b. Oct. 13, 1775; was a printer by trade, established himself in Boston, and was one of the publishing house of Munroe and Francis, and d. in Boston, unm., Feb. 9, 1854, aged 79.
181 | *Abigail*, b. Dec. 6, 1777; m. June 24, 1801, Joseph Locke, Jr. She d. May 14, 1838, aged 60. They resided at West Camb., and had eight children.

27–103– | WILLIAM MUNROE m. Anna Smith, dau. of Benjamin and Anna (Parker) Smith, b. March 31, 1743. She d. Jan. 2, 1781, aged 38, and he m. wid. Polly Rogers of Westford, whose first husband was killed at the Battle of Monmouth by the bursting of a cannon. William Munroe was orderly sergeant of Capt. Parker's co. in 1775; it was under his direction that a guard was posted at Mr. Clarke's house, on the evening of the 18th of April, 1775; and he paraded the men on the Common the next morning, in the very face of the British troops. The services he performed at the opening of the Revolution, were followed up by other services in the progress of the war. He was a lieutenant in the Northern army at the taking of Burgoyne, in 1777. He was a prominent citizen, and filled important town offices. He was selectman nine years, and represented the town two years. He was a colonel in the militia, and marched towards Springfield during Shay's Rebellion; but the dispersion of the insurgents enabled him to return in a short time. Col. Munroe kept the public house, long known as the "Munroe Tavern." Here the British regaled themselves, and committed many outrages on the 19th of April; here they shot down in cold blood John Raymond, who was about leaving the house; and here General Washington dined in 1789, when he visited the first battle field of the Revolution. Col. Munroe's portrait will be seen on the opposite page. He d. Oct. 30, 1827, aged 85; she d. Jan. 10, 1829, aged 73.

103–182 | *William*, b. May 28, 1768; m. Susan B. Grinnell of New Bedford. He was killed at Richmond, Va., by the upsetting of a stage, in 1814.
183 | *Anna*, b. May 9, 1771; m. Sept. 20, 1798, Rev. William Muzzy of Sullivan, N. H., and d. in Lex. 1850, aged 70.
184 | *Sarah*, b. Oct. 21, 1773; m. Jonathan Wheelock of Con., and d. aged about 77.
185 | *Lucinda*, b. April 9, 1776; d. unm. June 2, 1863, aged 87.
186 | †*Jonas*, b. June 11, 1778; m. March 17, 1814, Abigail C. Smith.
187 | *Edmund*, b. Oct. 29, 1780; m. first, Harriet Downes, second, Lydia Downes, third, Sophia Sewall. He was a broker in Boston, and d. April 17, 1865.

34–126– | PHILEMON MUNROE m. Feb. 17, 1784, Elizabeth Waite of Malden, b. Feb. 1750, and d. April 13, 1785. He m. second, Sept. 13,

1786, Rhoda Mead, b. July 8, 1758, who d. Jan. 18, 1824. Philemon Munroe was one of the heroic band who refused to disperse at the bidding of Maj. Pitcairn, on the 19th of April,—" not being afraid of the king's commandment." He had two children (twins), by his first wife, and six by his last. He d. Oct. 17, 1806, aged 53.

126–188   *Thomas*, b. March 30, 1785. He m. March 30, 1804, Elizabeth Jewett of Littleton. She d. Nov. 23, 1848, aged 63, and he m. Aug. 26, 1849, wid. Matilda (Jewett) Conant. His wives were sisters, and dau. of Joseph Jewett of Littleton. Mr. Munroe resided in Lex., Milton, and Dorchester, and then moved to Nashua, N. H., where he filled many important town offices, as well as those of notary and justice of the peace.

189   *Elizabeth*, b. March 30, 1785; m. April 24, 1804, Isaac Reed.
190   *Edwin*, b. April 3, 1788; m. Eliza Fowle, dau. of Henry and Rebecca Fowle of Med. They have resided in Lex., Med., Saugus, Charlestown, and Somerville.
191   *Josiah*, b. Nov. 25, 1789; d. Aug. 20, 1837, unm.
192   *Catharine*, b. July 24, 1791; m. Ira Thorp of Athol.
193   *Parnell*, b. Nov. 27, 1793; d. 1821, aged 28.
194   *Charles*, b. May 12, 1796; m. Maria Russell, r. at Somerville.
195   *H. G. Otis*, b. Nov. 29, 1798; m. Dec. 12, 1822, Sophia Harrington. They reside in Boston, where he does business.

34–127–   WILLIAM MUNROE m. 1781, Abigail Harrington, dau. of John and Mary (Wooton) Harrington. He d. April 30, 1837, aged 80; she d. Nov. 1, 1811.

127–196   *Susan*, b. Oct. 19, 1781; m. 1801, Nathan B. Foster.
197   *William*, b. May 18, 1785; m. Oct. 11, 1813, Lucy Frost. He moved to that part of Charlestown which is now Somerville.
198   *Enoch*, b. Sept. 9, 1787; d. May 18, 1814, in Boston, aged 26.
199   *Sarah*, b. Nov. 1789; m. Jesse Russell; r. in Woburn.
200   *Esther*, b. 1792; d. in Belfast, Me., 1811, aged 19. Her death was caused by her clothes taking fire.
201   *Hannah*, b. 1794; d. 1819, unm.
202   *Louisa*, b. 1796; m. Nov. 13, 1825, Thomas J. Buckman of Lynn.
203   *Mary*, b. 1798.   204 *Harriet*, b. 1805; d. 1822.

38–128–   GEORGE MUNROE m. Anna Bemis. She d. Mar. 8, 1815, aged 78.

128–205   *Anna*, bap. May 13, 1759; m. —— Sampson.
206   †*Thaddeus*, b. April 26, 1762; m. Oct. 1, 1820, Rebecca Locke, and d. 1846, aged 84.
207   *Abigail*, bap. July 26, 1767; m. June 8, 1788, Joseph Blodgett.
208   *Hannah*, bap. March 24, 1772; m. Bela Rice.
209   *Hepzibah*, bap. Sept. 17, 1775; m. April 24, 1791, Joshua Wyman. He d. and she m. —— Daniels.

38–129–   TIMOTHY MUNROE m. —— Eaton of Reading. He probably moved to Lynn or Danvers, where he had a family of children, who settled in that neighborhood. He marched with the Danvers company on the 19th of April, 1775, met the British at West Cambridge, where he and others were surrounded, when several of his comrades were killed, and he escaped with a ball in his thigh which he carried through life, and his garments riddled with bullet holes. He d. at Lynn, 1808, aged 72.

39-135- EBENEZER MUNROE m. March 29, 1771, Martha Smith, dau. of Benjamin and Anna (Parker) Smith, b. April 19, 1745. He was enrolled with Parker's patriots, and was in the battle of Lexington, in 1775, and was also in the campaign in the Jerseys, in 1776. He d. Aug. 22, 1826, aged 82; she d. Oct. 13, 1834, aged 86.

135-210 *Patty*, b. Feb. 19, 1772; m. Dec. 25, 1804, Isaac Pierce of Walt.
211 *Ebenezer*, b. Feb. 2, 1777; d. June 6, 1798, aged 21 years.
212 *Esther*, b. Oct. 1783; m. Jan. 19, 1806, David Tuttle; d. Oct. 14, 1809.
213 †*John*, b. April 28, 1785; m. Charlotte Bacon.

39-136- JOHN MUNROE m. Dec. 3, 1772, Rebecca Wellington, dau. of Thomas and Margaret, of Waltham. Like most of the young men of that day, he was one of the Lex. minute-men, and did service on the 19th of April, 1775. He lived on Woburn street. He d. April 4, 1831, aged 82; she d. Feb. 16, 1838, aged 90.

136-214 *Margaret*, b. July 31, 1773; m. Daniel Mixer of Walt., where they resided for a time, when they moved to Worcester. He d. and she returned to Lex. and m. April 4, 1793, Thomas Winship as a second wife. She d. 1789.
215 *Rebecca*, b. May 30, 1776; m. Feb. 1, 1795, Jonathan Whittemore of West Cambridge.
216 *Mary*, b. Aug. 30, 1779; m. Sept. 2, 1802, Seneca Harrington of Worcester. She was a wid. in Pepperell, 1858.
217 *Philena*, b. May 27, 1782; m. Feb. 2, 1804, David Johnson. She is living in Lex., at the age of 85.

44-146- JOSEPH MUNROE m. July 22, 1783, Rhoda Leathe of Wo. He resided on Woburn street, easterly of Col. Russell's. She d. Jan. 2, 1825; he d. Sept. 22, 1832, aged 74.

146-218 *Rhoda*, b. Dec. 24, 1784; m. —— Cobbett.
219 *Seth*, b. April 18, 1788.
220 *Lydia*, b. May 19, 1791; m. April 11, 1811, Joel Gleason of Bed.
221 *Jeptha*, b. June 15, 1793; resided in Woburn.
222 *Dennis*, b. Jan. 22, 1797; m. Elizabeth Fox.
223 *Lavinia*, b. March 11, 1806.

92-171- NATHAN MUNROE m. Susanna Loring. He d. in Concord, where he then resided.

171-224 *Elbridge*, b. July 28, 1804, at Lexington.
225 *Nathan*, b. July 28, 1808, at Concord.
226 *Jonas Clarke*, b. Sept. 22, 1812, at Lincoln.
227 *James*, b. Feb. 27, 1817, at Concord.

92-172- JONATHAN MUNROE m. Feb. 13, 1812, Rhoda Johnson, dau. of Frederick and Rhoda (Reed) Johnson. She d. July 19, 1865, aged 72; he d. Dec. 4, 1867, aged 85.

172-228 *William*, b. Dec. 17, 1812; m. Dec. 1846, Elvira Merriam of Con., dau. of Joseph Merriam. They r. at Southbridge.
229 *Elizabeth*, b. March 21, 1814; m. June 7, 1839, Francis Johnson of Wo. now Winchester, where they reside.
230 *Josiah*, b. Oct. 21, 1818; m. Oct. 10, 1847, Adeline Dodge of Boston. They reside in Roxbury.
231 *Faustina*, b. Feb. 1, 1821; m. June 12, 1859, Frederick Stimpson.

232 | *Albert*, b. May 2, 1824; m. April 12, 1850, Elizabeth Millet of Wo.
233 | *Julia Maria*, b. Dec. 31, 1832; d. Sept. 25, 1833.

103–186– | JONAS MUNROE m. March 17, 1814, Abigail C. Smith, dau. of Joseph and Lucy (Stone) Smith. He was a lieutenant in United States dragoons, in 1807, resigned his commission, and on the breaking out of the war of 1812, was commissioned as lieutenant of infantry, and was engaged for a short time in the recruiting service. He was drowned at Somerville, while bathing, July 2, 1860, aged 82. His wid. d. April 4, 1861, aged 68. He kept the "Munroe Tavern" and was extensively and favorably known to the traveling public.

186–234 | *William Henry*, b. Mar. 2, 1815. He is doing business in Philad.
235 | *Harriet*, b. Nov. 25, 1816; is now living, unm.
236 | *Abby Smith*, b. Aug. 28, 1819; d. Dec. 21, 1822. .
237 | †*James S.*, b. June 6, 1824; m. Alice B. Phinney.

128–206– | THADDEUS MUNROE m. Oct. 1, 1820, Rebecca Locke, dau. of Thomas and Lydia (Reed) Locke. He d. April 7, 1846, aged 84, and she d. July 23, 1846. He was a large landholder.

206–238 | †*George*, b. Feb. 25, 1822. He has been twice married.
239 | *Ann Rebecca*, b. July 10, 1825; m. March 19, 1846, John M. Randall, a lawyer, settled at Woburn. He is not living.

135–213– | JOHN MUNROE m. Dec. 11, 1811, Charlotte Bacon of Wo. He d. Feb. 17, 1865, aged 79. She is living, in her seventy-sixth year.

213–240 | *John Harrison*, b. June 3, 1813. He r. at Fall River.
241 | *Charles Henry*, b. Aug. 10, 1814; d. at Buffalo, July 17, 1850.
242 | *Harriet*, b. April 29, 1816; d. Feb. 2, 1835.
243 | †*Ebenezer*, b. Dec. 3, 1817; m. Margaret M. Wilson.
244 | *Jonas*, b. Sept. 10, 1819; d. Aug. 15, 1843.
245 | *Lavinia*, b. Oct. 16, 1821; m. April 4, 1839, Galen Allen. She d. April 22, 1865, and he d. Jan. 29, 1864.
246 | *Oliver*, b. April 10, 1825; d. May 4, 1857.
247 | *Charlotte*, b. March 28, 1827; m. George Mulliken. She d. Dec. 8, 1861.

186–237– | JAMES S. MUNROE m. May 23, 1854, Alice B. Phinney, dau. of Elias Phinney, Esq.

237–248 | *William*, b. March 23, 1855. 249 *John C.*, b. March 26, 1858.
250 | *James*, b. June 3, 1862.

206–238– | GEORGE MUNROE m. Dec. 13, 1846, Eliza Wood. She d. Aug. 7, 1852, and he m. Nov. 7, 1854, Susan P. Winning.

238–251 | *Rebecca Eliza*, b. Oct. 6, 1847. 252 *Georgiana*, b. Jan. 8, 1850.
253 | *George Warren*, b. Aug. 3, 1855; d. Sept. 2, 1857.
254 | *Mary Alice*, b. Sept. 7, 1857. 255 *Elmina*, b. Dec. 18, 1860.

213–243– | EBENEZER MUNROE m. Nov. 26, 1850, Margaret M. Wilson. She d. Feb. 4, 1860; he d. Jan. 5, 1868, aged 50.

243–256 | *Julia Maria*, b. April 17, 1852. 257 *Robert*, b. Aug. 10, 1854.
258 | *Anne S.*, b. Nov. 26, 1855; d. Jan. 28, 1856.

THE MUZZY FAMILY.

The Muzzys were early in Lexington, and were for a century and a half among the leading influential families in the place. The name is spelled Mussy, Muzzy, and the Lex. families have recently added the *e* in the last syllable, Muzzey.

1   Benjamin Muzzy of Malden m. Alice Dexter, and had *Benjamin*, b. April 16, 1657; *Joseph*, b. March 1, 1659. He may have been son of Robert of Ipswich, one of the first settlers of that town, who was made freeman, 1634.

1- 2   Benjamin Muzzy m. first, Sarah ——, who d. in Lex. Jan. 28, 1710, aged 50 years, and m. second, Jane ——. What time he came to Cambridge Farms, we are not able to say. We find a record of the birth of Mary Muzzy, dau. of Benjamin and Sarah, in Cambridge, in 1683; but whether he lived at that time in the old town or at the Farms, is uncertain. His name is found on the earliest records at the Farms or North Precinct,—he being one of the subscribers for the first meeting house, in 1692, and was one of the largest tax payers the following year. As he was a large land-holder in the centre of the town, at the organization of the Parish in 1693, it is probable that he had been in the place for some time. In 1693, he was placed on a committee with David Fiske, sen., Samuel Stone, sen., and others, to negotiate with Cambridge for the purchase of a tract of land for the support of the ministry. He was constable in 1694, and an assessor in 1700. He filled the dignified office of tythingman in 1716. In 1711, the inhabitants of the Precinct purchased of Benjamin Muzzy about two acres of land for a Common, and a site for a meeting house. This was done by subscription, in which he and his sons John and Richard participated. He resided on or near the spot where Rufus Merriam now resides. Here was opened the first public house in the place, his son John being licensed for that purpose in 1714. He d. May 12, 1732, possessed of a large landed property. The inventory of his estate mentions his mansion house, barn, cider mill, and a homestead of 111 acres. Among the articles appraised were three slaves,—a man, valued at £80, and a woman and child at £60. The record of his family is incomplete. He bought his homestead of Edward Pelham of Rhode Island, 1693. It is described as bounded by John Munroe, ministerial land, Matthew Bridge, and extending to Vine Brook.

2- 3   *Mary*, b. July 13, 1683.
4   †*John*, b. 1685; d. March 8, 1768.
5   †*Benjamin*, b. Feb. 20, 1689; m. Patience ——.
6   *Richard*, b. ——. He was drowned, in a pond in Maine, 1719, unm. He owned real estate in Lexington.
7   †*Amos*, bap. Jan. 7, 1699; m. Esther Green.
8   *Bethia*, bap. June 1701; m. Ebenezer Fiske, as his second wife.
9   *Thomas*, bap. Sept. 1, 1706; d. Nov. 26, 1740.

2-4-   John Muzzy m. first, July 12, 1709, Elizabeth Bradshaw of Med. She d. Feb. 22, 1722, aged 33 years. He m. second, Dec. 1, 1722, Rebecca Ingham, who d. July 12, 1731, aged about 40; and he m. third, Mary ——, who d. March 9, 1758, aged 66. He d. March 28, 1768, aged 83. He was either born in Lex., or came in with his father in early infancy. He opened the first public house in the place, in 1714, which he continued for a long period. He filled many town offices, being constable in 1727, school committee in 1733, selectman in 1741, '42, '44, and assessor in 1746. He was ad. to the ch. Aug. 24, 1735. In his will, dated 1764, and a codicil dated 1765, he mentions dau. Mary Hall, Sarah Hill, and Jane Stone, and sons John and Benjamin. He made his son-in-law, Samuel Stone, executor of his will. He not only owned land in Lex., but was an owner of land in Templeton, having as a proprietor, drawn a lot of forty acres in that township, in 1735. This land he gave to his sons Benjamin and John.

4-10   *Elizabeth*, bap. April 23, 1710; m. John Hovey and d. at Camb. Dec. 1729, aged 19.

11   *Mary*, bap. May 18, 1712; m. Stephen Hall.

12   *John*, b. May 12, 1714.

13   *Sarah*, b. July 6, 1716; m. Jacob Hill.

14   *Jane*, b. July 4, 1719; m. Samuel Stone.

15   *Elizabeth*, b. Dec. 17, 1734; m. April 29, 1756, Francis Falkner of Acton. She d. in three weeks after marriage.

16   *Benjamin*, b. Oct. 29, 1736; probably went to Sudbury, where he m. July 30, 1761, Elizabeth Witherbee of Stow.

17   *Abigail*, bap. May 10, 1739.

2-5-   BENJAMIN MUZZY m. Patience ——. He d. Jan. 29, 1764, aged 84, and she d. Oct. 7, 1767, aged 80. Their deaths are inscribed on one stone in the Lex. grave yard. He was frequently called to fill town offices, being from time to time chosen school committee, &c. His will, dated Feb. 19, 1763, and proved Feb. 13, 1764, mentions wife Patience, sons Joseph and John, and dau. Esther Merriam, Mary Reed, and grandsons Benjamin, James, Seth, and Benoni, sons of Benjamin, deceased. His son John was appointed executor of his will, and to him he gave all his land and buildings in Lex.

5-18   †*Joseph*, bap. March 19, 1710.

19   *Esther*, bap. Feb. 16, 1712; m. Nathaniel Merriam.

20   †*John*, bap. Feb. 12, 1716; d. Dec. 16, 1784.

21   *Mary*, bap. March 2, 1718; m. —— Reed.

22   *Benjamin*, b. ——; m. Feb. 19, 1752, Hannah Discom, and moved to Shrewsbury, where they were ad. to the ch. July, 1753. Their children were Benjamin and Hannah, a pair of twins, who were bap. Aug. 15, 1755, James, bap. Jan. 2, 1757, Seth, bap. Oct. 8, 1758, Benoni, bap. April 26, 1760.

2-7-   AMOS MUZZY m. Sept. 26, 1734, Esther Green, dau. of Samuel and Esther Green. He d. June 26, 1752. His wid. m. March 4, 1758, Thomas Prentice, Esq., of Newton. Mr. Muzzy died possessed of a large property for that period. Among his chattels were a male and female negro—the former inventoried at £350, and the latter at £100. His homestead is thus described: "The home land, containing by estimation eighty-two acres, with a mansion house and barn and corn house upon it, consisting of pasturage, mowing, ploughing, orchard, and woodland, lying upon both sides of the great county road leading to Concord." This mansion house was on or near the spot where David W. Muzzey now resides, and the land extended down upon Waltham street, to what is now called Grape Vine Corner. He also owned land in Woburn and Townsend. He was an assessor in 1744, and a selectman in 1750.

7-23   *Esther*, b. July 11, 1735; d. Oct. 9, 1789, unm.

24   *Sarah*, b. March 30, 1737; m. Oct. 19, 1758, Bezaleel Lawrence.

25   *Amos*, b. June 7, 1739; d. July, 1740.

26   †*Amos*, b. May 24, 1741; m. Nov. 29, 1764, Abigail Bowers.

27 ‡*William*, b. July 31, 1743; m. Lydia Reed.
28 *Samuel*, b. July 12, 1745; d. Aug. 23, 1747.
29 *Bethiah*, b. July 8, 1747; m. Nov. 16, 1769, Thaddeus Brown.
30 *Mary*, b. Sept. 8, 1749.
31 *Benjamin*, b. Jan. 25, 1752. He was grad. H. C. 1774, sailed from Boston, Sept. 1777, in the privateer Hero Revenge as chaplain, and was lost at sea.

5-18-   JOSEPH MUZZY m. Lois ——. We have been able to learn but little of this family. He was ad. to the ch. June 9, 1728. He was a house-holder in 1735, and was taxed the following years for real estate.

18-32 *Lois*, bap. Oct. 12, 1735.   33 *Sarah*, bap. Jan. 8, 1738.
34 *Joseph*, b. Aug. 26, 1740; probably went to Shrewsbury.
35 *Abigail*, bap. July 28, 1745.   36 *Nathan*, b. May 12, 1751.
They may have had other children. Some of these probably d. in infancy. In 1769, we have a record of the death of Joseph Muzzy's child.

5-20-   JOHN MUZZY m. first, Rebecca Reed, dau. of Maj. Benjamin and Rebecca Reed, who was b. Nov. 5, 1724. She d. Jan. 24, 1771, and he m. second, Aug. 19, 1773, Mrs. Rebecca Munroe, wid. of Jonas Munroe, a grandson of the first William. He d. Dec. 16, 1784, and she d. Jan. 14, 1839, aged 85. He was one of the Lex. company who met the enemy in 1775. He was also two months with the army at Cambridge, during the siege of Boston, in 1776.

20-37 *Isaac*, bap. Dec. 6, 1744. He was ad. to the ch. Nov. 17, 1771. He was one of the heroes who fell, a prey to British aggression, on the Common at Lex. April 19, 1775. His name is preserved on the Monument.
38 *Rebecca*, b. ——; d. unm.
39 *Mary*, b. June 3, 1748; m. Aug. 31, 1769, Silas Fuller.
40 ‡*Ebenezer*, bap. July 8, 1750; m. Betty Reed.
41 *Abigail*, b. ——; drowned in a tub of water, at the age of 2 years.
42 ‡*John*, b. ——, 1754.
43 *Abigail*, bap. Feb. 1, 1756; m. Nov. 20, 1780, Abel Winship. They resided in Bedford.
44 *Thaddeus*, bap. Sept. 25, 1757; d. 1785, unm.
45 *Eunice*, b. ——; m. Ebenezer Estabrook of Holden.
46 *Betty*, bap. Aug. 10, 1761; m. March 14, 1786, Joshua Stearns of Princeton. They moved to New Ipswich, N. H.
John Muzzy and his first wife had several other children, who d. in early infancy.

7-26-   AMOS MUZZY m. first, Aug. 29, 1764, Abigail Bowers of Billerica. They were ad. to the ch. June 26, 1766. She d. March 15, 1803, aged 58 years, and he m. second, Abigail Smith, wid. of Capt. Joseph Smith, Dec. 25, 1806. She d. Feb. 18, 1814, aged 63, and he d. Dec. 10, 1822, aged 82. Amos Muzzy and his two wives were placed in a tomb in the church yard in Lex., covered with a slab bearing this inscription: "The northwest corner of this tomb is reserved for Mr. Amos Muzzy and wives, and no other corpse to be laid there." He was in the Battle of Lex. 1775, and in 1776 was five months at Ticonderoga, and three months at Camb. 1778.

26-47 ‡*Amos*, b. April 19, 1766; m. Lydia Boutelle.
48 *Josiah*, bap. Nov. 7, 1767; d. Nov. 26, 1767.

49 | *Abigail*, b. May 27, 1769; m. 1800, Thomas Conant of Boston.
50 | †*William*, b. May 25, 1771; d. April 16, 1835.

7-27- | WILLIAM MUZZY m. Nov. 29, 1764, Lydia Reed of Charlestown. They were ad. to the ch. May 18, 1766. He d. Nov. 20, 1770.

27-51 | *Lydia*, bap. July 26, 1767; m. Dec. 25, 1788, Nathan Brown.
52 | *Mary*, bap. Jan. 7, 1770; m. Feb. 24, 1796, Daniel Marrett, minister in Standish, Me.

20-40- | EBENEZER MUZZY m. June 6, 1774, Betty Reed, dau. of Joshua and Susanna Reed. They commenced life in Lex., but afterwards moved to Rindge, N. H., where most of their children were born. They returned to Lex., where he d. March 29, 1804, and she d. March 12, 1846, at the advanced age of 91.

40-53 | †*Isaac*, b. April 5, 1775.
54 | *Betsey*, b. ——; m. Jonas Reed and moved to Heath.
55 | *Nabby*, b. ——; m. John Parker and moved to Phillipston, where she d. He afterwards came came back to Lex. and m. Esther Reed, dau. of Thaddeus Reed, and moved to Nashua, N. H.
56 | *Joshua*, b. ——. He was killed by falling from a tree, when about eight years of age.
57 | *Thaddeus*, b. 1784; m. Mrs. Mary Patch of Boston, where they lived. He was drowned in Boston Harbor, by the upsetting of a boat, June 15, 1815, aged 31 years. She d Dec. 7, 1816, aged 32.
58 | *John*, b. Nov. 19, 1794; m. Nov. 19, 1816, Lydia More, dau. of Thomas D. More of Boston. They resided in the city till 1854, when they came to Lex. They had two children,—the first d. in early infancy, the other, John M., b. July 18, 1819, and d. April 5, 1839, aged 20 years. He d. Dec. 30, 1864, aged 70 years; she d. Dec. 20, 1862, aged 66.

20-42- | JOHN MUZZY m. May 2, 1777, Rebecca, dau. of Jonas and Rebecca Munroe. She was the dau. of his step-mother. He was in the army in the Jerseys in 1776, and also at Ticonderoga the same year.

42-59 | *Mary*, b. Dec. 14, 1777; m. Aug. 30, 1798, Nathan Reed, Jr.
60 | †*John*, b. Dec. 22, 1780.
61 | †*Jonas M.*, b. July 18, 1782.

26-47- | AMOS MUZZY m. Lydia Boutelle, dau. of Timothy Boutelle of Leominster. They were ad. to the ch. April 28, 1798. He was chosen deacon April 14, 1822. He d. May 20, 1829; she d. Dec. 24, 1838.

47-62 | *Elmira*, b. Oct. 21, 1794; m. Oct. 12, 1817, Charles Reed.
63 | †*Benjamin*, b. Dec. 13, 1795; m. 1822, Elizabeth Wood.
64 | *Lydia*, b. June 11, 1799; m. Oct. 29, 1818, Samuel Chandler.
65 | *Artemas Bowers*, b. Sept. 21, 1802; he grad. H. C. 1824, studied theology, was ordained at Framingham, June 10, 1830, left in 1833, and in 1834 was installed at Cambridgeport, left in 1846, and the same year was settled over the Lee street ch. in Cambridgeport, resigned his situation, and in 1854 was settled over the Second Congregational Church in Concord, N. H. He m. June 26, 1831, Hepsabeth Patterson of Boston, dau. of Enoch Patterson, Esq., by whom he had several children. His oldest son, *Henry W. Muzzy*, read law, and is now in practice in Boston.

66 *Abigail*, b. Nov. 26, 1804; m. Sept. 11, 1834, Samuel Chandler.
67 *Amos Otis*, b. June 14, 1808; d. Jan. 20, 1812.

26-50— WILLIAM MUZZY m. Sept. 20, 1798, Anna Munroe. He was grad. H. C. 1793, and was ordained at Sullivan, N. H., Feb. 7, 1798. He left in 1828, and returned to Lex. with his family, where he d. April 16, 1835 and she d. June 19, 1850, aged 79. They had five children b. in Sullivan, two of whom d. 1814 of the spotted fever. *William*, b. June 30, 1801, lives at Philadelphia; *Emily*, b. Nov. 1800, d. unm.; *Abby Ann*, b. June 15, 1806, m. Aug. 4, 1835, Dea. William Brigham, resides in Lexington.

40-53— ISAAC MUZZY m. Mary Boutelle of Malden. He d. Aug. 1, 1842, and she d. Aug. 2, 1849, aged 71.

53-68 ‡*Charles*, b. May 12, 1804; d. Aug. 27, 1853.
69 *Thomas*, b. March, 1808.
70 *Mary Ann*, b. April 15, 1811; m. Ebenezer Hosmer.

42-60— JOHN MUZZY m. Oct. 1811, Rebecca Lincoln of Hingham, dau. of Seth and Mary (Fearing) Lincoln. She was b. Oct. 26, 1789, and was descended, both on her father's and mother's side, from two of the oldest families of that town. He resided on the Concord road, and d. Dec. 1843. After the death of her husband, she returned to Hingham, where she was living, 1859.

60-71 *Julia A.*, b. Nov. 4, 1815. She resides in Hingham with her mother, unmarried.

42-61— JONAS M. MUZZY m. June 12, 1816, Abigail Dunklee of Milford, N. H. He resided near the Common, in the house now occupied by Simon W. Robinson, Esq. He d. Dec. 10, 1846. His widow resides in Hingham.

61-72 *Louisa C.*, b. June 1, 1818; m. Dec. 22, 1836, Seth L. Hobart of Hingham, and has had *Alice L.*, b. 1837; *Caroline H.*, b. 1842; *Elsa W.*, b. 1846; *Marion L.*, b. 1854.
73 *William P.*, b. Feb. 14, 1822; d. July 16, 1844.
74 *Franseena S.*, b. April 25, 1833.

47-63— BENJAMIN MUZZEY m. June 19, 1822, Elizabeth Wood of Newburyport. He d. suddenly at the Exchange Coffee House in Boston, where he was called on business, April 21, 1848. He commenced business in Boston as a trader, where he remained till about 1830, when he came to Lex. He was a leading popular man in the town, filled important town offices, and was a justice of the peace. The Lexington railroad is a standing monument of his public spirit and energy of character.

63-75 *Charles O.*, b. in Boston, Aug. 17, 1824. He entered in the navy in the late rebellion, Nov. 1861, as secretary to Capt. Pickering, U. S. Steamer Kearsarge, was transferred to the steamer Housatonic, May, 1863, and was killed by the explosion of a torpedo in Charleston Harbor, which destroyed the ship, Feb. 18, 1864.
76 *Susan Elizabeth*, b. in Boston, July 21, 1826; d. Sept. 12, 1827.
77 *Helen Elizabeth*, b. in Boston, June 25, 1828; m. Nov. 22, 1854, Richard F. Hooper of Charlestown.
78 *Loring W.*, b. in Lex. Aug. 28, 1831. He entered the service in 1861, in the 12th Regt., promoted to Quartermaster, May, 1862—

to captain and commissary of subsistence, March, 1864—and to major and commissary of subsistence, July, 1865.

79 *David Wood*, b. July 10, 1833; m. Dec. 13, 1860, Anna W. Saville, dau. of David and Anna Saville. They have one child, viz., *Benjamin*, b. Sept. 19, 1866.

80 *George Eveleth*, b. Aug. 4, 1838. He entered the 12th Regt. Mass. Vols. 1861, was appointed quartermaster-sergeant 1862, promoted to first lieutenant, 1863, and quartermaster, 1864.

81 *Benjamin Lyman*, b. Nov. 14, 1840; d. March 13, 1855.
The three sons living are engaged in business in Boston.

53-68-   CHARLES MUZZY m. Feb. 3, 1827, Sarah Oakes of Malden. He was a trader, and moved to Philadelphia in 1829, and came back to West Camb. in 1834, where he was in trade at the "Foot of the Rocks," for several years, when he moved to Charlestown. In 1853, his health declining, he came to Lex., in hopes of recovery, but d. Aug. 27, 1853. They had but one child, *Sarah Elizabeth*, b. in Phil. June 6, 1834. She m. in Lex. April 5, 1855, George Tuttle, who d. Jan. 27, 1856, within a year of his marriage.

NASH.—JOSEPH NASH, of Weymouth, had among other children *Joseph*, who m. Eunice Ford, and had James, Joseph, Nathaniel, Charles, Atherton, and *Oran*, and several daughters.

ORAN NASH, the youngest son of Joseph and Eunice, b. March 19, 1805, m. Oct. 12, 1822, Lucy Cushing of Weymouth, dau. of Samuel and Elizabeth. They resided in Boston, where all their children but the youngest were born. They came to Lex. 1835. They have had five children, viz. *Emeline Augusta*, b. April 11, 1827; *Elizabeth*, b. April 7, 1829, d. 1830; *Howard A.*, b. July 18, 1831, m. Elizabeth Sutton, r. at Cincinnati, Ohio; *Rowena*, b. Dec. 30, 1833; *Ellen Louisa*, b. in Lex. Oct. 20, 1840.

THE NELSON FAMILY.

The name of Nelson appears first upon our records in 1722, when TABITHA NELSON, wife of Thomas, was ad. to the ch. In 1724, Thomas was chosen to a subordinate town office, which shows that he was an inhabitant of the town at that time; in 1730, he had a seat assigned in the meeting house, and in 1743, he was constable. He resided on the road to Concord, above what is now known as the old Viles Tavern, near what was then the line of Concord. When the town of Lincoln was created, in 1754, he and others were taken from Lex. to constitute that town. The Nelsons of Lincoln are from that stock. They were connected by marriage with the Hastings of Lex. The children of Thomas and Tabitha were *Thomas* and *Tabitha*, twins, b. Dec. 19, 1721, and *Josiah*, bap. in 1726.

Thomas Nelson first named was b. in Rowley, 1685; he was son of Thomas, b. in Rowley, 1661; who was son of Thomas, b. in Eng., who came over with his father, Thomas, in 1638, and settled in Rowley.

THE NORCROSS FAMILY.

JEREMIAH NORCROSS, who settled in Wat. as early as 1642, had *Richard*, who by wife Mary had *Nathaniel*, b. 1665, who m. Mehitabel Hager, and had a son bearing his own name. This *Nathaniel*,

b. 1695, m. 1717, Jemima Abbott, and had among other children, *Josiah*, b. 1734, m. Jan. 6, 1754, Elizabeth Child. They both died 1801. They had nine children. *John*, their sixth child, b. May, 1771, m. Margaret Everett. He d. 1823, and she d. 1843. They had Eliza, b. 1798, d. young; *John*, b. 1801, d. young; *John*, b. Sept. 28, 1803; Anna M., b. 1805, m. John English of Boston.

1   JOHN NORCROSS, son of John and Margaret, m. April 22, 1826, Eleanor Estabrook, dau. of Eliakim and Hannah Estabrook. He came to Lex. in 1846, and has been to the present day depot-master at East Lexington,—a term of service which furnishes the best evidence of his fitness and fidelity.

1- 2 *Eleanor M.*, b. Jan. 13, 1827; m. Dec. 14, 1848, James Prentice of West Cambridge.
3 *Eliza J.*, b. July 27, 1830; m. 1856, Leroy Chappell.
4 *Samuel T.*, b. Sept. 5, 1834. He was residing at the West, where he had accumulated some property. His health failing, he had converted his property into money and started, in a weak and enfeebled condition, for home. A villain, who had learned the facts in the case, ingratiated himself into his favor, and volunteered to become his protector; and when the train had arrived at a station in Altona, Pa., in the night time, he induced Norcross to leave the car and go with him, promising to conduct him to good quarters for the night; and when he had enticed him to a place of seclusion, he basely murdered him, Jan. 16, 1857. The murderer was ultimately arrested, tried, and executed.
5 *John Henry*, b. Oct. 29, 1841; m. June 6, 1866, Cynthia J. White of Medford, where they reside.

THE NUTTING FAMILY.

There was a family of *Nuttings* in Camb. Farms about the time the parish was organized. EBENEZER NUTTING was taxed in the parish in 1693. He and his wife owned the covenant in June, 1699, when *Jonathan*, *Lydia*, and *Sarah*, their children, were bap. *Ebenezer* and *James*, also children of Ebenezer, were bap. May 30, 1703. After this the name disappears on our records.

OVERING.—In 1729, *John Overing* of Boston, bought of William Russell of Lex., for £308, a tract of fifty-one acres of land, with buildings thereon, bounded on land of Jason and Philip Russell and Joseph Mason. In 1735 and 1737, he sold lands to Dea. Joseph Brown, and in 1738, he bought lands in Lex. of David Comee. John Overing of Lex. was probably a son of John Overing, Esq., of Boston. He probably came to Lex. about 1730. He must have been a man of some pretension, for in 1735 he was taxed in town for three houses, two slaves, three cows, and two horses, besides other personal and real estate. He probably left town about 1740. We find no records of his family, though he probably had one. We have a record of the death of three of the name, who were probably his children, or perhaps one of them was his wife. *Henry Overing*, d. Aug. 6, 1738; *Henrietta Overing*, d. Sept. 13, 1738; *George Overing*, d. Sept. 17, 1738.

THE PARKER FAMILY.

Parker has always been a common name in New England. Emigrants of that name were found in most of the early settlements. The oft repeated fiction of *three* brothers coming over and settling in three different towns, will not meet the present case; for we find Abraham and Amariah and Edmund and George and Jacob and James and Joseph and Matthew and Nicholas and Robert and Thomas and two or more Williams and as many Johns, appearing in nearly as many of the different settlements at an early day. This name has been common in Reading, Groton, Billerica, Woburn, and other towns in this vicinity. But it is believed that the Lexington Parkers are the descendants of

1   THOMAS PARKER of Lynn, who was made freeman in 1637. He embarked at London, March 11, 1635, and settled in Lynn the same year. He moved to Reading, where he aided in establishing a church, of which he was a deacon. He had by his wife, Amy, a family of eleven children. He d. 1683, aged 74 years, and consequently must have been born in 1609. She d. Jan. 15, 1690.

1- 2 | *Thomas*, b. 1636; d. June 9, 1699.
    3 | †*Hananiah*, b. 1638; d. March 10, 1724, aged 86.
    4 | *John*, b. 1640; d Feb. 28, 1699. 5 *Joseph*, b. 1642, d. 1644.
    6 | *Joseph*, b. 1645; d. 1646.   7 *Mary*, b. March 12, 1647.
    8 | *Martha*, b. March 14, 1649.   9 *Nathaniel*, b. May 16, 1651.
  10 | *Sarah*, b. Sept. 30, 1653; d. Oct. 16, 1656.
  11 | *Jonathan*, b. May 18, 1656; m. Sept. 24, 1677, Bethia Polly, and had fourteen children.
  12 | *Sarah*, b. May 23, 1658.

1-3-   HANANIAH PARKER m. Sept. 30, 1663, Elizabeth Brown. She d. 1698, and he m. second, Mrs. Mary Bright, widow of Dea. John of Wat. He d. March 10, 1724; she d. Jan. 4, 1736, aged 87. He lived and died in Reading, and had the honorable title of *Lieutenant.*

3-13 | †*John*, b. Aug. 3, 1664; m. Deliverance ——.
  14 | *Samuel*, b. Oct. 24, 1666.   15 *Elizabeth*, b. June, 1668.
  16 | *Sarah*, b. Feb. 6, 1672; d. Oct. 2, 1673.
  17 | *Hananiah*, b. Nov. 2, 1674; d. Oct. 2, 1675.
  18 | *Ebenezer*, b. Feb. 13, 1676; m. Rebecca ——.
  19 | *Mary*, b. —— ; m. —— Poole.
  20 | *Hananiah*, b. April 30, 1681.

3-12-   JOHN PARKER m. 1689, Deliverance ——. They came to Lex. about 1712, and settled in the south part of the town. By a deed, dated June 25, 1712, John Cutler sold to John Parker, then of Reading, land at Camb. Farms, containing " one small mansion house and sixty acres of land, bounded southerly on Watertown line," elsewhere by Daniel White, John Stone, and Thomas Cutler. He was chosen fence viewer in 1714, and tythingman in 1715 and 1721. He must have been a man of dignity of character; for in seating the meeting house, 1731, where they had reference to age, honor, and property, they placed him in the second seat below, with Ensign John Mason, Thomas Mead, and other highly respectable citizens. She d. March 10, 1718, and he d. June 22, 1741, aged 78. There is scarcely a prominent family in Lex. whose record in every period of its history is so incomplete. This accounts for any inaccuracy, if any should be found.

13-21 | *Hananiah*, b. Oct. 10, 1691 ; d. at Port Royal, 1711.
22 | †*Andrew*, b. Feb. 14, 1693 ; m. Aug. 2, 1720, Sarah Whitney.
23 | †*Josiah*, b. April 11, 1694 ; m. Dec. 8, 1718, Anna Stone.
24 | *Mary*, b. Dec. 4, 1695.
25 | *Eddie*, b. Aug. 19, 1697 ; d. 1709.

These births are recorded in Reading, where they occurred, and are also found on the Lex. records.

13-22- | ANDREW PARKER m. Aug. 2, 1720, Sarah Whitney, dau. of Josiah Whitney, b. April, 1703. Nov. 4, 1724, they made their peace with the ch., when three of their children were bap. They were ad. to the ch. 1728. She d. Dec. 18, 1774, aged 70, and he d. April 8, 1776, aged 83.

22-26 | *Sarah*, b. Feb. 9, 1721 ; m. June 21, 1739, Jabez Kendall.
27 | †*Jonas*, b. Feb. 6, 1722 ; m. Lucy ——.
28 | †*Amos*, b. July 27, 1723 ; m. Anna ——.
29 | *Elizabeth*, bap. Aug. 22, 1725 ; d. young.
30 | †*Thomas*, bap. Dec. 24, 1727 ; m. Jane Parrott of Bil. Mar. 8, 1750.
31 | *Abigail*, bap. July 27, 1729.
32 | *Lucy*, bap. April 4, 1731 ; m. May 24, 1750, Joshua Mead.
33 | *Elizabeth*, bap. June 22, 1735.
34 | †*Andrew*, bap. April 16, 1738 ; m. Nov. 29, 1759, Abigail Jennison of Weston.
35 | *Kezia*, bap. June 1, 1740 ; m. June 1, 1759, Joseph Wyman of Lunenburg.
36 | *Ebenezer*, bap. Feb. 28, 1742 ; probably d. 1743.
37 | *Mary*, bap. Oct. 21, 1744.

13-23- | JOSIAH PARKER m. Dec. 8, 1718, Anna Stone, dau. of John and Rachel (Shepard) Stone. Lieut. Parker, for he was honored with that title, was one of the most popular men in the town for a number of years. He filled almost every town office. He was an excellent penman, and filled the office of town clerk four years. He was an assessor nineteen years, from 1726 to 1755, with occasional intermissions, and was selectman seven years. He d. Oct. 9, 1756, aged 62 ; she d. Sept. 8, 1760. They were ad. to the ch. Aug. 13, 1719.

23-38 | *Anna*, b. Sept. 9, 1719 ; m. Nov. 6, 1737, Benjamin Smith.
39 | *Deliverance*, b. May 28, 1721 ; m. April 7, 1737, Marrett Munroe.
40 | *Mary*, b. July 3, 1723.
41 | †*Josiah*, b. April 11, 1725 ; m. Oct. 27, 1748, Mary Munroe, Weston.
42 | *Lois*, b. Aug. 20, 1727 ; d. July, 1735.
43 | †*John*, b. July 13, 1729 ; m. May 22, 1755, Lydia Moore.
44 | ‡*Thaddeus*, b. Sept. 2, 1731 ; m. May 29, 1759, Mary Reed.
45 | †*Joseph*, b. Nov. 28, 1733 ; m. July 5, 1759, Eunice Hobbs, Weston.

22-27- | JONAS PARKER m. Lucy ——. They made their peace with the ch. Sept. 15, 1745. He was one of the first martyrs of freedom who fell on the 19th of April, 1775. See History, p. 181 of this volume.

27-46 | *Nathan*, b. —— ; m. and had Abigail.
47 | *Lucy*, bap. Oct. 6, 1745.
48 | *Jonas*, bap. March 29, 1747 ; d. young.
49 | *Sarah*, bap. Sept. 4, 1748.
50 | †*Jonas*, b. July 10, 1753 ; m. Aug. 15, 1776, Martha Hosley of Bil.
51 | *Eunice*, bap. —— ; m. June 9, 1772, Asa Morse of Newton.

52 | *Prudence*, bap. April 27, 1757.
53 | *Elizabeth*, bap. March 18, 1759.   54 *Polly*, b. Jan. 4, 1761.
55 | *Philemon*, b. ———.

22-28- | AMOS PARKER m. Anna ———. They made their peace with the ch. Jan. 27, 1745. They probably left town in 1745, as his name disappears from the tax bill. He settled in Shrewsbury, where he had a child bap. 1750. They had *Amos*; *Sarah*, b. July 15, 1750; *Hollis*, b. Oct. 2, 1752; *Elisha*, b. Dec. 31, 1754; *Ephraim*, b. Oct. 4, 1757; *Frederick*, b. May 4, 1762; *Elizabeth*, b. March 29, 1769.

22-30- | THOMAS PARKER m. March 8, 1750, Jane Parrott of Chelmsford. They made their peace with the ch. in July, and their first child was bap. Aug. 19, 1750.

30-56 | †*Ebenezer*, bap. Aug. 19, 1750; m. Dec. 3, 1772, Dorcas Munroe.
57 | *William* ?, bap. Dec. 29, 1751.   58 *Mary*, bap. July 13, 1760.
| They buried two infant children, probably b. between William and Mary.

22-34- | ANDREW PARKER m. Nov. 29, 1759, Abigail Jennison of Weston. They made their peace with the ch. April 20, 1760. They removed about 1763 to Rutland, to the ch. of which place they were dismissed May 10, 1765. They had two children b. in Lexington.

34-59 | *Rhoda*, b. June 19, 1760.   60 *Abigail*, bap. Feb. 7, 1762.

23-41- | JOSIAH PARKER m. Oct. 27, 1748, Mary Munroe of Weston, dau. of Benjamin Munroe, son of the original William of Lex. He must have left town about the time of his marriage, as his name disappears from the tax bills after that time.

23-43- | JOHN PARKER m. May 25, 1755, Lydia Moore, dau. of Thomas and Mary Moore of Lexington. They were admitted to the church Oct. 31, 1756. John Parker was an assessor, 1764, '65, '66, and '74. But he was most distinguished for the part he acted at the opening of the Revolution. He commanded the company of minute men who stood firmly at their post on the 19th of April, 1775, when ordered to disperse by the impetuous Pitcairn, backed up, as he was, by eight hundred British regulars. He must have been a man of admitted character, to have been selected to command that Spartan band, containing, as it did, within its ranks, several veteran soldiers, and even officers who had seen service upon the " tented field." It has been said that he had served in the French war; but I have failed to find his name upon the rolls. On the Common on that trying occasion, he showed great coolness and bravery, ordering his men to load their pieces, but not to fire unless fired upon. And in the very face of the British regulars, when some of his men seemed to falter, he announced in a firm voice, that he would cause the first man to be shot down, who should quit the ranks or leave his post without orders. And though eight of his men were killed in the morning, and several were severely wounded, true to the spirit of freedom, he collected his company and marched to meet the enemy on their return from Concord, and poured a deadly fire into their ranks. While his health was feeble, and the disease which proved fatal in September of that year, was making a steady inroad upon his constitution, he obeyed the calls of patriotism, and marched with a portion of his co. to Cambridge on the 6th of May, and with a still larger detachment of them on the 17th of June. But though he performed a noble part in the opening scene of that glorious struggle, he did not live to witness its happy termination. He d. Sept. 17, 1775, aged 46. His wid. m Nov. 5, 1778, Ephraim Pierce of Waltham.

There are some incidents connected with the character and acts of Capt. Parker which deserve mention. We have seen the efforts made by the town, in 1774 and 1775, to arm and equip her company of minute-men. We have the receipt of Capt. Parker for two drums received of the town, which we will give verbatim, with a *fac-simile* of his signature.

" Agreeable to the vote of the Town, I have received by the hands of the Selectmen the drums provided by the Town for the use of the Military Company in this town, until the further order of the town.

John Parker

" Lexington, March 14, 1775."

There are two muskets, appropriate memorials of Capt. Parker, preserved in the State House, the gift of his grandson, Rev. Theodore Parker, to the State. On one is inscribed

" The First Fire Arm
Captured in the
War for Independence ; "

and on the other,

" This Firearm was used by
Capt. John Parker
in the Battle of Lexington,
April 19th,
1775."

These relics were received by the State authorities with due ceremony, and are conspicuously displayed in the Senate chamber for public view.

43–61 | *Lydia*, b. Nov. 8, 1756 ; d. in Rox. about 1810, unm.

62 | *Anna*, b. Jan. 11, 1759 ; m. March 16, 1780, Ephraim Pierce of Waltham.

63 | †*John*, b. Feb. 14, 1761 ; m. Feb. 17, 1785, Hannah Stearns.

64 | *Isaac*, b. May 11, 1763 ; moved to Charlestown, where he d.

65 | *Ruth*, b. Dec. 7, 1765 ; m. Nov. 14, 1787, David Bent ; moved to Nova Scotia.

66 | *Rebecca*, b. June 28, 1768 ; m. Peter Clarke of Wat.

67 | †*Robert*, b. April 15, 1771 ; m. Oct. 22, 1794, Elizabeth Simonds.

23–44– | THADDEUS PARKER m. May 27, 1759, Mary Reed, dau. of William and Abigail (Stone) Reed. He d. Feb. 10, 1789, aged 58 ; she d. Oct. 9, 1811, aged 73. She had the severe affliction of burying her husband and four children, in the short period of about eighteen months. Thaddeus Parker was one of the selectmen, 1770, '71, '73, '77,—a period when the most important duties were devolved upon that board. He was a member of the Lex. co. which stood undismayed before the British on the 19th of April, 1775, and was subsequently in the service eight months.

44–68 | *A child* born and died 1759.

69 | *Mary*, b. Sept. 26, 1760 ; d. June 3, 1787.

70 | *Sarah*, b. Aug. 24, 1762 ; d. Feb. 2, 1789.

71 | *Betty*, b. Aug. 28, 1764 ; d. Aug. 27, 1788.
72 | *Thaddeus*, b. July 10. 1767 ; d. June 14, 1789.
73 | *Josiah*, b. Sept. 19, 1770.

23–45– | JOSEPH PARKER m. July 5, 1759, Eunice Hobbs of Weston. After the birth of their first child, in 1760, they settled in Linc. As most of their children were bap. in Lex. we will give their birth.

45–74 | *Susanna*, b. Dec. 31, 1760.   75 *Levi*, b. April 16, 1762.
76 | *Lois*, b. Oct. 4, 1763.   77 *Aaron*, b. Dec. 5, 1765.
78 | *Joseph*, b. Nov. 17, 1767.   79 *Jonathan*, b. Oct. 17, 1769.
80 | *Elisha*, b. Dec. 9, 1772 ; d. in 1773.
81 | *Elisha*, } twins, b. Sept. 10, 1775.
82 | *Rebecca*, }

27–50– | JONAS PARKER m. Aug. 15, 1776, Martha Hosley of Bill. They were ad. to the ch. Feb. 28, 1779. He d. July 14, 1783, and Martha his wid. administered on his estate.

50–83 | *Patty*, bap. May 16, 1779.   84 *Betty*, bap. May 16, 1779.
85 | *John H.*, bap. Nov. 26, 1780.   86 *Jonas*, bap. March 2, 1783.

30–56– | EBENEZER PARKER m. Dec. 3, 1772, Dorcas Munroe. He was a corporal in Capt. Parker's co. and was with them on the 19th of April, the 6th of May, and the 17th of June, 1775. He and his wife were dismissed to the ch. in Princeton, Nov. 9, 1788. They had three children bap. in Lex. viz. *Abijah*, bap. May 30, 1773 ; *Quincy*, bap. April 30, 1775 ; *Lucy*, bap. July 22, 1781.

43–63– | JOHN PARKER m. Feb. 7, 1784, Hannah Stearns, dau. of Benjamin and Hannah (Seger) Stearns, b. May 21. 1764. He d. Nov. 3, 1835, aged 74 ; she d. May 15, 1823, aged 59.

63–87 | *Mary*, b. April 11, 1785 ; m. about 1816, Samuel Green, as his second wife,—he being the widower of her sister Hannah. She d. 1831.
88 | *John*, b. Oct. 12, 1786, m. Maria Green of West Camb.
89 | *Lydia*, b. April 2, 1789 ; d. April 25. 1791.
90 | *Hannah*, b. March 15, 1791 ; m. March 25, 1811, Samuel Green of Brighton. She d. Dec. 1, 1815, in Vt., and he m. her sister Mary.
91 | *Lydia*, b. July 1, 1793 ; m Isaac Herrick of Brighton and d. 1837.
92 | *Rebecca*, b. Dec. 10, 1795 ; d. Feb. 15, 1812, unm.
93 | †*Isaac*, b. Nov. 5, 1798 ; m. 1829, Martha M. Miller.
94 | *Ruth*, b. Nov. 12, 1800 ; d. Dec. 27, 1812.
95 | *Hiram S.*, b. Jan. 16, 1803 ; m. Nancy Leavitt of N. H.
96 | *Emily Ann*, b. May 11, 1806 ; m. Charles Miller of Somerville.
97 | †*Theodore*, b. Aug. 24, 1810 ; m. Lydia D. Cabot in 1837.

43–67– | ROBERT PARKER m. Oct. 22, 1794, Elizabeth Simonds, dau. of Joshua and Martha (Bowers) Simonds, b. July 4, 1772. He d. Dec. 31, 1840, aged 70. She d. April 11, 1849, aged 77.

67–98 | *Mary*, b. Dec. 26, 1794 ; m. April 11, 1822, Isaac W. Lawrence of West Camb. They have had four children.
99 | *Josiah*, b. July 6, 1798 ; d. Dec. 25, 1840, unm.
100 | *Thomas*, b. March 16, 1800 ; d. April 30, 1800.
101 | *Eliza Eleanor*, b. Sept. 20, 1804 ; m. April 12, 1829, Nathan Robbins of West Camb. They have had seven children.
102 | *Almira*, b Aug. 30, 1806 ; m. Oct. 1, 1837, Joshua Robbins of West Camb. They have had three children.

103 | *Jonathan Simonds*, b. Aug. 8, 1808; d. Feb. 13, 1813.
104 | †*Jonathan Simonds*, b. July 30, 1812; m. Dec. 29, 1835, Abigail Tuttle.
105 | *William Bowers*, b. Jan. 13, 1817; m. Nov. 30, 1843, Elizabeth Garfield. He settled in Charlestown, and has had seven children.

63-93—   ISAAC PARKER m. 1829, Martha M Miller, b. June 28, 1801, in Hillsborough, N. H. They settled in Waltham, but came to Lex. in 1832, and took up their abode on the old Parker Place in the south part of the town. Their first two children were born in Waltham.

93-106 | *Isaac Moore*, b. Nov. 10, 1829.
107 | *Martha Ann*, b. June 16, 1831; m. Oct. 28, 1855, William W. Durgee of York, Pa.
108 | *Frances Maria*, b. Jan. 21, 1833.
109 | *Charles M.*, b. Feb. 15, 1835. He enlisted for three years and served in the 24th Reg. Mass. Vols. in the late war.
110 | *James Theodore*, b. Sept. 18, 1837; d. April 2, 1838.
111 | *Emily R.*, b. April 7, 1839; d. Aug. 6, 1858.
112 | *Theodore James*, b. April 21, 1841.
113 | *George E.*, b. Jan. 2, 1843; d. Oct. 6, 1857.

63-97—   THEODORE PARKER m. April 20, 1837, Lydia D. Cabot of Boston, dau. of John and Lydia (Dodge) Cabot, b. Sept. 12, 1813. They had no children. In 1830 he entered H. C., but owing to his limited pecuniary means, he was not able to incur the expense of a life at the college, but remained at home pursuing his studies through the winter, and then engaged himself as a teacher. Not residing at the college and attending the daily exercises, he did not take his degree; though in 1840 he received from the University the honorary degree of A. M. Our limits will not permit us to give in detail the events of his laborious life. It is sufficient to say, that he raised himself to great distinction by his own unassisted industry and force of character. Without the usual advantages enjoyed by those who are destined to a literary life, by persevering industry he overcame all these disadvantages, and became a man of vast acquirements, procured and mastered an extensive library, and died in the midst of life with a reputation which few men ever acquire.

Giving his mind to religious subjects, he entered the theological school at Cambridge in 1834, and after graduating, he was first settled at West Roxbury, and subsequently became pastor of the Twenty-eighth Congregational Society which worshiped at Music Hall in Boston. By that incessant labor, which few constitutions can endure, he became somewhat enfeebled, and a hemorrhage from the lungs required him to suspend all labor. By the advice of his physician, and the entreaty of friends, he was induced to seek a more genial climate. In February, 1859, he embarked for the West Indies, where he remained for a time, when he sailed for the south of Europe. But neither medical skill, nor the balmy air of Italy, could stay the ravages of disease, and he d. at Florence, May 10, 1860. He was buried in a little Protestant cemetery outside the city walls. The grave is inclosed by a border of gray marble, and at the head is a plain stone of the same material, with this inscription:

THEODORE PARKER,
Born at Lexington, Mass.,
United States of America,
Aug. 24, 1810.
Died at Florence, May 10, 1860.

The unsparing censure which has been heaped, and the unlimited praise which has been bestowed upon Mr. Parker, will justify us in saying a few words upon his character. The leading characteristic of the man was his *thirst for knowledge*. This manifested itself in his persistant industry from his boyhood to the day of his death. His love of books became almost a passion, and he made himself acquainted with various languages, that he might read the best authors in their native tongue. Few men under the circumstances in which he was placed, have ever performed more labor, or accomplished as much. His moral character, as seen by the world, was above reproach. But to judge the man aright, we must look beneath the surface, and see the motives by which he was actuated. And here we find a stern sense of justice tempered with mercy, a strong love for the poor and down-trodden, and a warm sympathy for humanity, for whose elevation he was ready to spend, and be spent. And though he sometimes indulged in bitter denunciation, too common among reformers, we shall generally find that it was prompted by a strong sense of wrong or injustice committed against those he was laboring to elevate and improve.

But it is with reference to his religious character that the people have been most divided. Though it is not the object of this work to decide upon matters of faith, we will glance at this subject with that freedom which Mr. Parker himself always exercised, and with such a spirit as he, if present, would approve. Born of a pious and devout mother, whose instructions sank deep into his tender heart, and living under the influences of religious institutions founded upon the *broad basis of divine revelation*, he early imbibed enlightened views of the character of our Heavenly Father, and of our duty to love and adore him. These views he cherished through life: so that we can with justice pronounce him not only a *moral* but a *devout* man. But though we can endorse his moral and religious character, we are constrained to express our conviction that this character was the result of his early training and the natural goodness of his heart, rather than of his theological speculations. He was moral and devout in spite of his theory. This impression is strengthened by the fact that very many of those who embrace his speculations have but little sympathy with that devout spirit by which he was actuated.

That he was a man of extraordinary intellectual powers, all must admit. He had a keen perception of the evils which existed in society, but like many reformers had not constructive powers sufficient to supply the remedy. So in matters of faith, he could point out with a master's hand the incongruities of existing systems, but has never, as far as we can learn, been able to present a clear and well defined system of his own. We do not mean that he had no belief. He had certain doctrines which he inculcated with earnestness and in sincerity. But he has never, we believe, combined them so as to make a complete system,—*one harmonious whole.*

Thus much it seemed proper to say concerning one of the most distinguished men to whom Lexington has ever given birth. Mr. Parker has left a large number of ardent and devoted friends. They have erected a memorial stone in Lexington to his memory, on the spot where stood the old house in which he was born. The stone is of Concord granite, finished on all sides, three feet square, and three and a half feet high, resting on a base four feet square and one foot high. On the front face, in raised letters, is the simple inscription,

BIRTH-PLACE
of
THEODORE PARKER.
1810.

The farm has been in possession of the Parker family since 1712.
The following engraving shows the house in which he was born, and
the old belfry building which stood on the Common on the site of
the present monument, in 1775, from which went forth those peals
of alarm which called the patriots to arms on the morning of the 19th
of April. The old belfry was procured by the family and removed
to the Parker Place, where it is now standing.

67-101- JONATHAN S. PARKER m. Dec. 29, 1835, Abigail Tuttle, dau. of
David Tuttle. He d. July 5, 1859, and she d. April 4, 1860. He
was captain of the Lex. artillery, and filled the most important town
offices,—was treasurer five years, assessor four years, and selectman
three years.

104-114 *John Henry*, b. Sept. 16, 1836; d. Sept. 12, 1855.
   115 *Elizabeth S.*, b. Sept. 30, 1838. 116 *Esther T.*, b. Feb. 21, 1842.
   117 *Abby M.*, b. April 23, 1847.
   118 *Georgiana T.*, b. Oct. 12, 1849.
   119 *Emma Frances*, b. April 8, 1853. 120 *Ellen Henry*, b. June 28, 1858.

There was an OBADIAH PARKER in town for a few years, who by
his wife, Hepzibah, had at least two childen b. in Lex. *Almira*, b.
April 16, 1802, d. Nov. 14, 1802; *Almira*, b. Nov. 9, 1803. He
appears to have been a man of considerable talents. He was appointed to pronounce an eulogy on Washington in 1800, whose
death was noticed with appropriate solemnities. He opened a private
school in Lex., which was quite popular. He visited New York,
where for misconduct he found employment quite different from that
of teaching the young.

JAMES PARKER, another school-teacher, m. in Lex. Nov. 2, 1842, Adaline Reed, dau. of Isaac and Elizabeth (Munroe) Reed, b. Jan. 10, 1812. He settled in Lex. They have one child, *James Emery*, b. Aug. 30, 1845.

PARKHURST.—JOHN PARKHURST of Lex. m. Sept. 15, 1763, Elizabeth Bowers of Billerica. He came to Lex. from Chelmsford, and was probably a descendant of Joseph Parkhurst, of that town, who had Joseph, b. 1661, and perhaps other sons. He was in the campaign of White Plains in 1776. He was selectman, 1791. He resided on the Concord road, and built the house occupied by the late Col. John Parkhurst Merriam. He had no children. He d. July 2, 1812. His will, dated June 4, 1812, mentions wife Elizabeth, John White of Gardner, John Muzzey, and John P. Merriam, John Peake Hunt of Jaffrey, N. H., brother Jonathan, and sisters Hannah Parker, Mary Colburn, and Elizabeth Baldwin. His wid. d. July 9, 1822, aged 83 years.

PEAKE.—Jonas Stone in 1754, gave notice as then required by law, that *Philip Peake*, a child from Boston, came to Lexington to reside in his family. There were other Peakes in town, but I know not their origin.

JOHN PEAKE m. March 21, 1776, Hitty Hastings. They were ad. to the ch. Nov. 29, 1778. Their first child b. and d. 1777. *Mary*, bap. Jan. 17, 1779; *John*, bap. July 1, 1781; *Thomas*, bap. Dec. 28, 1783; *Sarah*, bap. June 3, 1787; *Hannah*, bap. Dec. 26, 1790; *Philip*, bap. April 22, 1794.—*Philip* d. at the age of 24. *Mary* m. Isaac Childs; *John* m. and moved to Sudbury; *Sarah* m. Nathan Priest of Jaffrey, N. H. *Thomas* m. Elizabeth ——; r. Vt.

Joseph Mason m. Oct. 19, 1769, *Elizabeth Peake*, who was ad. to the ch. Oct. 13, 1765.

PENNY.—DAVID PENNY and Sally Smith, both of Lex., were m. Sept. 30, 1779. They had *Sarah*, b. Feb. 20, 1780; *Polly*, b. Feb. 20, 1782, d. Feb. 23, 1782; *Jonathan*, b. March 12, 1783, d. Dec. 5, 1783; *Polly*, b. Nov. 12, 1785, d. 1829; *David*, b. March 25, 1788, m. May 12, 1822, Mary F. Sherman, she d. 1852; *Isaac*, b. July 20, 1790, d. 1809; *Samuel C.*, b. Dec. 13, 1793; *Hannah*, b. May 14, 1795, d. Feb. 21, 1860. David, sen., d. Jan. 1830. The absence of a record will prevent any fuller account of this family.

PERRY.—This name appears upon our records at different periods, and yet we are not able to give a connected view of the families. JOHN PERRY, by his wife, Deborah, had the following children: *John*, b. Dec. 19, 1720; *Thomas*, b. Dec. 19, 1722; *Joseph*, b. Oct. 3, 1724; *Millicent*, b. May 10, 1726; *Ebenezer* and *Jonathan*, twins, b. July 17, 1728, Jonathan m. Jan. 27, 1760, Mary Blodgett; *Thaddeus*, b. Dec. 26, 1730; *Abigail*, b. Aug. 10, 1735, m. Nov. 20, 1754, Abel Fox of Billerica. Deborah was ad. to the ch. June 29, 1735, and d. May 22, 1736. *Thomas Perry* was in the French war from Lex. in 1759 and 1762.

The name, which had faded out from the records, appeared again about 1800. NATHAN PERRY by his wife, Sally, had *Sullivan B.*, b. Feb. 1802; *Mary*, b. Oct. 1, 1803; *Sally*, b. Aug. 30, 1804; *Abijah H.*, b. Dec. 19, 1806; *Thomas W.*, b. May 1, 1808, d. Nov. 9, 1821; *Nahum S.*, b. March 28, 1810.

THE PHELPS FAMILY.

The early history of this family is but imperfectly known to us.

1   JONATHAN PHELPS came to this country early in the eighteenth century, and landed in Newport, R. I. From thence he came to Reading, Mass., where he reared a family of children. One of them (name unknown) came first to Beverly, and then to Salem, where he d. Dec. 1799, aged about 92. He had three sons, Jonathan, Henry, and William, and several daughters.

1- 2   HENRY PHELPS was a shipmaster, from the port of Salem, and was lost at sea, 1786. He m. and had children.

2- 3   HENRY PHELPS, son of the preceding, having bodily infirmities, which disqualified him from following his father's profession, fitted for college and entered Harvard, where he was graduated, 1788. He studied medicine, and settled in 1799, at Gloucester, as an apothecary and physician. He m. Mary Forbes, dau. of Peter Coffin, Esq., of Gloucester. He d. Feb. 18, 1852, aged 86, and hence was b. 1766. He acquired some practice as a doctor, but soon abandoned that branch of his business. He was many years postmaster, and the principal acting magistrate in the town. He continued to keep his shop till he was about eighty years of age. He had three wives and several children.

3- 4   WILLIAM DANE PHELPS, son of the foregoing, was b. at Gloucester, Feb. 14, 1802; m. Mary Ann Cushing, dau. of Henry Cushing of Boston. She d. Dec. 16, 1831, and he m. May 18, 1834, Lusanna T., dau. of Josiah and Sally (Wellington) Bryant of Lex. He came to Lex. to reside about the time of his second marriage.

His profession has been that of a mariner. He commenced early as a cabin-boy, and has worked his way through the different grades to master—making many voyages to Europe and the Levant, around Cape Horn and the Cape of Good Hope, in command of some of the finest ships of the times. He was wrecked once while a boy at the Cape of Good Hope, and once when captain at the entrance of Plymouth Harbor in the winter of 1836; which was one of the most distressing shipwrecks known for many years on our coast. The cold was intense, and the ship was unmanageable in consequence of the ice which accumulated upon her. Part of the crew perished by the cold, and those who were saved were badly bruised and frozen. In one of his early voyages, when he was before the mast, he was left with seven others on a desert island in the Indian Ocean to procure a cargo of sea elephant oil, and fur seal skins—the captain promising to return for them in nine months. But actuated probably by that thirst of gain which stifles every feeling of humanity, and believing that they could not subsist after the provision left with them was exhausted, and as the island was very rarely visited by voyagers, he thought he might touch there at a future day, and take his oil and furs without being troubled by having any men to pay off. But on his return twenty-eight months after, he found not only a full cargo of oil and furs, but his eight men all living. The island being in a high latitude, it was cold and desolate, not a tree or shrub sprang from its inhospitable bosom; and consequently these poor dwellers thereon had no fuel of the ordinary kind, but were compelled to burn the blubber of the sea elephant. The interior of the island was composed of barren volcanic ridges, but the shores abounded with sea fowl, penguin, and marine animals. Their nine months' provisions became exhausted, and for the remainder of the time they subsisted upon what the shore afforded, fish and fowls and their eggs. For clothing they supplied themselves with fur skins, and for shelter they sought the "caves and dens of the earth." After twenty-eight months, their unprincipled captain arrived—his being the first vessel which had been in sight for the whole period. He took his cargo and the men, who were glad to leave that inclement island. The subsequent conduct of this brutal captain, fully justified the suspicion that he had hoped that they had all perished before his return.

During this voyage, which to young Phelps was extended to more than six years, he, by the force of circumstances, left the ship, and was obliged to take service under the flags of various nations, visiting most of the parts of the Pacific, and the then known parts of Australia and Van Dieman's land, and returned home by way of Cape Horn in 1823, in good health, with considerable experience, but with empty pockets.

In 1840, in command of a large ship, he commenced a series of trading voyages to California, remaining there till he had disposed of his cargo and procured a cargo of hides. These voyages were generally of about three years' duration. San Francisco was then called Yerba Buena, and consisted of only three houses, where the famous city now stands. At that time the River Sacramento had never been visited from the sea, and Capt. Phelps with two of his boats and a part of his crew explored it about one hundred miles, and displayed the Stars and Stripes for the first time upon its placid waters. On his third voyage, the country was disturbed by the Mexican War, and being upon the coast he co-operated with Stockton and Fremont in various ways, and so contributed something to our gaining possession of the country. He visited the mines twice, handled some of the first specimens of gold, and returned home by the way of Panama, bringing some of the first specimens of gold, and reliable information in relation to the mines. The last voyage he performed was to California, the Sandwich Islands and China, and returned to New York in 1857. He has spent about forty years in a sea life, twenty-six of them in command of a ship. During that time, with one exception already mentioned, no Insurance Office has ever paid a dollar for damage to his ships or cargo; and with the same exception, he never lost a man by sickness or accident, until the last voyage, when two died of disease in China.

From this brief sketch, it will be seen that Capt. Phelps's life has been active and eventful. With no small degree of truth, we can say of him in the language of Campbell,

> "His march was o'er the mountain wave,
> His home was on the deep."

4– 5   *Lusanna*, b. Nov. 18, 1836.
   6   *Alice D.*, b. Oct. 18, 1838; m. Oct. 15, 1862, Charles C. Goodwin of Charlestown. They reside in Lex. and have one child, viz. George C., b. Nov. 24, 1863.
   7   *Edwin Buckingham*, b. April 14, 1845; d. Sept. 9, 1849.

THE PHINNEY FAMILY.

1   BENJAMIN PHINNEY, the first of the name in Lex., came into the town, 1787, from Granville, Nova Scotia. We have not been able to learn his birth or parentage. He and his wife, Susanna, were ad. to the ch. in Falmouth, Mass., May 10, 1772; at the same time two of their children, Chloe and Josiah, were bap. In Aug. 1774, their dau. Susanna was baptized; and they were dismissed from the Fal-

mouth church to the united church of Annapolis and Granville, Nova
Scotia. The Lexington church records, Oct. 14, 1787, recognize the
fact of their recommendation from Falmouth to Nova Scotia, "from
thence they came to reside in this town, and requested ch. privileges
with us." He d. 1843, aged 99, and hence must have been b. about
1744. She d. June 16, 1829.

1- 2   *Patience*, b. ———; m. Sept. 25, 1809, Eli Green of Boston.
   3   *Chloe*, bap. May 10, 1772; m. May 21, 1794, John Stearns of Walt.
   4   *Josiah*, bap. May 10, 1772.
   5   *Susanna*, bap. May 10, 1774; m. May 22, 1794, Peleg Stearns, Walt.
   6   *Joseph*, b. ———; was drowned.
   7   *Theodore*, b. ———; m. Ann Barrett in Cuba.
   8 †*Elias*, b. in Nova Scotia, 1780; m. June 6, 1809, Catharine Bartlett.
   9   *Benjamin*, bap. Oct. 14, 1787; d. Oct. 16, 1791.
 10   *Deidama*, bap. Aug. 20, 1788; m. Barnabas Fales of Washington
      city and d. soon after.

1-8-   ELIAS PHINNEY m. June 6, 1809, Catharine Bartlett, dau. of Dr.
Josiah and Elizabeth (Call) Bartlett of Charlestown. He grad. H.
C. 1801, read law, and commenced practice in Thomaston, Me.
He afterwards removed to Charlestown, where he had an office.
Having a taste for rural life, he came to Lex. in 1823, where he d.
July 24, 1849, aged 69. His wid. d. Aug. 2, 1864, aged 78. He
was a prominent man in the town and county, was for many years
clerk of the courts for the county of Middlesex, which office he held
at the time of his death. He was highly distinguished as an agriculturalist, being for many years a trustee of the State Agricultural
Society. His farm in the south part of the town was brought by him
to a high state of cultivation, and the farm, fruit trees, and stock
attracted visitors from a great distance; so that his scientific and
practical knowledge of husbandry exerted a wide influence over those
engaged in that department of human industry. In 1825, he published an interesting account of the Battle of Lexington, in which he
vindicated with great ability the claims of the town of Lexington
against certain pretensions set up by a few indiscreet men of Concord.

8-11 *Josiah B.*, b. April 1, 1810; m. Lucretia Beckford of Charlestown.
      He moved to Cuba, where they resided twelve or fifteen years,
      when he returned to the United States and settled in Illinois. He
      had two sons, one of whom is living.
 12 *Susan M.*, b. Sept. 30, 1812; m. Dec. 19, 1833, Isaac H. Spring.
      He resided in Boston, where he d. April 7, 1864. They had four
      daughters.
 13 *Catharine B.*, b. April 2, 1814; m. in 1837, Thomas Goodall. They
      resided in Vicksburg, Miss. He d. and she is now residing in
      Chicago. They had four children.
 14 *Elizabeth B.*, b. Dec. 29, 1816; m. Sept. 30, 1841, A. H. Nelson,
      who was a prominent member of the bar, and was raised to a
      judgeship. They resided first in Concord, and afterward in Wo.,
      where he d. 1857.
 15 *Mary P.*, b. Feb. 2, 1818; m. May 1, 1858, G. A. Olnhausen. He
      d. Sept. 7, 1860. They resided in Manchester, N. H. Mrs. Oln-
      hausen is a lady of great perseverance and force of character.
      After the death of her husband she returned to her friends, and
      on the breaking out of the Rebellion her sympathies were turned
      to the sick and wounded soldiers, who had left the comforts of
      home to sustain the liberties of the country. Her active sense of
      the worth of our institutions, and of the baseness of the attempt

to overthrow them; and her just appreciation of the devotion of the gallant men who had voluntarily taken their lives in their hands, and gone forth amidst the dangers of the field and the diseases of the camp, to uphold the government of our choice, prompted her to offer her services to her country. In August, 1862, she entered upon her duty as a hospital nurse, and served first at the Mansion House at Alexandria, from thence she was transferred to Morehead City, then to Beaufort, and at last to Smithville, N. C. Having entered for the war, she remained in the United States' service till 1865. She was associated with that well known philanthropist, Miss Dix; and being a regular nurse in the service, she was subject to the orders of the hospital department, or else she would have followed her inclination, and gone to the front, where she would have seen more of suffering, and where she believed, she could have been more useful. Mrs. Olnhausen acquired a high reputation at the hospitals as an active, skillful, and self-sacrificing nurse—always cool and collected, she devoted herself assiduously to the wants of her patients. By her kindness and fidelity she won the respect and esteem of all committed to her care. Many a poor sick or wounded soldier, far from the comforts and endearments of home, has found in her the care and watchfulness of a faithful mother, and the kindness and sympathy of an affectionate sister. We naturally extol the heroism of the gallant soldier who promptly faces danger on the field of battle; but it requires as much moral courage, as much self-sacrifice to brave the diseases of the hospitals, as it does to face the enemy in the field. Much praise is due to Mrs Olnhausen.

16 *Jane*, b Oct. 3, 1820.
17 *Charlotte B.*, b. July 17, 1822; m. April, 1842, Rev. William G. Swett, who was settled as a minister in Lexington. She had one dau. C. B. W. G. Swett, b. Feb. 8, 1843. He d. Feb. 15, 1843, and she m. June 1, 1863, Francis K. Simonds. They have two children.
18 *George P.*, b. Jan. 24, 1824; m. Kate Richardson of Woburn. He resides in Illinois, and has six children. She d. May, 1867.
19 *Alice B.*, b. Nov. 9, 1826; m. May 23, 1854, James S. Munroe; they reside in Lexington.
20 *B. Frank*, b, Jan. 28, 1829. He was a mariner—having entered on ship-board as a cabin boy, he passed through the different stages to that of captain. He d. in Brazil, 1855.

THE PIERCE FAMILY.

The Pierces (frequently spelt Peirce,) came to the country early, and settled in that great hive of emigrants, Watertown. It is somewhat difficult to trace the genealogy of the family, as they are quite numerous, and are scattered through several towns. There is also danger of confounding the Watertown families with the descendants of Robert Pierce, who settled at Dorchester as early as 1630.

1 JOHN PIERCE, a weaver of Wat. was ad. freeman March, 1638. He died, Aug. 19, 1661. His wid. Elizabeth, in her will dated March 5, and proved April 2, 1667, makes mention of sons Anthony, Robert and John, and dau. Esther Morse, and Mary Coldam. It is probable that Robert settled in Wo. where he d. Sept. 10, 1706, leaving a family of children.

1- 2 ANTHONY PIERCE, b. in England, 1609, and ad. freeman Sept. 3, 1634, was the ancestor of all or nearly all the families bearing that

name in the towns of Wat., Waltham, Weston, Lincoln, and Lex. He
m. first, Sarah ——— ; m. second, about 1638, Anne ———. He
d. May 9, 1678. His wid. d. Jan. 20, 1683.

2- 3 | *John*, b. ——— ; m. Ruth, dau. of Nathaniel Bishop. He d. without issue, and his wid. m. William Fuller.
4 | *Mary*, b. Oct. 20, 1633; d. young.
5 | *Mary*, b. 1636; m. Ralph Reed, son of William and Mabel Reed of Woburn.
6 | *Jacob*, b. Sept. 15, 1637; was living in 1683.
7 | †*Daniel*, b. Jan. 1, 1640; m. Elizabeth ———.
8 | *Martha*, b. April 24, 1641.
9 | †*Joseph*, b. ——— ; ad. freeman April 18, 1690.
10 | *Benjamin*, b. 1649; m. Jan. 15, 1677, Hannah Brooks of Concord.
11 | *Judith*, b. July 18, 1650; m. Feb. 1677, John Sawin.

2-7-   DANIEL PIERCE m. Elizabeth ——— ; b. 1642. He settled in Groton, where he had five children b. He returned to Wat. about 1681. He o. e. Jan. 16, 1687, when his wife and three children were baptized.

7-12 | *Elizabeth*, b. May 16, 1665; m. in Wat. Oct. 17, 1684, Isaac Mixer.
13 | *Daniel*, b. Nov. 28, 1666; m. Abigail ———, and lived in Groton.
14 | *John*, b. Aug. 18, 1668.   15 *Ephraim*, b. Oct. 15, 1673.
16 | *Josiah*, b. May 2, 1675.
17 | †*Joseph*, b. ——— ; mentioned in the will of sister Elizabeth.
18 | *Abigail*, b. Jan. 3, 1682.   19 *Hannah*, bap. Jan. 16, 1687.
20 | *Benjamin*, bap. Jan. 16, 1687.

2-9-   JOSEPH PIERCE m. Martha ———. She d. and he m. June 15, 1698, Mrs. Elizabeth Winship, wid. of Ephraim Winship of Camb. Farms.

9-21 | †*Joseph*, b. Oct. 2, 1669; was thrice m.
22 | *Francis*, b. July 27, 1671; lived in Weston, d. April 22, 1728.
23 | †*John*, b. May 27, 1673; m. Nov. 5, 1702, Elizabeth Smith.
24 | *Mary*, b. Nov. 26, 1674.
25 | *Benjamin*, b. March 25, 1677.
26 | *Jacob*, b. Dec. 25, 1678; m. Nov. 13, 1702, Hannah Lewis, and d. 1740.
27 | *Martha*, b. Dec. 24, 1681; m. May 17, 1706, William Whitney.
28 | *Stephen*, b. Oct. 1683; m. 1780, Abigail Bemis, lived in Weston.
29 | *Israel*, b. Oct. 7, 1685; m. Jan. 14, 1718, Sarah Holland. He moved to Camb. in 1721.
30 | *Elizabeth*, b. Sept. 9, 1687; m. Oct. 15, 1706, Joseph Bemis.

7-17-   JOSEPH PIERCE of Wat. m. Dec. 30, 1698, Mary Warren. He was selectman in Waltham, 1738, '39, '42.

17-31 | †*Isaac*, b. Sept. 19, 1700.   32 *Mary*, b. Feb. 28, 1703.
33 | *Elizabeth*, b. Feb. 23, 1704.   34 *Sarah*, b. Sept. 11, 1705.
35 | *Lydia*, b. March 11, 1707.   36 *Eunice*, b. Feb. 11, 1709.
37 | *Grace*, b. April 27, 1711.   38 *Prudence*, b. Aug. 2, 1713.
39 | *Lois*, b. Jan. 21, 1716.   40 *Ruhamah*, b. Jan. 12, 1718.

9-21-   JOSEPH PIERCE m. May 20, 1688, Ruth Holland. She d. and he m. about 1692, Hannah Munroe, dau. of William Munroe of Camb. Farms, the ancestor of all the Munroes in Lex. and the vicinity. His wife Hannah was ad. to the ch. in Lex. Feb. 1, 1699, and he was ad. Sept. 28, 1701. What time he came into the Precinct is uncertain; probably about 1700, as he had a child bap. 1699, and united with the ch. in 1701. He was a subscriber for the purchase of the Common in 1711, and filled the dignified office of tythingman in 1717. His wife Hannah d. and he m. third, Beriah, wid. of Daniel Child. He d. Mar. 13, 1753, and his wid. m. John Whitney of Westford.

21-41 ‡*Joseph*, b. Feb. 5, 1694; m. Abigail ——.
42 †*George*, b. Feb. 2, 1696; m. Hannah ——, moved to Lincoln.
43 ‡*John*, b. Mar. 11, 1699; m. Rachel ——.
44 *Martha*, b June 2, 1702.
45 *Mary*, b. March 28, 1705; m. June 24, 1725, Thomas Fiske.
46 †*William*, b. July 10, 1707; m. Abigail ——.
47 *Ruth*, b. April 8, 1710.
48 *David*, b. April 16, 1713; m. May 29, 1734, Sarah Piper of Con.

9-23- JOHN PIERCE m. Elizabeth Smith. She d. Sept. 20, 1747. They were m. Nov. 5, 1702.

23-49 *John*, b. Sept. 1, 1703; m. Rebecca ——.
50 †*Jonas*, b. Dec. 20, 1705; m. Jan. 4, 1728, Abigail Comee of Lex.
51 *Ezekiel*, b. March 7, 1709; m. Nov. 17, 1731, Mercy Wellington of Watertown.
52 *Samuel*, b. July 3, 1712.   53 *Elizabeth*, b. Jan. 3, 1716.
54 *Daniel*, b. Oct. 21, 1719; m. Martha ——.
55 *Jonathan*, b. Sept. 28, 1724.

17-31- ISAAC PIERCE m. Sept. 7, 1722, Susanna Bemis. They resided in Waltham.

31-56 *Josiah*, b. Feb. 13, 1723; m. March 14, 1744, Sarah Gale.
57 *Joseph*, b. Nov. 23, 1724; m. June 2, 1748, Ruth White.
58 *Abijah*, b. May 23, 1727; m. Thankful Brown, lived in Lincoln.
59 ‡*Ephraim*, b. Aug. 12, 1729.   60 *Susanna*, b. May 22, 1732.
61 *Mary*, b. June 22, 1735; m. April 22, 1757, Moses Harrington.
62 *Isaac*, b. March 24, 1739; m. 1764, Hannah Mason. He had a family of twelve children, the youngest of whom was Cyrus, b. Aug. 1, 1790; grad. at H. C. 1810; m. Sally Coffin, has no issue. He was the first teacher of the first Normal school in Massachusetts, which was established in Lexington. He d. 1860.

21-41- JOSEPH PIERCE, m. Abigail ——. He d. Feb. 12, 1737. He resided in Lex. He appears to have been the only male of the family which remained permanently in Lexington.

41-63 *Ebenezer*, b. Sept. 13, 1715.   64 *Jonas*, b. Oct. 15, 1717.
65 *Joseph*, b. Feb. 3, 1719.

21-42- GEORGE PIERCE m. Hannah ——. They were ad. to the ch. in Lex. May 28, 1738. They moved to Linc. though several of their children were bap. in Lex. They had nine children.

21-43- JOHN PIERCE m. Rachel ——. He must have left Lex. as he was not taxed in town in 1729, or after that time.

43-66 *Anthony*, b. Sept. 13, 1720.   67 *John*, b. Feb. 11, 1722.
68 *Lucy*, b. Jan. 28, 1728.

21-46-   WILLIAM PIERCE m. Abigail ——.   He was ad. to the ch. in Lex.
June 29, 1733. He probably left Lex., as his name does not appear
on the tax bills after 1735.

46-69 | *Abigail*, b. May 7, 1729.   70 *Bridget*, b. Oct. 23, 1730.
71 | *Abner*, bap. Jan. 6, 1733.   72 *Zebulon*, bap. Dec. 15, 1734.
73 | *Phebe ?*, bap. Aug. 21, 1737.

23-50-   JONAS PIERCE m. Jan. 4, 1728, Abigail Comee of Lex., dau. of
John and Martha (Munroe) Comee.

50-74 | *Jonas*, b. July 7, 1730.
75 | *Nathan*, b. Dec. 15, 1732; m. Dec. 26, 1753, Sarah Reed.
76 | *Elizabeth*, b. May 31, 1735.   77 *John*, b. July 14, 1736.
78 | *Thaddeus*, b. May 14, 1739.
79 | *Solomon*, b. June 15, 1742; m. Dec. 15, 1763, Amity Fessenden.
80 | *Abigail*, b. Aug. 3, 1744; m. March 30, 1762, Nathan Derby of
Westminster, where their descendants are at this day.
81 | *Mary*, b. Feb. 7, 1747.

31-59-   EPHRAIM PIERCE of Waltham m. May 8, 1753, Lydia White, who
d. May 6, 1777, aged 43, and he m. Nov. 5, 1778, Mrs. Lydia Parker, wid. of Capt. John Parker, who commanded the company on
Lex. Common on the memorable 19th of April, 1775. Ephraim Pierce
spent most of his days in Waltham, where he had his family, and
we mention him here, as we have several other families, because his
descendants settled in Lex. He came to Lex. to reside about the
time he m. his second wife. He d. Jan. 16, 1790.

59-82 | *Lois*, b. Feb. 2, 1754; m. Oct. 8, 1772, Joshua Stearns of Waltham.
83 | *Lucy*, b. March 27, 1755; m. Dec. 24, 1772, George Wellington of
Waltham.
84 | *Ephraim*, b. Sept. 27, 1757; m. March 16, 1780, Anna Parker, dau.
of Capt. John of Lex. He d. Dec. 12, 1811, aged 54.
85 | ‡*Reuben*, b. March 18, 1760; m. Susanna Smith of Lex.
86 | *Amos*, b. March 27, 1761; m. Betsey Hobbs of Weston, and moved
to Westford, where he d. Oct. 5, 1819.
87 | *Lydia*, b. April 15, 1763; m. Samuel Smith and moved to Salem.
88 | *Elijah*, b. Jan. 1, 1765; m. Dilley Munroe, dau. of Nathan and
Elizabeth Munroe. They resided in Wo., where he d. aged 54.
89 | ‡*Abner*, b. Sept. 1, 1766; m. Grace Harrington.
90 | *Avis*, b. Jan. 17, 1768; m. —— Cummings of Burlington.
91 | *Jonas*, b. July 24, 1771; m. Eunice Brown of Waltham, and resided
in Quincy, where he d. aged 57.
92 | *Susanna*, b. June 24, 1773; m. Jacob Smith of Lex. and d. April
9, 1835.
93 | *Jane*, b. Feb. 17, 1769; m. William Smith of Lexington.
94 | ‡*Loring*, b. Sept. 18, 1775; m. Sybil Wellington, dau. of William
Wellington of Waltham.

59-85-   REUBEN PIERCE m. Oct. 8, 1785, Susanna Smith, dau. of Josiah
and Hannah Smith. She d. March 22, 1819, aged 52, and he d.
Oct. 30, 1824, aged 64.

85-95 | *Reuben*, b. Dec. 5, 1786. He d. Jan. 15, 1860, aged 73, unm.
96 | ‡*Nathaniel*, b. Sept. 22, 1789; m. Abigail Wellington.
97 | ‡*Ebenezer*, b. April 18, 1792; m. Nabby Brown.
98 | *Susanna*, b. April 30, 1794; d. Dec. 18, 1796.
99 | ‡*Pelatiah P.*, b. March 13, 1806; m. Paulina Burbank.

59-89- | ABNER PIERCE m. July 22, 1792, Grace Harrington, dau. of Daniel and Anna (Munroe) Harrington. They commenced house-keeping in Lex., afterwards they moved to Medford, where they lived fourteen years, when they moved to Chelsea, where they remained fourteen years, and after an absence of twenty-eight years, came back to Lex., and took up their abode on the place occupied by the late Capt. Larkin Turner. He d. Sept. 12, 1837, aged 71; she d. Aug. 27, 1842.

89-100 | *Harriet*, b. Nov. 23, 1792; d. July 8, 1809.
101 | *Lucy*, b. Oct. 12, 1794; d. Sept. 25, 1796.
102 | *Abner*, b. Feb. 25, 1797; m. Sarah Buckman; she d. and he m. Eliza Tufts. They resided in West Cambridge, where he died.
103 | *Larkin*, b. May 10, 1798; d. July 12, 1801.
104 | *Lucy P.*, b. July 26, 1803; m. May 23, 1833, Larkin Turner.

59-94- | LORING PIERCE m. Sybil Wellington, dau. of William Wellington of Waltham. He moved to Lex. and took up his abode on Main street, where Loring S. Pierce now resides. He d. Oct. 11, 1857.

94-105 | *Catharine*, b. Oct 28, 1807; m. Phinehas Lawrence. He d. and she is now living, a widow.
· 106 | *Sybil*, b. Sept. 6, 1811; m. Amos Russell of West Camb., and d. March 17, 1837.
107 | *Almira*, b. Jan. 1, 1814; d. July 18, 1837, unm.
108 | *Loring*, b. Jan. 13, 1816; d. Jan. 26, 1816.
109 | †*Loring S.*, b. March 1, 1817; m. April 23, 1846, Frances A. Harrington.
110 | *Lois S.*, b. Nov. 11, 1819; m. Amos Russell, late husband of her sister Sybil, deceased.
111 | *Eleanor J.*, b. Sept. 14, 1823; m. William P. Locke of West Camb.

85-96- | NATHANIEL PIERCE m. Nov. 25, 1827, Abigail Wellington of Waltham, dau. of William and Avis (Fiske) Wellington, b. Feb. 11, 1806.

96-112 | *Harriet R.*, b. April 9, 1828; d. July 15, 1830.
113 | *Susan*, b. Oct. 27, 1829; m. May 8, 1854, Charles Nunn of West Roxbury, who moved to Lex. and resides near the junction of Main and Middle streets. They had first, Charles P., b. April 4, 1855, second, Leah A., b. July 4, 1857, third, Nathaniel, b. Feb. 23, 1859.
114 | *Nathaniel*, b. Aug. 26, 1831.
115 | *Abbie*, b. Nov. 15, 1835; m. Dec. 25, 1856, George Conant of Somerville. She d. suddenly Nov. 27, 1857.
116 | *Elizabeth*, b. Dec. 31, 1837.
117 | *Emma L.*, b. Nov. 26, 1840; d. July 19, 1843.
118 | *Willard E.*, b. March 17, 1843. 119 *Emma L.*, b. July 8, 1847.

85-97- | EBENEZER PIERCE m. Jan. 5, 1814, Nabby Brown, dau. of James and Betty (Reed) Brown.

97-120 | *Harrison*, b. Dec. 26, 1813; m. Harriet F. Penny. They have had Harriet Ann, b. Feb. 25, 1842, d. May 27, 1844; Harrison R., b. July 15, 1846, d. April 23, 1848; Alice W., b. Nov. 5, 1850.
121 | *Ella*, b. April 18, 1815.
122 | *Daniel*, b. June 27, 1817; d. Sept. 12, 1852.
123 | *Susan*, b. Oct. 28, 1819; d. Oct. 23, 1822.
124 | *Susan*, b. Sept. 10, 1823; m. Jonas Harrington; d. April 16, 1856.

125 | *Hiram*, b. May 1, 1826.
126 | *Ophelia*, b. 1829 ; d. Oct. 10, 1831.

85–99– | PELATIAH P. PIERCE m. Dec. 25, 1833, Paulina Burbank, dau. of Col. Sullivan Burbank.

99–127 | *Sullivan*, b. Nov. 6, 1834. He was drowned while skating on the ice, Dec. 15, 1849.
128 | *Ellen*, b. April 27, 1836.   129 *Paulina*, b. Nov. 5, 1838.
130 | *Emily R.*, b. 1841 ; d. Sept. 14, 1843.
131 | *Emily A.*, b. Feb. 20, 1845.   132 *Frank D.*, b. Jan. 2, 1851.

91–109– | LORING S. PIERCE m. April 23, 1846, Frances A. Harrington, dau. of Lewis and Sally (Dudley) Harrington. He has filled the office of selectman and assessor several years.

109–133 | *George L.*, b. Feb. 22, 1847.   134 *Gertrude*, b. April 2, 1853.
135 | *Alfred*, b. Feb. 10, 1858.

THE PLUMER FAMILY.

FRANCIS PLUMER was born in Newbury, Berkshire county, England. He and his two sons were of a party of twenty-three who came over in 1633, and settled in Ipswich. They moved, 1635, to the north side of Parker river, so named in honor of their pastor, Rev. Thomas Parker, and called the place Newbury. Francis Plumer was made freeman 1634, and d. July 17, 1672. The descendants have been quite distinguished—five of whom have been members of Congress. *Samuel*, his son, b. 1619, and d. 1682; *Sylvanus*, son of Samuel, b. 1658, d. 1724; *Samuel*, son of Sylvanus, was b. 1684, d. 1760; *Samuel*, son of Samuel, was b. 1722, d. 1803; *William*, son of Samuel, was b. 1759, and d. 1850. Samuel Plumer, with his son William, then but a lad, moved to Epping, N. H. William became one of the most prominent men in New Hampshire. He represented the State in the U. S. Senate, and also filled the Executive chair of the State. He was for many years one of the leading lawyers and statesmen, at a period when the State was not wanting in able men.

WILLIAM PLUMER, the son of Gov. William, was b. 1789, and d. 1854. He was honored by his fellow citizens with many offices of trust, and was elected to Congress.

1 | WILLIAM PLUMER, son of the preceding, was b. Nov. 29, 1823; grad. H. C. 1845, entered the law school, then in charge of Judge Story, and was admitted to the bar, 1848. Oct. 2, 1850, m. Emily J. Lord, dau. of Joseph H. and Judith M. Lord of Camb., and moved to Lex. During the late rebellion, he entered the service of the United States, and commanded a company of sharpshooters. He received an injury at the Battle of Gettysburg, which induced him to leave the service. His children were born in Lexington.

1– 2 | *William*, b. Sept. 5, 1851.
3 | *Edith Mansfield*, b. Feb. 27, 1853.
4 | *Margaret Frost*, b. Aug. 8, 1854. 5 *Grace Herbert*, b. Jan. 28, 1856.
6 | *Edward Lord*, b. Oct. 7, 1857 ; d. June 24, 1858.
7 | *Mary Elizabeth*, b. July 27, 1859. 8 *Annie Dow*, b. March 7, 1861.

THE POULTER FAMILY.

The Poulters were of German descent, though they came to this country from England. John Poulter was in Billerica 1676. He m. Rachel Eliot of Braintree. JOHN POULTER, who was at Cambrige Farms in 1693, was probably son of John of Billerica. He probably m. Hannah Hammond of Watertown. JONATHAN POULTER appears in the precinct about the same time as John. They were probably brothers. While we cannot give a full and connected view of the family, we can present the following.

JONATHAN POULTER and his wife, Elizabeth, were ad. to the ch. in Lex. 1697. They had at least seven children. *Abigail*, b. Sept. 3, 1692; *Elizabeth*, b. Feb. 5, 1694; *Hannah*, b. Nov. 12, 1697; *Mary*, b. Jan. 11, 1700; *Rachel*, b. May 11, 1702; *Jonathan*, b. Jan. 11, 1705, probably d. May 2, 1707; *Submit*, b. June 16, 1708. Jonathan, the father, d. May 27, 1708, and his wid. d. July 9, 1741.

JOHN POULTER m. Hannah Hammond and had a family, a perfect list of which we are unable to give. We find the following only. *Sarah Poulter*, bap. Dec. 30, 1799, John owning the covenant. Sarah m. about 1719, William Reed, 2d. Her mother being a *Hammond*, and her grandmother an Eliot, will account for those names in the Reed family. *Mary*, a dau. of John Poulter, was bap. Jan. 12, 1700. She was ad. to the ch. 1728. *Catharine*, bap. April 25, 1703, d. Aug. 19, 1705; *Eliot*, b. June 19, 1709. John Poulter, the father, d. July 22, 1744, and his wife d. Dec. 12, 1735. John Poulter was selectman, 1718. They resided in the neighborhood of the Reeds-

THE PRESTON FAMILY.

MARSHALL PRESTON came to Lex. from Billerica in 1849. His family record, as far as ascertained, is as follows:

1   AMARIAH PRESTON of Connecticut, m. Elizabeth Warren of Newton, Mass., and r. in Uxbridge. She d. about 1756, and he m. a second wife. He d. in Roxbury, Delaware Co., N. Y., Feb. 27, 1834, at the advanced age of 95. He had a son bearing his own name.

1- 2   AMARIAH PRESTON, b. Feb. 5, 1758; m. Oct. 18, 1790, Hannah Reed of Bedford. She d. Feb. 8, 1795, and he m. May 15, 1796, Ruhamah Lane, dau. of John and Rebecca, who d. Oct. 2, 1826. Mr. Preston had an eventful life. His mother dying when he was about two years old, he was *put out*, as the term was, and after living in Uxbridge, Mass., and Ashford, Conn., he went to Dighton, Mass , to learn a trade. In 1777, he entered the Continental army and served three years. In 1785, he commenced the study of medicine and established himself in Bedford, where he practiced forty-five years. His wife dying, and he being in the seventy-fifth year of his age, and not affluent in his circumstances, he left Bedford to reside with his son, Hervey N. Preston, then practicing medicine in Plymouth. His son dying soon after his arrival, he immediately entered upon his practice, and though advanced in life, he retrieved his fortune by continuing in practice till he was eighty-seven years of age. He then left Plymouth to reside with his son Marshall at Billerica. Soon after this his son removed to Lex., and the old gentleman came with him, where he spent the remainder of his days. He d. Oct. 29, 1853, aged 95 years, 8 months, and 24 days. He retained his faculties both bodily and mental to the last; and his whole life furnishes a remarkable instance of energy and perseverance.

2- 3 | †*Marshall*, b. June 5, 1792; m. Feb. 12, 1824, Maria Parker.
  4 | *Hannah*, b. Jan. 8, 1795; d. Aug. 8, 1810.
  5 | *Amariah*, b. June 21, 1798; d. March 22, 1831, in N. Y. State.
  6 | *Ezekiel Warren*, b. July 8, 1800; d. Sept. 7, same year.
  7 | *Ezekiel Warren*, b. Dec. 24, 1802; r. in N. Y. State.
  8 | *Hervey N.*, b. June 21, 1806; d. July 14, 1837.
  9 | *Lovice M.*, b. Feb. 19, 1809; d. June 18, 1843.

2–3– | MARSHALL PRESTON m. Feb. 12, 1824, Maria Parker of Billerica, dau. of John and Susan (Minot) Parker, b. Oct. 10, 1797. He read law with his uncle, Warren Preston, in Maine, and was admitted to the bar at Augusta. He subsequently established an office in Billerica, where he practiced till he came to Lex. in 1849. He held important town offices in Billerica, and was for many years assistant clerk of the courts in Middlesex county, which office he held till 1863, when his health failing, he retired from the place he had so faithfully filled. They are both living.

3–10 | *George Henry*, b. June 6, 1825; m. Jan. 1, 1855, Catharine R. Faulkner of Bil. He grad. at H. C. 1846, read law and practiced in Boston, where he resides. They have several children.
  11 | *Susan Crosby*, b. Sept. 21, 1831; d. Nov. 25, 1851.

PUFFER.—SYLVESTER PUFFER, b. in Sudbury, May 19, 1810; m. April 18, 1839, Catharine Brown of Burlington, b. June 29, 1819. She d. May 18, 1866, aged 46. They have had the following chil., all but the oldest b. in Lex. *George S.*, b. in Acton, Feb. 13, 1840; *Mary C.*, b. Jan. 12. 1842; *Charles H.*, b. Dec. 30, 1843; he entered the service of the United States in the late Rebellion, and d. at Alexandria, Va., of a wound received at Fredericksburg, Feb. 5, 1863; *William E.*, b. Jan. 28, 1846; *Sarah E.*, b. July 7, 1849; *Lucy A.*, b. June 22, 1852; *Reuben W.*, b. April 28, 1854, d. May 1, 1854; *Alvin H.*, b. Feb. 22, 1856. He came to Lex. about 1841.

THE RAYMOND FAMILY.

The Raymonds were never very numerous in Lexington, though at one time there were several of that name. We are not able to fix the time when they came to Lexington. We find upon the tax bill of 1733 the names of Jonathan Raymond and Jonathan Raymond, jr., and in the following year Jonathan, jr., was chosen one of the fence viewers in Lexington. Samuel Raymond and his wife, Sarah, were admitted to the church, Jan. 26, 1737, by a letter from the church in Beverly. Richard Raymond was in Salem in 1634, and the name was quite common in Beverly at an early day. As Samuel Raymond came from Beverly, it is highly probable that Jonathan came from the same place, as they were brothers. As Jonathan Raymond in 1733 bore the addition of jr., it is probable that his father was in the town also at that time.

1 | JONATHAN RAYMOND, sen., was the father both of Jonathan and Samuel. In his will, dated Aug. 16, 1742, and proved Nov. 22, 1742, he says, "To my beloved sons Jonathan Raymond and Samuel Raymond I give twenty shillings each, which, with what I have already possessed them with, is what I devise to them out of my

estate." He also mentions in his will his wife, Charity, to whom he gives among other things, " the use of my boy Robin." He mentions further, sons, Thomas, William, Bartholomew, and Josiah, and dau. Sarah Tidd, deceased, Mehitabel, and Charity. The birth of a part of these children are borne upon the Lexington records, though most of them were born before he came to Lexington. She d. March 9, 1768, aged 87.

1- 2 | †*Samuel*, b. ——— ; m. Sarah ———.
3 | †*Jonathan*, b. Feb. 27, 1702; m. Hepzibah ———.
4 | *Thomas*, b. ———.   5 *William*, b. ———.
6 | *Sarah*, b. ———.   7 *Josiah*, b. ———.
8 | *Bartholomew*, b. ———.
9 | *Mehitabel*, b. Oct. 12, 1721; ad. to the ch. in Lex. July 18, 1742; she m. Stephen Locke.
10 | *Charity*, b. Sept. 15, 1724; m. Thomas Blodgett.

1-2- | SAMUEL RAYMOND m. Sarah ———. They were ad. to the ch. in Lex. Jan. 26, 1737.

2-11 | *Sarah*, b. Nov. 6, 1730; m. April 12, 1753, Thomas Smith.
12 | *Charity*, b. Dec. 12, 1733.   13 *Samuel*, b. Dec. 4, 1735.
14 | *Jonah*, b. Sept. 18, 1738; m. March 23, 1762, Submit Whittemore.
15 | †*Bartholomew*, b. May 7, 1742.

1-3- | JONATHAN RAYMOND m. Hepzibah ———. They were ad. to the ch. in Lex. May 9, 1756, by a letter from Beverly. He d. Aug. 9, 1760, and she m. Dec. 29, 1763, Thomas Munroe of Concord.

3-16 | *Hepzibah*, b. Sept. 19, 1729; m. Dec. 13, 1751, Dr. Joseph Fiske.
17 | †*John*, b. Sept. 5, 1731. He was of Capt. Parker's co. in 1775.
18 | †*Jonathan*, b. Sept. 17, 1734; m. Oct. 4, 1756, Susannah White.
19 | *Elizabeth*, b. April 10, 1737; m. Aug. 17, 1756, Ebenezer Winship.
20 | *Mary*, b. Aug. 20, 1740; m. Feb. 2, 1757, Nathaniel Piper.
21 | *Hannah*, b. Aug. 27, 1742; m. Feb. 16, 1762, Samuel Reed.
22 | *Daniel*, b. March 18, 1744.   23 *Joseph*, b. May 31, 1747.
24 | *Ruth*, b. March 24, 1752.

2-15- | BARTHOLOMEW RAYMOND m. Mehitabel Mallett of Charlestown, to which place he removed before the opening of the Revolution. He run a ferry-boat across Charles River, before the building of Charles River Bridge. He d. 1831, aged 74; she d. 1828, aged 76.

15-25 | *Bartholomew*, b. Sept. 1, 1776.   26 *Mehitabel*, b. May 29, 1780.
27 | *William*, b. Aug. 8, 1786.
28 | *Samuel*, b. July 26, 1788. He m. a Miss Wheeler of Bolton. They are both dead.

3-17- | JOHN RAYMOND m. Rebecca ———. He was killed by the British soldiers on the 19th of April, in a brutal and cowardly manner. He was infirm, and was tending bar at the Munroe Tavern. The British entered the house and helped themselves to whatever the house afforded. They compelled Raymond to wait upon them, and after they had imbibed freely, they became noisy and tumultuous, and Raymond being alarmed for his personal safety, was in the act of leaving the house, when he was shot down by these vandals.

17-29 | *John*, b. Nov. 24, 1763.   30 *Eliakim*, b. July 29, 1765.
31 | *Rebecca*, b. Oct. 7, 1768; m. Ebenezer Danforth and went South.
32 | *Isaac*, b. March 9, 1770.   33 *Edmund*, b. Aug. 17, 1773.

3-18- | JONATHAN RAYMOND m. Oct. 4, 1756, Susanna White, dau. of Joseph and Hannah White. They probably lived for a short period in Wat., as we find the following record of the baptism of one of their children. " Baptized Mary Raymond, dau. of Jonathan, jr., the parents having owned the covenant in Watertown." They had a family of eleven children, six sons and five dau. Among them were Susanna, b. March 28, 1757; Mary, bap. Nov. 28, 1759; Hepzibah, bap. Jan. 3, 1762. They removed to Westminster about 1763, where most of his children were born, and where he d. about 1783. He was a soldier in the War of the Revolution. Some of his descendants are found in Westminster at the present day.

There are at the present time, Raymonds in town, but from a different family, though probably of the same original stock, and not till recently resident in this place.

1 | WILLIAM RAYMOND emigrated from England and settled first at Salem and afterward at Beverly. He had four children.

1- 2 | DANIEL RAYMOND, his second son, m. Abigail Balch, 1714. He moved to Marblehead. He and his eldest son died in the expedition to Louisburg, 1745.

2- 3 | FREEBORN RAYMOND, the youngest son of Daniel, b. Feb. 20, 1741, m. about 1761, Mary Young. She d. and he m. about 1778, Sarah Powers. He d. Feb. 11, 1817. He had sixteen children b. in Athol.

3- 4 | FREEBORN RAYMOND, eldest son of the foregoing, b. June 4, 1762, m first, Lucinda Graves, and had one son. She d. and he m. second, Lois Kendall, and third, Jane Rich, who d. March 15, 1865. He d. July 3, 1824. He had the following children.

5 | *Wyman*, b. Jan. 31, 1788.   6 *Freeman C.*, b. Dec. 13, 1801.
7 | *Louisa K.*, b. Sept. 2, 1803.
8 | *Freeborn F.*, b. Dec. 2, 1805; d. 1808.
9 | *Thatcher R.*, b. March 9, 1808; d. June 17, 1860.
10 | *Lucinda G.*, b. Nov. 20, 1810.
11 | †*Freeborn F.*, b. Oct. 19, 1812, at Athol.
12 | *Jane Y.*, b. Aug. 9, 1815, at Jaffrey, N. H.
13 | *Eliza Ann*, b. July 20, 1818; d. Nov. 11, 1837.
14 | *Joseph P.*, b. July 1, 1821, at Nashua, N. H.

4-11- | FREEBORN F. RAYMOND m. June 12, 1855, Sarah E. Richardson, dau. of A. P. and Betsey (Reed) Richardson of Lex. He took up his residence in Lex. about the time of his marriage, but does business in Boston. Their children are *Franklin F.*, b. May 2, 1856; *Helen E.*, b. May 25, 1859, d. Aug. 23, 1863; *Henry S.*, b. May 18, 1866.

THE REED FAMILY.

The Reeds came to Cambridge Farms from Woburn in 1686. They were in the country much earlier. There is considerable difficulty in tracing the residence of the first ancestor of this family, arising from the fact that there are several persons among the early emigrants of the same name. But there is evidence which we deem reliable, that William Reed and his wife, Mabel, with three of their children, viz., George, then six years old, Ralph, five years old, and

Justus, eighteen months, came to New England from London, in the ship Defence, in 1635. He was at that time forty-eight years old, and his wife thirty. He settled first at Dorchester; but like many of the early settlers moved from place to place, at least temporarily. In 1639, he sold his real estate in Dorchester and moved to Scituate, where he was constable in 1644. While there he sent his wife to Dorchester on horse-back with an infant to be baptized; he being a member of the church in that place. He was probably a resident at Muddy River (now Brookline) in 1648, when he purchased of Nicholas Davis a farm in Woburn of some sixty acres, "with all the barns, out-houses, fences, and all to the same belonging." He probably moved to Woburn soon after he made this purchase, and resided there a few years, when he and his wife returned to England, where he died at Newcastle-upon-Tyne in 1656. He made his will, appointing no executor, and Oliver Cromwell made his wife, Mabel, executrix, on the last day of October, 1656; and she returned to this country to their children, then in Woburn, Nov. 24, 1660. She m. Henry Sumner of Woburn, whom she survived, and d. in the family of her son George, June 15, 1690, aged 85 years. Most of the Reeds of Lexington descended from

1   WILLIAM REED and Mabel, his wife, whose maiden name was probably Kendall.

1- 2 | †*George*, b. in Eng. 1629; m. Oct. 4, 1652, Elizabeth Jennison.
3 | *Ralph*, b. in Eng. 1630; m. Mary Pierce of Wat. and d. in Woburn, Jan. 4, 1712, aged 84, and left issue.
4 | *Justus*, b. in Eng. 1633; d. before his parents went to England.
5 | *Abigail*, b. probably in Dor.; m. Oct. 2, 1650, Francis Wyman.
6 | *Bethia*, b. probably in Dorchester; m. Apr. 28, 1657, John Johnson, son of Capt. Edward, Author of "Wonder-Working Providence."
7 | *Israel*, b. 1642; m. Mary, dau. of Francis Kendall, his cousin.
8 | *Sarah*, b. ——— ; m. Sept. 10, 1662, Samuel Walker.
9 | *Rebecca*, b. ——— ; m. Joseph Winn.

The above named children all resided in Woburn. *George, Ralph,* and *Israel* had large families, making the name of Reed quite common in that town.

1-2-   GEORGE REED m. Oct. 4, 1652, Elizabeth Jennison, dau. of Robert Jennison of Wat. She was b. April 12, 1637, and d. Feb. 26, 1665. He m. Nov. 9, 1665, Hannah Rockwell of Charlestown. He had eight children by his first wife, and five by his last. He d. Feb. 21, 1706, aged 77.

2-10 | *Elizabeth*, b. July 29, 1653; m. Dec. 15, 1675, David Fiske of Wat.
11 | *Twins*, b. Nov. 14, 1654; d. without names.
12 | *Samuel*, b. April 29, 1656; m. April 19, 1679, Elizabeth Munsal.
13 | *Abigail*, b. June 27, 1658; m. Sept. 18, 1694, Nathaniel Richardson.
14 | *George*, b. Sept. 14, 1660; m. Feb. 18, 1684, Abigail Pierce. He was deacon of the church many years, and d. Jan. 20, 1756.
15 | †*William*, b. Sept. 22, 1662; m. May 24, 1686, Abigail Kendall.
16 | *Sarah*, b. Feb. 12, 1665; m. Dec. 12, 1685, ——— Robinson.
17 | *Hannah*, b. Feb. 18, 1669; m. ——— Elson.
18 | *John*, b. March 18, 1671; m. June 10, 1697, Ruth Johnson.
19 | *Mary*, b. June 15, 1674; m. 1697, Matthew Johnson.
20 | *Timothy*, b. Oct. 20, 1678; m. Persis Kendall.
21 | *Thomas*, b. July 15, 1682; m. Feb. 1, 1704, Sarah Sawyer.

2-15-   WILLIAM REED m. May 24, 1686, Abigail Kendall of Woburn. She had extra fingers and toes, and from this blood that excrescence has cropped out from generation to generation in some branches of the family. William Reed, or *Capt. Reed* as he was generally called, may be regarded as the ancestor of the greater part of the Reeds of Lexington, though there were others of the name, who will be noticed hereafter. He was one of the most prominent citizens of the precinct and town. He was a justice of the peace, filled the office of selectman, and represented the town in the General Court several years. He was equally prominent in the church, being one of the original members. He purchased land in the north-westerly part of the township, and located himself on what is now known as Bedford street, near the residence of the late Christopher Reed. He added to his real estate from time to time, and became a large land-holder, and so was able to leave a good farm to each of his three sons. A portion of his lands has remained in the family to the present day. The neighborhood of Capt. Reed's residence was at one time the most populous of any part of the town out of the village. In addition to the Reeds, which were quite numerous, the Hewses, Trasks, Poulters, Kendalls, Lawrences, Dunklees, and Fassetts all resided on or near Bedford street. No family of the early settlers has sustained its standing, through all periods of the town's history, better than the Reeds. He d. May 12, 1718, aged 56, and she d. Oct. 12, 1734.

———

15-22   *Abigail,* b. May 29, 1687: m. Jonathan Fiske and moved to Sud.
23   †*William,* b. July 18, 1693; m. Sarah Poulter.
24   *Mary,* b. April 8, 1695; m. April 8, 1714, Dea. John Stone, and d. Oct. 1, 1772.
25   †*Benjamin,* b. Oct. 22, 1696; m. Rebecca Stone.
26   *Samuel,* b. Oct. 20, 1699; d. April 3, 1711.
27   †*Joshua,* b. June 20, 1702; m. Elizabeth Russell.
28   *Hepzibah,* b. Dec. 10, 1705; m. April 19, 1724, Daniel Tidd.

15-23-   WILLIAM REED m. Sarah Poulter, dau. of John, about 1719. He was an active and efficient man, both in the church and in the town. He held for many years a commission of justice of the peace, and did considerable business in that capacity; and was well known in the town and vicinity by the appellation of *'Squire Reed.* He was very popular with the people, and received all the honors in their gift. Besides minor offices, he was selectman eleven years, and representative seventeen years. He was also a captain in the militia, and was out with a portion of his company in the French war, in 1755. He d. Feb. 11, 1778, aged 85; she d. Nov. 25, 1769. He resided in the house owned by the late Christopher Reed on Bedford street.

———

23-29   †*William,* b. Jan. 1, 1720; m. Jan. 1, 1741, Abigail Stone.
30   †*Samuel,* b. May 4, 1722; m. Eunice Stone.
31   *Sarah,* b. June 3, 1725; m. Dec. 23, 1742, Benjamin Brown.
32   *Mary,* b. March 10, 1728; m. May 4, 1753, William Bowman.
33   *Oliver,* b. March 25, 1730; m. April 11, 1754, Sarah Bridge, who was b. Dec. 21, 1735. They moved to Bedford, where they had *Oliver,* b. 1755, *Sarah,* b. 1757, *Reuben,* b. 1759, and *Mary,* b. 1763.
34   *John,* b. May 28, 1731; m. Ruhamah Brown; r. in Bedford, Jan. 18, 1753.
35   †*Hammon,* b. April 28, 1734; m. Betty Simonds.
36   *Eliot,* b. April 28, 1737; m. May 3, 1757, Joseph Bridge.
37   *Hannah,* b. Oct. 21, 1740; m. April 14, 1761, John Bridge.
38   †*Nathan,* b. Nov. 9, 1743; m. April 30, 1782, Mary Page.

15-25-   BENJAMIN REED m. Rebecca Stone, dau. of Samuel and Dorcas (Jones) Stone, b. 1696. She d. and he m. July 19, 1753, Mrs. Hannah Estabrook, wid. of Dea. Joseph Estabrook, and dau. of Joseph Bowman. He d. Dec. 25, 1765. Like his brother William, he was frequently called by his townsmen to places of honor and trust. He was constable, assessor, selectman nine years, and representative ten years. He was a major in the militia when that office was filled by the most prominent citizens. He was also justice of the peace. He d. July 13, 1789, aged 93; she d. April 1, 1768.

  25-39 | *Benjamin*, b. May 13, 1718; moved to Holden.
     40 | *Abigail*, b. March 30, 1720; d. Sept. 12, 1731.
     41 | *Jonas*, b. June 7, 1722; he was dismissed from the church in Lex. to the ch. in Rutland, Nov. 1763.
     42 | *Rebecca*, b. Nov. 25, 1724; m. John Muzzy.
     43 | ‡*Isaac*, b. July 30, 1727; m. April 22, 1754, Mary Bridge.
     44 | *Jonathan*, b. March 8, 1729; m. Jan. 30, 1754, Sarah Lawrence; r. at Littleton.
     45 | *Thaddeus*, b. June 17, 1732; d. April 21, 1741.
     46 | *Dorcas*, b. July 18, 1734; m. Oct. 15, 1750, David Cutler.
     47 | *Samuel*, b. April 3, 1737; m. Feb. 16, 1762, Hannah Raymond; r. at Littleton.
     48 | *Ruth*, b. Nov. 9, 1741; m. Dec. 13, 1759, Ebenezer Estabrook.

15-27-   JOSHUA REED m. Jan. 21, 1725, Elizabeth Russell, dau. of Jonathan and Elizabeth. She d. Feb. 29, 1744; he d. Oct. 15, 1755. The inventory of his estate shows the manners and customs of the times, by giving us a *warming-pan, flax-comb, box-heater, pillion*, &c.

  27-49 | *Elizabeth*, b. Feb. 28, 1726; m. Jonathan Winship.
     50 | *Hepzibah*, b. March 8, 1728; d. about 1754.
     51 | ‡*Joshua*, b. May 15, 1730; was twice married.
     52 | *James*, b. ————.
     53 | *Joseph*, b. June 21, 1739; r. at Rutland.
     54 | *Rebecca S.*, b. ————.

23-29-   WILLIAM REED m. Jan. 1, 1741, Abigail Stone. She d. Nov. 30, 1773, and he m. Lydia Ingalls. He d. Oct. 9, 1813, aged 93; she d. March 9, 1817.

  29-55 | ‡*William*, b. Oct. 2, 1742; m. Dec. 1, 1768, Elizabeth Davis.
     56 | *Abigail*, b. Sept. 22, 1744; m. Jan. 21, 1766, William Grimes.
     57 | *Sarah*, b. May 14, 1747; m. Dec. 6, 1770, Oliver Bacon.
     58 | *Nathaniel*, b. June 2, 1749; m. Jan. 16, 1772, Hepzibah Bateman of Bedford.
     59 | *Mary*, b. July 17, 1751; m. April 28, 1774, Moses Harrington.
     60 | *Beulah*, b. May 4, 1753; m. June 28, 1787, Abel Johnson of Boston.
     61 | ‡*Thaddeus*, b. Aug. 25, 1755; m. Anna Longley of Littleton.
     62 | *Josiah*, b. Aug. 25, 1757; was twice m.; d. without issue.
     63 | *Hannah*, b. Oct. 8, 1758; m. Nov. 28, 1782, James Danforth of Fitchburg.
     64 | *Milly*, b. April 26, 1762; d. unm. in Boston.
     65 | *Esther*, b. Oct. 25, 1765; d. unm. Nov. 24, 1786.

23-30-   SAMUEL REED m. Eunice Stone and moved to what is now Burlington, where he had a large family. Moses, one of his sons, m. April 23, 1770, Sarah Whittemore of Lex. and moved to this place, where they were ad. to the ch. Jan. 27, 1771. They had *Whittemore*, b. Feb. 18, 1771; *Moses*, b. Aug. 10, 1773; *Sarah*, b. April 1, 1775; *Abel*, b. May 8, 1777; and *Elizabeth*, b. Feb. 17, 1779.

23-35-   HAMMON REED m. April 13, 1757, Betty Simonds. He was one of the gallant band who struck for liberty, April 19, 1775. He filled several important town offices, being five years selectman during the most important period of our history, and was one of the Committee of Safety, 1778. She d. Feb. 2, 1815; he d. July 12, 1817.

35-66   *Betty*, b. Dec. 12, 1757; m. May 30, 1780, James Brown.
67   *Lydia*, b. July 11, 1760; m. Nov. 5, 1786, Thomas Locke of Wo.
68   †*Hammon*, b. Feb. 24, 1763; m. Oct. 26, 1786, Sarah Chandler.
69   *Patty*, b. Dec. 5, 1765; m. Nov. 28, 1786, Amos Marrett.
70   *Sarah*, b. June 22, 1770; d. young.
71   *Benjamin*, b. Oct. 22, 1774; d. young.

23-38-   NATHAN REED m. April 30, 1772, Mary Page of Bedford, dau. of Christopher and Susanna Page. He and his wife were ad. to the ch. Jan. 24, 1773. He was subsequently chosen deacon, which office he held from 1787 to 1808, when he resigned on account of ill health. He d. Nov. 17, 1811, aged 68; she d. May 17, 1831, aged 84. He was one of the band which faced the British in 1775. He served as selectman several years. He was a large land-holder in Lex. and elsewhere.

38-72   *Nathan*, b. Feb. 7, 1773; d. Aug. 1, 1775.
73   †*Nathan*, b. Sept. 15, 1776; m. Polly Muzzy.
74   *Mary*, b. Oct. 20, 1778; m. Dec. 3, 1799, John Merriam of Bed.
75   *Sarah*, b. July 1, 1781. She is living, in her eighty-seventh year.
76   *Hiram*, b. June 22, 1784; d. Feb. 8, 1808, unm.
77   *Susanna W.*, b. Dec. 10, 1786; m. 1815, John Chandler, and d. Dec. 19, 1863, leaving one dau. Sarah Chandler.
78   *Hannah*, b. Sept. 4, 1789; d. Aug. 30, 1854, unm.
79   †*Christopher*, b. March 18, 1792; m. Betsey Gibson of Francestown, N. H.

25-43-   ISAAC REED m. April 2, 1754, Mary Bridge, dau. of John Bridge, b. April 19, 1733. He had one child, *Isaac*, b. May 18, 1755, in Lex. He moved to Littleton.

27-51-   JOSHUA REED m. Nov. 27, 1753, Mrs. Susanna Houghton of Lancaster. He was one of Capt. Parker's co. 1775, and was one of the selectmen in the eventful period of the Revolution.

51-80   *Betty*, b. Nov. 26, 1754; m. Jan. 6, Ebenezer Muzzy.
81   ‡*Joshua*, b. Sept. 11, 1756; he was twice married.
82   *Susanna*, b. March 11, 1759; m. Jonas Bridge.
83   *Hepzibah*, b. Feb. 26, 1769; m. May 10, 1790, William Wait of Greenfield.
84   *James*, b. Dec. 15, 1771; m. Susanna Stone of Rindge, N. H.
85   *Rebecca*, bap. June 26, 1774; m. Feb. 22, 1801, David Wait of Deerfield, a brother of William, who married her sister.

29-55-   WILLIAM REED m. Dec. 1, 1768, Elizabeth Davis of Bed. He was in Parker's co. on the 19th of April, and marched with them to Camb. June 17, 1775.

55-86   *Elizabeth*, b. March 7, 1770.
87   *William*, b. May 11, 1772; d. April 3, 1776.
88   *Abigail*, b. May 8, 1774.   89 *Ruthy*, b. June 9, 1776.
90   *William*, b. April 5, 1778.
91   *Lydia*, b. Nov. 3, 1780; d. March 6, 1822, unm.

29-61- | THADDEUS REED m. Anna Longley of Littleton. His second son, William, came home from New York, 1824, with the small pox, and gave it to the family, of which both the parents, and his brother Thaddeus' wife, died. Luther Prescott, husband of their dau. Anna, also fell a victim to the same disease, the same year.

61-92 | *Edmund*, b. Oct. 20, 1788.
93 | *Esther*, b. Aug. 16, 1790; m. April 21, 1812, John Parker.
94 | *William*, b. Feb. 13, 1792.
95 | *Thaddeus*, b. Oct. 1, 1794; m. Dec. 8, 1819, Phebe Prescott of Con.
96 | *Anna*, b. Feb. 12, 1797; m. Jan. 6, 1819, Luther Prescott of Con.
97 | *Augustus*, b. June 27, 1799.
98 | *Levi*, b. July 24, 1801.

35-68- | HAMMON REED m. Oct. 25, 1786, Sarah Chandler, dau. of John and Beulah (Merriam) Chandler, b. Feb. 27, 1764. She d. April 24, 1854, aged 90; he d. Aug. 31, 1848, aged 85.

68- 99 | *Sarah*, b. May 17, 1788; d. Nov. 10, 1788.
100 | †*Benjamin*, b. Jan. 20, 1790; m. Bethia L. Webber.
101 | *Sally*, b. June 21, 1792; m. April, 1817, William Nichols of Bur.
102 | *Betsey*, b. June 15, 1799; m. June 26, 1823, Aaron P. Richardson.
103 | *Emily*, } twins, b. Jan. 26, 1804; { d. in early infancy.
104 | *Almira*, } { m. Jan. 29, 1829, Eben R. Smith.

38-73- | NATHAN REED m. Aug. 30, 1797, Mary Muzzey, dau. of John and Rebecca (Munroe) Muzzey. He d. July 20, 1836, aged 60.

73-105 | †*Cyrus*, b. Nov. 9, 1798; m. April 4, 1824, Sarah Jewett.
106 | *Nathan Horatio*, b. Sept. 28, 1805; m. April 20, 1841, Luzilla Meigs. They had one child, who is living in Wisconsin. He d. March 11, 1854; she d. Jan. 9, 1868.
107 | *Hiram*, b. Feb. 8, 1810; d. March 30, 1854, unm.
108 | *Marshall*, b. Oct. 4, 1815; d. July 31, 1837.

38-79- | CHRISTOPHER REED m. Betsey Gibson of Francestown, N. H. He d. Sept. 25, 1861. They had one child, *William Eustis*.

51-81- | JOSHUA REED m. Sept. 11, 1780, Susanna Leathers. She d. Sept. 8, 1802, and he m. Elizabeth Brooks of Line. He d. Sept. 8, 1826. He was a member of Capt. Parker's company.

81-109 | †*Charles*, b. July 10, 1781; m. Almira Muzzy.
110 | *Susanna*, b. Jan. 30, 1783; m. Nov. 30, 1813, John Mulliken.
111 | *Phebe*, b. Aug. 28, 1792; m. Oct. 2, 1822, Thomas Greenleaf.

68-100- | BENJAMIN REED m. Feb. 3, 1825, Bethia L. Webber of Bedford, dau. of John and Bethia (Lane) Webber. He was a prominent citizen, being one of the selectmen six years. He also held the commission of captain in the militia. He d. Oct. 16, 1860, aged 71 years.

100-112 | *Frances Walker*, b. Dec. 21, 1825; d. April 4, 1863, unm.
113 | *Hammon*, b. Sept. 25, 1829; m. Oct. 19, 1856, Sylvia Wadsworth of Milford, N. H., dau. of Samuel and Rhoda (Fitch) Wadsworth. He has filled the offices of overseer of the poor and of selectman several years, and also holds a commission of justice of the peace. They have three children, *George H.*, b. Jan. 31, 1858; *William W.*, b. June 28, 1859; *Sylvia B.*, b. May 21, 1864.

73-105-   CYRUS REED m. April 4, 1824, Sarah Jewett of Boxboro'.

105-114 *John Muzzy*, b. May 24, 1825; m. June 7, 1866, Alice L. Hobart of Hingham. They have one child, *Louisa Hobart*, b. April 19, 1867.

115 *George Henry*, b. May 7, 1831.

116 *Catharine Eliza*, b. Jan. 30, 1832.

81-109-   CHARLES REED m. Oct. 23, 1817, Almira Muzzy, dau. of Amos and Lydia (Boutelle) Muzzy. She d. Nov. 15, 1819, aged 25 years, and he m. June 28, 1821, Martha Wellington. He d. May 19, 1846, aged 65; she d. May 10, 1838. He was a popular and influential man. He held the office of selectman twelve years, assessor five years, town clerk seven years, and town treasurer seven years.

109-117 *Charles M.*, b. Sept. 12, 1819.   118 *Henry S.*, b. June 29, 1822.

     There is another family of Reeds in Lexington, which have been in the place several generations; and though they do not claim any relationship with the descendants of William Reed of Lexington, are nevertheless from the same stock. George Reed, the oldest son of the original emigrant, and father of William Reed, who settled in Cambridge Farms, now Lexington, had a large family, and among his children was

1   TIMOTHY REED (No. 20, in the Reed family) b. Oct. 20, 1678. He was a younger brother of William. He m. Persis Kendall and resided in Wo. They had among other children, Jacob, b. 1714.

1- 2   JACOB REED m. June 19, 1711, Elizabeth French of Billerica. He resided in Wo. They had a family of seven children.

2- 3   ISAAC REED, the youngest child of the foregoing, b. Aug. 9, 1756, m. April 27, 1780, Susanna Munroe, dau. of William Munroe. She d. 1828, aged 75; he d. April 20, 1848, aged 92.

3- 4 *‡Isaac*, b. Jan. 12, 1781; m. Elizabeth Munroe.

5 *Susan*, b. Oct. 16, 1782.

6 *William*, b. March 14, 1785; m. Rebecca Gardner. He d. 1851.

7 *Oliver*, b. Aug. 4, 1787; m. Sarah Thayer.

8 *Thomas*, b. Jan. 18, 1790; m. Relief Pratt, and d. 1829.

9 *‡Reuben*, b. March 25, 1792; was twice married.

10 *Hugh M.*, b. Dec. 23, 1793; d. 1821, unm.

11 *Enos*, b. Aug. 21, 1796; m. Sarah Gardner.

3-4-   ISAAC REED m. April 24, 1804, Elizabeth Munroe, dau. of Philemon and Elizabeth (Waite) Munroe. He probably came to Lex. about the time of his marriage. He d. Nov. 10, 1854, aged 73; she d. Oct. 24, 1865, aged 80 years.

4-12 *Emeline*, b. June 10, 1805; d. Dec. 22, 1822.

13 *Susan E.*, b. Dec. 16, 1807; m. April 9, 1855, William K. Fowle of Roxbury.

14 *Isaac E.*, b. Jan. 2, 1810; d. Dec. 31, 1836.

15 *Adeline*, b. Jan. 10, 1812; m. Nov. 2, 1842, James Parker. They have one child, James Emory, b. Aug. 30, 1845.

16 *‡William H. H.*, b. Nov. 26, 1813; m. Mary Crowningshield.

17 *Horatio*, b. Dec. 21, 1815; m. Mary Phipps; resides in New York.

18 *Parnell M.*, b. April 30, 1818; d. Oct. 16, 1821.

19 *Edwin*, b. Feb. 20, 1821; resides in Boston.

20 *Hugh M.*, b. March 27, 1824; m. Sophia C. Lawrence, dau. of Phinehas Lawrence; resides in Providence.

21 *Emeline P.*, b. Oct. 5, 1826; m. Dec. 20, 1860, William K. Fowle, the husband of her late sister Susan.

3-9- REUBEN REED m. Dec. 8, 1819, Sarah Russell of Camb. She d. Aug. 2, 1822, and he m. Feb. 26, 1824, Mary H. Willard of Harvard. She d. Feb. 14, 1860, aged 69; he d. March 4, 1864, aged 71.

9-22 *Reuben*, b. Feb. 5, 1821; d. June 22, 1822.

23 *Reuben Willard*, b. Jan. 12, 1825; m. Sept. 1854, Georgiana Ferren of Charlestown. They have *Emmie G.*, b. Nov. 10, 1856; *Mary Hattie*, b. Sept. 7, 1860, d. Oct. 15, 1864; *Lizzie Virginia*, b. April 27, 1866.

24 *Josiah Haskell*, b Feb. 12, 1827; m. Oct. 9, 1860, Clara Rebecca Gates, dau. of Howard Gates of Ashby. They have *Frank Haskell*, b. Dec. 26, 1862; *Alice Gates*, b. Aug. 21, 1864.

4-16- WILLIAM H HARRISON REED m. Sept. 5, 1850, Mary Crowningshield, dau. of A. W. Crowningshield of Lex. He now resides in Charlestown.

16-25 *Mary Ella*, b. March 9, 1852; d. Sept. 5, 1852.

26 *Julia Ella*, b. June 12, 1854.

27 *Mary Alice*, b. Nov. 30, 1855.

There was also another family of Reeds in Woburn and Lexington, which had no connection with the William and Mabel race. If we may believe tradition, and the statement is confirmed by many attendant circumstances, Swethern Reed came to this country from Ireland about 1725, and settled in Boston. After remaining there a few years, he removed to Woburn, and took up his abode in that part of the town which now constitutes Burlington.

1 SWETHERN REED probably m. Margery Collens, and had a number of children, of whose birth we have very imperfect records.

1- 2 †*James*, b. ——; m. Elizabeth Wellington of Camb. Sept. 24, 1778.

3 †*Robert*, b. ——; m. Elizabeth Hartwell of Bedford.

4 *Elizabeth*, b. April, 1740; m. Nov. 30, 1763, Thomas Fox.

5 *Susannah*, b. ——; m. Jedathan Wellington, 1775.

6 *Margery*, b. ——; m. —— Collens, and went to China.

7 *Nancy*, b. ——; m. Nov. 14, 1780, Nathaniel Trask.

8 *Ruth*, b. ——; m. June 5, 1777, Matthew Farrington.

1-2- JAMES REED m. Sept. 24, 1778, Elizabeth Wellington of Camb.

2- 9 *John*, b. Jan. 30, 1779; m. Susan Clapp.

10 *Elizabeth*, b. Oct. 4, 1780; m. Jedediah Stearns.

11 *James*, b. April 12, 1783; m. Susan Johnson.

12 *Susannah*, b. Aug. 10, 1785; m. —— Rugg of Boston.

13 *Joseph*, b. Sept. 9, 1787; m. first, Maria Walker, and second, Roxana Richardson.

14 *Luke*, b. Sept. 6, 1789; m. Barbara Ross of Augusta, Ga.

15 *Artemas*, b. Dec. 1, 1792; d. at the age of sixteen.

16 *Florinda*, b. Nov. 20, 1794; m. Thomas Hersey.

1-3- ROBERT REED m. Elizabeth Hartwell of Bedford. He m. as of Woburn. She d. May 8, 1792.

3-17 | *Swethern*, b. Aug. 13, 1771; m. Nov. 19, 1795, Anna Wyman. He
d. Oct. 28, 1834.
18 | *Elizabeth*, b. April 3, 1773.   19 *Robert*, b. Sept. 4, 1775.
20 | *Sarah*, b. Feb. 22, 1778.   21 *Daniel*, b. Dec. 11, 1781.

1 | SETH REED from Charlestown came to Lexington a young man.
He entered the army of the Revolution and served three years.
After his return, he m. June 26, 1796, Fanny Harrington, dau. of
Thaddeus and Lydia (Porter) Harrington. She d. and he m. Lydia
Harrington, sister of his first wife. After his marriage he moved to
Westminster, Vt., where he remained about two years, when he
returned to Lexington, where he d. Sept., 1815.

1- 2 | *Seth*, b. April 24, 1778; m. Eliza Frost of West Camb. He resides
in Wo., and is the father of Joseph G. Reed of Lex. who m.
June, 1851, Ann Murphy, and has Francis W., b. March 14, 1854.
3 | *Lewis*, b. ——; m. Mary Flint of North Reading.
4 | *Sylvestus S.*, b. ——; d. young.
5 | *Fanny*, b. ——; m. Warren Emerson of Woburn.
6 | *Lydia*, b. ——; m. Nathaniel Hutchinson of Woburn.
7 | *Rhoda*, b. ——; d. 1859, aged 30, unm.

Situated on the borders of Lexington, in Woburn and Burlington,
it is not at all strange that individuals and even families of the name
of Reed, should cross the line and live for a time in Lexington, or at
least should have their names upon our Records. I find several
such, and shall give them as I find them, without attempting to trace
their descent.

PETER REED m. Abigail, and had *Abigail*, b. May 23, 1727, d.
young; *Peter*, b. Feb. 16, 1729; *Abigail*, b. April 2, 1731; *Mary*, b.
April 3, 1733; *Sarah*, b. April 26, 1736; *Thomas*, b. Nov. 3,
1739; *Rebecca*, b. May 24, 1743.

DAVID REED m. Lois, and had *Philip*, b. April 5, 1736; *David*,
b. April 2, 1738; *Lydia*, b. June 28, 1740; *Silas*, b. Feb. 23, 1742;
Persis, b. April 11, 1745.

NEWHALL REED of Wo., m. Oct. 16, 1777, Mary Harrington of
Lex., dau. of Henry and Sarah (Laughton) Harrington, and had
Joel, b. May 13, 1777; *Abigail*, b. July 21, 1778, and d. same day;
Newhall, b. April 5, 1783, d. April 8, 1855, aged 73; *Nathan*, b.
Feb. 18, 1786; *Mary*, b. Sept. 20, 1790, and d. young; *Florinda*,
b. Nov. 24, 1793; *Abigail*, b. Nov. 21, 1795.

Whether the above named families resided in Lex. or only had
their associations here, we are unable to say. Their names are upon
Lexington Records.

THE RICHARDSON FAMILY.

Though the Richardsons have been numerous in Woburn and several other towns in the vicinity, there has been no permanent family
of that name in Lexington till within a comparatively recent period;
and the head of this family descended from a Newbury emigrant.

WILLIAM RICHARDSON was in Newbury early, and m. Aug. 23,
1654, Elizabeth Wiseman, and d. March 14, 1658. They had two
children. *Joseph*, b. May, 1655, m. July, 1681, Margaret, dau. of
Peter Godfrey and Mary Browne, who was the first white child b. in

Newbury. They had eight children. *Caleb*, their youngest child,
b. June 9, 1704, m. Tryphena, dau. of Capt. Daniel and Elizabeth
(Parker) Bodwell. They resided in Methuen, and had ten children.
Samuel, the sixth child of Caleb, b. Feb. 22, 1749, m Lucy Parker
of Westford. He was in the Revolutionary war. He d. July 15,
1836, aged 87; and she d. March 26, 1818, aged 64; they had eight
children b. in Methuen, viz. *Samuel*, b. July 4, 1781; *Lucy*, b. May
28, 1783, d. Oct. 19, 1812; *John C.*, b. May 4, 1785, d. Nov. 2,
1823; *Betsey P.*, b. March 13, 1787, is still living; *Achsa*, b. July
24, 1789, d. Nov. 7, 1819; *Aaron P.*, b. July 22, 1791; *William*, b.
April 26, 1794, d. Aug. 2, 1836; *Mary*, b. July 27, 1797.

---

1   AARON P. RICHARDSON, the third son of Samuel and Lucy, m.
June 26, 1823, Betsey Reed, dau. of Hammon and Sarah (Chandler) Reed, b. June 15, 1799. She d. April 24, 1856, aged 57. He
came to Lex. April, 1820.

1- 2   *Chandler R.*, b. April 10, 1825, m. Feb. 16, 1859, Elvira L. Richards of Pittsfield, only child of Alfred and Harmony H. Richards,
b. May 5, 1832.
3   *Sarah E.*, b. July 11, 1830; m. June 12, 1855, Freeborn F. Raymond.

THE ROBBINS FAMILY.

1   NATHANIEL ROBBINS and Mary Brazier, his wife, came to this
country from Scotland about 1670, and settled in Cambridge, where
he d. 1719, aged 70 years. He was married about the time of his
embarkation, and his children were all born in this country. He had
at least eight children.

1- 2 *Rebecca*, b. Jan. 6, 1671.	3 *Mary*, b. Dec. 31, 1673.

4   *Deborah*, b. June 6, 1674.
5   †*Nathaniel*, b. Feb. 28, 1677; m. Hannah Chandler.
6   *Jonathan*, b. Nov. 21, 1680. He lived in what is now Brighton.
7   *Thomas*, b. Nov. 6, 1683. When a young man, he was passing
    with a team from Boston to Cambridge, on a hot summer day,
    when he stopped to drink at a spring and died immediately. He
    was unmarried.
8   *Samuel*, b. May 30, 1686. He settled in Sudbury.
9   *Joseph*, b. Nov. 8, 1689.

1-5-   NATHANIEL ROBBINS m. Hannah Chandler. About 1700 he
moved to Charlestown, where he lived nearly thirty years, when he
returned to Camb., where he d. Jan. 16, 1741, in his 64th year.
His wife d. Sept. 15, 1738, aged 44 years. This family became
quite distinguished in several of its branches.

5-10   †*Nathaniel*, b. 1699.
11   *Mary*, b. July 22, 1701; m. Joseph Russell.
12   ‡*Thomas*, b. Aug. 11, 1703; d. in Lex. June 30, 1791, aged 88.
13   *Hannah*, b. June 30, 1705; m. Zebediah Johnson.
14   *Rebecca*, b. 1707; m. —— Patten.
15   †*Philemon*, b. Sept. 19, 1709; grad. H. C. 1729.
16   *Deborah*, b. March 24, 1712; m. Joseph Robbins.
17   *Sarah*, b. ——; m. —— Butterfield.

5-10-   NATHANIEL ROBBINS m. ———— and lived in Charlestown, where
at an early age he d., leaving two young children and a widow. He
was mowing in the field in perfect health, when he fell and expired
immediately.

5-12-   THOMAS ROBBINS m. Ruth Johnson, who d. June 27, 1737, in her
35th year, and he m. Exene Jackson. He and his wife, Exene, were
ad. to the ch. in Lex. May 9, 1754, by a letter of dismission from
the Second church of Camb. He came to Lex. about 1744, as his
name appears upon the tax bill in 1745. He was a soldier in the
French war from Lex. in 1758, and was enrolled in Capt. Parker's
co. in 1775. He was one of the assessors in 1746, and one of the
selectmen in 1749. Several of his children were born before he came
to Lex., and hence we have no full record of the family. His will,
dated 1789, and proved 1791, mentions eldest son Thomas, Stephen,
John, Nathaniel, and daughters Mary Mead, Susanna Wadsworth,
Deborah Williams, Exene, Ruth, and Hannah. He d. Jan. 30,
1791, aged 89; she d. Feb. 5, 1786, aged 79. The first six of the
children were by the first wife.

12-18   †Thomas, b. about 1723.
19   †Nathaniel, b. about 1727.
20   Mary, b. about 1730; m. ———— Mead.
21   †Stephen, b. about 1733; m. Dec. 8, 1753, Sarah Wooten.
22   Susanna, b. about 1735; m. ———— Wadsworth.
23   Esther, b. about 1737.
24   †John, b. about 1739; m. Oct. 14, 1761, Sarah Prentice of W. Camb.
25   Exene, b. in Lex. Sept. 15, 1749.
26   Deborah, b. Nov. 9, 1750; m. ———— Williams.
27   Ruth, b. Nov. 11, 1752.
28   Hannah, b. Dec. 1753.
29   †Philemon, b. about 1756; m. Sally ————.
30   Ebenezer, b. ————.

5-15-   PHILEMON ROBBINS grad. H. C. 1729, entered the ministry, and
was settled at Branford, Conn. He m. Hannah Foot, 1735. She d.
1776, and he m. wid. Jane Mills. He d. 1781. He had three sons,
—one d. while in college, the other two were ministers. Ammi
Ruhamah, grad. at Yale, 1760, settled at Norfolk, Conn., 1761. Two
of his sons were ministers. Thomas, one of them, grad. at Williams,
1796, settled at Mattapoisett. He was distinguished as an antiquary,
and had during his ministry collected a very extensive and valuable
library relating to American history, general history, and theology.
He had a large and rare collection of Bibles. He d. in 1856, aged
79, unm. Chandler Robbins, another son of Philemon, grad. at
Yale, 1756, was ordained at Plymouth, Mass., 1760. He was a man
of eminent talents, and his family was distinguished. His son
Chandler, grad. H. C. 1782, was judge of probate at Hallowell, Me.;
Samuel P., grad. H. C. 1798, was minister at Marietta, Ohio; Peter
G., was a physician at Roxbury, Mass. Chandler had sons Chandler,
who was a physician in Boston, and William, a lawyer at Fayetteville,
N. C., both graduates of Bowdoin College. Peter G. had sons
Chandler, who grad. H. C. 1829, ordained at the Old North Church
in Boston, 1833; and Samuel D., grad. Harv. Theolog. School, 1833,
settled in Lynn, afterwards at Framingham, and now at Wayland.

The Robbinses mentioned above have been highly distinguished,
and have received the first honors from our colleges.

RESIDENCE OF STEPHEN ROBBINS,

12-18- THOMAS ROBBINS was taxed in Lex. and filled important offices, but we find no record of wife or children; he may have remained single. He was selectman in 1772, '74, '78. He d. Dec. 2, 1804, aged 82.

12-19- NATHANIEL ROBBINS grad. H. C. 1747. He studied theology, settled at Milton, where he m. a Hutchinson, and d. 1795. One of his sons, Edward Hutchinson, b. Feb. 19, 1758, grad. H. C. 1775. He entered the legal profession, was chosen to represent the town in the Legislature. In 1793 was chosen speaker, an office which he held nine years; in 1812 was elected lieut.-governor; in 1814 was appointed judge of probate of Norfolk county. He d. Dec. 29, 1829.

12-21- STEPHEN ROBBINS m. Dec. 8, 1753, Sarah Wooten, dau. of Capt. Wooten. She d. Dec. 16, 1791.

21-31 *John*, b. ——; went to Pennsylvania.
32 *Sarah*, bap. March 14, 1756; m. Charles Cutter of West Camb.
33 †*Stephen*, bap. Feb. 5, 1758; m. Abigail Winship.
34 *Philemon*, bap. Nov. 11, 1759; d. May 30, 1829.
35 *Lucy*, bap. Dec. 27, 1761; d. unm.
36 *Nathan*, b. ——; m. a Prentice, resided in West Cambridge.
37 *Deborah*, bap. June 30, 1765; m. —— Blodgett.

12-24- JOHN ROBBINS m. Oct. 14, 1761, Sarah Prentice of West Camb. He was of Capt. Parker's co. in 1775.

24-38 *Sarah*, b. March 2, 1762.   39 *Elizabeth*, b. May 26, 1765.
40 *John*, b. Oct. 16, 1769.   41 *Anna*, b. March 27, 1772.
42 *Ruth*, b. July 9, 1774.   43 *Hannah*, b. March 14, 1778.

12-29- PHILEMON ROBBINS m. Sally ——.

29-44 *Sally*, b. Nov. 3, 1781.   45 *Philemon*, b. Dec. 9, 1783.
46 *Joshua*, b. May 25, 1785; d. Aug. 13, 1817.

21-33- STEPHEN ROBBINS m. Abigail Winship. He d. Oct. 12, 1847, aged 89; she d. March 31, 1850, aged 90. He was a fur dresser, and introduced that business into the East Village, which contributed greatly to the growth and prosperity of the place. He, and his son Eli after him, prosecuted that branch of industry, employing at times from eighty to one hundred hands. This of course would require dwellings, and many houses were erected in consequence of this business. Similar enterprise would be productive of benefit to the town in any section thereof at the present day.

33-47 *Stephen*, b. May 26, 1780; m. June 5, 1811, Mary Harrington. He d. in Boston, Aug. 25, 1846.
48 *Samuel*, b. Sept. 7, 1781. He went to Windsor, Vt., where he m.
49 *Nabby*, b. July 24, 1783; m. June 16, 1809, James H. Langdon of Vermont.
50 †*Eli*, b. Nov. 12, 1786; m. July 31, 1809, Hannah Simonds.
51 *Martin*, b. July 6, 1788; d. young.
52 *Lot*, b. March 28, 1790; is living, unmarried.
53 *Caira*, b. April 2, 1794.

33-50- ELI ROBBINS m. July 31, 1809, Hannah Simonds, dau. of Joshua and Martha (Bowers) Simonds. He d. Sept. 27, 1856, aged 70;

she d. Dec. 13, 1864, aged 78. He was a man of great activity and enterprise, and did much to build up the village in the east part of the town. He caused a tower to be erected on the high land in the rear of the settlement, which, together with his residence, will be seen in the following engraving.

50–54 *Hannah M.*, b. Aug. 12, 1812.

55 *Abigail*, b. Dec. 3, 1814; m. Dec. 23, 1839, Stillman L. Lothrop of Boston. He d. in the West Indies, Nov. 22, 1859, aged 49; he had two sons,—*Stillman Follen*, b. May 1, 1841; m. Nov. 18, 1867, Sarah Jane Holbrook of Winchester; *George Langdon*, b. Jan. 27, 1846. Mr. Lothrop, the father, is a descendant in a direct line from Mark Lothrop of Duxbury, b. 1656.

56 *Ellen A.*, b. May 21, 1817; m. Dec. 8, 1853, Abner Stone, b. in Lex. 1812. They were m. at Hartford, Conn., by Rev. Thomas Robbins. They have two children, *Ellen A.*, b. Oct. 7, 1854, and *Mary R.*, b. July 17, 1860.

57 *Julia Ann*, b. May 6, 1819; m. 1860, John Barrett of Concord.

58 *Mary L.*, b. March 23, 1824; d. 1832.

59 *Eli M.*, b. April 4, 1826; r. in New York, where he has a wife and one child, b. 1859.

60 *Martha*, b. Jan. 21, 1829; d. same month.

THE ROBINSON FAMILY.

This family has never been very numerous in Lexington, nor were they among the earliest settlers. The first of the name which appears on our Records was

1 | JONATHAN ROBINSON, son of William, b. in Cambridge, April 20, 1682. I find on a copy of the Will of Richard Cutler of Cambridge, made a short time before his death in 1693, this endorsement: "For the two Robinsons, grandsons to the deceased." This paper being found among the papers left by Jonathan Robinson, and Richard Cutler having several dau., one of them may have m. a Robinson, the father of Jonathan. It appears by a deed in possession of the family, that Isaac Powers of Camb., sold to Jonathan Robinson of Camb., weaver, in 1706, a lot of land at Camb. Farms, bounded northerly by Concord road, easterly by land of Joanna Winship, southerly by land of John Dickson, and westerly by land of the heirs of Samuel Winship. This and other deeds of land to Jonathan Robinson, bounded by the Winships, Whitmores, and Bowmans, leaves no doubt but that he resided on or near the place now occupied by Mr. Jonas Gammell, at the termination of Oak street. Jonathan Robinson m. Ruth ———, and probably came to the Farms about 1706. He d. 1753, and she d. April 25, 1759. He filled the honorable office of tythingman in 1735, and in 1744 was on a committee to "dignify and seat the meeting house."

1– 2 | †*Jonathan*, b. July 25. 1707.
3 | *Ruth*, b. June 29, 1709; d. Oct. 23, 1722.
4 | *Abigail*, b. Feb. 4, 1711; m. Nathaniel Bacon of Lexington.
5 | †*James*, b. Aug. 30, 1715; m. 1751, Anna Trask.
6 | *Lydia*, b. Aug. 29, 1718; m. Caleb Simonds.
7 | *Hannah*, b. Jan. 8, 1721; d. Oct. 24, 1721.

1-2– | JONATHAN ROBINSON m. Elizabeth ———. They were ad. to the ch. July 18, 1742. He d. 1748.

2– 8 | *Elizabeth*, b. June 20, 1732.   9 *Jonathan*, b. Sept. 29, 1733.
10 | †*Jacob*, b. Feb. 3, 1739.   11 *Submit*, bap. July 17, 1743.

1-5– | JAMES ROBINSON m. May 23, 1751, Anna Trask. She d. and he m. second, Margaret ———, by whom he had eight children. He was ad. to the ch. March 10, 1765. She d. Nov. 5, 1767, and he m. third, Elizabeth ———, by whom he had three children. He d. Aug. 12, 1774.

5-12 | *Ruth*, b. Jan. 28, 1753.
13 | †*Joseph*, b. March 18, 1755; m. Mrs. Betty Hadley.
14 | *Silas*, b. Feb. 20, 1757; m. and had a child which d. Dec. 17, 1777.
15 | *Asa*, b. Jan. 19, 1759; was in the campaign to N. Y., 1776.
16 | *James*, b. Nov. 26, 1760; m. May 25, 1787, Judith Reed of Woburn. He was a soldier in the Continental army.
17 | *Rhoda*, b. May 10, 1763; d. young.
18 | †*Ebenezer*, b. Feb. 14, 1765; d. in Vt., 1857, aged 92.
19 | *Persis*, bap. Feb. 1, 1767.
20 | *Rhoda*, bap. Oct. 20, 1771; m. May 24, 1781, Simeon Snow.
21 | *Lydia*, bap. Jan. 5, 1772.   22 *James*, bap. Dec. 1, 1773.

2-10– | JACOB ROBINSON m. Elizabeth Draper. They were ad. to the ch. March 21, 1775.

10-23 | †*Jacob*, b. Oct. 28, 1762; m. Hannah Simonds.
24 | *Elizabeth*, b. March 6, 1765; d. Dec. 29, 1767.
25 | †*Jesse*, b. July 14, 1767; m. Rebecca Tidd.
26 | †*Jonathan*, b. June 20, 1769; was twice married.
27 | *Betty*, b. Feb. 26, 1772; m. —— White of Watertown.

28   *Anna*, b. June 28, 1774 ; m. —— Gardner of Cambridge.
29   *Nathan*, b. Dec. 1, 1775 ; d. Sept. 22, 1776.

5-13-   Joseph Robinson m. Mrs. Betty Hadley, wid. of Samuel Hadley, who was killed April 19, 1775. He was a member of Capt. Parker's company, and joined in the first act of the Revolutionary drama. Nor did his zeal in the cause of liberty cease with the opening scene. He enlisted with the eight months' men in 1775, and served with the twelve months' men the year following, and subsequently entered the continental line. He lived to enjoy the bounty of his country, and to see her prosperous and happy, and d. April 14, 1830, aged 75. She d. Feb. 9, 1831.

13-30   *Rhoda*. b. May 17, 1781 ; m. May 17, 1810, John Gammell of Charlestown, and d. Sept. 11, 1861.
31   *Margaret*, b. Feb. 20, 1783.
32   *Nancy*, b. Jan. 30, 1785 ; m. July 20, 1809, Thomas Cutler of West Cambridge.
33   *Joseph*, b. July 14, 1787 ; m. Lydia Gair of Boston. He d. May 18, 1822.

5-18-   Ebenezer Robinson d. in South Reading, Vt., Oct. 31, 1857, in his 92d year. He was too young to take part in the opening scene of the Revolution ; but before he was sixteen he enlisted with others in a privateer. While on this voyage, having made two prizes, and sent them into Boston, they fell in with several armed ships, and after a desperate struggle in which he was slightly wounded, they were made prisoners. He was taken to New York, and confined in an old prison ship, where from the packed state of the ship, scanty supply of provision, and other inhuman treatment, he suffered every thing but death. After about six months' confinement in this loathsome prison, he was exchanged ; and in a weak, ragged, and penniless condition, was obliged to beg his way home to Lexington, suffering at one time the cold repulses and scoffings of the Tories, and cheered and encouraged at others, by the generosity of the Patriots. Having reached home, and recovered from his imprisonment and suffering, young Robinson enlisted into the Continental army for three years—being then seventeen years of age. For a few months he was stationed at West Point, and was then ordered to New York, where he was connected with the body guard of Washington. On the return of peace, having served about two years, he returned to Lexington, where he remained till 1788, when he in company with an older brother moved to South Reading, Vt., then an almost unbroken wilderness. In 1792, he erected a frame house, and m. Hannah Ackley, who had recently immigrated to that place from Connecticut. He was highly esteemed as a man and a citizen, and filled with honor several military and civil offices. He was always devoted to the cause of liberty, and died respected by his fellow-citizens.

10-23-   Jacob Robinson m. Aug. 26, 1790, Hannah Simonds, dau. of John and Mary (Tufts) Simonds. They were ad. to the ch. April 1, 1791. He d. Sept. 12, 1848, aged 84. She d. Oct. 18, 1853, aged 80. He was selectman in 1805 and 1806, and an assessor several years.

23-34   ‡*Jacob*, b. April 24, 1791 ; m. Ann Hall,
35   *Charles*, b. May 5, 1793 ; d. Sept. 24, 1801.

36 | *Hannah*, b. April 25, 1795; m. April 8, 1821, Charles Tufts of Charlestown, founder of Tufts College.
37 | *John*, b. April 30, 1797; d. Sept. 26, 1801.
38 | *George*, b. Dec. 2, 1799; d. Sept. 22, 1801.
39 | †*Charles*, b. May 5, 1802; m. Oct. 16, 1827, Mary Davis.
40 | *John*, b. Aug. 19, 1804. He has for many years labored under a quiet kind of insanity.
41 | *Harriet*, b. Nov. 6, 1806; m. Thomas C. Gilmor.
42 | *Mary Ann*, b. Feb. 2, 1812; m. May. 1841, Sylvester Harrington.

19-25— JESSE ROBINSON m. Nov. 24, 1793, Rebecca Tidd of Acton. They moved to Bedford, where they had several other children than the two mentioned below.

43 | *Rebecca*, b. Feb. 14, 1795.   44 *Jesse*, b. June 4, 1797.

10-26— JONATHAN ROBINSON m. Joanna Jennings. She d. and he m. May 1, 1831, Mary Jennings. He had no children.

23-34— JACOB ROBINSON m. Jan. 9, 1818, Ann Hall of Cambridge. She d. April 19, 1850, aged 57, and he m. Oct. 13, 1850, Lucinda Davis of Medford. He had no children by either wife. He was an assessor three years. He was also a of justice of the peace.

23-39— CHARLES ROBINSON m. Oct. 16, 1827, Mary Davis of Con., dau. of Abel and Lavinia (Hosmer) Davis. Lavinia Hosmer was a dau. of Joseph, who acted as adjutant at Concord, April 19, 1775. He has served as selectman several years.

39-45 | *Charles*, b. Nov. 6, 1829; m. July 4, 1858, Rebecca T. Ames of Charlestown, where he resides and does business as a lawyer. He has also been a trial justice, and mayor of the city.
46 | *George D.*, b. Jan. 20, 1834. He grad. H. C. 1856, and was engaged some eight or ten years as a teacher of the High School at Chicopee. He m. Nov. 24, 1859, Hannah E. Stevens, dau. of William and Nancy Stevens. She d. Sept. 5, 1864, aged 31 years. He read law with his brother, and is now in practice in Chicopee. He m. second, July 11, 1867, Susan E. Simonds of Lex., dau. of J. F. Simonds. He has Walter S., b. March 22, 1861.

There are other Robinsons in town not connected with the preceding family, whose descent as far as ascertained is as follows:

JONATHAN ROBINSON of New Market, N. H., m. Mary Chase of Exeter, by whom he had ten children. *Noah*, their seventh son b. in Stratham, May 7, 1757, m. for his first wife, Nancy Wiggin of Stratham. In 1790, after serving his country through the whole period of the Revolution, he moved to New Hampton in that State, which was then a howling wilderness. His wife dying, he m. June 26, 1805, Mrs. Elizabeth Brown of Portsmouth, N. H. He d. Feb. 10, 1827. He had by his two wives seven sons and two daughters.

SIMON W. ROBINSON, the fourth son of Capt. Noah, b. Feb. 19, 1792, m. Hannah T. Danforth of Billerica, by whom he had four children—two sons and two daughters, viz. *Sarah*, b. Aug. 6, 1817; *John B.*, b. May 30, 1819; *Henry B.*, b. Oct. 3, 1821, and d. March 25, 1826; *Hannah A.*, b. Dec. 22, 1823, d. Feb. 7, 1856. He came to Boston in 1813 and went into business, where he remained thirty-four years, when he came to Lex. in 1847. His wife d. Oct., 1843, and he m. 1847, Mrs. Elizabeth G. Little of Bucksport, Me. Mr. Robinson, when in Boston was elected to the Legislature, and has also represented the town of Lexington in that body. He has for many years held a commission of justice of the peace.

GEORGE W. ROBINSON, a son of Capt. Noah by his second wife, was b. Feb. 23, 1808, and m. Dec. 5, 1830, Maria Jewett, dau. of Nathaniel Jewett of Charlestown. He came to Lex. 1848, where the last three of his children were born. He is engaged in mercantile business in Boston. The following are his children. *George Henry*, b. Sept. 26, 1833, d. at sea on his passage home from the East Indies, Feb. 24, 1858; *Frances Maria*, b. Feb. 26, 1836; *Emily Hamblet*, b. March 1, 1840, d. Oct. 30, 1841; *Frederick Osborn*, b. May 11, 1842; he has spent several years in mercantile pursuits at the Mauritius; *Theodore Parker*, b. July 29, 1845; *William Howard*, b. June 13, 1848; *Sarah Elizabeth*, b. Nov. 24, 1852; *Edith Jewett*, b. May 28, 1858.

THE RUSSELL FAMILY.

1　WILLIAM RUSSELL and his wife Martha, the ancestors of the Lexington Russells came over from England early, and like many of the early emigrants, did not at once fix upon their location. They were in Camb. 1645, and were members of the church there. He d. Feb. 14, 1662. She m. March 24, 1665, Humphrey Bradshaw, and in 1683, Thomas Hall, and d. 1694. Several of their children were b. in England.

1- 2　†*Joseph*, b. 1636; m. June 23, 1662, Mary Belcher; d. June 26, 1691.
3　†*Benjamin*, probably b. in England; m. Rebecca ——.
4　*Phebe*, probably b. in England; d. July 8, 1642.
5　†*John*, b. Sept. 11, 1645; m. Elizabeth ——.
6　*Martha*, b. ——.
7　†*Philip*, b. 1650; m. April 19, 1680, Joanna Cutler.
8　†*William*, b. April 28, 1655; m. Abigail Winship.
9　†*Jason*, b. Nov. 14, 1658; m. June 27, 1684, Mary Hubbard.
10　*Joyce*, b. March 31, 1660; m. Oct. 13, 1680, Edmund Rice of Sud.

1-2-　JOSEPH RUSSELL m. June 23, 1662, Mary Belcher. They resided in Camb. She d. June 23, 1691.

2-11　*Mary*, b. Jan. 8, 1665.
12　*Martha*, b. June 27, 1666; d. May 26, 1691.
13　*Abigail*, b. May 12, 1668; m. Matthew Bridge.
14　*Prudence*, b. May 30, 1670.
15　*Joseph*, b. July 15, 1673; d. young.
16　*Walter*, b. May 30, 1676; m. Elizabeth Winship, dau. of Edward Winship, 2d. They resided at W. Camb. and had a large family.
17　†*Joseph*, ⎱ twins, b. June 21, 1680; ⎰ resided in Lexington.
18　*Jeremiah*, ⎰
19　*John*, b. May 5, 1683.　　　　21 *Samuel*, b. Sept. 9, 1685.

1-3-　BENJAMIN RUSSELL m. Rebecca ——. They resided in Camb. and had *Rebecca*, d. 1673; *Jason, Benjamin, William, Joyce*, and *Sarah*.

1-5-　JOHN RUSSELL m. Elizabeth ——. He was at Camb. Farms at the organization of the parish in 1693, and was the largest subscriber for the meeting house. He was one of the original members of the ch. in 1696, and his wife removed her relation from the ch. in Camb. to that of Lex, soon after. He was not only a man of wealth, but was an active and valuable citizen, and filled various offices under the parish and town organization. The record of his family is quite defective. Probably d. March 6, 1733.

5-22	†*John*, b. Nov. 9, 1671.	23	*Thomas*, b. Sept. 13, 1673.
24	*Martha*, b. Sept. 1, 1675; d. Dec. 7, 1675.		
25	*Benjamin*, b. April 2, 1677.	26	*Abigail*, b. April 18, 1686.
27	*Patience*, b. May 27, 1688.	27½	*Esther*, b. Dec. 19, 1700.

They probably had children between 1676 and 1686.

1-7-   PHILIP RUSSELL m. April 19, 1680, Joanna Cutler, dau. of James Cutler, b. 1660, and d. Nov. 26, 1703, aged 43; and he m. second, Oct. 18, 1705, Sarah Brooks of Med. The name of Philip Russell is borne upon our earliest parish and town records; and he appears to have enjoyed the confidence of the people, not only in the new settlement but in the old town. Though residing in the precinct, he was one of the selectmen of Old Camb. in 1700 and 1701. He was a subscriber for the meeting house at the Farms in 1692, and on the committee to "seat the meeting house," when it was ready for occupation. He d. Feb. 7, 1730, aged 80 years. The record of his family is imperfect, but from the probate files we have been enabled to present the following.

7-28	*Joanna*, b. Dec. 30, 1684; m. about 1716, William Munroe as his second wife. She was ad. to the ch. Dec. 24, 1727.
29	†*Philip*, b. Sept. 18, 1688; d. March 3, 1773, aged 85.
30	*Samuel*, b. Jan. 12, 1691.
31	*Jemima*, b. 1692; m. William Locke.
32	†*James*, b. ——; m. Mary ——.
33	‡*William*, b. ——; m. Elizabeth ——.
34	*Sarah*, b. ——; m. April 26, 1739, Joseph Russell.
35	*Abigail*, b. Oct. 27, 1700; m. —— Sprague.
36	*Susanna*, b. Oct. 27, 1706.

1-8-   WILLIAM RUSSELL m. March 18, 1685, Abigail Winship, dau of Lieut. Edward Winship of Camb. We have little knowledge of the family, as they probably never came to Lex. They had *William*, b. 1687, who m. Mary, and d. in Lex. Nov. 25, 1731; *Abigail*, b. Dec. 31, 1688, d. unm. June 20, 1710; *Edward*, b. 1694, d. June 21, 1695. They probably had other children.

1-9-   JASON RUSSELL m. May 27, 1684, Mary Hubbard of Camb., where they resided. They had *Jason*, b. 1687, *John*, *Martha*, *Hubbard*, *Thomas*, *Elizabeth*, and *Noah*. The late Col. Thomas Russell of W. Camb. was a descendant of this family, being a son of Thomas, son of Jason, son of Hubbard.

2-18-   JOSEPH RUSSELL m. Jane ——. He was in the French war. He d. Dec. 20, 1763. The want of records leaves us almost without knowledge of this family. The probate files furnish a few facts. They had at least Jabez, Ephraim, and Joseph. *Joseph* m. April 26, 1739, Sarah Russell, dau. of Philip Russell. They were cousins. They had two children, one b. Jan. 11, d. Jan. 13, 1740; *Sarah*, b. Feb. 28, 1740, and d. June 10, 1741. Sarah, the mother, d. May 29, 1742, and Joseph, the husband, d. March 23, 1743. Thus this family became extinct. Joseph, the husband of Jane, in his Will,

proved 1763, speaks of wife Jane, dau. Abigail Bowman, and sons
Thomas, Jabez, and Ephraim. Of the latter alone have we any
full record.

18-37   ‡*Ephraim*, b. 1730 ; m. Miriam Wheeler of Bedford.

5-22-   JOHN RUSSELL m. Rebecca ——. They were ad. to the ch. in
Lex. April 10, 1715. He d. June 14, 1746.

22-38 *Rebecca*, b. June 24, 1711.   39 *Adonijah*, b. Feb. 25, 1713.
    40 *Abigail*, b. Feb. 15, 1716.   41 *John*, b. April 26, 1719.
    42 *Solomon*, b. Aug. 5, 1723.   43 *Joseph*, b. Aug. 13, 1729.

7-29-   PHILIP RUSSELL m. Sarah ——. They were ad. to the ch. Oct.
5, 1718. She d. Dec. 17, 1767 ; he d. March 3, 1773. He was constable in 1733, and subsequently he served on the school committee.

29-44 *Sarah*, b. May 22, 1718.
    45 *Millicent*, b. Dec. 29, 1720 ; m. Joshua Bond.
    46 *Mary*, b. May 13, 1722 ; d. Aug. 12, 1736.
    47 *Phebe*, b. April 14, 1725 ; d. July 29, 1736.
    48 ‡*Philip*, b. April 5, 1727 ; m. April 24, 1750, Lydia Eaton of Read.
    49 ‡*Joseph*, b. June 19, 1729 ; m. Hannah ——.
    50 *Joanna*, b. Nov. 21, 1731.

7-32-   JAMES RUSSELL m. about 1706, Mary ——. They were ad. to the
ch. in Lex. May 24, 1719. He was one of the subscribers for the
purchase of the Common, 1711. He d. April 1, 1748.

32-51 *Mary*, bap. Aug. 3, 1707.   52 *James*, bap. Aug. 21, 1709.
    53 *Josiah*, bap. April 1, 1711 ; moved to Plainfield, Conn.
    54 *Samuel*, bap. Nov. 9, 1712.   55 *Joanna*, b. April 8, 1714.
    56 *Sarah*, b. Jan. 8, 1716.   57 *Abigail*, b. April 29, 1718.
    58 *Lucy*, b. April 15, 1720 ; m. Nov. 23, 1738, Moses Goodnow, Sud.

7-33-   WILLIAM RUSSELL m. Elizabeth ——. He was constable in 1722,
and 1723. He d. Nov. 25, 1731. He held a commission of captain.

33-59 *Nathaniel*, bap. Feb. 23, 1707 ; m. and had *Abigail*, b. Mar. 10, 1728.
    60 *Lydia*, bap. June 3, 1711.   61 *Submit*, bap. Dec. 28, 1712.
    62 *Joel*, b. Aug. 2, 1716.

18-37-   EPHRAIM RUSSELL m. Jan. 9, 1755, Miriam Wheeler of Bed.
They were ad. to the ch. in Lex. Dec. 5, 1756.

37-63 *Ephraim*, b. Nov. 1, 1755.   64 *Solomon*, b. Jan. 29, 1758.
    65 *Nathan*, bap. Dec. 9, 1759.   66 *Calvin*, bap. Jan. 17, 1762.
    67 *Joseph*, bap. Dec. 11, 1764.   67½ *Dorcas*, bap. March 30, 1766.

29-48-   PHILIP RUSSELL m. April 24, 1750, Lydia Eaton of Reading, by
whom he had one son, Amos. She d. Oct. 5, 1751, and he m. second, June 22, 1758, Lydia Dodge, by whom he had nine children.
He d. Jan. 19, 1816, aged 89; she d. Feb. 28, 1772. In his Will,
dated 1796, he mentions sons Amos, Nathan, and Jonas, and dau.
Phebe Merriam and Lucy Harrington.

48-68 *Amos*, b. Dec. 5, 1750 ; m. Feb. 23, 1773, Betty Munroe and moved
    to Gardner, where they had Samuel and Sarah. He d. in Lex.
    June 25, 1801.

69 | *Lydia*, b. Nov. 9, 1758; d. May 25, 1777, aged 19.
70 | †*Nathan*, b. March 1, 1760; m. June 18, 1795, Sybil Blood.
71 | *Sarah*, b. March 24, 1761; m. Dec. 21, 1780, Jonas Locke, and d. 1799.
72 | *Thomas*, b. April 10, 1762; d. Nov. 15, 1763.
73 | *Phebe*, b. May 24, 1764; m. 1783, Joseph Merriam of Bed. She d. May 29, 1845.
74 | *Thomas*, b. Feb. 18, 1766; d. May 14, 1766.
75 | *Jonas*, b. April 29. 1767; d. Nov. 21, 1847, aged 81.
76 | *Lucy*, b. Nov. 7, 1768; m. 1792, Joseph Harrington.
77 | *A child*, b. March 16, 1771; d. May 27, 1771.

20–49– | JOSEPH RUSSELL. m. Hannah ——. She d. Sept. 15, 1808, aged 83. He d. Oct. 17, 1802, aged 73. They had Hannah, b. Aug. 12, 1764. Her mother, her last-surviving parent, dying 1808, Hannah was left alone, and she lived about thirty years the sole occupant of the house, and d. 1838, unm., aged 74 years. Her house was near the present residence of Col. Philip Russell.

48–70– | NATHAN RUSSELL m. June 18, 1795, Sybil Blood of Carlisle, who was b. June 25, 1765. She d. Jan. 28, 1853, aged 88, and he d. Jan. 9, 1848, aged 88.

70–78 | †*Philip*, b. Aug. 6, 1796; m. March 16, 1837, Sabra Wood of Bur.
79 | *Nathan*, b. July 4, 1798; m. Mary A. Thayer of West Camb. She d. Feb. 12, 1830, and he m. second, Nov. 14, 1830, Elizabeth Farwell of Camb. She d. July 3, 1852, and he m. third, 1854, Abigail Whitney. His wives were all of Camb. where he resided, and died.
80 | *Thomas*, b. Feb. 2, 1800; m. July 24, 1828, Cynthia Jones. They resided in Cambridge.
81 | *Bowen*, b. March 24, 1802; m. first, May 12, 1825, Susan K. Locke. She d. Dec. 19, 1826, and he m. second, June 6, 1833, Mehitabel Locke. They resided at West Cambridge.
82 | *Mary*, b. Feb. 22, 1804; ⎰ m. Nov. 24, 1829, Isaac B. Smith.
83 | *Stephen*, b. Feb. 22, 1804. ⎱
84 | *Lydia*, b. Sept. 30, 1806; ⎰ d. Nov. 26, 1844, unm.
85 | *Sally*, b. Sept. 30, 1806; ⎱ m. Oct. 16, 1834, Thomas Joyce, whose name was afterwards changed to Thomas J. White. He resided in Cambridge.
86 | *Betsey*, b. May 2, 1808.

It is worthy of remark that in the above family there were nine children born in less than twelve years. This is explained by the remarkable fact that there were two pairs of twins in the family.

70–78– | PHILIP RUSSELL m. March 16, 1837, Sabra Wood of Burlington. She d. Oct. 10, 1862. The confidence reposed in him by his fellow citizens is manifest from the various offices he has been called to fill. He was selectman thirteen years, assessor five years, and representative nine years. He was also actively engaged in the military, and passed through the various grades till he enjoyed the title of colonel.

78–87 | *Sabra Ann*, b. Feb. 3, 1838; d. May 15, 1862.
88 | *Philip Marshall*, b. June 9, 1839; m. Rebecca ——. They have one child, Sabra, b. Oct. 12, 1866.
89 | *Henry Austin*, b. Nov. 16, 1841; d. March 15, 1866.
90 | *Martha Ella*, b. Nov. 18, 1850.

We have found more than ordinary difficulty in tracing the Russell family. There were Russells in town who probably did not descend from William and Martha. There were Russells in Charlestown and in Woburn, and probably some of the name came into Lexington. Early upon our records we find the name of *Jonathan Russell*, who appeared to have been a man of some note, as he filled the office of constable in 1717, and subsequently was otherwise noticed. He was ad. to the ch. Dec. 19, 1708. He may have come to Lex. from Wo.

1 | JONATHAN RUSSELL m. Elizabeth ——.

1- 2 | *Elizabeth*, b. July 15, 1702.   3 *Mary*, b. Jan. 1, 1705.
4 | *Jonathan*, b. April 5, 1707; dismissed to Acton, April, 1742.
5 | *Jane*, b. April 19, 1711; m. Feb. 11, 1735, Benjamin Lawrence.
6 | *Ruth*, b. May 24, 1714.   7 *Ebenezer*, b. May 1. 1717.
8 | *Samuel*, b. Feb. 3, 1723.   9 *Hester*, b. April 4, 1725.

1 | ELEAZER RUSSELL m. Nov. 23, 1738, Tabitha Prentice. They were ad. to the ch. of Lex. Aug. 19, 1739.

1- 2 | *Martha*, b. Feb. 1739.   3 *Thaddeus*, b. Jan. 27, 1742.

1 | DAVID RUSSELL m. Abigail ——. They were ad. to the ch. Dec. 19, 1708. He was an assessor, 1710. He may have come from Charlestown or Woburn.

1- 2 | *David*, bap. Oct. 29, 1699.   3 *John*, bap. Dec. 6, 1702.
4 | *Abigail*, bap. Sept. 9, 1705.   5 *Hannah*, bap. June 6, 1708.
6 | *Jason*, bap. July 23, 1710.   7 *Elizabeth*, b. July 1, 1716.

The following baptisms we are unable to classify.

1 | *William Russell*, bap. Feb. 12, 1716.
2 | *Martha*, ⎫ twins, bap. Feb. 17, 1716.
3 | *Mary*, ⎭
4 | *Eleazer*, bap. May 12, 1717.   5 *Esther*, bap. May 23, 1725.
6 | *Isaac*, bap. Sept. 1, 1729.   7 *Keziah*, bap. Nov. 22, 1730.
8 | *Jonathan*, bap. May 11, 1735.   9 *James*, bap. April 22, 1739.
10 | *Azubah*, bap. May 22, 1741.   11 *Ebenezer*, bap. Aug. 9, 1741.
12 | *Mary*, bap. April 3, 1748.

The following transient baptisms of the Russells do not fall in with any consecutive record.

Mary, of James Russell, jr., bap. Aug. 25, 1734; probably d. young.
Mary, of James, jr., b. April, 1736.

Thomas Russell, of Josiah, bap. May 25, 1739.
Hannah Russell, of Josiah, bap. July 28, 1745.

May have been the children of Josiah Russell, the son of James, (No. 35). Josiah (No. 63) was at one time in Connecticut. He might have returned.

Col. JOSHUA RUSSELL from Wo. resided for a time in Lex., but has no descendants in town at the present day.

JOHN A. RUSSELL, son of Jeremiah Russell of West Camb., b. Jan. 17, 1813; m. Oct. 11, 1840, Lydia M. Locke, dau. of Jonas and Abigail (White) Locke, b. May 3, 1816. He came to Lex. 1833. They have Leonora, b. Aug. 3, 1843; John Adams, b. May 5, 1846; Amy M., b. June 3, 1849, d. Sept. 10, 1863; Celia, b. July 4, 1851.

THE SAVILLE FAMILY.

EDWARD SAVILLE of Weymouth, and WILLIAM SAVILLE of Braintree, were both in the country as early as 1640. But it is not known from which, if from either, the family we design to trace descended.

THOMAS SAVILLE, said to have come from Malden, settled in Gloucester, in a part of the town called Squam, where he d. at the age of 84. He m. 1722, Mary Haraden. They had several children, among whom was *Jesse*, who was one of his majesty's custom house officers in 1770. The opposition to British taxation rendered every officer of the crown unpopular. Saville shared the fate of all such officers. His house was assailed, and he was treated with violence. It does not appear, however, that he espoused the cause of Great Britain. Babson in his History of Gloucester, says of him, "He lived a useful and retired life, and d. March 11, 1823, at an advanced age." He had several sons; *John* went to sea and was taken prisoner and carried to England, and never returned; *Oliver*, d. on a voyage to India; *David*, was lost at sea. Besides these, he had *Thomas*, *James*, and *William*.

1   THOMAS SAVILLE b. Aug. 18, 1764; m. May 10, 1787, Betsey Haraden, b. June 15, 1764. He d. May 7, 1845; she d. Sept. 23, 1836. They had several children who d. in infancy. Besides they had the following.

1- 2	*Betsey*, b. 1788; d. 1816.	3 *Thomas*, b. 1791; d. 1809.
4	*John*, b. 1793; d. 1833.	5 *Martha B.*, b. April 22, 1802.
6	†*David*, b. June 2, 1804; m. Sept. 12, 1830, Ann W. Leonard.	
7	*James*, b. Jan. 29, 1808.	8 *Laura*, b. April 5, 1810.

1-6-   DAVID SAVILLE m. Sept. 12, 1830, Ann W. Leonard, dau. of Rev. Ezra and Nancy (Woodbury) Leonard, b. July 19, 1808. Mr. Leonard, the father-in-law of Mr. Saville, was a Congregationalist clergyman in Gloucester. In the course of his ministry he embraced the doctrine of universal salvation, and such was his influence in his parish, and such his hold upon their esteem and affections, that his whole congregation either adopted his views, or quietly tolerated them, so that no rupture occurred in the society, and he continued to be their pastor. Mr. Saville resided in Gloucester till 1845, when he moved to Charlestown, and in 1849 he removed to Lexington. His father being a seafaring man, he accompanied him on voyages at an early age, and continued in the calling of a mariner till he became master of a vessel. He was taken prisoner on the coast of Chili by a privateer and set on shore, where he was forced into the army, from which he escaped and shipped on board a whaler. In his voyages he visited different parts of both continents. He was in the West India and South American trade; made voyages to the Baltic and the Mediterranean, and left the sea about 1835. In 1836 and 1838, he represented his native town in the Legislature, and was for some years an inspector in the Boston Custom House. Since 1849, he has spent most of his time in California, keeping up his residence in Lexington, where his family reside.

6- 9 | *Leonard A.*, b. Jan. 31, 1833; m. June 5, 1862, Rebecca H. Gould, dau. of James Gould of Lex. He has spent five years in California. They have two children, *Fred Clifford*, b. Feb. 21, 1865; *Anna Muzzey*, b. Sept. 19, 1866. He is in trade in Lex.; was chosen town clerk, 1868.

10 | *John*, b. July 7, 1835; d. Jan. 6, 1838.

11 | *Annie W.*, b. July 8, 1838; m. Dec. 13, 1860, David W. Muzzey.

12 | *Clifford*, b. July 19, 1840. He was nine months in the service in North Carolina in the late Rebellion.

13 | *David*, b. May 8, 1843; he was killed at Gloucester, Sept 29, 1853, by the accidental discharge of a gun.

14 | *Frank Edward*, b. Dec. 24, 1846. He was b. in Charlestown, while his brothers and sisters were all b. in Gloucester.

THE SIMONDS FAMILY.

The Simondses of Lexington, originated in Woburn, and came to this place about 1680. The first notice of them in the Woburn records, is in 1644. When they came to the country is unknown.

1 | WILLIAM SIMONDS of Wo. m. Jan. 28, 1644, Judith Hayward, dau. of James Hayward. He settled in Wo., about a mile and a half westerly of the centre of the town, where he built a house which was used as a fort during the Indian wars. He was one of the proprietors of the town, and became a considerable landholder. He was denominated a planter. He served, as most of the men at that day did, in the military movements of the times. He was admitted a freeman in 1670. He d. in 1670, leaving a wife and a large family of children. His widow survived him twenty years, and d. Jan. 5, 1690.

1- 2 | *Sarah*, b. Aug. 8, 1644.   3 *Judith*, b. May 13, 1646.

4 | *Mary*, b Jan. 19, 1648.

5 | *Caleb*, b. Aug. 26, 1649; m. Sept. 1677, Sarah Bacon.

6 | *William*, b. April 25, 1651.

7 | †*Joseph*, b. Sept. 28, 1652; d. Aug. 12, 1733, in Lexington.

8 | *Benjamin*, b. March 28, 1654; m Rebecca ———.

9 | *Tabatha*, b. July 30, 1656; d. same day.

10 | *James*, b. Oct. 11, 1657; m. Feb. 19, 1685, Susanna Blodgett.

11 | *Bethiah*, b. Feb. 11, 1659; m. Aug. 13, 1696, John Walker.

12 | *Huldah*, b. Jan. 23, 1660; m. May 10, 1683, Samuel Blodgett.

1-7- | JOSEPH SIMONDS m. March 7, 1681, Mary Tidd, dau. of John and Rebecca (Wood) Tidd. Mr. Simonds and his father-in-law both came from Wo. and settled in the same neighborhood, near where Mr. Charles Johnson now resides. The locality is marked by the huge and venerable elms which have braved the tempests of nearly two centuries. His name is found on the earliest records of Lex., he being a subscriber to the first meeting house in 1692. His name is also borne on the first tax bill in 1693, and was among the eight or ten highest tax payers on the list. In 1695, we find the name of Sergeant Joseph Simonds among the assessors, along with Sergeant Thomas Cutler and Corporal William Reed, so that at that early day he seems to have been on the high road of military promotion. He was one of the selectmen at the first organization under the town charter, in 1713. He subsequently served on the school committee, and filled other important offices in the town. He and his wife, Mary, were admitted to the church under Mr. Estabrook, in 1698. He d. Aug. 12, 1733, aged 86, and his wife d. Jan. 4, 1732, aged 77.

One stone in the grave yard bears the names of both of them. The record of this family is very imperfect,—the birth of only four of their children is recorded. His Will, dated Jan. 16, 1733, and proved Sept. 21, 1733, mentions sons Joshua, Joseph, Daniel, and Jonathan, and dau. Rebecca Wellington, Mary Grimes, Abigail Knight, and Elizabeth Brown. Daniel was made executor of his Will.

———

7-13   *Rebecca*, b. June 11, 1682; m. Thomas Wellington of Watertown.
14   *Mary*, b. Dec. 15, 1684; m. William Grimes.
15   †*Joshua*, b. Jan. 23, 1687; d. Nov. 3, 1768, aged 82.
16   *Joseph*, b. June 8, 1689.
17   †*Daniel*, b. 1692; d. April 3, 1776.
18   †*Jonathan*, b. ——; d. Dec. 22, 1748.
19   *Abigail*, b. ——; m. —— Knight.
20   *Elizabeth*, bap. Nov. 13, 1698; m. Jonathan Brown.

———

7-15-   JOSHUA SIMONDS m. Hannah Poulter of Lex. He was constable in 1728, school committee in 1732, and selectman in 1733 and 1746. He d. Nov. 3, 1768, aged 82; and she d. Nov. 11, 1789, at the advanced age of 96. His Will, dated June 29, 1767, and proved Nov. 22, 1768, mentions Hannah, his wife, and his sons Joshua and Joseph, and his dau. Sarah Bowman, Hannah Brooks and Betty Reed. He made ample provision for his wife, which I will notice, as it shows the habits and customs of the times. After describing the portion of his house which she might occupy, he provides that she shall be furnished with a good horse, two good cows, six bushels of corn, three of rye, two of wheat, two of malt, fifty pounds of pork, hundred pounds of beef, two barrels of good cider, three bushels of winter apples, a sufficiency of suitable sauce, twelve pounds of flax, six pounds of wool, and six cords of wood, to be furnished annually during her life.

———

15-21   *Joshua*, b. Feb. 11, 1721; d. Aug. 29, 1724.
22   *John*, b. Aug. 1, 1724; d. Sept. 1, 1728.
23   *Sarah*, b. Aug. 11, 1727; m. June 24, 1756, Francis Bowman, Bed.
24   *Hannah*, b. Oct. 17. 1729; m. —— Brooks.
25   *Betty*, b. Jan. 22, 1732; m. April 13. 1757, Hammon Reed.
26   †*Joshua*; b. May 26, 1736; m. Martha Bowers.
27   †*Joseph*, b. Oct. 1, 1739; m. March 2, 1769, Elizabeth Stone.

———

7-17-   DANIEL SIMONDS m. Nov. 29, 1716, Abigail Smith of Waltham. The same year, according to the good old custom, he was chosen hogreeve. To him this was a rising-post, for subsequently, viz. in 1740 and 1755, we find his name among the selectmen. He and his wife united with the church in Lexington, 1751. He d. April 3, 1776, aged 83.

———

17-28   *Mary*, b. March 20, 1718.
29   †*Daniel*, b. Nov. 28, 1719; m. Nov. 13, 1750, Mary Mixter.
30   †*Nathan*, b. Sept. 10, 1722.
31   *Jane*, b. Dec. 1724; d. March 12, 1725.
32   *Abigail*, b. April 22, 1732; d. Nov. 2, 1734.
33   *Abigail*, b. Aug. 30, 1736; m. May 29, 1753, Isaiah Tay of Woburn.
34   *Sarah*, b. April 25, 1739; m. April 22, 1756, Abraham Merriam of Concord.

———

7-18-   JONATHAN SIMONDS m. Lydia Bowman. He appears to have been a considerable landholder. His homestead contained one hundred and two acres, bounded easterly on land of Thomas Blodgett, Robert Fiske, and Woburn line, westerly by land of Joshua Simonds and the town road, northerly on land of Joshua Simonds, Jonathan Robinson, and Thomas Hadley, and southerly on land of Joshua Simonds, Samuel Raymond, Robert Fiske, and Thomas Blodgett. His whole estate at his decease was valued in the currency of the day at £3,251. This description of his homestead fixes his residence in the north-easterly part of the town, near the present corner of Wo. and Bur. He d. Dec. 22, 1748. He was one of the selectmen in 1732.

———

18-35   *Jonathan*, b. April 26, 1715.
36   *Lemuel*, b. June 1, 1717; d. June 2, 1764.
37   *Joseph*, b. June 7, 1721.
38   *Frances,* } twins, b. Feb. 1, 1724; { d. in early infancy.
39   *Amos,*   }   { d. 1750.
40   *Francis*, b. July 12, 1726.
41   ‡*John*, b. Jan. 5, 1730; m. Mary Tufts.
42   *Ebenezer*, b. May 30, 1735.

15-26-   JOSHUA SIMONDS m. Martha Bowers of Billerica. They were admitted to the church, Sept. 7, 1756. He was a large landholder, owning real estate not only in Lex. and other towns in Massachusetts, but in Hollis, N. H. He d. July 24, 1805, aged 69; she d. June 24, 1819, aged 77. He was among the brave men who met the British on the 19th of April, 1775. He went into the meeting house for powder, and finding himself cut off from his company, cocked his gun and placed the muzzle on an open cask of powder, resolved to blow up the house in case the British should enter it.

———

26-43   *Martha*, b. Oct. 1, 1766; m. Aug. 18, 1785, Rufus Merriam.
44   *Elizabeth*, b. May 24, 1768; d. young.
45   ‡*Joshua*, b. Jan. 1, 1770; m. Abigail Cutler.
46   *Elizabeth*, b. July 4, 1772; m. Robert Parker.
47   †*William*, b. Aug. 18, 1774; m. Susan Pierce.
48   *Lucy*, b. Dec. 15, 1776; d. Nov. 4, 1824, unm.
49   ‡*Jonathan*, b. Feb. 22, 1779; m. Mrs. Hill of Boston.
50   *Hannah*, b. July, 1786; m. July 31, 1809, Eli Robbins.

15-27-   JOSEPH SIMONDS m. March 2, 1769, Elizabeth Stone. They were admitted to the church, April 15, 1770. He d. March 18, 1813, aged 73; she d. June 10, 1806, aged 63. He was an ensign in Capt. Parker's company in 1775.

———

27-51   *Betty*, b. May 30, 1769; d. Aug. 6, 1795, aged 26.
52   †*Joseph*, b. Sept. 29, 1771; m. Mary Viles.

17-29-   DANIEL SIMONDS m. Nov. 13, 1750, Mary Mixer, dau. of Maj. Joseph and Mary (Ball) Mixer. He d. Feb. 9, 1761, and his wid. m. May 26, 1763, Andrew Munroe.

———

29-53   *Daniel*, b. Nov. 26, 1751; d. Feb. 9, 1761.
54   *Mary*, b. Nov. 9, 1753.   55 *Abigail*, b. Feb. 15, 1756.
56   *Joseph*, b. April 2, 1758.
57   *Lucy*, b. Aug. 18, 1761, about six months after the death of her father. Her mother m. Andrew Munroe, by whom she had two sons, the last of whom was born one month after the death of his father.

17-30-   NATHAN SIMONDS m. —— Smith of Walt. She d. and he m. Abigail Cutler of Bur. He resided at one time in Wo. In 1762, Nathan Simonds, wife, and children, came from Wo. to Lex. and resided in the house of Daniel Simonds. He was one of the selectmen in 1776.

30-58   *Jonas*, b. ——. He entered the army of the United States, rose to a coloncley, and d. in the service.
59   †*David*, b. 1769; m. July 23, 1795, Jerusha Locke.
60   *Supply*, b. ——; m. Betsey Brown of Boston. He was drowned in Boston.
61   *Nathaniel*, b. ——; m. Sept. 21, 1800, Dolly Johnson, dau. of Francis Johnson of Wo. and d. in Charlestown, where he resided.
62   *Joel*, b. ——; m. Susan Hammond of Marblehead. They resided in Charlestown, where he died.
63   *Abigail*, b. ——; m. Nathaniel Hill of West Cambridge.

18-41-   JOHN SIMONDS m. Mary Tufts. dau. of Benjamin and Mary (Hutchinson) Tufts of Med. They lived at the corner of Burlington and Grove streets. Their first six children were all bap. at one time, viz. March 11, 1770. He d. Dec. 6, 1812, aged 83.

41-64   *Lydia*, b. Jan. 13, 1757; m. James Wyman.
65   †*Ebenezer*, b. Aug. 15, 1758; m. Anne Bradbury.
66   *Mary*, b. July 19, 1761; m. July 28, 1794, John Angier of Malden.
67   *Rebecca*, b. Aug. 1, 1763; m. William Diamond.
68   †*Lemuel*, b. Aug. 26, 1765; m. Mary Maxwell of Bedford.
69   *Hannah*, b. Aug. 7, 1767; m. Aug 26, 1790, Jacob Robinson.
70   *Sarah*, b. Nov. 26, 1776; m. Nov. 3, 1800, Jonathan Locke.

26-45-   JOSHUA SIMONDS m. Jan. 5, 1794, Abigail Cutler, dau of Thomas Cutler. She was b. May 2, 1771, and d. Aug. 1837, aged 66. He d. Jan. 1, 1858, aged 88. He kept a public house in Lex. about fifty-eight years, at the foot of Fiske Hill, so called, on Monument street; and the rest of the period, commencing with 1802, at his late residence on Bedford street.

45-71   *Joseph*, b. March 1, 1795.
72   *Abigail*, b. March 14, 1797; m. June 3, 1837, Michael Crosby of Bed. as his second wife.
73   *Franklin*, b. June 10, 1799; went to Walpole, N. H. where he m. —— Spaulding.
74   †*Joshua*, b. May 29, 1801; m. Lucy J. Winn of Salem
75   *Maria*, b. June 30, 1807; d. unmarried.
76   *Otis*, b. April 17, 1810; m. Ellen Crosby, dau. of Michael Crosby, the husband of his sister Abigail by his first wife. Otis Simonds resides in Connecticut.

26-47-   WILLIAM SIMONDS m Aug. 18, 1799, Susan Pierce. dau. of Isaac and Hannah Pierce of Walt. She d. Feb. 4, 1847, in her 68th year, and he d. 1858. They were ad. to the ch. June 13, 1813. He kept a tavern on Concord avenue eighteen years, commencing with 1810.

47-77   *Their first child*, b. Dec. 13, 1799, and d. the next day.
78   *Humphrey*, b. June 6, 1801; m. Emeline Gizeley. He went to New Orleans, where he d. Sept. 7, 1835, leaving a wife and two children in Lexington.
79   *Cyrus*, b. May 9, 1803; d. April 17, 1805, by his clothes taking fire.

80 | *William*, b. Oct. 21, 1805; moved to Walt. where he m. 1836, Martha Pierce.
81 | *Jonathan Bowers*, b. Aug. 2, 1807; m. 1832, Harriet Childs of Walt. where they reside.
82 | *Susan*, b. July 18, 1809; d. Aug. 18, 1813.
83 | *Alice*, b. Dec. 3, 1811; d. March 3, 1815.
84 | *Their eighth child*, b. March 15, 1814; d. same day.
85 | †*Cyrus P.*, b. April 10, 1815; m. Mary Ann Russell.
86 | †*Eli*, b. Aug. 4, 1817; m. Elizabeth Swan.
87 | *Isaac Mason*, b. Oct. 15, 1819; d. March 21, 1821.
88 | *Rufus*, b. Feb. 10, 1822; d Dec. 17, 1832.

26–49– JONATHAN SIMONDS m. Dec. 8, 1816, Mrs. Patty Hills, wid. of Capt. S. C. Hills, and daughter of Erasmus Pierce of Boston. He fitted for college, but prefering a more active life, went to Boston. About 1809, he entered the army of the United States, was stationed at Burlington, Vt., where he was promoted to a captaincy. In 1811, he resigned his commission and returned to Boston, where he established himself as a broker, and where he d. He had two children, Albert, b. April 17, 1817, and George W., b. March 1, 1820, who resided for some years with his uncle, Eli Robbins, at East Lex. He has since gone to New York.

27–52– JOSEPH SIMONDS m. Mary Viles, dau. of Joel and Mary (Bowman) Viles. He d. Nov. 21, 1834, and she d. March 5, 1867, in her 92d year. He was representative sixteen years, selectman five years, and assessor three years. He was often placed on important committees, and was one of the leading men of the town.

52–89 | *Twins*, b. 1803; d. soon.
90 | *Eliza*, b. March 26, 1804; m. July 21, 1831, Abraham French, lives in Lowell.
91 | *Mary Ann*, b. June 6, 1806; living, unmarried.
92 | †*Joseph Frederick*, b. Oct. 26, 1810; m. Susan Mulliken.
93 | *Marcellus*, b. 1812; d. 1849, aged 36. He m. May 12, 1846, Maria Augusta Ball of Con., by whom he had Marcella Augusta. His wid. m. William Heard of Con. and now lives in Detroit.

30–59– DAVID SIMONDS m. July 23, 1795, Jerusha Locke, dau. of Reuben and Jerusha (Richardson) Locke. She d. March, 1867, aged 93.

59–94 | *Nabby*, b. Dec. 17, 1795; m. James Bailey.
95 | *Betsey*, b. June 4, 1797; m. June 6, 1819, William Walker.
96 | *Bradley*, b. Dec. 19, 1799; m. May 26, 1823, Mary A. Pierce of Wo. and moved to Ashby.
97 | *Lydia*, b. Feb. 15, 1802; d. unmarried.
98 | *Nathan*, b. April 16, 1816; m. Amanda Parks of Linc. and moved to California.

41–65– EBENEZER SIMONDS went to Med. about 1780. where he m. April 30, 1785, Anne Bradbury of that place. His children were all born in Med. On the death of his father in 1812, he returned to Lex. and took up his abode on the old homestead. He d. Aug. 23, 1845, aged 87, and she d. July 12, 1820, aged 61. They were severely afflicted in the loss of their children. He was one of the patriotic band who defied British aggression on the 19th of April, 1775.

65– 99 | *Nancy*, b. Jan. 18, 1786; d. Jan. 29, 1800.
100 | *Mary*, b. May 4, 1788; m. Thomas Hadley of Peterboro', N. H., and d. 1823.

101 | *Abigail*, b. Aug. 21, 1790; d. June 18, 1817.
102 | *Judith*, b. Aug. 27, 1792; d. May 15, 1815.
103 | †*Ebenezer*, b Feb. 6, 1795; m. Rachel Nichols, and d. Jan. 27, 1867.
104 | *Henry*, b. Dec. 22, 1797; d. Dec. 15, 1842.
105 | *Charles*, b. Aug. 6, 1801; d. Aug. 6, 1815.
106 | *Elizabeth*, } twins, b. Jan. 25, 1804; } d. Oct. 10, 1804.
107 | *William*, }
108 | *John*, b. Feb. 8, 1807; d. Dec. 30, 1823.

41–68– | LEMUEL SIMONDS m. Mary Maxwell of Bedford.

68–109 | *Betsey*, b. ———; m. William Holden of Woburn.
110 | *Daniel*, b. ———; m. Susan Stearns of Linc. where he lived and d.
111 | *Mary*, b. ———; m. ——— Jones of Boston.
112 | *Harriet*, b. ———; m. George Blake and moved into the country.
113 | *Benjamin*, b. ———; d. 1838, unmarried.
114 | *Abigail*, b. ———; m. and moved into the country.
115 | †*George*, b. Oct. 11, 1807; m. Jan. 5, 1835, Hannah Estabrook.

45–74– | JOSHUA SIMONDS m. Dec. 25, 1842, Lucy J. Winn of Salem, who was b. April 18, 1818.

71–116 | *Marcus*, b. Oct. 1, 1843.   117 *Abbie Jane*, b. Ap. 25, 1849.

47–86– | CYRUS P. SIMONDS m. June 6, 1841, Mary Ann Russell, dau. of Bill Russell of Woburn.

85–118 | *Rufus*, b. Oct. 6, 1843.   119 *Marietta G.*, b. July 18, 1845.
120 | *Cyrus W.*, b. May 26, 1848.

47–85– | ELI SIMONDS m. Sept. 4, 1842, Elizabeth Swan of West Camb. He resides on his father's homestead on Concord avenue. He has filled the principal town offices,—overseer, selectman, &c.

85–121 | *Alice*, b. June 8, 1843.
122 | *William Henry*, b. Nov. 1, 1844. 123 *Frank*, b. May 12, 1848.

52–92– | JOSEPH FREDERICK SIMONDS m. May 7, 1835, Susan Mulliken, dau. of John and Susan (Reed) Mulliken. He was selectman, 1848, '49, and assessor, 1857.

92–124 | *Mary Caroline*, b. April 1, 1836; m. Nov. 27, 1862, Dr. W. S. Miller of Boston.
125 | *Charles Frederick*, b. March 11, 1837; d. Aug. 4, 1842.
126 | *Ellen E.*, b. July 23, 1838.
127 | *Joseph*, b. July 24, 1840. He entered the U. S. service, 1861, was wounded at Malvern Hill, Va., and d. of the wound in N. Y. Hospital, Oct. 1862.
128 | *Susan*, b. Oct. 15, 1842; m. July, 1867, George D. Robinson, as his second wife.
129 | *Charles Frederick*, b. July 7, 1844.
130 | *Clara Maria*, b. Dec. 4, 1846.   131 *Augusta D.*, b. Aug. 4, 1852.

65–103– | EBENEZER SIMONDS m. Feb. 15, 1824, Rachel Nichols, dau. of Adna Nichols and Sarah (Loring), b. Aug. 7, 1797. He d. Jan. 27, 1867, aged 72.

103–132 | *Susan*, b. Dec. 8, 1824; d. Oct. 7, 1825.
133 | *Henry L.*, b. March 28, 1826; unmarried.

134 | *Francis K.*, b. Aug. 22, 1828; m. June 1, 1853, Charlotte B. Swett, wid. of Rev. William Gray Swett, and dau. of Elias Phinney, Esq. Their children are *Henry*, b. July 10, 1854, in Burlington, Vt., where they then resided, and *Franklin P.*, b. in Lex. June 25, 1856. She had by her first husband one dau. C. B. W. G. Swett, b. Feb. 8, 1843.

135 | *Susan L.*, b. March 25, 1832; d. March 5, 1839.
136 | *Rachel Ann,* } twins, b. March 10, 1836; { d. March 7, 1839.
137 | *Mary E.,* } { d. Oct. 14, 1838.

68-115- | GEORGE SIMONDS m. Jan. 5, 1835, Hannah Estabrook, dau. of Attai Estabrook.

115-138 | *John*, b. April 23, 1836; m. Katy Louisa Nichols of Charlestown, where they reside.
139 | *George*, b. June 14, 1838; m. Dec. 28, 1863, Mary E. Bannoñ.
140 | *Phidelia*, b. Dec. 21, 1840.   141 *Rosanna*, b. Dec. 16, 1842.
142 | *Anna*, b. March 29, 1848.   143 *Ella*, b. Nov. 25, 1853.

THE SMITH FAMILY.

In looking into the early records of almost any town in the Commonwealth, we should naturally expect to find the name of *Smith*; and if *John* himself was not there, we should infer that he had left his kinsmen, *Joseph*, and *Thomas*, and *Samuel*, and had gone on a tour to visit his old friend, Mr. *Jones*. In regard to Lex. we are not left to matters of inference; for in looking at the first tax ever imposed by the parish, in 1693, we find that both *John* and *Thomas* are there, acting the part of good citizens, by contributing to the support of religious institutions. But though we have record evidence that John and Thomas were at Camb. Farms in 1693, we are not so certain whence they came or who were their ancestors. The Smiths were so numerous in Wat., Lex., and other neighboring towns, and the Christian names of John and Joseph and Thomas and Samuel being so common in all the families, it becomes exceedingly difficult to trace them and preserve the personal identity, or even the family to which any one of them belongs. Living as they did, and still do, on the borders of the town, near the line of Wat. and Walt., there will, almost as a matter of course, be some passing and repassing of the town line, which increases the difficulty in making the genealogy perfectly accurate.

According to the best information we can obtain, the Lex. Smiths came from Wat. On the earliest list of proprietors of that town, in 1636, are four of the name of Smith, viz., John, sen., John, jr., Thomas, and Francis.

1 | JOHN SMITH, sen., had a wife by the name of Isabella, who d. Oct. 12, 1639, aged 60 years. It is probable that John and Isabella were the parents of John, jr., and Thomas, and perhaps of Francis and Daniel. John, sen., d. July 12, 1639, aged 60.

1- 2 | *John*, ad. freeman, May 22, 1639. He may have been the John Smith who d. in Lancaster in 1669.
3 | *Francis* was ad. freeman, May 18, 1631.
4 | *Daniel* was a resident in Wat. as early as 1642.
5 | †*Thomas* came to America in the summer of 1635, and was ad. freeman, May 17, 1637.

1-5- | THOMAS SMITH m. Mary, dau. of William Knapp. He d. March 10, 1693, aged 92.

5- 6 | *James*, b. Sept. 18, 1637; he moved to Lancaster.
7 | *John*, b. and d. Nov. 1639.
8 | †*Thomas*, b. Aug. 26, 1640; d. in Lex. Dec. 25, 1727.
9 | †*John*, b. Dec. 10, 1641; m: Mary Reeves.
10 | †*Joseph*, b. June 10, 1643; d. June, 1711.
11 | *Mary*. b. ——; m. 1667, John Stratton.
12 | *Ephraim*, b. —— blind, a town charge from 1707 to 1737.
13 | *Jonathan*, b. 1659; ad. freeman 1690.
14 | *Sarah*, d. before her father, leaving children.

5-8- | THOMAS SMITH m. 1663, Mary Hosmer, dau. of James Hosmer of Con., where his eldest three children were born. He moved to Lex., where he and his wife were ad. to the ch. June, 1701, by a letter of dismission from Weymouth. He was taxed here in 1693, and in 1700 we find honorable mention of him. In the delicate work of seating the meeting house, we find that John Stone and Thomas Smith, "were Plast in y° fore seatt of y° body of seats." He d. Dec. 25, 1727, aged 88, and she d. Oct. 1, 1719, aged 64. Their names and deaths are inscribed on one stone in the Lex. Old Grave Yard.

8-15 | †*Thomas*, b. Concord; m. Mary ——.
16 | *James*, b. in Concord; d. of casualty in Wat. in 1674.
17 | *John*, b. in Concord.
18 | *Samuel*, bap. in Wat.; d. April 22, 1670.
19 | †*Joseph*, b. March 4, 1687; bap. in Wat.; m. Hannah Tidd.
20 | †*Benjamin*, b. Sept. 24, 1689.

5-9- | JOHN SMITH m. April 1, 1665, Mary Beers.

9-21 | *Mary*, b. June 15, 1667.
22 | †*John*, b. Aug. 8, 1668.　　　23 *Abigail*, b. June 29, 1670.
24 | *Hannah*, b. Dec. 27, 1672; m. Oct. 20, 1693, William Fiske.
25 | *Sarah*, b. June 7, 1675.　　　25½ *Samuel*, b. March 10, 1680.

5-10- | JOSEPH SMITH m. Dec. 1, 1674, Hannah Tidd, dau. of John and Rebecca Tidd, then of Wo. but afterwards of Lexington.

10-26 | *Joseph*, b. April 19, 1677.
27 | *John*, b. April 5, 1678; m. Jan. 15, 1713, Jane Barnard. She d. in Lex. Sept. 16, 1763, aged 86; said to be of Waltham.
28 | †*Daniel*, b. Sept. 26, 1681; m. 1708, Mary Burridge of Newton.
29 | *Hannah*, bap. Dec. 4, 1687; m. 1708, David Mead.
30 | *Rebecca*, bap. Dec. 4, 1687.

8-15- | THOMAS SMITH m. Mary ——. They were ad. to the ch. in Lex. March 12, 1710. It is supposed that he returned to Wat. and probably m. a second wife, Abigail, by whom he had *Abigail* and *Ruth*, and d. 1736.

8-19- | JOSEPH SMITH m. Oct. 14, 1701, Mary Richards, b. May 15, 1680, dau. of William and Mary Richards of Wat. They were in Lex. as early as 1702, their first child being bap. that year.

19-31 | *Mary*, b. April 3, 1701.
32 | *William*, b. June 25, 1703; d. Feb. 7, 1728.

33   †*Hezekiah*, b. April 2, 1706; m. Feb. 24, 1725, Elizabeth Wellington.
34   ‡*Ebenezer*, b. Aug. 15, 1708; m. Abigail, wid. of Benjamin Wellington, jr.
35   *Joseph*, b. Aug. 30, 1711; d. young.
36   †*Samuel*, b. June 14, 1714; d. May 4, 1760.
37   *Hannah*, b. Jan. 21, 1716; m. Feb. 19, 1737, Timothy Davis, Bed.
38   *Joseph*, b. June 4, 1719; d. Nov. 11, 1740.
39   *Abigail*, b. Sept. 6, 1722; m. Feb. 22, 1746, Henry Gale of Weston.
40   †*Josiah*, b. July 6, 1724; m. Sarah Francis.

8-20-   BENJAMIN SMITH m. July 9, 1713, Martha Comee. She d. Nov. 19, 1749, and he m. May 3, 1750, Mrs. Esther Green. He d. Dec. 9, 1779, aged 90. He was for a long time very popular with his townsmen, being often elected to public office. He was twelve years on the board of selectmen. They had the misfortune to lose five of their children young.

20-41   †*Benjamin*, b. July 20, 1714; m. Anna Parker.
42   *Daniel*, b. Dec. 15, 1715; d. Feb. 8, 1740.
43   *Ezekiel*, b. April 28, 1717; d. Dec. 12, 1739.
44   *Martha*, b. June 3, 1720; d. Sept. 26, 1728.
45   *Thomas*, b. Aug. 11, 1723; d. May 27, 1726.
46   *Solomon*, b. Sept. 11, 1725; d. July 26, 1733.
47   †*Thomas*, b. April 15, 1727.

9-22-   JOHN SMITH m. Mary ——. He was probably the John Smith who was taxed at Camb. Farms in 1793; but did not reside there permanently till some time after, as his name is not upon the tax bills for several of the subsequent years. Probably the John Smith who d. Feb. 4, 1743.

22-48   *Isaac*, b. Sept. 20, 1695.   49   *Sarah*, b. Feb. 3, 1698.
50   *Eunice*, b. Sept. 1, 1704.   51   *Obadiah*, b. May 10, 1708.
52   †*Jesse*, b. April 1, 1711; m. April 26, 1733, Experience Ward of Westboro'.

10-28-   DANIEL SMITH m. May 25, 1708, Mary Burridge of Newton. She was ad. to the ch. in Lex. May 26, 1717, and four of their children were bap., viz., Mary, Jonathan, Betsey, and Lydia, Nov. 2, 1718. He d. March 5, 1757.

28-53   *Mary*, b. March 13, 1709; m. Dec. 30, 1730, Jabez Wyman of Wo.
54   *Daniel*, b. March 10, 1711.
55   †*Jonathan*, b. Oct. 15, 1713; m. Abigail Stratton.
56   *Betsey*, b. Feb. 11, 1715.   57   *Lydia*, b. May 3, 1718.
58   *Sarah*, b. July 28, 1723; m. Jan. 14, 1742, Abiel Richardson.
59   *Lucy*, b. June 3, 1725; m. Benjamin Wellington of Brookfield.
60   *Abigail*, b. Feb. 22, 1728.
61   *Eunice*, b. June 4, 1730; m. Jan. 4, 1750, Joseph Underwood.

19-33-   HEZEKIAH SMITH m. Feb. 14, 1726, Elizabeth Wellington of Wat. He d. Oct. 16, 1760, and his wid. m. May 18, 1762, Dea. James Brown. They were ad. to the ch. Sept. 26, 1736. He was selectman, 1756.

33-62   †*Abijah*, b. Feb. 26, 1727; m. Jan. 18, 1750, Mary Lawrence.
63   *Elizabeth*, b. July 9, 1728; m. 1750, Amos Tidd.
64   *Kezia*, b. Nov. 30, 1734; m. April 3, 1751, Samuel Green.
65   †*William*, b. Jan. 16, 1736; m. Abigail Smith.

66 †*Joseph*, b. May 21, 1743; m. first, Lucy Stone, second, Abigail Ingoldsby.

67 *Sarah*, b. March 28, 1746.   68 *Amos*, b. April 14, 1748.

69 *Hannah*, b. April 14, 1750.

19-34-   EBENEZER SMITH m. Abigail Wellington, wid. of Benjamin Wellington, jr. They were very unfortunate in their children, having lost four in three years. He was a member of Capt. Parker's co. in 1775, and was called to Camb. May 10, and June 17, 1775.

34-70 †*Ebenezer*, b. Sept. 20, 1740; m. Dec. 29, 1763, Priscilla Diamond.

71 *Mary*, b. Dec. 23, 1743; d. Dec. 1, 1756.

72 *Abigail*, b. Dec. 2, 1746; d. June 28, 1753.

73 *Thaddeus*, b. Nov. 24, 1748; d. 1753.

74 *Ezekiel*, b. April 15, 1751; d. June 26, 1753.

75 *Thaddeus*, b. Sept. 25, 1753; one of Capt. Parker's company.

19-36-   SAMUEL SMITH m. Mary ——. He d. May 1, 1760, aged 46 years, and she d. Sept. 8, 1763, aged 46 years. We find no record of the birth of their first seven children, yet the papers connected with the settlement of his estate, show that he had the children named below, and their birth must have been nearly as set down.

36-76 *Mary*, b. about 1737.

77 *Lucy*, b. about 1739; m. Benjamin Wellington of Brookfield.

78 †*Samuel*, b. about 1741; m. Aug. 30, 1764, Abigail Harrington.

79 *Anna*, b. about 1743; m. April 10, 1764, Simeon Leonard of Bridgewater.

80 *Amos*, b. about 1746.   81 *Jonathan*, b. about 1748.

82 *Elizabeth*, b. about 1751.

83 *Abigail*, b. March 27, 1754; d. June 1, 1757.

84 †*John*, b. Aug. 21, 1756; m. Nov. 15, 1781, Sarah Lawrence of Lex.

85 *Abigail*, b. April 3, 1759.

19-40-   JOSIAH SMITH m. Nov. 15, 1750, Sarah Francis of Medford. She d. April 27, 1757, and he m. Jan. 1, 1758, Hannah Brown. He was one of the brave defenders of his country's rights on the 19th of April, 1775. He was selectman several years.

40-86 *Josiah*, b. Dec. 1, 1751; d. July 1, 1753.

87 †*Josiah*, b. Nov. 26, 1753; m. Feb. 6, 1777, Polly Barber.

88 †*Abraham*, b. July 23, 1755; m. Martha Bowman.

89 *Ebenezer*, b. Dec. 4, 1758; d. unm. Sept. 1777.

90 *Sarah*, b. July 26, 1760; m. Sept. 30, 1779, David Penney.

91 *Hannah*, b. July 13, 1762.

92 †*Isaac*, b. Feb. 1, 1764; m. Aug. 6, 1798, Sally Iles.

93 †*Jacob*, b. June 24, 1765; m. Susan Pierce of Waltham.

94 *Susanna*, b. May 22, 1767; m. Reuben Pierce.

95 *Elijah*, b. May 28, 1769; m. Lydia Stearns of Walt.; d. in Med.

96 †*Joel*, b. June 1, 1771.

20-41-   BENJAMIN SMITH m. Nov. 17, 1734, Anna Parker, who d. a wid. in Walt. June 10, 1768.

41-97 *Solomon*, b. Oct. 27, 1738; d. April 16, 1741.

98 †*Benjamin*, b. March 11, 1741.

99 *Anna*, b. March 31, 1743; m. William Munroe, son of William and Sarah.

100 *Martha*, b. April 19, 1745; m. May 27, 1771, Ebenezer Munroe.

101 | *Esther*, b. April 10, 1751; m. Simeon Snow of Holden, and d. Jan. 14, 1780.
102 | *David*, b. Aug. 15, 1756. He was a member of Capt. Parker's co.
103 | *Thomas*, b. July 24, 1760; m. Oct. 3, 1782, Sarah Taylor, Charlest.

20–17– | THOMAS SMITH m. April 12, 1753, Sarah Raymond. They lived probably in Wo. now Burlington; for in 1751, they were ad. to the ch. in Lex. by a letter of dismission from the second church in Wo.

47–104 | *Solomon*, b. June 12, 1754.
105 | *Ezekiel*, b. Nov. 24, 1755. 106 perhaps *Sarah*, b. ———.

22–52– | JESSE SMITH m. April 26, 1733, Experience Ward of Westboro', dau. of Oliver and Hannah (Brigham) Ward of Northboro'.

52–107 | *Abiezer*, b. May 2, 1734.
108 | *Israel*, b. Aug. 26, 1735. 109 *Elizabeth*,?

28–55– | JONATHAN SMITH m. Aug. 30, 1738, Abigail Stratton of Walt. He d. March 23, 1801, aged 88. He was one of the sons of liberty in the Battle of Lexington, and was called to Camb. on the 17th of June, 1775. He was on the board of selectmen, 1771. He was a lieutenant in the militia.

55–110 | *Abigail*, b. May 29, 1739; m. William Smith.
111 | *John*, b. Aug. 12, 1743.
112 | *Dorcas*, b. June 3, 1746; m. April 4, 1764, John Wood of Camb.
113 | †*Jonathan*, b. Oct. 4, 1748; d. Nov. 29, 1819, aged 71.
114 | *Phinehas*, b. Feb. 7, 1751; d. in Charlestown.
115 | *Timothy*, b. Aug. 11, 1753; ad. to the ch. Sept. 17, 1775.
116 | *Susanna*, b. Jan. 7, 1756; m. March 25, 1784, Lydia Pierce, Walt.
117 | *Daniel*, bap. April 24, 1758; m. and d. in Charlestown.
118 | *Amasa*, bap. May 9, 1762; d. Oct. 10, 1812.
119 | *Nathan*, bap. March 25, 1764; m. April 24, 1794, Katharine Bacon. They moved to Fitzwilliam, N. H., where he d. 1853.

33–62– | ABIJAH SMITH m. Jan. 18, 1750, Mary Lawrence, dau. of Jonathan and Elizabeth Lawrence, b. Nov. 30, 1729. She d. May 22, 1775. He was generally known as "Lieut. Smith."

62–120 | *Abijah*, bap. Sept. 1, 1750.
121 | *A child*, which d. Oct. 8, 1760. 122 *Mary*, bap. Jan. 11, 1761.

33–65– | WILLIAM SMITH m. Oct. 20, 1757, Abigail Smith, dau. of Jonathan and Abigail (Stratton) Smith of Lex. He d. 1811, aged 75. He was a member of Capt. Parker's co., and was in service both on the 19th of April, and on the 17th of June, 1775.

65–123 | *Abigail*, bap. Aug. 20, 1758; m. Sylvanus Wood of Burlington.
124 | †*William*, bap. Dec. 27, 1761; m. Jan. 22, 1789, Jane Pierce, Walt.
125 | *Lydia*, b. July 3, 1764; m. May 21, 1789, Abner Matthews of Line.
126 | *Betty*, bap. Dec. 4, 1765; m. Jonas Bacon of Bed. They moved to Billerica.
127 | *Amos*, bap. Oct. 8, 1775; d. in infancy.

33–66– | JOSEPH SMITH m. Jan. 17, 1765, Lucy Stone. She d. June 29, 1772, and he m. second, March 13, 1777, Abigail Ingoldsby of Lex., b. Oct. 13, 1750. He was on the Common on the 19th of April, when the British fired upon the Americans, was afterwards captain, and d. Aug. 19, 1805.

66-128 *Joseph*, b. Nov. 8, 1765; d. Feb. 26, 1766.
129 *Joseph*, b. Jan. 26, 1767; m. Susan Dakin of Maine.
130 *Hezekiah*, b. April 17, 1769. He went to Providence.
131 †*Jonas*, b. March 19, 1771; m. Polly Underwood.
132 *Lucy*, b. Feb. 25, 1778; m. Enoch Cory of Marlboro'.
133 *John Ingoldsby*, b. Aug. 30, 1779. He moved to Providence.
134 *Betsey*, b. Sept. 14, 1781. She m. a Tileston and moved to Windsor, Vt.
135 †*Amos*, b. Feb. 12, 1784; m. Catharine S. Langdon of Boston.
136 *Timothy*, b. Oct. 27, 1786.
137 *James Milledge*, b. April 4, 1790.
138 *Abigail Cook*, b. June 29, 1792; m. Jonas Munroe.
139 *Ralph*, b. March 26, 1795; m. 1816, Rebecca Belcher. She d. Aug. 1, 1829, and he m. March 4, 1830, Mrs. Anna M. (Adams) Hopkins. He d. June 2, 1853. He resided in Boston. He had a family of eleven children, seven of whom are married.
140 †*Billings*, b. Oct. 6, 1797; d. May 3, 1847.

34-70- EBENEZER SMITH m. Dec. 29, 1763, Priscilla Diamond. He was one who was called to Camb. during the Battle of Bunker Hill. She d. Sept. 18, 1773.

70-141 *Mary*, b. Oct. 17, 1764. 142 *Diamond*, b. Nov. 25, 1767.
143 *Ezekiel*, b. March 26, 1769.
144 *Edmund*, b. June 21, 1771; d. Jan. 16, 1772.
145 *Lucy*, b. April 11, 1773.

36-78- SAMUEL SMITH m. Aug. 30, 1764, Elizabeth Harrington. They were ad. to the ch. Nov. 25, 1764, when their first child was bap. About 1768, they removed to New Hampshire. In 1772, Samuel and Elizabeth Smith were dismissed to "Mason, N. H., in order to the gathering of a church there." They may have had other children.

78-146 *Samuel*, bap. Nov. 25, 1764. 147 *Elizabeth*, bap. Feb. 1, 1767.

36-84- JOHN SMITH m. Nov. 15, 1784, Sarah Lawrence, dau. of Bezaleel Lawrence. We confess our inability to trace *John Smith*, or to keep a record of his whereabout. His name appears on the tax bill from 1784 to 1788; but in 1789, we find that the assessors of that year, inserted his name as though he was an inhabitant, and erased it as though he was not.

40-87- JOSIAH SMITH m. Feb. 6, 1777, Polly Barber of Lex. He d. Nov. 20, 1826, of leprosy, aged 73. He and his wife were ad. to the ch. May 14, 1780. She was a dau. of a captain in the British service. She d. May 10, 1838, aged 84. He was in Capt. Parker's co. at the opening of the Revolution. He was an asssessor six or eight years.

87-148 *Polly*, b. Jan. 2, 1777; m. March 7, 1799, Abijah Pierce of Lex.
149 †*Ebenezer*, b. Dec. 1, 1780; m. Anna Underwood.
150 *Sarah*, b. Nov. 29, 1785; m. Feb. 4, 1808, Abner B. Phelps of Derby, Vt.
151 †*Josiah*, b. April 17, 1789; m Lucinda Wyman of Medford.
152 †*Elias*, b. July 21, 1792; m. Harriet Hastings.
153 *Maria*, b. Jan. 17, 1796; m. June 20, 1814, Nathan Brooks of Wo.

40-88- ABRAHAM SMITH m. May 8, 1788, Martha Bowman. He was ad. to the ch. May 25, 1777. He d. Jan. 9, 1826, aged 70, and she d. Aug. 22, 1839, aged 81. He was one of the heroes of the opening scene of the Revolution in 1775.

88-154 *Oliver*, bap. April 19, 1789; he is now living, in his 79th year.
155 *William Bowman*, bap. Feb. 23, 1794; m. Dec. 10, 1835, Mary Smith, dau. of Isaac and Mary. He d. Nov. 7, 1867. Children, Abram B., b. May 18, 1836, m. March 23, 1862, Annette A. Allen, and has Mary L., b. Dec. 8, 1862, Lottie A., b. March 10, 1865; Edwin Oliver, b. March 23, 1839, d. Sept. 10, 1849; Martha B. b. June 28, 1831.

40-92- ISAAC SMITH m. Aug. 6, 1798, Sally Iles. He d. Dec. 6, 1840, aged 77. She d. Sept. 25, 1861, aged 86.

92-156 *Eliza*, b. Jan. 22, 1800; m. March 24, 1831, Charles Blodgett.
157 *Susan Pierce*, b. July 21, 1801; m. May 18, 1823, Francis Kittridge Dudley of Weston.
158 *Mary*, b. Jan. 16, 1803; m. 1835, William Bowman Smith.
159 †*John*, b. Oct. 17, 1804; m. Oct. 16, 1831, Hannah Fillebrown.
160 *Martha Bowman*, b. Jan. 20, 1809; d. May 30, 1851, unm.

40-93- JACOB SMITH m. Susan Pierce of Walt. She d. April 9, 1735, aged 62; he d. Aug. 3, 1844, aged 79.

93-161 *Isaac Brooks*, b. Jan. 16, 1803; m. Nov. 24, 1829, Mary Russell, dau. of Nathan and Sybil Russell. She d. May 15, 1849, aged 45, and he m. second, May 19, 1850, Sarah Poor. He had by his first wife *Mary Frances*, b. Sept. 10, 1830, d. April 26, 1847; *Susan Pierce*, b. March 9, 1836, d. Sept. 21, 1849.
162 †*William Henry*, b. Jan. 7, 1809; m. Susan B. Cutter.

40-96- JOEL SMITH m. Sept. 21, 1794, Elizabeth Stearns of Walt. She d. April 1, 1836, and he m. second, June 9, 1839, wid. Zerviah Hall of Brewster.

96-163 *Lois*, b. Feb. 18, 1795; m. first, June 9, 1822, Jonathan Sanderson, and second, June 19, 1832, Patrick Sullivan.
164 †*Joshua Stearns*, b. May 9, 1796; m. April 24, 1822, Maria Lawrence.
165 *Levi*, b. Aug. 10, 1798; d. Feb. 8, 1799.
166 *Levi*, b. Aug. 5, 1800; d. Oct. 5, same year.
167 *Isaac*, b. Aug. 31, 1803. He r. in Manchester, N. H.
168 *Eli Francis*, b. Nov. 24, 1805; m. wid. Livermore, r. in Waltham.
169 *Priscilla*, b. Oct. 14, 1808; m. Darius Wellington of Waltham.
170 *James*, b. Dec. 2, 1813; d. unmarried.

41-98- BENJAMIN SMITH m. Mary Lee. They were ad. to the ch. June 24, 1768.

98-171 *Anna*, b. April 2, 1770; m. Abijah Wyman of Burlington.
172 *Benjamin*, b. Sept. 1, 1774. He went to Townsend, where he m. a Turner, and was killed by the upsetting of a cart.
173 *David*, b. Sept. 29, 1776. He went to Ashby and m. a Foster.

41-103- THOMAS SMITH m. Oct. 3, 1782, Sarah Taylor of Charlestown, b. March 12, 1760. He d. Aug. 11, 1807.

103-174 *Sarah*, b. Oct. 17, 1783; m. John Underwood.
175 *Abigail*, b. March 30, 1785; m. Sept. 27, 1809, David Tuttle.

176 | *Thomas*, b. June 12, 1788; d. Aug. 12. 1809, unm.
177 | *William Taylor*, b. Aug. 3, 1789; m. May 27, 1812, Cynthia Child of Gardner. They are both living. No issue.
178 | *Charles*, b. July 27, 1791; m. Hannah Hammond.
179 | *Patty*, b. Aug. 10, 1793; m. David Tuttle as his second wife.
180 | *Jonas Leonard*, b. June 11, 1795; d. March 16, 1801.
181 | *Larkin*, b. Oct. 15, 1797; m. Lucy S. Smith, dau. of Jonas.
182 | †*Ebenezer R.*, b. Dec. 3, 1799; m. Almira Reed.
183 | *Jonas Leonard*, b. April 10, 1803; m. Sarah Cowley of Wat. They had a child which d. young. He d. Dec. 10, 1815.

55–113– JONATHAN SMITH m. first, June 15, 1771. Lydia Muzzy. She d. Nov. 7, 1785, and he m. second, Oct. 16, 1788, Abigail Marrett. She d. March 30, 1794, and he m. third, March 17, 1795, Ruth Fiske, dau. of Dr. Joseph and Hepzibah Fiske. He had four children by his first wife, three by his second, and four by his third. He d. Nov. 29, 1819, aged 71. He resided on Main street, on the place owned by Mr. Cotterell. He was a tanner.

113–184 | *Susanna*, b. March 4, 1772; m. Nov. 27, 1794, Joshua Russell.
185 | *Rhoda*, b. April 29, 1774; d. same day.
186 | *Samuel*, b. Feb. 6, 1778; d. same day.
187 | *Samuel*, b. April 15, 1780.
188 | *Harriet*, b. Jan. 6, 1791; m. Jan. 1, 1823, Imla Parker.
189 | *Cyrus*, a twin, b. Dec. 20, 1792. He went to Boston, where he had a family.
190 | *Augustus*, a twin, b. Dec. 20, 1792; he was found drowned in a watering trough, unmarried.
191 | *Hepzibah*, b. Oct. 5, 1795; m. April 19, 1821, Benjamin Eaton of Woburn.
192 | *Abigail*, b. May 16, 1797; m. Joseph Johnson.
193 | *Ruth*, b. June 30, 1799; m. Lot Eaton of Woburn.
194 | *Jonathan*, b. May 16, 1802; left Lex. and never returned.

65–124– WILLIAM SMITH m. Jan. 22, 1789, Jane Pierce of Walt. dau. of Ephraim and Lucy (White) Pierce. Record very defective. He d. Oct. 13, 1846, aged 85. She d. March 11, 1850, aged 81.

124–195 | *Abigail*, b. ———.
196 | *Lovina*, b. ———; m. Oliver Locke.

66–131– JONAS SMITH m. March 26, 1798, Polly Underwood. He d. Sept. 12, 1811.

131–197 | *Mary Munroe*, b. Oct. 28, 1798; m. John C. Bracket of Woburn.
198 | *Lucy Stone*, b. July 29, 1802; m. Dec. 26, 1824, Larkin Smith.
199 | *Sophronia*, b. Sept. 6, 1807; m. Orin Knapp of Somerville.

66–135– AMOS SMITH m. April 7, 1808, Catharine S. Langdon, dau. of Judge Timothy Langdon of Wiscasset, Me. He went to Boston, when a young man, and was in trade as a druggist. He d. July 19, 1816, aged 32: she d. May 20, 1857, aged 83 years.

135–200 | *Sarah Langdon*, b. July 21, 1809; d. July 18, 1825.
201 | *Lucy Catharine*, b. Oct. 1, 1811; m. Oct. 6, 1831, John H. Rogers.

203 | *Amos*, b. Nov. 29, 1816, after the death of his father. He grad. H. C. 1838, entered the ministry, and was settled in Boston, Dec. 7, 1842, colleague with Rev. Dr. Parkman. In 1848, he left Boston, and was settled, Nov. 26 of that year, at Leominster. In 1856, he left Leominster, and took charge of a new society at Belmont. He was installed over that society, April 26, 1857.

66-140- | BILLINGS SMITH m. Nov. 19, 1820, Sarah C. Blodgett. She d. May 30, 1836, aged 35, and he m. second, March 8, 1837, Maria A. Winship. He d. May 3, 1847, aged 50. He was a captain.

140-204 | †*Billings*, b. Sept. 25, 1821; m. Feb. 10, 1847, Martha Child, Walt.
205 | *Ellen A.*, b. July 29, 1824; m. Feb. 10, 1846, Joseph A. Wellington.
206 | *James M.*, b. June 8, 1827; d. in California.
207 | *Sarah C.*, b. May 9, 1836.
208 | *George M.*, b. July 15, 1842; d. Sept. 24, 1843.

87-149- | EBENEZER SMITH m. Dec. 5, 1807, Anna Underwood. She d. Sept. 6, 1849, aged 65. He d. June 15, 1860, aged 79.

149-209 | *Mary Ann*, b. April 21, 1811; m. April 7, 1835, Isaac Childs. She d. 1859.
210 | *Emily Jane*, b. Sept. 20, 1813; d. Sept. 20, 1817.
211 | *Maria*, b. Jan. 10, 1816; m. Feb. 20, 1834, W. F. Adams of Acton. She m. second, Jonas Hanscomb of Moultonboro', N. H.
212 | *Emily Jane*, b. July 18, 1818; d. June 28, 1820.
213 | *Elizabeth Nichols*, b. Aug. 8, 1820; m. Ap. 8, 1841, Alonzo Goddard.
214 | *Adeline,* b. Oct. 28, 1822; m. May 1, 1842, Sam. Cooper of Charlest.
215 | *Addison,* b. Oct. 28, 1822; m. June 22, 1846, Dorcas Ireland of Som.
216 | *Dorcas Wade*, b. Sept. 5, 1824; m. Elbridge Farmer of W. Camb.
217 | *Josiah*, b. July 23, 1827; m. Nov. 22, 1849, Aurilla Snow.

81-151- | JOSIAH SMITH m. May, 1817, Lucinda Wyman of Med. She d. April 4, 1853, aged 60. He is living, in the 79th year of his age, as spry and active as most men at sixty. He has been long and extensively known as a master of the fife. Commencing at an early age, he has played nearly seventy years for military companies. Such has been his reputation as a fifer, that he has been engaged by some of the most celebrated companies in the State, to play for them on their annual parades and on festive occasions. The Ancient and Honorable Artillery Company have been regaled by his music on their annual parade for the last half century, and thousands of our citizens, from Bangor, Me., to Alexandria, Va., have been excited to patriotic emotions by the piercing notes of his favorite instrument. Nor has his labor in this line been confined to the " piping times of peace." In the war of 1812, he was three months in the service, and in the late war many a soldier has left the Commonwealth to defend our free institutions, with his breast heaving with patriotism excited by the music of this venerable fifer.

151-218 | *James T.*, b. April 19, 1819; d. Aug. 11, 1821.
219 | *Oliver*, b. Dec. 6, 1820; m. Dec. 20, 1849, Louisa Porter.
220 | *Emeline L.*, b. Aug. 17, 1822; m. Jan. 21, 1841, Charles Clark.
221 | *Caroline*, b. July 9, 1824; m. March 3, 1844, John Earle, jr.
222 | *George H.*, b. June 11, 1826; m. Jan. 9, 1851, Eliza Melvin.
223 | *Charles C.*, b. May 2, 1829; d. April 6, 1830.
224 | *Charles C.*, b. Jan. 5, 1831; m. Lucinda Brown.

225 | *Josiah Granville*, b. June 16, 1833; m. Oct. 29, 1862, Georgia L. Houghton.

226 | *Ethalinda Jane*, b. May 25, 1840; m. Aug. 15, 1861, Francis M. Sawyer.

87-152- | ELIAS SMITH m. Aug. 8, 1819, Harriet Hastings, dau. of Samuel and Lydia Hastings, b. July 12, 1795.

152-227 | *Sarah Phelps*, b. May 8, 1820; m. March 28, 1839, Ebenezer Whittum. They reside in Boston, and have one child.

228 | *Mary Robbins*, b. Aug. 5, 1821; m. Oct. 7, 1846, David Hall of Walpole. They r. in Lexington.

229 | *Julia Ann*, b. July 31, 1823; m. Dec. 3, 1846, George Arnold of Charlestown.

230 | *James Hastings*, b. Aug. 11, 1825; m. June, 1849, Eliza A. Arenburg of Lunenburg, Nova Scotia.

231 | *Elias Everett*, b. Aug. 7, 1827; m. May 27, 1854, Melvina J. Meers of Hartford, Vt.; r. in Belmont.

232 | *Albert Bradford*, b. June 9, 1829; m. Sarah A. Bryant. They have Etta A., b. Sept. 4, 1863.

92-159- | JOHN SMITH m. Oct. 16, 1831, Hannah Fillebrown of W. Camb.

159-233 | *Adeline R.*, b. Sept. 15, 1832; m. Sept. 12, 1858, Francis H. Kneeland of Sweden, Me.; r. in Lex. He served three years in the late war. They have Ada F., b. July 19, 1861.

234 | *John F.*, b. Nov. 20, 1834; d. Aug. 24, 1856.

93-162- | WILLIAM HENRY SMITH m. Nov. 29, 1834, Susan B. Cutter, dau. of Stephen and Sally (Barker) Cutter. She d. Sept. 18, 1857, aged 48.

162-235 | *George Henry*, b. May 11, 1841. He was three years in the service of the United States in the Rebellion.

236 | *Susan Rebecca*, b. June 29, 1843.

237 | *Sarah Jane*, b. March 11, 1846.

238 | *Mary Frances*, b. July 8, 1848.

96-164- | JOSHUA S. Smith m. April 24, 1822, Maria Lawrence, dau. of Phinehas Lawrence. He d. Jan. 7, 1865.

164-239 | *Levi James*, b. May 15, 1823; m. Laura A. George of Cornish, Vt.; r. in Lex. till about 1852.

240 | *Charles L.*, b. Nov. 16, 1824; m. Patience Clarke of Me. They are now residing in Charlton.

241 | *Alden Bradford*, b. Aug. 1, 1829; m. Hannah Clarke of East Camb. r. in Lexington.

242 | *Meline Augusta*, b. Jan. 28, 1830.

243 | *Maria Louisa*, b. Dec. 6, 1832; d. Jan. 21, 1852.

244 | *Windsor*, b. April 19, 1836; m. Anna Ford of Provincetown; r. in Boston.

245 | *Anna Arbelle*, b. Oct. 25, 1840; d. Oct. 7, 1854.

246 | *Marshall Brown*, b. March 8, 1843.

103-182- | EBENEZER R. SMITH m. Jan. 29, 1829, Almira Reed. She d. Feb. 12, 1860, aged 56.

182-247 | *Sarah E.*, b. Oct. 27, 1829; m. April 23, 1851, Edmund Reed, Bur.

248 | *Eustis R.*, b. March 6, 1832; d. Dec. 10, 1832.

249 | *Almira J.*, b. Oct. 1, 1833; d. Nov. 22, 1834.
250 | *Almira Jane*, b. Oct. 24, 1835.   251 *Eustis Reed*, b. June 30, 1839.
252 | *Octavia*, b. July 16, 1841.

140-204- | BILLINGS SMITH m. Feb. 10, 1847, Martha Childs, dau. of Isaac Childs of Walt. He traded several years in Lexington, where he now resides, but is doing business in Boston, in the grain line.

204-253 | *Billings*, b. July 19, 1848.   254 *Lucy R.*, b. Nov. 18, 1850.
255 | *Martha E.*, b. April 29, 1853.   256 *Ralph*, b. Sept. 28, 1857.
257 | *Alice M.*, b. Feb. 24, 1867.

1 | WILLIAM SMITH b. May 26, 1794, in Walt.; came to Lex. Jan. 8, 1819, m. April, 1820, Mary Fiske, dau. of Isaac and Sarah (Flagg) Fiske of Walt. She d. March 19, 1823, leaving one child. He m. July 22, 1824, Mary C. Green, dau. of Jonas and Hannah (Child) Green of Walt. She d. Feb. 13, 1829. She had two children. He m. Nov. 1832, Joan, wid. of Oliver Locke. Capt. William Smith, though not a Lexington man by birth, is from the same parent stock as the families above traced. He was son of *Elijah* Smith, b Jan. 30, 1760, who was the son of *Jonas* Smith, b. June 7, 1719, who was the son of *Zachariah* Smith, b. May 16, 1687, who was the son of *Jonathan* (No. 13 in the foregoing table of the Smith family), and Jonathan was a brother of *Thomas, John,* and *Joseph,* who settled in Lex., and they were sons of Thomas, who was born in England and came to this country, 1635, with his father, John.

1- 2 | *William H.*, b. Dec. 22, 1820; he resides in Boston.
3 | *Franklin G.*, b. May 23, 1825; d. Sept. 19, 1826.
4 | *Charles G.*, b. Sept. 25, 1827; d. March 25, 1829.
5 | *Mary E. B.*, b. Jan. 3, 1834; m. May 21, 1861, William P. F. Meserve. They reside in Boston, and have three chil., Josephine C., b. Nov. 2, 1862; William S., b. June 28, 1864; Harry F., b. May 7, 1867.

WEBSTER SMITH, like Capt. William above. is a Lexington man by adoption, but is of the same parent stock as the Lexington families. His father, *Jonas* Smith, b. Feb. 6, 1788, was son of *Zachariah*, b. Aug. 22, 1749, who was son of *Jonas*, b. June 7, 1719. Here the ancestors of William and Webster unite; and by tracing them back through *Zachariah*, we come to *Jonathan* (No. 13 in the foregoing register of the Smiths), and thence to the first emigrant. These Smiths generally resided in Waltham.

JONAS SMITH of Line. m. 1815, Abigail Fiske, dau. of Phinehas. She d. April 13, 1862. They have had *Abigail*, d. in infancy; *Francis*, b. April 8, 1822, m. Abigail Baker; *Webster*, b. May 24, 1825; *Sarah Caroline*, b. June 7, 1828, m. Samuel Pierce.

WEBSTER SMITH, the second son of Jonas, purchased the well known Phinney Place, and came to Lex. about 1852. He m. April 5, 1863, Caroline Cormie, dau. of Peter and Mary Cormie of Pictou, Nova Scotia. They have one child, *Abbie Fiske*, b. July 4, 1865. He was one of the selectmen during the Rebellion, when many important duties were devolved upon that Board.

There are other Smiths in Lexington, who have come into town recently, but do not belong to the same original stock.

1 WILLIAM L. SMITH came to Lex. from Sterling about 1820. He m. Hannah Lane of Bed. He d. July, 1857, aged 60.

1- 2 *William H.*, b. Dec. 10, 1820; m. May 20, 1849, Susan L. Holbrook. He was a trader in the East Village. He was killed by falling from his wagon, 1867. He had one child, George Edwin, b. July 27, 1854.

3 *Adeline A.*, b. June 20, 1827; m. May 1, 1846, Horatio Locke of West Cambridge.

4 *George O.*, b. Jan. 5, 1832; is in business in Boston.

There is still another family of *Smiths* in Lexington.

SYLVANUS W. SMITH came to Lex. from Newton, 1831. *Abiel Smith* of Smithfield, R. I., removed to Needham, Mass., where he d. Feb. 1861. His son, *Enoch Smith*, was b. in Needham, but settled in Newton, where he d. Nov. 25, 1851. He m. Elizabeth Woods, dau. of George Woods of Rox. She d. Oct. 11, 1848. SYLVANUS W. SMITH, son of Enoch and Elizabeth, was b. in Newton, Aug. 2, 1808, and m. July 6, 1834, Catharine Adams of Lex., dau. of Zabdiel and Susan, b. April 26, 1813. They have had three children, *Susan E.*, b. July 9, 1835; *Ellen E.*, b. Nov. 25, 1837, d. Aug. 7, 1848; *Emma A.*, b. Oct. 5, 1848. Sylvanus W. Smith has served several years as overseer of the poor and as selectman. He is also a magistrate.

THE SPAULDING FAMILY.

Though the name of *Spaulding* is quite common, no family of that name has resided in Lexington till a period comparatively recent. The Spauldings probably originated in Braintree, where Edward and his wife Margaret settled, and where she d. 1640. He had *Edward* and *Benjamin* b. in Braintree before 1644, and *Andrew* b. Nov. 19, 1653 in Chelmsford, to which place he had removed. Andrew was a deacon of the church there. The descendants of *Edward Spaulding* became numerous in that and some of the neighboring towns. Edward Spaulding was chosen into office in Chelmsford in 1654, and is said to have planted the first orchard in the town. The late Dr. Spaulding of Lexington descended from this stock.

1 STILLMAN SPAULDING, son of Job and Sarah (Proctor) Spaulding of Chelmsford, m. May 13, 1819, Lucy Butterfield, dau. of John and Rebecca (Kendall) Butterfield of the same town. Having studied medicine, he established himself in Lex. about 1820, and continued in practice to the time of his death, May 26, 1860. He was in his 72d year.

1- 2 *John B.*, b. June 29, 1823; d. May 4, 1832.

3 *Susan B.*, b. July 31, 1826; m. Jan. 23, 1845, William J. Currier, who is in practice of medicine in Lexington.

4 *Nathaniel E.*, b. Nov. 23, 1829; m. June 14, 1858, Henrietta D. Palfrey of Boston.

5 *Louisa B.*, b. Feb. 16, 1833; d. next day.

6 *John B.*, b. Sept. 11, 1836; m. Oct. 3, 1861, Mary Bates Saville of Gloucester.

There are other Spauldings in Lexington, from whom no returns have been received.

STAPLES.— Rev. Nahor Augustus Staples, who was settled in Lexington, was son of Jason and Phila (Tuft) Staples of Mendon. He was b. Aug. 24, 1830; m. Sept. 24, 1854, Margaret Shipping, dau. of Charles and Martha (Eddawes) Shipping of Philadelphia, Pa. He grad. at Meadville Theological School in 1854, and was ordained at Lexington, Sept. 20, 1854. He was dismissed at his own request, Nov. 30, 1856, and was settled over a new society formed in Milwaukee, Ill. After the breaking out of the Rebellion, he united himself with one of the Illinois regiments as chaplain. His health became impaired and he left the service. Having partially recovered his health, he settled over a society in Brooklyn, N. Y. His zeal and unsparing devotion to his profession gradually undermined his constitution, and he d. Feb. 5, 1864. Mr. Staples was a man of brilliant talents, and though he died young, had acquired a high reputation as a preacher. Their first child, *Frederick A.* Staples, was b. in Lex. Dec. 11, 1855.

THE STEARNS FAMILY.

There have been a few Stearnses in Lexington in every period of her history, and yet it is impossible to give a connected genealogy of them. This arises from the fact that the first family of that name became nearly if not quite extinct, and also from the fact that they descended from two distinct families.

1 Isaac Stearns came to this country in 1630, probably in the same ship with Gov. Winthrop and Richard Saltonstall, and settled in Wat., near Mount Auburn. He was made freeman, 1630, which is the earliest date of any such admissions. He was selectman several years, and d. June 19, 1671, leaving a wid., Mary, who d. April 2, 1677. Two or three of their children were born in England. Isaac Stearns, in his Will, dated only a few days before his death, says, "My will is that my kinsman, Charles Stearns, shall have ten pounds of my estate." This Charles Stearns is the ancestor of a portion of the Lex. Stearnses.

1- 2 | *Mary,* b. in Eng.; m. July 9, 1646, Isaac Learned of Woburn.
3 | *Hannah,* b. in Eng.; m. in Wat. Dec. 25, 1650, Henry Freeman.
4 | *John,* b. in Eng.; settled in Billerica, where he d. 1668.
5 | ‡*Isaac,* b. Jan 6, 1633; m. June 24, 1660, Sarah Beers.
6 | *Sarah,* b. Sept. 22, 1635; m. June 7, 1655, Dea. Samuel Stone of Camb. She d. Oct. 6, 1700.
7 | *Samuel,* b. April 24, 1638; d. Aug. 3, 1683.
8 | *Elizabeth,* b. ——; m. April 13, 1664, Samuel Manning of Camb.; r. in Billerica.
9 | *Abigail,* b. ——; m. April 27, 1666, Dea. John Morse.

1-5- Isaac Stearns m. June 24, 1660, Sarah Beers, and settled in Lex. He d. Aug. 2, 1676, and his wid. m. July 23, 1677, Thomas Wheeler of Concord.

5-10 | *Sarah,* b. Jan. 14, 1662; m. Dec. 27, 1678, John Wheeler of Con.
11 | *Mary,* b. Oct. 8, 1663; m. Jan. 1, 1694, John Cutler.
12 | ‡*Isaac,* b. April 26, 1666; m. Elizabeth ——.
13 | ‡*Samuel,* b. Jan. 11, 1668; m. Phebe ——.
14 | *Abigail,* b. ——; m. Nov. 29, 1692, Samuel Hartwell, and d. May 11, 1709.
15 | *John,* b. 1675. He r. in Con., afterwards in Bil., where he d. 1734.

5-12- ISAAC STEARNS m. Elizabeth ——. He was a subscriber to the first meeting house, 1692, and was taxed the year following. He was ad. to the ch. May 8, 1699, by a letter from the ch. in Wat. He was constable in 1710. His first four children were recorded in Camb., the others in Lex. His children settled in Stoughton.

12-16 Isaac, } twins, b. Oct. 19, 1697; both went to Stoughton.
17 Simon, }
18 Jabesh, b. Jan. 27, 1700; d. April 30, 1700.
19 Jonathan, b. Nov. 20, 1701; r. in Stoughton.
20 Hannah, b. Jan. 26, 1704.
21 Mary, b. Nov. 10, 1706; m. about 1729, Dr. Edward Esty of Stoughton, who lived to be one hundred years old. They had fourteen children, twelve died without families.
22 Martha, bap. Feb. 7, 1709; m. Nov. 1, 1734, Daniel Talbot of Stoughton.
23 Ebenezer, bap. July 8, 1711; was a Baptist clergyman in Stoughton.
24 Abigail, bap. Nov. 12, 1713.

5-13- SAMUEL STEARNS m. Phebe ——. He was in the precinct at its organization, and was taxed 1694, was an assessor 1711, '13, '17, and was a tythingman, 1718. He was killed by a casualty, Nov. 19, 1721, and his widow settled his estate. She moved to Littleton in 1730, with a portion of her children. The rest appeared to have scattered in different directions.

13-25 Sarah, b. Jan. 15, 1697; m. May 21, 1729, William Wheeler of Stoughton.
26 Mary, b. June 27, 1699; m. John Powers of Shutesbury.
27 Abigail, b. Feb. 18, 1700; m. Joseph Temple of Con.
28 Samuel, b. March 7, 1702; resided in Hollis, N. H.
29 Ruth, b. May 25, 1704; m. Feb. 5, 1724, Oliver Lawrence of Wat. and d. 1725.
30 Phebe, b. Feb. 23, 1706; m. —— Cummings of Uxbridge.
31 Rebecca, b. April 15, 1708; m. —— Whittemore.
32 Thomas, b. July 4, 1710; resided in Littleton.
33 John, b. July 23, 1712; r. in Dedham and Attleboro'.
34 Joseph, bap. April 15, 1715.
35 Benjamin, b. Jan. 6, 1720; resided in Rutland.

This branch of the Stearns family appears to have become extinct in Lexington; though other branches from time to time crop out in the town.

1 PHINEHAS STEARNS of Waltham, b. Feb. 28, 1738, son of Dea. Isaac, m. July 9, 1761, Mary Wellington, who d. Feb. 13, 1790. He moved to Lexington as early as 1768. A part of their children were b. in Lex., and several of them m. into Lex. families. He was in the Revolution. He was selectman 1781 and 1782.

1- 2 Sarah, b. Dec. 24, 1761; m. Isaac Hastings of Lexington.
3 Mary, b. March 6, 1764; m. William Stearns, and d. 1814.
4 Peleg, b. April 25, 1766; m. May 22, 1794, Susan Phinney.
5 John, bap. April 24, 1768; m. May 22, 1794, Chloe Phinney.
The foregoing two brothers were m. at the same time, and their wives were sisters, dau. of Benjamin Phinney of Lexington.
6 Phinehas, bap. June 1, 1770; d. young.
7 Susanna, b. Aug. 8, 1774; m. 1800, James Wyeth of Camb.
8 Isaac, b. Nov. 3, 1776; d. young.

9 | *Rebecca*, b. Aug. 24, 1778; m. April 11, 1805, David Wellington.
10 | *Dorcas*, b. May 8, 1780; m. Dec. 11, 1808, Luke Child.

SAMUEL STEARNS b. Oct. 23, 1761, son of Samuel of Walt., m. 1799, Elizabeth Brown, dau. of Capt. Francis Brown of Lex., resided for a short time in Lex., where he d. June 15, 1805. They had *Samuel*, b. in Walt. Aug. 20, 1800; and *Charles* and *Edwin*, twins, b. in Lex. May 22, 1804. Charles d. in Boston, 1830, unm. and Edwin went to Middletown, Conn., where he became prominent, having been bank commissioner, aide to the Governor, representative and senator, and State treasurer.

1 | CHARLES STEARNS of Wat. was admitted freeman, May 6, 1646. He was "kinsman" of Isaac Stearns, mentioned in his Will, 1671. In 1680, he was elected constable in Wat., but declined serving. It is supposed that soon after this he moved to Lynn End (now Lynnfield) with his son, Shubael. His first wife, Hannah, d. in Wat. 1651, and he m. second, June 22, 1654, Rebecca Gibson, dau. of John Gibson of Cambridge.

1- 2 | *Samuel*, b. in Wat. June 2, 1650; settled in Watertown.
3 | *Shubael*, b. in Camb. Sept. 20, 1655; settled in Lynnfield.
4 | †*John*, b. in Camb. Jan. 24, 1657; r. in Lexington.
5 | *Isaac*, b. ———; settled in Salem, and d. previous to 1692.
6 | *Charles*, b. ———; slain in the King's service prior to 1695.
7 | *Rebecca*, b. ———; m. Jan. 25, 1693, Thomas Traine.
8 | *Martha*, b. ———; m. ——— Hutchinson.

1-4- | JOHN STEARNS m. Judith Lawrence. She d. and he m. April 2, 1713, Mary Norcross. He resided in Lex., where he was taxed in the first tax list, 1693. He d. Feb. 22, 1722. Living near the line of Wat., most of his children were bap. in that town.

4- 9 | *Rebecca*, b. March 21, 1682.   10 *Judith*, bap. June 22, 1690.
11 | *Sarah*, bap. June 22, 1690.
12 | *George*, bap. June 22, 1690; d. June 26, 1760; r. in Waltham.
13 | †*Benjamin*, bap. June 22, 1690; m. Hepzibah Shattuck.
14 | *John*, bap. May 11, 1701; m. Deliverance Bigelow; r. in Worcester.
15 | *Thomas*, bap. May 11, 1701; he settled in Worcester, and kept a public house.
16 | *Daniel*, bap. May 11, 1701.
17 | *Isaac*, bap. May 11, 1701; m. Mehitabel Frost; r. in Boston.
18 | *Mary*, bap. May 11, 1701.   19 *Elizabeth*, bap. May 11, 1701.
20 | *Abigail*, b. in Lex. May 12, 1700; m. April 2, 1724, Jonas Harrington.
21 | *Charles*, b. in Lex. Oct. 22, 1702; he was ad. to the ch. Jan. 15, 1721, and dismissed April 13, 1729, to a church in Carolina.

4-13- | BENJAMIN STEARNS m. Sept. 6, 1721, Hepzibah Shattuck, wid. of Nathaniel. Her maiden name was Hastings.

13-22 | *Hepzibah*, bap. Sept. 1, 1722; d. 1723.
23 | *Benjamin*, b. 1723; d. 1724.
24 | *Hepzibah*, b. March 7, 1725; m. 1744, Josiah Smith of Weston.
25 | *Lucy*, b. Jan. 24, 1727; m. Feb. 28, 1748, James Smith of Weston.
26 | †*Benjamin*, b. Dec. 27, 1728; m. in Newton, Hannah Seger.

13-26- | BENJAMIN STEARNS m. Sept. 11, 1754, Hannah Seger of Newton. They were ad. to the ch. in Lex. June 22, 1766. On the 13th of

July of that year, five of their children were baptized. He d. May 26, 1801, aged 73; she d. Nov. 25, 1805, aged 69. He was in the campaign to White Plains, in 1776.

26-27 †*Asahel*, bap. July 13, 1766; m. Mary Smith.
28 *Habakkuk*, bap. July 13, 1766; m. April 18, 1785, Eunice Child, and settled in Linc., where he d. Feb. 15, 1822, and his wid. d. Nov. 1822.
29 *Nahum*, bap. July 13, 1766.
30 *Martha*, bap. July 13, 1766; d. May 9, 1791.
31 *Ishmael*, bap. July 13, 1766; r. in Walt. and d. 1820.
32 *Noah*, bap. Sept. 21, 1766; m. June 5, 1806, Prudence Winship of Lexington.
33 *Hannah*, bap. Sept. 21, 1766; m. Feb. 17, 1785, John Parker. They were the parents of Rev. Theodore Parker.
34 *Hiram*, bap. Oct. 16, 1768.
35 *Jeptha*, m. in Weston, Nov. 1, 1798, Sally Fiske.
36 *Ammi*, b. ———; m. in Boston, Jan. 31, 1804, Polly Stearns.
37 *Elisha*, bap. April 27, 1777.

26-27- ASAHEL STEARNS m. Mary Smith. They made their peace with the ch. in Lex. Sept. 25, 1785, and two of their children were bap. Oct. 2, 1785. He was a member of Capt. Parker's co. 1775, was one of the eight months' men in 1775, and was in the continental line.

27-38 *Nathan*, bap. Oct. 2, 1785; m. May 21, 1807, Susanna Adams. He d. 1845.
39 *Moses*, bap. Aug. 13, 1786; m. ——— Harthan; resided in Lex.
40 *Amos*, bap. July 6, 1788; m. Nancy Blodgett; r. in Lowell.
41 †*Joel*, bap. June 20, 1790; m. Betsey Parker.
42 *Matthew*, bap. June 17, 1792; m. Nabby Brooks.
43 *Rhoda*, bap. July 27, 1794; m. Charles Gove.
44 *Leonard*, bap. Aug. 28, 1796; m. Hannah Wilson; r. in Belmont.
45 *Marshall*, bap. Aug. 26, 1798; m. Elvira Flagg.
46 *Luther*, bap. Sept 12, 1800; m. Oct. 5, 1830, Lydia Varnum. They had four children, who d. young.
47 *Otis*, bap. Nov. 14, 1802; m. Lydia ———.

27-41- JOEL STEARNS m. Betsey Parker.

41-48 *John*, b. about 1816; r. in Charlestown.
49 †*George*, b. Nov. 3, 1818; m. Lavinia Hadley.
50 *David*, b. ———; m. Adeline Withington; r. in Charlestown.
51 *Almira*, b. about 1822; m. George Webber of Waltham.
52 *Ambrose M.*, b. 1824; m. Cynthia Viles of Walt.; r. in Charlest.
53 *Abner*, b. ———; m. Charlotte Bigelow of Linc.; r. in Charlest.
54 *Henry*, b. ———; m. Marie Piper of Walt.; resides there.
55 *Jane*, b. ———; m. Sept. 22, 1844, Nathan Boynton; r. Westboro'.
56 *Edward*, b. ———; d. 1863.
57 *Ophelia*, b. ———; m. George Rawson; r. in Boston.
58 *Albert*, b. ———; m. Lizzie Grace; r. in Waltham.
There being no record of the family, they may not be arranged in the order of their birth.

41-49- GEORGE STEARNS m. Dec. 25, 1844, Lavinia Hadley, dau. of Sewell Hadley.

49-59 *George Arthur*, b. March 12, 1846.
60 *Adelaide*, b. Dec. 16, 1848.
61 *Charles Herbert*, b. Dec. 7, 1854.

THE STETSON FAMILY.

CALEB STETSON is a son of Thomas Stetson of Kingston, and was b. July 12, 1793. He grad. H. C. 1822, and was settled as a clergyman at Medford, Feb. 28, 1827. He left Medford, and was settled at South Scituate. Mr. Stetson is a lineal descendant from the original emigrant, *Robert Stetson*, who settled in Scituate, commonly called "Cornet Robert," he being a cornet of the first company of horse in Plymouth Colony. He was seventeen years a deputy to the General Court, and was active in King Philip's War. He d. Feb. 1, 1702, aged 90 years. *Thomas*, his third son, had a family of twelve children. *Elisha*, the fifth son of Thomas, bap. 1686, m. about 1706, Abigail Brewster, by whom he had five children. *Elisha*, his only son, b. 1718, m. 1742, Sarah Adams, and had ten children. *Thomas*, his third son, b. March 9, 1752, m. Sept. 3, 1778, Elizabeth Cook of Kingston, and had eleven children. He was a shipmaster about thirty years, when he left the sea, and settled on a farm in Harvard, where he d. 1820. His children, of whom *Caleb* was the ninth, were born in Kingston.

1   CALEB STETSON m. Aug. 22, 1827, Julia Ann Merriam, dau. of Rufus and Martha (Simonds) Merriam of Lexington. After leaving South Scituate, he came to Lex. to reside on the old homestead of his father-in-law, in 1860.

1- 2   *Frederic D.*, b. July, 1828; went abroad for his health, and was lost at sea on his passage from Palermo, March 10, 1846.

3   *Thomas M.*, b. June 15, 1830; grad. H. C. 1849, read law, and is in practice at New Bedford. He m. Sept. 10, 1856, Caroline Dawes, dau. of Hon. Thomas D. Elliott of New Bedford.

4   *Julia*, b. April 1, 1834; m. Dec. 5, 1867, Sergeant C. Whitcher of Boston; r. in Lexington.

5   *Osgood*, b. Oct. 5, 1837; d. Oct. 9, 1838.

6   *Edward G.*, b. Nov. 4, 1840; grad. H. C. 1863, is studying law.

7   *Abby*, b. Sept. 10, 1844; m. March 8, 1866, A. Augustus Griffing.

8   *Ellen W.*, b. July 31, 1847.

STEVENS.—The family here traced is said to have descended from *John Stevens*, one of the first settlers of Andover, but in the absence of the records we are unable to fill up the line of descent.

CYRUS STEVENS of Gloucester m. about 1796, Hannah Elwell of that town. They had *Caroline*, b. 1797; *William*, b. 1799; two children who d. in early infancy; *George*, b. 1802; *Henry*, b. 1804; *James*, b. 1807.

WILLIAM STEVENS, son of Cyrus and Hannah, m. May 13, 1822, Nancy Pierce, dau. of Henry and Abigail (Knights) Pierce. He settled in Gloucester and subsequently in Charlestown, and from thence came to Lex. about 1845. He engaged in mercantile pursuits, and afterwards was a clerk in the Boston Custom House twelve years. He d. Aug. 28, 1862, aged 63. They had the following children, *Anna P.*, b. Dec. 29, 1823, d. Oct. 8, 1824; *William H.*, b. April 13, 1826, m. June 5, 1848, Caroline E. Goodrich of Charlestown, they reside in California, and have two children; *Thomasine L.*, b. March 25, 1828; *Ann C.*, b. Feb. 28, 1831, m. June 2, 1852, Horace B. Davis, and has two children; *Hannah E.*, b. June 2, 1833, m. Nov. 27, 1857, George D. Robinson, and d. April 5, 1864, leaving one child; *Mary*, b. Nov. 12, 1844.

Caleb Stetson.

THE STONE FAMILY.

The Stones were early in the country, and have become very numerous in all parts of the State. They were among the early settlers in Lexington, and were numerous, respectable, and influential. There were so many of the same name, that they were in many instances in the Lex. Records, designated by their geographical position, as John Stone *East* and John Stone *West*, Samuel Stone *East* and Samuel Stone *West*. But the family are now, and for some time have been, nearly or quite extinct in the town.

1   GREGORY STONE, their original ancestor, came to this country with his family in 1635, and settled in Cambridge. He was one of the members of the first church, and was one of its deacons. He had six children, four sons and two daughters. He was also step-father of John and Lydia Cooper, two children of his wife by her first husband in England. Dea. Stone d. Nov. 30, 1672, aged 82. She d. June 24, 1674. He was ad. freeman, 1636; was one of the proprietors of Watertown, and a representative in 1638.

1- 2 *John*, b. in Eng. about 1619; m. Anne ———. He was one of the proprietors of Sudbury, had several grants of land there, and settled on the Sudbury river near the Falls, being the place where the village of Saxonville, in Framingham, is now situated. He had twelve children, and his descendants have been numerous in Sudbury, Framingham, and other towns in that neighborhood. None of them came to Lexington.

3 *Daniel*, was a "chirurgeon," and resided in Boston.

4 †*David*, settled on his father's "Cambridge Farms," where he owned a large tract in the southwestern part of the town, including what is now a part of Lincoln, where Gregory Stone, one of his descendants lived on the old homestead.

5 *Samuel*, like his brother David, settled on his father's large tract, residing about a mile easterly of his brother, near the junction of our present Lincoln and Weston streets, where stood the old mansion, occupied by the Stones for more than a century.

6 *Elizabeth*, m. ——— Potter, and resided in Ipswich.

7 *Sarah*, m. July 12, 1653, Joseph Merriam of Con. and was the mother of Joseph, John, Robert, and Thomas Merriam, who settled in Lex. in the immediate neighborhood of the Stones. She d. in Lex. April 8, 1704, aged 71, and hence was born 1633.

1-4- DAVID STONE m. Elizabeth ——— about 1648, and had David, but the mother and child soon d., and he m. second, Dorcas ———, and had several children, 1647. He was made freeman, 1647. He d. Jan. 16, 1704, and she d. Aug. 13, 1704. His name does not appear upon the first records of the precinct, except as a tax payer, and his tax being small, he had probably disposed of most of his property to his sons, and had in a manner retired from business, as he was between seventy and eighty years of age. The record of his family, and that of his sons, is exceedingly defective, and hence I can give no full account of them.

4- 8 †*David*, b. April 9, 1650; m. Dec. 31, 1674, Sarah Hildreth.

9 †*Daniel*, b. ———.   10 *Dorcas*, b. Dec. 18, 1652.

11 †*John*, b. 1654; m. Mary ———.

12 †*Samuel*, b. June 19, 1656; m. Hannah ———.

13 *Nathaniel*, b. ———.

1-5-   SAMUEL STONE was b. 1635, the year his father came to the country. He m. June 7, 1655, Sarah Stearns of Wat., by whom he had
ten or twelve children, about half of whom d. young.   It is difficult
to say at what time Samuel Stone and his brother David came to
Cambridge Farms, but it is probable that they settled here about the
time of their marriage, that is, about 1648 and 1655 respectively;
and as the country was at that time unsettled, they would naturally
precede their families, and so may have been here a year earlier.
They were at all events among the first settlers.
    Samuel's name is borne upon our first records, being a subscriber
for the first meeting house in 1692, and was taxed on the precinct
tax bill in 1693, where his tax was higher than that of any other
citizen, showing that he was a man of large landed property.
    At the first organization of the precinct, no man was more promi-
nent than Samuel Stone, Sen. He was chosen deacon at the organization of the ch., was assessor, and was on almost every important
committee. He d. Sept. 27, 1715, aged 80 years and 7 months.
His first wife, Sarah, d. Oct. 4, 1700, and he m. second, Abigail
———, who d. in Wo., 1728, aged 71.

5-14   †Samuel, b. Oct. 1, 1656; m. Dorcas Jones of Concord.
  15   Sarah, b. Feb. 5, 1660; m. Edward Converse of Woburn, where
        she was living 1709.
  16   †John, b. May 12, 1663; m. Rachel Shepard of Concord.
  17   Lydia, b. Nov. 25, 1665; m. Francis Bowman.
  18   †Joseph, b. 1671; m. Sarah Wait. ?
  19   Anna, b. June 30, 1673; m. it is supposed, John Merry.

4-8-   DAVID STONE m. Dec. 31, 1674, Sarah Hildreth. In the absence
of any connected record, I shall not attempt to give any connected
genealogy of this family. He probably d. Sept. 21, 1679.

8-20   Sarah, b. March 6, 1676.   21 Elizabeth, b. Jan. 6, 1679.

4-9-   DANIEL STONE m. Sarah ———. The following is all that can be
gleaned of this family from the Lex. Records. Daniel Stone was a
subscriber for the meeting house in 1692, and was taxed in the precinct the year following. I find no record of the birth of his children. In 1700, Gregory Stone, Lydia Stone, and Susanna Stone,
children of Daniel Stone, were baptized. With this meagre record,
we dismiss the family, observing that there is a marked difference
between the Stones denominated East and those denominated West;
the former kept up a good record in the town and church, while the
latter did not.

4-11-   JOHN STONE m. Mary ———. Of this family but little appears of
record. John Stone West, was a subscriber for the meeting house in
1692, and his name appears subsequently in the precinct tax bills.
His wife was ad. to the ch. June 14, 1699.

11-22 Mary, bap. Nov. 13, 1698.
  23   Abigail, bap. Nov. 13, 1698; m. Jan. 9, 1724, John Cutler.
  24   Benjamin, bap. Feb. 1702; probably m., as we find Mary of Ben-
        jamin Stone, bap. Oct. 13, 1728.

4-12-   SAMUEL STONE m. Hannah ———. David, his father, in 1699,
deeded him land on which Samuel's house stood. He subscribed for

the first meeting house, designating himself "David's son." The records give very little information concerning his family.

25 *Mary*, bap. Nov. 13, 1698.

5-14- SAMUEL STONE m. June 12, 1679, Dorcas Jones of Concord. He was designated Samuel Stone *East*, to distinguish him from his cousin Samuel, who was called Samuel Stone *West*. He was one of the original members of the church in 1696, and his wife was received in 1698, from the church in Concord. He d. June 17, 1743, aged 87; she d. Sept. 24, 1746, aged 87. He was chosen deacon of the ch. Nov. 1715, to fill the vacancy in that office occasioned by the death of his father. He was selectman, 1714, '15, '23.

14-26 ‡*Samuel*, b. Aug. 12, 1684; m. Abigail Reed of Woburn.
27 †*Joseph*, b. Feb. 8, 1687; m. Mary ——.
28 †*Jonathan*, b. Feb. 2, 1689; m. Chary Adams.
29 *Sarah*, b. ——; m. Thomas Cutler.
30 *Elizabeth*, b. 1693; m. March 18, 1710, John Lawrence.
31 *Rebecca*, b. 1696; m. Benjamin Reed.

5-16- JOHN STONE m. April 27, 1687, Rachel Shepard of Con. He was a subscriber for the first meeting house, and to distinguish him from his cousin, and to show that he was on the high road of military promotion, he was designated *corporal*. They were admitted to the church Jan. 18, 1708. He d. Feb. 3, 1713, in his 49th year.

16-32 *Rachel*, b. 1688; d. Aug. 31, 1695.
33 ‡*John*, b. Dec. 15, 1689; m. April 8, 1714, Mary Reed.
34 *Mary*, b. Sept. 26, 1692; m. John Bowman.
35 *Anna*, b. Nov. 27, 1694; m. Dec. 8, 1718, Josiah Parker.
36 *Rachel*, b. June 6, 1697; m. Jan. 1721, Jonathan Butterfield of Cambridge.
37 *Ruth*, b. Aug. 27, 1700.

5-18- JOSEPH STONE m. Sarah Wait. He d. Jan. 17, 1703, aged 32. He was taxed in the precinct, 1693.

18-38 *Lydia*, b. about 1693.
39 *Isaac*, b. about 1695; m. July 24, 1722, Elizabeth Brown of Sudbury. He moved to Shrewsbury.
40 *Joseph*, b. about 1697; m. Lydia Parkhurst of Weston, and resided in Framingham.
41 *Abigail*, bap. Jan. 1, 1699; m. Jan. 9, 1723, John Cutler.
42 *Sarah*, bap. Nov. 1700; m. Nov. 5, 1719, Joseph Blodgett.
43 *Tabitha*, bap. Jan. 3, 1703; m. in Weston, Aug. 26, 1728, Samuel Warren.

14-26- SAMUEL STONE m. April 3, 1706, Abigail Reed of Wo. dau. of Dea. George Reed. June 8, 1718. Samuel Stone and wife were dismissed from the ch. of Lex. to the ch. of Sud., where they then lived; subsequently they removed to Rutland. Afterwards they returned to Lex. and were readmitted, Nov. 11, 1744. He d. April 5, 1769; she d. Jan. 16, 1767.

26-44 *Abigail*, b. April 21, 1707; m. April 2, 1724, Micah Stone of Framingham.
45 *Samuel*, b. Dec. 8, 1708; m. Oct. 20, 1732, Mindwell Stevens of Rutland, where he settled and had a family.

46 †*Jonas*, b. Dec. 3, 1710 ; he was twice married.
47 *Elizabeth*, b. Dec. 21, 1713 ; m. Jan. 12, 1731, John Stone, settled in Rutland.
48 *Tabitha*, b. Jan. 9, 1716 ; m. John Noyes of Sudbury.
49 *Mary*, b. March 9, 1718 ; m. Thomas Bent of Sudbury.
50 *Susanna*, b. April 24, 1720 ; m. Elijah Bent of Sudbury.

14-27- JOSEPH STONE m. Mary ——. His Will was proved May 21, 1753. He was selectman, 1743.

27-51 *Ephraim*, b. Nov. 20, 1710 ; resided in Stow.
52 *Mary*, } b. June 26, 1714 ; m. William Keyes of Harvard.
53 *Joseph*. } b. June 26, 1714 ; r. in Brookfield.
54 *Abigail*. b. Sept. 26, 1716 ; m. Josiah Shattuck of Cambridge.
55 †*Samuel*, b. Aug. 13, 1718 ; m. Jane ——.
56 *Sarah*, b. Feb. 29, 1720 ; m. Dea. Jonas Stone as his second wife.
57 *James*, b. Aug. 7, 1722 ; resided in Weston, dismissed to that church 1749.
58 *Elizabeth*, b. Feb. 7, 1724 ; m. Jan. 15, 1752, Benjamin Sampson of Leominster.
59 *Dorcas*, b. April 11, 1725 ; m. Benjamin Stone of Harvard.
60 *Bartholomew*, b. June 19, 1727 ; d. young.

14-28- JONATHAN STONE m. Nov. 17, 1712, Chary Adams of Concord.

28-61 *Margaret*, b. Oct. 25, 1713 ; d. Dec. 30, 1713.
62 *Dorcas*, b. March 25, 1715 ; m. Nov. 13, 1733, Joseph Wellington.
63 *Margaret*, b. Sept. 15, 1718 ; m. March 13, 1735, Thomas Wellington, jr.
64 *Rebecca*, } b. Jan. 7, 1723 ; m. Timothy Wellington.
65 *Love*, } b. Jan. 7, 1723 ; m. June 11, 1747, Samuel Whittemore of Cambridge.
66 *Jonathan*, bap. March 14, 1725 ; m. 1747, Martha Cutler of West Cambridge.
67 *Samuel*, b. June 10, 1727 ; m. first, Martha Earle of Boston, second, Mrs. Eunice Underwood of Lexington.
68 *Josiah*, b. Nov. 10, 1729 ; m. Abigail ——.

16-33- JOHN STONE m. April 8, 1714, Mary Reed, dau. of Capt. William Reed. He d. Aug. 7, 1762, aged 73, and she d. Oct. 16, 1772, aged 78. In his Will, dated Nov. 11, 1756, he gave £5 to the church, of which he was deacon. He was selectman 1734, and for eight subsequent years, and assessor 1746.

33-69 *John*, b. July 11, 1715 ; d. March 22, 1736, aged 21 years.
70 *Mary*, b. Feb. 26, 1717 ; she was insane.
71 *Anna*, b. Nov. 22, 1718 ; m. July 28, 1737, Robert Munroe, who was killed on the Common, April 19, 1775.
72 *Nathan*, b. Sept. 21, 1723 ; d. July 13, 1740, aged 16 years.
73 *Ruth*, b. July 5, 1725 ; d. July 19, 1740, aged 15 years.
74 *Lydia*, b. Sept. 20, 1729 ; m. June 6, 1751, Nathaniel Mulliken, who d. Nov. 23, 1767, aged 46, and she m. Jonathan Harrington. She d. Nov. 13, 1785.

26-46- JONAS STONE m. Elizabeth Adams. He moved to Rutland, where his wife d. April 3, 1751, when he returned to Lexington, where he m. May 12, 1752, his cousin, Sarah Stone, dau. of Joseph. He d. Oct. 29, 1790, aged 80, and she d. Nov. 4, 1780, aged 61. He was selectman thirteen years, assessor nine years, and treasurer from

1755 to 1778; was on the committee of correspondence in 1773 and 1776, was representative from 1771 to 1777, delegate to the first and second Provincial Congresses in 1774 and 1775.

46-75 | *Elizabeth*, b. 1733; d. Dec. 27, 1752.
76 | *Deborah*, b. 1736; m. April 13, 1753, Samuel Bass of Boston.
77 | †*Jonas*, b. 1741; m. June 12, 1756. Sarah Buckman.
78 | *Lucy*, b. 1743; m. Jan. 17, 1765, Joseph Smith.
79 | *Hannah*, b. 1746; m. June 29, 1769, Thomas Barrett of Concord.
80 | *Zerviah*, b. 1749; d. Dec. 27, 1752.

27-55- | SAMUEL STONE m. Jane ——, who d. 1786, aged 66, and he d. in Lex. March 31, 1768. They had two children recorded, *Elizabeth*, b. June 5, 1743; *Ruth*, b. Nov. 26, 1744, m. July 21, 1768, John Buckman, jr.

46-77- | JONAS STONE m. June 12, 1766, Sarah Buckman. He d. April 24, 1814, aged 73, and she d. Sept. 24, 1825, aged 78. He was a member of Capt. Parker's company in 1775.

77-81 | *Sarah*, b. Dec. 1767.
82 | *Samuel*, b. Dec. 27, 1769; m. Sally Child. He d. Oct. 11, 1824, and she d. Oct. 9, 1824. They were both buried in the same grave, the same day. They had Samuel, b. March 27, 1794, who m. Mary Spaulding.
83 | *Elizabeth*, b. Nov. 13, 1770.

The Stones of Lexington seemed to disappear rather suddenly, and to have left a record so imperfect, that it is impossible to state their genealogy, or the place to which they removed. It would be injustice, however, not to mention the generous act of one of that name, whose family we are unable to trace. At a town meeting in Lex. held June 15, 1761, "Mr. *Isaac Stone* came into said meeting and gave the Town a Bell for the Town's use forever; which Bell was there, and weighed four hundred sixty-three pounds, for which the Moderator in the name of the Town returned him thanks."

THE STOWE FAMILY.

1 | WILLIAM STOWE was born in New Haven, Conn. and m. Emeline Thomas of that place. Like many other young men, he was thrown in early life upon his own resources. He entered the army and served several years. mostly upon the frontier. After his discharge, he returned to his native place, and by his own personal efforts qualified himself to enter the Newton Theological School. When he left that institution, he commenced preaching as a Baptist clergyman in Charlestown, Mass. After laboring there about eight years, he went to Martha's Vineyard. He subsequently united with the Episcopalians, and settled at Bristol, R. I. After a ministry of six or seven years. he received a call at Port Huron, Mich., which he accepted, and where he still remains. Though in a great degree self-taught, he has become quite a proficient in some departments of science and literature. He has had eight children, two of whom d. young.

1- 2 | REV. WILLIAM T. STOWE, his oldest son, was b. Aug. 30, 1841. He qualified himself by his own efforts to enter the law school at Albany, from which he graduated, and was admitted to the bar in that city in 1860. Having a desire to enter the ministry, he turned his attention to the Gospel rather than to the law, and commenced preaching under the auspices of the Universalists. In 1862, he was settled in Brattleboro', Vt., where he remained till he came to Lex. in 1864. Since that time he has preached for the United Societies in the East Village. He m. June 7, 1861, Maria Hartness, dau. of John Hartness of Albany.

2- 3 | *William H.*, b. in Brat. March 28, 1862.
4 | *Mary Blasdel*, b. in Lex. June 11, 1865.
5 | *John*, b. in Lex. July 25, 1867.

SUMNER.—WILLIAM SUMNER, son of Roger of England, came to this country about 1635, with his wife Mary, by whom he had a family in Dorchester. *William*, one of his sons, m. Elizabeth Clement, and had among other children, *Clement*, b. Sept. 6, 1671, who m. May 18, 1698, Margaret Harris, and had *Benjamin*, b. May 28, 1711, who m. Mercy ——. He d. July 21, 1795. His wife d. Feb. 22, 1768. *James*, a son of Benjamin and Mercy, was b. 1740, and d. 1814. He m. first, Alice Waldron, second, —— Byles, and third, Hannah Ridgeway. By his wife Alice he had *James*, b. 1763, who m. Elizabeth Foster of Beverly, and d. Oct. 23, 1814. James and Elizabeth had a son, *James*, b. May 4, 1788, and d. April, 1849. He m. Sarah Badger of Boston. They had six children b. in Boston, where their ancestors for several generations had resided, viz., *James D.*, b. 1816; *Elizabeth*, b. March, 1818, m. Charles Southack; *Sarah Ann*, b. Jan. 27, 1820, m. May 9, 1839, Charles Brown of Lex.; *Mary B.*, b. 1822, m. John Tilton; *Catharine*, b. —, d. young.

JAMES DUDLEY SUMNER, the eldest child of James, was b. May 14, 1816, and m. Feb. 13, 1840, Sarah Maria Johnson, b. April 22, 1816. They r. in Lex. and have had *Maria Carlton*, b. Dec. 17, 1842, d. April 13, 1856, and *James Frank*, b. Aug. 18, 1857.

THORNING.—In December, 1781, Thomas Cutler, in conformity to the law then existing, gave notice to the selectmen, that he had taken into his house to reside *John Thorning* and wife, and their dau. *Sarah*, with Eunice Philips, also *William Thorning*; and that they came from Lincoln. JOHN THORNING by his wife Betsey had, in addition to *Sarah*, *Frederick A.*, b. Dec. 27, 1790. WILLIAM THORNING, who came to Lex. with John, m. June 18, 1782, Eunice Phillips, who came to Lex. with John, and had a large family. They resided on Wood street, in the house now occupied by Mr. Medill. He d. March 23, 1829, aged 72; she d. Feb. 10, 1849, aged 93. His children were *William*, b. March 21, 1783; *Abigail*, b. April 26, 1784; *John*, b. June 29, 1785; *Eunice*, b. Jan. 28, 1787; *Sally*, b. Dec. 29, 1788, d. Aug. 27, 1846, aged 57, unm.; *Polly*, b. Nov. 2, 1790, m. Sept. 10, 1823, Leonard Wood of Wo.; *Dorcas*, b. June 14, 1792, m. Aug. 25, 1821, William Child of Groton; *Isaac*, b. June 7, 1794; *Cyrus*, b. June 18, 1796; *Leonard*, b. Aug. 8, 1799, m. May 17, 1827, Almira Whitney.

THE TIDD FAMILY.

There is some obscurity in the early history of the Tidds in this country.

1 | JOHN TIDD, the original ancestor of the family, it is probable, came over and settled in Charlestown in 1637. He moved to

Woburn in 1640, and d. Aug. 3, 1643. His name was spelled *Tead*, and sometimes *Teed*, which was the common spelling in the early Lexington records. Most if not all his children were born abroad. His Will, dated Jan. 4, 1642, and proved Sept. 5, 1643, mentions sons John and Joseph, and dau. Mary, who probably m. Francis Kendall, and three grand-children, the youngest children of Ebenezer, deceased. His son John came to Lex., and is the ancestor of the Tidds of this town.

1- 2   JOHN TIDD, b. 1625, and m. in Wo. April 14, 1650, Rebecca Wood of that town. She d. Jan. 10, 1717, aged 92. He moved to Camb. Farms, 1686, and settled upon the farm where Mr. Charles Tidd now resides. He appears to have been somewhat extensively engaged in dealing in real estate. He became one of the proprietors of Camb., for in the division of the land in 1683 above the "eight mile line," John Tidd received his distributive share. He also purchased lands of David Mackgeney, William Carly, David Fiske, and others. The homestead appears to have been bought of David Fiske, and conveyed by deed dated June 1, 1686. It was a lot of forty acres. Here the first house for the Tidds was probably erected, and the property remains in the hands of the lineal descendants at the present day,—a period of more than one hundred and eighty years.

On our earliest records, viz., a subscription for building a meeting house, in 1692, we find the name of John Tidd, or *Teed*, as the name was frequently spelt, and also the names of his sons Joseph and Samuel; and on the tax bill for 1693, we find the names of John and his sons Joseph, Samuel, and Daniel. The same year John Tidd was chosen one of the assessors, and one of a committee to purchase of the town of Cambridge a tract of land for the support of the ministry. He d. April 12, 1703, aged 78. His Will, dated Aug. 7, 1701, and proved May 31, 1703, gives a general view of his descendants. He gives a considerable portion of his property to his son John, with a provision that he shall pay a certain sum to Daniel and Mary Tidd, the children of his son Daniel, deceased. He gives twenty shillings to each of his four oldest grand-sons (not including Daniel mentioned above), viz., Joseph Smith, John Tidd, Thomas Blodgett, and Joseph Simonds. He also makes a bequest to his four oldest grand-daughters, viz., Elizabeth Tidd, Rebecca Simonds, Hannah Smith, and Rebecca Blodgett. His children were all born in Woburn.

2- 3   *Hannah*, b. Sept 21, 1652; m. Dec. 1, 1674, Joseph Smith of Wat.
    4   *John*, b. Feb. 26, 1654; m. about 1678, Elizabeth ——, by whom he had between 1679 and 1691 five children, Elizabeth, John, Joseph, Rebecca, and Mary. None of them probably ever came to Lex. to reside.
    5   *Mary*, b. Nov. 13, 1656; m. Joshua Simonds of Lexington.
    6   *Samuel*, b. June 16, 1659; d. May 9, 1699, unm. His heirs signed an agreement about his property, by which it appears that his brothers, John and Joseph, and his sisters, Hannah Smith, Mary Simonds, and Rebecca Blodgett, were living at his decease; that his brother Daniel died before him, leaving two children, Daniel and Mary, and their mother, Lydia. Samuel Tidd was in the ill-fated expedition to Canada, in 1690.
    7   †*Joseph*, b. Jan. 20, 1660; d. Dec. 26, 1730.
    8   †*Daniel*, b. about 1662; d. Nov. 29, 1696.
    9   *Rebecca*, b. about 1665; m. Nov. 11, 1685, Thomas Blodgett of Wo. They subsequently removed to Lex. and were the ancestors of most of the Blodgetts which have ever resided in the town.

2-7-   JOSEPH TIDD m. Mary ——, who d. Jan. 23, 1694, aged 23.
Their child d. Jan. 23, 1696. He m. second, Mary ——, who d. Jan.
9, 1718, aged 32. By her he had at least six children ; of the birth of
some of them we find no record. He m. third, Mary ——. He d.
Dec. 26, 1730, and she d. Jan. 4, 1731. Tradition says they both d.
of the small pox. He was a man of handsome property for that day.
His son Joseph administered upon his estate, which was inventoried
at £ 967, 10s. 6d, his real estate being £809 of that sum. He was
constable in 1699, was appointed on several important committees,
and was one of the selectmen in 1714.

7-10   A child, b. ——— ; d. Feb. 3, 1703.
11   †Joseph, bap. May, 1707 ; d. Sept. 2, 1772.
12   Samuel, b. May 29, 1709 ; settled in Western (now Warren).
13   Sarah, b. Nov. 19, 1711 ; m. John Bridge, and d. March 14, 1754.
14   Betty, b. May 29, 1714 ; m. Gershom Flagg of Woburn.
15   Mary, b. ——— ; m. David Cutler of Lex.

2-8-   DANIEL TIDD m. Dec. 4, 1694, Lydia Carter of Camb. He was
residing in Lex.. and was upon the tax bill in 1694, '95, '96, but d.
on the 29th of Feb. of the last year, leaving a widow, who d. Aug.
15, 1727, aged 55.

8-16   †Daniel, b. about 1695 ; m. Hepzibah Reed.
17   Mary, b. about 1697.

7-11-   JOSEPH TIDD m. July 31, 1731, Dorothy Stickney. He d. Sept.
2, 1772, aged 66, and she d. 1790, aged 78. They were ad. to
the ch. in Lex. Aug. 1, 1756. He resided upon the old homestead. He was a large owner of real estate, having lands not only
in Lex. but in New Braintree, Woburn, Templeton, and Phillipston.
His Will, dated Oct. 4, 1770, and proved Dec. 15, 1772, mentions
wife Dorothy, sons Benjamin, John, Joseph, and Ebenezer, and
dau. Mary Jennison and Sarah Joslin. He made Benjamin and
John executors of his Will, and gave them the greater part of his
property,—they to pay out certain legacies and provide for their
mother. The provisions of his Will in relation to the support of his
wid. cast some light upon the manners, customs, and mode of living
at that day, and hence we will give a few items. After mentioning
a certain portion of the house which she should occupy, it is provided
that John and Benjamin shall furnish her annually six cords of wood,
cut fit for the fire, at the front door of the house, two barrels of cider,
one bushel of malt, six bushels of Indian meal or corn, six bushels of
rye, one hundred pounds of pork, seventy pounds of beef, four pounds
of good wool, ten pounds of flax, &c. He was selectman, 1761,
'66, '67.

11-18   Mary, b. Jan. 7, 1732 ; m. Feb. 12, 1756, Josiah Jennison of Lex.
19   Joseph, b. May 11, 1734 ; m. Dec. 7, 1762, Sarah Munroe, dau. of
William and Sarah (Mason) Munroe. He moved to New Braintree, where he was a lieutenant, when that title implied more than
it does at present.
20   Ebenezer, b. Aug. 16, 1737 ; he moved to New Braintree in 1768,
where he resided. Among his children was Ebenezer, who was a
prominent man in his day. He was a captain of a company of
cavalry, served many years as selectman, and filled other town
offices. His son, Hollis Tidd (grand-son of Ebenezer of Lex.),
has for many years been a leading citizen in that small but very
intelligent town. He was an aide to Gen. Crawford, served on the

school committee more than thirty years, as one of the selectmen and as one of the assessors some fifteen or sixteen years each, represented the town in the legislature two years, and has for many years held the office of justice of the peace.

21 *Sarah*, b. March 8, 1739; m. Nov. 23, 1763, Samuel Joslin of New Braintree.
22 †*Benjamin*, b. June 21, 1742; m. Joanna Fitch of Bedford.
23 †*John*, b. Oct. 26, 1749; m. Elizabeth Reed.

8-16- DANIEL TIDD m. April 19, 1742, Hepzibah Reed, dau. of Capt. William and Abigail (Kendall) Reed. He d. Jan. 16, 1776, aged 81; she d. April 11, 1777, aged 72. He was on the board of selectmen nine years, on the board of assessors ten years, and town clerk nine years.

16-24 *A son*, b. Jan. 22; d. Jan. 24, 1725.
25 *Daniel*, b. Feb. 26, 1726; d. Jan. 31, 1759.
26 †*Amos*, b. Jan. 12, 1729; m. Elizabeth Smith.
27 *Hepzibah*, b. Aug. 22, 1730; d. April 11, 1777.
28 *Lydia*, b. July 6, 1732; m. Feb. 16, 1775, Samuel Hastings.
29 *John*, b. Sept. 13, 1734; d. Nov. 27, 1743.
30 †*William*, b. July 11, 1736; m. Jan. 9, 1766, Ruth Munroe.
31 *Abigail*, b. Jan. 12, 1738; m. Dec. 4, 1760, Amos Marrett of Camb.
32 †*Samuel*, b. Jan. 12, 1741; m. Feb. 28, 1771, Rebecca Simonds.
33 *Betty*, b. Oct. 24, 1742; m. July 15, 1766, Uriah Cotting of Walt.

11-22- BENJAMIN TIDD m. Jan. 6, 1774, Joanna Fitch. They were ad. to the ch. Oct. 13, 1776, and were dismissed to the ch. at New Braintree, Oct. 24, 1790, to which place they had removed, and where land was left him by his father's Will. Several of his family had already located themselves in that town, where their descendants are at the present day. Benjamin Tidd remained in Lexington till after the close of the Revolutionary struggle, and like most of the citizens of the town, was enrolled in that patriotic band commanded by Parker. He was on the Common on the 19th of April, and marched to Cambridge on the memorable 17th of June, 1775; and served at Dorchester the year following. He was one of the committee of correspondence in 1780. The three children mentioned below were baptized in Lex. They probably removed with their parents to New Braintree, where other children may have been added to the family.

22-34 *Benjamin*, bap. Nov. 10, 1776.   35 *Sarah*, bap. Sept. 20, 1778.
36 *Lydia*, bap. Sept. 16, 1781.

11-23- JOHN TIDD m. Elizabeth, dau. of Isaac and Elizabeth Reed of Wo. She d. Sept. 18, 1799, and he m. 1802, Susannah Tidd of Rindge, N. H. She d. Sept. 12, 1824, aged 68. He d. March 29, 1812, aged 63. John and Elizabeth Tidd were ad. to the ch. May 29, 1791, when three of their children were baptized. John Tidd was a member of Capt. Parker's company, and was upon the Common at the opening scene of the American Revolution. He was among the last to leave the ground, and was pursued by a British officer on horseback and struck down by a sword; and while he was senseless upon the ground, the British robbed him of his arms, and left him for dead.

23-37 †*John*, b. March 2, 1779; m. Esther Hayward of Acton.
38 *Joseph*, b. May 9, 1783; d. Nov. 13, 1798.
39 *Jacob*, b. March 14, 1785; settled in Boston as a merchant, and d. March 20, 1835, aged 50. He m. Martha F. Adams.

16-26-   AMOS TIDD m. Elizabeth Smith, dau. of Hezekiah and Elizabeth
          (Wellington) Smith, who was b. July 9, 1728. They were m. 1750.

26-40 *Amos*, bap. Dec. 1, 1751.   41 *John*, bap. July 15, 1753.
   42 *Nathan*, bap. Aug. 1, 1755.   43 *Oliver*, bap. March 28, 1758.
   44 *Daniel*, bap. Feb. 10, 1760.   45 *Abijah*, bap. Sept. 4, 1763.
   46 *Thaddeus*, bap. O   30, 1768.

16-30-   WILLIAM TIDD ... Jan. 9, 1766, Ruth Munroe, dau. of Robert
          and Anna Munroe. They were ad. to the ch. Dec. 28, 1766. He
          was a lieutenant under Capt. Parker, in the company which dared
          to stand on their own parade ground in the face of ten times their
          number of British regulars, though commanded to throw down their
          arms and disperse. In affidavit taken in 1824, after describing the
          fire of the British on that morning, he says, "I then retreated up
          the north road, (Hancock street,) and was pursued by an officer on
          horseback (supposed to be Maj. Pitcairn) calling out to me, 'Damn
          you, stop or you are a dead man.' I found I could not escape him,
          unless I left the road. I therefore sprang over a pair of bars, and
          made a stand, and discharged my gun at him; upon which he imme-
          diately returned to the main body, which shortly after took up their
          march for Concord."
              Lieut. Tidd was also one of a detachment of Parker's company
          which marched to Cambridge on the 17th of June, at the time of the
          battle of Bunker Hill, where they remained two days, when they
          were dismissed. But his public service was not confined to the
          military alone. He filled various civil offices in town, being an
          assessor in 1776, '79, '80, '91, and one of the selectmen at the time
          of the Revolution, when great responsibility rested upon that board.
          He d. Oct. 25, 1826, aged 91. Ruth, his wife, d. May 14, 1839, at
          the advanced age of 97.

30-47 *Ruth*, bap. Jan. 11, 1767; m. Oct. 4, 1785, Nathan Chandler. She
          was an only child, and d. Sept. 15, 1846, aged 80.

16-32-   SAMUEL TIDD m. Feb. 28, 1771, Rebecca Simonds of Bedford.
          Like his brother William he took part in the events of the 19th of
          April and the 17th of June, 1775. They were ad. to the ch. Sept.
          29, 1771. In 1805, they were dismissed to the ch. of Bedford. He
          afterwards returned to Lexington. He was one of the committee
          of safety and correspondence in 1781.

32-48 *Betty*, bap. Jan. 5, 1772; m. 1821, Noah Stearns.
   49 *Rebecca*, bap. Feb. 2, 1777.

23-37-   JOHN TIDD m. Esther Hayward of Acton. They were ad. to the
          ch. May 6, 1810, when two of their children were baptized. He d.
          Jan. 9, 1842, and she d. April 24, 1852.

37-50 *Elizabeth*, b. June 2, 1800; d. Aug. 26, 1801.
   51 *Elizabeth*, b. Oct. 26, 1801; m. George P. Elliot of Lowell, by
          whom she had three children. George Henry, one of them, was
          graduated at West Point, entered the service of the United States
          as a lieutenant. She d. Jan. 19, 1835.
   52 †*Charles*, b. Jan. 6, 1807. He has been twice married.
   53 *Mary H.*, b. July 22, 1812; m. Daniel T. Watson, and moved to
          Franklin, N. H. She d. Aug. 30, 1864, at Miller's Farm, Penn.

37-52-   CHARLES TIDD m. June 7, 1830, Rebecca M. Nurse of Water-
          ford, Me. She d. Jan. 1847, and he m. second, Jan. 6, 1848,

RESIDENCE OF MR. WILLIAM A. TOWER.

Rebecca W. B. Trask, widow of Rev. William G. Trask of Taunton, and dau. of Col. Daniel Brooks of Lincoln. Mr. Tidd was town clerk from 1832 to 1838. He has taken an active part in the cause of education, has served many years on the school committee, and has been engaged as a teacher of youth more than thirty years, the last twenty-five of which were in Lexington. He resides upon the old homestead, in a house a part of which must have stood at least one hundred and seventy-five years, and was erected, not by his great-grandfather, as stated by mistake in page 433, but by the grandfather of his great-grandfather.

52-54   *Charles Eustis*, b. March 24, 1831; d. Aug. 25, 1833.
55   *Jacob Henry*, b. March 20, 1833; d. Jan. 30, 1851, in California.
56   *Charles Lowell*, b. Feb. 12, 1838; m. March 28, 1866, Ellen A. Gooking of Portsmouth, N. H. He served nine months as a volunteer in the late war.
57   *Esther Mary*, b. April 26, 1841.

TOWER.—This name appears early in New England. *John Tower* was in Hingham in 1637, and came from Hingham, Eng. He m. Margaret Ibrook, and had at least three sons. He was engaged in settling Lancaster, and some of his descendants may have located in that town. At any rate we find the Towers somewhat numerous in the western portion of Middlesex county, and in the northern portion of Worcester.

WILLIAM A. TOWER, son of Oren and Harriet Tower, was b. in Petersham, Feb. 26, 1825, and m. April 29, 1847, Julia Davis, dau. of Austin and Sally Davis of Lancaster. He came to Lex. in Oct. 1855. He is engaged in business in Boston. He represented the Lexington District in the General Court in 1863. They have four children, *Ellen M.*, b. in Lancaster, Feb. 28, 1848; *Charlotte G.*, b. in Camb. Feb. 12, 1851; *Augustus C.*, b. in Camb. July 3, 1853; *Richard G.*, b. in Lex. Oct. 11, 1857.

THE TRASK FAMILY.

About 1715, a family by the name of *Trask* came to Lex. and located themselves on the northwesterly side of the meadow, beyond Captain Reed's, near the line of Bedford. The place from whence they came is not certainly known; but as the first of that name settled in Salem and Beverly, it is presumed that the family in Lexington are of the same stock.

1   NATHANIEL TRASK and his wife, Anna, had a dau. here as early as 1716; and he was chosen a highway surveyor in 1720. He was also one of the assessors in 1726, '39, and '40. He was a man of considerable property, standing on the tax bill for 1729 the tenth in point of amount. He d. Aug. 4, 1753, aged 59, and hence must have come to Lex. when he was a young man. She was living in Lex. and was taxed in 1779. His property at his death was inventoried at £7,596. He had two hundred acres of land, and was a proprietor in Narraganset Township No. 6, now Templeton. From the imperfect record of the family we glean the following.

1- 2 *Anna*, b. May 20, 1716; m. Joseph Hill of Billerica.
3   †*John*, b. Feb. 8, 1717; was of Wo. in 1754.
4   *Mary*, b. Nov. 19, 1719.
5   †*Nathaniel*, b. March 18, 1723; d. at Epping, N. H., 1789.

6 | *Elizabeth*, b. April 21, 1725; m. 1751, James Robinson.
7 | *Lydia*, b. Nov. 27, 1730; m. Nov. 6, 1760, William Morris of Brentwood.
8 | *Hannah*, b. March 28, 1733; m. Samuel Stearns of Billerica.
9 | †*Jonathan*, b. Dec. 12, 1735; d. April 10, 1768, aged 33.

1-3- JOHN TRASK m. Mary Green, b. Jan. 6, 1723. She was from Conn., and was sister to Henry Harrington's second wife. He lived at one time in Wo., and d. Nov. 20, 1786, aged 69.

3-10 | *Mary*, b. Nov. 7, 1742.
11 | *Isaac*, b. Jan. 3, 1744; m. April 6, 1767, Elizabeth Humble. He was a soldier in the French War.
12 | *John*, b. Feb. 28, 1746.   13 *Sarah*, b. April 3, 1748.
14 | †*Joseph*, b. June 28, 1751; m. Eunice Tufts.
15 | †*Nathaniel*, b. about 1753; m. Nancy Reed.
16 | †*Elijah*, b. about 1755; m. Sept. 8, 1793, Sally Benney.
17 | *Lucy*, b. about 1758; m. May 20, 1786, Daniel Bemis of Boston, to which place they moved.

1-5- NATHANIEL TRASK was grad. H. C. 1742, studied theology, and was settled at Keesboro', now Epping, N. H., 1747. He was dismissed from the Lex. ch. to Keesboro'; and to show their respect for him, Capt. William Reed, Capt. Benjamin Reed, and Mr. Jonathan Lawrence, three of his old neighbors, were sent as delegates to his ordination. He d. 1789, aged 66.

1-9- JONATHAN TRASK m. Chloe ——. He d. April 10, 1768, aged 33, and she m. April 16, 1781, Robert Harrington. She was ad. to the ch. 1775, when the two children mentioned below were baptized.

9-18 | *Lydia*, b. 1767.
19 | †*Jonathan*, b. 1768; m. Ruth Wood of Woburn.

3-14- JOSEPH TRASK m. March 26, 1776, Eunice Tufts of Med. He resided at first in Lex., but afterwards moved to Billerica, where he died. They had *Nathan, Katharine, Eunice Tufts, Joseph*, and perhaps other children. Joseph went South, where he died.

3-15- NATHANIEL TRASK m. Nov. 14, 1780, Nancy Reed, dau. of Swethern Reed of Bur. He resided first in Lex., then in Charlestown, where he d. He had *Nathaniel, Nancy*, and *Lydia*. Nathaniel had the misfortune to lose one of his hands in a mill. She d. July 20, 1789.

3-16- ELIJAH TRASK m. Sept. 8, 1793, Sally Benney. They moved to Boston, where he died at an advanced age.

9-19- JONATHAN TRASK m. Sept. 8, 1790, Ruth Wood of Wo. The records furnish no information concerning their family. Tradition furnishes a few facts. They had children as follows: *Jonathan; Charles*, went to Charlestown; *Chloe*, m. David Fiske; *Ruth*, d. unm.; *Josiah*, r. in Philadelphia. The records and the Trask family seemed to fade out together in Lexington.

TUCKER.—JOSEPH TUCKER of Milton m. Mary Dana of Pomfret, Conn. *Joseph*, son of Joseph and Mary, b. about 1758, m. Sarah Hill of Stoughton. He d. 1819, aged 61; she d. May, 1828, aged 73. They had five children. *Seth*, son of Joseph and Sarah,

b. 1786, m. Oct. 13, 1808, Eliza Kent of Concord, N. H. She was b. April 15, 1790. He d. Dec. 15, 1837, aged 51; she d. March 11, 1848, aged 58. They r. in New Hampshire, and had nine children.

CHARLES K. TUCKER, b. in Con. May 11, 1811, m. Nov. 27, 1836, Nancy S Poor of Wolfboro', N. H., b. March 24, 1814. He settled in Charlestown, Mass., where he remained till 1842, when he removed to Lexington. He was captain of the artillery co in Charlestown. He has served in Lex. on the board of overseers of the poor, and represented the district in the Legislature in 1858. They have children.

THE TUFTS FAMILY.

Though the Tuftses came into Lex. late, we are able to trace them to the original emigrant. PETER TUFTS was born in England, 1617. He came to this country about 1638, and settled in Malden. He was the ancestor of a numerous family of that name settled in Malden, Medford, and other towns. He was a large landholder in several towns in the vicinity. He had among other sons, *John*, b. 1657, who m. Mary Putnam Their son *Peter*, b. 1696, m. Lydia Buckman, and settled in Milk Row, Charlestown. His son *Peter*, b. April 24, 1728, m. April 19, 1750, Anne Adams. They had a family of ten children, among whom was the first of the name who came to Lex.

1   THOMAS TUFTS, b. May 18, 1766, m. Nov. 29, 1791, Rebecca Adams of Lincoln, b. Feb. 28, 1767. He d. June 10, 1830, aged 64. She d Feb. 20, 1858, aged 91. He was selectman, 1799 and 1800.

1- 2 *Thomas*, b Dec. 16, 1792. He was drowned in Ky., Oct. 8, 1817.
3   *Rebecca*, b. Aug. 31, 1797; d. Sept. 13, 1826.
4   *Marshall*, b. Sept. 26, 1802; was grad. H. C. 1827, studied theology with Dr. Holmes of Camb. Owing to mental aberration, he never officiated any length of time in his calling. He had great peculiarities of character and conduct. He wrote and published several small volumes, one of which was, "The Shores of Vespucci," a romance; he also attempted a translation of the Iliad, which, though following pretty closely the translation of Pope, bore strong marks of the state of his mind, wandering on poetic feet. The unfortunate man d. May 17, 1855.
5   *Eveline*, b. Sept. 16, 1804; m. John Rochester of Logan, Hocking Co., Ohio, where she resides.
6   †*Bowen A.*, b. Jan. 29, 1807.

1-6-   BOWEN A. TUFTS m. Jan. 1, 1831, Sarah Ann Mead, dau. of Stephen Mead of Waltham. He lived upon his father's homestead, near the junction of Weston street and Concord avenue. He d. May 28, 1867, aged 60.

6- 7 *Bowen Russell*, b. Dec. 20, 1831; d. Dec. 29, 1831.
8   *Sarah Eleanor*, b. Nov. 17, 1832; d. April 14, 1850.
9   *Bowen Russell*, b. April 3, 1834; d. March 20, 1836.
10   *Thomas Edward*, b. Oct. 16, 1836; d. Nov. 14, 1852.
11   *Abby Bright*, b. Aug. 4, 1838.
12   *Martha Emily*, b. May 10, 1840; m. June 20, 1866, Selwin Z. Bowman.
13   *Albert Nelson*, b. March 17, 1842.
14   *Ada Elizabeth*, b. April 12, 1843; d. Nov. 25, 1843.
15   *Kate*, b. Feb. 10, 1845; d. Dec. 9, 1852.
16   *Alice Ames*, b. Feb. 10, 1847.
17   *Arthur*, b. Dec. 23, 1849; d. Dec. 2, 1852.

THE TURNER FAMILY.

HUMPHREY TURNER, the emigrant ancestor of the late Captain
Turner of Lex., came to this country about 1628, and settled in
Scituate. He m. Lydia Garner, who was b. in England, where they
were married. Their son *John* m. 1645, Mary Brewster. She d.
and he m. 1649, Ann James. He had nine children. *Japheth*, their
oldest child, b. 1650, m. Hannah Hudson. He d. 1699. They had
four children. *Japheth*, their third child, b. 1682, m. Hannah Hatch,
and had four children. *Japheth*, their first child, m. 1725, Elizabeth
Morse, and had eight children. *Joseph*, their fifth child, b. July 23,
1734, m. Oct. 5, 1756, Mercy French, in Chester, Vt. He is said to
have held a commission, and died in the French war, 1757. *Joshua*,
their only child, b. Dec. 13, 1757, m. Aug. 22, 1781, Lydia Drury
of Grafton, Mass. He d. Dec. 21, 1820, and she d. March 25, 1849,
aged 86. They had a family of ten children.

1   LARKIN TURNER, the oldest child of Joshua and Lydia, was b. in
Grafton, Dec. 7, 1781, and m. Sept. 11, 1808, Sally Gould of Reading, b. March 17, 1791. She d. April 24, 1832, in Charlestown,
where they resided, and he m. May 23, 1833, Lucy P. Pierce of Lex.,
dau. of Abner and Grace Pierce, b. July 25, 1803. He d. Feb. 2,
1861, aged 79. Capt. Turner was literally the architect of his own
fortune. With limited early advantages, he entered upon a seafaring life at the age of sixteen, and passing through all grades, at
the age of twenty-two he took the command of a vessel fitted out by
that prince of merchants, William Gray, Esq. During nearly forty
years he followed the seas, and there were but few parts of the commercial world to which he had not navigated, with unusual success.
Though he commenced his career with a very limited education, by
industry and application he so informed himself, as to be enabled, as
a merchant and shipmaster, to take a high rank in his calling. By
his modest and gentlemanly bearing he gained many friends. In
1831, John Randolph, then minister to Russia, did him the honor to
make him his confidential agent and friend,—Capt. Turner at that
time being at the Russian capital. During his voyages he made
Charlestown the place of his residence, and in 1836 and 1837, he
represented that town in the legislature. About 1840, he came to
Lexington, where he spent the remainder of his days. All his children but the last were born in Charlestown.

1- 2   *Sarah E.*, b. June 22, 1810; m. Jan. 24, 1832, Isaac W. Smith.
3   *Thomas L.*, b. Aug. 17, 1812; m. April 3, 1843, Elizabeth E.
Whiton; r. in Boston.
4   *Lydia D.*, b. Feb. 20, 1820; m. Aug. 23, 1838, George I. Browne.
5   *Helen Georgiana*, b. July 18, 1826; r. in Charlestown.
6   *Josephine Maria*, b. Sept. 6, 1831; d. July 26, 1834.
7   *Harriet Josephine*, b. July 18, 1834; m. June 21, 1865, Edward L.
Nicoll of Wheeling, Va. They have one child, b. Aug. 1867.
8   *Grace Ardelle*, b. July 1, 1838; m. Dec. 8, 1859, H. B. Sampson.
They have one child, George Walter, b. March 25, 1865.
9   *Eugene Drury*, b. Dec. 30, 1842; d. Nov. 4, 1843.

THE TUTTLE FAMILY.

JOHN TUTTLE came to this country in the ship Planter, in 1635,
and settled in Ipswich. He was b. in 1596, and hence was thirty-
nine years old when he came to this country. He was made free-

man in 1639, and was representative in 1644. He d. 1656. He had four children when he came to America. *Simon*, his oldest son, b. 1631, m. Sarah Cogswell of Ipswich, and d. 1692. They had a family of eleven children. *Charles*, their second son, b. March 31, 1679, m. Ann Burnham. Their son, *Charles*, b. 1708, m. Ann Jewett, and had four children.

———

1   JEDEDIAH TUTTLE, son of Charles and Ann, was b. Nov. 24, 1753, m. Lucia Smith of Leominster, b. Dec. 30, 1755. Her mother was a *Rogers*, said to have been a lineal descendant from *John*, the martyr. He d. Sept. 9, 1833, aged 80 years; she d. Dec. 17, 1844, aged 89 years. They settled in Winchendon. He was in the Revolutionary war; was at the Battle of Bunker Hill and at the taking of Burgoyne.

1- 2 *James*, b. Aug. 10, 1780; settled in Hopkinton, N. H.
3 †*David*, b. Dec. 2, 1782; d. April 10, 1845.
4 *Jedediah*, b. April 18, 1785; d. Sept. 15, 1847.
5 *Frances*, b. March 9, 1788; m. —— Dexter.
6 *Clarissa*, b. Nov. 2, 1790; m. —— Lord.
7 *Electus*, b. Feb. 8, 1793; d. Sept. 1800.
8 *Silas*, b. Nov. 8, 1795; d. July, 1798.
9 *Eli*, b. July 5, 1797; d. 1797.
10 *Ainsworth*, b. June 1, 1799; d. Sept. 1800.
11 *Sarah*, b. Jan. 5, 1802; m. and is living.

1-3-   DAVID TUTTLE m. Jan. 19, 1806, Esther Munroe, dau. of Ebenezer Munroe of Lex. She d. Oct. 14, 1809, aged 26; he m. second, Sept. 27, 1810, Abigail, dau. of Thomas and Sarah (Taylor) Smith. She d. Dec. 15, 1816, aged 32 years, and he m. third, May 21, 1818, Patty Smith, sister of his second wife. She d. Feb. 17, 1833, aged 40, and he m. Jan. 8, 1835, Hannah Viles. He d. April 10, 1845, aged 62 years. He came to Lex. in 1804.

———

3-12 *Esther*, b. Aug. 3, 1812; m. 1833, Caleb S. Tuttle; settled in Alton, Ill.
13 *Abigail*, b. Aug. 2, 1814; m. Dec. 29, 1835, Jonathan S. Parker.
14 *David*, b. March 28, and d. April 30, 1819.
15 †*David Ainsworth*, b. May 28, 1820; m. Susan S. Johnson.
16 *George*, b. Nov. 30, 1821; m. April 5, 1855, Sarah E. Muzzey. He d. Jan. 27, 1856.
17 *Martha*, b. Jan. 30, 1824; m. Nov. 26, 1846, Charles Hastings of East Cambridge.
18 *Eliza J.*, b. April 17, 1830; m. Dec. 25, 1851, William Macintosh of Lincoln.
19 *Emily A.*, b. June 15, 1832.

3-15-   DAVID A. TUTTLE m. Dec. 30, 1846, Susan S. Johnson, dau. of Thomas Johnson. He has served several years as selectman. They have two children. *Henry Eugene*, b. May 11, 1849; *Herbert Ainsworth*, b. Nov. 14, 1853.

THE UNDERWOOD FAMILY.

There is great difficulty in tracing the genealogy of this family, both before and after they came to Lexington. They have left a very incomplete record, and it seems that they were rather migratory in their habits.

1 | THOMAS UNDERWOOD of Hingham was ad. freeman in 1637. He represented that town in 1636 and 1638. He afterwards moved to Wat., where he was selectman in 1656. His Will, dated Feb. 15, 1668, and proved April 7, 1668, mentions wife, brother Joseph, and several nephews and nieces, and prominently among them *Thomas*, son of his brother Joseph, then living with him.

2 | JOSEPH UNDERWOOD, brother of Thomas, first settled in Hingham, but afterwards moved to Wat. and was ad. freeman, 1645. He d. prior to 1677. On the files of the court is a paper relating to his estate, naming his children, *Joseph, Sarah, Hannah, Elizabeth, Thomas,* and *Martha.* It is pretty evident that they are not named in the order of their birth.

2- 3 | †*Thomas*, b. ———; d. 1680.
4 | †*Joseph*, b. 1650.   5 *Sarah*, b. ———.
6 | *Mary*, b. ———; m. May 18, 1670, Isaac Ong.?
7 | *Martha*, b. ———.
8 | *Hannah*, b. ———; m. Oct. 14, 1680, John Gibson.
9 | *Elizabeth*, b. ———; m. Sept. 13, 1693, William Bull.

2-3- | THOMAS UNDERWOOD m. Magdalen ——— as her second husband. He probably d. soon after his marriage. His Will, dated July 19, 1679, and proved Oct. 5, 1680, mentions but one child.

3-10 | †*Thomas*, b. ———; m. Nov. 19, 1679, Mary Palmer.

2-4- | JOSEPH UNDERWOOD m. Elizabeth ———. He was ad. freeman 1690, and d. the year following. His Will, dated Feb. 16, 1691, and proved April 7, 1691, mentions wife Elizabeth, sons John, Joseph, Jonathan, and Joshua, and dau. Mary, Hannah, and Elizabeth.

4-11 | *John*, b. March 6, 1677; m. Nov. 19, 1701, Rebecca Shattuck. About 1714 he moved to Charlestown.
12 | *Elizabeth*, b. May 8, 1679.
13 | †*Joseph*, b. May 28, 1681; settled in Lexington.
14 | *Joshua*, b. Jan. 31, 1683; settled in Sherborn.
15 | *Sarah*, b. Feb. 9, 1687.   16 *Hannah*, bap. April 13, 1690.

3-10- | THOMAS UNDERWOOD m. Nov. 19, 1679, Mary Palmer. He d. June 17, 1691. Probably lived in Cambridge.

10-17. | *Thomas*, b. Oct. 20, 1680.   18 *Mary*, b. June 5, 1682.
. 19 | *Elizabeth*, b. Aug. 13, 1684; m. March 25, 1709, Jonathan Hewes of Cambridge.
20 | †*Jonathan*, b. Aug. 18, 1686; m. Nov. 17, 1709, Ruth Holland.
21 | *Abigail*, b. March 26, 1688.
22 | *Martha*, b. June 20, 1689.   23 *Thomas*, b. June 3, 1691.

4-13- | JOSEPH UNDERWOOD. We find no record of his marriage. He was in Lex. 1719, when he was chosen to a subordinate town office. He o. c. in 1723, when Joseph, probably their first child, was baptized. His name is borne upon the first town tax bill extant, 1729. He was taxed in Lex. 1745, and in 1748 and '49 as a non-resident. He probably left town between those periods.

13-24 | †*Joseph*, bap. March 3, 1723. He was twice married.
25 | †*Joshua*, bap. June 6, 1725; m. Abigail Stone.
26 | *Elijah*, bap. May 5, 1728.

27 | *Peter*, bap. May 25, 1729.   28 *Ruth*, bap. April 4, 1731.
29 | *Israel*, bap. June 23, 1734; was in the French War, 1758 and '59.
30 | *Moses*, bap. Aug. 17, 1735.   31 *Susanna*, bap. Sept. 2, 1739.

10-20-   JONATHAN UNDERWOOD m. Nov. 17, 1709, Ruth Holland, and settled in Lexington. They made their peace with the ch. Sept. 2, 1711, and Ruth, probably their first child, was bap. soon after.

20-32 | *Ruth*, bap. Sept. 23, 1711; she united with the ch. Oct. 4, 1728.
33 | *Thomas*, bap. Feb. 10, 1712; d. Feb. 16, 1743.
34 | *Sarah*, bap. May 23, 1714.   35 *Jonathan*, bap. Jan. 27, 1717.

13-24-   JOSEPH UNDERWOOD m. Feb. 26, 1744, Anna Baker of Waltham. She d. May 30, 1749, and he m. June 4, 1750, Eunice Smith, dau. of Daniel and Mary Smith. He d. April 25, 1760. She was ad. to the ch. July 6, 1760.

24-36 | *Samuel*, b. Nov. 21, 1744.
37 | †*Joseph*, b. April 30, 1749; m. March 21, 1771, Mary Munroe.
38 | *Eunice*, b. Dec. 10, 1751.
39 | †*Nathan*, b. Aug. 3, 1753; grad. H. C. 1788.
40 | *Bettie*, b. Aug. 16, 1755.   41 *Anna*, b. May 22, 1757.
42 | *Sarah*, b. March 25, 1759.

13-25-   JOSHUA UNDERWOOD m. June 6, 1765, Abigail Stone.

25-43 | *Daniel*, bap. April 24, 1774; m. Aug. 1, 1798, Mary Mason.

24-37-   JOSEPH UNDERWOOD m. March 21, 1771, Mary Munroe, dau. of Marrett and Deliverance (Parker) Munroe. They were ad. to the ch. March 22, 1772. He d. Feb. 27, 1829, aged 80; she d. July 10, 1802. He was a member of Capt. Parker's company, and marched with a detachment to Cambridge, May 10, and also June 17, 1775.

37-44 | †*Joseph*, bap. July 5, 1772; m. March 2, 1800, Eusebia Harrington.
45 | *Mary*, bap. Feb. 27, 1774.
46 | *Anna*, bap. April 7, 1776; d. young.
47 | *Polly*, bap. Dec. 7, 1777; m. March 26, 1798, James Smith.
48 | †*John*, bap. March 26, 1780; m. Sarah ——.
49 | *Nathan*, bap. April 14, 1782; d. unm.
50 | *Anna*, bap. July 25, 1784.   51 *Betsey*, bap. Sept. 30, 1787.
52 | *Dorcas*, bap. April 15, 1790.

24-39-   NATHAN UNDERWOOD grad. H. C. 1788, studied divinity, and was ordained at Harwich, Nov. 21, 1792. He m. Sept. 26, 1793, Susanna Lawrence of Waltham. He d. 1841.

37-44-   JOSEPH UNDERWOOD m. March 2, 1800, Eusebia Harrington, dau. of Daniel and Anna (Munroe) Harrington. No issue. He d. Sept. 6, 1845, aged 73; she d. Dec. 22, 1859, aged 82. He was selectman, 1809.

37-48-   JOHN UNDERWOOD m. Sarah Smith, dau. of Thomas and Sarah (Taylor) Smith, b. Oct. 17, 1783. They were ad. to the ch. July 5, 1812. He d. Aug. 8, 1855, aged 76; she d. Jan. 25, 1848, aged 64.

48-53 | *Mary*, b. ——; d. 1814.   *Napoleon*, b. ——.
54 | *Abigail*, b. ——; m. Nov. 22, 1836, John Fillebrown of West Cambridge.

55 | *Mary*, bap. May 21, 1815.
66 | *Sarah*, bap. Sept. 4, 1817; d. young.
57 | *Joseph*, bap. Jan. 24, 1819.
58 | *Sarah*, bap. July 9, 1820; m. Feb. 9, 1843, John A. Tufts of Camb.
59 | *Nathan*, bap. Aug. 17, 1823.

The Underwoods, with their record, disappear suddenly, leaving only a few fragmentary notices of the name upon our books.

THE VILES FAMILY.

The Vileses have never been very numerous in Lexington, nor were they among the earliest families. They originated in Waltham, then a part of Watertown, where they were as early as 1729, and perhaps earlier.

1 | JOHN VILES m. July 2, 1731, Susanna Bemis. He d. Feb. 4, 1774; she d. Nov. 28, 1785. They were both quite advanced in age. They had a family of thirteen children.

1- 2 | *Abigail*, b. Oct. 26, 1731; m. Dec. 1752, Jonas Barnard of Wat.
3 | *John*, b. March 16, 1733; d. young.
4 | *Susan*, b. Nov. 17, 1734; m. —— Call.
5 | *Dinah*, b. June 10, 1738; m. April 9, 1761, John Watson.
6 | †*Nathan*, b. Dec. 30, 1739; m. Oct. 14, 1784, Mrs. Sarah Hagar.
7 | *Kezia*, b. Dec. 10, 1741; m. Jan. 16, 1770, John Watson of Read.
8 | †*Joel*, b. Dec. 14, 1743; m. June 27, 1775, Mary Bowman.
9 | *Jonas*, b. July 3, 1746; he was twice married.
10 | *Sarah*, b. July 3, 1748; m. Jan. 24, 1768, Jonathan Dix.
11 | *John*, b. June 12, 1750; m. Nov. 1, 1775, Hannah Warren. She d. April 5, 1784, aged 30, and he m. Aug. 26, 1784, Mary Warren of Weston, where he resided.
12 | *David*, b. Nov. 7, 1752; d. Nov. 11, 1754.
13 | *Lydia*, b. May 18, 1755; m. Jan. 25, 1775, David Wilson.
14 | *Lizza*, b. Feb. 27, 1757; m. May 22, 1777, Moses Mead.

1-6- | NATHAN VILES m. Oct. 14, 1784, Mrs. Sarah Hagar. She d. May 12, 1787, aged 33 years. They had one child, Nathan, b. Aug. 14, 1786, who d. Nov. 26, of the same year. He d. March 6, 1788, aged 49. His wife and child dying before him, he gave his property to his brothers and sisters, all of whom are mentioned in his Will, but Jonas and David, who had previously deceased.

1-8- | JOEL VILES m. June 27, 1775, Mary Bowman, dau. of William and Mary (Reed) Bowman. The precise time he came to Lex. we are not able to fix, but as he was chosen one of the hog-reeves in 1771, he must have been an inhabitant of the town at that time. He was a corporal in Capt. Parker's co. 1775. Was in the detachment which marched to Camb. May 10 and June 17 of that year. He was also in the service two months in 1776.

8-15 | *Mary*, b. Nov. 10, 1775; m. Joseph Simonds, and d. March 5, 1867, aged 92.
16 | *Susanna*, b. May 11, 1777; m. Jonas Coburn of Weston.
17 | *William*, b. Feb. 6, 1779; d. unm.
18 | *Bowman*, b. Dec. 7, 1780; moved to Lynnfield, where he died.
19 | †*John*, b. Aug. 11, 1782; m. Jan. 12, 1806, Sally Dudley.
20 | †*Elias*, b. Sept. 17, 1784; m. Betsey Fessenden.
21 | *Hannah*, b. Oct. 28, 1786; m. Amos Teel; she is living in Charlest.

22 | *Nathan*, b. Aug. 24, 1789; m. Nancy Reed; lives in Boston.
23 | *Lucy*, b. Sept. 11, 1791; m. March 18, 1820, John Nelson of Linc.
24 | ‡*Joel*, b. Oct. 21, 1793; m. April 12, 1821, Sally Smith, an adopted
    dau. of Jacob Smith.

8-19- | JOHN VILES m. Jan. 12, 1806, Sally Dudley, dau. of Nathan and
Sarah (Munroe) Dudley. He d. Sept. 28, 1858, aged 74.

19-25 | *Franklin*, b. July 25, 1807; d. June 23, 1836, unm.
26 | *Sarah A.*, b. March 17, 1810; m. Sept. 3, 1834, Charles A. Butters,
    son of Joshua and Susan Butters, b. Aug. 7, 1809. They have
    Frank, b. April 8, 1837; *S. Louisa*, b. July 3, 1839; *Ella F.*, b.
    Sept. 15, 1844.
27 | *William*, b. Dec. 12, 1812; unm.
28 | *John*, b. Feb. 14, 1819; m. Catharine R. Nelson, an adopted dau.
    of Dr. Nelson of Wo. They resided in Richmond, Va., where
    she died.
29 | *Martha A.*, b. May 10, 1821; m. John D. Tidd of Woburn.
30 | *Rebecca D.*, b. May 12, 1824.
31 | *Mary B.*, b. Feb. 17, 1831; m. Jan. 1860, B. F. Tenney of Boston.

8-20- | ELIAS VILES m. April 11, 1818, Betsey A. Fessenden, dau. of
Thomas and Hannah (Prentice) Fessenden. He d. and she m. 1833,
Jonathan Hartwell of Montague.

20-32 | *Emeline*, b. Feb. 24, 1819; m. John Ward of Montague, where
they reside.

8-24- | JOEL VILES m. Jan. 12, 1821, Sally Smith, and adopted dau. of
Jacob Smith. He represented the town in the convention to revise
the Constitution, in 1853. He has been selectman ten years.

24-33 | *Elias*, b. June 25, 1822; d. April 21, 1849, unmarried.
34 | *Susan P.*, b. Dec. 17, 1823; m. Oct. 7, 1849, Nathan Stiles. He
    ran a locomotive engine ten or twelve years; r. at Waterville, Me.
35 | *Joel Augustus*, b. March 15, 1825; d. Feb. 11, 1850, in California.
36 | *Andrew*, b. Oct. 27, 1827; d. Sept. 21, 1852.
37 | *Clinton*, b. Jan. 13, 1828; r. in Boston.
38 | *Adeline*, b. Nov. 25, 1830; m. Sept. 14, 1856, Oliver C. Robinson.
39 | *Sarah S.*, b. March 17, 1832; m. Jan. 8, 1853, George A. Stimson,
    and d. Dec. 23, 1853.
40 | *Jacob Smith*, b. July 16, 1840; r. in Boston.

THE WELLINGTON FAMILY.

The Wellingtons, though they have been quite numerous in Lexington, were not among the earliest settlers of the place. The name first appears on our records in 1705. They removed from Watertown to Cambridge Farms; and as they settled in the southeasterly part of Lexington, near the Watertown and Waltham line, and some portions of the families were frequently moving across the lines, it is somewhat difficult to trace the Lexington families. We give their origin and descent as near as we can; and in doing this, it would not be strange if in some cases, we should place some individuals on the wrong side of the town line.

1 | ROGER WELLINGTON, a planter, b. about 1609 or 10, was one of the early proprietors of Watertown. He probably removed to that place from Boston, for the Boston records contain the names of his

children. Though he was in Watertown as early as 1642, he was
not admitted freeman till 1690. He m. Mary, eldest dau. of Dr.
Richard of Charlestown. He d. March 11, 1698. He mentions in
his Will, his sons John, Joseph, Benjamin, Oliver and Palgrave.

1- 2 *John,* b. July 25, 1638; admitted freeman Dec. 1677. He was a
farmer in Camb.; m. Susanna Straight, and d. Aug. 23, 1726,
aged 88. He left no children.

3 *Mary,* b. Feb. 10, 1641; m. May 21, 1662, Henry Maddock, and
after his death m. John Cooledge—having one child by each
husband.

4 †*Joseph,* b. Oct. 9, 1643; admitted freeman, 1677.

5 †*Benjamin,* b. ———; admitted freeman, 1677.

6 *Oliver,* b. Nov. 23, 1648; admitted freeman, 1677; m. wid. Anna
Livermore, and d. Aug. 30, 1727, without issue.

7 *Palgrave,* admitted freeman, 1690; m. Sarah Bond, dau. of William
Bond, Esq., and d. about 1715, without issue.

1-4-   JOSEPH WELLINGTON was twice m. and had three daughters and
one son.

4- 8 ‡*Thomas,* b. Nov. 10, 1686; m. Rebecca Whittemore.

1-5-   BENJAMIN WELLINGTON m. Dec. 7, 1671, Elizabeth Sweetman of
Cambridge. He d. Jan. 8, 1710.

5- 9 *Elizabeth,* b. Dec. 29, 1673; m. John Fay of Marlboro'.

10 †*Benjamin,* b. June 21, 1676; d. in Lex. Nov. 15, 1738.

11 *John,* b. July 26, 1678; d. Nov. 30, 1717.

12 *Ebenezer,* b. ———; m. Jan. 28, 1704, Deliverance Bond.. He
probably settled in Lexington, where his first two children were
baptized. *Elizabeth,* bap. Aug. 26, 1705. *Ebenezer,* bap. March
13, 1709, and grad. H. C. 1727. He subsequently removed to
Watertown, where he kept a public house in 1715-17. The birth
of the rest of his children is found upon the Wat. Records.

13 *Ruhamah,* b. ———; m. Nov. 15, 1699, Dea. Joseph Brown, then of
Wat., but afterwards of Lexington. She d. July 1, 1772, aged 92.

14 *Mehitabel,* bap. March 4, 1688; m. Sept. 13, 1715, William Sherman
of Newton. She was the mother of the celebrated Roger Sherman
of Connecticut, of Revolutionary memory.

15 *Joseph,* bap. Jan. 4, 1691.

16 *Roger,* the youngest son, birth not recorded.

4—8   THOMAS WELLINGTON m. Rebecca Whittemore, and had five
children, two sons and three daughters. His sons were—

8-17 †*Joseph,* b. Nov. 21, 1711.

18 *Thomas,* b. Aug. 6, 1714; d. Nov. 4, 1783.

5-10-   BENJAMIN WELLINGTON m. Jan. 16, 1699, Lydia Brown, and
settled in Lexington, where they were ad. to the ch. June 10, 1705.
She d. May 13, 1711, and he m. second, Dec. 25, 1712, Elizabeth
Phelps. She d. Jan. 7, 1730, aged 54, and he m. third, Mary Whitney. He d. Nov. 19, 1738, aged 63. He was for many years one
of the most popular men in the town—having been elected assessor,
sixteen years, town clerk, fifteen years, treasurer, three years, and
representative, three years.

10-19 †*Benjamin,* b. May 21, 1702; d. Nov. 15, 1738.

20 *Lydia,* b. Aug. 24, 1704; d. Aug. 10, 1718.

21 | *Kezia*, b. March 28, 1707.
22 | *John*, b. Nov. 12, 1709; d. Sept. 22, 1728.
23 | *Abigail*, b. July 14, 1715; m. Feb. 19, 1734, David Munroe.
24 | †*Timothy*, b. July 27, 1719; d. previous to 1760.
25 | *Mary*, b. Oct. 20, 1732.   26 *Oliver*, b. April 14, 1735.

8-17- | JOSEPH WELLINGTON m. Nov. 13, 1733, Dorcas Stone.

17-27 | *Joseph*, b. Nov. 13, 1734; d. 1819.
28 | *Rebecca*, b. Sept. 4, 1737; m. Feb. 10, 1757, Zachariah Hill.
29 | *Dorcas*, b. May 31, 1740; d. unmarried.
30 | *Mary*, b. Nov. 29, 1742; m. July 6, 1761, Phinehas Stearns.
31 | *Hannah*, bap. 1745.
32 | *Margaret*, b. Aug. 22, 1745; m. Timothy Page, who was killed at the battle of White Plains.
33 | *Palgrave*, b. March 12, 1748. He moved to Alstead, N. H.
34 | *Jeduthan*, b. Sept. 4, 1750; settled on the homestead.
35 | *Elizabeth*, b. Nov. 6, 1753.   36 *Enoch*, b. Sept. 1, 1756.

10-19- | BENJAMIN WELLINGTON m. first, Lydia ——. He m. second, Abigail Fessenden, b. July 13, 1713, dau. of Thomas and Abigail (Poulter) Fessenden. He d. Nov. 15, 1738, and his wid. m. Ebenezer Smith of Lexington.

19-37 | *Lydia*, b. Dec. 22, 1722.
38 | *Roger*, b. June 22, 1733; m. in Waltham, March 10, 1757, Abigail Stearns. They had a son, Oliver, b. in Lexington, Jan. 19, 1758. They were admitted to the church in Lex. Dec. 25, 1757, and were dismissed in 1760 to the Second Church in Brookfield.
39 | *John*, b. April 18, 1736; removed to Townsend, Vt.
40 | *Benjamin*, b. April 22, 1738; m. Sept. 5, 1763, Lucy Smith. He removed to Brookfield, and in 1777 to Ashby.

10-24- | TIMOTHY WELLINGTON m. Rebecca Stone who was b. Jan. 22, 1721, dau. of Jonathan and Chary (Adams) Stone of Lex. He d. and his wid. m. Feb. 14, 1754, John Dix of Waltham.

24-41 | †*Benjamin*, b. Aug. 7, 1743; m. Martha Ball.
42 | *Chary*, b. July 12, 1745.
43 | †*Timothy*, b. April 15, 1747; d. April, 1809.
44 | *Abigail*, b. March 14, 1749; m. Dec. 29, 1768, Daniel Cotting of Waltham.
45 | *Ruhamon*, b. Sept. 4, 1751.

24-41- | BENJAMIN WELLINGTON m. Dec. 4, 1766, Martha Ball of Walt. He was selectman 1785 and 1792. He d. Sept. 14, 1812, aged 69. He was a member of Capt. Parker's company in 1775, and on coming to the Common that morning, was taken by the British and disarmed. He was detained but a short time, when he was discharged, so that he partook of the honors and dangers of that day. He was at the taking of Burgoyne in 1777. He was the first prisoner taken in the Revolution.

41-46 | *Mary*, b. Sept. 22, 1767; m. Dec. 31, 1789, Asa Baldwin Locke.
47 | *Abigail*, bap. in Walt. Oct. 1, 1769.
48 | *Benjamin*, bap. in Walt. July 13, 1772.
49 | *Oliver*, bap. in Walt. Nov. 13, 1774.
50 | †*Benjamin Oliver*, b. Aug. 23, 1778; d. Nov. 10, 1853, aged 75.
51 | †*Peter*, b. May 31, 1781; m. 1813, Hepzibah Hastings.

52 | *Richard*, b. July 14, 1783; d. Dec. 11, 1836, aged 53.
53 | *James*, b. Dec. 12, 1785; m. Nov. 18, 1820, Susanna Jacobs, b. Aug. 7, 1801, dau. of Braddock Jacobs of Lit.
54 | *Patty*, twin with James, b. Dec. 12, 1785.
55 | *Isaac*, b. Dec. 5, 1787; m. Nov. 18, 1824, Mary Wilder Jacobs and resided in Medford.

24-43-   TIMOTHY WELLINGTON, b. April 15, 1747; d. April, 1809: m. May 1, 1776, Hannah W. Abbott, b. Dec. 10, 1758, d. 1785. They were both admitted to the ch. in Lex. March 30, 1777. He was a member of the patriotic company which shed the first blood of the Revolution; he was subsequently in the service at Camb. some five months.

43-56 | *Rebecca Stone*, b. Feb. 5, 1777; m. April 22, 1799, John K. Coolidge, and moved to Cincinnati, Ohio.
       Timothy, b. March 29, 1778; drowned April 8, 1781.
57 | †*Nehemiah*, b. Jan. 1, 1780; m. May 16, 1805, Nancy Stearns.
58 | *Timothy*, b. Oct. 8, 1781; m. first, 1813, Mary E. Law, who d.
59 | March, 1816, and he m. second, 1820. Lydia Yates. He was grad. H. C. 1806, M. D. He settled in West Cambridge, where he d. 1853.
60 | *Hannah*, b. July 4, 1783; d. aged 17 or 18 years.
61 | *Joseph Abbott*, b. July 14, 1785.

41-50-   BENJAMIN OLIVER WELLINGTON m. in Lincoln, May 20, 1811, Patty Hastings, b. April 10, 1789, dau. of Major Samuel and Lydia (Nelson) Hastings. He was a military man, and rose to the rank of major. He was a leading influential citizen, and filled most of the important offices in the gift of his townsmen. He was selectman several years, and filled other places of honor and trust. He d. Dec. 10, 1853, aged 75. He and his wife were ad. to the ch. May 2, 1813. He lived and died upon the place which had been in possession of the family about one hundred and fifty years. He was the first man in the town who established a milk dairy for the supply of the Boston market,—which has since become a very important branch of husbandry in the town.

50-62 | *Oliver Hastings*, b. Feb. 23, 1812; d. March 1, 1813.
63 | *Oliver Hastings*, b. Aug. 19, 1813; m. Aug. 29, 1838, Charlotte Augusta, dau. of William Kent, Esq., of Concord, N. H., and had Mary C., William A., Arthur M., Lucy M. D.
64 | *Mary Jane*, b. July 5, 1815; m. April 17, 1845, James H. Danforth of Boston.
65 | *Albert*, b. June 1, 1817; m. in Boston, where he is a merchant.
66 | *Ambrose*, b. April 11, 1819; grad. H. C. 1841; m. May, 1845, Lucy J. Kent. He is a lawyer in Boston.
67 | *Martha*, b. April 11, 1821; d. Jan. 1863.
68 | *Benjamin*, b. March 21, 1823; resides in Buffalo.
69 | *Dorcas Ann*, b. April 20, 1825; m. Dr. Geo. H. Taylor.
70 | *Laura*, b. Dec. 26, 1826; d. Dec. 30, 1843.
71 | *Winslow*, b. May 16, 1829.
72 | *Edward*, b. March 3, 1831; drowned in Fresh Pond, July 6, 1852, while a member of the Lawrence Scientific School, a department of Harvard College.

41-51-   PETER WELLINGTON m. in Lincoln, May 26, 1813, Hepzibah Hastings, b. May 24, 1793. She was sister to his brother Benjamin

O.'s wife. He and his brother not only married sisters, but they resided in the same house, and each have had large families. He is living, and has nearly closed his eighty-seventh year.

51-73 *Henry Wakefield*, b. Feb. 25, 1814; m. June 1, 1836, Martha S. Small.
74 *Darius*, b. Oct. 9, 1815; m. Dec. 28, 1844, Hannah Duville.
75 *Isabella*, b. May 23, 1817; m. April 23, 1845, Herman Snow, and d. Aug. 3, 1848.
76 *Abby*, b. March 29, 1819; m. June 4, 1844, James Blodgett; d. Oct. 12, 1845.
77 *Caroline*, b. Dec. 3, 1820.
78 *Andrew*, b. Dec. 23, 1822; m. Leah L. Nichols.
79 *Eliza*, b. Dec. 6, 1824.
80 *Elbridge Gerry*, b. July 29, 1826; d. Oct. 23, 1849, in California.
81 *Cornelius*, b. May 23, 1828.
82 *Emily*, b. Feb. 24, 1830; d. April 13, 1850.
83 *Samuel Hastings*, b. Aug. 6, 1832; d. April 7, 1833.
84 *Louisa Maria*, b. April 20, 1834; m. May 24, 1863, Lucius H. Peaslee of Boston.
85 *Charles Austin*, b. Dec. 2, 1837.

43-82- NEHEMIAH WELLINGTON m. May 16, 1805, Nancy Stearns, dau. of Joshua of Waltham. He d. May 11, 1857, aged 77. He was selectman 1841, assessor 1840, and representative 1836 and 1838.

82-86 *Anna Eliza*, b. March 2, 1806; d. Oct. 3, 1822.
87 †*Augustus*, b. June 15, 1807.
88 *Hannah Maria*, b. Nov. 17, 1809; m. June 15, 1835, Samuel Bridge.
89 *Timothy W.*, b. July 4, 1811; m. Nov. 4, 1835, Susanna Ray, who d. April 28, 1847, and he m. Sept. 3, 1848, Augusta Fiske, dau. of Samuel Fiske. They reside in Worcester. At the breaking out of the Rebellion, Mr. Wellington took an active part in sustaining the Government by all the means in his power. Two of his oldest sons, *Edward W.* and *Frank W.*, enlisted as privates in the 25th Regt. of Mass. Vols., and after serving through Burnside's campaign in North Carolina, Edward was promoted to a lieutenancy in Col. Lowell's cavalry; but his health failing, he resigned his position. Frank W. was detailed to the commissary department, and was stationed at Newberne, N. C., where he remained till his three years expired. *George*, a younger son of Timothy, at the age of seventeen, enlisted in the 2d Mass. Heavy Artillery, was taken prisoner at Plymouth, N. C., sent to Andersonville, where he died, a victim to Rebel barbarity. *Charles*, a twin brother of George, enlisted in the navy, and served fifteen months.

Mr. Wellington not only sent four sons to the war, but he provided, at his own expense, a hospital at Worcester for the sick and disabled soldiers, which he supported about five months, and dispensed favors to fifty or sixty patriotic soldiers. Mr. Wellington represented the twenty-seventh Worcester district in the legislature of 1864.

90 †*Sullivan*, b. Nov. 8, 1813; he has been thrice married.
91 *Jonas Clarke*, b. Nov. 30, 1815; m. Oct. 17, 1839, Harriet Bosworth, dau. of Nathaniel Bosworth of Attleboro'. He left Lexington in 1856, and took up his residence in Camb. During the late rebellion, he took a deep interest in the welfare of the soldiers, often visiting our armies in the field, and in the winter of 1863-4, he visited New Orleans, as agent from Massachusetts, to attend to

the want of the soldiers. His oldest son, *Austin C.*, enlisted in the 38th Regt., was made sergeant, and detailed as acting adjutant, which position he held till the rebellion closed. He was in the Shenandoah Valley under Sheridan, during his brilliant career. Jonas Clarke was an assessor in Lex. 1852–54, and town treasurer in 1855.

92 | *Horatio*, b. Sept. 6, 1817; m. Dec. 16, 1841, Mary Bowman Teel, dau. of Amos Teel of Charlestown, to which place he removed in 1850. His eldest son, *Arthur*, seventeen years of age, enlisted in the 13th Regt., was discharged for disability, re-enlisted in the 36th Regt., was taken prisoner and paroled, and again discharged for disability. Mr. W. represented the first Middlesex district in the legislature of 1864.

93 | *Aris M.*, b. June 27, 1819; m. Oct. 17, 1850, Emory Abbott Mulliken.

94 | *Joseph A.*, b. June 12, 1821; m. Feb. 10, 1846, Ellen A. Smith, dau. of Billings Smith. He moved to Camb. 1854, where he now resides.

82–87– | Augustus Wellington m. first, March 3, 1835, Tryphena M. Winship, dau. of Stephen Winship. She d. Dec. 26, 1841, aged 34, and he m. second. Sept. 18, 1842, Mrs. Martha Hastings, who d. suddenly, April 20, 1852, aged 46. He m. third, Sept. 8, 1852, Sarah Bisbee of Boston.

87–95 | *Henry A.*, b. July 10, 1839; m. March 16, 1862, Angeline E. Moore of Canaan, Me.

96 | *Tryphena*, b. 1841; d. Aug. 16, 1846.

97 | *Charles B.*, b. Sept. 28, 1849; d. Aug. 27, 1850.

98 | *Grace Standish*, b. Sept. 30, 1853.

99 | *Herbert Lyman*, b. Oct. 9, 1856.

82–90– | Sullivan Wellington m. April 12, 1844, Isabella L. Hastings, dau. of Charles and Martha Hastings of Waltham. She d. March 29, 1853, aged 26, and he m. second, March 1, 1855, Antoinette Holten, dau. of Jeremiah and Mary Holten of Boothbay, Me. She d. May 4, 1859, aged 33, and he m. third, June 20, 1860, Louisa Robinson, dau. of Moses and Hannah Robinson of Rockland, Me.

90–100 | *Ellen J.*, b. March 11, 1846; m. Feb. 23, 1868, R. Russell Simonds.

101 | *Martha Antoinette.* } b. Jan. 25, 1856; d. Feb. 9, 1856.

102 | *Mary Lizzie.* } b. Jan. 25, 1856; d. Aug. 30, 1863.

103 | *Clifford Holten*, b. April 28, 1859; d. Dec. 25, 1859.

104 | *Charles Sumner*, b. Sept. 21, 1862.

105 | *Ernest Hathorn*, b. Nov. 2, 1864.

There is another branch of the Wellington family, several of whom have settled in Lexington, though their ancestors for some generations have been of Waltham or Watertown.

1 | William Wellington of Waltham, who was b. July 28, 1746, and who was son of Thomas Jr., of Waltham, b. Aug. 6, 1714, and grandson of Thomas (No. 18 in the preceding table of Wellingtons) m. Aug. 18, 1764, Mary Whitney. He had a family of fourteen children, many of whom were remarkable for their longevity. William was a prominent citizen in Waltham; was selectman seventeen years. Many of his children settled in Lexington, or were connected with Lexington families.

1– 2 | ‡*William*, b. Dec. 11, 1769, first of Walt., but afterwards of Lex.

3 | ‡*David*, b. Nov. 1, 1771; m. Rebecca Stearns.

4 | *Abraham*, b. March 22, 1774; m. Elizabeth Lawrence.
5 | *Polly*, b. April 16, 1776; m. Phinehas Lawrence.
6 | *Isaac*, b. Feb. 20, 1778; drowned in Fresh Pond, Nov. 1798, then a member of the senior class, H. C.
7 | *Charles*, b. Feb. 20, 1780; grad. H. C. 1802; settled a clergyman in Templeton.
8 | *Alice*, b. Oct. 31, 1781; m. March 3, 1803, Jonas Clarke.
9 | *Betsey*, b. Feb. 4, 1784; m. June 28, 1804, Capt. Isaac Child.
10 | *Seth*, b. Nov. 18, 1785; m. Louisa Miles and Mrs. Sabra Stone.
11 | *Sybil*, b. Sept. 24, 1787; m. Dec. 18, 1806, Loring Pierce.
12 | †*Marshall*, b. Sept. 26 1789; m. March 9, 1815, Elizabeth Kimball.
13 | *Darius*, b. Jan. 14, 1794; was twice married.
14 | *Almira*, b. Aug. 1, 1795; m. Francis Bowman.
15 | *Isaac*, b. Nov. 12, 1796.

1-2- | WILLIAM WELLINGTON m. May 3, 1798, Avis Fiske. He resided first in Waltham, and afterwards came to Lexington. He d. Aug. 24, 1861, aged 92 years and 8 months. She d. Jan. 5, 1863, aged 84 years and 9 months.

2-16 | *Mary*, b. Feb. 11, 1799; m. May 8, 1825, Aaron Holbrook.
17 | *Jonathan F.*, b. Jan. 5, 1801; m. March, 1825, Abigail Cope of Quincy.
18 | *Adeline*, b. March 8, 1803; m. Dec. 13, 1827, Nathaniel W. Stearns of Waltham.
19 | *Abigail*, b. July 15, 1805; d. Oct. 15, 1806.
20 | *Abigail*, b. Feb. 11, 1807; m. Nov. 25, 1827, Nathaniel Pierce of Lexington.
21 | *William*, b. March 29, 1808; m. Dec. 1, 1833, Rebecca Ames of Pembroke.

1-3- | DAVID WELLINGTON m. April 11, 1805, Rebecca Stearns. They were ad. to the ch. in Lex. June 6, 1806. She d. Feb. 18, 1821. He d. March 10, 1860, aged 88 years.

3-22 | *Hiram*, b. March 14, 1806; grad. H. C. 1834, m. Oct. 23, 1851, Ann A. Hudson. He is a lawyer in Boston.
23 | *Rebecca*, b. April 11, 1808.
24 | *David*, b. Aug. 15, 1810; a merchant in Boston.
25 | *Mary*, b. March 31, 1813; m. Oct. 31, 1840, George S. Cary, son of Jonathan.
26 | *Francis*, b. Aug. 27, 1815. 27 *Susan Wyeth*, b. Aug. 28, 1818.
28 | *Avery*, b. Feb. 14, 1821; m. Dec. 17, 1851, Martha L. Kidder.

1-12- | MARSHALL WELLINGTON m. March 9, 1815, Elizabeth Kimball. He d. July 10, 1866, aged 76.

12-29 | *Marshall Kimball*, b. in Lex. March 24, 1817; m. May 20, 1843, Joanna Carrol.
30 | *Elizabeth*, b. Jan. 16, 1820; m. May 9, 1838, Albert W. Bryant. She d. July 15, 1840.
31 | *Nancy*, b. March 1, 1822; m. Aug. 23, 1841, Albert W. Bryant, widower of her late sister Elizabeth.
32 | *Walter*, b. Dec. 3, 1824; m. Dec. 3, 1847, Martha W. Hastings, dau. of Charles and Martha of Waltham. She d. June 18, 1849, and he m. Jan. 6, 1852, Hannah M. Parker. They have had *Charles*, b. Oct. 13, 1853; *A. Elizabeth*, b. Feb. 1, 1856, d. Nov. 9, 1865; *Marion L.*, b. Oct. 17, 1866.

THE WESTCOTT FAMILY.

REV. HENRY WESTCOTT was b. in Warwick, R. I., Oct. 30, 1831; m. June 10, 1863, Sarah A. Read, dau. of William Read of Cambridge, Mass. He graduated at Brown University, 1853, and after pursuing his theological studies, was settled in Barre, Mass., where he remained five years. After leaving Barre, he supplied the society at West Dedham one year, when he came to Lexington, where he was installed June 26, 1867. He was son of Josiah and Mary H. (Tibbetts) Westcott of Warwick, R. I., who was a direct descendant from *Stukely Westcott*, who came to this country about 1635, and settled in Salem. Entertaining religious opinions differing from the puritans in general, a controversy arose, and Stukely Westcott was excommunicated, in 1639, with Roger Williams and others, who had already gone to Providence to found a colony there. Westcott settled in Warwick, where his descendants are found at the present day.

THE WHITE FAMILY.

1   DANIEL WHITE was in Cambridge Farms as early as 1696, when his name appears on the tax bill. He was constable in 1713 and 1714. He must have been a man of some dignity of character; for in seating the meeting house in 1731, he was placed in the second seat below. He m. Mary ——; she d. and he m. second, Hannah ——. His Will, 1738, mentions wife Hannah, sons Joseph, John, Stephen, and Samuel, and dau. Sybil Mansfield and Sarah Locke.

1- 2 *Daniel*, b. Oct. 29, 1695.
3   *Mary*, b. Oct. 24, 1697; probably d. young.
4   †*John*, b. Feb. 16, 1699.   5 *Mary*, bap. Sept. 8, 1700.
6   *Thomas*, b. Feb. 22, 1702; d. March 22, 1718.
7   †*Joseph*, b. April 17, 1704.
8   *Sybil*, b. May 12, 1706; m. Dec. 25, 1734, Theophilus Mansfield of Watertown.
9   *Stephen*, b. April 27, 1709.
10 *Sarah*, b. Aug. 23, 1711; m. —— Locke.
11 *Samuel*, bap. Sept. 12, 1714; m. Sept. 13, 1736, Dinah Ward.

1-4-   JOHN WHITE m. Susanna ——. He and his wife made their peace with the ch. Oct. 10, 1735, and the next Sabbath, John, their first child, was bap. We find no other record of his family. He appears to have been a military character. He was in service as a corporal among the King's troops in 1725, and was also in the French and Indian wars, 1757 and 1760. As there is no further record of him in Lex., he probably never returned to reside in that place.

1-7-   JOSEPH WHITE m. Hannah —— about 1727. She d. April 7, 1731, and he m. Mary ——, He d. Aug. 4, 1777, aged 73, and she d. Oct. 20, 1780.

7-12 *Hannah*, b. Dec. 10, 1728; m. May 24, 1752, Joseph Abbot.
13   *Mary*, b. March 25, 1731.
14   *Susanna*, b. Oct. 10, 1735; m. Oct. 4, 1756, Jonathan Raymond.
15   *Joseph*, b. Oct. 11, 1737.
16   *William*, b. April 25, 1740; m. Feb. 9, 1767, Tabitha Ener of Walt.
17   *Thomas*, b. April 15, 1742.   18 *Benjamin*, b. May 9, 1744.
19   †*Ebenezer*, b. July 10, 1746; m. Elizabeth Harrington.
20   *John*, b. June 1, 1748.   21 *Nathan*, b. June 16, 1750.

6-19-   Ebenezer White m. Feb. 12, 1767, Elizabeth Harrington. He took an early part in the Revolutionary struggle, being with the Lex. minute men on the Common on the 19th of April 1775. He also marched to Camb. on the 6th of May that year, and also on the day of the battle of Bunker Hill. At that time he held a sergeant's warrant. He subsequently held a commission, and enlisted into the Continental army. He d. Oct. 6, 1777.

19-22 | *Nathan*, b. July 27, 1767.   23 *Jonas*, b. Jan. 20, 1768.
24 | *Joseph*, b. Nov. 30, 1770; m. Nov. 29, 1792, Polly Harrington.
25 | *Sally*, bap. Dec. 28, 1772; d. in infancy.
26 | *Ebenezer*, b. April 7, 1775; d. Dec. 13, 1819, aged 44.

THE WHITMAN FAMILY.

John Whitman, one of the early settlers of Weymouth, was probably the ancestor of nearly all the Whitmans in the country. He was in New England before 1638, as he was made freeman that year. He filled several public offices in Weymouth. He had nine children. *Thomas*, his eldest son, probably came to this country with his mother, about 1641, being at that time twelve years of age; and hence was b. in England, 1629. He was made freeman 1653. In 1655, he m. Abigail Byram. He and his father-in-law moved to Bridgewater. He d. 1712, aged 83. He had three sons and four daughters. *Nicholas*, the third son of Thomas, m. Sarah Vining of Weymouth, and had by her four sons. She d. and he m. Mary Conant, by whom he had several other children. He was killed by being run over by a cart. *John*, the second son of Nicholas by his first wife, was b. 1704, and m. Mary Richards, by whom he had no children. She d. and he m. Elizabeth Cary, by whom he had Samuel and John. He m. a third wife, by whom he had other children. He d. 1792, aged 88 years.

1   John Whitman, of John, m. Lydia Snow. He resided in Bridgewater on the patrimonial farm. By his first wife he had three children. She d. and he m. his cousin, Abigail Whitman, dau. of Josiah Whitman, by whom he had eleven children. He was deacon of the church, and d. 1842, at the advanced age of 107 years.

1- 2 | *Lydia*, b. 1765; m. Ebenezer Whitman of Windsor. She d. 1826.
3 | *Elizabeth*, b. 1767; m. —— Trowbridge of Middleboro'; d. 1791.
4 | *James*, b. 1769; resided in Belchertown. He d. 1855.
5 | *Catharine*, b. 1775; d. Dec. 1793.
6 | *Bathsheba*, b. 1777; d. unm. in Lex. Aug. 20, 1864, aged 87. Miss Whitman was engaged as a teacher in private and public schools, nearly all the time from 1794 to 1845. She was a woman of superior mind, and retained her faculties to the last. After she was eighty years old, she wrote an excellent round hand, without the least tremor. She was highly respected, and d. in full faith of a happy immortality.
7 | *Josiah*, b. 1779; resided in Wellfleet.
8 | *Alfred*, b. 1781; d. Aug. 1842.
9 | *Obadiah*, b. 1783; removed to New Gloucester.
10 | *Nathaniel*, b. 1785; grad. H. C. 1809, settled as a clergyman at Billerica.
11 | *Hosea*, b. 1788; resided in Waltham; d. 1859.
12 | *John*, b. 1790; deceased 1822.
13 | *Abigail*, b. 1793; deceased 1818.

91

14 | *Bernard*, b. 1796; he was a clergyman, and d. in Waltham, 1834.
15 | †*Jason*, b. April 30, 1799; d. in Portland, 1858.

1-15- | JASON WHITMAN m. March, 1832. Mary Fairfield of Saco; grad. H. C. 1825; read Theology and settled at Saco, Me., 1830. In 1834, was appointed General Agent of the American Unitarian Association. Subsequently he was settled in Portland. In 1845, he was invited to Lexington, where he was installed July 30, of that year. In December, 1847, he and his wife went to Saco, to attend the funeral of her brother, and in Portland he was taken suddenly ill, and d. Jan. 25, 1858. His wid. is still living in Lexington.

15-16 | *Sarah*, b. April 8, 1833; d. Feb. 21, 1846.
17 | *Bernard*, b. Sept. 15, 1834; he has spent some ten years in South America.
18 | *Catharine*, b. July 18, 1836.
19 | *John*, b. May 28, 1838. He had followed the seas some years in the merchant service, and in the midst of the late rebellion he entered the navy, and served to the end of the war.
20 | *Martha*, b. July 13, 1840.

The Whitmans have been remarkable for longevity. In the brief line we have traced, there are four persons whose aggregate age is three hundred and sixty-five years, giving the average of ninety-one years to each.

THE WHITMORE FAMILY.

Though Whitmore has never been a very common name in Lex., it is immediately connected with the earliest records, and is mentioned in connection with the boundary of the parish, when it was incorporated in 1693. The Great and General Court, in setting off the Farms as a precinct, described the dividing line between the old town of Cambridge and the North Parish as follows: " Beginning at the first run of water or swampy place, over which is a kind of a bridge in the way or road, on the southerly side of Francis Whitmore's house, towards the town of Cambridge."

This vague and indefinite description was again adopted when the precinct was erected into a town, in 1713, and remains to this day the boundary between Lexington and Arlington. But though this description is not very definite, it fixes with a good degree of certainty the location of the Whitmore house. It must have been situated on Main street, below Cutler's Tavern, near the line of the town. But while this house was within the precinct, it is not certain that Francis Whitmore ever resided in it, though it was owned by him and bore his name. He certainly could not have resided there at the incorporation of the precinct, for he had then been dead several years. The house was probably occupied by his son, Samuel, whose name is found upon the parish tax bills, back to the incorporation of the parish.

1 | FRANCIS WHITMORE was born about 1625. He lived in Camb., and was a large landholder in that and the neighboring towns. He m. Isabel Parke, dau. of Richard Parke of Camb. She d. March 31, 1665, and he m. Nov. 10, 1666, Margaret Harty. He d. Oct. 12, 1685, aged 62. He served in the Indian War under Major Willard, as the treasurer's books show.

1- 2 | *Elizabeth*, b. May 2, 1649; m. Nov. 3, 1669, Daniel Markham.
3 | *Francis*, b. Oct. 12, 1650; removed to Connecticut.

4 | *John*, b Oct. 1, 1654; lived in Medford, and d. Feb. 22, 1739.
5 | †*Samuel*, b. May 1, 1658; m. Rebecca Gardner.
6 | *Abigail*, b. July 3, 1660; m. —— Wilcox.
7 | *Sarah*, b. May 7, 1662; m. May 29, 1683, William Locke.
8 | *Margaret*, b. Sept. 9, 1668; m. Thomas Carter.
9 | *Frances*, b. March 3, 1671; m. Jonathan Thompson.
10 | ‡*Thomas*, b. 1673; m. Mary, dau. of Samuel Waters.
11 | †*Joseph*, b. 1675; lived in Woburn.

He had also *Margery*, bap. March 27, 1664, and *Hannah*, bap. Feb. 15, 1667, but both died young.

1-5- | SAMUEL WHITMORE m. March 31, 1686, Rebecca Gardner. His name is found upon our earliest records, being a subscriber for the erection of a meeting house in 1692, and one of a committee, in 1693, for making taxes. He was an assessor in 1700 and 1708, and a tythingman in 1712. He was one of the original members of the ch. gathered in 1696, and his wife, Rebecca, was admitted Jan. 16, 1700. She d. June 6, 1709, aged 43, and he m. Mrs. Mary, wid. of Abraham Watson; she d. Nov. 14, 1730, aged 60. He d. May 22, 1724, aged 66.

5-12 | †*Francis*, b. Dec. 9, 1686.
13 | ‡*Samuel*, b. April 1, 1688; m. Jan. 7, 1720, Bethia Page.
14 | *Rebecca*, b. Feb. 9, 1690; d. June 12, 1709.
15 | *John*, b. June 5, 1692; d. May 5, 1714.
16 | *Benjamin*, bap. Nov. 27, 1698, moved to Newton.
17 | *Abigail*, bap. Nov. 27, 1698.   18 *Sarah*, b. April 10, 1701.
19 | *Nathaniel*, b. May 7, 1702, moved to Newton.
20 | *Mary*, b. May 4, 1704.
21 | *John*, b. Jan. 25, 1714. John and his wife, Lydia, of Camb. sold land in Lex. in 1735, to Jonathan Robinson.

1-10- | THOMAS WHITMORE m. Mary, dau. of Samuel Waters of Woburn. She was ad. to the church in Lex. April 10, 1709. In May following eight of their children were bap. It is uncertain how long Thomas Whitmore resided in Lex. In 1696, Hugh Day of Camb. Farms, sold land in Camb. Farms to Thomas Whitmore of Wat. This purchase included a house and twenty acres of land. In 1698, Thomas Whitmore of Camb. Farms, sold the same land to Josiah Whitney. He had seven acres given him, in 1707, by the proprietors of Billerica. He removed to Killingly, Conn., and is said to have died there, Jan. 23, 1751; but we suspect an error in the date.

10-22 | *Thomas*, b. Nov. 4, 1694.   23 *Francis*, b. Sept. 5, 1696.
24 | *Samuel*, b. Sept. 22, 1698.   25 *Mary*, b. Sept. 4, 1700.
26 | *Daniel*, b. Feb. 22, 1702.
27 | *Hannah*, ⎫ bap. with another ⎧ m. Oct. 22, 1722, David Cady.
28 | *Ephraim*, ⎬ sister, *Abigail*, ⎨
29 | *Sarah*, ⎭ May 29, 1709; ⎩ m. May, 1730, Benj. Lovejoy.

1-11- | JOSEPH WHITMORE m. Feb. 13, 1699, Mary, dau. of Thomas Kendall. May 9, 1703, he and his wife were ad. to the ch. in Lex., and on the 6th of June following, Joseph, probably their first child, was bap., being b. Feb. 17, 1700. As he was subsequently of Wo. he may have resided there at this time. They were dismissed to the ch. in Wo. Feb. 20, 1704.

5-12- | FRANCIS WHITMORE. Though he was chosen hog-reeve in 1714, a significant intimation that he may have changed his situation in life, we find no record of his marriage or of any children, and hence infer that he was never married. He d. Dec. 20, 1758.

5-13-   SAMUEL WHITMORE m. Jan. 7, 1720, Bethia Page. She was ad. to the ch. June 14, 1724. He was a tythingman in 1723, which shows that he was a man of sobriety of character. He d. Aug. 17, 1724, about three months after his father.

13-30   *Rebecca*, bap. Jan. 15, 1721.
    31   *Daniel*, b. Feb. 21, 1725. He was a posthumous son. He m. 1746, Elizabeth Townsend, and lived in Boston, where, in 1748, they executed a deed of their land in Lex. to Jonathan Robinson. He probably left no sons, and possibly no issue.

By deaths and removals from town, the name of Whitmore has long since become extinct in Lex. In 1852, *Charles O. Whitmore*, a wealthy merchant in Boston, purchased him a summer residence in Lex., which he has fitted up in fine style, and rendered it one of the most spacious and attractive dwellings in the town. He is a direct descendant of the fifth generation from John, the second son of the original Francis Whitmore.

    1   CHARLES O. WHITMORE, son of William D. and Rhoda (Woodward) Whitmore, was b. Nov. 2, 1807, in Bath, Me. He m. Lovice Ayres. She d. Sept. 27, 1849, and he m. Oct. 30, 1851, Mary E. Blake, wid. of George Blake, Jr. of Boston. He had by his first wife the following children.

1- 2   *Charles J.*, b. April 27, 1834; m. June 8, 1858, Sarah Olcott Murdoch Blake, dau. of the above mentioned Geo. Blake, Jr., and has four children.
    3   *William H.*, b. Sept. 6, 1836. To him the writer is indebted for information concerning this family.
    4   *Martha H.*, b. Sept. 5, 1838.
    5   *Anna L.*, b. Sept. 16, 1840; m. Nov. 7, 1867, Philip L. Van Rensselaer of New York.
    6   *Charlotte R.*, b. March 9, 1843.
    7   *Creighton*, b. Dec. 16, 1845; d. April 25, 1848.

THE WHITNEY FAMILY.

This name, like the preceding, appears early upon the Lex. records, but does not continue long. ELEAZER WHITNEY was taxed at the Farms in 1693, '94, '95, and '96; and d. Feb. 1697.

    1   ISAIAH WHITNEY and wife, Sarah, owned the covenant May 4, 1696, when one of their children, probably their first, was bap. He d. Jan. 7, 1712.

1- 2   *Mary*, bap. May 4, 1696.   3 *Isaiah*, bap. July, 1700.
    4   *Sarah*, bap. April 22, 1703; m. Aug. 2, 1720, Andrew Parker.
    5   *Elijah*, bap. April 3, 1707; m. Dec. 8, 1736, Rebecca Winship.
    6   *Abraham*, bap. Feb. 19, 1710.   7 *Jonas*, bap. Nov. 25, 1711.

THE WHITTEMORE FAMILY.

THOMAS WHITTEMORE came to Malden at an early day, where he owned real estate, and had a family. He is supposed to be the ancestor of the Lex. Whittemores.

1 | NATHANIEL WHITTEMORE, a grandson of Thomas, and son of Nathaniel and Mary, was b. Sept. 26, 1670. He m. Sarah French. He and his wife were ad. to the ch. in Lex. April 24, 1720. She d. Aug. 15, 1734, and he m. Abigail ——. He d. 1754. His Will, dated Feb. 22, 1752, and proved Jan. 6, 1755, mentions wife Abigail, sons Nathaniel and Jacob, and sister Rebecca. He was an assessor in 1719, and constable 1720. He resided on the Concord road, near the Concord line, in the neighborhood of Thomas Nelson. He was an almanac maker, and published about 1707. He was a man of more than ordinary education for that day ; was often employed as a surveyor. He also sold drugs, and hence is often denominated Doctor, in the records. One number of his almanacs has its position in the scale of time thus fixed : " For the Year of Our Lord 1707, being third after leap year. From the Creation, 5656 ; from Noah's Flood, 4000 ; from the building of London, 2814 ; from the death of Alex. the Great, 2030 ; from the Discovery of America, 215 ; The reign of our Gracious Queen Anne the 6th." Another, of 1724, shows his loyalty, and the spirit of the times, thus : " O Heaven, crown our Great and Gracious King with length of days and lasting peace. Beneath his feet let all his foes stoop down ; let him be a nursing father, while on earth he reigns ; and of God's church great care may he take, and Christ will him reward with lasting gain. God save the King."

1- 2 | *Thomas,* b. Sept. 21, 1718.
3 | †*Jacob,* b. March 3, 1722.
4 | *Sarah,* bap. April 4, 1724 ; d. Aug. 15, 1734.
5 | *Abigail,* b. Dec. 8, 1725.
6 | *John,* b. Aug. 27, 1727 ; d. the Jan. following.
7 | †*Nathaniel,* b. June 26, 1729 ; m. Jemima Dunton of Bedford.

1-3- | JACOB WHITTEMORE m. Oct. 28, 1746, Esther Whittemore of Con. She d. 1753, and he m second, Dec. 5, 1754, Elizabeth Hoar of Con. She d. and he m. third, Oct. 19, 1759, Deborah Flagg. He d. Jan. 21, 1780. His Will, proved June 16, 1780, mentions dau. Esther Brown, Sarah Reed, and wife Elizabeth. Jacob Whittemore was ad. to the ch. in Lex. March 21, 1754, being dismissed from the ch. in Concord.

3- 8 | *Esther,* b. Oct. 24, 1748 ; m. June 12, 1769, Benj. Brown of Templeton.
9 | *Jonathan,* b. Aug. 22, 1750.
10 | *Sarah,* b. Nov. 1, 1751 ; m. April 23, 1770, Moses Reed of Wo. He had two other children by his first wife, who d. in early infancy.

1-7- | NATHANIEL WHITTEMORE m. Nov. 1, 1752, Jemima Dunton of Bed. There is some difficulty in fixing the residence and marriage of Nathaniel Whittemore. The Bedford record, in giving the marriage as above, speaks of him as " of Lexington." The Lexington ch. records have the following, under date of June 6, 1756 : " Baptized, Abigail Whittemore of Nathaniel, the father having owned the covenant at Lincoln." He also had Jemima, bap. at Linc. Aug. 7, 1763. Ward, in his History of Shrewsbury, gives the following : " Nathaniel Whittemore, (supposed originally from Weston or vicinity,) Aug. 17, 1753, m. Sarah, dau. of Luke Rice. He was then called of Shrewsbury. Chil. *Sarah,* b. July 18, 1754 ; *Nathaniel,* b. March 9, 1756 ; *Lydia,* b. Feb. 15, 1758 ; *Paul,* b. May 24, 1760 ; *Eber,* b. April 24, 1762. Nathaniel Whittemore d. in 1765, and his wid. m. March 31, 1774, George Harrington of Brookfield." There was a Nathaniel Whittemore and his wife, Mary, in Charlestown, in 1670, who had a son, Nathaniel, b. Sept. 26, 1670; these probably were the parents of the Nathaniel who settled in Lexington.

There were other Whittemores in Lexington, from time to time, but we can give no connected view of them.

Pelatiah Whittemore, ad. to the ch. April 14, 1728.
Nathan Whittemore, bap. Feb. 7, 1750.
Deborah Whittemore, ad. to the ch. April 21, 1751.
Sarah Whittemore, of Deborah, bap. Nov. 3, 1751.
Submit Whittemore, ad. to the ch. Jan. 18, 1756; m. March 23, 1762, Jonas Mason.
Jonas Whitney, of Narragansett No. 2 (now Westminster), and *Sarah Whittemore* of Lexington were united in marriage, Sept. 27, 1757.
Joel Whittemore was taxed in Lex. from 1750 to 1752 inclusive. He may have gone to Shrewsbury, and m. April 28, 1761, Rezinah Rand.

The name of *Whittemore*, should never be confounded with *Whitmore*, as the families are believed to be distinct.

THE WILLIAMS FAMILY.

1   REV. AVERY WILLIAMS, formerly a clergyman in Lex., was b. Jan. 9, 1782, in Guildford, Vt. His father, Rev. Henry Williams, being then pastor of the church at that place, but afterwards removing to Leverett, Mass., Avery's childhood and youth were passed there. He grad. Dartmouth C. 1804, studied Theology at Princeton, N. J. He m. Feb. 25, 1807, Clarissa Grennell of Greenfield, and was settled in Lex. Dec. 30, 1807. He left Lex. in 1815, in consequence of ill health, and went South in hopes of relief; but disease had so far impaired his constitution, that his journey was unavailing. He d. at Spartansburg, S. C., Feb. 4, 1816. His widow was living in Greenfield a few years since. He published a Century Sermon on the anniversary of the incorporation of the town of Lexington, which shows him a man of good talents, careful research, and faithful as a historian.

1- 2   *Clarissa G.*, b. April 14, 1810.
3   *Lydia Maria*, b. April 1, 1812; died in childhood.
4   *Mary D.*, b. Feb. 11, 1814; resides at Greenfield.
5   *Avery*, b. Feb. 14, 1816; m. Eliza Squire of Lanesboro'. He studied medicine and was residing, when last heard from, at Buffalo, N. Y.

THE WILSON FAMILY.

1   JAMES WILSON was in Camb. Farms, 1693, when he was taxed for the purchase of the ministerial land. He was assessor in 1703, and constable in 1713. He m. Deborah ——. They were ad. to the ch. Feb. 6, 1699. They buried a child in 1696, and two in 1703. There was also a John Wilson taxed in 1696, but this is the only record we find of him. The Wilsons probably left town early, as no one of the name appears on the earliest town tax bills extant, viz., 1729 and 1735. James Wilson, from Lexington, settled in Leicester, 1721. This was probably the family.

1-2	*James*, bap. Aug. 1699; probably settled in Bed. and d. 1753.		
3	*Deborah*, bap. Aug. 1699; d. Dec. 14, 1703.		
4	*Abigail*, bap. Aug. 1699.	5	*Ebenezer*, bap. Oct. 8, 1699.
6	*John*, bap. Sept. 17, 1704.	7	*William*, bap. May 27, 1705.
8	*Margaret*, bap. Nov. 24, 1706.	9	*Hannah*, bap. July 20, 1708.
10	*Thomas*, bap. May 14, 1710.	11	*Phebe*, bap. May 29, 1713.
12	*Jonathan*, bap. Oct. 31, 1714.		

The name appears several times in connection with the history of Lexington, but it is uncertain whether they were related to this family. Hezekiah Dunkley m. *Damaris Wilson*, Oct. 17, 1734. Sergeant *Robert Wilson*, *Robert Wilson, Jr.*, and *Barnabas Wilson* were in the French War from Lex. in 1756, and Robert also in 1758. *James Wilson* was in the Continental army from Lex. in the Revolution.

THE WINSHIP FAMILY.

The Winships were among the first settlers in Lexington, and were for a long period among the most numerous and respectable families. They were the descendants of

1   EDWARD WINSHIP of Cambridge. He was made freeman in 1635, was a member of the Ancient and Honorable Artillery Co., 1638, was selectman of Cambridge eleven years, between 1637 and 1684. He was representative in 1663, '64, '81 and '86. He also held a commission in the militia, and was dignified with the title of *Lieutenant* Winship. He was also an active and honored member of the church. He was twice married. His first wife was Jane, who d. between 1648 and 1651; his second wife was Elizabeth. He d. Dec. 2, 1688, in the 76th year of his age, and his widow, Elizabeth, d. Sept. 19, 1690, in her 58th year. It is believed that all the Winships in the vicinity descended from Lieutenant Edward. His Will was dated 1685, and as it casts considerable light upon this family, I will cite the portions which relate to the Lexington branches.

1. "I give to my son *Ephraim*, the lot of land whereon his house standeth, both all the meadow and upland he hath now in his possession."

2. "I give to my son *Edward*, all my land that lieth on the east side of the brook, whereon a sawmill standeth, except that which I bought of Edward Methelson, and twelve acres in my own Great Meadow."

3. "I give to my son *Samuel*, one hundred acres of land or thereabouts, some of it measured by David Fiske, about eighty acres upon the west side of Concord way, next to his brother Ephraim's line, and another tract of land on the east side of Concord way."

4. He gave land on Alewife brook to *Joseph*, another son; and mentions *Mary*, *Elizabeth* and *Abigail*, his daughters.

His widow's Will, dated 1689, mentions dau. Elizabeth, Abigail, Margery and Mehitabel.

Lieutenant Winship was a large landholder, not only in Old Cambridge, but at the Farms, where he had land assigned him as early as 1642. He owned, as will be seen by his Will, a large tract of land within the present limits of Lexington, extending from Lowell street across the brook to the hill west of Main street, upon the present line of Arlington, including the mill site, Mount Ephraim, and a portion of the Great Meadow. Living as his descendants did, upon the borders of Lexington and Cambridge, their association was partly with one town, and partly with the other; and hence the record of the family is sometimes in one town, and sometimes in the other, which makes it very difficult to trace the families.

1- 2   *Mary*, b. June 8, 1638; d. young.
   3   *Sarah*, b. 1639.   4 *Mary*, b. Aug. 5, 1641.
   5 †*Ephraim*, b. July 9, 1643; d. Oct. 19, 1696.
   6 ‡*Joanna*, b. Aug. 1, 1645; d. Nov. 19, 1707.
   7 *Edward*, b. June 18, 1648; d. same day.
   8 *Elizabeth*, b. April 15, 1652.
   9 ‡*Edward*, b. March 3, 1654.
  10 *Abigail*, b. Feb. 13, 1656; m. William Russell, May 8, 1683.
  11 ‡*Samuel*, b. Oct. 24, 1658; m. April 12, 1687, Mary Powers.
  12 ‡*Joseph*, b. June 21, 1661; m. Sarah Harrington.
  13 *Margery*, b. Dec. 10, 1664; m. May 12, 1687, John Dixon.
  14 *Mehitabel*, b. Nov. 19, 1667.

1-5-   EPHRAIM WINSHIP m. April 7, 1670, Hannah Rogers, who d. Dec. 20, 1674. He m. second, Dec. 19, 1675, Elizabeth Kendall of Woburn. He resided on the place described in his father's Will, in the extreme easterly part of the town. He must have come to the place early. He was a subscriber for the meeting house in 1692, and on the organization of the parish in 1693, he was one of the assessors. He was also a member of the committee chosen to treat with the town of Cambridge in relation to the purchase of land for the ministry, and an assessor, 1694. He d. at Lexington, Oct. 19, 1696. His widow removed her relation to the ch. in Lex. from that of Woburn, immediately after the death of her husband. He had the honor of giving his name to a swell of land near his residence, which is to this day known as "Mount Ephraim." He probably had no children. In the settlement of his estate, mention is made of Sarah Reed, their adopted dau. His widow, Elizabeth, administered upon the estate. She subsequently m. Joseph Pierce of Watertown.

1-6-   JOANNA WINSHIP d. unm. Nov. 19, 1707, aged 62. She was famous in her day as a school teacher; and as our ancestors knew how to appreciate the character of a good school ma'am, they, under the influence of the muses, inscribed upon her monumental stone, this plaintive strain—this melting elegy:

> "This good school Dame
> No longer school must keep,
> Which gives us cause
> For children's sake, to weep."

1-9-   EDWARD WINSHIP m. May 14, 1683, Rebecca Barsham, who d. Aug. 1717, aged 61. He d. in Camb. June 10, 1718, aged 64. He was selectman of Camb. 1691, '93, '95 and 1701. Though he owned land in Cambridge Farms, he resided on the Cambridge side of the line. He d. testate; and by his Will, proved 1718, and by an instrument signed by his heirs, it appears that he had seven children living at the time of his death. He gave to his oldest son Edward, "the house he dwelleth in, and fifty acres of land adjoining, bounded as follows: beginning near the town road leading from old Mr. Munroe's, towards Menotomy," &c. (This is the present Lowell street.) He gave to his son Ephraim, "all that parcel of land whereon he dwells, and the interest I have in the house he now dwells in, which was formerly my brother Ephraim's, lying on the southwest side of the county road." Both of these bequests were of land lying in Lexington, and they show that his sons Edward and Ephraim were then living in Lexington.

9–15 | †*Edward*, b. Jan. 9, 1684; m. Sarah Manning.
16 | *Elizabeth*, b. June 1, 1686; m. April 3, 1706, Walter Russell.
17 | †*Ephraim*, b. Feb. 4, 1688; m. June 17, 1708, Hannah Cutler.
18 | †*Nathaniel*, b. Feb. 16, 1689; m. Feb. 11, 1713, Rebecca Pierce of Woburn.
19 | *William*, b. ———.
20 | †*John*, b. ———; m. Oct. 2, 1718, Elizabeth Wyeth.
21 | *Jason*, b. 1699.

1–11– | SAMUEL WINSHIP m. April 12, 1687, Mary Powers of Medford. He resided in the precinct, and was a subscriber for the meeting house in 1692, and for the purchase of the Common in 1711, and his name is upon the tax bills from the first. He was selectman in 1728, '29, '30, '32 and '33. He d. June 18, 1696.

11–22 | †*Samuel*, b. Jan. 8, 1688; m. June 10, 1712, Jane Fessenden.
23 | *Mary*, b. Dec. 12, 1689.   24 *Elizabeth*, b. Dec. 26, 1691.

1–12– | JOSEPH WINSHIP m. Nov. 24, 1687, Sarah Harrington of Watertown. She d. Nov. 28, 1710. They resided in West Cambridge, where he d. Sept. 18, 1725. They had the following and probably other children.

12–25 | *Joanna*, b. Jan. 14, 1689; d. Dec. 17, 1716.
26 | *Joseph*, b. Feb. 28, 1701; m. about 1722, Anne ———.
27 | *Margaret*, b. Aug. 8, 1703.

9–15– | EDWARD WINSHIP m. about 1705, Sarah Manning. He was a tythingman in Lexington, 1714; fence viewer, 1716; constable, 1717. He o. c. in Lex. Sept. 1, 1706. He d. May 15, 1763, aged 88 years.

15–28 | †*Edward*, b. Aug. 25, 1706.
29 | *Rebecca*, b. Aug. 22, 1709; m. June 16, 1728, John Manning.
30 | *Sarah*, b. June 28, 1712.
31 | *Jonathan*, b. May 28, 1713; d. young.
32 | *Mary*, b. June 25, 1716.
33 | †*Jonathan*, b. May 28, 1719; m. Elizabeth Cutler.
34 | †*Isaac*, b. June 8, 1724.

9–17– | EPHRAIM WINSHIP m. June 17, 1708, Hannah Cutler. He was a subscriber for the purchase of the Common in 1711. In 1717, he was chosen surveyor of highways, tythingman in 1721, constable, 1728. Not Ephraim alone was employed by the town, but his wife, by vote of the inhabitants, was employed to keep a school in her part of the town. He and his wife were ad. to the ch. Oct. 12, 1718. She d. April 9, 1764, aged 77. He d. July 16, 1757, aged 70.

17–35 | †*Ephraim*, b. May 23, 1709; m. Aug. 28, 1735, Mehitabel Cutler.
36 | †*Richard*, b. July 25, 1711.
37 | *Daniel*, b. Aug. 27, 1713; d. Dec. 8, same year.
38 | *Joshua*, b. Feb. 17, 1715; was in the West India service, 1740.
39 | *Hannah*, b. Aug. 18, 1718.
40 | *Moses*, b. Sept. 18, 1720; m. Lucy Hastings of Waltham, 1746.
41 | *Bethiah*, b. Feb. 11, 1724; d. March 19, 1740.

9–18– | NATHANIEL WINSHIP, m. Feb. 11, 1713, Rebecca Pierce of Wo.

18–42 | *Elizabeth*, b. Oct. 13, 1714.   43 *Nathaniel*, b. Dec. 27, 1716.
44 | *Rebecca*, b. Dec. 7, 1717; m. Dec. 8, 1736, Elijah Whitney.

92

45 | *Martha*, b. June 21, 1720; d. July 8, 1746, unm.
46 | *Abigail*, b. March 25, 1722; d. July same year.

9-20- | JOHN WINSHIP m. Oct. 2, 1718, Elizabeth Wyeth. He probably m. as a second wife, about 1730, Bethiah ——. He d. July 18, 1747.

20-47 | *Josiah*, b. Oct. 1, 1719; d. young.
48 | *Elizabeth*, b. March 24, 1721.   49 *Ruth*, b. June 14, 1726.
50 | *John*, b. Nov. 8, 1728.
51 | *Thaddeus*, b. March 8, 1731; d. June 3, 1747.
52 | *James*, b. Sept. 27, 1733; m. April 15, 1762, Lydia Phillips of West Cambridge.
53 | *Ebenezer*, b. Sept. 30, 1735; m. Aug. 19, 1756, Elizabeth Raymond.
54 | *Bethiah*, b. March 19, 1739; d. March 18, 1740.
55 | *Josiah*, b. July 18, 1741.
56 | *Eliot*, b. 1743; m. June 16, 1768, Edward Crafts of Boston.

11-22- | SAMUEL WINSHIP m. June 10, 1711, Jane Fessenden, dau. of Nicholas and Margaret Fessenden. He was High Sheriff of Middlesex co. He o. c. Sept. 21, 1712, when his first child was bap. His wife d. Jan. 12, 1771; he d. Feb. 13, 1776, aged 88.

22-57 | †*Samuel*, b. Sept. 25, 1712; m. May 22, 1735, Hannah Loring.
58 | *Martha*, b. Dec. 27, 1714; m. William Bowers of Billerica.
59 | *Margaret*, b. Dec. 25, 1718; d. May 25, 1791, unm.

15-28- | EDWARD WINSHIP m. Esther ——. She d. Oct. 10, 1785; he d. Dec. 7, 1773, aged 69.

28-60 | †*Thomas*, b. Oct. 25, 1729; m. May 28, 1755, Sarah Harrington.
61 | *Benjamin*, b. April 12, 1731.
62 | †*Edward*, b. Jan. 18, 1733; m. Feb. 9, 1757, Hepzibah Laughton.
63 | †*Joel*, b. Nov. 13, 1734; m. Elizabeth Grant of Sudbury.
64 | *Amos*, b. Dec. 12, 1736; d. May 9, 1740.
65 | *Mary*, bap. 1738.
66 | *Esther*, b. Jan. 21, 1739; d. April 28, 1789, unm.
67 | *Evebell*, b. Feb. 2, 1743.   68 *Joshua*, b. Jan. 27, 1748.

15-33- | JONATHAN WINSHIP m. Dec. 3, 1741, Isabel Cutler of Camb. She d. and he m. about 1746, Elizabeth ——. He was ad. to the ch. by a letter from the ch. in Camb. May 21, 1754. She was ad. June 18, 1758.

33-69 | *Jonathan*, b. Jan. 18, 1747; dismissed, 1772, to the ch. in Mason, N. H.
70 | *Joshua*, b. June 27, 1748.   71 *Amos*, b. Dec. 19, 1750.
72 | *Hepzibah*, b. Feb. 15, 1753.   73 *Mary*, b. Feb. 18, 1755.
74 | *Elizabeth*, b. May 23, 1757.   75 *Lucy*, b. Feb. 9, 1760.
76 | *Nathaniel*, b. June 23, 1762.
77 | *Edmund*, b. Oct. 2, 1765; m. Nov. 22, 1789, Lucy Learned.

15-34- | ISAAC WINSHIP m. Hannah ——. He was in the French and Indian war, in 1755. He d. April 8, 1783, and his son, Isaac, administered upon his estate.

34-78 | *Hannah*, b. Dec. 26, 1746; d. July 23, 1749.
79 | †*Isaac*, b. April 7, 1749; m. Sarah Fessenden.
80 | *Hannah*, b. May 4, 1752; d. young.
81 | *Sarah*, b. May 12, 1754.

82 | *Phebe*, b. July 23, 1755; m. May 11, 1779, Ebenezer Hadley.
83 | *Hannah*, b. April 25, 1757; m. May, 1779, Jonathan Marble.
84 | *Eunice*, b. Feb. 28, 1758.   85 *Grace*, b. May 17, 1759.
86 | *Rebecca*, b. May 20, 1760.
87 | *Richard*, b. Nov. 30, 1762; he was a soldier in the Revolution.
88 | *Martha*, b. Feb. 12, 1764   89 *Prudence*, b. May 2, 1765.
90 | *Benjamin*, bap. Oct. 12, 1766. 91 *Nehemiah*, b. April 4, 1767.
92 | *Lydia*, b. April 3, 1769.

17–35–   EPHRAIM WINSHIP m. Aug. 28, 1735, Mehitabel Cutler. He moved to New Marblehead, now the town of Windham, Me., about 1740. This place suffered severely from the Indians, from 1747 to 1763. On the 14th of May, 1756, Ephraim Winship and Ezra Brown, both of Windham, left the fort (for safety required them to live in garrisons) for the purpose of laboring upon Brown's lot, about a mile distant. Knowing that the Indians were lurking about in the region, they took the precaution to engage a guard of four men and four lads. In passing through a thick wood, when Winship and Brown were about fifty rods in advance of the guard, they were fired upon by fifteen or twenty Indians, who lay in ambush. Brown fell dead upon the spot. Winship received two balls, one in the eye, and another in the arm and fell to the ground,—where both were scalped by the Indians. A portion of the guard fled to the fort to give the alarm, while the remainder, and among them Gershom Winship, the oldest son of Ephraim, who was born before the family left Lexington, and then about twenty years of age, boldly rushed upon the savages, who were more than three times their number, and finally put them to flight. The Indians were led by Poland, their chief. When the guard approached, the Indians concealed themselves behind the trees, that they might be secure from the shots of their pursuers, and that they might step from their hiding places and fire upon the citizens, before they were aware of their presence. Poland was the first to break the silence; he stepped from behind the tree, discharged his musket, and immediately concealed himself again to reload. In his eagerness to reload his piece, that he might have another shot, his body became partially exposed, and he received a fatal shot from one of their pursuers. The Indians gathered around their fallen chief, and gave one of their infernal yells, which was answered by a volley from the little Spartan band, which killed or mortally wounded two more of their number. The Indians immediately fled, carrying off their dead and wounded.

At the time Winship received these wounds, he was a widower, his wife, Mehitabel, having died, leaving six children. Winship recovered from his wounds, though the Indians had taken two scalps from his head, and given him a blow with a hatchet, leaving him for dead. They took the two scalps in consequence of his having, as is sometimes the case, two crowns upon his head. In taking the scalps, they left a narrow strip of skin from his forehead directly over the top of his head. This ever afterwards gave him a very singular appearance. After this misfortune he m. a second wife, by whom he had five more children. He d. at Windham, June 4, 1766, aged 55. These facts were obtained from the Centennial Address of T. L. Smith, Esq., delivered at Windham, July 4, 1839, which contains much valuable information. Two children of Ephraim Winship were b. before he left Lex., viz., *Gershom*, b. May 10, 1736, and *Mehitabel*, b. July 28, 1738.

17–36–   RICHARD WINSHIP m. Prudence Estabrook, dau. of John and Prudence (Harrington) Estabrook, b. March 28, 1724. His Will, dated Nov. 28, 1768, and proved Jan. 7, 1769, mentions eight children then living, viz., Abigail, Ephraim, Hannah, Grace, Rebecca, Richard, Prudence, and Nehemiah. He d. Dec. 13, 1768, aged 58; she d. 1776, and Nehemiah Estabrook administered upon her estate. He was constable in 1750, and tythingman in 1758.

36- 93 *Prudence*, b. March 12, 1749; d. Oct. 2, 1751.
94 *Abigail*, b. Jan. 2, 1751.
95 *Ephraim*, b. June 25, 1753; m. April 8, 1777, Susanna Marion.
96 *Prudence*, b. July 16, 1756; d. young.
97 *Hannah*, b. April 25, 1757.
98 *Grace*, b. May 17, 1759; probably m. Simon Childs of Cambridge.
99 *Rebecca*, b. May 20, 1760. 100 *Richard*, b. Nov. 30, 1762.
101 *Prudence*, b. May 2, 1765. 102 *Nehemiah*, b. April 23, 1767.

22-57- SAMUEL WINSHIP m. May 22, 1735, Hannah Loring, dau. of Joseph and Lydia (Fiske) Loring. She d. July 27, 1747, and he m. May 5, 1748, Abigail Crosby of Billerica. He d. Feb. 16, 1780, aged 68.

57-103 *Hannah*, b. April 26, 1736; m. March 20, 1760, Richard Francis of Medford.
104 *Lydia*, b. Feb. 14, 1738; d. May, 1754.
105 *Elizabeth*, b. May 23, 1740.
106 *Martha*, b. May 12, 1742; d. Jan. 8, 1746.
107 *Samuel*, b. April 17, 1744; m. July 4, 1771, Rebecca Johnson of Lynn.
108 *Loring*, b. Dec. 10, 1746; d. May 11, 1754.
109 †*Simon*, b. Nov. 2, 1749; m. May 21, 1776, Joanna Abbott of Bil.
110 *John*, b. June 16, 1752; d. April 7, 1754.
111 †*John*, b. May 12, 1754; m. Deliverance ——.
112 †*Stephen*, b. Feb. 23, 1756; m. Feb. 5, 1787, Edith Merriam.
113 *Abigail*, b. May 18, 1759.

28-60- THOMAS WINSHIP m. May 28, 1755, Sarah Harrington, dau. of Henry and Sarah Harrington. He probably had one child before Henry, mentioned below. He d. Aug. 4, 1796. He was one of the brave band who rallied under Capt. Parker, April 19, 1775. He was selectman, 1779 and '81; assessor six years.

60-114 *Henry*, bap. Nov. 11, 1759. 115 *Isabel*, b. March 29, 1762.
116 *Anna*, b. April 18, 1764.
117 †*Thomas*, b. April 12, 1766; m. April 11, 1793, Anna Harrington.
118 *Moses*, b. June 20, 1768.
119 †*Jonathan*, b. Sept. 14, 1770; m. first, Martha ——, and second, Elizabeth Coggen.
120 *Joel*, b. April 18, 1773; m. Nov. 14, 1792, Phebe Hill of Camb.
121 *Eunice*, b. ——; m. Nov. 2, 1800, Jonas Locke.

28-62- EDWARD WINSHIP m. Feb. 9, 1757, Hepzibah Laughton, dau. of Dea. John and Sarah Laughton.

62-122 *Amos*, b. Feb. 6, 1758. 123 *Esther*, b. March 4, 1760.
124 *John*, b. Feb. 16, 1762. 125 *Edward*, b. Oct. 15, 1764.
126 *Oliver*, b. May 8, 1767.

28-63- JOEL WINSHIP m. Jan. 15, 1755, Elizabeth Grant of Sud. They moved to Royalston.

127 *Elizabeth*, b. March 14, 1755; m. —— Fiske; went to Barre.
128 *Dorcas*, b. June 24, 1758; d. 1807, unm.
129 *Joel*, b. May 1, 1761; went to Queensburg, N. Y.

34-79- ISAAC WINSHIP m. March 4, 1773, Sarah Fessenden. He was m. as of Medford, where he resided at the time. When he returned to Lex. does not appear; but as he was taxed in 1785, it is probable that he returned soon after the death of his father, which occurred in 1783, and his son, Isaac, administered upon the estate. He d. Nov. 29, 1834, aged 85; she d. Feb. 12, 1834, aged 80. He was an assessor from 1793 to 1814, inclusive. We can find no record of his family, and have to depend upon the imperfect recollection of one of his descendants.

79-130 *Isaac*, b. ——; moved to Portland.
131 *Jonas*, b. ——; lived in Portland, was twice married.
132 *Sarah*, b. ——; m. John Frost.
133 *Thaddeus*, b. ——; m. Mary Walker. He had a family, but left no record.
134 *Hannah*, b. ——; m. Leonard Johnson.
135 *Lydia*, b. ——; m. John Frost.
136 †*Oliver*, b. Nov. 12, 1794; has been twice married.

57-109- SIMON WINSHIP m. May 21, 1776, Joanna Abbott of Billerica. They o. c. July 20, 1777, when their first child, Joanna, was baptized. He d. Jan. 4, 1813, and Elias Maynard of Boston was appointed guardian of his widow, as a *non compos*. She d. Feb. 2, 1826. He was in service in the Jersies, in 1776, and sergeant in 1777.

109-137 *Joanna*, b. May 4, 1777.
138 *Oliver Abbott*, b. March 5, 1779; d. Oct. 11, 1792.

57-111- JOHN WINSHIP m. Deliverance ——. He d. in West Camb. April, 1825, and his widow administered upon his estate. He was a soldier in Capt. Parker's co. 1775, also served in the first campaign of eight months and twelve months, New York.

111-139 *John*, b. Dec. 28, 1779.   140 *Stephen*, b. July 15, 1782.
141 *Charles*, b. June 30, 1784.   142 *Sally*, b. July 23, 1786.
143 *Polly*, b. April 26, 1788.   144 *Henry*, b. June 28, 1790.
145 *Magus*, b. Aug. 4, 1793.

57-112- STEPHEN WINSHIP m. Feb. 5, 1787, Edith Merriam, dau. of Benjamin and Ginger (Porter) Merriam, b. Aug. 20, 1763. He d. Nov. 16, 1839, aged 84; she d. Feb. 20, 1839, aged 73.

112-146 *Stephen*, b. Sept. 25, 1787; d. April 18, 1788.
147 *Edith*, b. Jan. 16, 1789; m. Sept. 2, 1806, Isaac Adams of Boston.
148 *Cynthia*, b. May 10, 1791; lives in Camb.
149 *Stephen*, b. April 16, 1793; d. Aug. 27, 1864, aged 71.
150 *Sophia*, b. March 3, 1795; lives at Cambridgeport.
151 *Philenia*, b. April 30, 1798; d. Jan. 16, 1819, unm.
152 *Lavinia*, b. Feb. 22, 1800; m. March 26, 1822, P. R. L. Stone.
153 *Maria Antonette*, b. March 8, 1802; m. March 8, 1837, Billings Smith.
154 *Archibald*, b. Aug. 6, 1804.
155 *Tryphena Merriam*, b. March 16, 1808; m. March 3, 1835, Augustus Wellington, and d. Dec. 26, 1811, aged 34.

60-117- THOMAS WINSHIP m. April 11, 1793, Anna Harrington. They were ad. to the ch. April, 1795. He d. March 2, 1830, aged 64; she d. July 15, 1821, aged 55.

117-156 *Lucebia*, b. May 2, 1794; m. Lot Reed.
157 *Emily*, bap. Jan. 29, 1797; m. Otis Reed of Bedford.

60-119- JONATHAN WINSHIP m. Martha ——. She d. Jan. 10, 1799, and he m. May 12, 1800, Elizabeth Coggen of Natick. She d. June 13, 1823, aged 49; he d. July 22, 1825.

119-158 *Esther*, b. May 21, 1796; d. Aug. 15, 1810.
159 *Moses*, b. Sept. 20, 1798; d. Feb. 4, 1799.
160 *Eliza*, b. Feb. 3, 1801; d. Feb. 18, 1801.
161 *Mary,* } b. May 3, 1803; } d. Nov. 6, 1807.
162 *Eliza.* }
163 *Thomas Jefferson*, b. May 6, 1805; d. Jan. 18, 1827.
164 *Anna*, b. March 10, 1807.
165 *Henry Coggen*, b. Sept. 6, 1810.

79-136- OLIVER WINSHIP m. Sept. 10, 1820, Anna Fiske. She d. Oct. 15, 1851, and he m. March 25, 1853, Amanda F. Chamberlain.

136-166 *Isaac A.*, b. July 4, 1822; m. in Cal. Elizabeth Brooks.
167 *Oliver M.*, b. March 6, 1823.
168 *Mary E.*, b. March 13, 1825; m. Dec. 31, 1846, William Daley of Cambridge.
169 *Charles F.*, b. July 16, 1828; m. Mary Holbrook. They have one child, Eddy Bigelow.
170 *Sarah*, b. July 16, 1828, twin; m. Oct. 1866, George Hager; r. in California.

The records of many of the Winship families are so imperfect, that it is impossible to trace their genealogy. Some families have neglected their record altogether, and hence it is impossible to bring them down to the present day.

THE WINTER FAMILY.

1 JOHN WINTER was a proprietor of Wat. in 1636, and d. in that place, 1662. His Will, dated March 4, 1661, and proved June, 1662, mentions sons Richard and Thomas, late of London, dau. Alice Lockman of London, and son John of Wat., to whom he gave his landed property. He probably came from Camb. to Lex. He had land assigned between the eight mile line and Concord, in 1683.

1- 2 JOHN WINTER lived at Camb. Farms, where he d. Jan. 18, 1690. His Will, dated Dec. 12, 1689, makes no mention of his wife, who probably d. before him, but speaks of sons John, Thomas, and Samuel, and dau. Sarah, Hannah, and Mary.

2- 3 *Joseph*, b. ——; d. at Camb. Farms, Dec. 10, 1690, being the first death mentioned in the Lex. records.
4 †*John*, b. ——; owned the covenant at Wat. June 22, 1690.
5 *Thomas*, b. ——.   6 *Samuel*, b. ——.
7 *Sarah*, b. ——; d. Jan. 19, 1690, one day after her father.
8 *Hannah*, b. ——; m. Nov. 17, 1681, John Harrington.
9 *Mary*, b. ——.

2-4-

JOHN WINTER m. Abigail ——. He was a subscriber for the erection of a meeting house in Lex. 1692, following the example of his father, who had subscribed for the same object before his death. She was ad. to the ch. April 9, 1699. They had *Joseph*, bap. April 2, 1699; *Benjamin*, bap. Oct. 8, 1699; *Ruth*, bap. Sept. 22, 1702; *Lydia*, bap. Aug. 15, 1703; *James*, bap. Sept. 30, 1705; *Isaac*, bap. Nov. 3, 1706; *Elizabeth*, bap. Jan. 20, 1708.

As the tax bills of 1729 and 1735 do not contain the name of Winter, and as no place was assigned when the meeting house was seated, in 1731, we infer that they had all left town before that period.

WRIGHT.—ELISHA WRIGHT came to Lex. about 1855. He was b. in Washington, N. H., 1811, and m. Dec. 1836, Harriet Farmer, b. Feb. 22, 1814. He was son of *Nathan*, b. Feb. 1786, who was son of *Jacob*, b. Dec. 1758, who served in the Revolution, and m. Patty Reed. Jacob was son *Jacob*, of whose birth we have no record, but whose death occurred in 1763. Elisha, by his wife Harriet, has five children, three sons, all of whom were in the U. S. service in the late Rebellion, and two daughters, as follows:

Walter R., b. Aug. 22, 1838; m. Nov. 1860, Lydia Kenniston, and has Minnie, b. Feb. 8, 1862, and Charles C. He served nine months in the army, in North Carolina. *Willis L.*, b. Sept. 14, 1841; he was nine months in the service. *George W.*, b. June 30, 1843. Like his two brothers, he was one of the nine months' men who served in North Carolina to put down the rebellion. *Hattie A.*, b. June 9, 1850. *Emma E. H.*, b. Oct. 22, 1852. The first three children were b. in Washington, N. H., the last two in Camb. Mass.

There is another Wright family in town, which originated in Ashby, having no connection with the family above.

ABEL WRIGHT of Ashby, m. first, —— Hayward of Acton. She d. and he m. second, —— Rice of Ashburnham. He had a family of nineteen children. *Isaac*, their first child, b. Feb. 12, 1799, m. Arvilla Kendall, dau. of Oliver Kendall of Ashby. They had nine children. He d. May 25, 1864.

LUKE W. WRIGHT, son of Isaac, b. Sept. 27, 1821; m. April 7, 1846, Abigail Estabrook, dau. of Attai and Polly (Pierce) Estabrook of Lex. b. Dec. 16, 1819. He came to Lex. 1843. They have had the following children. *Sarah Arvilla*, b. Oct. 5, 1848; *Abbie Elizabeth*, b. Dec. 11, 1849; *Arthur E.*, b. Sept. 29, 1854, d. Jan. 22, 1859; *Alice Arthuretta*, b. Jan. 29, 1861.

THE WYMAN FAMILY.

The name of Wyman is of German origin, and was at first spelt Weyman. Two individuals, who were the progenitors of most of the Wymans, appear on the Charlestown records as signers of "town orders," Dec. 18, 1640. This was coeval with the settlement of Woburn. We find John and Francis Wyman in Woburn immediately after. They were Tanners; and thus was laid early the foundation of the shoe and leather business, for which Woburn has always been more or less distinguished. John m. in Wo. 1644, Sarah Nutt.

1 | FRANCIS WYMAN, from whom our Lex. Wymans descended, m. Jan. 30, 1645, Judith Pierce of Wo. She dying, he m. second, Oct. 2, 1650, Abigail Reed.

1- 2 | *Judith*, b. Sept. 29, 1652; d. Dec. 22, 1652.
3 | *Francis*, b. about 1654; d. unm. Aug. 26, 1676.
4 | *William*, b. about 1656; m. Prudence Putnam, and d. 1705.
5 | *Abigail*, b. about 1658; m. Stephen Richardson.
6 | *Timothy*, b. Sept. 15, 1661; m. Hannah ——.
7 | *Joseph*, b. Nov. 9, 1663; d. July 24, 1714, unm.
8 | *Nathaniel*, b. Nov. 25, 1665; m. Mary Winn, and d. 1691.
9 | *Samuel*, b. Nov. 29, 1667; m. 1692, Rebecca Johnson.
10 | *Thomas*, b. April 1, 1671; m. May 5, 1696, Mary Richardson.
11 | †*Benjamin*, b. Aug. 25, 1674; m. Elizabeth Hancock of Cambridge.
12 | *Stephen*, b. June 2, 1676; d. Aug. 19, 1676.
13 | *Judith*, b. Jan. 15, 1679; m. Nathaniel Bacon.

1-11- | BENJAMIN WYMAN m. Jan. 20, 1702, Elizabeth Hancock of Camb. He d. Dec. 19, 1735, and she m. Aug. 22, 1739, Jonathan Brown of Bed. and d. 1749. Though Benjamin Wyman may not have resided long in Lex., he and his wife o. c. in the place, June 24, 1705, when Elizabeth, their first child, was bap. Mrs. Wyman was probably sister to Rev. Mr. Hancock; which would account for their attending ch. in Lex., though their residence might have been out of town.

11-14 | *Elizabeth*, b. May 1, 1705; m. June 11, 1724, Jacob Richardson.
15 | †*Benjamin*, b. Nov. 13, or Dec. 17, 1706.
16 | *Lucy*, b. April 17, 1708; m. Nathaniel Davenport.
17 | *Zedekiah*, bap. Oct. 30, 1709.

11-15- | BENJAMIN WYMAN m. Esther, dau. of Jacob Richardson of Wo. He was dignified by the title of captain. He resided in Wo. where he had a family, among whom was James, the immediate ancestor of the Lexington branch of the Wyman family.

15-18- | JAMES WYMAN b. June 29, 1741; m. Jan. 14, 1766, Anna Porter. He came from Wo. to Lex. in 1763, and so was m. as of Lex. She d. and he m. second, Lydia Simonds. He d. Nov. 13, 1822.

18-19 | *Anna*, b. March 8, 1768; m. Nov. 19, 1795, Sweethen Reed.
20 | †*James*, b. Sept. 26, 1769.
21 | *William*, b. Dec. 11, 1771; moved to Westminster, Vt.
22 | *Benjamin*, b. March 20, 1774; m. Lucy Gardner, and d. 1849. No issue.
23 | *Phebe*, b. Feb. 9, 1776; d. April 8, 1805.
24 | *Sally*, b. Oct. 18, 1778; d. April 7, 1782.
25 | *Lydia*, b. Feb. 9, 1781; d. unm. Dec. 1, 1861.
26 | *Sally*, b. June 20, 1783; m. March 13, 1810, John Crapo of Lynn.
27 | *Lucy*, bap. Nov. 27, 1785; d. young.
28 | *Francis*, b. April 11, 1789; m. Mrs. Margaret Wyman.

18-20- | JAMES WYMAN m. Jan. 25, 1798, Betsey Locke, dau. of Reuben Locke. He d. April 19, 1835, aged 67. She was burned to death in a house which took fire, when she was left in it alone, too infirm to help herself.

20-29 | *James*, b. April 18, 1798. He was for some time a partner in the mercantile house of Kittridge & Wyman, Boston. He m. Dec. 10, 1823, Margaret Center, dau. of Cotton Center. She was divorced

from him, 1851, and m. Feb. 19, 1852, Francis Wyman of Lex.
an uncle of her first husband. James Wyman m. a second wife.

30 | *Emelia,* b. Oct. 18, 1801; d. May 9, 1803.
31 | *Emelia,* b. June 10, 1803; m. March 31, 1825, John Johnson, 2d.
32 | *Elbridge,* b. March 1, 1805; formerly a merchant in Boston.
33 | *William,* b. Dec. 6, 1808; a machinist in Woburn.
34 | *Anna P.,* b. ———.
35 | *Benjamin,* b. July 1, 1816; m. Nov. 17, 1840, Lucy Ann Puffer of
Waltham.
36 | *John G.,* b. ———.
37 | *Susan E.,* b. Aug. 17, 1820; m. Jan. 17, 1838, Jewett B. Streeter
of Lowell.
38 | *Lucy A.,* b. April 2, 1825. 39 *Francis S.,* b. April 7, 1827.

There were other Wymans in Lex. from time to time, all from the
same original stock, but through other branches; nor was their residence permanently in the town.

JAMES WYMAN, the eldest son of David, of James, who was a
great grand-son of the original Francis, was b. Feb. 8, 1825; m. in
Lex. as his second wife, Abigail S. Harrington, who d. 1827. His
first wife was Rhoda Robbins, and his third wife was Sophia Grover.
He had ten sons and three dau. He resided in Lex., Burlington,
and Danvers.

HENRY WYMAN of Lancaster, a great grand-son of Francis of
Wo., m. 1767, Sarah Mason of Lexington.

INCREASE WYMAN, second son of Nathaniel, son of Francis of
Wo., was in Lex. 1756–59; was also of Lincoln, Burlington, and
Billerica. He had a family of eight children by his wife, Deborah
Pierce. *Nathaniel,* his second and youngest son, was killed in Lex.
near the Common, on the morning of the 19th of April, 1775, aged
24 years.

WILLIS.—JOHN WILLIS and his wife Elizabeth were in Duxbury
as early as 1637. He was one of the first settlers of Bridgewater,
was a deacon there, and filled important town offices, and represented
the town in the court of the colony some twenty years. He m. Mrs.
Elizabeth Palmer, and had six children. *Benjamin,* son of John, m.
Susanna, dau. of Thomas Whitman, by whom he had Thomas and
Benjamin, Susanna and Elizabeth. *Thomas,* son of Benjamin, m.
Mary, dau. of Samuel Kingsly, and had eight children. *Thomas,*
son of Thomas and Mary, m. Susannah, dau. of Thomas Ames, and
had six children. *Thomas,* one of their sons, m. first, a Hunt, and
second, a Dean; among his children he kept up the family name, and
called one of his sons *Thomas,* who m. Frances Willis, dau. of
Ephraim Willis, by whom he had four sons, *Royal B., Stillman D.,
Sidney D.,* and *Martin W.*

ROYAL B WILLIS, son of Thomas and Frances, was b. at Easton,
Sept. 3, 1812; m. Sept. 16, 1833, Phebe C., dau. of Peter Webster
of Methuen. He commenced business in Boston in 1834, and represented the city in the Legislature, 1844 and 1845. In 1846, he
removed to Lexington, continuing his business in Boston. He has
held a commission of justice of the peace. For several years past,
he has been engaged in the furniture business in Cincinnati, Ohio,
keeping up his family residence in Lexington. They have had three
children—*George Franklin,* b. in Methuen, July 17, 1834, d. Sept.
13, 1834; *Francis Royal,* b. in Boston, Feb. 22, 1838; *Julia Augusta,* b. in Boston, June 26, 1842.

The Genealogy of the following families was obtained too late to be inserted in the appropriate alphabetical place in the Register, and is here appended.

CUMMINGS.—DANIEL CUMMINGS, son of Ebenezer Cummings of Woburn, was b. Jan. 7, 1797; m. Abigail Wright of Woburn, dau. of Jacob Wright, b. April 28, 1797. They resided first in Bedford, where their first three children were born, and afterwards in Lexington. They have *Daniel*, b. Aug. 3, 1817, m. —— Fowle; *Abigail*, b. July 17, 1819, m. Charles Flagg of Wo.; *William*, b. Feb. 22, 1822; *George*, b. Nov. 24, 1833; *Oliver Waterman*, b. Dec. 23, 1836. Mr. Cummings resides at the extreme part of the town, where Burlington and Bedford corner upon Lexington.

THE CURRIER FAMILY.

RICHARD CURRIER was in Salisbury in 1640, and by his wife Ann had several children. *Samuel Currier*, perhaps son of Richard, was in Haverhill, and built him a cottage on the common land in 1668, and in 1670, m. Mary Hardy. I have no record of his death or of his children. In 1727, a school was kept at the house of widow Currier, and in 1732 the school was described as being at the house of Reuben Currier. From this imperfect record it is inferred that Samuel d. before 1727, and that *Reuben* was his son. Reuben Currier was a lieutenant in Haverhill in 1757. He m. and had at least two sons, Reuben and Jonathan. He moved to Bow, N. H., about 1760. *Jonathan*, m. Nancy Sargent of Haverhill, and among other children had

1   JONATHAN CURRIER b. 1787; m. Jan. 1, 1814, Cynthia Whitney, b. April 14, 1792. He d. Oct. 15, 1859, aged 72, and she d. in Lexington, Nov. 10, 1866.

1- 2   ‡*William Jackson*, b. Feb. 21, 1815; m. Susan B. Spaulding.
    3   *Charles Whitney*, b. March 9, 1817; d. 1838, in Nashville, Texas.
    4   *Simon Pender*, b. Aug. 19, 1822; m. and r. in the State of N. Y.

1-2-   WILLIAM J. CURRIER m. Jan. 23, 1845, Susan B. Spaulding, dau. of Dr. Stillman and Lucy (Butterfield) Spaulding of Lexington. He studied medicine with Dr. Stedman at the Marine Hospital in Chelsea, and with Dr. Chaplin in Cambridge. He attended lectures at Pittsfield and at Boston, and grad. 1839, at the Berkshire Medical Institute. He is a member of the Mass. Medical Society. He came to Lexington in 1840, and established himself in his profession. They have two children, *Charles Wingate*, b. April 1, 1850; *William B.*, b. July 2, 1859.

DOW.—DARIUS DOW, son of Levi and Catharine (Haynes) Dow, was b. in Sudbury, Jan. 16, 1825; m. Oct. 14, 1851, Abbie Lovewell of Weston, b. Nov. 8, 1830. He came to Lexington about 1853. They have had *Darius A.*, b. Dec. 28, 1852, in Waltham; *George H.*, b. in Lex. Nov. 4, 1855; *Hattie L.*, b. Nov. 22, 1856, d. June 14, 1857; *Henrietta J.*, b. March 6, 1862.

FITCH.—DAVID FITCH b. in Billerica, March 3, 1832. His father, David Fitch, was son of David of Bedford. *David* of Lex. came to this town about 1858, and m. Jan., 1858, S. M. Williams of Rox. He entered the 45th Reg. in the late Rebellion, and served in

N. C. as a soldier from Lex. His brother Albert enlisted from Burlington for three years, and was killed at the battle of Chancellorsville. David has four children, the first two born in Burlington, the last two in Lexington. *David Warren*, b. Oct. 20, 1858; *Joseph Henry*, b. Feb. 12, 1861; *Ellen L.*, b. Aug. 31, 1864; *Eliza Jane*, b. Sept. 19, 1866.

FOWLE.—This name has been common in some of the neighboring towns, and a few persons of that name have from time to time appeared upon our records.

ISAAC FOWLE of Medford m. Nancy Hall, and had a family of eleven children. *William Henry*, one of his sons, b. July 9, 1815, m. April 8, 1835, Susan E. Reed, dau. of Isaac Reed of Lex. She d. July 29, 1859, and he m. Dec. 20, 1860, Emeline P. Reed, sister of his first wife. He came to Lexington with his family, 1857. His father and brother John came with them. The father is now living in his 85th year. William H. Fowle d. Aug. 8, 1862. He had two children by his first wife—Susan Elizabeth, b. Aug. 11, 1839; Emma S., b. Sept. 3, 1844; m. July 2, 1865, George D. Estabrook.

HILDRETH.—SAMUEL HILDRETH b. March 1, 1797, son of James Hildreth of Westford, m. July 3, 1823, Sophia Doloph of Candia, N. H. They resided in Boston and Dorchester, and came to Lex. 1855. They have had eleven children, viz. *Sophia A.*, d. young; *Samuel B.*, b. 1825, r. in Boston; *Prescott P.*, b. 1827, and *Rufus H.*, b. 1828, reside in Dorchester; *Sophia A.*, b. 1830, r. in Quincy; *John*, b. 1832, d. young; *Mary E.*, b. 1833; *Joseph W.*, b. 1835; *Eliza Jane* and *Jane Eliza*, twins, b. 1837, the latter d. young; *Harriet P.*, b. Dec. 26, 1838, m. Nov. 26, 1863, Thomas W. Child, r. in Lex. and have two children; George O., b. 1843; Benjamin F., b. 1847, d. young.

HOLBROOK.—MOSES HOLBROOK was b. in Marlborough, Nov. 24, 1745, and m. Rachael ——, b. May 8, 1748. He d. in Templeton, where they resided, June 28, 1810; and she d. July 18, 1797. They had *Rachael*, b. May 5, 1775; *Patty*, b. June 9, 1778, d. 1812; *Cynthia*, b. July 17, 1781, d. Aug. 1855; *Rufus*, b. April 11, 1784, d. 1824; *Aaron*, b. Dec. 18, 1788, d. 1841; *Moses*, twin of Aaron, d. young.

1   AARON HOLBROOK m. May 7, 1818, Susan Miles. She d. and he m. Mary Wellington of Waltham.

1- 2   *Aaron*, b. March 19, 1819.
3   *Susan L.*, b. June 8, 1822; m. May 20, 1849, William Henry Smith of Lexington.
4   *Mary A.*, b. May 28, 1826; m. Charles F. Winship of Lexington.
5   *Henry C.*, b. May 14, 1828; r. in Georgia.
6   †*Rufus W.*, b. March 29, 1830; m. Sarah E. Stocker.
7   *Edwin W.*, b. July 21, 1832; r. in New York.

1-6-   RUFUS W. HOLBROOK m. April 28, 1857, Sarah E. Stocker of Saugus. They have two children, *Abbie Pierce*, b. Aug. 11, 1858; *Nellie*, b. April 29, 1861. The Holbrook family came to Lex. 1840.

JEWETT.—NATHANIEL JEWETT came to Lexington about 1835 from Charlestown. He was son of Jedediah, who was a direct descendant of Maximilian Jewett of Rowley, who came to the country early and was made a freeman, and was chosen deacon in Rowley in 1640. He had numerous descendants in Rowley, Ipswich and the neighboring towns.

NATHANIEL JEWETT was b. Oct. 23, 1780, and m. Nov. 22, 1807, Betsey Hamblet, b. May 3, 1783. He d. in Lex. Oct. 26, 1861, aged 81. She d. March 27, 1857, aged 74. They had six children, viz. *Amory*, b. Aug. 14, 1808, m. Lucy E. Duade; r. in Boston. *Louisa*, b. June 15, 1810, m. George F. Tuttle, r. at Woodstock, Vt. *Maria*, b. March 13, 1812, m. Dec. 5, 1830, George W. Robinson; r. in Lex. *Eliza*, b. Feb., 1814, m. Charles Brown; r. in Linc. *Elias K.*, b. Dec. 15, 1817, d. Jan. 27, 1855, in California by the explosion of a steamboat boiler. *Gorham*, b. Aug. 3, 1819, m. March 11, 1857, Caroline R. Farnsworth. They have Caroline F., b. Aug. 6, 1858.

JONES.—SAMUEL JONES, son of Samuel of Quincy, was b. Feb. 14, 1809. He came to Lex. about 1833, and m. Nov. 28, 1834, Sarah Fogg, from N. H. They have had *Sarah A.*, b. Nov. 19, 1836, d. April 20, 1842; *Samuel H.*, b. Nov. 13, 1838. He entered the service of the United States, and was nine months in North Carolina. Subsequently he re-enlisted in the Heavy Artillery and served till the close of the war. *Lydia A.*, b. April 5, 1842, m. Aug. 10, 1860, Alexander Corey, and has three children; *George A.*, b. May 6, 1859.

KEITH.—JOHN KEITH came to Boston from Scotland about 1790. He m. Deborah Thayer of Braintree. They had *Robert*, b. 1793; *Ann*, b. 1795; *William*, b. 1797. He d. 1801.

1   WILLIAM KEITH m. 1820, Priscilla W. Whiston of Boston, dau. of Francis and Elizabeth (Downes) Whiston.

1– 2   ‡*William W.*, b. Feb. 10, 1822; m. Cordelia Bryant.
   3   *Elizabeth W.*, b. Aug. 20, 1823; d. 1849.
   4   *Amos B.*, b. June 10, 1825; m. 1846, Catharine E. Marsh of Lynn.
   5   *John H.*, b. Jan. 20, 1827; m. Mary E. Foster of Salem; r. there.
   6   *Priscilla W.*, b. April 23, 1829; m. James Annin of Leroy, N. Y.
   7   *Edward H.*, b. May 6, 1831; m. 1849, Mary ——; r. in Chicago.
   8   *Harriet A.*, b. June 10, 1833; d. 1854.

1-2–   WILLIAM W. KEITH m. May 18, 1848, Cordelia Bryant, dau. of Nathaniel and Clarissa (Blodgett) Bryant, b. April 9, 1821. They came to Lexington, 1859. He is a broker in Boston. They have four children, *Harry H.*, b. Nov. 15, 1851; *William W.*, b. June 22, 1857; *Lillian B.*, b. May 12, 1860; *Walter B.*, b. Dec. 13, 1862.

THE KNIGHT FAMILY.

1   LOAMMI KNIGHT, son of Aaron and Rebecca (Adams) Knight was b. in Hancock, N. H., Oct. 14, 1803. He came to Lexington, 1821, and m. May 3, 1829, Mary Robbins, dau. of Stephen Robbins, and d. Jan. 5, 1868. He was devoted to the militia, and rose to the rank of Major.

1– 2   *Mary*, b. April 2, 1830; d. April 6, 1830.
   3   †*Francis H.*, b. May 11, 1831; has been twice married.

4 *Mary R.*, b. Nov. 17, 1833; m. Nov. 25, 1852, Joshua Hobart, and has had one child, Mary L., b. July 9, 1855.

5 *Franklin*, b. Sept. 29, 1835.

6 *Melinda*, b. July 19, 1838; m. Nov. 22, 1866, John D. Smith of Charlestown.

7 *Helen Augusta*, b. May 1, 1841; m. Sept. 25, 1861, Franklin E. Melvin of Charlestown.

8 *Annie Maria*, b. March 8, 1844.

1-3- FRANCIS H. KNIGHT m. Aug. 15, 1855, Loenza L. Hills, dau. of Joseph and Olive K. Hills of Hancock, N. H. She d. Oct. 25, 1859, and he m. Nov. 15, 1860, Lizzie H. Collamer, dau. of Horace and M. E. Collamer of Woburn. They moved to Reading, 1862. His children are *Clarence C.*, b. July 21, 1858; *Lizzie Loenza*, b. Oct. 6, 1861; *Mary C.*, b. June 24, 1864; *Nellie Winslow*, b. Oct. 23, 1867.

LEWIS.—JOSHUA LEWIS, a Baptist clergyman, came from Wales about 1780 and settled in Conn. His son *Joshua*, likewise a Baptist clergyman, resided in Conn. and R. I. His son *Joshua* removed to Saratoga, N. Y., where he m. —— Grinnell. His son *John* moved to the neighborhood of Auburn, N. Y., where he m. Delecta Barbour, and became a farmer. They had five children.

DIO LEWIS, son of John, was b. 1825; m. July 11, 1849, Hellen C. Clarke, dau. of Dr. Peter Clarke of Montezuma, N. Y. He studied medicine in Auburn, and attended a course of lectures in the Medical Department of Harvard University, and afterwards took his diploma from the Medical College at Cleveland, Ohio. He settled in Buffalo, N. Y., where he followed his profession several years, and edited a Medical Magazine. After traveling some years at home and abroad, and giving himself to the development of a new system of physical culture, he came to Boston in 1860, and established a Normal Institute for physical education. To his labors as President of that institution, he added the establishment and conduct of a Young Ladies' Seminary, which he opened in Lexington, 1864. Of this school, and of the success of his system we have spoken elsewhere. See History, pp. 375, 376.

RHODES.—THOMAS H. RHODES, son of Cyrus Rhodes, was b. in Antrim, N. H., March 7, 1816. He came to Lexington in 1840, and m. Feb. 3, 1841, Jane M. Taylor of Boston, b. March 7, 1821. She was dau. of Eli Taylor. They have had the following children. *Sarah Elizabeth*, b. March 27, 1842; m. May 1, 1864, Joshua L. Johnson from Me. They reside in Charlestown, and have one child. *George H.*, b. May 2, 1844, d. Aug. of the same year. *Rebecca J.*, b. Aug. 1, 1845. *Henry*, b. April, 1847, d. young. *Silas Edwin*, b. Oct. 6, 1851. *Charles Henry*, b. Jan. 23, 1858.

SIMONDS.—CALVIN SIMONDS, son of Bradley, and grandson of David Simonds, (No. 59 in the Simonds family,) was b. in Ashby, June 5, 1836, and m. April 11, 1859, Julia A. Petigrew, b. March 8, 1834. They came to Lex. in 1860. They have had *Carrie A.*, b. Jan. 5, 1861; *Mary Ella*, b. Jan. 7, 1863, d. March 11, 1863; *George Francis*, b. Nov. 21, 1864; *Jennie Maria*, b. Oct. 12, 1866.

TYLER.—EDWARD TYLER was b. Nov. 10, 1776; m. 1799, first, Mary G. Thomas, b. 1779. She d. and he m. second, Susanna Thomas, 1808; she d. July 21, 1811, and he m. third, Alma E.

Holden. He d. Dec. 26, 1827. He had *Mary*, b. 1805; *Edward
L.*, b. Aug. 5, 1806; *Alma E.*, b. 1815; *Susan*, b. 1816; *John F.*,
b. 1818; *Harriet N.* and *James R.*, (twins,) b. 1820; *Elizabeth*, b.
1823. They r. in Harvard.

1   EDWARD L. TYLER, son of Capt. Edward and Mary, m. April 16,
1832, Rachel Stevens. She d. April 3, 1839, and he m. Nov. 13,
1839, Martha T. Savage. He came to Lexington about 1828, and
d. March 23, 1864, in his 58th year. He had two children by each
wife.

1- 2 *Edward F.*, b. Nov. 13, 1834.
  3 *Mary S.*, b. Feb. 7, 1838; m. Ap. 2, 1865, Marshall Lee of Carlisle.
  4 *Henry H.*, b. Nov. 22, 1840.   5 *Arthur F.*, b. March 12, 1852.

NOTE.—In the multiplicity of names and dates it is almost impossible to
avoid mistakes. A few errors have been detected since the sheets passed the
Press, which are here corrected, and a few slight additions made.

In the History:

> Page 321, line 20 from the top, for 'Barnes,' read 'Bowes.'
> "   397, line 14 from the bottom, for '1861,' on the left margin, read
>   '1862.'
> "   398, line 15 from the bottom, insert on the left margin against
>   Alvin Cole, '1862.'

In the Genealogy:

> Page 11, line 2 from the bottom, for Charles 'Hawes,' read Charles
>   'Harvey.'
> "   31, first line, for 'Susanna,' read 'Lusanna.'
> "   43, line 11 from the top, for 'Brown,' read 'Bowen.'
> "   125, line 22 from the top, for '1738,' read '1838.'
> "   149, line 18 in a few copies, for '1747' and '1749,' read '1647' and
>   '1849.'
> "   179, line 11 from bottom, after 'Lusanna,' insert 'T.'
> "   181, line 32 from the top, for '1863,' read '1853.'
> "   217, line 17 from the bottom, after 1857, add '1861,' and '1863—
>   1865.'
> "   230, line 8 and 9 from the top, for 'Illinois,' read 'Wisconsin.'
> "   244, line 29 from top, for 'Viles,' read 'Teal.'
> "   262, line 10 from top, for '1858,' read '1848.'

INDEX TO THE GENEALOGIES.

In the following Index, the names of the Families, which are arranged in alphabetical order, are printed in SMALL CAPITALS, and the page or pages occupied by each family, respectively, are set against them. The names which follow the families, and are arranged in alphabetical order, are of those, whether male or female, who have intermarried with some member of the family, and the figures set against their name refer to the consecutive number of each family, against which the name will be found. Names having more than one number against them, denote that different persons, of the same surname, married into the family. In a few instances, distinct families of the same name, have the same numbers. Hence both numbers should be consulted. Persons marrying those of the same surname are omitted in the index. In the introduction of the families, the name of the wife is sometimes given before the consecutive numbers commence; and in some of the small families the numbers are omitted altogether. In such cases, the name of the person intermarrying will be found inserted below, without any number annexed, but can easily be found under the head of the family where they occur.

Bowman, 32
Bridge, 33, 36, 37, 43, 82
Brooks, 81
Brown, 31, 34, 66
Chandler, 68, 77
Cutler, 46
Danforth, 63
Davis, 55
Elson, 17
Estabrook, 25, 48
Fiske, 10, 22
Gibson, 79
Greenleaf, 111
Grimes, 56
Harrington, 59
Hobart, 114
Houghton, 51
Ingalls, 29
Jennison, 2
Jewett, 105
Johnson, 6, 18, 19, 60
Kendall, 1, 7, 15, 20
Lawrence, 44
Leathers, 81
Locke, 67
Longley, 61
Marrett, 69
Meigs, 106
Merriam, 74
Mulliken, 110
Munsal, 12
Muzzy, 42, 73, 80, 109
Nichols, 101
Page, 38
Parker, 93
Pierce, 3, 14
Poulter, 23
Prescott, 95, 96
Raymond, 47
Richardson, 13, 102
Robinson, 16
Rockwell, 2
Russell, 27
Sawyer, 21
Simonds, 35
Smith, 104
Stone, 24, 25, 29, 30, 84
Tidd, 28
Wadsworth, 113
Waite, 83, 85
Walker, 8 ⁓.
Webber, 100
Wellington, 109
Whittemore, 30
Winn, 9
Winship, 49
Wyman, 5

TIMOTHY REED, 196, 197
Crowningshield, 16
Ferren, 23
Fowle, 13, 21
French, 2
Gardner, 6, 11
Gates, 24
Kendall, 1
Lawrence, 20
Munroe, 3, 4
Parker, 15
Phipps, 17
Pratt, 8
Russell, 9

Thayer, 7
Willard, 9

SWETHERN AND OTHER
   REEDS, 197, 198
Clapp, 9
Collens, 1, 6
Emerson, 5
Farrington, 8
Flint, 3
Fox, 4
Frost, 2
Harrington, 1
Hartwell, 3
Hersey, 16
Hutchinson, 6
Johnson, 11
Murphy, 2
Reed, 13
Ross, 14
Rugg, 12
Stearns, 10
Trask, 7
Walker, 13
Wellington, 2, 5
Wyman, 17

RHODES, 231
Johnson.
Taylor.

RICHARDSON, 198, 199
Bodwell.
Browne.
Godfrey.
Parker.
Raymond, 3
Reed, 1
Richards, 2
Wiseman.

ROBBINS, 199—202
Barrett, 57
Blodgett, 37
Brazier, 1
Butterfield, 17
Chandler, 5
Cutter, 32
Foot, 15
Harrington, 47
Holbrook, 55
Hutchinson, 19
Jackson, 12
Johnson, 12, 13
Langdon, 49
Lothrop, 55
Mead, 20
Mills, 15
Patten, 14
Prentice, 24, 36
Russell, 11
Simonds, 50
Stone, 56
Wadsworth, 22
Williams, 26
Winship, 33
Wooten, 21

ROBINSON, 202—206
Ackley, 18
Ames, 45
Bacon, 4

Brown.
Chase.
Cutler, 32
Danforth.
Davis, 34, 39
Draper, 10
Gair, 33
Gammell, 30
Gardner, 28
Gilmor, 41
Hadley, 13
Hall, 34
Harrington, 42
Hosmer, 39
Jennings, 26
Jewett.
Little.
Reed, 16
Simonds, 6, 23, 46
Snow, 20
Stevens, 46
Tidd, 25
Trask, 5
Tufts, 36
White, 27
Wiggin.

RUSSELL, 206—211
Belcher, 2
Blood, 70
Bond, 45
Bradshaw, 1
Bridge, 13
Brooks, 7
Cutler, 7
Dodge, 48
Eaton, 48
Farwell, 79
Goodnow, 58
Harrington, 76
Hubbard, 9
Jones, 80
Joyce, 85
Lawrence, 5
Locke, 31, 71, 81
Merriam, 73
Munroe, 28, 68
Prentice, 1
Rice, 10
Smith, 82
Sprague, 35
Thayer, 79
Wheeler, 37
White, 85
Whitney, 79
Winship, 8, 16
Wood, 78

SAVILLE, 211, 212
Gould, 9
Haraden, 1
Leonard, 6
Muzzey, 11

SIMONDS, 212—218
Angier, 66
Bacon, 5
Bailey, 94
Ball, 93
Bannon, 139
Blake, 112
Blodgett, 10, 12